Fodor's

COSTA RICA

WELCOME TO COSTA RICA

Costa Rica has it all: nowhere else can you gaze upon a volcano while soaking in a hot spring one day, hike deep into a rain forest the next, and end your trip learning to surf at a luxurious seaside resort. Miles of pristine beaches on the Pacific and Caribbean coasts, fabulous national parks with plentiful opportunities for wildlife viewing, and world-renowned eco-lodges have made this one of the hottest destinations around. The welcoming people of Costa Rica, and their mellow *pura vida* lifestyle, add warmth to every visit.

TOP REASONS TO GO

★ **Active Volcanoes:** Five imposing behemoths exude, fume, seethe, and smolder.

★ **Beaches:** From pristine secluded hideaways to palm-fringed resort strands.

★ **Coffee:** A plantation tour shows you what makes the country tick.

★ **Eco-friendly Hotels:** Wilderness lodges set the standard for green tourism with style.

★ **Outdoor Adventure:** Zip lining, canopy tours, hiking, and surfing are all top notch.

★ **Wildlife Galore:** Monkeys, sloths, and turtles abound, and the birding is superb.

Fodor's COSTA RICA

Publisher: Amanda D'Acierno, *Senior Vice President*

Design: Tina Malaney, *Associate Art Director*; Erica Cuoco, *Production Designer*

Photography: Jennifer Arnow, *Senior Photo Editor*; Mary Robnett, *Photo Researcher*

Maps: Rebecca Baer, *Senior Map Editor*; David Lindroth, Mark Stroud (Moon Street Cartography), *Cartographers*

Production: Angela L. McLean, *Senior Production Manager*

Sales: Jacqueline Lebow, *Sales Director*

Marketing & Publicity: Heather Dalton, *Marketing Director*; Katherine Punia, *Publicity Director*

Business & Operations: Susan Livingston, *Senior Vice President, Strategic Business Planning*; Sue Daulton, *Vice President, Operations*

Fodors.com: Megan Bell, *Executive Director, Revenue & Business Development*; Yasmin Marinaro, *Senior Director, Marketing & Partnerships*

Copyright © 2017 by Fodor's Travel, a division of Penguin Random House LLC

Writers: Marlise Kast-Myers, Dorothy MacKinnon, Jeffrey Van Fleet

Editor: Teddy Minford

Production Editor: Jennifer DePrima

18th Edition

ISBN 978–1–101–87998–6

ISSN 1522–6131

All details in this book are based on information supplied to us at press time. Always confirm information when it matters, especially if you're making a detour to visit a specific place. Fodor's expressly disclaims any liability, loss, or risk, personal or otherwise, that is incurred as a consequence of the use of any of the contents of this book.

SPECIAL SALES

This book is available at special discounts for bulk purchases for sales promotions or premiums. For more information, e-mail specialmarkets@penguinrandomhouse.com.

PRINTED IN THE UNITED STATES OF AMERICA

10 9 8 7 6 5 4 3 2 1

CONTENTS

CONTENTS

ABOUT THIS GUIDE

Fodor's Recommendations

Everything in this guide is worth doing—we don't cover what isn't—but exceptional sights, hotels, and restaurants are recognized with additional accolades. **Fodor's Choice★** indicates our top recommendations.

Trip Costs

We list prices wherever possible to help you budget well. Hotel and restaurant price categories from $ to $$$$ are noted alongside each recommendation. For hotels, we include the lowest cost of a standard double room in high season. For restaurants, we cite the average price of a main course at dinner or, if dinner isn't served, at lunch. For attractions, we always list adult admission fees; discounts are usually available for children, students, and senior citizens.

Hotels

Our local writers vet every hotel to recommend the best overnights in each price category, from budget to expensive. Unless otherwise specified, you can expect private bath, phone, and TV in your room. For expanded hotel reviews visit Fodors.com.

Top Picks
★ **Fodor's**Choice

Listings
⊠ Address
⊠ Branch address
☏ Telephone
🖷 Fax
⊕ Website
✉ E-mail
🎟 Admission fee
☉ Open/closed times
Ⓜ Subway
⊹ Directions or Map coordinates

Hotels & Restaurants
🛏 Hotel
↘ Number of rooms
🍽 Meal plans
✕ Restaurant
✍ Reservations
👗 Dress code
▭ No credit cards
$ Price

Other
⇨ See also
☞ Take note
🏌 Golf facilities

Restaurants

Unless we state otherwise, restaurants are open for lunch and dinner daily. We mention dress code only when there's a specific requirement and reservations only when they're essential or not accepted.

Credit Cards

The hotels and restaurants in this guide typically accept credit cards. If not, we'll say so.

EUGENE FODOR

Hungarian-born Eugene Fodor (1905–91) began his travel career as an interpreter on a French cruise ship. The experience inspired him to write *On the Continent* (1936), the first guidebook to receive annual updates and discuss a country's way of life as well as its sights. Fodor later joined the U.S. Army and worked for the OSS in World War II. After the war, he kept up his intelligence work while expanding his guidebook series. During the Cold War, many guides were written by fellow agents who understood the value of insider information. Today's guides continue Fodor's legacy by providing travelers with timely coverage, insider tips, and cultural context.

EXPERIENCE
COSTA RICA

WHAT'S WHERE

1 San José. Do you know the way to San José? You will soon enough. Almost everyone passes through on their way to the beach or the mountains. This capital city isn't much to look at, but it has great restaurants and nightlife, and fascinating museums dedicated to gold and jade.

2 The Central Valley. You likely won't linger long in the Central Valley, as it lacks any of the country's big-name attractions. But there are quite a few day-trip possibilities from San José, including exploring mountain villages, rafting through white-water rapids, and gaping into the mouths of some of the country's most accessible active volcanoes.

3 Arenal, Monteverde, and the Northern Lowlands. This part of Costa Rica attracts those who don't like sitting still. After zipping along cables through the misty jungle of Monteverde Cloud Forest, windsurfing on glittering Lake Arenal, or taking in the majesty of the Arenal Volcano, you can reward yourself with a dip in the bubbly waters of Tabacón Hot Springs.

4 Guanacaste and the Nicoya Peninsula. If you came for beaches, this area is for you. Each has a unique personality: Flamingo's endless stretch of sand draws

Elevation	
12,500	3,810
10,000	3,048
7,500	2,286
5,000	1,525
4,000	1,220
3,000	915
2,500	762
2,000	610
1,500	457
1,000	305
750	230
500	152
250	75
100	30
feet	meters

Barra del Colorado
Barra del Colorado
Wildlife Refuge

Tortuguero
Tortuguero
National Park

Caribbean Sea

Puerto Viejo
de Sarapiquí

7

Guápiles

Siquirres

Moín
Limón

Congo
Poás

2

Braulio Carillo
National Park

Turrialba

Alajuela   Irazú
Heredia

☆ San José

Turrialba

Cahuita
National Park

Cahuita
Puerto Viejo
de Talamanca

Escazú

Cartago

Santa María

Orosi

Cerro Chirripó
National Park

1

Bribri

San Gerardo
de Dota

CORDILLERA

Chirripó   La Amistad
National Park

Parrita

San Isidro de
El General

Ulyum

PANAMA

Quepos

DE TALAMANCA

Buenos
Aires

Nai

Bine

Manuel Antonio
National Park   Dominical

VALLE DE EL GENERAL

Paso Real

San
Vito

Uvita

Río Terraba

Ciudad Cortés

Palmar Norte

Piedras Blancas
National Park

Ciudad
Neily

Drake
Drake Bay

Rincón

Golfito

OSA PENINSULA

Puerto
Jiménez

Paso
Canoas

6

Zancudo

Corcovado
National Park

Carate   Dulce
Gulf

Pavones

Ocean

Matapalo

0   30 mi

0   30 km

sun worshippers; Tamarindo's
nightlife is legendary; Avellanas's strong swells challenge
surfers; Ostional's nesting sea
turtles bring nature lovers;
and the Papagayo Peninsula's
all-inclusive resorts provide
every creature comfort.

**5 Manuel Antonio and
the Central Pacific Coast.**
The area's not just for spring
breakers, although it does
include funky surf towns like
Jacó. Drive down the coast to
the cluster of small hotels and
restaurants at Manuel Antonio.
The national park, on a peninsula jutting into the ocean, has
the easiest wildlife viewing on
the planet and is the country's
most visited attraction.

**6 The Osa Peninsula
and the South Pacific.**
Rustic lodges in the Osa
Peninsula sit on the edge of
the country's wildest region,
consisting almost entirely
of Corcovado National
Park. Hikes reveal toucans
and scarlet macaws in the
treetops, and boating trips
often include swimming with
whales and dolphins.

**7 Tortuguero and the
Caribbean Coast.** Come
here for the spirited music,
the tasty food, the chance to
mix with the Afro-Caribbean
population, and the turtle-
watching at Tortuguero
National Park.

NEED TO KNOW

AT A GLANCE

Capital: San José

Population: 4,814,144

Currency: Costa Rican colón

Money: ATMs common but cash more common than credit; tourist prices in USD

Language: Spanish

Country Code: 506

Emergencies: 911

Driving: On the right

Electricity: 120v/60 cycles; plugs are U.S. standard two- and three-prong

Time: Two hours behind New York during daylight savings; one hour behind otherwise

Documents: Up to 90 days with valid passport

Mobile Phones: GSM (850 and 1800 bands)

Major Mobile Companies: Kölbi (ICE), Movistar, Claro

WEBSITES

Instituto Costarricense de Turismo:
⊕ www.visitcostarica.com

Anywhere Costa Rica:
⊕ www.anywherecostarica.com/travel-guide

Costa Rica Map: ⊕ www.costaricamap.com

GETTING AROUND

✈ **Air Travel:** Two international airports and 16 domestic airfields make getting to and around Costa Rica by air a breeze.

🚌 **Bus Travel:** All Costa Rican towns are connected by reliable and inexpensive bus service. Tickets are sold at bus stations and on buses.

🚗 **Car Travel:** Renting a car is a good yet expensive choice if you're destination hopping or going off the beaten path. Special insurance is mandatory and 4WD suggested.

PLAN YOUR BUDGET

	HOTEL ROOM	MEAL	ATTRACTIONS
Low Budget	$100	$10	Irazú Volcano, $15
Mid Budget	$200	$20	Café Britt Coffee Tour, $22
High Budget	$300	$30	White-water rafting in Turrialba, $99

WAYS TO SAVE

Load up at lunch. *Almuerzo* (lunch) is the biggest meal of the day for Costa Ricans, and savvy travelers know that lunch specials are the biggest bargain of the day.

Rent a house. Rental houses are common all over Costa Rica, and popular in the Pacific coast destinations; they can accommodate a family for less.

Book domestic flights in advance. Small airlines Nature Air and SANSA serve many tourist hot spots in Costa Rica. Flights are dirt cheap, if booked far in advance.

Book attractions with transport. Many attractions offer an affordable transport option providing door-to-door service.

Hassle Factor	Low. Flights to San José and Liberia are frequent from several U.S. gateways.
3 days	Relax poolside or beachside at a resort on the Pacific coast and visit the rain forest to search for wildlife. Or visit a volcano and coffee farm outside San José.
1 week	Split your time between the Pacific coast and the country's stunning interior, either Arenal or Monteverde Cloud Forest.
2 weeks	You have time to see three major highlights of the Pacific coast: sunny Papagayo Peninsula, the rain forest of Manuel Antonio, and the unspoiled Osa Peninsula. Visit a remote eco-lodge in the Osa.

WHEN TO GO

High Season: The sunniest, driest season in most of the country occurs from mid-December through April, with Christmas and Easter bracketing the busiest tourist season. March and April are sweltering in lowland areas, with temperatures in the arid North Pacific frequently exceeding 90°F.

Low Season: Afternoon showers kick in by May and last through November, with a brief drier season in June and July. Rain or not, North American and European summer vacations do increase the influx of visitors from June through August. Rains become heavy in September and October.

Value Season: The transition periods between rainy and dry seasons and back again make a marvelous time to visit Costa Rica. Visitor numbers are smaller and the threat of rain is minimal.

BIG EVENTS

January: Costa Rica's largest traditional fiesta, Fiestas Palmares, takes place in Palmares over 11 nights.

March–April: From Palm Sunday through Easter Sunday, Holy Week sees parties up and down the coasts.

August: Día de la Virgen de los Ángeles celebrates Costa Rica's patron saint on August 2.

September: Parades mark Independence Day in most communities on September 15.

READ THIS

■ *Monkeys Are Made of Chocolate,* Jack Ewing. A naturalist's take on human interaction with Costa Rica's abundant flora and fauna.

■ *Radical Sabbatical,* Laura Berger. An expat couple's life in Costa Rica.

■ *Pura Vida (Love Has No Boundaries),* Sara Alva. Young love on the Costa Rican coast.

WATCH THIS

■ *Jurassic Park.* Set in Costa Rica, but filmed in Hawaii.

■ *Runner, Runner.* Costa Rica is the backdrop for this thriller starring Justin Timberlake.

■ *After Earth.* Will Smith sci-fi flick features Arenal Volcano.

EAT THIS

■ **Gallo pinto:** cilantro-and-onion-flavored black beans with rice and salsa lizano

■ **Casado:** rice, cabbage salad, plantains, and a meat

■ **Olla de carne:** stew of beef and vegetables

■ **Rondón:** stew of fish or meat, plantains, breadfruit, and yam

■ **Sopa negra:** black-bean soup with a poached egg

■ **Ensalada de palmito:** shaved heart of palm with mayo

COSTA RICA
TOP ATTRACTIONS

Arenal Volcano

(A) Costa Rica has five active volcanoes, with Arenal being its most visited. The behemoth has settled into a less active phase these days—likely temporary—but its sinister, majestic, perfectly shaped cone never fails to impress, if the clouds part long enough for you to get a view.

Tortuguero

(B) Even the most curmudgeonly visitor marvels at the sight of recently hatched sea turtles scurrying from their nests to the ocean, and Tortuguero is Costa Rica's premier site to witness this age-old spectacle. This roadless region epitomizes the old adage that "Getting there is half the fun"—boat and plane are your only options—and the lodges up here can fix you up.

Manuel Antonio National Park

(C) Some of the country's most thrilling views can be seen from the trails through Manuel Antonio National Park. As you emerge from the rain forest, don't be surprised to find yourself alone on a palm-shaded beach. Make sure to look up—sloths and three types of monkey make their home in the canopy, and on a good day you might see them all.

Corcovado National Park

(D) Bird-watchers come to this vast and pristine rain forest with hopes of catching a glimpse of the endangered harpy eagle. It's notoriously difficult to see, but other feathered friends—like the scarlet macaw, the orange-bellied trogon, and the golden-hooded tanager—practically pose for pictures. No need to head off into the rain forest with your binoculars; dozens of hummingbirds are likely to dart around you as you relax by the pool.

Playa Carrillo

(E) This long, picturesque beach, backed by a line of swaying palms and protective cliffs, is certainly one of the most beautiful stretches of sand in the country. Perfect for swimming, snorkeling, or just walking, the beach isn't marred by a single building. Visit on a weekday and it's possible that you may have the entire shore to yourself.

Nicoya Peninsula

(F) Popular with the sun-and-fun crowd, the peninsula still has a yet-to-be-discovered feel. Maybe that's because its sandy shores are never covered with a checkerboard of beach blankets. Drive a few miles in any direction and you can find a spot all to yourself. But civilization isn't far away—some of the country's best restaurants are within reach.

Turrialba

(G) Heavy rainfall, steep mountains, and rocky terrain make this region a magnet for white-water rafters, and there's a river to match everyone's level of expertise. Not far from San José, the Central Valley has outfitters who offer everything from easy day trips to challenging multiday excursions. Many of these companies congregate around Turrialba, the country's white-water capital and close to the Río Pacuare and Río Reventazón.

Monteverde Cloud Forest Biological Reserve

(H) The roads leading here are terrible, but you won't mind once you see the mist-covered reserve. Because of the constant moisture, this private park is unbelievably lush. It's gorgeous during the day, but many prefer night hikes, when you can see colorful birds asleep in the branches, hairy tarantulas in search of prey, and nocturnal mammals like the wide-eyed kinkajou.

COSTA RICA MADE EASY

Do I need any special documents to get into the country?

Aside from a passport that's valid for at least six months after date of entry and a round-trip/outbound ticket, you don't need anything else to enter the country. You'll be given a 90-day tourist visa as you pass through immigration. You're no longer required to have your passport with you at all times during your trip, but you must carry a photocopy while you're out and about.

How difficult is it to travel around the country?

It's extremely easy. Thanks to the domestic airlines, getting to your ultimate destination takes far less time than just a few years ago; almost every worthwhile spot is within an hour of San José. Long-distance buses and vans are usually very comfortable, so don't overlook these as a way to get to far-flung destinations. Renting a car is a great way to get around, because you're not tied to somebody else's schedule. Alas, roads are not always well marked. It's good to have a detailed map if you're driving in rural areas, as it's easy to miss a turn.

Are the roads as bad as they say?

Yes and no. You'll still find potholes the size of bathtubs on the road leading to Monteverde Cloud Forest Biological Reserve, and the gravel roads on the Nicoya Peninsula are often so grooved by the rain that they feel like an endless series of speed bumps. But roads are improving. The most dramatic improvements have been made near the resort area of Lake Arenal. Repairs to the road between Nuevo Arenal and La Fortuna have cut your travel time almost in half. During and immediately after the rainy season is the worst time for driving. The constant deluge takes its toll on the pavement.

Should I rent a four-wheel-drive vehicle?

Probably. If your trip will take you mostly to the beaches, you won't necessarily need a 4WD vehicle. If you're headed to more-mountainous areas, such as any destination in the Northern Plains, you'll definitely want one. But even on the most badly maintained roads through the mountains, you'll see locals getting around just fine in their beat-up sedans. There's usually only a minor difference in the cost, so there's no reason not to go for the 4WD. Keep in mind, though, manual-transmission cars are standard, so if you have to drive an automatic, you'll pay a good bit extra for it.

Should I get insurance on the rental car?

Even if your own insurance covers rental cars, go ahead and take full insurance. The cost is often less than $10 a day. For that you get the peace of mind of knowing that you're not going to be hassled for a scratch on the fender or a crack in the windshield. One traveler reported returning a rental car with a front bumper completely detached, but because he had full insurance the clerk just smiled and wished him a good trip home.

Should I consider a package tour?

If you're terrified of traveling on your own, sign up for a tour. But Costa Rica is such an easy place to get around that there's really no need. Part of the fun is the exploring—finding a secluded beach, hiking down to a hidden waterfall, discovering a great crafts shop—and that's just not going to happen on a tour. If you're more comfortable with a package tour, pick one with a specific focus, like bird-watching or boating, so that you're less likely to get a generic tour.

Do I need a local guide?

Guides are a great idea for the first-time visitor in search of wildlife. A good guide will know where to find the animals, and will bring along a telescope so that you can get an up-close look at that sloth high in the trees or the howler monkeys across the clearing. After the first day, however, you'll probably grab your binoculars and head out on your own. It's much more gratifying to tell the folks back home that you discovered that banded anteater all by yourself.

Will I have trouble if I don't speak Spanish?

No problema. Most people in businesses catering to tourists speak at least some English. If you encounter someone who doesn't speak English, they'll probably point you to a coworker who does. Even if you're in a far-flung destination, locals will go out of their way to find somebody who speaks your language.

Can I drink the water?

Costa Rica is the only Central American country where you don't have to get stressed out about drinking the water. The water is potable in all but the most remote regions. That said, many people don't like the taste of the tap water and prefer bottled water.

Are there any worries about the food?

None whatsoever. Even the humblest roadside establishment is likely to be scrupulously clean. If you have any doubts about a place, just move on to the next one. There's no problem enjoying fruit, cheese, bread, or other local products sold from the stands set up along the roads.

Do I need to get any shots?

You probably don't have to get any vaccinations or take any special medications. Be up to date on the same routine vaccinations you would get back home. For longer trips, typhoid and hepatitis A immunizations may be warranted; check with your doctor. The U.S. Centers for Disease Control (CDC) no longer recommends taking antimalarial medications for travel here.

Should I be concerned about Zika and pregnancy?

The mosquito-borne Zika virus has been detected in Costa Rica and has been associated with fetal abnormalities. The CDC recommends that pregnant women or those trying to become pregnant, along with their partners, defer non-essential travel to Costa Rica. It's a matter best discussed with your doctor.

Can I use my ATM card?

Most ATMs are on both the Cirrus and Plus networks, so they accept debit and credit cards issued by U.S. banks. Some might accept cards with just the MasterCard or just the Visa logo; if that's the case, try a machine at a different bank. Know the exchange rate before you use an ATM for the first time so that you know about how much local currency you want to withdraw.

Do most places take credit cards?

Almost all tourist-oriented businesses accept credit cards. Smaller restaurants and hotels may not accept them at all. Some businesses don't like to accept credit cards because their banks charge them exorbitant fees for credit-card transactions. They will usually relent and charge you a small fee for the privilege.

Do I need a plug adaptor?

Outlets in Costa Rica are 120 volts, with standard U.S. two-prong plugs, three prongs if grounded, so U.S. appliances will work without adaptors.

COSTA RICA TODAY

Government

Costa Rica is a democratic republic whose structure will be familiar to any citizen of the United States. The 1949 constitution divides the government into independent executive, legislative, and judicial branches. All citizens are guaranteed equality before the law, the right to own property, freedom of speech, and freedom of religion.

Costa Rica elected its first female president for a four-year term in 2010, the fifth of, now, six Latin American countries to take such a step. Now a former occupant of the office, Laura Chinchilla became the first person here to hold the title "La Presidenta."

The country is famous for lacking an army, which was abolished when the constitution was ratified in 1949. The country's stable government and economy have made this possible, even as its neighbors were embroiled in civil war. Costa Rica does maintain a small national guard.

Economy

By the mid-1990s, Costa Rica had diversified its economy beyond agriculture, and tourism was bringing in more money than its three major cash crops: coffee, bananas, and pineapples. High-tech companies such as Intel, Hewlett-Packard, and Motorola; Internet purveyor Amazon; and pharmaceutical companies like Procter & Gamble and GlaxoSmithKline have now opened plants and service centers in Costa Rica, providing well-paid jobs for educated professionals. The U.S. chains and big-box stores have arrived, too, most notably Walmart, which operates eight supercenters here.

Costa Rica has staked hopes on international free-trade agreements in recent years, most notably with Canada (2002), the United States (2008), the European Union (2010), and China (2011). Opponents of the treaties are wary of how much benefit they provide for the country, however.

The economy continues to bedevil Costa Rica. Although economic growth is on the rise, it still has a $4.1 billion trade deficit and annual inflation just under 5%. Unemployment stands at 8.6%.

Tourism

Today Costa Rica faces the challenge of conserving its natural resources while still permitting modern development. The government has been unable or unwilling to control illegal logging, an industry that threatens to destroy the country's old-growth forests. Urban sprawl in the communities surrounding San José and the development of megaresorts along the Pacific coast threaten forests, wildlife, and the slow pace of life that makes Costa Rica so desirable.

Although tourism injects much-needed foreign cash into the economy, the government has not fully decided the best way to promote its natural wonders. The buzzwords now are not just ecotourism and sustainable development, but also adventure tourism and extreme sports. The two sides do not always see eye to eye.

Religion

Because it was a Spanish colony, Costa Rica continues to have a close relationship to the Catholic Church. Catholicism was made the country's official religion in the constitution. Because of this, priests are the only type of clergy authorized to perform civil marriages. (Others require the assistance of a legal official.)

More than 70% of Costa Ricans consider themselves Catholics. But even among this group, most people do not have a strong identification with the church or with its teachings. The live-and-let-live attitude of most Costa Ricans does not mesh well with religious doctrine. That's also probably why the evangelical churches that have made huge inroads in neighboring countries are not as prevalent here.

Every village has a church on its main square, always hopping once a year—when the town's patron saint is honored. These are times for food, music, and dancing in the streets. If the celebrations lack much religious fervor—well, that's Costa Rica for you.

Sports

Like everyone else on this soccer-mad isthmus, Costa Ricans take their game seriously, and passions bubble over when it comes to their beloved national team.

On the national level, the big local rivalry is between LD Alajuelense (*La Liga*, or The League) and Deportivo Saprissa (*El Monstruo Morado*, or The Purple Monster). They have won the Costa Rican championship 29 and 32 times, respectively, which makes the rivalry particularly intense. You can tell how important the sport is when you fly into the country. As your plane flies across the Central Valley, you'll notice that every village, no matter how small, has a soccer field.

Cash Crops

If nearby Honduras was the original "Banana Republic," 19th-century Costa Rica was a "Coffee Republic." Coffee remains inexorably entwined with the country, with economists paying close attention to world prices and kids in rural areas still taking class time off to help with the harvest.

The irony is that it's hard to get a decent cup of the stuff here. True to economic realities of developing countries, the high-quality product gets exported, with the inferior coffee staying behind for the local market. (The same is true of bananas, Costa Rica's other signature agricultural product.) The best places to get a cup of high-quality Costa Rican coffee are upscale restaurants and hotels. Owners understand foreign tastes and have export-quality coffee on hand. Gift shops sell the superior product as well.

The Central Valley is where you'll find many of the coffee plantations. You'll recognize them immediately by the rows of brilliant green plants covered in red berries. Because many of these plants are sensitive to light, they are often shaded by tall trees or even by canopies of fabric. Tours of the plantations are a great way to get to know the local cash crop.

In recent years, the producers of coffee have focused on quality rather than quantity. That's why bananas are now the top agricultural export, followed by pineapples. Both grow in sunny lowland areas, which are abundant on both the Atlantic and Pacific coasts. These crops are treated with just as much care as coffee. You're likely to see bunches of bananas wrapped in plastic bags—while still on the tree. This prevents blemishes that make them less appealing to foreign consumers.

ECOTOURISM IN COSTA RICA

Perhaps more than anyone else, it was the two writers of a field guide about tropical birds that were responsible for the ecotourism movement in Costa Rica.

Environmental officials frequently identify the 1989 publication of *A Guide to the Birds of Costa Rica* by F. Gary Stiles and Alexander Skutch as drawing the first flock of bird-watchers to the country. The rest, as they say, is history.

The country's leaders, seeing so many of its primary growth forests being felled at an alarming rate by loggers and farmers, established its national park system in 1970. But it wasn't until nearly two decades later, when the birding guide was published, that they realized that the land they had set aside could help transform the tiny country's economy. (Lasting peace finally coming to neighboring countries was key to overcoming visitors' apprehensions about travel to Central America, too.)

Of the 2.6 million people who travel each year to Costa Rica, many are bird-watchers who come in search of the keel-billed toucan, the scarlet-rumped tanager, or any of the 850 other species of birds. Other travelers are in search of animals, such as two types of sloth, three types of anteater, and four species of monkey, all of them surprisingly easy to spot in the country's national parks and private reserves.

But other people come to Costa Rica to go white-water rafting on the rivers, soar through the treetops attached to zip lines, or take a spin in a motorboat. And many people combine a little bit of everything into their itineraries.

Which raises a few questions: Is the person coming to see the wildlife practicing ecotourism? Is the adventure traveler? And exactly what is the definition of ecotourism, anyway?

Defining Ecotourism

Ecotourism has become the buzzword of Costa Rica's travel industry. From the original concept revolving around travel to enjoy nature, it has morphed into everything from hiking through the rain forest to rumbling over hillsides in all-terrain vehicles. We'll go with the oft-stated definition that ecotourism is "environmentally responsible travel." Costa Rica does itself proud in the domain of adventure tourism and extreme sports, but those activities sometimes conflict with that lofty ecotourism goal. That is not to say that adventure sports can't be part of a green vacation. It all depends what impact they have on the environment and the local community.

Going Green

Over the past decade, the concept of ecotourism has made a strong impression on the average traveler. Many people now realize that mass tourism can be damaging to environmentally sensitive places like Costa Rica but that much can be done to alleviate the negative effects. At the same time, *ecotourism* has become a marketing term used to attract customers who have the best intentions.

In addition to giving travelers the chance to observe and learn about wildlife, ecotourism should accomplish three things: refrain from damaging the environment, strengthen conservation efforts, and improve the lives of local people.

The last part might seem a bit beside the point, but environmentalists point out that much of the deforestation in Costa Rica and other countries is by poor people trying to eke out a living through sustenance farming. Providing them with other ways to make a living is the best way to prevent this.

What Can You Do?

Make sure the hotel you choose is eco-friendly. A great place to start is the Costa Rican Tourism Board (⊕ *www.turismo-sostenible.co.cr*). It has a rating system for hotels and lodges called the Certification for Sustainable Tourism. The New York–based Rainforest Alliance (⊕ *www.rainforest-alliance.org*) has a convenient searchable database of sustainable lodges. The International Ecotourism Society (⊕ *www.ecotourism.org*) also has a database of tour companies, hotels, and other travel services that are committed to sustainable practices.

Use locally owned lodges, car-rental agencies, or tour companies. Eat in local restaurants, shop in local markets, and attend local events. Enrich your experience and support the community by hiring local guides.

Make sure your tour company follows sustainable policies, including contributing to conservation efforts, hiring and training locals for most jobs, educating visitors about the local ecology and culture, and taking steps to mitigate negative impacts on the environment.

Don't be overly aggressive if you bargain for souvenirs, and don't shortchange local people on payments or tips for services.

Stray from the beaten path—by visiting areas where few tourists go, you can avoid adding to the stress on hot spots.

Support conservation by paying entrance fees to parks and protected sites. You can go a few steps further by making donations to local or international conservations groups such as Conservation International, the Rainforest Alliance, and the World Wide Fund for Nature.

Top Eco-Lodges in Costa Rica

The term *eco-lodge* conjures up images of staying in a remote place with no electricity at the end of a mud road—and indeed, Costa Rica offers such accommodation. But this country also shows that *eco* can be comfy or rustic, flashy or utilitarian, remote or close, large or small.

Arenal Observatory Lodge. You'll rub shoulders with research biologists at this environmentally conscious lodging near the summit of Arenal Volcano.

Finca Rosa Blanca. Sumptuous accommodation on a working coffee plantation with eco-friendly practices.

Hotel Lagarta Lodge. A tiny hotel with a large private biological reserve keeps an eagle eye on its water and energy consumption and environmental impact.

Hotel Sí Como No. Its meticulous recycling, minimal energy consumption, and community outreach prove that a snazzy resort hotel can be eco-friendly, too.

Laguna del Lagarto Lodge. Rustic and remote, this smallish property offers a variety of nature-themed activities that rival those of the big players.

La Selva. A working biological station gives room priority to researchers, but its impressive slate of environmental educational programs is open to all.

Lapa Ríos. Costa Rica's pioneer eco-lodge manages a large forest reserve and spearheads environmental outreach to the local community.

Rancho Naturalista. The Central Valley's prime address for birding enthusiasts offers you the chance to check 450 species off your life list.

IF YOU LIKE

Yoga

With Costa Rica's focus on natural healing, there are dozens of yoga spots where you can power-up and down-dog your way to a healthy mind, body, and spirit. Most yoga retreats are situated in nature and include organic cuisine, and optional excursions so you can explore the country and meet locals.

If you're not quite sure about turning your vacation into a nam-a-stay, start by booking a hotel where yoga classes are available. Many mid- to high-end properties have on-site yoga instructors with sessions averaging $15 per class.

RipJack Inn, Playa Grande. In addition to retreats and certification programs, this hotel hosts a variety of daily classes.

Harmony Hotel, Nosara. Start your day at this property with sunrise yoga and morning meditation, followed by fruit smoothies and a detoxing massage. This holistic retreat holds 3–5 daily classes in a jungle studio and is one of the few places in Costa Rica where you can find aerial yoga—a method that involves being suspended from a hammock.

Mystica Lodge, Arenal. This jungle lodge boasts classes, retreats, and workshops that combine yoga and treetop therapies of healing, massage, and psychotherapy. Weeklong retreats include yoga, lodging, meals, transportation, and excursions.

Encantada Ocean Cottages, Playa Esterillos. At these peaceful and sweet beachfront cottages, you can spend the morning honing your yoga skills, or simply stretch out those achy muscles after a surf session. They occasionally host retreats in addition to morning classes.

Coffee

Costa Rica B.C. (before coffee) was a poor country with scant infrastructure and little income. Coffee production changed that and was instrumental in the development of a solid middle class, transforming the country into the wealthiest and most stable in Central America.

Ever wonder where your morning cup of coffee comes from? A few purveyors give informative tours of their facilities and acquaint you with the country's favorite beverage. Tours guide you through the plant-to-crop process in English and Spanish, taking you from picking to drying to roasting to packing to brewing. Reservations are essential.

Café Britt, Barva, Heredia. Britt incorporates a small theater production into its informative tour, presenting the history of Costa Rican coffee in song and dance.

Coopedota Santa María, Santa Maria de Dota. A tour here acquaints you with the standard bean-to-bag experience, as well as the cooperative's pioneering environmental practices.

Doka Coffee Estate, Alajuela. Doka offers a comprehensive tour through the entire growing and drying process and lets you sample the local brew.

Don Juan Coffee Tour, Monteverde. A personalized excursion with a small group is the hallmark of this tour to a coffee plantation a few miles outside the town of Santa Elena.

Monteverde Coffee Tour, Monteverde. A tour here offers you some hands-on experience. Depending on the time of year, you can help with picking, drying, roasting, or packing.

Wildlife

Your trip to Costa Rica won't be an African safari, but several protected areas in this narrow land bridge between the two Americas will impress you with their wildlife populations. This country, the size of Vermont and New Hampshire combined, hosts a surprising variety of terrains and habitats and, consequently, of wildlife.

Corcovado National Park. *National Geographic* dubbed this park "biologically intense." Do the math: 140 species of mammals, 370 of birds, and 116 of reptiles and amphibians call the place home all or part of the year. Included in those numbers are the country's largest concentrations of jaguars and scarlet macaws.

Manuel Antonio National Park. You need not travel to the ends of the earth here for a terrific wildlife experience. The country's most visited national park brims with sloths and capuchin and squirrel monkeys. The excellent nearby tourism infrastructure hasn't threatened their habitats—not too much, at least, although that is the age-old concern.

San Gerardo de Dota. At 7,000 to 10,000 feet, San Gerardo's misty heights are Costa Rica at its most mountainous. This cloud forest par excellence is much less crowded than its better-known counterpart at Monteverde, and you stand a better chance here of glimpsing the resplendent quetzal, that Holy Grail among bird-watchers.

Tortuguero National Park. Four species of sea turtles nest on the beaches at this isolated park on the north Caribbean coast. The nighttime spectacle of laying and hatching—in the company of a guide only—never fails to impress.

Local Culture

It's a cliché, but Costa Ricans are some of the friendliest people on earth. For all its world-class rain forests, volcanoes, and beaches, Costa Rica will charm you with its culture. The grand monuments found elsewhere in Latin America don't exist here. The country revels in the understated, sometimes quirky, things instead.

Street art, San José. They take some searching, but some downright whimsical sculptures tuck themselves away among the congested streets of the capital. You'll find monuments to street sweepers, peasants, buxom rural women, Holocaust figure Anne Frank, and Beatle John Lennon.

La Carreta, Sarchí. Oxcarts still transport coffee and sugarcane in rural areas of the Central Valley, and this means of conveyance has become a symbol of Costa Rica. Sarchí pays homage to the oxcart with the world's largest, which looms over its central park.

Magmática, Cartago. Earthquakes have rattled Costa Rica for centuries, although stringent building codes provide a reassuring cushion of safety these days. A Cartago museum fills you in on the hows and whys of tremors and the musts of preparedness. If you're up for it, you can experience the feel of a simulated earthquake, too.

Guaitil pottery, Nicoya. You'll swear the entire village of Guaitil, in the Nicoya peninsula, is populated by artisans who create clay pottery in the style of their indigenous Chorotegan ancestors. You can buy their works in high-end souvenir shops around Costa Rica, but nothing compares to seeing the pieces created at their source.

COSTA RICA OUTDOOR ADVENTURES

ZIP LINING AND CANOPY TOURS

Costa Rica gave the world the so-called canopy tour, a series of zip lines that let you glide through the treetops, attached to a secure harness. Although billed as a way to get up close and personal with nature, your focus and attention will likely be on the ride rather than spotting that elusive resplendent quetzal. No matter. Zip lining has become one of Costa Rica's signature activities for visitors. The term "canopy tour" has expanded to include hanging bridges and elevated trams where you walk or ride through the forest canopy. The latter two really are more effective ways to view all the nature the treetops have to offer.

Zip lines are a fast-paced, thrilling experience. You're attached to a zip line with a safety harness, and then you "fly" at about 15–40 miles per hour from one tree platform to the next. (You may be anywhere from 60 to 300 feet above the forest floor.) Tree-to-tree zip lines date from the 19th century and have been a bona fide activity for visitors to Costa Rica since the mid-1990s when the first tour opened in Monteverde. These tours are tremendous fun, but you won't see any animals. An average fitness level—and above-average level of intrepidness—are all you need. Be brutally frank in assessing your desire and ability to do this, and remember that once you start, there's no turning back.

Bridges and trams are canopy tours in a literal sense, where you walk along suspension bridges, ride along in a tram, or are hoisted up to a platform to get a closer look at birds, monkeys, and sloths. They're also called hanging-bridges tours, sky walks, or platform tours. If seeing nature at a more leisurely pace is your goal, opt for these, especially the bridge excursions. Early mornings are the best time for animal sightings—at 50–250 feet above ground, the views are stupendous.

Best Canopy Tours

El Santuario Canopy Adventure Tour, Manuel Antonio National Park. The mile-plus cable in the system here is Costa Rica's longest single zip line.

Original Canopy Tour, Limón. A branch of Costa Rica's first zip-line tour is the highlight of a nature-themed park near the Caribbean coast.

Osa Canopy Tour, Uvita. One of the South Pacific's few such operations combines zip lines with rappelling stations and a Tarzan swing.

Rain Forest Adventures, Braulio Carrillo National Park. These folks pioneered the concept of guided gondola rides through the canopy.

Rincón de la Vieja Canopy, Rincón de la Vieja National Park. Combine zip lines with horseback riding and sulfur springs on the summit of northern Costa Rica's best-known volcano.

Selvatura, Monteverde Cloud Forest. Some of the longest zip lines in the country are here. There is also an extensive bridge system that lets you walk through the canopy at your own pace.

SPORTFISHING

Adventurous anglers flock to Costa Rica to test their will—and patience—against an assortment of feisty fresh- and saltwater fish. Just remember: catch-and-release is sometimes expected, so the pleasure's all in the pursuit. With so many options, the hardest decision is where to go. Inshore fishing in the country's rivers and lakes yields roosterfish, snapper, barracuda, jacks, and snook. Fly-fishing aficionados love the extra-large tarpon and snook because of their sheer size and fight. The country's coasts swarm with a multitude of bigger game, including the majestic billfish—the marlin and the sailfish. There are many top-notch fishing outfitters up and down both coasts and around rivers and lakes, so planning a fishing trip is easy. Charter boats range from 22 feet to 60 feet in length. With a good captain, a boat in the 22- to 26-foot range for up to three anglers can cost from $500 to $800 a day. A 28- to 32-foot boat fits four and costs from $800 to $1,400 per day. A boat for six people costs $1,400 to $1,800 and measures between 36 and 47 feet. A 60-foot boat for up to 10 anglers costs about $3,000 a day. A good charter boat company employs experienced captains and offers good equipment, bait, and food and beverages.

You're guaranteed a few good catches no matter what the season, as demonstrated by the cadre of sportsmen who circle the coasts year-round chasing that perfect catch. If your heart is set on an area or a type of fish, do your research ahead of time and plan accordingly. Costa Rica teems with a constant supply of fish, some of which might seem unique to North Americans.

Northern Lowlands: Lake Arenal and Caño Negro are great freshwater spots to snag extra-large tarpon, snook, and the ugly-but-fascinating guapote bass. Start your fishing journey in nearby La Fortuna.

Guanacaste: Tamarindo is the main departure point for anglers looking to find big game, including tuna, roosterfish, and marlin. Boats also leave from Playas del Coco, Ocotal, Tambor, and Flamingo Beach, which are best fished May through August. All are close to the well-stocked northern Papagayo Gulf.

Central Pacific coast: If you're hunting sailfish and marlin between December and April, head to the Central Pacific coast around Los Sueños and Quepos, where up to 10 sailfish are caught per boat.

South Pacific: Puerto Jiménez, Golfito, and Zancudo are less developed than the other Pacific regions and are famous for their excellent inshore fishing for snapper and roosterfish, though offshore big game is also good in the area, especially November through January.

Caribbean coast: Barra del Colorado is a popular sportfishing hub and a great departure point for freshwater fishing on the Caribbean side of the country. Fly fishers looking for the ultimate challenge head to the San Juan River for its legendary tarpon. The Colorado River lures anglers with jack, tuna, snook, tarpon, and dorado. Transportation and tours can be arranged by the hotels listed in Tortuguero or Puerto Viejo de Sarapiquí.

SCUBA DIVING AND SNORKELING

For snorkelers and scuba divers, Costa Rica is synonymous with swarms of fish and stretches of coral that hug the country's 802 miles of coastline. Submerge yourself in crystalline waters and enter another world, with bull sharks, brain coral, and toothy green eels. The variety and abundance of marine life are awe-inspiring.

Beach towns on both coasts are riddled with diving schools and equipment-rental shops. Look for outfitters that are PADI (Professional Association of Diving Instructors) trained or give PADI certifications. If you're a first-timer and plan to go diving just once, taking a basic half-day class isn't difficult, and it will allow you to dive up to 40 feet with an instructor. A three- or four-day certification course gets you a lifetime license and allows you to dive up to 130 feet and without a guide.

The Pacific tends to be clearer than the Caribbean, and the fish are bigger and more abundant. Northern waters are generally best May through July, after winds die down and the water turns bluer and warmer. The southern Osa Peninsula is popular during the dry season, from January to April. The Caribbean, known for its diverse coral and small fish, is good for beginners because it has less surge. The best months are September and October, when the ocean is as calm and flat as a swimming pool. April and May also offer decent conditions, but steer clear during the rest of the year, when rain and strong waves cloud the water.

Cahuita. Mounds of coral and a barrier reef (dubbed Long Shoal) run from Cahuita to Punta Mona, along 25 km (15 miles) of Caribbean coastline. Arches, tunnels, and canyons in the reef form a playground for small fish, crabs, and lobsters. Even though sediment and waste water have damaged much of the coral, the healthy sections are dense, colorful, and delightfully shaped. Gentle pools right off the beach allow for some of the country's best snorkeling.

Golfo de Papagayo (Papagayo Gulf). This northern gulf has Costa Rica's highest concentration of snorkel and dive shops. Calm, protected waters make it the best place for beginner divers on the Pacific.

Isla del Coco (Cocos Island). One of the world's premier sites for advanced divers lies 295 nautical miles and a 36-hour sail from Puntarenas. Visibility is good all year, and hammerhead and white-tipped reef sharks are the main attractions.

Isla de Caño (Caño Island). With visibility of 20 to 80 feet, strong currents, and very changeable conditions, Caño is best suited for advanced divers. The huge schools of large fish and potential shark sightings are the attractions here. Novice snorkelers can frolic in the Coral Garden, a shallow area on the north side of this biological reserve.

Isla Santa Catalina (Santa Catalina Island). Known for sightings of golden cownose rays and giant mantas, these big rocks near Playa Flamingo have spots for beginner and advanced divers. Snorkelers should head to shallower waters near the beach.

Isla Murciélago (Bat Island). Located inside Santa Rosa National Park, this cluster of rocks is good for advanced divers and famous for its fearsome bull sharks.

BIRD-WATCHING

Even if you've never seen yourself as a bird-watcher, Costa Rica will get you hooked. Waking you before dawn, calling to you throughout the day, and serenading you through tropical nights, birds are impossible to ignore here. Luckily, Costa Rica has a wealth of world-class ornithologists and local bird guides who can answer all your questions. Every licensed naturalist guide also has some birding expertise, so many tours you take in the country will include some bird-watching.

The sheer variety and abundance of birds here make bird-watching a daily pastime—with less than 0.03% of the planet's surface, Costa Rica counts some 900 bird species, more than the United States and Canada combined. You don't have to stray far from your hotel or even need binoculars to spot, for instance, a kaleidoscopic-colored keel-billed toucan, the bird of Fruit Loops cereal fame. But armed with a pair of binoculars and a birding guide, the sky is literally the limit for the numbers of birds you can see. Catching sight of a brilliantly colored bird is exciting; being able to identify it after a couple of encounters is even more thrilling. For kids, spotting birds makes a great game. With their sharp, young eyes, they're usually very good at it—plus it's wildly educational. About 10% of Costa Rica's birds are endemic, so this is a mecca for bird-watchers intent on compiling an impressive life list.

The best time to bird is November to May, when local species are joined by winter migrants. Breeding season, which varies by species throughout the year, is the easiest time to spot birds, as males put on displays for females, followed by frequent flights to gather nesting material and then food for the chicks. Also keep your eye on fruit-bearing trees that attract hungry birds.

The most sought-after bird is the aptly named resplendent quetzal, sporting brilliant blue, green, and red plumage and long tail feathers. The best places to spot it are **Los Quetzales National Park** in the **Cerro de la Muerte** highlands, the **San Gerardo de Dota** valley, and the **Monteverde Cloud Forest Reserve.** Another bird high on many bird-watchers' lists is the scarlet macaw, the largest of the parrot family here. You'll see pairs performing aerial ballets and munching in beach almond trees in **Corcovado National Park,** along the Osa Peninsula's coastline, and around **Carara National Park** in the Central Pacific region. The **Tempisque River** delta's salty waters, at the north end of the Gulf of Nicoya, are famous for a wealth of water birds, notably wood storks, glossy ibis, and roseate spoonbills. Farther north, in **Palo Verde** and **Caño Negro National Parks,** look for the rarest and largest of wading birds, the Jabiru. The network of jungle-edged natural canals in **Tortuguero National Park,** in the northern Caribbean, is home to a host of herons, including the spectacular rufescent tiger heron and the multi-hued agami heron. More than 50 species of hummingbirds hover around every part of the country. Look for them around feeders at lodges in the **Cerro de la Muerte** area, Monteverde, and the Turrialba region.

BEACHES

Tourism data suggests that about three-fourths of tourists to Costa Rica visit a beach, and with over 800 miles of coastline, you'll find plenty of strands of sand to choose from. From pulverized volcanic rock and steady waves to soft sand and idyllic settings, each of Costa Rica's beaches has its own distinct merits and personality. Some have dominant nationalities too, based on the expat communities who have settled there: Nosara leans German and Swiss, Ojochal is French and Québécois, Potrero is Canadian, and Flamingo is red-white-and-blue American. All are Costa Rican, of course, and all beaches are public here.

We should cite a couple of drawbacks. Costa Rica is neither Cancún nor Bora Bora; beaches here skew toward the dark-sand end of the spectrum. Also, riptides can be dangerous and hardly any Costa Rican beaches have lifeguards; get information from your hotel about where to swim safely. The conditions that make Costa Rican beaches touchy for swimmers make for great surfing, and the country is one of the world's premier destinations for surfers.

Guanacaste and Nicoya Peninsula. Costa Rica's driest climate makes the North Pacific coast the country's Beach Central. Popular luxury resorts line the beaches of the Papagayo Peninsula. Lively Tamarindo is a hyped-up surfing and watersports beach with solid nightlife. Playas Hermosa and Sámara are family-friendly spots with swimmable waters; and Playas Langosta and Pelada are made for contemplative walks. Montezuma's off-beat town is as much a draw as its bayside beach. Some of the largest surfing waves in Costa Rica are at Malpaís.

Central Pacific. Two powerhouse beaches anchor this easily accessible stretch of coast closest to San José, and your fellow tourists here are just as likely to be Costa Ricans, making reservations a must during high-season weekends. A terrific national park and a lively tourist scene—straight and gay—make the palm-lined beaches collectively known as "Manuel Antonio" Costa Rica's most popular tourist destination. Farther up the coast, Jacó gets mixed reviews; it has acquired cachet in surfing circles but others bemoan its unchecked development. In between, surfers, Ticos, and foreigners have laid claim to the smaller beaches at Herradura, Hermosa, Bejuco, and Esterillos.

South Pacific. The long southern coast begins at the friendly, somewhat ramshackle beach town of Dominical. Once quite remote, up-and-coming Playas Uvita and Ballena are more accessible than ever, thanks to the construction of a new coastal highway. Each passing year sees the addition of snazzy new dining and lodging options. There's an end-of-the-world feel in the air if you make it to remote, rocky, black-sand Playa Pavones, down near the Panamanian border.

Caribbean. European backpackers discovered the dark-sand beaches at Cahuita and Puerto Viejo de Talamanca decades ago. Neither place has entirely outgrown those party roots, although both brim with more grown-up offerings too. The north Caribbean coast proffers a different kind of "nightlife" in the form of the age-old spectacle of nocturnal nesting of four species of sea turtle.

SURFING

Costa Rica's big surfing community, consistent waves, and not-too-crowded beaches make surfing accessible to anyone who is curious enough to paddle into the line up; surf schools and board rentals are plentiful.

At many of Costa Rica's top surf spots, a wide range of ages and skills can be found bobbing together in the water. With the right board—ideally a foam longboard for first timers—and good instruction, just about anybody can stand up and ride. Trained instructors can adapt lessons to different levels, ages, and body types. If you want to get a head start before your vacation, practice pop-ups at home (YouTube has dozens of tutorials) or swim laps at your local pool to get in shape before your first wipe out.

With warm water, offshore winds, and friendly locals, you really can't find a better place to learn the sport. Costa Ricans are known for their pura vida attitude, and this usually translates into a welcoming vibe in the water. Just steer clear of the hot shots until you know local protocol.

On the Pacific, waves are consistent from December through April. As you move southward, the breaks are best from May to November. On the Caribbean side, conditions are best January through April.

Dominical, Pacific Coast. A long set of fast, powerful breaks that are great for advanced levels. When waves get too big, head south to Dominicalito.

Esterillos, Pacific Coast. Divided into three beaches, this wide stretch of coast is uncrowded to the point of desolation. The surf and currents can be tough for beginners, and Este and Centro have waves much like Hermosa. Oeste has softer waves.

Jacó, Pacific Coast. Unless the surf gets too big, the consistent beach breaks produce forgiving waves that are good for beginner to intermediate surfers.

Malpaís, Pacific Coast. A variety of beach breaks plus a point break that's good when waves are pumping.

Manuel Antonio, Pacific Coast. Playitas, at the national park's north end, is perhaps the most consistent spot here. It's only good at high tide, about three hours per day, and usually flat September through December.

Pavones, Pacific Coast. This advanced and fickle spot is said to be one of the world's longest lefts, lasting nearly three minutes.

Playa Cocles, Caribbean Coast. Plenty of beach breaks and good for all levels, but beware of riptides.

Playa Guiones, Pacific Coast. If not the best surf in the vicinity of Nosara, it's the best beach break for beginners and longboarders, with plenty of long rights and lefts.

Playa Hermosa, Pacific Coast. A steep beach break just south of Jacó with some of the country's best barrels and surfers. Waves can get big, mean, hollow, and thunderously heavy.

Salsa Brava, Caribbean Coast. When it's on, this is arguably Costa Rica's best and most powerful wave, breaking right over a shallow coral reef.

Sámara, Pacific Coast. Protected, mellow beach breaks great for beginners, yet close to advanced spots like Playa Camaronal.

Tamarindo, Pacific Coast. Surfer's paradise for all levels, with famous breaks like Ollie's Point, Playa Avellanas and Playa Negra (south), and Witch's Rock (north). Solid waves are formed at a point break called Pico Pequeño and at the river mouth called El Estero at the beach's north end.

WEDDINGS AND HONEYMOONS

Ever dreamed of getting married on a sandy beach shaded by palm trees? Many people who envision such a scene immediately think of the Caribbean. But Costa Rica is fast becoming a favored destination for tropical nuptials.

Compared with the complicated procedures in many other destinations, getting married in Costa Rica is easy. There are no residency restrictions or blood-test requirements. At least a month in advance, couples of the opposite sex who are over 18 should provide their local wedding planner with a copy of their birth certificates and passports so they can be submitted to the local authorities. Same-sex unions have no legal status in Costa Rica—the matter is under consideration—but wedding planners here have arranged commitment ceremonies.

Any previous marriage complicates things a bit. The couple needs to provide documentation that the marriage was terminated. Divorce papers or death certificate of a previous spouse must be translated into Spanish and notarized.

The Big Day

Judges, attorneys, and Catholic priests have legal authority to certify a marriage in Costa Rica. (Most foreign couples avoid the latter because a Catholic wedding requires months of preparation.) The official ceremony is simple, but couples are free to add their own vows or anything else they would like. The officiant will register the marriage with the civil registry and the couple's embassy.

At the wedding, the couple needs to have at least two witnesses who are not family members. Many couples choose their best man and maid of honor. If necessary, the wedding planner can provide witnesses.

The license itself takes three months to issue and is sent to the couple's home address. For an extra fee, couples can ask for the process to be expedited. Virtually all Western countries recognize the legality of a Costa Rican marriage.

Beautiful Backdrops

Although Costa Rica offers no shortage of impressive backdrops for a ceremony, the Central Pacific coast sees the most tourist weddings and honeymoons. May and June are the most popular months for foreigners, but many people choose January or February because you are virtually guaranteed sunny skies. (Costa Ricans favor December weddings.) Manuel Antonio's Makanda by the Sea, La Mariposa, Sí Como No, and Punta Leona's Villa Caletas are among the many lodgings here with events staff well versed in planning ceremonies and tending to the legalities.

There are many details to attend to: flowers, music, and photography. Most large hotels have on-staff wedding planners to walk you through the process. Couples can also hire their own wedding planner, which is often less expensive. Either way, wedding planners have a wide range of services available, and couples can pick and choose.

Honeymoons

As far as honeymoons go, no place in Costa Rica is inappropriate. Although honeymoons on the beach, especially along the Northern Pacific and Central Pacific coasts, are popular, many couples opt for treks to the mountains or the rain forests. Dozens of newlyweds choose offbeat adventures, such as spotting sea turtles along the Caribbean coast or swimming with pilot whales off the Osa Peninsula.

THE PEOPLE OF COSTA RICA

Unlike many of its neighbors, Costa Rica never had a dominant indigenous population. When Christopher Columbus arrived in the early 16th century, he didn't encounter empires like those in present-day Mexico and Peru. Instead, a small contingent of indigenous Caribs rowed out in canoes to meet his ship. The heavy gold bands the indigenous peoples wore led to Columbus mistakenly calling the land Costa Rica, or "Rich Coast."

On the mainland, the Spanish encountered disparate peoples like the Chorotega, Bribri, Cabécar, and Boruca peoples. Archaeological evidence shows that they had lived in the region for thousands of years. But that would change with breathtaking speed. European diseases felled many of their members, and the brutality of slavery imposed by the colonial power drove most of those remaining into the mountains.

Some of these peoples still exist, although in relatively small communities. Several thousand Bribri, Kekoldi, and other peoples live in villages scattered around Talamanca, a mountainous region close to the border of Panama. Although many traditions have been lost over the years, some have managed to retain their own languages and religions. If you're interested in seeing the local culture, tour companies in the coastal communities of Limón and Puerto Viejo de Talamanca can arrange visits to these villages.

That isn't to say that there's no local culture. More than 90% of the country's residents are *mestizos*, or mixed-race descendants of the Spanish. But few people express any pride in their Spanish heritage. Perhaps that is because Spain had little interest in Costa Rica, the smallest and poorest of its Central American colonies. Instead, the people here created a unique culture that mixes parts of Europe, Latin America, and the Caribbean. There's a strong emphasis on education, and the 95% literacy rate is by far the highest in the region. There's a laid-back attitude toward life, typified by the common greeting of *pura vida*, which translates literally as "pure life" but means something between "no worries" and "don't sweat the small stuff."

It sounds like a cliché, but Costa Ricans are an incredibly welcoming people. Anyone who has visited other Central American countries will be surprised at how Ticos seem genuinely happy to greet newcomers. If you ever find yourself lost in a town or village, you may find locals more than willing to not only point you in the right direction but walk you all the way to your destination.

Other cultures have added their own spice to Costa Rica. On the Caribbean coast you'll find Afro-Caribbean peoples, descendants of Jamaicans who arrived in the late 19th century to build the railroad and remained to work on banana and cacao plantations. In the seaside town of Limón, cruise ships frequently call, and the passengers who hurry down the gangplank encounter steel-drum music, braided hair, and rickety houses painted every color of the rainbow. They may think that they have discovered the "real" Costa Rica, and they have, in a way. But they also have barely scratched the surface.

FLAVORS OF COSTA RICA

A common misconception among first-time visitors to Costa Rica is that all south-of-the-U.S.-border cuisine is the same. This is absolutely not the case—the only place you'll dine on tacos and fajitas here is in a Mexican restaurant. Although Costa Rican food is not spicy, you'll frequently find homemade *chilero* sauces—cauliflower, carrots, onions, and hot peppers pickled in vinegar—in a jar on tables in local restaurants to spoon onto your food for more of a kick. It's always optional, of course. Costa Rican cuisine is hearty and mild, but certainly not the country's biggest draw. *Comida típica,* or "typical food," consists primarily of chicken, pork, beans, and rice, although kitchens around the country serve sophisticated Thai, Indian, Italian, and Lebanese cuisine.

Start with the Staples

The cilantro-and-onion-flavored pot of black beans cooked with yesterday's rice, known as *gallo pinto* (literally "spotted rooster"), is synonymous with all things Costa Rican—"As Tico as gallo pinto" is a common expression here. Mounds of this hearty dish, served with scrambled eggs, tortillas, and sour cream, can be had in all of the quintessential local eateries called *sodas.* (Costa Rican Spanish calls a carbonated beverage a *gaseosa.*) Gallo pinto usually serves as a breakfast staple—even McDonald's has embraced the dish on its morning menu—but it shows up for lunch and dinner in Costa Rican homes, too. The ubiquitous Salsa Lizano just might deserve to be classified as its own Costa Rican food group. No self-respecting Costa Rican kitchen is without this condiment resembling a thick Worcestershire sauce.

Lunch is typically the biggest meal of the day here. If you're watching your budget, follow that lead; you'll find omnipresent midday restaurant specials, and upscale restaurants go equally posh in their lunchtime terminology, offering an *almuerzo ejecutivo* or "executive lunch" special. *Casado* (married) is a plate that "marries" rice with cabbage salad, fried plantains, and a main entrée of beef, chicken, pork, or fish; it's always the lunchtime bargain in mom-and-pop Costa Rican restaurants. Hearty dishes of *olla de carne* (a beef and vegetable stew) and *sopa negra* (a black-bean soup with a poached egg) will fortify you for an afternoon of sightseeing, too. The mildly seasoned *arroz con pollo* (chicken with rice) makes a good choice if you're not feeling too adventurous. Few visitors develop a taste for *chicharrones,* fried pork rinds.

Add the Bounty of the Land

You've never seen so many fruits and vegetables. The usual suspects like bananas, oranges, pineapples, lemons, mangoes, potatoes, and cabbage are all ubiquitous, but a walk through any Costa Rican market turns up new products you won't find back home. Most visitors develop a fondness for *carambola,* or star fruit, a mildly sweet treat that's perfect on a warm day.

Don't try eating plantains raw—*plátanos* should always be cooked. They end up as a side dish in casados around the country. The Caribbean coast always marches to its own drummer, of course, and cooks there mash them, fry them, and serve them as *patacones* with a touch of salt. Plátanos, along with breadfruit and yams, also get mixed in with fish or meat to make *rondón,* a hearty Caribbean stew. Coconut (*coco*) infuses Caribbean cuisine, most notably the long-simmering rice and beans—the name is always in English—that bears no resemblance to the gallo pinto you've been eating elsewhere in Costa Rica. Roadside vendors around the country will whack a coconut in half with a machete, insert a straw, and, voilà, you have a refreshing drink called *agua de pipa*.

Costa Rica is one of the world's top exporters of *palmito,* the heart of palm that is a staple in salads here. The starchy palm fruit *pejibaye* is cooked and served with a dollop of mayonnaise. *Ensalada rusa,* the so-called Russian salad, mixes beets with potatoes, eggs, and mayonnaise, and is a must-have in the arsenal of any Costa Rican cook. *Elote,* or roasted corn on the cob, is a favorite at any small-town Costa Rican celebration. The hearty, gourdlike *chayote* and the starchy cassava root *yuca* taste bland on their own, but as ingredients in other dishes, assume a variety of flavors.

Wash It Down

Café con leche mixes strongly brewed coffee with milk and lots of sugar for breakfast. Your best bet for a decent cup of coffee, however, is always an upscale restaurant that's attuned to foreign tastes. It will keep export-quality product on hand. Costa Rica's signature beverage takes center stage again mid-afternoon when seemingly the entire country takes a coffee break. Natural fruit juices, called *frescos,* also come with teeth-shattering amounts of sugar, but the variety of flavors is astounding. If you're watching your own or your child's intake, request one with only a little sugar (*con poco azúcar*); chances are it will be sweet enough, but you can always top it off if need be. For a less sweet alternative, try an *horchata,* a beverage made of cornmeal and flavored with cinnamon. It's a Guanacaste specialty.

Cervecería Costa Rica, the country's sole large brewery, has a virtual monopoly on beer production, but makes some respectable lagers that pair well with beach lounging. Iconic Imperial (known by the red, black, and yellow eagle logo that adorns bar signs and tourist T-shirts) is everybody's favorite. The slightly bitter Pilsen is a close runner-up, followed by the gold, dark, and light variations of Bavaria. Feeling brave? *Guaro,* the locally distilled sugarcane firewater, really packs a punch; surprisingly, its distillation is exclusively a state enterprise. The various rums of the locally made Ron Centenario are respectable, but less well-known outside of Costa Rica—and even here, Nicaragua's famous Flor de Caña rum has made huge inroads. House wines are typically a low-end Chilean choice (this simply isn't wine-drinking country). Our advice? Go tropical! The country's abundant tropical fruit juices mix refreshingly well with local rums or, in a pinch, with a dash of guaro.

Leave Room for Dessert

You'll soon realize that Costa Ricans like things sweet; the country has one of the world's highest rates of sugar consumption—and, alas, also a high incidence of type 2 diabetes. *Tres leches* mixes three milks (evaporated, condensed, and whole)—the name means "three milks"—into a very sweet sponge cake. As an alternative, *cajeta de coco* is a tasty coconut fudge. *Pan de maíz* translates literally as "corn bread," but all the sugar in the recipe makes it more like a corn cake instead.

GREAT ITINERARIES

Costa Rica looks disarmingly small on the map. This country the size of Vermont and New Hampshire combined *should* be easy to take in, right? Arrive here and you'll see that a mountainous spine transects the country and dirt roads make driving downright abysmal. Ambitious plans to see the entire country never materialize. Rather than rushing around—and rushing is something you can't easily do here—pick and choose a couple of destinations and get to know them well.

Lay of the Land

San José and the Central Valley. Costa Rica's congested capital sits smack-dab in the center of the country. Since it's the country's transportation hub, you'll likely pass through, even if only on your first and last days here. Coming to Costa Rica on business? You'll probably get to know the city well. San José gives way to bustling suburbs, then smaller towns, then pastoral countryside ringing the capital in a mountain valley (elevation 3,000–5,000 feet). Take in the valley as day trips from the city or base yourself out here. San José's Aeropuerto Internacional Juan Santamaría sits in the Central Valley, too.

The North. Transportation is straightforward in the vast, mostly flat northern one-third of the country that makes up the Northern Lowlands. This area has two of Costa Rica's biggest attractions, Arenal Volcano and Monteverde Cloud Forest. Roads are decent here, with the exception of the notoriously awful route to Monteverde—and, even here, paving is on the drawing board. You'd think a highway, north to south, would line the northern Pacific coast, making it easy to bop among this region's famed beaches and down through the Nicoya Peninsula. However, you frequently have to head back inland to get to the next strand of sand down the coast. If this area is your sole destination, book your flights to Liberia's Aeropuerto Internacional Daniel Oduber Quirós, rather than down in San José.

Manuel Antonio and the Central Pacific Coast. A spiffy highway puts San José an hour or two from the beaches along this section of the coast. That's great for the tourism industry here, but you should book space for holidays and high-season weekends in advance: Costa Ricans love to take mini-breaks to this region, too.

The Osa Peninsula and the South Pacific. The south is rarely first-timer's territory—even most Costa Ricans have never ventured to the southern third of their country, a land of remote beaches, mountains, and wilderness eco-lodges. Transportation is improving to and within this splendid region, but can still be a chore. Sample it, though, and you might count yourself among the growing number of fans.

Tortuguero and the Caribbean Coast. Once you get over the hump of the mountains north of San José, a good road puts you directly en route to the sultry, tropical, southern Caribbean coast, still largely the province of European visitors and less known in American circles. The northern Caribbean coast near Tortuguero National Park is a different story entirely: no roads exist up here, making boat or plane your only travel options.

Timing

Costa Rican Tourist Board surveys show that U.S. visitors spend an average of nine days on a trip here. That's ample occasion to take in destinations in a couple of regions, and it accounts for time to get from one place to the other. (Depending on the places you choose, that last part can be more of a chore than you may

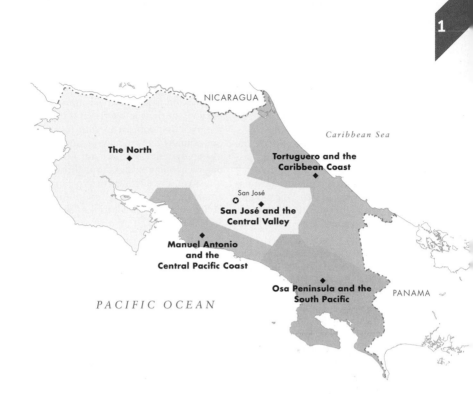

NICARAGUA

Caribbean Sea

The North
◆

Tortuguero and the
Caribbean Coast
◆

San José
✪

San José and the
Central Valley
◆

Manuel Antonio
and the
Central Pacific Coast
◆

Osa Peninsula and the
South Pacific
◆

PANAMA

PACIFIC OCEAN

realize.) Rather than packing too much in, keep repeating that most Costa Rican of expressions: *si Dios lo quiere.* If God is willing, you'll get back here to partake of what you didn't see the first time around.

Itineraries

We proffer five possible itineraries, each taking in a small slice of the country and showcasing some of the crowd-pleasing destinations for which Costa Rica is known. The San José, Central Valley, and Tortuguero itinerary leans more toward the "leave the driving to them" end of the spectrum; the Osa Peninsula itinerary incorporates domestic air travel. If you have time, these itineraries can be combined or broken apart and reassembled to suit your needs. If you are doing the driving, remember the sun sets here around 5:30 pm all year long, give or take about 15 minutes. Always plan to arrive at your destination before dark.

Peak Season: December to April

The Christmas-to-Easter period essentially defines Costa Rica's high season. With little rain and temperatures in the 80s and higher, the country makes an ideal escape for North Americans and Europeans fleeing those frigid winters.

GREAT ITINERARIES

BEST OF COSTA RICA: 7-DAY ITINERARY

Volcanoes and beaches are two of the things Costa Rica does best, so the classic first-timer's itinerary to Costa Rica takes in two of its most popular destinations: the impressive Arenal Volcano and the beaches of the Central Pacific coast's lovely Manuel Antonio.

DAY 1: SAN JOSÉ

Arrive in **San José's Aeropuerto Internacional Juan Santamaría** (most arrivals are in the evening) and head straight to one of the small hotels north of the city in the **Central Valley.** The airport lies northwest of the capital, so staying in San José requires a bit of backtracking. The **Hampton Inn** just across from the airport lets you ease into your Costa Rican experience in familiar surroundings; the **Xandari Resort & Spa** offers a far more local, and pricier, first night here. Brace yourself for lines at immigration if you arrive in the evening along with several other large flights from North America. Try to get a seat near the front of the plane, and don't dawdle when disembarking.

DAY 2: POÁS VOLCANO AND TABACÓN HOT SPRINGS

(45 minutes by paved road from airport to Poás Volcano; 2½ hours by paved road from airport to La Fortuna)

If you have the time, set out early for **Poás Volcano,** where you can peer over the edge of the crater. It makes an interesting start to your first full day in Costa Rica. Fortify yourself with the fruits, jellies, and chocolates sold by vendors on the road up to the summit. Otherwise, get going to the Arenal area right away. Set out on the scenic drive—turn north at San Ramón—to **La Fortuna,** which sits at the foot of **Arenal**

Volcano and is its hub. Bear in mind that portions of the route twist and turn and fog over by noon. Drop your luggage at one of many fantastic hotels, and partake of the myriad activities here. Take a zipline or hanging-bridges tour through the forest canopy north of the volcano with amazing views of the mountain itself. Follow up with a visit to the **Tabacón Hot Springs & Resort** to pamper yourself with a spa treatment. Finish the day by sinking into a volcanically heated mineral bath with a cocktail at your side as the sun sets behind Volcán Arenal.

Shuttle vans have hotel-to-hotel service, usually from the Hampton Inn to many Arenal-area hotels. You can stay right at Tabacón and have access to facilities there not open to day or evening visitors. **Nayara Hotel & Spa** also offers terrific views of Arenal Volcano.

DAY 3: CAÑO NEGRO WILDLIFE REFUGE

(90 minutes by paved road from La Fortuna)

Spend the day in the **Caño Negro Wildlife Refuge,** a lowland forest reserve replete with waterfowl near the Nicaraguan border. Book your trip the night before; tour operators in La Fortuna keep evening hours for exactly that reason. All transport is included, and it's far easier than trying to visit the refuge on your own.

DAY 4: SCENIC DRIVE TO THE CENTRAL PACIFIC

(4–4½ hours by paved road from La Fortuna)

Today's a traveling day—a chance to really see the country's famous landscape. Four hours' drive from Arenal takes you to fabled **Manuel Antonio** on the Central Pacific coast. Beyond-beautiful hotels are the norm here, and you have your choice of seaside luxury—we like the **Arenas del**

Los Chiles

Caño Negro
Wildlife Refuge

NICARAGUA

Caribbean
Sea

Tabacón Hot Springs & Resort / Nayara Hotel & Spa
Arenal Volcano   La Fortuna

Poás Volcano

San Ramón   Alajuela   Central
Atenas   Valley

Juan Santamaria
International Airport   San José

PACIFIC OCEAN

Jacó

Quepos

Manuel Antonio
National Park/
Beaches

Mar Beachfront and Nature Resort—or tree-shrouded lodges like **Villas Nicolás.**

Hotel-to-hotel shuttle-van services can get you from Arenal to Manuel Antonio. If you drive instead, start out as early as possible. You'll pass again through the mountainous stretch between La Fortuna and San Ramón—that's the way you came—to get back to the main highway heading east. Exit at **Atenas,** a pleasant town that makes a good lunch stop. South of Atenas, hook up with the Pacific Highway—follow the signs directing you to Caldera. The Jacó exit takes you on the fairly good road to Manuel Antonio.

DAY 5: MANUEL ANTONIO NATIONAL PARK
(10–20 minutes from most area lodgings)

Manuel Antonio is Costa Rica's most famous national park for a reason: it has beaches, lush rain forest, mangrove swamps, and rocky coves with abundant marine life. You can—and should—spend an entire day exploring the park, home to capuchin monkeys, sloths, agoutis, and 200 species of birds. It's also one of two locales in the country where you'll see squirrel monkeys. Almost all Manuel Antonio hotels have transport to the park. If yours doesn't, taxis are plentiful and cheap. Don't forget: the park is closed on Monday.

DAY 6: BEACHES
(10–20 minutes from most area lodgings)

Days 1 through 5 were on-the-go days. Reward yourself today with lots of relaxation. One of Costa Rica's most popular strands of sand, **Playa Espadilla** hums with activity on weekends and holidays. Alas, riptides can make swimming risky here. Within the national park, **Playa Manuel Antonio** and **Playa Espadilla Sur** offer more seclusion, but no real facilities. Manuel Antonio and its neighboring town, **Quepos,** have the best selection of restaurants of any beach community in the country.

DAY 7: SAN JOSÉ
(2–2½ hours by paved road from Manuel Antonio)

An easy morning drive back to San José gives you time to spend the afternoon in the city. Visit the **Teatro Nacional** and the **Museo de Oro Precolombino,** and save time for late-afternoon shopping. An evening dinner caps off your trip before you turn in early to get ready for tomorrow morning's departure. We recommend that you check in three hours before your flight.

GREAT ITINERARIES

DAY TRIPS FROM PLAYA HERMOSA: 6-DAY ITINERARY

The province of Guanacaste and the Nicoya Peninsula are known as Costa Rica's "fun in the sun" destination. Kids and adults alike enjoy the region's huge variety of land- and water-based activities.

DAYS 1 AND 2: PLAYA HERMOSA
(30 minutes by paved road from Liberia airport)

Most arrivals to **Liberia's Aeropuerto Internacional Daniel Oduber Quirós,** Costa Rica's second international airport, are in the early afternoon. You can't go wrong with any North Pacific beach, but we like **Playa Hermosa** for its location about 30 minutes from the airport—it's convenient as a base for visiting area attractions. The smaller lodgings here make the perfect antidote to the megaresorts that are not too far away. They can arrange to have transport waiting at the airport, with advance notice. **Hotel La Finisterra** perches above the ocean; the pricier **Hotel Playa Hermosa Bosque del Mar** hugs the beach itself. The big all-inclusives up here have their own minivans to whisk you in air-conditioned comfort from airport to resort. Otherwise, the airport contains the full selection of car-rental counters.

Start Day 2 off lazing on the beach. Morning is a great time of day to hit the beach in this part of Costa Rica—the breezes are refreshingly cool and the sun hasn't started to beat down yet. After lunch, explore Playa Hermosa's "metropolis," the small town of **Playas del Coco.** Quite frankly, Coco is our least favorite beach up here. But we like the town for its little souvenir shops, restaurants, and local color.

Taxis are the easiest way to travel between Playa Hermosa and Coco, about 10 minutes away. Have your hotel call one, and flag one down on the street in town when it's time to return.

DAY 3: RINCÓN DE LA VIEJA VOLCANO
(1½-hour drive from Playa Hermosa, the last 45 minutes by dirt and stone road)

The top of **Rincón de la Vieja Volcano,** with its steaming, bubbling, oozing fumaroles, lies about 90 minutes from Hermosa. Lather on the sunscreen and head for the **Hacienda Guachipelín**—tours are open to non-hotel guests, too—and its volcano-viewing hikes, canopy tours, rappelling, horseback riding, mountain biking, and river tubing. Cap off the day with a spa treatment, complete with thermal mud bath.

If you don't have a rental car, book a private driver for the day, which can usually be arranged through your hotel. The region has seen an increase in tour operators who can take you to area attractions, too, which your hotel can arrange.

If you are driving yourself, you may wish to spend the night up here and not trek back down to the coast the same day. Hacienda Guachipelín itself is a solid lodging value.

DAY 4: GOLF OR DIVING
(30 minutes by paved road from Playa Hermosa to Papagayo Golf & Country Club; 10 minutes by paved road from Playa Hermosa to Playas del Coco)

Golf is big up here. The 18-hole **Papagayo Golf & Country Club** is just southeast of Playas del Coco. The other popular, slightly pricey, sport here is scuba diving. Dive operators are based in nearby Playas del Coco—we like **Rich Coast Diving**—or Playa Panamá. A daylong diving course won't certify you, but gives you a taste of the

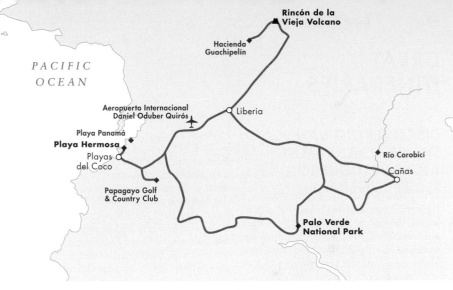

PACIFIC
OCEAN

Rincón de la
Vieja Volcano

Hacienda
Guachipelín

Aeropuerto Internacional
Daniel Oduber Quirós

Liberia

Playa Panamá
Playa Hermosa
Playas
del Coco

Río Corobicí

Cañas

Papagayo Golf
& Country Club

**Palo Verde
National Park**

deep. A taxi can transport you to and from the golf course, and dive operators will pick you up from and return you to your hotel.

DAY 5: PALO VERDE NATIONAL PARK
(1½ hours by paved road from Playa Hermosa to Palo Verde, the last 45 minutes by dirt road)

Start with a morning guided tour at **Palo Verde National Park,** one of the last remaining dry tropical forests in Central America. The **Organization for Tropical Studies,** which operates the biological station here, has terrific guides. Spend the afternoon observing nature in a more relaxed fashion with a float (easy Class I and II rapids) down the nearby Río Corobicí. The aptly named **Safaris Corobicí,** near Cañas on the Pan-American Highway, specializes in the floating trips. This excursion is a bit roundabout, so this is the day your own vehicle would come in handiest. But you can also hire a private driver or get a tour operator to fix you up (arranged through your hotel). Bring water to drink: it gets hot here.

DAY 6: DEPARTURE
(30 minutes by paved road from Playa Hermosa)

Grab a last dip in the ocean this morning, because your flight departs from Liberia

TIPS

■ A car is ideal for this itinerary, yet many area attractions and tour operators provide transport to and from area lodging if you aren't too far afield.

■ All-inclusive resorts do a good job of organizing local excursions with local operators, so if you're staying at one, take advantage of them.

■ Getting from beach to beach often requires travel back inland. There is no real (i.e., navigable) coastal road.

■ If ever there were a case for an off-season vacation, this is it. This driest, hottest part of the country gets very dry and hot from January through April. We prefer the region during the low season after April.

in the early afternoon. The airport terminal is modern and spacious, but you should still allow yourself plenty of time for check-in.

GREAT ITINERARIES

DISCOVERING SAN JOSÉ, THE CENTRAL VALLEY, AND TORTUGUERO: 7-DAY ITINERARY

It's entirely possible to take in a mix of urban, suburban, and remote Costa Rica without having to rent a car with this let-someone-else-do-the-driving itinerary. Tortuguero, on the Caribbean coast, is accessible only by boat.

DAY 1: ARRIVAL

Following your evening arrival in **San José,** head to one of the many in-town lodgings. **Hotel Grano de Oro,** west of downtown, or **Hôtel Le Bergerac,** east of downtown, are good options. Your hotel can arrange for transport with advance notice. The big players have their own hotel shuttle vans, but smaller lodgings can arrange for a taxi. Otherwise, grab one of the official orange airport cabs at the customs exit. Plan on spending $25–$30 for a taxi ride into the city.

DAY 2: SAN JOSÉ

A full day in the city gives you time to spend the morning visiting the **Teatro Nacional** and the **Museo de Oro Precolombino**—they're on the same block. Duck into the **Museo del Jade** in the afternoon, especially if it's raining, or partake of some late-afternoon crafts shopping. An evening dinner at one of San José's fine restaurants caps off the day. Asian restaurant **Tin Jo** is one of the country's top dining experiences.

DAY 3: DAY TOURS TO THE CENTRAL VALLEY

San José's location makes it the perfect place from which to fan out to the Central Valley's many sights. The list of things to see and do in the valley is impressive:

learn all about coffee at the installations of **Café Britt,** near Heredia, or the **Doka Estate,** near Alajuela; peer over the rim into bubbling cauldrons of the **Poás** or **Irazú** volcanoes; wander among fluttering butterflies at the **Butterfly Farm** in Alajuela; step back into history in the **Orosi Valley;** learn what makes nature tick at **INBioparque,** in Santo Domingo; or shop for crafts in **Sarchí,** the country's signature artisan town. Hitting all the attractions in one day is next to impossible, of course—Café Britt and INBioparque lie 30 minutes or less from the capital, but plan on up to an hour to reach the others. San José's several tour operators offer half- or full-day excursions that incorporate various Central Valley attractions, or can tailor one that fits your interests. Plan to be picked up from your hotel between 7 and 8 in the morning and return after midday for a half-day tour, or around 5 for a daylong excursion.

DAYS 4 AND 5: TORTUGUERO

(2 hours by paved road plus 2–2½ hours by boat from San José)

An early-morning pickup at your San José hotel and you are off to one of Costa Rica's most remote destinations. Once you traverse **Braulio Carrillo National Park** north of the capital, you switch from van to boat at a put-in point in the Caribbean lowlands. The final stretch to **Tortuguero** takes place by boat; this is a roadless part of Costa Rica. Arrive at your lodge by mid-afternoon. Rest and get cleaned up for a sumptuous buffet dinner.

Although you can do Tortuguero on your own, most visitors opt for an all-inclusive tour. **Pachira Lodge,** along the main canal, or the more secluded **Evergreen Lodge** are good options.

The knock at the door comes early in the morning of Day 5 as you are roused out of bed to go on a prebreakfast bird-watching excursion in **Tortuguero National Park.** (Remember: there are no roads, so transport is by boat.) The day entails a guided hike in the national park and a stroll through the tiny village of the same name. Evenings give way to turtle-watching during the nesting season (July through October).

Tortuguero is the rainiest spot in Costa Rica, and the rains spread evenly throughout the year. Plan to get wet (it's half the fun). Most of the lodges here provide ponchos and rain boots.

DAY 6: BACK TO SAN JOSÉ
(60–90 minutes by boat plus 2 hours by paved road from Tortuguero)

Day 6 is your fourth day in reverse. After a hearty breakfast at your lodge, you board the launches back to civilization. The boat travels faster than it did on the way up here. You transfer to a waiting van at the put-in point and head back to your city hotel, arriving in the afternoon. Tortuguero lodges do offer two-day/one-night excursions, but go for the extra day if your schedule permits.

TIPS

■ Tortuguero has no roads. Forget the car and let someone else take care of your transportation needs.

■ Many San José hotels will allow you to leave your things while you're touring outside the city, a particular boon when you're headed to Tortuguero. Space inside the small boats is limited.

■ July through October is prime turtle-nesting season in Tortuguero.

■ If you have more money than time, the Tortuguero lodges can arrange for you to fly to and from San José on domestic airlines Nature Air or SANSA.

DAY 7: DEPARTURE
(30–45 minutes from San José)

Most international flights depart Aeropuerto Internacional Juan Santamaría in the morning. Recommended check-in time is always three hours in advance of departure.

GREAT ITINERARIES

THE WILD OSA PENINSULA: 8-DAY ITINERARY

Most travelers who make it this far south already have a trip to Costa Rica under their belts, but feel free to break that rule. All you need is a spirit of adventure.

DAY 1: ARRIVAL

Following your arrival in **San José,** head to one of the several lodgings near the airport. We recommend staying out here rather than heading into San José itself, about 30 minutes away; you need to be back at the airport the next morning for your flight to the Osa Peninsula, and you'll appreciate the extra time. You cannot get closer to the airport than the **Hampton Inn,** just across the highway. Wherever you stay, your hotel can arrange for transport with advance notice, whether its own shuttle vans or sending a taxi for you. Otherwise, grab one of the official orange airport cabs as you exit customs.

DAY 2: SAN JOSÉ TO PUERTO JIMÉNEZ TO CABO MATAPALO

(1 hour by air to Puerto Jiménez and 1 hour by gravel road)

You're back at the airport for your hour-long flight to Puerto Jiménez on either of the country's two domestic airlines: Nature Air is inside the international terminal; SANSA has its own building. Check-in is a leisurely affair, but you should arrive at the airport at least 45 minutes before departure. Arrival at the airstrip in Puerto Jiménez, Osa's "metropolis," is even more low-key. Our recommended lodgings in Cabo Matapalo, 21 km (14 miles) south, can arrange for transfers. Each has its own style: **Lapa Ríos** rates as one of the world's premier eco-lodges; **El Remanso** is quiet and intimate;

Bosque del Cabo draws an engaging, sociable clientele.

DAYS 3 AND 4: NATURE EXCURSIONS

The Cabo Matapalo lodges offer their own nature-themed activities. They range from quiet hikes to snorkeling to horseback riding to more strenuous rappelling and climbing. Highly regarded local tour operator **Everyday Adventures** takes you on excursions that skew toward the adrenaline-rush end of the spectrum. The end of the day puts you back at your lodge, chatting with other guests well into the evening about what you saw that day.

DAY 5: CABO MATAPALO TO CARATE

(1 hour by road)

Carate is literally Osa's end of the road. The lodges here can arrange for an overland transfer from Cabo Matapalo or all the way from Puerto Jiménez if you're skipping Matapalo entirely. Accommodations here have their own personalities, too: **Finca Exótica** caters to nature lovers, **Luna Lodge** is for the yoga or wellness devotee. A trip to the beach rounds out your day. Alas, as is the case elsewhere in Costa Rica, riptides are dangerous here.

DAY 6: CORCOVADO NATIONAL PARK

(45-minute hike to La Leona park entrance from Carate; half day or full day of hiking in park)

If you've come this far, Costa Rica's famed **Corcovado National Park** should be on your agenda. The lodges here can arrange for guided walks to the park—it's the only way to approach Corcovado from this direction. You must enter Corcovado accompanied by a guide and you must pay your entry fee in advance. Accommodation inside the park—advance reservations are mandatory—is rustic. Any overnights would necessitate adding extra days onto this itinerary. No one ever tires of repeating the platitudes about Corcovado, most often citing *National Geographic*'s description of the park as "the most biologically intense place on earth in terms of biodiversity."

DAYS 7 AND 8: CARATE TO PUERTO JIMÉNEZ TO SAN JOSÉ
(2 hours by road and 1 hour by air to San José)

The lodges here can arrange for an overland transfer back to Puerto Jiménez, or you can take the *colectivo*, the public transport here. Carate does have its own tiny airstrip with charter planes making the quick jaunt back to Puerto Jiménez. If timing does not coincide with Nature Air or SANSA's schedules, a night in Puerto Jiménez gives you a dose of civilization again in the style of a tropical frontier town. You can catch a flight back to San José the next morning, from where you can depart for other destinations in Costa Rica.

TIPS

■ Opt for morning flights during the rainy season.

■ Same-day international-to-domestic and domestic-to-international air connections are risky; both Nature Air and SANSA advise against them.

■ Domestic airlines limit your luggage to anywhere from 15 to 40 pounds, depending on your fare. Pack lightly, or make advance arrangements with your hotel.

■ September and October are the wettest months of the rainy season and Osa roads occasionally become impassable.

■ Lodges and tour operators here can take care of your advance fee payment to enter Corcovado National Park. Visitor numbers are limited; make arrangements far in advance.

■ You *can* do this trip overland with your own 4WD vehicle or by public bus, but it's a long slog down here. If you choose the land option, add an extra full day at the beginning and end of this itinerary.

GREAT ITINERARIES

COSTA RICA OFF THE BEATEN PATH: 9-DAY ITINERARY

Avoid the crowds in lesser-known, but up-and-coming destinations.

DAY 1: ARRIVAL

Following your evening arrival at Juan Santamaría International Airport, head into San José. The airport lies northwest of the capital, and since you'll be heading east out of the city the next morning, this gets you well on your way there. The west-side Hotel Grano de Oro or the east-side Hotel Casa Cambranes are tried-and-true favorites and make for wonderful ways to ease into your Costa Rican experience.

DAY 2: SAN JOSÉ TO CARTAGO TO THE OROSI VALLEY
(1 hour by road)

Allow yourself a leisurely breakfast at your hotel and avoid San José's morning rush hour. Get going by 10 and you'll be fine. A half-hour drive takes you to Cartago and its two must-see sights: tradition holds that the Basílica de Nuestra Señora de los Ángeles was the site of a 17th-century apparition of the Virgin Mary; and Magmática fills you in on all you wanted to know about earthquakes and lets you shake and rattle in a simulated tremor. A leisurely drive east takes you to Paraíso. Just before Paraíso lies the Jardín Botánico Lankester, a must for orchid lovers. Turn south at the center of town and descend steeply into the Orosi Valley. Spend the night at the rustic, but smart, Hotel Quelitales or the sumptuous La Casona del Cafetal.

TIPS

A very early departure from San José on Day 2 would let you squeeze in a morning visit to the Irazú Volcano. The early bird always catches the best volcano views in Costa Rica, of course, and the volcano is only a short detour from Cartago. A stop at Dominical, one of the country's quintessential beach towns, could add an extra day or two onto this itinerary. While the Costanera is a modern highway by Costa Rican standards, do be careful navigating its ever-growing truck traffic.

DAY 3: OROSI VALLEY

A loop road lets you easily navigate the entire valley. Ujarrás houses the ruins of Costa Rica's first church. The town of Orosi itself contains the Church of San José de Orosi, the country's oldest house of worship still in use. Whether you stay there or not, La Casona del Cafetal is one of Costa Rica's most famous lunch stops. Expect a long wait on weekends.

DAY 4: OROSI VALLEY TO SAN GERARDO DE DOTA
(2 hours by road)

For optimal driving conditions, get an early start today. Head back toward Paraíso and Cartago, then south on the Pan-American Highway. You'll pass over the ominously named Cerro de la Muerte ("hill of death"). You'll be fine, but the high-elevation stretch of highway fogs over by noon. At Km. 80, turn off to San Gerardo de Dota and navigate the steep descent carefully. You'll welcome the sight of the Savegre Hotel or Dantica Lodge, both wonderful places to spend a couple of nights.

DAY 5: SAN GERARDO DE DOTA

San Gerardo means bird-watching. The activity generally requires some hiking here. The two lodges we suggest both have top-notch, on-site guides. If you're not a birder, don't forget that this is one of Costa Rica's premier trout-fishing and horseback destinations.

DAY 6: SAN GERARDO DE DOTA TO COSTA BALLENA

(2 hours by road)

Another early start today and it's back up the road and back down the Pan-American Highway. The highway descends to the hub city of San Isidro de El General, a good refueling stop. An hour-long descent to the coast takes you to the beach town of Dominical. Your reward for the rugged highway conditions you've endured so far is the so-called Costanera, a modern highway that hugs the Pacific Ocean. Head south along the coast.

DAYS 7 AND 8: COSTA BALLENA AND BALLENA NATIONAL MARINE PARK

A couple of days of exploring this stretch of coast between Dominical and Ojochal allow you to experience up-and-coming Costa Rica. El Castillo Luxury Boutique Hotel and Kura Design Villas offer some amazing luxury down here, but Villas Gaia and Río Tico Safari Lodge provide comfort at affordable prices. Ballena National Marine Park, the region's original sine qua non, provides whale- and dolphin-watching tours, along with terrific sunsets and sections with swimming—a treat hard to come by at many of the country's beaches.

DAY 9: COSTA BALLENA TO SAN JOSÉ

(3–4 hours by road)

You need not return to San José the same way you came. At Dominical, the Costanera continues northwest to Quepos and Jacó, from where you can catch the tolled Carretera a Caldera (Highway 27) back to the capital with much better road conditions.

KIDS AND FAMILIES

With so much to keep them interested and occupied, Costa Rica is a blast with kids. The activities here are things the whole family can do together: discovering a waterfall in a rain forest, snorkeling with sea turtles, or white-water rafting down a roaring river. There are also activities for kids that will allow parents time to stroll hand-in-hand down a deserted beach.

Choosing a Destination

Basing yourself in one place for several days is a great idea. Climbing into the car every day or two not only makes the kids miserable but means that the best part of the day is spent traveling. (Kids who are prone to carsickness won't do well on the winding, twisting roads, like the road to Monteverde Cloud Forest.) The good news is that there are many destinations where you could stay for a week and still not do and see everything.

Headed to the beach? Remember that for families, not all beaches are created equal. Choose a destination with a range of activities. Manuel Antonio, on the Central Pacific coast, is your best bet. The proximity to the national park is the main selling point, but you're also close to other nature preserves. As for activities, there's everything from snorkeling and surfing lessons to kayaking excursions to zip-line adventures. And the range of kid-friendly restaurants is unmatched anywhere in the country. On the Nicoya Peninsula, Playas del Coco and Playa Tamarindo have a decent amount of activities for the small fry.

Santa Elena, the closest town to Monteverde Cloud Forest Biological Reserve, is another great base. There are several nature preserves in the area, and they offer both day and night hikes. If skies are cloudy—as they often are—there are

indoor attractions like the display of slithering snakes. The town is compact and walkable, and has many eateries with children's menus. La Fortuna, the gateway to the Lake Arenal area, has activities from waterfall hikes to canopy tours. The town itself isn't attractive, so you'll want to choose a place nearby.

Believe it or not, the San José area is not a bad base. Activities like white-water rafting are nearby, and on rainy days you can visit the city's excellent museums dedicated to gold and jade. The hotels in the surrounding countryside are often a long drive from good restaurants. We prefer the hotels in the city, as dozens of restaurants line the pedestrian-only streets.

Kid-Friendly Activities

You can't beat the beach in Costa Rica. Avoid those without lifeguards, and take warning signs about rip currents very seriously. Snorkeling and surfing lessons are great for older kids, but stick with a licensed company rather than that enthusiastic young person who approaches you on the beach.

Canopy tours are good for kids of all ages. Ask the staff about how long a tour will take, because once you set out on a hike over a series of hanging bridges, you often have no choice but to continue on to the end. Zip lines are appropriate for older teens, who should always be accompanied by an adult.

For the smallest of the small fry, the butterfly enclosures and hummingbird gardens that you find near many resort areas are wonderful diversions. Indoor activities, like the display of frogs at Santa Elena, fascinate youngsters. And don't avoid the easier hikes in the national parks. Seeing animals in the wild is likely to start a lifelong love of animals.

BIODIVERSITY

Updated by
Jeff Van Fleet

Costa Rica's forests hold an array of flora and fauna so vast and diverse that scientists haven't even named thousands of the species found here. The country covers less than 0.03% of Earth's surface, yet it contains nearly 5% of the planet's plant and animal species. Costa Rica has at least 9,000 plant species, including more than 1,200 types of orchids, some 2,000 kinds of butterflies, and 876 bird species.

Costa Rica acts as a natural land bridge between North and South America, so there is a lot of intercontinental exchange. But the country's flora and fauna add up to more than what has passed between the continents. Costa Rica's biological diversity is the result of its tropical location, its varied topography, and the many microclimates resulting from the combination of mountains, valleys, and lowlands. The isthmus also acts as a hospitable haven to many species that couldn't complete the journey from one hemisphere to the other. The rain forests of Costa Rica's Caribbean and southwestern lowlands are the most northerly home of such southern species as the crab-eating raccoon. The tropical dry forests of the northern Pacific slope are the southern limit for such North American species as the Virginia opossum. And then there are the dozens of northern bird species that spend their winter holidays here.

Research and planning go a long way in a place like Costa Rica. A short trip around the country can put you in one landscape after another, each with its own array of plants and animals. The country's renowned national park system holds examples of all of its major ecosystems, and some of its most impressive sights. In terms of activities, there's more interesting stuff to do here than could possibly ever fit into one vacation. But keep in mind that somewhere around three-fourths of the country has been urbanized or converted to agriculture, so if you want to see the spectacular nature that we describe in this book, you need to know where to go. *In addition to this section on biodiversity, you'll find regional planning information, national park highlights, and a list of our favorite eco-lodges at the front of each chapter.*

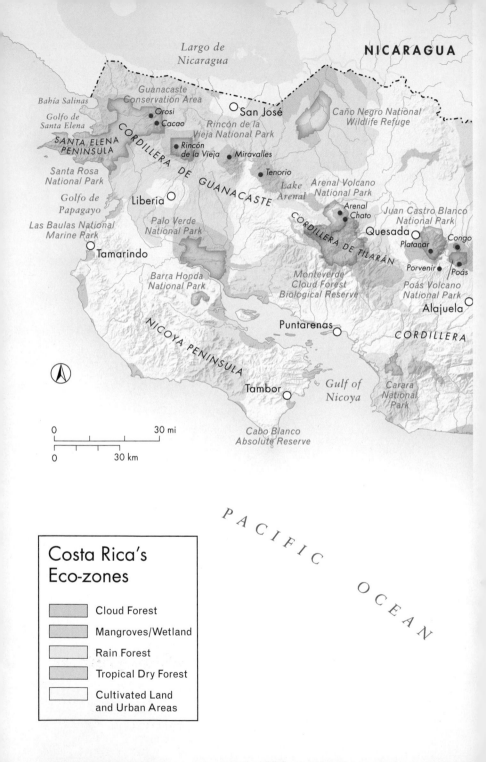

Largo de
Nicaragua

NICARAGUA

Bahía Salinas

Golfo de
Santa Elena

Guanacaste
Conservation Area

● Orosi
● Cacao

○ San José

Caño Negro National
Wildlife Refuge

SANTA ELENA
PENINSULA

Rincón de la
Vieja National Park

CORDILLERA

● Rincón
de la Vieja ● Miravalles

Santa Rosa
National Park

DE

● Tenorio

Lake
Arenal

Arenal Volcano
National Park

Golfo de
Papagayo

Liberia ○

GUANACASTE

Arenal
● Chato

Juan Castro Blanco
National Park

Las Baulas National
Marine Park

Palo Verde
National Park

CORDILLERA

Quesada ○

Congo

Tamarindo

DE TILARÁN

Platanar

Porvenir ● | Poás

Barra Honda
National Park

Monteverde
Cloud Forest
Biological Reserve

Poás Volcano
National Park

Alajuela ○

NICOYA

PENINSULA

Puntarenas ○

CORDILLERA

Tambor ○

Gulf of
Nicoya

Carara
National
Park

0 ————————— 30 mi

Cabo Blanco
Absolute Reserve

0 ————————— 30 km

PACIFIC

OCEAN

Costa Rica's Eco-zones

Cloud Forest

Mangroves/Wetland

Rain Forest

Tropical Dry Forest

Cultivated Land
and Urban Areas

Costa Rica's Eco-zones

Barra del Colorado Wildlife Refuge

Caribbean Sea

La Selva
○ **La Virgen**
Braulio Carrillo National Park

Tortuguero National Park

● *Cacho Negro*
● *Barva*

○ **Heredia**

Turrialba Volcano National Park
● *Turrialba*
● *Irazú*

○ **Limón**

⭐ **SAN JOSÉ**
○ **Cartago**

Irazú Volcano National Park

CENTRAL

Cahuita National Park

Chirripó National Park

La Amistad International Biosphere

Chirripó *(Highest point in Costa Rica 3,810 m)* ▲

San Gerardo de Dota

○ **Quepos**

CORDILLERA
▲ *Eli*
▲ *Ena*
DE
▲ *Utyum*
TALAMANCA
▲ *Nai*

PANAMA

○ **San Isidro de El General**

Manuel Antonio National Park

○ **Buenos Aires**

VALLE DE EL GENERAL

▲ *Bine*

Ballena National Marine Park

Río Terraba

○ **Drake**
Drake Bay

○ **Golfito**

Piedras Blancas National Park

OSA PENINSULA

Golfo Dulce

Corcovado National Park

RAIN FOREST

Warm and wet, Costa Rica's rain forest is the quintessential dripping, squawking, chirping, buzzing jungle. In this sultry landscape of green on green, birds flap and screech overhead and twigs snap under the steps of unseen creatures. All the ingredients for life—water, sunlight, and more water—drench these areas.

WORD OF MOUTH

"We were on the Osa in July and surprisingly didn't get a drop of rain. I'd avoid going in September and October. Our guide told us that it can rain for days without a break."

—volcanogirl

The amount of rain in a rain forest is stunning. The enormous swath of forest in the Caribbean lowlands averages more than 4 meters (13 feet) of rain a year. Corcovado National Park, on the Osa Peninsula, can get 5½ meters (18 feet).

The soaring canopy soaks up the lion's share of sunlight, seriously depriving the plants below. Underneath the highest trees are several distinct layers of growth. The understory is made up of smaller and younger trees, shaded but also protected from harsh winds and rainfall. Shrubby species and even younger trees stand farther below, and small plants, fungus, dead trees, and fallen leaves cover the constantly decomposing forest floor.

Light rarely passes through these layers and layers of growth. At the forest floor, plants lie poised, in a stasis of sorts, waiting for one of the giants above to fall and open a patch of sky. When this does happen, an incredible spectacle occurs as the waiting plants unveil an arsenal of evolutionary tricks. Vines twist out, looking for other trees to pull themselves up along, shoots explode from hidden bulbs, and ferns and lianas battle for height and access to the sun.

But as competitive as the jungle sounds, it is essentially a series of ecosystems based on interdependence and cooperation. Trees depend on the animals that eat their fruit to disperse their seeds. Fungi feed off the nutrients produced by the decomposing forest floor. From death comes life—an abundance of life.

Costa Rica's rain forests have suffered from incursions by agriculture, logging, and cattle farming, but they're still home to the majority of the nation's biodiversity, with more species per square mile than anywhere else.

ADVENTURE HIGHLIGHTS

■ Novice bird-watchers can enroll in La Selva's Birding 101 class. It's taught by some of the finest naturalists in the country.

■ Join the folks at Brisas del Nara, 32 km (20 miles) outside Manuel Antonio, for an all-day horseback-riding excursion through the protected Cerro Nara mountain zone. It ends with a swim in a natural pool with a 107-meter (350-foot) waterfall.

■ Stray way off the beaten path on a multiday hike through Corcovado National Park with tropical biologist Mike Boston from Osa Aventura.

TOP DESTINATIONS

Most of Costa Rica's rain forest can be found across the Caribbean lowlands and on the South Pacific coast.

CORCOVADO NATIONAL PARK

At the other end of the spectrum is Corcovado National Park, the remote, untamed jewel of Costa Rica's biodiversity crown. Covering one-third of the Osa Peninsula, Corcovado National Park holds about one-quarter of all tree species in Costa Rica and at least 140 identified species of mammals. Covering 445 square km (172 square miles), the park includes Central America's largest tract of lowland Pacific rain forest, including some old-growth areas. Corcovado is home to the largest concentration of jaguars left in the country, and the biggest population of scarlet macaw. There are at least 116 species of amphibians and reptiles, and about 370 bird species. Ranger stations and campsites are available for the more adventurous, and luxurious eco-lodges surround the park for those who don't like to rough it. (⇨ *See Chapter 8.*)

LA SELVA

If anybody knows anything about the rain forest, it is the researchers at La Selva biological station, situated in the midst of 3,900 acres of protected forest in northern Costa Rica. The station, run by the Organization for Tropical Studies,

A green and black poison frog, La Selva

was founded by famed biologist Leslie Holdridge in 1954 and is one of the most important sites worldwide for research on tropical rain forests. The research station can sleep up to 80 people in dormitory-style rooms and two-room family cabins, and feed as many as 100 in the dining hall. More than 50 km (31 miles) of trails provide access to a variety of ecosystems. (⇨ *See Chapter 9.*)

MANUEL ANTONIO NATIONAL PARK

For a tame, up-close glimpse of the rain forest and some of its more photogenic inhabitants, Manuel Antonio National Park is a favorite. Located on the Central Pacific coast, Manuel Antonio is one of Costa Rica's most visited—and smallest—national parks. Capuchin monkeys are used to humans to the point of practically ignoring them, unless a snack is poking out from an unattended backpack. The highly endangered squirrel monkeys are less bold, but can be seen at the park or from nearby hotels. Sloths are a common sight along the trail, as are a host of exotic birds and other creatures. But despite the apparent vibrancy of life found here, Manuel Antonio is isolated, with no biological bridges to other forests, and threatened by encroaching development. (⇨ *See Chapter 7.*)

Squirrel Monkey; danmike, Fodors.com member

EXPERIENCING A RAIN FOREST

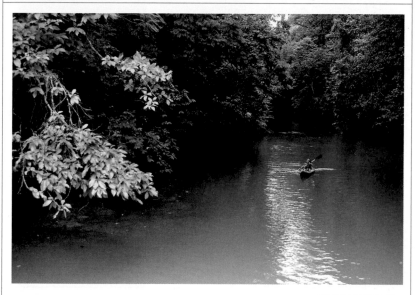

Kayaking in Drake Bay

There are a variety of ways to explore and experience the rain forest, which is only fitting given the diversity of the rain-forest ecosystem.

CANOPY TOURS
Canopy tours are a wonderful way to get a bird's-eye—or sloth's—view of the rain forest. Suspension bridges and zip lines, originally used for canopy research, offer a fantastic glimpse into the upper reaches of the forest. If you're not very mobile or don't feel like walking, go on a rain-forest tram; it's a small, slow-moving gondola that carries passengers gently through the jungle canopy.

HIKING
Hiking or walking through any one of Costa Rica's numerous national parks is an easy way to fully experience the vibrancy of the life found there. And we can't say this too many times: guided hikes are the way to go for anyone who hopes to catch a glimpse of the more exotic and hard-to-find species or better understand the complexity of the surrounding ecosystems.

MOUNTAIN BIKING
During the dry season, some parks open up trails for mountain bikers. But once the rains begin, a bike trip can turn into a long slog through the mud. Before you rent a bike, ask about the conditions of the trails.

RAFTING
Gentle, slow-moving rivers beg to be explored by canoe or kayak. It's a wonderful way to experience the deep calm of the jungle, and stealthy enough to increase your chances of seeing wildlife. If you're more of a thrill seeker, choose from any of the white-water rafting tours that pass through rain forests.

FLORA

To enter into a Costa Rican rain forest is to be overwhelmed by the diversity and intensity of life. A single hectare (2½ acres) contains almost 100 species of trees, and many of the more than 1,000 species of orchids are nested in their branches.

FALSE BIRD OF PARADISE

No avid photographer will return from Costa Rica without snapping a few shots of a heliconia, one of the most vibrant families of plants in the rain forest. This genus of flowering plant, containing between 100 and 200 species, includes the false bird of paradise (*Heliconia rostrata*), a dangling, impossibly colorful flower of alternating bulbous protrusions, colored red and tipped with green and yellow. Its vibrant colors and nectar make it a favorite for hummingbirds.

False Bird of Paradise

GUARIA MORADA

Almost every tree here plays host to lichens, woody vines called lianas, and rootless epiphytes, including the national flower, guaria morada (*Guarianthe skinneri*). Because this is an orchid species, you'll find it in several different shapes and colors: the flowers can be from pure white to deep magenta, and the base of its lip can range from yellow to white. There can be anywhere from 4 to 14 flowers per stem.

Guaria morada

SILK COTTON TREE

The silk cotton tree (*Ceiba pentandra*), known locally as *ceiba*, is one of the most easily recognizable of the rain-forest giants. Growing nearly 60 meters (200 feet) tall, it can be identified close to the ground by its tall, winding, and narrow roots, which act as buttresses to support the enormous trunk.

The Silk Cotton Tree

STRANGLER FIG

Aptly called matapalo in Spanish, meaning "tree killer," the strangler fig begins its life as an epiphyte, living high in the branches of another tree. Over several years, it grows dangling roots to the forest floor that capture nutrients from the soil, thicken, and slowly meld onto the host tree. Eventually—it might take as long as 100 years—the strangler completely engulfs its host. In time the "strangled" tree decomposes and disintegrates, leaving the strangler fig—replete with branches, leaves, flowers, and fruit—standing hollow but victorious.

Strangler Fig

Harpy Eagle

FAUNA

Keep an eye out for three-wattled bellbirds, chestnut-mandibled toucans, or the secretive Baird's tapir. A host of wildcats include the ocelot, jaguarundi, puma, margay, and rarely seen jaguar.

HARPY EAGLE

The endangered harpy eagle, nearly extinct from Costa Rica, is the country's largest and most powerful raptor. It's named for the Greek spirits that carried the dead to the underworld of Hades, who are said to have the faces of humans but the bodies of eagles. Harpy eagles are huge—females are more than 0.6 meters (2 feet) in length and have a 1.8-meter (6-foot) wingspan. They hunt above the canopy, searching for large mammals or, occasionally, for large birds like the macaw.

Blue Morpho

MORPHO BUTTERFLY

The bright blue morpho butterfly bounces through the jungle like a small piece of sky on a string. The entire life cycle, from egg to death, is approximately 137 days, and the adult butterflies live for only about a month. Once they emerge from the cocoon, morphos have few predators, thanks to the poisonous compounds that they retain from feeding habits back in their caterpillar days. In fact, the hairy brown tufts on the morpho caterpillar have been known to irritate human skin.

SCARLET MACAWS

Every bit the pirate's crimson parrot, these large and noisy birds mate for life, travel in pairs or large groups, and can often be found gathered in almond trees in low-elevation forests of the central and southern Pacific coast. Their cousin, the critically endangered great green macaw, travels across the Caribbean lowlands, following the ripening of the mountain almond.

Scarlet Macaw

THREE-TOED OR TWO-TOED SLOTH

Though difficult for us to spot, the barely moving three-toed sloth and two-toed sloth are principal meals for the harpy eagle. This animal's fur is a small self-sustaining ecosystem unto itself: because the forest is so wet and the sloth so inert, two species of blue-green algae thrive on its fur and provide it with needed camouflage. Non-parasitic insects also live here, feeding off the algae and keeping the growth under control.

■TIP➜ The vibrantly colored red-eyed tree frog, like the white tent bat, sometimes rests on the underside of large jungle leaves. If you're lucky, your guide may be able to coax one out for you to see.

Three-toed-sloth

VOLCANOES

As part of the Pacific Ring of Fire, the country has three volcanic mountain ranges: Guanacaste, Central, and Tilarán. There are around 300 volcanic points in Costa Rica, but only 5 have formed volcanoes that have erupted in recent memory: Turrialba, Irazú, Poás, Rincón de la Vieja, and Arenal.

Costa Rica's volcanoes are the result of friction between two enormous tectonic plates—the Cocos plate and the Caribbean plate. As these plates rub against each other, the friction partially melts rock. Although everyone uses the term "lava," pyroclastic flow, or hot gas and rock, more accurately describes the product spewed from the volcanoes here. The flow is forced toward the surface, leaking through cracks or weak spots in the crust along with volcanic gas. In Rincón de la Vieja, gas escapes through craters high on the volcano, as well as seeping up through the surrounding ground, creating bubbling mud pits, hot springs, and fumaroles.

The volcanic mountain ranges divide the country's Pacific and Caribbean slopes and are responsible for the differences in climate between each side. Rain-laden trade winds blowing westward can't pass over these ranges without shedding their precipitation and rising. This creates Guanacaste's rain shadow: the dry plains and tropical dry forest that lie leeward, or west of the mountains. The mountains block the rain-producing weather system and cast a "shadow" of dryness.

Costa Rica's volcanic lakes occur when there is no natural drainage from a crater. The chemicals, minerals, and gases from below the earth's crust infuse the water and vibrantly color it. Irazú's lake is neon green; the baby-blue lagoon in Poás is extremely acidic and gives off toxic sulfur clouds and massive amounts of carbon dioxide.

The surface ecology of a volcano varies. Rincón de la Vieja is skirted by Guanacaste's signature grasslands and tropical dry forest. Poás Volcano is blanketed with rain forest and tipped with cloud forest. Some of the country's best coffee is grown on the slopes of Poás.

ADVENTURE HIGHLIGHTS

■ A hike through lush cloud forest will take you to the five magnificent waterfalls at La Paz Waterfall Gardens near Poás Volcano National Park.

■ Anglers love the guapote, tilapia, and machaca pulled from Lake Arenal.

■ The Arenal area is the jumping-off point for Class II–IV white-water rafting trips on the Blancas, Arenal, Toro, and San Carlos rivers.

■ Take the tough hike to La Fortuna Waterfall, near Arenal. Swimming under the waterfall is a slice of paradise.

TOP DESTINATIONS

Costa Rica's volcanoes are often the centerpieces of large national parks.

On the Road to Arenal; piper35w, Fodors.com member

ARENAL VOLCANO

At 1,680 meters (5,512 feet), Arenal Volcano, rising on the northwestern plains of San Carlos, is every bit an awesome sight. Tall and perfectly conical, its sides are scarred by a history of violent eruptions and textured by decades of pyroclastic flow. Located at the northern end of the Tilarán Mountain Range, northwest of the capital, it is Costa Rica's best-known volcano. Arenal has settled into a less active phase these days. It's likely temporary: research suggests that Arenal has a 400-year cycle of major eruptions, and the activity since the 1968 explosion is small in comparison with what it's capable of. (⇨ *See Chapter 5.*)

POÁS VOLCANO

Poás Volcano is Costa Rica's most visited national park, in part because it is the closest active volcano to the capital of San José and the Aeropuerto Internacional Juan Santamaría. Located in the Cordillera Volcánica Central Mountain Range, Poás is topped by three craters, the tallest reaching 2,708 meters (8,885 feet) above sea level. Only the main cone has shown any volcanic eruptions in the

Gaudy Leaf Frog; Marco13, Fodors.com member

last 200 years. You can get a good look at the crater from the viewing deck. (⇨ *See Chapter 4.*)

Note: Costa Rica's hot spot (literally) these days is the Turrialba Volcano, which occasionally spews ash over the metro area and periodically closes the international airport. Authorities currently prohibit entry to the national park.

RINCÓN DE LA VIEJA

A mass of slopes, craters, and biodiversity that bridges the Continental Divide, Rincón de la Vieja is in Costa Rica's arid northwest. It's not the classic conical volcano, but rather a ridge made of a series of craters that include bare, rocky bowls with brilliantly colored lakes, and velvety cones covered in rain forest. Scientists believe Rincón de la Vieja was born of simultaneous volcanic activity at nine different eruption points. The Rincón de la Vieja National Park covers nearly 35,000 acres and is a wonderland of volcanic activity that includes bubbling mud pits, hot springs, and geysers, as well as refreshing lagoons and spectacular waterfalls. (⇨ *See Chapter 6.*)

EXPERIENCING THE VOLCANOES

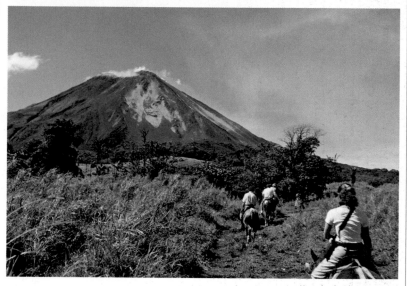

Horseback riding in Arenal

The Guatuso people believed that the fire god lived inside the Arenal Volcano—and in 1968, the gods were not happy. After 500 years of dormancy, Arenal erupted savagely, burying three small villages and killing 87 people. Today, thousands live at its base in the thriving town of La Fortuna, which is literally in Arenal's shadow.

HIKING
Volcano tourism is a major draw for international visitors, but given the dangers at the active sites, activities at the top are limited. The parks have hiking trails. For your safety, we recommend hiking with a guide, especially at Arenal. The volcano has settled into a less active phase these days, but it's still one of those you-never-know situations, and a knowledgeable guide knows where not to tread. At Poás and Irazú, you can go right up to the summit and peer inside.

HORSEBACK RIDING
All of Costa Rica's active volcanoes are the centerpieces of national parks. Arenal and Poás have good horseback-riding trails and many outfitters, especially in Arenal. For safety's sake and the well-being of the animals, stick with the operators we recommend.

GEOTHERMAL WONDERS
Volcanic activity is not limited to a volcano's peak. The underground heat that fuels these giants also results in hot springs, bubbling mud pits, and geysers, among other geological wonders. Minerals from the dormant Tenorio Volcano create a fascinating effect in one of the rivers running down its side, the Río Celeste, giving it a baby-blue tint.

FLORA

The habitat and ecology of these geologic giants is influenced mostly by their surrounding ecology zones and elevation. Conditions around the crater of an active volcano are intensely harsh, but some tougher species do manage to survive.

FERN
Contrary to popular stereotypes, ferns don't necessarily grow in shady, moist environments. The tongue fern (*Elaphoglossum lingua*) extends long, rubbery, tongue-shape leaves and has evolved to grow around volcanic rock and hardened ash. You'll find it around the top of the Poás Volcano. Farther down, you'll find other types of ferns adapted to friendlier conditions.

MYRTLE
Myrtle (*Myrtaceae*) and other low-lying shrubs survive this environment thanks to their slow growth rate. Myrtle, poor man's umbrella (*Gunnera insignis*), papelillo (*Senecio oerstedianus*), and other shrubs and ferns cover the higher bluffs around Irazú's crater. Mistletoe (*Psittacanthus*) can be found near the major volcanoes in the Central Valley. These flowering plants are interesting because they attach to trees by haustoria, special structures that penetrate the host plant and absorb its water and nutrients. When the mistletoe dies, it leaves a mark on the tree, a woodrose or rosa de palo.

OAK
Forests in Costa Rica's higher mountain areas share some plant species with cloud forests. However, the plants here have adapted to live in cold temperatures and, if the volcano is active, in compacted ash. Surrounding the Botos Lagoon, on the south side of the principal Poás crater, is high-elevation cloud forest of oak (*Quercus costaricensis and Q. copeyensis*), small cedar (*Brunellia costaricensis*), and flowering cypress (*Escallonia poasana*)—trees that are typically crowded with epiphytes, bromeliads, and mosses.

WILD BALSAM
Wild balsam, oak, and poor man's umbrella carpet the inactive cones around Rincón de la Vieja. Tropical dry-forest species grow farther down. Look for the guanacaste tree (*Enterolobium cyclocarpum*), Spanish cedar (*Cedrela odorata*), oak (*Q. oocarpa*), and the country's largest wild population of the guardia morada orchid, Costa Rica's national flower.

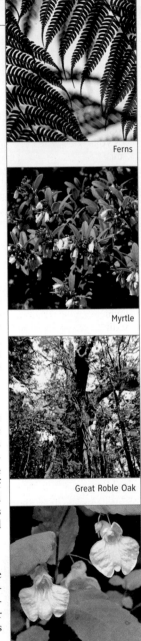

Ferns

Myrtle

Great Roble Oak

Wild Balsam aka
Touch-me-not Balsam

2

FAUNA

Like the flora around a volcano, the wildlife diversity of this region is dictated by the ecology around the mountain. Also, the more humans there are, the fewer animals you'll see.

FIERY-THROATED HUMMINGBIRD

Birds are one of the most populous types of creature to live on the flanks of Poás and many more of Costa Rica's volcanoes. The fiery-throated hummingbird, the summer tanager, the sooty robin, and the emerald toucanet are among the 79 bird species that have been recorded at Poás. The fiery-throated hummingbird is recognizable by its forecrown, throat, and breast colors, as well as its bluish hump and blue-black tail.

Fiery-Throated Hummingbird

NINE-BANDED ARMADILLO

Irazú is home to smaller creatures such as the nine-banded armadillo, the eastern cottontail, and the little spotted cat. The nine-banded armadillo has a long snout and fantastic sense of smell. It can hold its breath for up to six minutes. This helps it keep dirt out of its nostrils while digging. Under stressful conditions, a female armadillo can prolong her pregnancy for up to three years by delaying the implantation of the fertilized egg into the uterus wall.

Nine-banded armadillo

NORTH AMERICAN PORCUPINE

The much drier region of Rincón de la Vieja has a distinctly different—and broader—set of animal inhabitants, including the North American porcupine and the agouti (a large, short-legged relative of the guinea pig). Pumas, ocelots, raccoons, and three species of monkeys (the howler, the white-faced capuchin, and the Central American spider monkey) are among the larger mammals. More than 300 bird species have been recorded there, including the collared aracari, the bare-necked umbrella bird, and the three-wattled bellbird.

North American Porcupine

PUMA

In the Barva region, pumas (also called mountain lions and cougars), and even jaguars still stalk the more remote forests, searching for the tapir or an unlucky spider monkey. The puma is an excellent climber and can jump to branches 5 meters (16 feet) off the ground, essentially giving monkeys nowhere to hide. Pumas have never been hunted for their pelts, but are suffering from habitat destruction. In Costa Rica, they are rarely found outside protected areas.

Puma

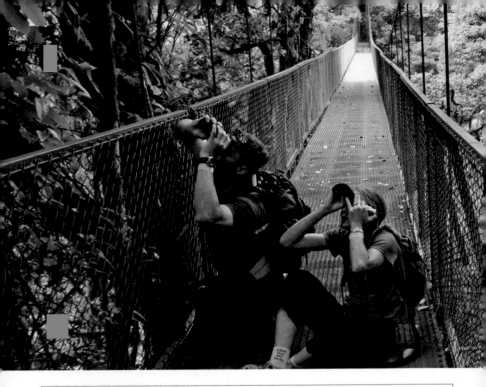

CLOUD FOREST

The four mountain ranges that make up Costa Rica's own piece of the Continental Divide split the country into its Caribbean and Pacific regions. At these higher altitudes, temperatures cool, clouds settle, and rainfall increases. The forests found here are shrouded in mist and rich in biodiversity. Welcome to Costa Rica's famed cloud forests.

Like their lowland rain-forest cousins, cloud forests are packed with plant and animal species, thanks largely to their water-drenched conditions. There's an average of 5 meters (16 feet) of rainfall a year, but that number doubles when you factor in the amount of moisture gleaned from the clouds and fog that drift through every day. As in rain forests, giant hardwoods reaching as high as almost 60 meters (200 feet) set the ceiling for this ecology zone, while a variety of smaller trees, ferns, shrubs, and other plants fill the understories. Epiphytes flourish here, as do mosses, lichens, and liverwort. These plants cling to passing moisture and capture it like sponges. As a result, cloud forests are constantly soaking wet even when there is no rain.

Because conditions in a cloud forest can be harsh, many of the tougher and more adaptable rain-forest species make their home here. The relentless, heavy cloud cover can block sunlight even from the highest reaches of the forest, and deeper inside, light is rare. Photosynthesis and growth are slower, so the plants tend to be smaller with thicker trunks and stems. These unique conditions also produce an unusually high number of endemic and rare species.

The Monteverde Cloud Forest Preserve, one of the world's most famous protected cloud forests, shelters innumerable life-forms. There are more than 100 mammal species; 400 bird species, including at least 30 species of hummingbird; 500-plus species of butterfly; and more than 2,500 plant species, including 420 types of orchids. There are only a handful of protected cloud forests here and worldwide, and this type of ecozone is increasingly threatened by human encroachment.

ADVENTURE HIGHLIGHTS

■ Leave the car at home and travel on horseback to or from the Arenal Volcano area and Monteverde Cloud Forest. Contact Desafío Adventures, the only guides we recommend for this journey.

■ The good folks at the Savegre Hotel will give you an education on one of their daylong natural-history hikes around San Gerardo de Dota cloud forest.

■ Selvatura, right next to Monteverde, is the only canopy tour in the area with a zip line built entirely inside the cloud forest.

TOP DESTINATIONS

Regardless of which cloud forest you visit, bring a raincoat and go with a guide if you want to see wildlife. You'll marvel at their ability to spot a sloth at a hundred paces.

Banded Anteater; maddytem, Fodors.com member

BRAULIO CARRILLO NATIONAL PARK
Descending from the Cordillera Volcánica Central Mountain Range, Braulio Carrillo National Park is an awesome, intimidating, and rugged landscape of dense cloud forest that stretches toward the rain forests of the Caribbean lowlands. The enormous park encompasses 117,580 acres of untamed jungle and is less than an hour's drive from San José. The country's principal eastbound highway cuts a path straight through it. Elusive (and endangered) jaguars and pumas are among the many animal species here, and scenic viewpoints are plentiful along the highway. A handful of trails, including the easy-to-access loop trails at the Quebrada González station, can be taken a short distance into the park's interior. (⇨ *See Chapter 9.*)

MONTEVERDE CLOUD FOREST BIOLOGICAL RESERVE
Costa Rica's most famous cloud forest reserve is packed with an astonishing variety of life: 2,500 plant species,

400 species of birds, 500 types of butterflies, and more than 100 different mammals—many of them bats—have been cataloged so far. The reserve reaches 1,535 meters (5,032 feet) above sea level, spans the Tilarán Mountain Range, and encompasses 9,885 acres of cloud forest and rain forest. There are 13 km (8 miles) of well-marked trails, zip-line tours, and suspended bridges for canopy viewing, as well as bird tours, guided night walks, and a field research station with an amphibian aquarium. Allow a generous slice of time for leisurely hiking; longer hikes are made possible by some strategically placed overnight refuges along the way. (⇨ *See Chapter 5.*)

SAN GERARDO DE DOTA
One of Costa Rica's premier nature destinations, San Gerardo de Dota is a damp, epiphyte-laden forest of giant oak trees and an astonishing number of resplendent quetzals. Outdoors enthusiasts may never want to leave these parts—some of the country's best hiking is in this valley, and it's popular with bird-watchers. It's also great for horseback riding and trout fly-fishing. (⇨ *See Chapter 8.*)

Braulio Carrillo National Park

EXPERIENCING A CLOUD FOREST

2

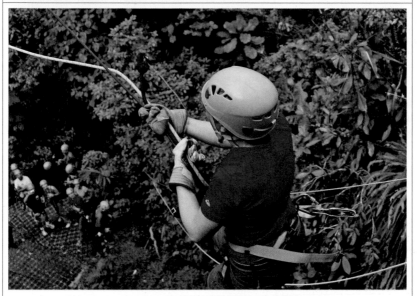

Gearing up for the Tarzan swing at the end of the zip line tour at Selvatura.

You may need to get down and dirty—well, more like wet and muddy—to experience a cloud forest's natural wonders, but then, that's half the fun.

BIRD-WATCHING

Bird-watching is rewarding in the cloud forest, where some of the most vibrant and peculiar of nature's winged creatures can be found. Rise early, enjoy some locally grown coffee, and check the aguacatillo trees for quetzals. If you opt to go without a guide, bring along waterproof binoculars and a good guidebook (we recommend *The Birds of Costa Rica*, by Richard Garrigues and Robert Dean) for spotting and identifying birds.

CANOPY TOURS

Canopy tours and suspended bridges run right through the upper reaches of the cloud forest—an ecosystem in its own right. Spot birds, monkeys, and exotic orchids from a viewpoint that was once nearly impossible to reach. Get even closer to butterflies, amphibians, snakes, and insects at various exhibits in the parks' research centers.

FISHING

If freshwater fishing in spectacular surroundings is right up your alley, check out the Savegre River, in the San Gerardo de Dota Valley. It's been stocked with rainbow trout since the 1950s.

HIKING

Well-guided hikes through this eerie landscape, draped with moss and vines, make it easier to spot the less obvious features of this complex ecosystem. Compared with the barren tropical dry forest and colorful rain forest, cloud forests don't easily offer up their secrets. Binoculars and a good guide will go a long way toward making your hike and wildlife spotting richer experiences.

FLORA

A typical hectare (2½ acres) of cloud forest might be home to nearly 100 species of trees. Contrast that with a mere 30 in the richest forests of North America.

EPIPHYTES

Epiphytes thrive in cloud and rain forests, thanks to all the moisture and nutrients in the air. The *stanhopea* orchid is interesting because of its clever pollination tricks. The blossoms' sweet smell attracts bees, but the flower's waxy surface is slippery so they slide down inside. As they slowly work their way out, they brush up against the flower's column and collect pollen. This pollen is then transferred to the sticky stigma of other flowers.

Bromeliads, another family of flowering plants, compete with epiphytes for space on the branches and trunks of the forest's trees. The spiraling leaves form caches for water, falling plant material, and insect excretions. These are mineral-rich little ponds for insects and amphibians, and drinking and bathing water for birds and other animals.

POOR MAN'S UMBRELLA

If you're caught in the rain, take cover under a poor man's umbrella (*Gunnera insignis and Gunnera talamancana*), whose broad and sturdy leaves sometimes grow large enough to shelter an entire family. These shrubby plants love the dark, moist interior of the cloud forest.

ROBLE TREE

Majestic roble, or oak—principally the white oak (*Quercus copeyensis*) and black oak (*Quercus costarricensis*)—is the dominant tree of Costa Rica's cloud forests and grows to 60 meters (200 feet). The deciduous hardwood cedro dulce, or Spanish cedar (*Cedrela tonduzii*), is also a giant at 40 meters (147 feet). These two are joined by evergreens like the *jaúl*, or alder, and the *aguacatillo*, a name meaning "little avocado" that's given to a variety of trees from the *lauracea* family.

STAR ORCHID

The star orchid (*Epidendrum radicans*) is one of the few orchids that is not an epiphyte. It grows on land and mimics in color and shape other nectar-filled flowers in order to attract butterflies who unwittingly become pollinators.

Epiphyte Stanhopea

Poor Man's Umbrella

White Oak Tree

Star Orchid

FAUNA

The resplendent quetzal, the blue-crowned motmot, the orange-bellied trogon, and the emerald toucanet are just some of the hundreds of species that can be logged in a cloud forest.

COLLARED TROGON

The collared trogon and the orange-bellied trogon are in the same family as the quetzal. They all share square black-and-white tail plumage and bright orange or yellow chest feathers. The collared trogon perches very quietly and is easy to miss. Luckily, it doesn't fly far, so its flight is easy to follow.

Collared Trogon

GLASS FROGS

One of the more bizarre amphibians is the tiny, transparent glass frog of the *Centrolenellu* genus, whose internal organs can be seen through its skin. It lives in trees and bushes and can often be heard at night near the rivers and streams. Cloud forests have fewer amphibian species than rain forests, but amphibian populations worldwide have plummeted in recent decades. No one knows the cause yet. Some blame acid rain and pesticides; others believe it is yet another sign of coming ecological disaster.

Glass Frogs

HOWLER MONKEYS

One of the largest New World monkeys, howlers are named for their loud, barking roar that can be heard for miles. If you want to spot a howler, be sure to scan the treetops; their diet consists mainly of canopy leaves, and they rarely leave the protection of the trees. Other cloud-forest mammals include the white-faced capuchin monkey, white-nosed coatis, porcupines, red brocket deer, and Alston's singing mouse.

Howler Monkey

RESPLENDENT QUETZAL

Perhaps the most famed resident of Costa Rica's cloud forests is the illustrious resplendent quetzal. Every year, bird-watchers come to Costa Rica hoping to spot the green, red, and turquoise plumage of this elusive trogon. Considered a sacred creature by the Maya and the namesake of Guatemala's currency, the quetzal spends much of its time perched in its favorite tree, the *aguacatillo*.

Resplendent Quetzal

TROPICAL DRY FOREST

The most endangered biome in the world, these seasonal forests swing between two climate extremes—from drenching wet to bone dry. To survive, plants undergo a drastic physical transformation: forests burst into life during the rainy months, and are brown, leafless, and seemingly dead during the dry season.

For about half the year, northwestern Costa Rica is as wet as the rest of the country. The weather blows in from the Pacific, and it can rain every day. During the dry season, from January to April, weather patterns change, winds shift, and the land becomes parched.

Tall deciduous hardwoods are the giants in this ecology zone, with spindly branches creating a seasonal canopy as high as 30 meters (100 feet). A thorny and rambling understory of smaller trees and bushes thrives thanks to the plentiful light permitted once the canopy leaves fall to the forest floor. The challenges of the dry months

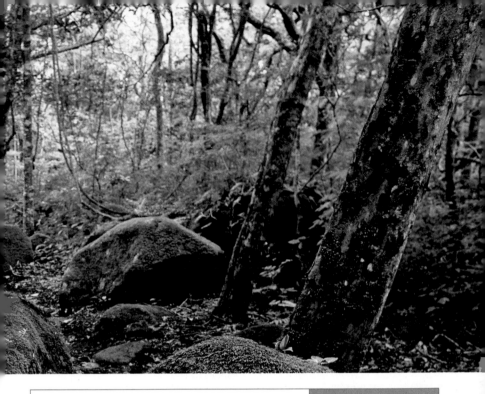

have forced plants to specialize. The hardwoods are solitary and diffuse, their seeds spread far and wide by animals and insects. Some even flower progressively through the dry season, depending on the plant species and the particular bees and birds that have evolved to pollinate them.

Dry season is perfect for bird- and animal-watching since the lack of foliage makes wildlife spotting easy. Keep your eyes peeled for monkeys, parrots, lizards, coyotes, rabbits, snakes, and even jaguars.

There was once one great, uninterrupted swath of dry forest that began in southern Mexico, rolled across Mesoamerica, and ended in northwest Costa Rica. Today, less than 2% of the Central American tropical dry forest remains, the majority of it in Costa Rica. But even here, the forest is fractured into biologically isolated islands, thanks to decades of logging and agriculture. The Guanacaste Conservation Area has managed to corral off large chunks of land for preservation, and private and government efforts are under way to create biological corridors between isolated dry forests so that animals and plants can roam farther and deepen their gene pools, so critical to their survival.

ADVENTURE HIGHLIGHTS

■ Adrenaline-spiked tours with Hacienda Guachipelín (bordering Rincón de la Vieja National Park) include river tubing, rappelling, zip lines, and a Tarzan swing.

■ Let the knowledgeable folks from the Organization for Tropical Studies take you on a guided bird-watching tour through Palo Verde National Park. Boat rides float you past hundreds of waterfowl.

■ Take the kids on a bird- and monkey-watching journey down the Río Corobicí, in Palo Verde National Park.

TOP DESTINATIONS

Most of Costa Rica's remaining tropical dry forests are located in the northwest of the country, not too far from the Nicaragua border.

GUANACASTE CONSERVATION AREA

Santa Rosa is part of the larger Guanacaste Conservation Area, which is composed of some tropical dry forest and former farmland that's being regenerated to its natural state. The park is intended to serve as a much-needed biological corridor from Santa Rosa up to the cloud forests of the Orosi and Cacao volcanoes, to the east. Park infrastructure is generally lacking, though three biological stations offer some accommodations to student groups and researchers. (⇨ *See Chapter 6.*)

PALO VERDE NATIONAL PARK

Farther south, Palo Verde National Park skirts the northeastern side of the Río Tempisque, straddling some of the country's most spectacular wetlands and tropical dry forest. Thanks to these two very different ecology zones, Palo Verde is packed with very diverse bird, plant, and animal species—bird-watchers love this park. The Organization for Tropical Studies has a biological station at Palo Verde and offers tours and accommodations. Park guards also maintain

Hummingbird Nesting; reedjoella, Fodors.com member

a ranger station with rustic overnight accommodations. (⇨ *See Chapter 6.*)

RINCÓN DE LA VIEJA NATIONAL PARK

More tropical dry forest can be found inside the Rincón de la Vieja National Park, ringing the base of the two volcanoes of this protected area—the dormant Santa María and the active Rincón de la Vieja. The park hosts some 300 bird species as well as cougars, kinkajous, and the shy, elusive jaguar. A handful of lodges inside the park and the proximity to the city of Liberia make Rincón an easy destination to visit. (⇨ *See Chapter 6.*)

SANTA ROSA NATIONAL PARK

The largest piece of tropical dry forest under government protection in Central America spreads out over Santa Rosa National Park, about 35 km (22 miles) north of Guanacaste's capital, Liberia. The park, which covers 380 square km (146 square miles), also includes two beaches and coastal mangrove forest. Thanks to trails and equipped campsites, you can venture deep into the park. During the dry season, visibility is excellent and chances are good in terms of spotting some of the hundreds of bird and animal species there. (⇨ *See Chapter 6.*)

Canopy Tour at Rincón de la Vieja National Park

EXPERIENCING A DRY TROPICAL FOREST

Rincón de la Vieja National Park

Many of Costa Rica's roads are rough at best, and tropical forests are often remote. We recommend renting a four-wheel-drive vehicle for getting around.

BIKING
Some parks allow biking, but again, this is certainly something you don't want to do during the rains. Contact the park that you'll be visiting ahead of time for trail and rental information.

BIRD- AND WILDLIFE-WATCHING
Most people come to these areas for bird-watching and wildlife spotting, but it's best done during the dry season, when all the foliage drops from the trees. Bring a good bird or wildlife guide, binoculars, lots of water (we can't stress this enough), and plenty of patience. It's a good idea to find a watering hole and just hunker down and let the animals come to you. If you don't want to explore the forest alone, tours can be arranged through hotels, ranger stations, and private research centers inside the parks. In terms of bird and wildlife guides, we recommend *The Birds of Costa Rica* by Richard Garrigues and Robert Dean and *The Mammals of Costa Rica* by Mark Wainwright. If you'd like to know more about plants, pick up *Tropical Plants of Costa Rica* by Willow Zuchowski.

HIKING
The best way to experience these endangered woods is to strap on your hiking boots, grab a hat and lots of water, and get out and walk. Most of the dry forests are protected lands and found in Guanacaste's national parks. Some have road access, making it possible to drive through the park, but most are accessible only by hiking trails. During the rainy season, roads become mud pits and hiking trails are almost impassable.

FLORA

Among other types of flora, tropical dry forests are filled with deciduous hardwoods, such as mahogany (*Swietenia macrophylla*), black laurel (*Cordia gerascanthus*), ronrón (*Astronium graveolens*), and cocobolo (*Dalbergia retusa*). Much of the wood is highly prized for furniture and houses, so many of these trees are facing extinction outside national parks and protected areas.

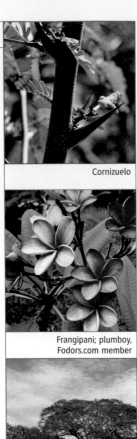
Cornizuelo

CORNIZUELO
The spiky *cornizuelo* (*Acacia collinsii*) is an intriguing resident of the lower levels because of its symbiotic relationship with ants. This small evergreen tree puts out large thorns that serve as a home for a certain ant species. In exchange for food and shelter, the ants provide the tree protection from other leaf-munching insects or vines. Sometimes the ants will even cut down encroaching vegetation on the forest floor, allowing the tree to thrive.

FRANGIPANI TREE
The frangipani tree (*Plumeria rubra*) can grow up to 8 meters (26 feet) and has meaty pink, white, or yellow blossoms. The flowers are most fragrant at night to lure sphinx moths. Unfortunately for the moth, the blooms don't produce nectar. The plant simply dupes their pollinators into hopping from bloom to bloom and tree to tree in a fruitless search for food.

Frangipani; plumboy,
Fodors.com member

GUANACASTE
Perhaps the most striking and easy-to-spot resident of Costa Rica's tropical dry forest is the *guanacaste* (*Enterolobium cyclocarpum*), an imposing tree with an enormous, spherical canopy that seems straight out of the African savanna. The guanacaste is the northwest province's namesake and Costa Rica's national tree. It is most easily identified standing alone in pastures. Without the competition of the forest, a pasture guanacaste sends massive branches out low from its trunk, creating an arching crown of foliage close to the ground. The ear-shaped seedpods are also a distinct marker; the hard seeds inside are popular with local artisan jewelers.

Guanacaste

GUMBO-LIMBO
Costa Ricans call the gumbo-limbo tree (*Bursera simaruba*) *indio desnudo* (naked Indian) because of its red, peeling bark. This tree is also found in Florida, and the wood has historically been used for making carousel horses in the United States.

Gumbo-limbo

FAUNA

Tropical dry forests are literally crawling with life. Bark scorpions, giant cockroaches, and tarantulas scuttle along the forest floor, and the buzz from wasps and cicadas gives the air an almost electric feel. A careful eye may be able to pick out walking sticks frozen still among the twigs. The jaguar, and one of its favorite prey, the endangered tapir, also stalk these forests.

Black-headed Trogon

BLACK-HEADED TROGON
With an open canopy for much of the year, and plentiful ground rodents and reptiles, these forests are great hunting grounds for birds of prey like the roadside hawk and the spectacled owl. The white-throated magpie jay travels in noisy mobs, while the scissor-tailed flycatcher migrates from as far north as the southern United States. The rufous-naped wren builds its nest in the spiky acacia trees. The black-headed trogon, with its bright yellow breast, and the elegant trogon both nest exclusively in Costa Rica's tropical dry forest.

Coyote

COYOTE
Nearly unique to the dry tropical forest is the coyote, which feeds on rodents, lizards, and an assortment of small mammals, as well as sea turtle eggs (when near the beach) and other improvised meals. Like the Virginia opossum and the white-tailed deer, the coyote is believed to have traveled south from North America through the once-interconnected tropical dry forest of Mesoamerica.

NEOTROPICAL RATTLESNAKE
The venomous neotropical rattlesnake and the exquisite painted wood turtle are among the reptiles that exclusively call this region home. Salvin's spiny pocket mouse, the eastern cottontail rabbit, and both the spotted and hooded skunk are also unique to Costa Rica's dry forests.

Neotropical Rattlesnake

WHITE-FACED CAPUCHIN
Monkeys are common all over Costa Rica, and the dry forests are home to three species: the howler monkeys, with their leathery black faces and deep barking call, are the loudest of the forest's mammals; the white-faced capuchin travel in playful packs; and the endangered spider monkey requires large, undisturbed tracts of forest for a healthy population to survive. This last group is in steep decline—another indicator of the overall health of this eco-region.

White-faced capuchin

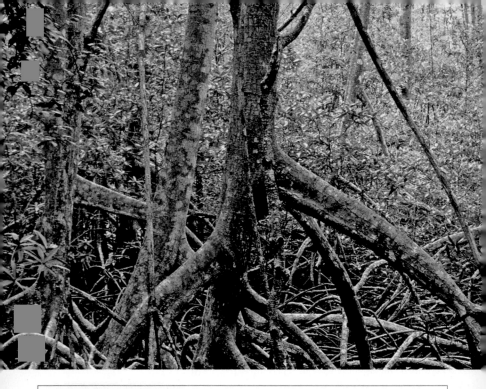

WETLANDS AND MANGROVES

Wetlands are any low-lying areas that are perpetually saturated with water. Their complex ecosystems support a variety of living things—both endemic species unique to the area and visitors who travel halfway around the hemisphere to get here. Here, land species have evolved to live much of their lives in water.

One common type of wetland in Costa Rica is a floodplain, created when a river or stream regularly overflows its banks, either because of heavy rains or ocean tides. Thanks to huge deposits of sediment that are left as the floodwaters recede, the ground is extremely fertile and plants thrive, as do the animals that feed here.

Mangroves are a unique type of wetland and cover 1% of the country. They are found at the edges of tidal areas, such as ocean inlets, estuaries, and canals where saltwater mixes with fresh. Mangrove forests are made

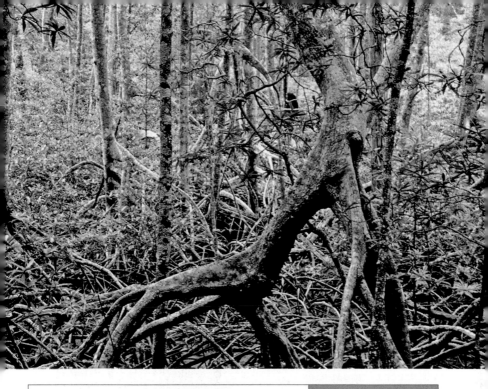

up of a small variety of plants, principally mangrove trees, but attract a huge variety of animals.

Mangrove trees are able to survive in this stressful habitat because they have developed the ability to cope with constant flooding, tolerate a lack of oxygen, and thrive in a mix of salt- and freshwater thanks to uniquely adapted roots and leaves. The nutrient-rich sediment and mud that build up around these trees and between their prop roots create habitat for plankton, algae, crabs, oysters, and shrimp. These, in turn, attract larger and larger animals that come to feed, giving mangrove forests a remarkable level of biodiversity.

These thick coastal forests are protective barriers for inland ecosystems; they dissipate the force of storm winds and sudden surges in tides or floods triggered by coastal storms or tsunamis.

Sadly, coastal development is a big threat to mangroves. It is illegal to clear mangrove forests, but enforcement is weak, and beachfront developers have been caught doing it. Wetlands are also threatened by the diversion of water for agriculture.

ADVENTURE HIGHLIGHTS

■ Witness the spectacle of nesting turtles at Tortuguero National Park. Turtle-watching excursions require a certified guide and take place only between February and November.

■ Anglers can hook mackerel, tarpon, snook, calba, and snapper in the canals and along the coast of Tortuguero and Barra Colorado.

■ Take a kayaking tour through the mangrove estuary of Isla Damas, near Manuel Antonio. You'll probably see monkeys, crocodiles, and numerous birds.

TOP DESTINATIONS

The Ramsar Convention on Wetlands is an intergovernmental treaty to provide a framework for the conservation of the world's wetlands. There are 11 Ramsar wetlands in Costa Rica: all are impressive, but we've listed only our top three.

CAÑO NEGRO NATIONAL WILDLIFE REFUGE

One Ramsar wetland is found in the Caño Negro National Wildlife Refuge, in the more remote northern plains close to the border with Nicaragua. Caño Negro has a seasonal lake that can cover as many as 1,975 acres and grow as deep as 3 meters (10 feet). The lake is actually a pool created by the Frio River that dries up to nearly nothing between February and May. The park also has marshes, semipermanently flooded old-growth forest, and other wetland habitats. (⇨ *See Chapter 5.*)

PALO VERDE NATIONAL PARK

Within the Palo Verde National Park is perhaps Costa Rica's best-known wetland—a system that includes shallow, permanent freshwater lagoons, marshes, mangroves, and woodlands that are seasonally flooded by the Tempisque River. A good portion of this 45,511-acre park is covered by tropical dry forest. In fact, this park has 12 different habitats, creating one of the most diverse collections

Alpha Howler Monkey; Liz Stuart, Fodors.com member

of life in the country. At least 55 aquatic plants and 150 tree species have been identified here, and the largest number of aquatic and wading birds in all of Mesoamerica can be found at Palo Verde wetlands. A total of 279 bird species have been recorded within Palo Verde, so little surprise that it's listed by the Ramsar Convention as a wetland of international importance. The Organization for Tropical Studies maintains a research station at the park with limited accommodations but great views of the marshes, as well as extremely knowledgeable guides. (⇨ *See Chapter 6.*)

TORTUGUERO NATIONAL PARK

Ninety-nine percent of mangrove forests are found on Costa Rica's Pacific coast. But the best place to see some of the remaining 1% on the Caribbean side is Tortuguero National Park. Like Palo Verde, Tortuguero is home to a wide variety of life—11 distinct habitats in total, including extensive wetlands and mangrove forests. Beach-nesting turtles (*tortugas*) are the main attraction here, but the park is included in the Ramsar list of internationally important wetlands. Many of the species listed here can be spotted along the banks of Tortuguero's famous canals. (⇨ *See Chapter 9.*)

Tortuguero; StupFD, Fodors.com member

EXPERIENCING THE WETLANDS AND MANGROVES

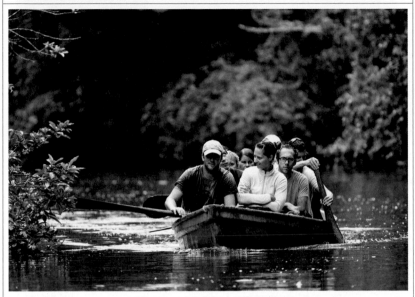

Paddling through Tortuguero at dawn; Thornton Cohen, Fodors.com member

Wildlife viewing in general can be very rewarding in these areas, because a wide variety of creatures come together and share the habitat.

BIRD-WATCHING

The most populous and diverse of the creatures that live in and depend on wetlands and mangroves are birds, so bring some binoculars and your field guide, and prepare to check off some species. For good photos, take a long lens and tripod, and get an early start—midday sun reflecting off the ubiquitous water can make your photos washed out or create some challenging reflections.

BOATING

The best way to see Costa Rica's remaining mangrove forests is by boat—we recommend using a kayak or canoe. These vessels allow you to slip along canals and protected coastlines in near silence, increasing your chance of creeping up on

many of the more impressive creatures that call this habitat home. A guided boat tour is also recommended—a good naturalist or biologist, or even a knowledgeable local, will know where creatures habitually hang out and will be able to distinguish between thick branches and a knotted boa at the top of a shoreside tree.

FISHING

Canals that are not part of protected areas can be ripe for fishing—another, tastier way to get a close-up look at some of the local fauna. Make sure to ask about what's biting, as well as local fishing regulations.

VIEWING PLATFORMS

Hiking can be more difficult in these areas because wetlands are by definition largely underwater. But some areas have elevated platforms that make for great up-close viewing of the interior parts of marshes and shallow lagoons.

FLORA

Wetland and mangrove plants share an ability to live in soggy conditions. However, not all wetland plants are able to survive brackish water in the way coastal mangrove flora can.

Black Mangrove

BLACK MANGROVE

The black mangrove can grow as tall as 12 meters (40 feet) and has adapted to survive in its habitat by excreting salt through special glands in its leaves. It grows on the banks above the high-tide line and has evolved to breathe through small roots it sends up vertically in case of flooding.

RED MANGROVE

Costa Rica has seven species of mangrove trees, including red mangrove (*Rhizophora mangle*), black mangrove (*Avicennia germinans*), white mangrove (*Laguncularia racemosa*), and the rarer tea mangrove (*Pelliciera rhizophorae*). Red mangrove is easily identified by its tall arching prop roots that give it a firm foothold against wind and waves. The tidal land is also unstable, so all mangroves need a lot of root just to keep upright. As a result, many have more living matter underwater than aboveground. They also depend on their prop roots for extra nutrients and oxygen; the red mangrove filters salt at its roots.

Red Mangrove

THORNY SENSITIVE PLANT

Aquatic grasses and herbs grow along the shallower edges of swamps and marshlands where they can take root underwater and still reach the air above. The curious dormilona, or thorny sensitive plant (*Mimosa pigra*), is another invasive wetland shrub and can be identified by the way its fernlike leaves wilt shyly to the touch, only to straighten out a little later.

Thorny sensitive plant

WATER HYACINTH

The succulent, floating water hyacinth (*Eichornia crassipes*) is recognizable by its lavender-pink flowers that are sometimes bundled at 8 to 15 per single stalk. The stems rise from a bed of thick, floating green leaves, whereas the plant's feathery roots hang free in the still freshwater. The water hyacinth is prolific and invasive; they've even been known to clog the canals of Tortuguero.

Water Hyacinth

FAUNA

Though the diversity of plant life in mangrove swamps and wetlands is small compared with other ecozones, this habitat attracts an extremely wide variety of fauna.

BLACK-BELLIED WHISTLING DUCK
Bird-watchers love the wide-open wetlands and marshes, with flocks of thousands of migrating and resident species. In these tropical floodplains pink-tinged roseate spoonbills will be found stalking the shallow water alongside the majestic great egret and the bizarre and endangered jabiru stork. Keep an eye out for the black-bellied whistling duck, which actually perches and nests in trees. These migrant ducks can also be found in some southern U.S. states.

BLACK-CROWNED NIGHT HERON
Mangroves are critical nesting habitats for a number of birds, including the endangered mangrove hummingbird, the yellow-billed continga, the Amazon kingfisher, and the black-crowned night heron. Interestingly, black-crowned night herons don't distinguish between their own young and those from other nests, so they willingly brood strange chicks.

CRAB-EATING RACCOON
Bigger creatures are attracted to these mangroves precisely because of the veritable buffet of sea snacks. The crab-eating raccoon will prowl the canopy of the mangrove forests as well as the floor, feeding on crabs and mollusks. The endangered American crocodile and the spectacled caiman can be found lurking in still waters or sunning themselves on the banks of mangrove habitat.

RAINBOW PARROT FISH
Rainbow parrot fish, in addition to many other fish species, spend time as juveniles in mangrove areas, feeding in the relative safety of the roots until they're big enough to venture out into more open water. Parrot fish have a few unusual abilities: they are hermaphroditic and can change sex in response to population density; at night they wrap themselves in a protective mucus cocoon; and they eat algae off the coral and excrete a fine white sand. One parrot fish can create up to 200 pounds of sand per year, which ultimately washes ashore. Think about it the next time you're lying on the beach.

Black-Bellied Whistling Duck

Black-Crowned Night Heron

Crab-eating Raccoon

Rainbow Parrot Fish

2

SHORELINE

Costa Rica has a whopping 1,290-km-long (799-mile-long) coastline that varies from expansive beaches to tranquil bays, muddy estuaries, and rocky outcroppings. They're backed by mangrove, rain, transitional, and tropical dry forests.

Each of Costa Rica's coastal environments, as well as the currents and the wind, has its own distinct impact on the ecology of the beach.

Costa Rica's sand beaches come in different shades and textures: pulverized black volcanic rock (Playa Negra), crushed white shells (Playa Conchal), finely ground white coral and quartz (Playa Carrillo), and gray rock sediment (many stretches along both coasts). These strips of sand may seem devoid of life, but they're actually ecological hotbeds, where mammals, birds, and amphibians live, feed, or reproduce. The hardiest of creatures can be found in the tidal pools that form on rockier beaches; keep an eye out for colorful fish, starfish, and sea urchins, all of which endure pounding waves, powerful tides, broiling sun, and predator attacks from the air, land, or sea.

By law, all of Costa Rica's beaches are public, but beaches near population centers get strewn with trash quite quickly. It's one of the great ironies of Costa Rica that a country renowned for its environmental achievements litters with such laissez-faire. Limited access tends to make for more scenic beaches. If you're worried about pollution, keep an eye out for Blue Flag beaches (marked on our maps with blue flags), an ecological rating system that evaluates water quality—both ocean and drinking water—trash cleanup, waste management, security, signage, and environmental education. Blue flags are awarded to communities rather than to individual hotels, which feeds a sense of cooperation. In 2002, the competition was opened to inland communities.

ADVENTURE HIGHLIGHTS

■ From October 15 to February 15, Playa Grande sees lumbering, huge leatherback turtles come ashore to nest. Sixty days later, the hatchlings will scramble toward the water.

■ Gentle, consistent waves and a couple of good surfing schools make Sámara, on the North Pacific coast, a good choice for first-timers hoping to catch a wave.

■ Snorkeling is phenomenal near Cahuita's coral reef and at Punta Uva on the Caribbean coast. Look for colorful blue parrot fish, angelfish, sponges, and seaweeds.

TOP DESTINATIONS

Costa Rica's beach scenes are wildly diverse, so a little planning can go a long way.

WHALE MARINE NATIONAL PARK

This unique park is along one of the more remote stretches of coastline, on the southern end of the Central Pacific region, and encompasses several beaches. Parque Nacional Marino Ballena (*ballena* is Spanish for "whale") gets its name from the humpback whales who feed here, and for a peculiar sandbar formation at Playa Uvita that goes straight out toward the ocean before splitting and curving in two directions, much like a whale's tail. (⇨ *See Chapter 8.*)

THE CARIBBEAN

This coast has an entirely different feel from the Pacific. North of Limón, there are miles of undeveloped, protected beaches where green sea turtles come from July to October to lay eggs. There have also been sightings of the loggerhead, hawksbill, and leatherback turtles. The currents here are strong, so don't plan on swimming.

To the south of Limón, beaches are bordered by dense green vegetation all year long, and the quality of the sand can change dramatically as you wander from cove to cove. Some of the country's

Uvita Beach; Toronto Jeff, Fodors.com member

healthiest living coral reefs are offshore, so snorkeling is worthwhile. Beaches of note are Cahuita's Playa Negra and Playa Blanca, and Puerto Viejo de Talamanca's Punta Uva. (⇨ *See Chapter 9.*)

MANUEL ANTONIO NATIONAL PARK

On the northern end of the Pacific coast, Manuel Antonio National Park shelters some of the country's more precious beaches. A series of half-moon bays with sparkling sands are fronted by transitional forest—a combination of flora and fauna from the tropical dry forests farther north and the tropical rain forests that stretch south. Wildlife is abundant at Manuel Antonio, and the towering jungle at the beach's edge can give the area a wild and paradisiacal feel. (⇨ *See Chapter 7.*)

THE NICOYA PENINSULA

A succession of incredible beaches are scattered along this region of the Pacific coast, from Playa Panama in the north all the way south to Montezuma, including Avellanas, Guiones, and Sámara. Ostional, just north of Guiones, offers something none of the others can: the turtle arribada. The beach is part of the Ostional Wildlife Refuge, granting an extra level of protection to the area. (⇨ *See Chapter 6.*)

Montezuma; Justin Hubbell, Fodors.com member

EXPERIENCING THE SHORELINE

Nesting Olive Ridley Turtles at Ostional Wildlife Refuge

Costa Rica's beaches have tons of activities. If you like getting wet, the ocean is bathwater warm and there are water-sports outfitters just about everywhere. There are also plenty of hammocks and cafés.

HORSEBACK RIDING

Horseback riding on the beach is great fun, but you can't do it everywhere. Many of the most popular beaches have outlawed it for health reasons, especially if it's where a lot of people swim.

SURFING

Costa Rica is a world-class surfing destination, and the Pacific coast in particular has enough surf spots to satisfy both pros and novices. You can arrange lessons in most beach towns. Surfing is an activity that involves a lot of floating, so it allows for plenty of wildlife watching: keep a weather eye for jumping fish, stingrays, dolphins, and squads of brown pelicans.

TURTLE TOURS

Witnessing the nesting ritual of Costa Rica's visiting sea turtles is a truly unforgettable experience. Various organizations oversee the nesting beaches and arrange tours. The onslaught of mother turtles is most intense throughout the night, so setting out just before dawn is the best way to see and take pictures of the phenomenon in progress at first light.

■ TIP→ Take great care at beaches that drop off steeply as you enter the water. This is an indicator not only of large waves that crash straight onto the shore but also of strong currents.

FLORA

The plants along the coast play an important role in maintaining the dunes and preventing erosion in the face of heavy winds and other forces.

COCONUT PALMS

Coconut palm trees are the most distinctive plants in any tropical setting. No postcard photo of a white-sand beach would be complete without at least one palm tilting precariously over the shore. Palm trees (from the *Arecaceae* family) require a lot of sunlight and, thanks to their strong root system, will often grow at nearly horizontal angles to escape the shade of beachside forests. The coconut palm is also the proud parent of the world's largest seed—the delicious coconut—which can float long distances across the ocean, washing up on a foreign shore and sprouting a new tree from the sand.

Coconut Palms

MANGROVE

Mangrove swamps are rich, murky forests that thrive in brackish waters up and down Costa Rica's coasts. They grow in what's known as the intertidal zone, the part of the coast that's above sea level at low tide and submerged at high tide. Mangrove trees (*rhizophora*) are just one of the species that live in these coastal swamps—you can recognize them by their stilt roots, the long tendril-like roots that allow the tree to breathe even when it's partially submerged. These forests are vibrant and complex ecosystems in their own right.

Mangrove tree

MANZANILLO DE PLAYA

Steer clear of the poisonous manchineel, or *manzanillo de playa* (*Hippomane mancinella*), the most toxic tree in Costa Rica. Its fruit and bark secrete a white latex that's highly irritating to the touch and poisonous—even fatal—if ingested. Don't burn it either, because the smoke can also cause allergic reactions. The tree can be identified by its small, yellowish apples and bright green leaves. It's found along the North Pacific coast, stretches of the Nicoya Peninsula, the Central Pacific's Manuel Antonio National Park, and on the Osa Peninsula.

Manzaniillo de playa

SEA GRAPE

Sea grape (*Coccoloba uvifera*) and similar types of shrubby, ground-hugging vegetation grow closer to the water, around the edges of the beach. These plants play a part in keeping the beach stable and preventing erosion.

Seagrape

FAUNA

Beaches are tough environments where few animals actually make their home. But as we all know, you don't have to live on the beach to enjoy it.

Brown Pelican

BROWN PELICAN

Brown pelicans fly in tight formation, dropping low over the sea and running parallel with the swells in search of shoals of fish. Browns are unique in that they're the only pelican species that plunge from the air to catch their food. After a successful dive, they have to guard against gulls, who will actually try to pluck the freshly caught fish from their pouch.

IGUANAS

A common sight on Costa Rica's sandy shores are iguanas. The green iguana (*Iguana iguana*) and the black spiny-tailed iguana, or black iguana (*Ctenosaura simi*), are often found sunning themselves on rocks or a few feet from the shade (and protection) of trees. Interestingly, the green iguana has been known to lay eggs and share nests with American crocodiles and spectacled caimans.

Iguanas

OLIVE RIDLEY TURTLE

At 34 to 45 kilos (75 to 100 pounds) the olive ridley (*Lepidochelys olivacea*) is the smallest of the five marine turtles that nest in Costa Rica. During mass nesting times (arribada), anywhere from tens to hundreds of thousands of females drag themselves ashore, gasping audibly, to lay their eggs. Between dusk and dawn, the prehistoric creatures crawl over the beach, sometimes even over one another, on their way between the ocean and their nests. People who are lucky enough to witness the event never forget it. Costa Rica's shores are also visited by the green turtle, the hawksbill, the loggerhead, and the leatherback turtle.

Olive Ridley Turtle

PAINTED GHOST CRAB

These intriguingly named crabs are called "ghosts" because they move so quickly that they seem to disappear. They're also one of the few creatures that actually live full-time on the beach. Sun beats down, wind is strong, danger lurks everywhere, and there's little to no cover, but painted ghost crabs (*Ocypode cuadrata*) survive all this by burrowing deep under the sand where the temperature and humidity are more constant and there's safe protection from surface threats like the black iguana.

Painted Ghost Crab

SAN JOSÉ

WELCOME TO SAN JOSÉ

TOP REASONS TO GO

★ **Eating out:** Instead of relying on mostly rice and beans and chicken like the rest of Costa Rica, San José's diverse restaurants offer a welcome change of pace.

★ **Gold and Jade museums:** For a sense of indigenous Costa Rica, frequently forgotten during the nation's march to modernity, the country's two best museums are must-sees.

★ **Historic Barrios Amón and Otoya:** These northern neighborhoods abutting and sometimes overlapping downtown have tree-lined streets and century-old houses turned into trendy hotels and restaurants.

★ **Location, location, location:** From the capital's pivotal position, you can be on a coffee tour, at the peak of a giant volcano, or riding river rapids in an hour or less.

★ **Shopping:** San José is the best place to stock up on both essentials and souvenirs. Look for leather-and-wood rocking chairs, ceramics, textiles, and, of course, wonderful coffee.

1 Downtown. This area holds San José's historic and commercial districts and many top attractions: the Museo del Jade (Jade Museum), Museo del Oro Precolombino (Gold Museum), Mercado Central (Central Market), and Teatro Nacional (National Theater).

2 West of Downtown. The mostly residential neighborhoods here are anchored by large Parque Metropolitano La Sabana (La Sabana Park) and the Museo de Arte Costarricense (Museum of Costa Rican Art).

3

GETTING ORIENTED

The metropolitan area holds around 2.2 million residents, but the city proper is small, with some 288,000 people living in its 44 square km (17 square miles). Most sights are concentrated in three downtown neighborhoods—La Soledad, La Merced, and El Carmen—named for their anchor churches. Borders are fuzzy: one *barrio* (neighborhood) flows into the next, districts overlap, and the city itself melts into its suburbs with nary a sign to denote where one community ends and another begins.

3 North of Downtown.
Historic barrios Amón and Otoya and the Museo de los Niños (Children's Museum) are a few of the attractions to the north.

4 East of Downtown.
Several good restaurants and hotels and the Universidad de Costa Rica (University of Costa Rica) are ensconced in the San Pedro suburb.

SOUVENIR SHOPPING IN SAN JOSÉ

San José's shops and markets can be crowded, but they're great fun for the savvy shopper and a great way to explore. The city's bustling downtown is compact enough to make it easy to visit a few markets in a day, or even an afternoon.

Coffee. The most authentic modern-day Costa Rica souvenir, and the most appreciated back home. Load up on whole bean (*grano entero*), or, if you prefer ground (*molido*), buy the *puro*, otherwise it might have pre-added sugar. Café Britt is the most famous brand (¢2,500/lb).

Coffee brewers. The original Costa Rican coffeemaker is called a *chorreador*. It's a simple wooden stand that's fitted with cloth sock-like filters. Finely ground coffee is dumped in the sock, and hot water is filtered into the mug beneath. Unadorned ones in sleek cherry wood cost around ¢5,000. Don't forget extra filters (¢250).

Local libations. If you don't have room for a six-pack, be sure to take home the Imperial beer label on a stein or T-shirt (both ¢2,500). Or, snag a bottle of Costa Rica's signature sugarcane liquor, *guaro.*

Mayan ocarinas. Calling the ocarina two-faced would be an insult, but only because you wouldn't be giving it nearly enough credit. The Mayan resonant vessel flutes (¢2,500–¢7,000) depict over a half-dozen animal faces when flipped around and were often given as gifts to travelers by the Chorotega indigenous group in northwestern Guanacaste.

Hammocks. Swinging in one of these is the official *pura vida* posture. Structured hammocks with wooden dowels on the ends (¢12,000 and up) are optimal, but dowel-less, cocoon-like hammocks (¢10,000 and up) are infinitely more packable. Get a chair hammock (¢10,000) if you have limited space back home.

Oxcarts. From the Sarchí region, the oxcart has become Costa Rica's most iconic craftsman artifact. Full-size ones can run several hundred dollars, and dealers can arrange to have them shipped. There's also a coffee table–size version (¢20,000) or, better yet, an oxcart napkin holder (¢2,000).

Boruca Ceremonial Masks. The Boruca people, one of the country's last active indigenous groups, don these masks in their annual end-of-the-year festival, Dansa de los Diablitos (Dance of the Devils). Cheaper imitations abound, but Galería Namu has the best—and most authentic—selection (¢65,000 to ¢100,000).

Machetes. Knives and machetes are commonly used in the country's rural jungle areas and happily sold in leather slings to travelers (¢7,000). Also, knives (¢2,000–3,000) and other items, like frogs and butterflies made out of colored resin, might not be considered traditional but represent the Rastafarian side of the country.

Jewelry. Go for oversized wooden hoop earrings (¢3,000), wire-wrought gold and silver baubles (¢3,500), or

plaster-molded earrings adorned with toucans, frogs, and pineapples (¢1,500). Jewelry made from carved-out coco shells is popular, too.

Tropical woods and papers. Sleek mango-wood vases (¢8,500), inlaid rosewood cutting boards (¢8,000), and hand-painted rum wood mugs (¢4,000) are among the many elegant woodworks here. There are also scratch-and-sniff writing materials that would make Willy Wonka proud, with banana, mango, lemon, and coffee-scented stationery sets (¢3,700).

Folkloric dresses and shirts. While they're often only pulled out on national holidays like Independence Day, a flounced dress (¢8,000 and up) or pinafore (¢5,000) might be just the kitschy gift you're looking for. Ranchero-style shirts (¢8,000) and straw hats (¢2,000) are also an option.

Updated by
Jeffrey Van
Fleet

San José is the center of all that is Costa Rica, and—to Ticos in the countryside at least—it glitters every bit as much as New York City. True to developing-country patterns, everything—politics, business, art, cuisine, nightlife, and culture—converges here in the capital. It may not be the center of your trip to Costa Rica—those rain forests and volcanoes have your name written on them. But the city is worth a day or two of exploring, as a way to ease into Costa Rica at the start of a visit or to wrap things up with a well-deserved dose of civilization following your adventures to more remote parts of the country.

Amid the noise and traffic, shady parks, well-maintained museums, lively plazas, terrific restaurants, and great hotels do exist. Further, the city makes a great base for day trips: from downtown it's a mere 30- to 40-minute drive to the tranquil countryside and myriad outdoor activities of the surrounding Central Valley.

You'd never know San José is as old as it is—given the complete absence of colonial architecture—but settlers migrating from then-provincial-capital Cartago founded the city in 1737. After independence in 1821, San José cemented its position as the new nation's capital after struggles and a brief civil war with fellow Central Valley cities Cartago, Alajuela, and Heredia. Revenues from the coffee and banana industries financed the construction of stately homes, theaters, and a trolley system (later abandoned and now visible only in old sepia photographs).

As recently as the mid-1900s, San José was no larger than the present-day downtown area; old-timers remember the vast coffee and cane plantations that extended beyond its borders. The city began to mushroom only after World War II, when old buildings were razed to make room for concrete monstrosities. The sprawl eventually connected the capital with nearby cities.

San José has attracted people from all over Costa Rica, yet it remains, in many ways, a collection of distinct neighborhoods where residents maintain friendly small-town ways. For you, this might mean the driver you're following will decide to abruptly stop his vehicle to buy a lottery ticket or chat with a friend on the street. Or it might mean you have to navigate a maze of fruit-vendor stands on a crowded sidewalk. But this is part of what keeps San José a big small town.

PLANNING

WHEN TO GO
HIGH SEASON: MID-DECEMBER TO APRIL
San José's 3,800-foot altitude keeps temperatures pleasant and spring-like year-round. The capital's status as a business-travel destination means lodging rates rarely vary throughout the year. The dry season literally blows in with a change in wind patterns that make December and January brisk, but sunny. February warms up; by March and April, the heat and dust pick up considerably.

LOW SEASON: MAY TO MID-NOVEMBER
The wet season moves in gradually, with manageable brief afternoon showers from May through July. August becomes wetter. September and October might mean constant rain for days at a time, and navigating a traffic-clogged city in a torrential rush-hour downpour is little fun.

SHOULDER SEASON: MID-NOVEMBER TO MID-DECEMBER
Rains wind down by mid-November and you'll even experience a bit of a nip in the air—it's still the tropics, though—as the city decks itself out for the holidays. The big influx of tourists won't arrive until just before Christmas, so this is the time to enjoy the capital at its best.

PLANNING YOUR TIME
SAN JOSÉ IN A DAY
If you have only a day to spend in San José, the must-see stops are the Teatro Nacional (National Theater) and the Museo del Oro Precolombino (Pre-Columbian Gold Museum). It's easy to accomplish this because they sit on the same block.

With more time, take in the Museo del Jade (Jade Museum) and Museo Nacional (National Museum). The Museo de los Niños (Children's Museum) is a kid pleaser. It's in a dicey part of the barrio El Carmen, more north of downtown than actually in downtown; take a taxi.

BYPASS SAN JOSÉ?
San José isn't necessarily the Costa Rica you came to see. Those beaches and rain forests beckon, after all. If that is, indeed, the case, you can avoid the city altogether.

The international airport actually lies just outside the city of Alajuela, about 30 minutes northwest of the capital. Look for lodgings in Alajuela, San Antonio de Belén, Escazú, or Santa Ana—all within striking distance of the airport. Or head west. ⇨ *For information about lodgings near Aeropuerto Internacional Juan Santamaría, see Chapter 4.*

Few international flights arrive in the morning, but they do exist, especially via Miami. Get here early and you can head out of town immediately.

Another option is to join the growing number of visitors flying into Daniel Oduber International Airport in Liberia, where Costa Rica's northern and western reaches (including the North Pacific) are nearby.

DAY TRIPS FROM THE CAPITAL

The capital sits smack-dab in the middle of the country in the fertile Central Valley. Although a day trip to either coast would be grueling—despite Costa Rica's small size, it takes longer than you think to get from place to place—you can easily pop out to the Central Valley's major sights and be back in the city in time for dinner. Several of these attractions provide pickup service in San José, some for a nominal additional cost. Alternatively, tour operators include many of these attractions on their itineraries.

DESTINATION	FROM SAN JOSÉ (BY CAR)
Basílica de Nuestra Señora de los Ángeles	30 mins southeast
Café Britt	30 mins north
Carara National Park	2 hrs southwest
Doka Coffee Estate	1 hr west
Guayabo National Monument	2 hrs southeast, 4WD necessary
INBioparque	15 mins north
Irazú Volcano	60 mins east
La Paz Waterfall Gardens	2 hrs north
Orosi Valley	60 mins southeast
Poás Volcano	60 mins northwest
Rainforest Adventures	45 mins north
River Rafting	2–2½ hrs southeast or north
Sarchí	60 mins northwest
Tortuga Island	3 hrs west
Tropical Bungee	60 mins west
Zoo Ave	45 mins west

GETTING HERE AND AROUND

AIR TRAVEL

Aeropuerto Internacional Juan Santamaría, 16 km (10 miles) northwest of downtown, receives international flights and those of domestic airlines SANSA and Nature Air.

BUS TRAVEL

San José's public bus stations are all in sketchy neighborhoods. Always take a taxi to and from them. Even better: use air-conditioned minivan shuttles operated by Grayline and Interbus instead of buses to travel between the capital and key tourist destinations.

City buses are cheap (¢40–¢60) and easy to use. For Paseo Colón and La Sabana, take buses marked "Sabana–Cementerio" from stops at Avenida 2 between Calles 5 and 7 or Avenida 3 next to the post office. For Los Yoses and San Pedro, take the various "San Pedro" buses from Avenida Central between Calles 9 and 11.

Bus Terminals Gran Terminal del Caribe. ⊠ *C. Central, Avda. 13, Barrio Tournón.* **Terminal 7-10.** ⊠ *C. 10, Avda. 7, Barrio La Merced* ⊹ *across from former Cine Líbano.* **Terminal Atlántico Norte.** ⊠ *C. 12, Avda. 9, Barrio La Merced.* **Terminal Coca-Cola.** ⊠ *Avda. 1, C. 16, Barrio La Merced.* **Terminal San Ramón.** ⊠ *C. 16, Avda. 12, Barrio La Merced.* **Terminal Tracopa.** ⊠ *C. 5, Avda. 20, Barrio El Pacífico* ☎ *2221–4214.*

Shuttle Companies Grayline. ☎ *2291–2222* ⊕ *www.graylinecostarica.com.* **Interbus.** ☎ *4100–0888* ⊕ *www.interbusonline.com.*

CAR TRAVEL

Paved roads fan out from Paseo Colón west to Escazú and northwest to the airport and Heredia. For the North Pacific coast, Guanacaste, and on to Nicaragua, take the Pan-American Highway north (CA1). The Carretera a Caldera (Highway 27) takes you to Escazú, Santa Ana, and beyond to the Central Pacific coast. Calle 3 runs north into the highway to Guápiles, Limón, and the Atlantic coast through Braulio Carrillo National Park, with a turnoff to Sarapiquí. Follow Avenida Central or 2 east through San Pedro to enter the Pan-American Highway south (CA2), which has a turnoff for Cartago, Volcán Irazú, and Turrialba before it heads toward the South Pacific coast and Panama.

Avoid driving in the city if you can help it. Streets are narrow, rush hour (7 to 9 am and 5 to 7 pm) traffic is horrible, and drivers can be reckless. What's more, San José and neighboring San Pedro enforce rigid weekday driving restrictions (6 am–7 pm) for all private vehicles, including your rental car. The last digit of your license plate determines your no-driving day: Monday (1 and 2), Tuesday (3 and 4), Wednesday (5 and 6), Thursday (7 and 8), and Friday (9 and 0).

Driving is forbidden on 44 blocks in the center city—sections of Avenidas Central and 4, and Calles 2, 3, 8, 9, and 17—which have been turned into pleasant pedestrian-only thoroughfares. More of these *bulevares* are on the drawing board. Thank China and the European Union for much of the funding.

TAXI TRAVEL

You can hail cabs on the street or call for one. Licensed cabs are red with a gold triangle on the front doors. Taxis Unidos Aeropuerto—which go to the airport—are orange. A 3-km (2-mile) ride costs around $3; tipping isn't customary. By law cabbies must use *marías* (meters) within the metropolitan area; the meter starts at about $1.15. Cab drivers hate it if you slam the door; close the door gently.

The ride service Uber operates in San José and surrounding suburbs. At 90 cents for the first kilometer and 60 cents for each additional kilometer with a minimum fare of $2, it is cheaper than licensed taxis. Uber does adopt supplemental "surge pricing" at peak times, namely during rush hour, weekend nights, and rainy weather.

TUNE IN: COSTA RICAN RADIO

Take Costa Rican radio along if you're driving to your adventures out of San José. The airwaves here are filled with the hottest Latin hits or a hefty dose of religion, be it Catholic or evangelical. Below are a few of our favorite stations that break that mold:

Radio Sinfonola (90.3 FM): vintage Spanish romantic music of the *Bésame Mucho* type.

Radio 95.Cinco (95.5): hottest Latin-jazz fusion from Miami to Rio.

Radio Universidad (96.7 FM): Bach, Beethoven, Brahms, and more, with commentary in Spanish.

Radio Dos (99.5 FM): American and British pop hits of the '70s, '80s, and '90s, with Spanish-speaking DJs. (English-speaking jocks handle 6 to 9 am and 5 to 7 pm drive times.)

Taxis Alfaro. ☎ *2223–3373.* **Coopetaxi.** ☎ *2235–9966.* **San Jorge.** ☎ *2221–3434.* **Taxi Aeropuerto.** ☎ *2221–6865* ⊕ *www.taxiaeropuerto.com.* **Uber.** ⊕ *www.uber.com/cities/san-jose.*

HEALTH AND SAFETY

San José is safer than other Latin American capitals. Violent crime is rare; the greatest threat you're likely to face is petty theft. Standard big-city precautions apply:

Exchange money only at banks. Street money changers slip counterfeit bills into their stash, or doctor their calculators to compute unfavorable rates. In the extreme, they might grab your cash and run off.

Select ATMs in well-lighted areas. Better still, use a bank's ATM during opening hours, when a guard will likely be present. Go with a buddy, and conceal cash immediately.

Use only licensed red taxis with yellow triangles on the front doors. The license plate of an official taxi begins with TSJ ("Taxi San José").

Park in guarded, well-lighted lots ($2 an hour). If you must park on the street, make sure informal *guachimen* (watchmen) are present. Usually this is someone with a big stick who will expect payment of about $1 per hour. Never leave anything valuable in your parked vehicle.

Medical Assistance Clínica Bíblica. ⊠ *Avda. 14, Cs. Central–1, Barrio El Pacífico* ☎ *2522–1000* ⊕ *www.clinicabiblica.com.* **Hospital La Católica.** ⊠ *C. Esquivel Bonilla, Guadalupe* ☎ *2246–3000* ⊕ *www.hospitallacatolica.com.*

MONEY MATTERS

It's a bad sign when San José banks have televisions to watch while you pass the time in the horrendous lines. Bypass that process and get cash with your ATM card instead. Cash machines inside a bank, during the day while a guard keeps watch, are your safest bet.

Banks/ATMs BAC San José. ⊠ *Avda. 2, Cs. Central–1, Barrio El Carmen* ☎ *2295–9797* ⊕ *www.bac.net.* **Banco Nacional.** ⊠ *Avda. 1, Cs. 2–4, Barrio La Merced* ☎ *2212–2000* ⊕ *www.bncr.fi.cr.* **Scotiabank.** ⊠ *C. 5, Avdas. Central–2, behind Teatro Nacional, Barrio La Soledad* ☎ *2521–5680* ⊕ *www.scotiabankcr.com.*

TOURS

Barrio Bird Walking Tours. Despite the name, the focus of this company is not birding but rather two-hour walking tours of the city, with a focus on sights, art, and food. ☎ *6280–6169* ⊕ *www.toursanjosecostarica. com* ✉ *From $32.*

City Square Tours. A guided hop-on, hop-off bus tour lets you choose two routes: the Orange Line focuses on six stops in the center city; the Blue Line takes you from downtown to the western suburb of Escazú in the Central Valley. Tickets are valid for 24 or 48 hours. ☎ *4030-4125* ⊕ *www.costaricacitysquaretour.com* ✉ *From $30.*

Gray Line Costa Rica. This respected international company operates sightseeing and shopping tours, as well as excursions to the surrounding Central Valley. ✉ *San José* ☎ *2220–2106 in Costa Rica, 800/719–3905 in North America* ⊕ *www.graylinecostarica.com* ✉ *From $48.*

VIP City Bus. You'll see the city between downtown and La Sabana Park from the vantage point of a double-decker bus on VIP's four-hour tours that include snacks and commentary from bilingual guides. ☎ *2282-0240* ⊕ *www.vipcitybus.com* ✉ *From $70.* .

VISITOR INFORMATION

The ubiquitous "Tourist Information" signs you see around downtown are really private travel agencies looking to sell you tours rather than provide unbiased information. The Instituto Costarricense de Turismo, the official tourist office, operates an office on Avenida Central and a booth in the arrivals area of the international airport. The staff here is not allowed to make specific recommendations, so answers to questions sometimes come across as vague and lackadaisical.

Visitor Information Instituto Costarricense de Turismo (ICT). ✉ *Avda. Central, Cs. 1–3* ☎ *2222–1090* ⊕ *www.visitcostarica.com.*

EXPLORING

In San José some streets have names, but no one seems to know or use them. Streets in the center of the capital are laid out in a grid, with *avenidas* (avenues) running east and west, and *calles* (streets) north and south. Odd-number avenues increase in number north of Avenida Central; even-number avenues, south. Streets east of Calle Central have odd numbers; those to the west are even. Locals rarely use the numbers, however.

Costa Ricans rely instead on a charming and exasperating system of designating addresses by the distance from landmarks, as in "100 meters north and 50 meters west of the school." Another quirk: "100 meters" always refers to one city block, regardless of how long it actually is. Likewise, "200 meters" is two blocks, and so on. (As you can imagine, getting a pizza delivered here is quite a challenge.)

Historically, the reference point was the church, but these days it might be a bar, a Taco Bell, or even a quirky landmark: the eastern suburb of San Pedro uses the *higuerón,* a prominent fig tree. The city has embarked on an ambitious project to name all its streets once and

for all. Even after it's completed, it's improbable that anybody will know or use the names. Your best bet is to follow the time-honored practice of *ir y preguntar* (keep walking and keep asking). ⇨ *See the Vocabulary section in Understanding Costa Rica for help asking for directions in Spanish.*

DOWNTOWN

It's a trend seen the world over: businesses and residents flee city centers for the space, blissful quiet, and lower-priced real estate of the burbs. Although Costa Rica's capital is experiencing this phenomenon, downtown still remains the city's historic and vibrant (if noisy and congested) heart. Government offices have largely stayed put here, as have most attractions. It's impossible to sightsee without finding yourself downtown.

Boundaries are fuzzy. For example, the sub-neighborhoods of El Carmen, La Merced, and La Soledad are anchored in downtown but sprawl outward from the center city. And, in an effort to seem trendier, several establishments in downtown's northern fringes prefer to say that they're in the more fashionable barrios of Amón or Otoya.

TOP ATTRACTIONS

Fodor's Choice
★ **Museo del Jade** (*Jade Museum*). San José's starkly modern Jade Museum displays the world's largest collection of the green gemstone. The holdings log in at 5,000-plus pieces, and are, in a word, fabulous. Nearly all the items on display were produced in pre-Columbian times, and most of the jade (pronounced *hah*-day in Spanish) dates from 300 BC to AD 700. A series of drawings explains how this extremely hard stone was cut using string saws with quartz-and-sand abrasive. Jade was sometimes used in jewelry designs, but it was most often carved into oblong pendants. The museum also has other pre-Columbian artifacts, such as polychrome vases and three-legged *metates* (small stone tables for grinding corn), as well as a gallery of modern art. Also included on the tour is a startling display of ceramic fertility symbols. A glossy, photo-filled English-language guide to the museum sells for $15; the Spanish version is only $3. ☒ *Avda. Central, C. 13, Downtown* ☎ *2287–6034* ☏ *$15* ☾ *Daily 10–5.*

Fodor's Choice
★ **Museo del Oro Precolombino** (*Pre-Columbian Gold Museum*). This dazzling, modern museum in a three-story underground structure beneath the Plaza de la Cultura contains Central America's largest collection of pre-Columbian gold jewelry—20,000 troy ounces in more than 1,600 individual pieces—all owned by the Banco Central (the country's central bank) and displayed attractively in bilingual exhibits. Many pieces are in the form of frogs and eagles, two animals perceived by the region's early cultures to have great spiritual significance. A spiffy illumination system makes the pieces sparkle. All that glitters here is not gold: most spectacular are the various shaman figurines, which represent the human connection to animal deities. One of the halls houses the Museo Numismática (Coin Museum), a repository of historic coins and bills and other objects used as legal tender throughout the country's history. Rotating art exhibitions happen on another level. For an extra $7,

TO
AIRPORT

Gran Terminal
del Caribe

AVENIDA 13

MÉXICO

TOURNÓN

Avenida 11

22

Avenida 3

Avda. 9

Terminal
Atlántico
Norte

Río Torres

Avenida 11

Avenida 5

Avenida 9

Avenida 7

AMÓN

Calle 24

Calle 20

Calle 14

Calle 12

Calle 10

Calle 8

Calle 6

Calle 4

Avenida 5

Calle 1

EL CARMEN

Terminal
Coca-
Cola

Calle 22

COCA-
COLA

Avenida 3

Avenida 1

LA MERCED

4

20 21

19

Paseo Colón

18

17

Gran
Hotel
Costa Rica

Avenida Central

16 ICT

1

Avenida 2

2

Avenida 4

15

14

3

Avenida 4

12

Avenida 6

Avenida 6

13

Calle 20

Calle 16

Calle 14

Avenida 8

SANTA
LUCÍA

Avenida 10

Calle 2

Calle Central

LA
SOLEDAD

Terminal de
Puntarenas

Avenida 12

BOLÍVAR

DOLOROSA

Calle 3

Calle 5

Calle 7

Calle 9

A. Pochet e Odio

Avenida 14

Calle 16

Avenida 16

Hospital
Clínica
Bíblica

Avda. 20

Calle 18

Avenida 18

Avenida 20

0   300 yards

Avda. 22

PACIFICO

0   300 meters

Avenida 22

San José Exploring

SAN FRANCISCO
108

23

OTOYA

Casa Amarilla
7
5   8

CUESTA DE MORAS
9

Avenida 1

Avenida Central
6   11   10

TO GUADALUPE

Avenida 15

MIRAFLORES

TO SAN PEDRO, UNIVERSIDAD DE COSTA RICA
202

Avenida 11
Avenida 13

Avenida 11
Avenida 9
Avda. 7

ARANJUEZ

ESCALANTE
Avenida 5

LA CALIFORNIA

Calle 16
Calle 17
Calle 19

Calle 25

Avenida 6

Avenida 8

Avenida 10

MILFLOR

Avenida Central

LOS YOSES

Avenida 8

Avenida 10

Avenida 12

Calle 11
Calle 13

Calle José Martí

Calle 21
Calle 23
Calle 23bis

204

Avenida 16bis

CERRITO

you can take a guided tour via an app you download at the museum on your smartphone. However, the exhibits are well marked, both in English and Spanish, so there's little need for the app. ⊠ *C. 5, Avdas. Central–2, Downtown* ✛ *eastern end of Plaza de la Cultura* ☎ *2243-4202* 💳 *$11, includes Museo Numismática* ☉ *Daily 9:15–5.*

NEED A BREAK?

A slew of unnamed *sodas*—that's the Costa Rican term for a mom-and-pop eatery—populate the heart of the Mercado Central. Grab a quick bite while you explore. It's all very informal.

Fodor's Choice
★

Teatro Nacional. The National Theater is Costa Rica at its most enchanting. Chagrined that touring prima donna Adelina Patti bypassed San José in 1890 for lack of a suitable venue, wealthy coffee merchants raised import taxes and hired Belgian architects to design this building, lavish with cast iron and Italian marble. The theater was inaugurated in 1897 with a performance of Gounod's *Faust,* featuring an international cast. The sandstone exterior is marked by Italianate arched windows, marble columns with bronze capitals, and statues of strange bedfellows Ludwig van Beethoven (1770–1827) and 17th-century Spanish Golden Age playwright Pedro Calderón de la Barca (1600–81). The Muses of Dance, Music, and Fame are silhouetted in front of an iron cupola. French designer Alain Guilhot created the building's nighttime external illumination system (he did the same for the Eiffel Tower). The soft coppers, golds, and whites highlight the theater's exterior nightly from 6 pm to 5 am. A project funded by the German government has restored the theater's cupola to its original red color.

The sumptuous neo-baroque interior is of interest, too. Given the provenance of the building funds, it's not surprising that frescoes on the stairway inside depict coffee and banana production. Note Italian painter Aleardo Villa's famous ceiling mural *Alegoría del Café y Banano* (*Allegory of Coffee and Bananas*), a joyful harvest scene that appeared on Costa Rica's old 5-colón note. (The now-defunct bill is prized by collectors and by visitors as a souvenir, and is often sold by vendors in the plaza between the theater and the Gran Hotel Costa Rica next door.) You can see the theater's interior by attending one of the performances that take place several nights a week (tickets are reasonably priced); intermission gives you a chance to nose around. Stop at the *boletería* (box office) in the lobby and see what strikes your fancy. Don't worry if you left your tuxedo or evening gown back home; as long as you don't show up for a performance wearing shorts, jeans, or a T-shirt, no one will care.

For a nominal fee you can also move beyond the lobby for a guided tour; note that the theater is sometimes closed for rehearsals, so call before you go. If you're downtown on a Tuesday between February and Christmas, take in one of the Teatro al Mediodía (Theater at Midday) performances that begin at noon. It might be a chamber-music recital or a one-act play in Spanish. A similar program called Música al Atardecer (Music at Dusk) takes place each Thursday at 5 pm. Admission for either is $2, and both are presented in the second-floor foyer. ⊠ *Plaza de la Cultura, C. 3, Avda. 2, Downtown* ☎ *2221–5341* ⊕ *www.teatronacional.go.cr* ⊠ *$10* ☉ *Jan.–Apr., daily 9–4; May–Dec., Mon.–Sat. 9–4.*

3

NEED A BREAK?

Alma de Café. Duck into the Teatro Nacional's sumptuous café, off the theater lobby, to sit at a marble table and sip a hazelnut mocha beneath frescoed ceilings. The frescoes are part of an allegory celebrating the 1897 opening of the theater. Coffee runs from $3 to $5, depending on how much alcohol or ice cream is added. Sandwiches and cakes are $4 to $8. ⊠ *Teatro Nacional, C.3, Avda. 2, Downtown* ⊕ *www.almadecafe.net* ☉ *Jan.–Apr., daily 9–4; May–Dec., Mon.–Sat. 9–4; and before evening productions and during intermission.*

WORTH NOTING

Barrio Chino. We should get one thing straight about the capital's Chinatown: San José is not San Francisco. But the Chinese government has financed the transformation of five blocks of Calle 9 into a pleasant pedestrian mall. A large arch modeled on the architecture of the Tang Dynasty marks the north entrance to the street and several Chinese–Costa Rican businesses line the walkway. ⊠ *C. 9, Avdas. 2–12, Downtown.*

Catedral Metropolitana (*Metropolitan Cathedral*). Built in 1871 and completely refurbished in the late 1990s to repair earthquake damage, the neoclassical cathedral, topped by a corrugated tin dome, isn't terribly interesting outside. But inside are patterned floor tiles, stained-glass windows depicting various saints and apostles, and framed polychrome bas-reliefs illustrating the Stations of the Cross. A magnificent 1891 Belgian pipe organ fills the church with music. The renovation did away with one small time-honored tradition: rather than light real votive candles, the faithful now deposit a 100-colón coin illuminating a bulb in a row of tiny electric candles.

The interior of the small Capilla del Santísimo (Chapel of the Host) on the cathedral's north side evokes ornate old Catholicism, much more so than the main sanctuary itself. A marble statue of Pope John Paul II stands guard over the garden on the building's north side. Masses are held throughout the day on Sunday starting at 7 am, with one in English each Saturday at 4 pm. Although not technically part of the cathedral complex, a small statue of Holocaust victim Anne Frank graces the pedestrian mall on the building's south side. It was donated by the Embassy of the Netherlands. ⊠ *C. Central, Avdas. 2–4, Downtown* ☎ *2221–3820* ☉ *Mon.–Sat. 6:30–6, Sun. 6:30 am–9 pm.*

Centro Nacional de la Cultura (*National Cultural Center*). Rather than tear it down, the Ministry of Culture converted the sloped-surface, double-block 1853 Fábrica Nacional de Licores (National Liquor Factory) into this 14,000-square-meter (150,694-square-foot) cultural center, with government offices, two theaters, and a museum. It might seem strange that the liquor factory was state run, but the Costa Rican government also owns the light and water utility, phone company, Internet service provider, as well as banking, insurance, and hospital sectors. The National Liquor Factory was housed here until 1981, when it moved to a modern facility in the Central Valley. The stone-block storage depot next to the water towers at the southeast side of the complex became the Museo de Arte y Diseño Contemporáneo. A stone gate and sundial grace the entrance nearest the museum. The complex sits amid government offices, at the point where downtown's northern reaches fade into the more residential neighborhood of Barrio Otoya. ⊠ *C. 13, Avdas. 3–5, Downtown* ☎ *2257-5524* ⊕ *www.mcj.go.cr* ✉ *Tours free* ☉ *Weekdays 8–5, Sat. 10–5; tours Feb.–Nov., Wed. at 11.*

Teatro 1887. The clay-brick theater is devoted to performances by the National Dance Company. What is now the theater's lobby was once a chemical testing lab. ⊠ *C. 13, Avdas. 3–5, Downtown* ☎ *2222-2974* ⊕ *www.mcj.go.cr.*

Teatro FANAL. The metal Teatro FANAL hosts frequent theater and music performances. ⊠ *C. 13, Avdas. 3–5, Downtown* ☎ *2222-2974* ⊕ *www.mcj.go.cr.*

Correos de Costa Rica (*Central Post Office*). The handsome, carved exterior of the post office, dating from 1917, is hard to miss among the bland buildings surrounding it. The lobby and the small pedestrian plaza in front are a perpetual hive of activity. ⊠ *C. 2, Avdas. 1–3, Downtown* ☎ *2202-2900* ⊕ *www.correos.go.cr* ☉ *Weekdays 7:30–6, Sat. 8–noon.*

Estatua de John Lennon (*Statue of John Lennon*). A whimsical statue of John Lennon sits on a small, slightly out-of-the-way plaza across from La Soledad church. Sculptor José Ramón Villa's work marks the spot where, in 1966, Costa Ricans smashed Beatles records in protest of Lennon's statement that the iconic pop group was "more popular than Jesus." The official name of the statue is *Imagine All the People Living Life in Peace*, evoking the lyrics of Lennon's song *Imagine*. After nearly five decades, bygones are apparently bygones: residents and tourists alike enjoy having their photos taken sitting with the casually seated figure. ⊠ *C. 9, Avda. 4, Downtown.*

Mercado Central (*Central Market*). This block-long melting pot is a warren of dark, narrow passages flanked by stalls packed with spices (some purported to have medicinal value), fish, fruit, flowers, pets, and wood and leather crafts. The 1880 structure is a kinder, gentler introduction to a Central American market; there are no pigs or chickens or their accompanying smells to be found here. A few stands selling tourist souvenirs congregate near the entrances, but this is primarily a place where the average Costa Rican comes to shop. There are dozens of cheap restaurants and snack stalls, including the country's first ice-cream vendor. Be warned: the concentration of shoppers makes this a hot spot for pickpockets, purse snatchers, and backpack slitters. Enter and exit at the southeast corner of the building (Avenida Central at Calle 6).

A GOOD WALK

This walk lasts about an hour at a stroll. If you take a more leisurely approach, lingering at the parks or museums, it could take hours. Since the city's parks are best avoided at night, complete the walk by 5 pm, before the sun goes down.

Everyone finds a way to the **Plaza de la Cultura,** a favorite meeting spot in the heart of the city, and it makes a good kick-off point for the walk. The ornate **Teatro Nacional** sits on the south side of the plaza. Pop in and buy a ticket for an evening performance, or grab a cup of coffee at the lobby café. The **Museo del Oro Precolombino** lies under the plaza. The gold collection could easily captivate you for an hour or two. From here, head two blocks north on Calle 5 to **Parque Morazán** whose centerpiece Templo de Música is the symbol of the city. Traffic is particularly dangerous here, so take heed. The Edificio Metálico, a metal building that serves as a school, fronts the park's north side.

Continue just east of the park on Avenida 3 to the small **Parque España,** one of the city's most pleasant green spaces. The ornate building on the park's north side is the Andrew Carnegie–funded Casa Amarilla. The Ministry of Culture complex, the **Centro Nacional de la Cultura,** fronts the park's east side. From Parque España, walk one long block east to the **Parque Nacional.** Two blocks south on Calle 17 is a pleasant pedestrian mall.

Pass the Asamblea Legislativa, where Costa Rica's Congress meets, to reach the **Museo Nacional.** The entrance is on the museum's west side and is one of the higher levels on the Plaza de la Democracia, a great vantage point for sunsets. On the opposite side of the plaza sits the famed **Museo del Jade,** with its extensive American jade collection. Avenida Central fronts the plaza's north side. Head back downhill, into the city center. The avenue becomes a lively pedestrian mall at Calle 9, and three blocks later you return to the Plaza de la Cultura.

The green-and-white *"salida"* signs direct you to other exits, but they spill onto slightly less-safe streets. Use the image of the Sacred Heart of Jesus, the market's patron and protector, near the center of the building, as your guide; it faces that safer corner by which you should exit. (We doubt it was planned that way.) ⊠ *Bordered by Avdas. Central–1 and Cs. 6–8, Downtown* ☉ *Mon.–Sat. 6–6.*

NEED A BREAK?

Pops. To sample the crème de la crème of locally made ice cream, head to Pops. Mango is a favorite flavor. After a long walk on crowded sidewalks, it may be just what the doctor ordered. You'll find several outlets downtown, as well as around the country and Central America. This longtime institution is now Colombian owned. ⊠ *C. 3, Avda. Central, Downtown* ☎ *2222–2336* ⊕ *www.pops.co.cr.*

Museo de Arte y Diseño Contemporáneo (*Museum of Contemporary Art and Design*). This wonderfully minimalist space is perfect as the country's premier modern-art venue. The MADC, as it's known around town, hosts changing exhibits by artists and designers from all over Latin America. While the museum holds a permanent collection, space constraints mean that even that must rotate. You will probably not recognize the artists here, but names such as Miguel Hernández and Florencia Urbina tower over the field of contemporary art in Costa Rica. You can arrange for a guided visit with a couple of days' notice. The museum occupies part of a government-office complex in the Centro Nacional de la Cultura (CENAC). ⊠ *Centro Nacional de la Cultura, C. 15, Avdas. 3–5, Downtown* ☎ *2257-7202* ⊕ *www.madc.cr* ✉ *$3* ⊙ *Tues.–Sat. 9:30–5.*

Museo Nacional (*National Museum*). In the mango-color Bellavista Fortress, which dates from 1870, the museum gives you a quick and insightful lesson in English and Spanish on Costa Rican culture from pre-Columbian times to the present. Cases display pre-Columbian artifacts, period dress, colonial furniture, religious art, and photographs. Some of the country's foremost ethnographers and anthropologists are on the museum's staff. Nearly 1,000 pre-Columbian Costa Rican stone and ceramic objects dating from about AD 1000 are on display here. The artifacts were taken from the country in the late 19th century by businessman Minor Keith during the construction of the Atlantic Railroad and were repatriated from the Brooklyn Museum in 2012. Outside are a veranda and a pleasant, manicured courtyard garden. A former army headquarters, this now-tranquil building saw fierce fighting during a 1931 army mutiny and the 1948 revolution, as the bullet holes pocking its turrets attest. But it was also here that three-time president José Figueres abolished the country's military in 1949. ⊠ *Bellavista Fortress, C. 15, Avdas. Central–2, Downtown* ✛ *eastern end of Plaza de la Democracia* ☎ *2257-1433* ⊕ *www.museocostarica.go.cr* ✉ *$8* ⊙ *Tues.–Sat. 8:30–4:30, Sun. 9–4.*

Parque Central (*Central Park*). At the city's nucleus, the tree-shaded Central Park is more plaza than park. A life-size bronze statue of a street sweeper (*El Barrendero*) cleans up some bronze litter; look also for *Armonía* (*Harmony*), a sculpture of three street musicians. In the center of the park is a spiderlike gazebo donated by onetime Nicaraguan dictator Anastasio Somoza. ⊠ *Bordered by Avdas. 2–4 and Cs. 2–Central, Downtown.*

Parque España. This shady little park is a favorite spot. A bronze statue of Costa Rica's Spanish founder, Juan Vásquez de Coronado, overlooks an elevated fountain on its southwest corner; the opposite corner has a lovely tiled guardhouse. A bust of Queen Isabella of Castile stares at the yellow compound to the east of the park, the Centro Nacional de la Cultura. Just west of the park is a two-story, metal-sided elementary school made in Belgium and shipped to Costa Rica in pieces more than a century ago. Local lore holds that the intended destination for the appropriately named Edificio Metálico (Metal Building) was really Chile, but that Costa Rica decided to keep the mistakenly shipped building components. The bright yellow colonial-style building to the east of the modern INS building is the 1912 Casa Amarilla, home of Costa Rica's Foreign Ministry. The massive ceiba tree in front, planted by John F. Kennedy and the presidents of all the Central American nations in

TWO LAST NAMES

The immigration form you're given to fill out on your flight to Costa Rica has a space asking for your *segundo apellido* (second last name). We doubt you'll have one, but Costa Ricans all do.

If a Pedro Castillo marries an Ana Morales, and they have a son, Juan, his full legal name will consist of surnames from both his mother and his father: Juan Castillo Morales (although for the purposes of shorthand, he'll probably go by "Juan Castillo"). When Juan grows up and marries, his children will take his Castillo surname and his future wife's first surname. Juan's Morales name is lost to future generations. However, like most Costa Rican women, Ana likely decided to keep her own last names when she married, and not take Pedro's, a tradition that existed here long before liberated North American and European women adopted such customs. Of course, if Ana wants to show off her marital status, she might call herself Ana Morales de Castillo ("of Castillo"), a convention often seen only among wealthy women.

1963, gives you an idea of how quickly things grow in the tropics. A garden around the corner on Calle 13 contains a 6-foot-wide section of the Berlin Wall donated by Germany's Foreign Ministry after reunification. Ask the guard to let you into the garden if you want a closer look. ⊠ *Bordered by Avdas. 7–3 and Cs. 11–17, Downtown.*

Parque Morazán. Anchored by the 1920 Templo de Música (Temple of Music), a neoclassical bandstand that has become the symbol of the city, downtown's largest park is somewhat barren, though the pink-and-gold trumpet trees on its northwest corner brighten things up when they bloom in the dry months. The park is named for Honduran general Francisco Morazán, whose dream of a united Central America failed in the 1830s. Avoid the park late at night, when a rough crowd appears. ⊠ *Avda. 3, Cs. 5–9, Downtown.*

Parque Nacional (*National Park*). A bronze monument commemorating Central America's battles against North American invader William Walker in 1856 forms the centerpiece of the large, leafy park. Five Amazons, representing the five nations of the isthmus, attack Walker, who shields his face from the onslaught. Costa Rica maintains the lead and shelters a veiled Nicaragua, the country most devastated by the war. Guatemala, Honduras, and El Salvador might dispute this version of events, but this is how Costa Rica chose to commission the work by French sculptor Louis Carrier Belleuse, a student of Rodin, in 1895. Bas-relief murals on the monument's pedestal depict key battles in the war against the Americans. As with all San José parks, you should avoid the space after dark. ⊠ *Bordered by Avdas. 1–3 and Cs. 15–19, Downtown.*

Plaza de la Cultura. The crowds of people, vendors, and street entertainers at the plaza—it's a favored spot for marimba bands, clowns, jugglers, and colorfully dressed South Americans playing Andean music—hide the fact that the expanse is really just a mass of concrete. The ornate

The Museo del Oro Precolombino has the largest collection of pre-Columbian gold jewelry in Central America.

Teatro Nacional dominates the plaza's southern half. The Museo del Oro Precolombino, with its highly visited exhibits of gold, lies under the plaza. The plaza's western edge is defined by the Gran Hotel Costa Rica, with its pleasant Café 1930. ⊠ *Bordered by Avdas. Central–2 and Cs. 3–5, Downtown.*

Plaza de la Democracia. President Oscar Arias built this terraced space west of the Museo Nacional to mark 100 years of democracy and to receive dignitaries during a 1989 hemispheric summit. The view west toward the dark green Cerros de Escazú is nice in the morning and fabulous at sunset. Jewelry, T-shirts, and crafts from Costa Rica, Guatemala, and South America are sold in a string of stalls along the western edge. The city has been threatening to move the vendors to another location for years, but nothing has come of it. ⊠ *Bordered by Avdas. Central–2 and Cs. 13–15, Downtown.*

Plaza del Banco Central. A widening of Avenida Central, this plaza is popular with hawkers, money changers, and retired men, and can be a good place to get a shoe shine and listen to street musicians. Outside the western end of Costa Rica's modern federal-reserve bank building, don't miss *Presentes*, 10 sculpted, smaller-than-life figures of bedraggled *campesinos* (peasants). *La Chola*, a bronze statue of a buxom rural woman, resides at sidewalk level on the small, shady plaza south of the bank. It's public art at its best. Beware: the money changers here are notorious for circulating counterfeit bills and using doctored calculators to shortchange unwitting tourists. Avoid them. ⊠ *Bordered by Avdas. Central–1 and Cs. 2–4, Downtown.*

Teatro Popular Melico Salazar. Across Avenida 2 on the north side of Parque Central stands San José's second major performance hall (after the Teatro Nacional). The 1928 building is on the site of a 19th-century military barracks felled by an earthquake. The venue was later named for Costa Rican operatic tenor Manuel "Melico" Salazar (1887–1950). It was constructed specifically to provide a less highbrow alternative to the Teatro Nacional. (*Popular* in Spanish refers to something "common" or "for the people," rather than meaning "widely liked.") These days the Melico provides the capital with a steady diet of music and dance performances. ✉ *Avda. 2, C. 2, Downtown* ☎ *2295–6000* ⊕ *www.teatromelico.go.cr.*

3

WEST OF DOWNTOWN

Paseo Colón, one of San José's major boulevards, heads due west from downtown and leads to vast La Sabana Park, the city's largest parcel of green space. La Sabana anchors the even vaster west side of the city. A block or two off its exhaust-ridden avenues are quiet residential streets, and you'll find the U.S., Canadian, and British embassies here.

Museo de Arte Costarricense. Located in La Sabana Park, which was once Costa Rica's international airport, this—the country's foremost art museum—was once its terminal and control tower. A splendid collection of 19th- and 20th-century Costa Rican art, labeled in Spanish and English, is housed in 12 exhibition halls. Be sure to visit the top-floor Salón Dorado to see the stucco, bronze-plate bas-relief mural depicting Costa Rican history, created by French sculptor Louis Feron. Guided tours are offered Tuesday through Friday from 10 to 3. Wander into the sculpture garden in back and take in Jorge Jiménez's 22-foot-tall *Imagen Cósmica*, which depicts pre-Columbian traditions. ✉ *Parque La Sabana, C. 42, Paseo Colón, Paseo Colón* ☎ *2256–1281* ⊕ *www. musarco.go.cr* 🖙 *Free* ☉ *Tues.–Sun. 9–4.*

FAMILY **Parque La Sabana.** Though it isn't centrally located, La Sabana ("the savannah") comes the closest of San José's green spaces to achieving the same function and spirit as New York's Central Park. A statue of 1930s president León Cortes greets you at the principal entrance at the west end of Paseo Colón. Behind the statue, a 16-foot-tall menorah is illuminated each night during Hanukkah. La Sabana was once San José's airport, and the whitewashed Museo de Arte Costarricense, just south of the Cortes statue, served as its terminal and control tower.

The round Gimnasio Nacional (National Gymnasium) sits at the park's southeast corner and hosts sporting events and the occasional concert. The Estadio Nacional, a 40,000-seat stadium—a controversial gift from the government of China, which decided to use its own construction workers rather than employ locals—looms over the park's northwest corner. It hosts soccer matches primarily, but Paul McCartney, Elton John, Shakira, and Lady Gaga have all played in the stadium. In between are acres of space for soccer, basketball, tennis, swimming, jogging, picnicking, and kite flying. The park hums with activity on weekend days. You're welcome to join in the early-morning outdoor aerobics classes on Saturday and Sunday. A years-long project is under way to replace many of the park's eucalyptus trees with more bird-friendly species native to Costa Rica. Unsavory characters populate the park at night. The stadium grounds are fine, but avoid walking through the rest of the park after the sun goes down. ⊠ *Bordered by C. 42 and 68, Avda. de las Américas, and Carretera a Caldera, Paseo Colón.*

NORTH AND EAST OF DOWNTOWN

Immediately northeast of downtown lie Barrio Amón and Barrio Otoya. Both neighborhoods are repositories of historic houses that have escaped the wrecking ball; many now serve as hotels, restaurants, galleries, and offices—a few are even private residences. Where these barrios begin and end depends on who's doing the talking. Locales on the fringes of the city center prefer to be associated with these "good neighborhoods" rather than with downtown. Barrio Escalante, to the east, isn't quite as gentrified but is fast becoming fashionable.

The sprawling suburb of San Pedro begins several blocks east of downtown San José. It's home to the University of Costa Rica and all the intellect and cheap eats and nightlife and copy shops that a student or student wannabe could desire. But away from the heart of the university, San Pedro is awash with malls, fast-food restaurants, and car dealerships—although it manages to mix in such stately districts as Los Yoses for good measure. To get to San Pedro, take a $3 taxi ride from downtown and get off in front of Banco Nacional, just beyond the rotunda with the fountain at its center.

FAMILY   **Jardín de Mariposas Spyrogyra** (*Spyrogyra Butterfly Garden*). Spending an hour or two at this magical butterfly garden is entertaining and educational for nature lovers of all ages. Self-guided tours enlighten you on butterfly ecology and let you see the winged creatures close up. After an 18-minute video introduction, you're free to wander screened-in gardens along a numbered trail. Some 30 species of colorful butterflies flutter about, accompanied by six types of hummingbirds. Try to come when it's sunny, as butterflies are most active then. A small, moderately priced café borders the garden and serves sandwiches and Tico fare. ⊠ *Barrio Tournón* ✛ *50 m east and 150 m south of main entrance to El Pueblo shopping center* 🕾 *2222–2937* ⊕ *www.butterflygardencr.com* 🕾 *$7* ⊙ *Weekdays 9–2, weekends 9–3.*

FAMILY   **Museo de los Niños** (*Children's Museum*). Three halls of this museum are filled with eye-catching seasonal exhibits for kids, ranging in subject from local ecology to outer space. The exhibits are in Spanish, but most are interactive, so language shouldn't be much of a problem. The museum's most popular resident is the Egyptian exhibit's sarcophagus; the mummy draws "oohs" and "aahs." Located in a former prison, big kids may want to check it out just to marvel at the castlelike architecture and the old cells that have been preserved in an exhibit about life behind bars. The complex that houses the museum is called the Centro Costarricense de Ciencia y Cultura (Costa Rican Center of Science and Culture), and that will be the sign that greets you on the front of the building. Though just a short distance from downtown, a walk here takes you through a dodgy neighborhood. Always take a taxi to and

CLOSE UP

Are You Ready for Some Fútbol?

Sports mean one thing in San José: soccer. Very young boys (and a slowly increasing number of girls) kick around a ball—or some other object if no ball is available—in street pickup games, and they grow into fans passionate about their local team. But everyone puts aside regional differences when the reputation of Costa Rica's national team is on the line, as it is during the World Cup.

Consult the Spanish-language daily *La Nación* or ask at your hotel for details on upcoming games—you simply show up at the stadium box office. Prices range from $4 to $15.

Sombra numerado (shaded seats) are the most expensive.

Professional soccer matches are usually played on Sunday morning or Wednesday night in either of two San José stadiums. The Estadio Ricardo Saprissa (next to the Clínica Integrada de Tibás) is home to Saprissa, the capital's beloved hometown team, and is in the northern suburb of Tibás; the spanking-new, Chinese-built Estadio Nacional sits at the northwest corner of La Sabana Park and hosts visiting national teams who come to take on La Sele, Costa Rica's own national squad.

from. ⊠ *Centro Costarricense de Ciencia y Cultura, north end of C. 4, Barrio Tournón* ☎ *2258–4929* ⊕ *www.museocr.org* 🎫 *$4* ⊙ *Feb.–mid-Dec., Tues.–Fri. 8–4:30, weekends 9:30–5; mid-Dec.–Jan., weekdays 9–5, weekends 9:30–5.*

NEED A BREAK?

Giacomín. We have to admit that Costa Rican baked goods tend toward the dry-as-dust end of the spectrum. But Italian-style bakery Giacomín, near the University of Costa Rica, is an exception—a touch of liqueur added to the batter makes all the difference. Stand European-style at the downstairs espresso bar or take your goodies to the tables and chairs on the upstairs balcony. You'll also find branches in the eastern suburb of Curridabat and in Escazú, Santa Ana, and Heredia out in the Central Valley. ⊠ *Los Yoses* ✛ *Next to Automercado supermarket* ☎ *4001–7478* ⊕ *www. pasteleriagiacomin.com* ⊙ *Mon.-Sat. 8-7, Sun. 10-7.*

WHERE TO EAT

Costa Rica's capital beckons with the country's most varied and cosmopolitan restaurant scene. Italian, Spanish, Asian, French, Middle Eastern, Peruvian—they're all here, along with upscale Costa Rican cuisine.

Wherever you eat in San José, be it a small *soda* or a sophisticated restaurant, dress is casual. Meals tend to be taken earlier than in other Latin American countries; few restaurants serve past 9 or 10 pm. Local cafés usually open for breakfast at 7 am and remain open until 7 or 8 in the evening. Restaurants serving international cuisine are usually open from 11 am to 9 pm. Some cafés that serve mainly San José office

San José's ornate Correos de Costa Rica building houses a stamp museum on the second floor.

workers limit evening hours and close entirely on Sunday. Restaurants that do open on Sunday do a brisk business: it's the traditional family day out (and the maid's day off). ⚠ **Watch your things, no matter where you dine. Even at the best restaurants, thieves occasionally target purses slung over chair arms or placed under chairs.**

WHAT IT COSTS IN DOLLARS				
	$	$$	$$$	$$$$
Restaurants	under $10	$10–$15	$16–$25	over $25

Prices in the reviews are the average cost of a main course at dinner or, if dinner is not served, at lunch.

DOWNTOWN

$ ✕ **Café de la Posada.** The lack of alfresco dining in this tropical city is
CAFÉ disappointing, but this café's covered terrace with tables fronting the pedestrian-only Calle 17 is a pleasant exception. The folks here know how to make a great cappuccino. Salads, quiches, and empanadas are specialties. The best bargains are the four rotating *platos del día* (daily specials), with entrée, salad, and dessert for $10. If you opt for dinner, make it an early one: the café closes at 6. ⑤ *Average main: $9* ⊠ *C. 17, Avdas. 2–4, Downtown* ☏ *2258–1027* ⊕ *www.hotelposadadelmuseo. com* ⊘ *Closed weekends* ✛ *H4.*

$ ╳ **Chelles.** Part bar, part *soda*, this downtown San José institution has been
COSTA RICAN dishing up tasty, filling, and huge portions of *tipico* food for a century.
Empanadas, arroz con pollo (chicken with rice), and monster ham-and-cheese Cuban sandwiches lead the fare. The folks here speak barely a word
of English, but they'll figure out what you want even if your restaurant
Spanish is nonexistent. There's also Wi-Fi available. Chelles is open 24
hours, but do exercise care if you're out and about on the streets at 3 am.
⑤ *Average main: $7* ✉ *Avda. Ctrl, C. 9, Downtown* ☎ *2221-1369* ✛ *G4.*

$$ ╳ **Don Wang.** In a country where "Chinese cuisine" often means rice and
CHINESE vegetables bearing a suspicious resemblance to *gallo pinto* (the typical
Costa Rican dish of beans and rice), Don Wang's authenticity is a treat.
Cantonese cuisine is the mainstay—the owner comes from that region
of China—but these folks will Szechuan it up a bit if you ask. Don
Wang is known for its immensely popular dim sum, called *desayuno
chino*, literally "Chinese breakfast." You can order it all day (bearing
in mind that this place doesn't open until 11 am). The dining area is built
around a stone garden and small waterfall. ⑤ *Average main: $13* ✉ *C.
11, Avdas. 6–8, Downtown* ☎ *2233–6484* ⊕ *www.donwangrestaurant.
com* ▭ *No credit cards* ✛ *G4.*

$ ╳ **La Criollita.** Kick off your day with breakfast here. Mornings are the
COSTA RICAN perfect time to snag one of the precious tables in the back garden, an
unexpected refuge from noise and traffic. Platters come with eggs on
the side: the *americano* has pancakes and toast; the *tico* comes with
bread, fried bananas, and *natilla* (sour cream); and the huge *criollita*
has ham or pork chops. Government workers from nearby offices start
arriving late in the morning, and the lunchtime decibel level increases
appreciably. (This is the one time of day we recommend avoiding the
place.) Everyone filters out about 2 pm, and once again, you have a
quiet place for coffee and dessert. If you come here for dinner, make it
an early one; the place closes at 7. ⑤ *Average main: $9* ✉ *Avda. 7, Cs.
7–9, Downtown* ☎ *2256–6511* �) *No dinner weekends* ✛ *G3.*

$ ╳ **Nuestra Tierra.** Except for the traffic zipping by on one of San José's
COSTA RICAN busiest thoroughfares—opt for a table on the side facing less busy Calle
15—you might think you're out in the rural Central Valley. Bunches
of onions and peppers dangle from the ceiling, recalling a provincial
ranch. The generous homemade meals are delicious, and the incredibly
friendly waitstaff, who epitomize Costa Rican hospitality and dress in
folkloric clothing, prepare your coffee filtered through the traditional
cloth *chorreador*. The place is open until midnight, just in case those
late-night gallo pinto pangs hit. Some disparage the restaurant as "too
touristy." Perhaps it is, but it's also fun. ⑤ *Average main: $9* ✉ *Avda.
2-4, C. 13, Downtown* ☎ *2258–6500* ✛ *G4.*

$ ╳ **Shakti.** The baskets of fruit and vegetables at the entrance and the wall
VEGETARIAN of herbal teas, health-food books, and fresh herbs for sale by the register
signal that you're in a vegetarian-friendly joint. The bright and airy mac-
robiotic restaurant serves breakfast, lunch, and an early dinner, closing
at 7 pm weekdays and 6 pm Saturday. Homemade bread, soy burgers,
pita sandwiches (veggie or, for carnivorous dining companions, chicken),
fruit shakes, and a hearty plato del día that comes with soup, green salad,
and a beverage fill out the menu. The *ensalada mixta* is a meal in itself,

3

packed with root vegetables native to Costa Rica. $ *Average main: $8* ⊠ *Avda. 8, C. 11-13, Downtown* ☎ *2222–4475* ⊘ *Closed Sun.* ✛ *G5.*

$$$
ASIAN
Fodor's Choice
★

✕ **Tin Jo.** The colorful dining rooms of this converted house just southeast of downtown evoke Japan, India, China, Indonesia, and Thailand. In the Thai Room, a 39-foot mural depicts a Buddhist temple. You can select from all the above cuisines—there are a few Filipino and Vietnamese dishes, too—with menus to match the various dining areas. Start with a powerful Singapore sling (brandy and fruit juices) before trying such treats as *kaeng* (Thai shrimp and pineapple curry in coconut milk), *mu shu* (a beef, chicken, or vegetable stir-fry with crepes), samosas (stuffed savory Indian pastries), and sushi rolls. The vegetarian menu is extensive. Tin Jo stands out with always-exceptional food, attention to detail, and attentive service that make it, hands down, the country's top Asian restaurant. $ *Average main: $18* ⊠ *C. 11, Avdas. 6–8, Downtown* ☎ *2257–3622* ⊕ *www.tinjo.com* ✛ *G4.*

WEST OF DOWNTOWN

$$
PIZZA

✕ **The Corner.** Although this part of town is a bit off the standard tourist track, the pizza here is worth the trip. In true Costa Rican, no-real-addresses style, the directions are given—unironically—as "100 meters south of Pizza Hut." This homey spot contains a few wooden tables, a small outdoor patio, and a large picture window. The crusts are neither too thin nor excessively thick, and lots of cheese goes into the toppings. Enjoy a glass of the house wine with your meal, and top things off with flan or tiramisu for dessert. $ *Average main: $14* ⊠ *C. 28, Avda. 2, Paseo Colón* ☎ *2255–3333* ⊘ *Closed Sun.* ✛ *A3.*

$$$
ECLECTIC
Fodor's Choice
★

✕ **Grano de Oro Restaurant.** One of the city's premier lodgings, the Grano de Oro also houses one of San Jose's top dining destinations. The hotel's splendid restaurant sits to the left as you enter the lobby and wraps around a lovely indoor patio and bromeliad-filled garden. The garden area is a perfect spot for lunch on a warm day—choose from among a variety of light sandwiches and salads. Cooler evenings are the time to migrate to the elegant indoor dining area for dishes like corvina macadamia (breaded sea bass with orange sauce and macadamia nuts) or *cerdo en salsa tamarindo* (roasted pork in tamarind sauce). An impressive selection of 100-plus wines and decadent dessert menu—the coffee-cream "Pie Grano de Oro" is the must-try option here—round out the offerings. Although elegance is the word in this grand coffee-plantation-house-turned-hotel, you'll see everything from diners in business attire to guests in casual garb just back from the hinterlands. $ *Average main: $25* ⊠ *C. 30, Avdas. 2–4, Paseo Colón* ☎ *2255–3322* ⊕ *www. hotelgranodeoro.com* ▭ *No credit cards* ✛ *A4.*

$$$
ITALIAN

✕ **L'Olivo.** The same owners behind the west-side lodging Suites Cristina also operate this little bit of Tuscany a few blocks north of La Sabana Park. The restaurant is most easily entered from around the corner, however—it's physically separate from the hotel. Vaulted ceilings and a vineyard mural on one wall evoke old Italy. Homemade pastas—spinach cannelloni and linguine with clam sauce are popular dishes—make up the fare here, and an extensive wine list rounds out the offerings. Service is attentive—the chef makes the rounds to ensure that you're satisfied. The scant dozen tables mean that reservations are a good idea for dinner. The smallness of the restaurant does create one drawback: it can be difficult to carry on a conversation when things get busy, although that does add to the liveliness of the place. $ *Average main: $17* ✉ *Paseo Colón* ✛ *300 m north and 50 m east of ICE Bldg.* ☏ *2220–0453* ⊕ *www.apartotelcristina.com* ⊟ *No credit cards* ☉ *Closed Sun.* ⟴ *Reservations essential* ✛ *A3.*

$$
MIDDLE EASTERN
✕ **Lubnan.** Negotiate the quirky wrought-iron-and-burlap revolving door at the entrance and you've made it into one of San José's few Middle Eastern restaurants. The Lebanese owners serve a wide variety of dishes from their native region, so if you can't decide, the *mezza* serves two people and gives you a little bit of everything. For your own individual dish, try the juicy shish kebab *de cordero* (of lamb), or, if you're feeling especially adventurous, the raw ground-meat *kebbe naye* (with wheat meal) and *kafta naye* (without wheat meal). A hip bar in the back serves the same menu. On Wednesday night there is live synthesizer music; on Thursday night check out the immensely popular 8:30 pm belly-dancing show. $ *Average main: $12* ✉ *Cs. 22–24, Paseo Colón* ☏ *2257–6071* ☉ *Closed Mon. No dinner Sun.* ✛ *B3.*

$$
PERUVIAN
✕ **Machu Picchu.** A few travel posters and a net holding crab and lobster shells are the only props used to evoke Peru, but no matter: the food is anything but plain, and the seafood is excellent. The *pique especial de mariscos* (special seafood platter), big enough for two, presents you with shrimp, conch, and squid cooked four ways. The ceviche is quite different from, and better than, that served in the rest of the country. A blazing Peruvian hot sauce served on the side adds zip to any dish, but be careful—apply it by the drop. One more warning: the pisco sours from the bar go down very easily. $ *Average main: $13* ✉ *C. 32, Paseo Colón* ✛ *130 m north of KFC* ☏ *2222–7384* ☉ *No dinner Sun.* ✛ *A3.*

$$$
ECLECTIC
✕ **Park Café.** Set within an antiques shop, the all-tapas menu includes Thai-style tuna salad, red-snapper couscous, and other tasty dishes. Don't let appearances deceive you: the colonial-style house is only about a decade old, but attention to architectural detail and antique furnishings make you think the building was transplanted from Antigua or Granada. The menu varies from year to year, depending on what the owners have uncovered during their annual two-month European buying trip. Space is limited, so reservations are a must. The January through April dry season takes the pressure off a bit, allowing seating to spill over from the covered veranda to the open courtyard. You dine among the many antiques for sale here, so small children are not allowed. $ *Average main: $24* ✉ *Sabana Norte* ✛ *100 m north of Rosti Pollos* ☏ *2290–6324* ⊕ *parkcafecostarica.blogspot.com* ☉ *Closed Sun., Mon., and Sept. and Oct. No lunch* ⟴ *Reservations essential* ✛ *A3.*

$
COSTA RICAN
✕ **Soda Tapia.** One of San José's most popular restaurants fronts the east side of La Sabana Park. Don't expect anything fancy, but food here is cheap and filling. The ubiquitous gallo pinto for breakfast and casados (meat, fish, or poultry, accompanied by rice, cabbage salad, and dessert) for lunch are on the menu. The dinner menu has a variety of sandwiches and burgers. You can dine outdoors, but you'll have to contend with the traffic noise and the sight of the guard flagging cars in and out of

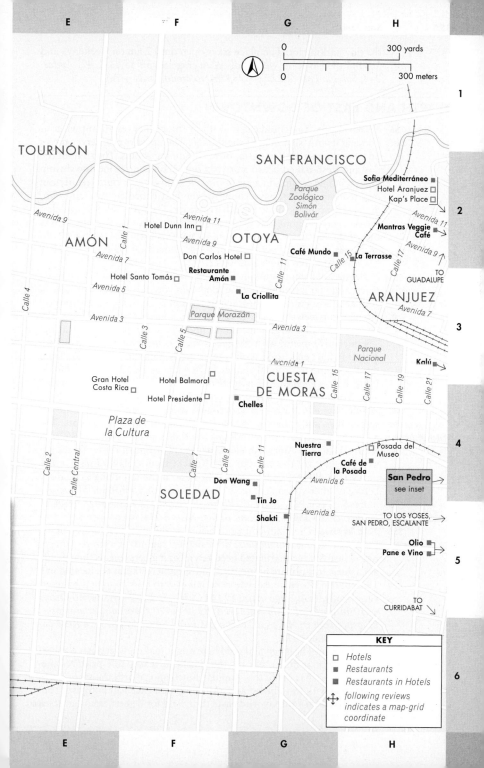

E   F   G   H

0   300 yards

0   300 meters

1

TOURNÓN

SAN FRANCISCO

Parque
Zoológico
Simón
Bolivár

Sofia Mediterráneo ■
Hotel Aranjuez □
Kap's Place □

Avenida 9

Avenida 11

Hotel Dunn Inn □

Avenida 9

OTOYA

Mantras Veggie
Café

Avenida 11

2

AMÓN

Avenida 7

Calle 1

Don Carlos Hotel □

Café Mundo ■

Calle 15

La Terrasse

Avenida 9

Calle 17

TO
GUADALUPE

Hotel Santo Tomás □

Restaurante
Amón ■

Calle 11

ARANJUEZ

Avenida 5

La Criollita ■

Avenida 7

Calle 4

Avenida 3

Parque Morazán

Calle 3

Calle 5

Avenida 3

Parque
Nacional

Kalú ■

3

Avenida 1

CUESTA
DE MORAS

Calle 15

Calle 17

Calle 19

Calle 21

Gran Hotel
Costa Rica □

Hotel Balmoral □

Hotel Presidente □

Chelles ■

Plaza de
la Cultura

Calle 2

Calle Central

Calle 7

Calle 9

Calle 11

Nuestra
Tierra ■

Posada del
Museo □

San Pedro
see inset

4

Café de
la Posada ■

Don Wang ■

Avenida 6

SOLEDAD

Tin Jo ■

Shakti ■

Avenida 8

TO LOS YOSES,
SAN PEDRO, ESCALANTE

Olio ■
Pane e Vino ■

5

TO
CURRIDABAT

6

KEY	
□	*Hotels*
■	*Restaurants*
■	*Restaurants in Hotels*
↔	*following reviews indicates a map-grid coordinate*

E   F   G   H

the tiny parking lot. The place stays open until 2 am on weekdays and around the clock on weekends. $ *Average main: $5* ⊠ *C. 42, Avdas. 2–4, Sabana Este* ☎ *2222–6734* ▬ *No credit cards* ✛ *A3.*

NORTH AND EAST OF DOWNTOWN

$$ ✗ **Café Mundo.** You could easily walk by this corner restaurant without
CAFÉ   noticing its tiny sign behind the foliage. The upstairs café serves meals on a porch, on a garden patio, or in two dining rooms. The soup of the day and fresh-baked bread start you out; main courses include shrimp in a vegetable cream sauce or *lomito en salsa de vino tinto* (tenderloin in a red-wine sauce). Save room for the best chocolate cake in town, drizzled with homemade blackberry sauce. Café Mundo is a popular, low-key gay hangout that draws a mixed gay-straight clientele. This is one of the few center-city restaurants with its own parking lot. $ *Average main: $13* ⊠ *C. 15, Avda. 9-11, Barrio Otoya* ☎ *2222–6190* ◷ *Closed Sun. No lunch Sat.* ✛ *G2.*

$$$ ✗ **Jürgen's.** A common haunt for *políticos,* Jürgen's attracts San José's
ECLECTIC   elites, and you'll feel pretty elite too when you dine here. Decorated in
Fodor's Choice   gold and terra-cotta with leather-and-wood accents, the contemporary
★   dining room feels more like a lounge than a fine restaurant. In fact, the classy bar, with a large selection of fine wines, is a prominent feature. The inventive menu, with delicacies such as medallions of roast duck and tuna fillet encrusted with sesame seeds, sets this place apart from the city's more traditional venues. $ *Average main: $23* ⊠ *Blvd. Barrio Dent, Barrio Dent* ✛ *250 m north of Grupo Q* ☎ *2283–2239* ◷ *Closed Sun. No lunch Sat.* ✛ *B5.*

$$$ ✗ **Kalú.** Camille Ratton, a longtime fixture on San José's restaurant
ECLECTIC   scene, owns and manages one of the capital's hippest dining spots. The
Fodor's Choice   panini and pastas are the standouts, but Kalú's menu incorporates Costa
★   Rican, Thai, and American elements, too. For one of those American-ized touches, try the *hamburguesa* Kalú with portobello mushrooms, mozzarella cheese, and hummus. Browse in the adjoining art gallery before or after your meal, or while you wait for your food. $ *Average main: $19* ⊠ *C. 31, Avda. 5, Barrio Escalante* ☎ *2253–8426* ⊕ *www. kalu.co.cr* ◷ *Closed Mon., no dinner Sun.* ✛ *H3.*

$$$ ✗ **La Terrasse.** The main-course offerings at this cozy restaurant rotate,
FRENCH   but might include a *blanquette de veau* (veal ragout) or a *daube proven-çale* (a hearty wine-marinated beef stew). Dining here feels as though you are a guest in a private home, and, indeed, the restaurant is located in a 1927 Barrio Otoya house, whose sign is easy to miss. Dining is by reservation only. $ *Average main: $24* ⊠ *C. 15, Avdas. 9–9A, Barrio Otoya* ✛ *50 m north of Café Mundo* ☎ *8939–8470* ⊕ *restaurantlaterrasse. blogspot.com* ▬ *No credit cards* ◷ *Closed Sun. No lunch* ⌔ *Reservations essential* ✛ *H2.*

$$ ✗ **La Trattoria.** The green and gold here might make a Green Bay Packers
ITALIAN   fan feel right at home, but it's the excellent, reasonably priced home-made pastas that make this popular lunch spot worth the stop. Begin your meal with fresh bread and any number of excellent antipasti, continuing on with your favorite pasta dish. And for dessert, who can resist

SAN JOSÉ'S CAFÉS

Costa Ricans are serious about *tomando café* (taking a coffee break), but most places they do so in the city feel pretty basic and institutional. A *cafetería* is the generic term for a coffee shop in Spanish. The venues below capture that trendy café feel and serve export-quality coffee.

Café 1930. The café under the arcades at the entrance to the Grand Hotel Costa Rica pulls duty as a pleasant place for a drink or coffee. Listen to live music on the grand piano each night from 6 to 8 pm. ☒ *Gran Hotel Costa Rica, Avda. 2, C. 3, Barrio La Soledad* ☎ *2221–4011.*

Café del Barista. The rain does get a bit loud on the metal roof, but the wide selection of coffee drinks here is worth the occasional racket. ☒ *C. 19, Avda. 11, Barrio Aranjuez* ☎ *2221–4712* ⊕ *www.cafedelbarista. com* ⊘ *Weekdays 7–6, Sat. 8–6.*

Café Miel Costa Rica. A scant two tables and a small counter are the only seating at this tiny place, which serves up coffee from its own *finca* in Tarrazú in the Los Santos region. ☒ *Avda. 9, C. 13, Barrio Otoya* ☎ *No phone* ⊘ *Mon.–Sat. 9–6.*

Cafeoteca. This café sits at the entrance to the trendy Kalú restaurant and blends and roasts its own coffee on-site. ☒ *C. 31, Avda. 5, Barrio Escalante* ☎ *2253-8426* ⊕ *www.kalu.co.cr.*

Club Unión. The elevated, glassed-in café here lets you survey the ongoing hive of activity on the small, shaded plaza in front of the post office. ☒ *C. 2, Avdas. 1–3, Barrio La Merced* ☎ *2257–1555* ⊘ *Weekdays 8–7, Sat. 10–6.*

Juan Valdez Café. This sleek, modern coffee shop is an island of all-Colombian products in Costa Rica. ☒ *Sabana Norte* ✛ *Northwest corner of La Sabana park* ☎ *4700-2361* ⊕ *www.juanvaldezcafe.com.*

Q'Café. There's lots of chrome at this downtown second-floor café that brews its own coffee from the Tarrazú and Naranjo regions. Grab a seat and survey the activity on Avenida Central. ☒ *Avda. Central, C. 2* ☎ *4056-5604* ⊕ *www.quecafe.com* ⊘ *Daily 10-7.*

Saboreaté y Café. It's as much about the tea as it is about the coffee at this small, cozy downtown café, a branch of a Spanish chain. ☒ *C. 5, Avda. 1A* ☎ *7205-5191* ⊕ *www.saboreateycafe.com* ⊘ *Mon.–Sat. 8-7.*

Starbucks. The coffee and bakery selections are just like back in the United States at the Costa Rican outlets of the ubiquitous chain. You'll find five branches (and counting) in the metro area. ☒ *Pavas* ✛ *100 m south of Scotiabank* ☎ *2208-2700* ⊕ *www.starbucks.co.cr.*

tiramisu? ⑤ *Average main: $10* ☒ *Barrio Dent* ✛ *Behind Automercado* ☎ *2224–7065* ⊘ *No dinner Sun.* ✛ *B5.*

$$$$
FRENCH
Fodor'sChoice
★

✕ **Le Chandelier.** San José doesn't get classier than this restaurant, where formal service and traditional sauce-heavy French dishes are part of the experience. The dining room is elegant, with wicker chairs, tile floors, and original paintings. The Swiss chef might start you off with saffron ravioli stuffed with ricotta cheese and walnuts. Main courses include such unique dishes as corvina in a *pejibaye* (peach palm) sauce or hearts of palm and veal chops glazed in a sweet port-wine sauce. The more familiar *pato a la naranja* (duck à l'orange) gets a tropical twist as *pato a la maracuyá* (duck in passion fruit). $ *Average main: $30* ☒ *C. 49, San Pedro* ✢ *50 m west and 100 m south of ICE Bldg.* ☎ *2225–3980* ⊕ *www.lechandeliercr.com* ☉ *Closed Sun. No lunch Sat.* ⌨ *Reservations essential* ✢ *C6.*

$ ✗ **Mantras Veggie Café.** This newest
VEGETARIAN   entry in the San José veggie-dining scene is more homey and less institutional than its competitors, and it's become all the rage among fans of meatless cuisine. The menu is extensive—try the cannelloni filled with mushrooms and mozzarella and topped with a zesty sauce, or the whole-wheat pita filled with couscous and tomato. A *natural* (a fruit drink) and green salad are included in the daily lunch special—a bargain at $6. $ *Average main: $8* ☒ *C. 35, Avda. 13, Barrio Escalante* ✢ *200 m east and 25 m south of the Farolito* ☎ *2253–6715* ☉ *No dinner* ✢ *H2.*

$$ ✗ **Olio.** Although this combination pub and restaurant serves the full
MEDITERRANEAN   contingent of Mediterranean cuisine, it's best for drinks and Spanish-style tapas. The century-old redbrick house with stained-glass windows draws everybody from tie-clad business executives to university students. Groups liven up the large front room—the quieter, smaller back rooms maintain a bit more romance. There are umbrella-covered tables on the sidewalk to enjoy warm evenings. Olio is extremely proud that it offers a copy of its menu in braille. $ *Average main: $11* ☒ *C. 33, Avda. 3, Barrio Escalante* ☎ *2281–0541* ☉ *Closed Sun. No lunch Sat.* ✢ *H5.*

$$ ✗ **Pane e Vino.** Look closely at the extensive menu here: there are 40 vari-
PIZZA   eties of the capital's best thin-crust pizza, and no one will rush you if you spend time pondering what you want. This lively two-level restaurant rounds out its offerings with a complete selection of pastas. You can dine until midnight daily, except on Sunday, when you'll have to finish dinner by 10 pm. The Pizza Allessandre—topped with prosciutto, mozzarella, and olives—is the most popular dish, and for good reason. Pane e Vino has become a small chain—it's even expanded to Ecuador—but this is the original of its nine Costa Rican locations. $ *Average main: $11* ☒ *San Pedro* ✢ *50 m west and 15 m south of Más X Menos supermarket* ☎ *2280–2869* ⊕ *www.paneevino.co.cr* ▭ *No credit cards* ✢ *H5.*

$ ✗ **Restaurante Amón.** Reasonable prices and hearty breakfast of gallo
COSTA RICAN   pinto, scrambled eggs, bread, and coffee will fortify you for a morning of sightseeing here. The bargain $6 lunch special consists of the standard *casado*—choose from fish, chicken, beef, or pork—accompanied by rice, beans, vegetable, salad, and dessert. This place is far from your typical mom-and-pop *soda* (a small Costa Rican restaurant), though. The exposed brick walls in this old Barrio Amón house serve as a

showcase for rotating art exhibits. ⑤ *Average main: $4* ⊠ *C. 7, Avdas. 7-9, Barrio Amón* ☎ *2221-2960* ⊙ *Closed weekends. No dinner* ✢ *F3.*

$$ ✕ **Sofía Mediterráneo.** Natives of Istanbul, the chef and owner rely on
MEDITERRANEAN   authentic recipes for excellent red peppers stuffed with spicy beef and rice, eggplant-tomato salad, and other Mediterranean treats. You'll find a good selection of vegetarian salads, too. Desserts include a scrumptious yogurt-and-honey *revani* cake and the beloved baklava. Top it off with a coffee, Turkish or otherwise. ⑤ *Average main: $14* ⊠ *C. 33, Avda. 3, Barrio Escalante* ☎ *2224–5050* ⊙ *Closed Mon. No dinner Sun.* ✢ *H2.*

3

WHERE TO STAY

San José may be a big city, but it truly shines in its selection of small to medium-size inns. They're all locally owned, and their friendly, attentive staff will make you feel as if you're staying in an oasis in the middle of Costa Rica's noisy, congested capital.

San José has plenty of chains, including Best Western, Holiday Inn, Radisson, Quality Inn, Meliá, and Barceló (the last two are Spanish). But it also has historic houses with traditional architecture that have been converted into small lodgings.

The historic houses are usually without concierge or pool and are found mainly in Barrios Amón and Otoya, and in the eastern suburb of San Pedro. The city also has a lower tier of lodgings with the simplicity (and prices) beloved of backpackers. Most smaller hotels don't have air-conditioning, but it rarely gets hot enough at this altitude to warrant it.

Many lodgings operate at near-full occupancy in high season (December–April), but the capital's status as a business-travel destination means the lodging rates remain constant year-round. Reconfirm all reservations 24 hours in advance. If you're flying out early in the morning and prefer to stay near the airport, consider booking a hotel near Alajuela or San Antonio de Belén in the Central Valley. (➪ *See Chapter 4.*)

Hotel reviews have been shortened. For full information, visit Fodors.com.

WHAT IT COSTS IN DOLLARS			
$	**$$**	**$$$**	**$$$$**
Hotels under $75	$75–$150	$151–$250	over $250

Hotel prices are the lowest cost of a standard double room in high season.

DOWNTOWN

Staying in the downtown area allows you to travel around the city as most Ticos do: on foot. Stroll the parks, museums, and shops, and then retire to one of the many character-filled small or historic hotels.

$$ 🏨 **Gran Hotel Costa Rica.** You cannot find a more central location than
HOTEL   at this grande dame of San José lodgings. **Pros:** central location; good value; great people-watching from ground-floor café. **Cons:** some street

noise from the adjoining plaza; some rooms have thin walls; no on-site parking. $ *Rooms from: $115* ⊠ *Avda. 2, C. 3, Downtown* ☎ *2221–4000, 800/949–0592 in U.S.* ⊕ *www.granhotelcostarica.com* ➦ *107 rooms, 5 suites* ⍻ *Breakfast* ✛ *F3.*

$$ ⊡ **Hotel Balmoral.** One of the capital's landmark hotels has recently com-
HOTEL pleted a top-to-toe remodeling, revealing a much-appreciated modern-ization of its guest rooms. **Pros:** central location; good restaurant; close to downtown sights. **Cons:** some street noise. $ *Rooms from: $109* ⊠ *C. 7, Avdas. Central–1, Downtown* ☎ *2222–5022, 800/691–4865 in North America* ⊕ *www.balmoral.co.cr* ➦ *112 rooms, 8 suites* ⍻ *Break-fast* ✛ *F3.*

$$ ⊡ **Hotel Presidente.** This hotel offers standard, medium-price, busi-
HOTEL ness-class accommodations, although plenty of leisure travelers base themselves here as well. **Pros:** central location; eco-friendly; close to downtown sights. **Cons:** some street noise; some rooms have thin walls. $ *Rooms from: $129* ⊠ *Avda. Central, C. 7, Downtown* ☎ *2010–0000, 877/540–1790 in North America* ⊕ *www.hotel-presidente.com* ➦ *80 rooms, 12 suites* ⍻ *Breakfast* ✛ *F4.*

$ ⊡ **Posada del Museo.** Painted a pretty shade of yellow, this wooden Vic-
B&B/INN torian-style house dating from 1928 is a great place to stay if you're bound for San José's museums (hence the name)—it's diagonally across the street from the Museo Nacional. **Pros:** cozy rooms; near the sights. **Cons:** rush-hour train passes by; fronts busy street. $ *Rooms from: $60* ⊠ *Avda. 2, C. 17, Downtown* ☎ *2258–1027* ⊕ *www.hotelposadadelmuseo.com* ➦ *7 rooms, 3 suites* ⍻ *Breakfast* ✛ *H4.*

WEST OF DOWNTOWN

San José's vast west side contains only a smattering of lodgings, but among them are two of the city's best, Hotel Grano de Oro and the Park Inn by Radisson.

$$ ⊡ **Hilton Garden Inn San José La Sabana.** The newest U.S. chain to set up
HOTEL shop in the capital manages to provide all the modern amenities of its well-known brand while incorporating local touches. **Pros:** mountain views; inviting pool; comfortable rooms. **Cons:** located in an office building; some of the sameness of a chain hotel in the rooms. $ *Rooms from: $119* ⊠ *Blvd. Rohrmoser, Sabana Norte* ✛ *Northwest corner of La Sabana park* ☎ *2520-6000, 800/445-8667 in North America* ⊕ *www.hilton.com* ➦ *115 rooms* ⍻ *Breakfast* ✛ *A4.*

$$$ ⊡ **Hotel Grano de Oro.** Two wooden houses have been converted into
HOTEL one of the city's most charming inns, decorated throughout with old
Fodor's Choice photos of the capital and paintings by local artists; head up to your
★   room for the old coffee-plantation feel for which the hotel is known. **Pros:** friendly management; top-notch service; superb, elegant restau-rant. **Cons:** far from downtown sights; need taxi to get here. $ *Rooms from: $215* ⊠ *C. 30, Avdas. 2–4, Paseo Colón* ☎ *2255–3322* ⊕ *www.hotelgranodeoro.com* ➦ *39 rooms, 3 suites* ⍻ *No meals* ✛ *A4.*

$$ ⊡ **Hotel Plaza Real.** Rooms in this Tuscan-style hotel are spacious and
HOTEL comfortable, with microwave ovens and safes, but the hotel is located in a busy commercial neighborhood far from the sights. **Pros:** helpful

staff; ample breakfasts. **Cons:** difficult to find; far from sights. $ *Rooms from: $83* ⊠ *La Uruca* ✛ *100 m south and 100 m east of Kia dealership* ☎ *2290–6409, 866/978–4556* ⊕ *www.plazareal.cr* ⟿ *30 rooms* ⦿ *No meals* ✛ *A3.*

$$ ⛨ **Park Inn by Radisson.** This chain lodging incorporates local flair—
HOTEL bright, fresh primary colors and a rotating selection of Costa Rican
Fodor's Choice art throughout—while providing business amenities in a clean, mod-
★ ern hotel. **Pros:** impeccable service; friendly staff; quiet neighborhood; local style despite being a chain hotel; pool. **Cons:** far from downtown sights. $ *Rooms from: $125* ⊠ *Avda. 6, Cs. 28–30, Paseo Colón* ☎ *2257–1011, 800/670–7215 in North America* ⊕ *www.parkinn.com* ⟿ *108 rooms, 9 suites* ⦿ *Breakfast* ✛ *A4.*

$$ ⛨ **Parque del Lago Boutique Hotel.** This west-side lodging away from the
HOTEL hubbub of downtown is mainly for business travelers, but makes a good base for leisure visitors too. **Pros:** lots of business amenities; friendly service; ample parking. **Cons:** far from downtown sights. $ *Rooms from: $125* ⊠ *C. 40, Avda. 2-Paseo Colón, Paseo Colón* ☎ *2547-2000* ⊕ *www.parquedellago.com* ⟿ *30 rooms, 10 suites* ⦿ *Breakfast* ✛ *A4.*

$$ ⛨ **Suites Cristina.** Our favorite of the capital's many *apartotels*—part
HOTEL apartment house, part hotel—sits on a quiet, out-of-the-way street north of La Sabana Park. **Pros:** friendly staff; quiet street; terrific rates for what is offered. **Cons:** far from downtown sights and center of town. $ *Rooms from: $76* ⊠ *Sabana Norte* ✛ *300 m north of ICE Bldg.* ☎ *2220–0453, 773/253–5965* ⊕ *www.apartotelcristina.com* ⟿ *50 suites* ⦿ *Breakfast* ✛ *A4.*

NORTH AND EAST OF DOWNTOWN

Just north of downtown, old homes converted into small lodgings populate Barrios Amón and Otoya, two of the capital's most historic neighborhoods. The small properties 10 minutes by cab east of downtown, toward the university, offer personalized service and lots of peace and quiet. Plenty of restaurants and bars are within easy reach.

$$ ⛨ **Don Carlos Hotel.** One of the city's first guesthouses (technically, it's
B&B/INN three houses), this is the kind of place where you'll meet fellow travelers and swap stories about what you've seen. **Pros:** good value; good place to meet kindred spirits. **Cons:** some noise in interior rooms; some reports of long waits in restaurant. $ *Rooms from: $80* ⊠ *C. 9, Avda. 9, Downtown* ☎ *2221–6707, 866/675–9259 in North America* ⊕ *www.doncarloshotel.com* ⟿ *30 rooms* ⦿ *Breakfast* ✛ *G2.*

$ ⛨ **Hotel Aranjuez.** Several 1940s-era houses with extensive gardens and
HOTEL lively common areas—visitors swap travel advice here—make up this family-run lodging. **Pros:** good budget value; great place to meet other budget travelers; excellent complimentary breakfast. **Cons:** cumbersome reservations system; far from sights; can be hard to find space in high season. $ *Rooms from: $58* ⊠ *C. 19, Avdas. 11–13, Barrio Aranjuez* ☎ *2256–1825* ⊕ *www.hotelaranjuez.com* ⟿ *35 rooms, 29 with bath* ⦿ *Breakfast* ✛ *H2.*

"Our first full day in San José was full of wandering through the streets and markets. We happened upon this friendly artist who shared his paintings with us." —Photo by Liz Stuart, Fodors.com member

$$ **HOTEL** **Fodor's Choice** **★** 🖼 **Hotel Boutique Jade.** The European owners of this small east-side lodging have instilled a standard for attentive service in their staff and the result is a devoted return clientele, mostly from Europe. **Pros:** friendly service; quiet street; close to lots of shopping. **Cons:** can be difficult to find; far from sights. 💲 *Rooms from: $136* ⊠ *Blvd. Dent, Barrio Dent* ✛ *250 m north of Grupo Q* ☎ *2224-2455* ⊕ *www.hotelboutiquejade. com* ⇨ *27 rooms, 2 suites* ⟟⊙⟨ *Breakfast* ✛ *B5.*

$$ **B&B/INN** **Fodor's Choice** **★** 🖼 **Hotel Casa Cambranes.** The friendly hosts are what make your stay a real treat at this comfy San Pedro lodging. **Pros:** friendly, gracious owners on-site; close to west-side shopping and nightlife; attentive service. **Cons:** can be difficult to find; no on-site parking; resident cat, so not a place to go if you dislike felines. 💲 *Rooms from: $85* ⊠ *C. 47. Avda. 10-10A, San Pedro* ✛ *across from Fátima church* ☎ *2253-8858, 877/798-5158 in North America* ⊕ *www.casacambranes.com* ⇨ *12 rooms* ⟟⊙⟨ *Breakfast* ✛ *C6.*

$ **B&B/INN** 🖼 **Hotel Dunn Inn.** Adjoining 1926 and 1933 houses fuse to create the cozy Barrio Amón experience at bargain prices. **Pros:** good value; friendly staff; many online specials. **Cons:** difficult to get reservations; interior rooms catch noise from lobby and bar; sits at bottom of steep street. 💲 *Rooms from: $74* ⊠ *Avda. 11, C. 5, Barrio Amón* ☎ *2222-3232, 800/545-4801 in North America* ⊕ *www.hoteldunninn.com* ⇨ *28 rooms* ⟟⊙⟨ *Breakfast* ✛ *F2.*

$ **B&B/INN** 🖼 **Hotel Santo Tomás.** The front of this century-old former coffee-plantation house is along a busy street, but close the front door behind you and you'll find an oasis of quiet in the center of the city. **Pros:** good value; friendly staff; central location. **Cons:** difficult parking; borders on sketchy neighborhood; small rooms. $ *Rooms from: $64* ⊠ *Avda. 7, Cs. 3–5, Barrio Amón* ☎ *2255–0448, 877/446–0658 in North America* ⊕ *www.hotelsantotomas.com* ⟿ *30 rooms* �’⊖❘ *Breakfast* ✛ *F3.*

$

B&B/INN

⌅ **Kap's Place.** The owners of this multibuilding lodging are committed to maintaining a family atmosphere, and you'll be guaranteed peace and quiet during your stay here. **Pros:** good budget value; quiet atmosphere. **Cons:** far from sights; small rooms; you can pay with a credit card if you stay in the main building, but not in one of the annexes. $ *Rooms from: $55* ⊠ *C. 19, Avdas. 11–13, Barrio Aranjuez* ✛ *200 m west and 50 m north of Shell station* ☎ *2221–1169* ⊕ *www.kapsplace.com* ⟿ *32 rooms, 20 with bath* ❘⊖❘ *Breakfast* ✛ *H2.*

NIGHTLIFE AND PERFORMING ARTS

NIGHTLIFE

The metro area's hottest nightlife has migrated to the Central Valley suburbs of Escazú and Heredia these days. (⇨ *See Chapter 4.*) Both are about 20- to 30-minute taxi rides from downtown San José. The capital isn't devoid of places to go in the evening, however. There are still plenty of bars, dance clubs, and restaurants and cafés where you can spend the evening. Take taxis to and from when you go; it's the safest option if you're out after dark. Most places will be happy to call you a cab—or, if there's a guard, he can hail you one—when it's time to call it a night. Remember that all venues are nonsmoking.

No one could accuse San José of having too few watering holes, but aside from the hotels there aren't many places to have a quiet drink, especially downtown. Barrios Amón and Otoya have little in the way of nightlife outside the occasional hotel bar.

The young and the restless hang out in the student-oriented places around the University of Costa Rica in the eastern suburb of San Pedro. The Calle de la Amargura (Street of Bitterness), named for the route Jesus took to the crucifixion, is much more secular than its name suggests and rocks loudly each night. (Nighttime robberies have occurred on "The Calle," so be wary.)

Don't write off every place around the university as rowdy. There are a few quiet bars and cafés where you can carry on a real conversation. Barrios La California and Escalante, an area anchored by the Santa Teresita church, connect central San José with San Pedro, and house some of the city's trendiest nightspots.

DOWNTOWN
GAY AND LESBIAN
La Avispa. A gay and lesbian crowd frequents La Avispa, which has two dance floors with videos and karaoke, as well as a quieter upstairs bar with pool tables. The last Friday of each month is ladies' night. ⊠ *C. 1, Avda. 8, Downtown* ☎ *2223–5343* ⊕ *www.laavispa.com* ☉ *Thurs.– Sun. 8 pm–1 am.*

WEST OF DOWNTOWN

BARS

La Bodeguita del Medio. The mojitos flow and the chips and guacamole keep coming at this west-side restaurant that showcases live (usually Cuban) music most evenings after 9. ⊠ *Avda. 4, C. 40, Paseo Colón* ✛ *200 m. south of Banco de Costa Rica* ☎ *2255-8383.*

Mac's American Bar. An older expat crowd hangs out at Mac's, which always has the TV tuned to a sporting event. It might even have the city's best burger. ⊠ *Sabana Sur* ✛ *South side of La Sabana Park, next to the Costa Rica Tennis Club* ☎ *2234-3145* ⊙ *Daily 9 am–2 am.*

NORTH AND EAST OF DOWNTOWN

BARS

> ### BE AWARE
>
> A few gems really do populate the downtown area, but several bars there double as prostitute pickup joints or are just boozy places where patrons go to pick fights. If you're downtown at night, drink at your hotel or one of the places we recommend, and don't wander directly south or west of Parque Central on foot.
>
> Also avoid the Centro Comercial El Pueblo (usually known simply as El Pueblo), north of downtown. There have been problems with security at this entertainment-and-shopping complex.

El Observatorio. El Observatorio strikes an unusual balance between casual and formal: it's the kind of place where folks over 30 go to watch a soccer game but wear ties. Something is on here every night except Sunday, usually a selection of stand-up comedy, live music, or karaoke. ⊠ *C. 23, Barrio La California* ✛ *across from Cine Magaly* ☎ *2223-0725* ⊕ *www.elobservatorio.tv* ⊙ *Mon.–Sat. 6 pm–2 am.*

Jazz Café San Pedro. This place draws big crowds for the nightly live music (except Sunday). Although the staple here is jazz, rock and funk acts play here as well—check the website to see what's on. You'll find a branch in the Central Valley suburb of Escazú as well. ⊠ *Avda. Central, San Pedro* ✛ *next to Banco Popular* ☎ *2253-8933* ⊕ *www. jazzcafecostarica.com* ⊙ *Mon.–Sat. 6 pm–1 am.*

Vyrus. There is occasionally live music at Vyrus on the weekend, which draws a mixed college student and young professional crowd. Videos from the '60s, '70s, '80s provide the backdrop other nights. Inside is dark, coupley, and kissy; the outdoor balcony is much more conducive to singing along to that Duran Duran song you haven't heard in ages. ⊠ *San Pedro* ✛ *100 m west of Spoon restaurant* ☎ *2280-5890* ⊙ *Mon.–Sat. 4 pm–2 am.*

CAFÉS

Café Mundo. The highly recommended restaurant Café Mundo is a quiet spot for a drink or bite to eat and is frequented by gay and bohemian crowds. ⊠ *C. 15, Avda. 9, Barrio Otoya* ☎ *2222-6190.*

Olio. Fill up on Spanish-style tapas at the Mediterranean bar and restaurant Olio. It draws a mix of professionals and older college students. ⊠ *C. 33, Avda. 3, Barrio Escalante* ☎ *2281-0541* ⊕ *www. oliorestaurante.com* ⊙ *Mon.–Sat. 6 pm–2 am.*

Omar Khayyam. Smack-dab in the center of the campus nightlife, Omar Khayyam is a blissfully quiet refuge. Share a jug of wine and falafel or hummus with fried yuca on the covered patio. ⊠ *C. de la Amargura, San Pedro* ☎ *2253–8455* ⊙ *Mon.–Sat. 10 am–2 am.*

DANCE

Merecumbé. Step into a San José nightclub and you might think Costa Ricans are born dancing. They aren't, but most learn to merengue, rumba, mambo, cha-cha, and swing (called *cumbia* elsewhere) as children. Play catch-up at dance school Merecumbé, which has 16 branches around Costa Rica. With a few days' notice you can arrange a private lesson with an English-speaking instructor. An hour or two is all you need to grasp the fundamentals of merengue and bolero, both of which are easy to master and work with the pop music you're likely to hear back home. ⊠ *100 m south and 25 m west of Banco Popular, San Pedro* ☎ *2224–3531* ⊕ *www.merecumbe.net.*

SOUTH OF DOWNTOWN
FOLKLORIC SHOWS

Ram Luna. In the far, far southern suburbs, Ram Luna is most famous for the views—the lights of the Central Valley sparkle at your feet—and the music. Make reservations if you plan to be here for Wednesday or Thursday evening's folklore show—a bilingual emcee fills you in on the cultural background of what you're enjoying—or Friday evening's dancing to live music. ⊠ *Aserrí* ✛ *15 km (9 miles) south of San José between Aserrí and Tabarca* ☎ *2230–3022* ⊕ *www.restauranteramluna. com* ⊙ *Mon. and Tues. 5–10, Wed. and Thurs. 7–10, Fri. 5–11, Sat. noon–11, Sun. noon–9.*

PERFORMING ARTS

The best source for theater, dance, film, and arts information is the "Viva" entertainment section of the Spanish-language daily *La Nación*. The paper also publishes the "Tiempo Libre" section each Friday, highlighting what's going on over the weekend. *GAM Cultural*, a free monthly flyer found in many upscale hotels and restaurants, publishes features about what's going on around town. Listings in both publications are in Spanish but are easy to decipher. The website of the English-language *The Tico Times* (⊕ *www.ticotimes.net*) lists many events of interest to visitors and the expat community.

Unfortunately, arts offerings in the city are nearly nonexistent during the high-season weeks from mid-December through early February. That's school vacation time.

FILM

Dubbing of movies is rare; films are screened in their original language, usually English, and subtitled in Spanish. Children's movies, however, *are* dubbed (*doblada*), although a multiplex cinema may offer some *hablada en inglés*, or screenings in English. Plan to pay $6 for a ticket. Don't expect anything too avant-garde in most theaters; month-old Hollywood releases are the norm. Following trends seen elsewhere, theaters have fled downtown for the suburban malls.

Sala Garbo. This theater shows arty films, often in languages other than English, with Spanish subtitles. ✉ *Avda. 2, C. 28, Paseo Colón* ☎ *2222–1034* ⊕ *www.salagarbocr.com.*

THEATER AND MUSIC

More than a dozen theater groups (many of which perform slapstick comedies) hold forth in smaller theaters around town. If your Spanish is up to it, call for a reservation. The curtain rises at 8 pm, Friday through Sunday, with some companies staging performances on Thursday night, too. If your Spanish isn't quite theater-ready, there are plenty of dance and musical performances.

Centro Nacional de la Cultura. There are frequent dance performances and concerts in the Teatro FANAL and Teatro 1887, both in the Centro Nacional de la Cultura. ✉ *C. 13, Avdas. 3–5, Barrio Otoya* ☎ *2257–5524* ⊕ *www.mcj.go.cr.*

Eugene O'Neill Theater. This theater has chamber concerts and plays most weekend evenings. The cultural center is a great place to meet North American expatriates. ✉ *Centro Cultural Costarricense–Norteamericano, Avda. 1, C. 37, Barrio Dent* ☎ *2207–7554* ⊕ *www.centrocultural.cr.*

Teatro La Aduana. You'll find frequent dance and stage performances at this theater, and it is home to the Compañía Nacional de Teatro (National Theater Company). ✉ *C. 25, Avda. 3, Barrio La California* ☎ *2257–8305* ⊕ *www.mcj.go.cr.*

Teatro Nacional (*National Theater*). This baroque theater is the home of the excellent National Symphony Orchestra, which performs on several Friday evenings and Sunday mornings between March and November. The theater also hosts visiting musical groups and dance companies. Tickets are $5–$50—far less than you'd pay for a comparable production back home. ✉ *Plaza de la Cultura, Barrio La Soledad* ☎ *2010–1100* ⊕ *www.teatronacional.go.cr.*

Teatro Popular Melico Salazar. San José's second-most-popular theater has a full calendar of music and dance shows, as well as a few offbeat productions. There is always something on several nights a week; tickets are $5–$25. ✉ *Avda. 2, Cs. Central–2, Barrio La Merced* ☎ *2233–5424* ⊕ *www.teatromelico.go.cr.*

SHOPPING

Although it might seem more "authentic" to buy your souvenirs at their source, you can find everything in the city, a real bonus if you're pressed for time. If the capital has any real tourist shopping district, it's found loosely in the cluster of streets around Parque Morazán, just north of downtown, an area bounded roughly by Avenidas 1 and 7 and Calles 5 and 9. Stroll and search, because many other businesses congregate in the area as well.

The northeastern suburb of Moravia has a cluster of high-quality crafts and artisan shops—for good reason very popular with tour groups—in the three blocks heading north from the Colegio María Inmaculada high school. The street is two blocks behind the city's church.

DID YOU KNOW?

The auditorium floor in the Teatro Nacional was designed to be hoisted up to stage level by a manual winch so that it could also be used as a ballroom.

Prices in shops are fixed and fair. You may be able to bargain at Mercado Central and the Calle Nacional de Artesania y Pintura, but bargaining isn't the sport it is in other countries. Haggling, even if not ill-intended, will come off as rude. Your best bet for getting a deal is to simply suggest you'll come back later and walk away. If the vendors really want to lower the price, they will.

MALLS

Several huge enclosed centers anchor the metro area. These are complemented by dozens of smaller strip malls. Expect all the comforts of home—food courts and movie theaters included. The large Mall San Pedro in the eastern suburb of San Pedro has had a few issues with safety; we recommend avoiding it.

Terramall. The mammoth, three-level,161-store Terramall is the far eastern suburbs' prime shopping destination. ⊠ *Autopista Florencio del Castillo, Tres Ríos* ☎ *2278–6970* ⊕ *www.terramall.co.cr.*

DOWNTOWN

BOOKS AND MAGAZINES

Casa de las Revistas. With several locations around the metro area, Casa de las Revistas has San José's best selection of magazines in English. ⊠ *C. 7, Avdas. Central–1, Downtown* ☎ *2256–8251.*

CRAFTS

Congo. Congo offers a good selection of wood carvings and ceramic bowls and vases made by local artisans. It's a small four-store chain. ⊠ *Arcade in Hotel Balmoral, C. Central, Avdas. 7–9, Downtown* ☎ *2010–7274* ⊕ *www.costaricacongo.com.*

Fodor's Choice
★

Galería Namu. Downtown San José's must-stop shop is Galería Namu, which sells the best indigenous crafts in town. Its inventory brims with colorful creations by the Guaymí, Boruca, Bribri, Chorotega, Huetar, and Maleku peoples—all Costa Rican indigenous groups. Such crafts used to be the exclusive domain of male artisans, but a growing number of works by women are on display here these days. You can also find exquisitely carved ivory-nut tagua figurines, dolls, and baskets made by the Wounan people from Panama's Darién region and Tuno textiles and Lenca pottery from Honduras. Take note of carved balsa masks, woven cotton blankets, and hand-painted ceramics.

The store looks expensive—and indeed, the sky's the limit in terms of prices—but if your budget is not so flush, say so: the good folks here can help you find something in the $15–$25 range that will make a cherished souvenir. As a bonus you'll get an information sheet describing your work's creator and art style. Namu has a reputation for fair prices for customers, and for fair pay to artists and artisans. ⊠ *Avda. 7, Cs. 5–7, Downtown* ☎ *2256–3412* ⊕ *www.galerianamu.com.*

AIRPORT SOUVENIR SHOPS

If you really didn't have time to shop, never fear. Aeropuerto Internacional Juan Santamaría has five noteworthy souvenir shops—**Britt Shop Costa Rica, Colibrí, Travel Zone, Casa Tica**, and **Green Trails**—for those last-minute purchases. All are in the boarding area past airport security. Choose from various blends of coffee ($5 per pound), hand-carved bowls and jewelry, aromatherapy candles, and banana-paper stationery. There's nary another store in the country carrying such variety all in one place. The catch is that the airport shops charge U.S.-level prices.

The airport's **IMAS Duty Free** shops carry all the standard merchandise you find in such outlets around the world. Costa Ricans, who get socked with high taxes on imported goods, love the prices; we doubt you'll find any bargains that you can't get back home.

MUSIC

Universal. In addition to selling everything else imaginable, downtown department store Universal stocks a good selection of Latin CDs in its first-floor music department. ⊠ *Avda. Central, Cs. Central–1, Downtown* ☎ *2222–2222* ⊕ *www.universalcr.com.*

SOUVENIRS

Calle Nacional de Artesanía y Pintura (*National Street of Artisanry and Painting*). Some 100 souvenir vendors congregate in a block-long covered walkway on the west side of the Plaza de la Democracia. As you approach, the whole affair looks like a string of metal shacks, but some of the sellers offer bargains in hammocks, wood carvings, and clothing. In a perpetual tug-of-war, the city proposes moving the stalls to a less visible location at Avenida 4 and Calle 7. The vendors balk and the city relents, only to have the dispute come up again a few months later. ⊠ *C. 13, Avdas. Central–2, Downtown* ✛ *western side of Plaza de la Democracia.*

Don Carlos Hotel. The gift shop at the Hotel Don Carlos has a good selection of popular souvenirs and CDs of Costa Rican music. ⊠ *Don Carlos Hotel, C. 9, Avda. 9, Downtown* ☎ *2221–6707* ⊕ *www.doncarloshotel.com.*

La Traviata. The small shop off the lobby of the National Theater has a terrific selection of thespian-themed postcards, tote bags, and glassware. You can access the shop without an admission ticket to a theater production. In addition to being open Monday through Saturday during the day, the shop is also open before evening performances and during intermission. ⊠ *Teatro Nacional, Plaza de la Cultura, Downtown* ☎ *2010–1118* ⊕ *www.latraviata.co.cr.*

Mercado Central. This maze of passageways is where the average Costa Rican comes to stock up on day-to-day necessities, but a few stalls of interest to tourists congregate near the entrances. ⊠ *Bordered by Avdas. Central–1 and Cs. 6–8, Downtown.*

Museo del Jade (*Jade Museum*). The small shop in the Jade Museum sells replicas of many of the pieces in the museum collection. The shop is accessible only if you've paid the museum admission. ⊠ *Avda. Central, C. 13, Downtown* ☎ *2287–6034.*

Museo del Oro Precolombino. The shop at the entrance of the Museo del Oro Precolombino offers a great selection of pre-Columbian-theme jewelry, art, exclusively designed T-shirts, coin key chains, notebooks, and mouse pads. You can access the shop without paying the museum admission. ⊠ *C. 5, Avdas. Central–2, Downtown* ☎ *2243–4217.*

WEST OF DOWNTOWN

CRAFTS

Hotel Grano de Oro. The small gift shop at the Hotel Grano de Oro has an impressive selection of carvings and jewelry on hand. ⊠ *C. 30, Avdas. 2–4, Paseo Colón* ☎ *2255–3322* ⊕ *www.hotelgranodeoro.com.*

NORTH AND EAST OF DOWNTOWN

BOOKS AND MAGAZINES

Librería Internacional. The city's largest bookstore evokes that Barnes & Noble ambience, though on a much smaller scale. It stocks English translations of Latin American literature, as well as myriad coffee-table books on Costa Rica. There are 22 other smaller branches around San José and the Central Valley. ⊠ *Plaza Antares, Blvd. Dent and Rotonda La Bandera, Barrio Dent* ☎ *2253–9553* ⊕ *www.libreriainternacional.com.*

CRAFTS

Kiosco SJO. Ensconced inside Barrio Escalante's trendy Kalú restaurant, equally trendy Kiosco SJO proffers a good selection of locally made woodwork, fabrics, and ceramics. ⊠ *Kalú, C. 31, Avda. 5, Barrio Escalante* ☎ *2253–8426.*

Mi Pueblo Verde. This is a standout among the Moravia shops for its fine carvings made from native *cocobolo* and *guápinol* wood. The salad bowls are especially unusual in their design. ⊠ *Moravia* ⊹ *50 m north of Colegio María Inmaculada* ☎ *2235–5742.*

FARMERS' MARKET

Feria Verde. It's a tad out of the way, but just up the street from the Hotel Aranjuez is the city's best Saturday-morning farmers' market. Stock up on organic fruits and veggies and take in the local scene. For something tropical, try some coconut milk—you'll get a coconut whacked in half by a machete and you can sip the water through a straw. Things get under way at 7 am and wind down around 1 pm. ⊠ *North end of C. 19, Barrio Aranjuez* ⊹ *150 m north of Hotel Aranjuez, then downhill to the left* ⊕ *www.feriaverde.org.*

SOUVENIRS

Artesanías Zurquí. You'll find a well-rounded selection of ceramics, wood, and leather at Artesanías Zurquí. ⊠ *Moravia* ⊹ *50 m north of Colegio María Inmaculada* ☎ *2240–5342.*

Mundo de Recuerdos. If you can't find it at Mundo de Recuerdos, it probably doesn't exist. Here's the largest of the Moravia shops with simply everything—at least of standard souvenir fare—you could ask for under one roof. ⊠ *Moravia* ⊹ *Across from Colegio María Inmaculada* ☎ *2240–8990.*

4

THE CENTRAL VALLEY

WELCOME TO THE CENTRAL VALLEY

TOP REASONS TO GO

★ **Avian adventures:** Flock to Tapantí National Park to see emerald toucanets, resplendent quetzals (if you're lucky), and nearly every species of Costa Rican hummingbird. Rancho Naturalista is the bird lover's hotel of choice.

★ **Coffee:** Get up close and personal with harvesting and processing on coffee tours at two of the valley's many plantations: Café Britt and Doka Estate.

★ **Poás Volcano:** Peer right down into the witches' cauldron that is the Poás Volcano.

★ **The Orosi Valley:** Spectacular views and quiet, bucolic towns make this area a great day trip or overnight from San José.

★ **Rafting the Pacuare River:** Brave the rapids as you descend through tropical forest on one of the best white-water rivers in Central America.

1 West of San José. The communities immediately west of San José are the capital's booming, upscale suburbs. Things turn more pastoral the farther west you go, and you'll find one of the country's best craft communities, Sarchí, and some luxurious countryside lodges near Grecia and San Ramón. Atenas, a thriving agricultural center known for its coffee plantations and livestock, offers a glimpse into a quintessential Costa Rican town. Heading farther west toward the Central Pacific coast, Carara National Park is home to an impressive collection of plants and animals.

2 North of San José. Coffee farms and small valley towns dominate the area north of San José. Their beautiful hotels attract visitors on their first and last nights in the country. Coffee plantations Café Britt and Doka Estate are both here, as is the international airport, near Alajuela. North of Alajuela, Poás Volcano's turquoise crater lake and steaming main

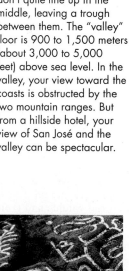

Santa Clara

Turrialba Volcano
Irazú Volcano
Potrero Cerrado
Turrialba
Guayabo National Monument
Jabillos
Pavones
Cartago
Juan Viñas
La Suiza
Moravia
Paraíso
Tuís
Bajo Pacuare
Orosi Valley
Río Macho
CARTAGO
Tapantí National Park
Pacuare River
Tres de Junio
Salsipuedes
Villa Mills

0   10 mi
0   15 km

CORDILLERA CENTRAL
TALAMANCA

GETTING ORIENTED

The Central Valley is something of a misnomer, and its Spanish name, the *meseta central* (central plateau) isn't entirely accurate either. The two contiguous mountain ranges that run the length of the country—the Cordillera Central range (which includes Poás, Barva, Irazú, and Turrialba volcanoes) to the north and the Cordillera de Talamanca to the south—don't quite line up in the middle, leaving a trough between them. The "valley" floor is 900 to 1,500 meters (about 3,000 to 5,000 feet) above sea level. In the valley, your view toward the coasts is obstructed by the two mountain ranges. But from a hillside hotel, your view of San José and the valley can be spectacular.

4

crater make it many visitors' favorite volcano stop.

3 East of San José. The less visited eastern Central Valley holds Cartago, older than San José, with a couple of historic attractions. Irazú is Costa Rica's tallest volcano. On a clear day you can see both the Atlantic and Pacific oceans from its peak. The nearby Orosi Valley is an often overlooked beauty. The

drive into the valley is simply gorgeous, and a tranquil way to spend a day. Birding destination Tapantí National Park is at the southern edge of the valley. Rafting trips on the Pacuare and Reventazón are based in bustling, growing Turrialba. The nearby Guayabo National Monument, ruins of a city deserted in AD 1400, is Costa Rica's only significant archaeological site.

CARARA NATIONAL PARK

One of the last remnants of an ecological transition zone between Costa Rica's drier northwest and more humid southwest, Carara National Park holds a tremendous collection of plants and animals.

Squeezed into its 47 square km (18 square miles) is a mixed habitat of evergreen and deciduous forest, river, lagoon, and marshland. Much of the park's terrain is blanketed with dramatic primary forest, massive trees laden with vines and epiphytes. This is a birder's and plant lover's haven. The sparse undergrowth makes terrestrial wildlife and ground birds easier to see. The most famous denizens—aside from the crocodiles in the adjoining Río Tárcoles—are the park's colorful and noisy scarlet macaws, which always travel in pairs. An oxbow lake (a U-shaped body of water that was once part of a river) adds an extra wildlife dimension, attracting turtles and waterfowl—and the crocodiles that dine on them. Bring lots of drinking water; this park can get very hot and humid. *(For more information, see the review in this chapter.)*

BEST TIME TO GO

Dry season, January to April, is the best time to visit. The trails get very muddy during the rainy season and usually close in the wettest months. This small park can feel crowded at the trailheads, so arrive early and walk far. Bird-watchers can call the day before to arrange early admission.

FUN FACT

The crowning glory of Carara is the successful conservation program that has doubled its scarlet macaw population. You can't miss these long-tailed, noisy parrots—look for streaks of brilliant blue and red in the sky.

BEST WAYS TO EXPLORE

BIRD-WATCHING

With more than 400 species recorded here, Carara is on every bird-watcher's must-visit list. It's an especially good place to see elusive ground birds, such as antpittas (a small ground-dwelling bird that eats ants), early in the morning and late in the afternoon. Around the lake and in the marshy areas, you may also spot roseate spoonbills, northern jacanas, and stately boat-billed herons. The park's most famous fliers are the scarlet macaws. Once almost absent from the area, a decades-long conservation program has revitalized the local population.

HIKING

The best and really only way to explore this park is on foot. Rubber boots or waterproof shoes are essential in the rainy season, and a good idea in the drier months as well. Trails are well marked and maintained but the ground is often muddy—this is rain forest, after all. The shortest—and most popular—loop trail can be done in only 15 minutes. But if you venture farther afield, you'll quickly be on your own, except for the wildlife you're bound to encounter. The longer trail that connects with the Quebrada Bonita loop takes about 90 minutes to hike. There is also a short wheelchair-accessible route that starts at the main entrance. It goes deep enough into the forest to give visitors a sense of its drama and diversity.

WILDLIFE-WATCHING

Carara is famous for an amazing variety of wildlife, given its relatively small area. Keep alert (and quiet) while walking and you'll have a good chance of spotting big and small lizards, coatimundis (a member of the raccoon family), and sloths. You're almost guaranteed to see white-faced monkeys and, with luck, howler and spider monkeys, too. You may even surprise a nine-banded armadillo snuffling along the ground or a northern tamandua (anteater) patrolling low branches.

TOP REASONS TO GO

4

Birds
With a varied habitat that attracts both forest and water birds, Carara is a treasure trove for birders. Even if you're not a birder, you'll get a thrill hearing the raucous crowing of beautiful scarlet macaws as they soar over the forest canopy.

The Jungle
The forest here is simply magnificent. Even if you don't spot a single bird or animal, you will experience the true meaning of jungle. Carara has one of the most diverse collections of trees in the country. Breathe deeply, be alert to the symphony of forest sounds, and bask in a totally natural world.

Wildlife
For most visitors, wildlife is the park's main attraction. You can count on seeing monkeys and lots of lizards as you walk the trails. Although they are a little harder to spot, look for anteaters, sloths, and armadillos.

POÁS VOLCANO

Towering north of Alajuela, the verdant Poás Volcano is covered with a quilt of farms and topped by a dark green shawl of cloud forest.

That pastoral scene disappears once you get to the 2,708-meter (8,885-foot) summit, and you gaze into the steaming, bubbling crater with smoking fumaroles and a gurgling, gray-turquoise sulfurous lake. You'll swear you're peering over the edge of a giant witches' cauldron. That basin, 2 km (1 mile) in diameter and nearly 305 meters (1,000 feet) deep, is thought to be the largest active volcanic crater in the world.

Poás is one of Costa Rica's five active volcanoes—it has erupted 40 times since the early 1800s—and is one of those rare places that permit you to see volcanic energy this close with minimal risk to your safety. Authorities closely monitor Poás's activity following several eruptions in March 2006, the first significant increase in activity since 1994. The most recent activity took place in February 2014 and produced clouds of smoke. Access is normally open, but park officials close the route up here when there is evidence of any activity they deem "irregular." *(For more information, see the review in this chapter.)*

BEST TIME TO GO

The peak is frequently shrouded in mist, and you might see little beyond the lip of the crater. Be patient and wait awhile, especially if some wind is blowing—the clouds can disappear quickly. Aim to get here before 10 am. The earlier in the day you arrive, the better the visibility.

FUN FACT

Forgot your umbrella? (It gets wet up here.) Duck under a *sombrilla de pobre* (poor man's umbrella) plant. These giant leaves can grow to diameters of 1 to 1½ meters (3 to 5 feet)— plenty big enough to shelter a few hikers caught out in the rain.

BEST WAYS TO EXPLORE

BIRD-WATCHING

Although birding can be a little frustrating here because of cloud and mist, more than 330 bird species call Poás home. One of the most comical birds you'll see in Costa Rica is usually spotted foraging in plain sight on the ground: the big-footed finch, whose oversized feet give it a clownish walk. Its cousin, the yellow-thighed finch, is easy to recognize by its bright yellow, er . . . thighs. Arrive early and bird around the gate before the park opens, and stop along the road to the visitor center wherever you see a likely birding area. In the underbrush you may find spotted wood quail or the elusive, buffy-crowned wood-partridge. The trees along the road are a favorite haunt of both black-and-yellow and long-tailed silky flycatchers.

HIKING

From the summit, two trails head into the forest. The second trail, on the right just before the crater, winds through a thick mesh of shrubs and dwarf trees to the eerie but beautiful Botos Lake (Laguna Botos), which occupies an extinct crater. It takes 30 minutes to walk here and back, but you'll be huffing and puffing if you're not used to this altitude.

VOLCANIC TIPS

A paved road leads all the way from Alajuela to Poás's summit. No one is allowed to venture into the crater or walk along its edge. ■TIP→ Take periodic breaks from viewing: step back at least every 10 minutes, so that the sulfur fumes don't overcome you. Be sure to bring a sweater or a jacket—it can be surprisingly chilly and wet up here.

TOP REASONS TO GO

A+ Facilities
You're on your own in many Costa Rican national parks, most of which are lacking in facilities, but this wheelchair-accessible park is a pleasant exception, with an attractive visitor center containing exhibits, a cafeteria, gift shop, and restrooms.

Lava and Ash
"Up close and personal with nature" takes on a whole new meaning here. Costa Rica forms part of the Pacific Rim's so-called Ring of Fire, and a visit to the volcano's summit gives you a close-up view of a region of the earth that is still in formation.

Location, Location, Location
Poás's proximity to San José and the western Central Valley makes it an easy half-day trip.

More Than a Volcano
The park is not just about its namesake volcano. A few kilometers of hiking trails wind around the summit and let you take in the cloud forest's lichens, ferns, and bromeliads.

IRAZÚ VOLCANO

The word *Irazú* is likely a corruption of Iztaru, a long-ago indigenous community whose name translated as "hill of thunder." The name is apt.

Volcán Irazú, as it's known in Spanish, is considered active, but the gases and steam that billow from fumaroles on the northwestern slope are rarely visible from the peak above the crater lookouts. The mountain's first recorded eruption took place in 1723; the most recent was a series of eruptions that lasted from 1963 to 1965. Boulders and mud rained down on the countryside, damming rivers and causing serious floods, and the volcano dumped up to 20 inches of ash on sections of the Central Valley.

When conditions are clear, you can see the chartreuse lake inside the Cráter Principal. The stark moonscape of the summit contrasts markedly with the lush vegetation of Irazú's lower slopes, home to porcupines, armadillos, coyotes, and mountain hares. Listen for the low-pitched, throaty song of the *yigüirro*, or clay-color thrush, Costa Rica's national bird. Its call is most pronounced just before the start of the rainy season. *(For more information, see the review in this chapter.)*

BEST TIME TO GO

Early morning, especially in the January–April dry season, affords the best views, both of the craters and the surrounding countryside. Clouds move in by late morning. Wear warm, waterproof clothing if you get here that early; although rare, temperatures have dropped down close to freezing around dawn.

FUN FACT

Irazú has dumped a lot of ash over the centuries. The most recent eruptive period began on the day that John F. Kennedy arrived in Costa Rica in March 1963. The "ash storm" that ensued lasted on and off for two years.

BEST WAYS TO EXPLORE

BIRD-WATCHING

The road to Irazú provides some of the best roadside birding opportunities in the country, especially on a weekday when there isn't a constant parade of cars and buses heading up to the crater. Some of the most fruitful areas are on either side of the bridges you'll pass over. Reliable bird species that inhabit these roadsides are acorn and hairy woodpeckers; the brilliant flame-throated warbler; buzzing around blossoms, the fiery-throated, green violet-ear; and (aptly named) volcano hummingbirds. Once past the main entrance, there are also plenty of opportunities to stop and bird-watch roadside. Look for volcano juncos on the ground and slaty flowerpiercers visiting flowering shrubs.

HIKING

Even before you get to the main entrance, check out the park's Prusia Sector, which has hiking trails that pass through majestic oak and pine forests and picnic areas. They're popular with Tico families on weekends, so if you want the woods to yourself, come on a weekday. Trails in the park are well marked; avoid heading down any paths marked with *"paso restringido"* ("passage restricted") signs.

VOLCANIC TIPS

A paved road leads all the way to the summit, where a small coffee shop sells hot beverages, and a persistent pair of coatis cruise the picnic tables for handouts. (Please resist the urge to feed them!) The road to the top climbs past vegetable fields, pastures, and native oak forests. You pass through the villages of Potrero Cerrado and San Juan de Chicuá before reaching the summit's bleak but beautiful main crater.

TOP REASONS TO GO

Easy to Get to
Irazú's proximity to San José and the entire eastern Central Valley makes it an easy half-day or day trip. Public transportation from the capital, frequently a cumbersome option to most of the country's national parks, is straightforward.

The View
How many places in the world let you peer directly into the crater of an active volcano? Costa Rica offers you two: here at Irazú and at Poás Volcano. Poás's steaming cauldron is spookier, but Irazú's crater lake with colors that change according to the light is nonetheless impressive.

More Views
"On a clear day, you can see forever," goes the old song from the musical of the same name. Irazú is one of the few places in Costa Rica that lets you glimpse both the Pacific and Atlantic (Caribbean) oceans at once. "Clear" is the key term here: clouds frequently obscure the view. Early morning gives you your best shot.

Updated by
Jeffrey Van
Fleet

San José sits in a mile-high mountain valley ringed by volcanoes whose ash has fertilized the soil and turned the region into Costa Rica's historic breadbasket. This will always be the land that coffee built, and the small cities of the Central Valley exhibit a tidiness and prosperity you don't see in the rest of the country. The valley is chock-full of activities and is Costa Rica at its most *típico*, giving you the best sense of what makes the country tick.

You can't find a more ideal climate than out here in the valley. When people refer to Costa Rica's proverbial "eternal spring," they're talking about this part of the country, which lacks the oppressive seasonal heat and rain of other regions. It's no wonder the Central Valley has drawn a growing number of North American and European retirees.

There's no shortage of terrific lodgings out here—everything from family-run boutique hotels to the big international chains are yours for the night. It used to be that everyone stayed in San José and took in the various attractions in the Central Valley on day trips. With the good selection of quality accommodations out here, why not base yourself in the Central Valley, and make San José your day trip instead?

PLANNING

WHEN TO GO
HIGH SEASON: MID-DECEMBER TO APRIL
The Central Valley's elevation keeps temperatures pleasant and spring-like year-round, slightly warmer to the west and slightly cooler to the east. Turrialba and the Orosi Valley represent a transition zone between the valley and the Caribbean slope; expect warmer temperatures there. December and January kick off the dry season with sunny days and brisk nights. February, March, and April warm up considerably. Some hotels here keep rates constant throughout the year; others follow high-season/low-season fluctuations.

LOW SEASON: MAY TO MID-NOVEMBER
The rainy season moves in gradually with afternoon showers from May through July. August becomes wetter, and September and October can mean prolonged downpours. The valley's western sector—Alajuela, San Antonio de Belén, Escazú, and Santa Ana—always catches a tad less rain than its eastern counterpart.

SHOULDER SEASON: MID-NOVEMBER TO MID-DECEMBER
Rains start to wind down by mid-November, and the month before Christmas is a terrific time to enjoy the Central Valley at its most lush and green, and before the big influx of tourists arrives. As an added bonus, the coffee harvest is under way in earnest in this part of the country, too—always a bustling, fascinating spectacle.

PLANNING YOUR TIME
You could spend an entire week here without getting bored, but if you have only a week or two in Costa Rica, we recommend a maximum of two days before heading to rain forests and beaches in other parts of the country. Spending a day after you arrive, then another day or two before you fly out gives you a taste of the region, breaks up the travel time, and makes your last day interesting, rather than spent in transit back to San José. The drive between just about any two points in the Central Valley is two hours or usually less, so it's ideal for short trips. Tour operators in and around San José offer daylong excursions that mix and match the valley's sights, perhaps a volcano visit in the morning and a coffee tour in the afternoon.

GETTING HERE AND AROUND
AIR TRAVEL
Although Aeropuerto Internacional Juan Santamaría is billed as San José's airport, it sits just outside the city of Alajuela in the near northwestern part of the valley. You can get taxis from the airport to any point in the Central Valley for $8–$80. Some hotels arrange pickup.

BUS TRAVEL
Many visitors never consider taking a local bus to get around, but doing so puts you in close contact with locals—an experience you miss out on if you travel by taxi or tour bus. It's also cheap. Always opt for a taxi at night or when you're in a hurry.

CAR TRAVEL
All points in the western Central Valley can be reached by car. For San Antonio de Belén, Heredia, Alajuela, and points north of San José, turn right at the west end of Paseo Colón onto the Pan-American Highway (Autopista General Cañas). The eastern Central Valley is accessible from San José by driving east on Avenidas 2, then Central, through San Pedro, then following signs from the intersection to Cartago. To get to the Orosi Valley, head straight through Cartago, turn right at the Basílica de Los Angeles, and follow the signs to Paraíso. The road through Cartago and Paraíso continues east to Turrialba. Driving from one side of the valley to the other means you need to get across San José. There's no truly efficient way to bypass the capital.

The best way to get around the Central Valley is by car. Most of the car-rental agencies in San José have offices at or near the airport in

Alajuela. They will deliver vehicles to many area hotels, but not those in Turrialba and the Orosi Valley.

TAXI TRAVEL

All Central Valley towns have taxis, which usually wait for fares along their central parks. The rideshare service Uber operates in a few of the larger suburbs—Escazú, Santa Ana, Alajuela, and Heredia—in the Central Valley.

Uber. ⊕ *www.uber.com/cities/san-jose.*

RESTAURANTS

Growing Escazú has become as metropolitan as San José and has the restaurant selection to prove it. Elsewhere, as befits this cradle of the country's tradition, typical Costa Rican cuisine still reigns.

HOTELS

Most international flights come into Costa Rica in the evening and head out early in the morning, meaning you likely have to stay your first and last nights in or near San José, and the Central Valley can be considered "near." For getting away from it all and still being close to the country's main airport, the lodgings around San José make splendid alternatives to staying in the city itself. It may pain you to tear yourself away from that beach villa or rain-forest lodge, but you can still come back to something distinctive here on your last night in Costa Rica. Small mom-and-pop places, sprawling coffee plantations, nature lodges, and hilltop villas with expansive views are some of your options. The large chains are here as well, but the real gems are the boutique hotels, many of which are family-run places and have unique designs that take advantage of exceptional countryside locations. Subtropical gardens are the norm, rather than the exception. The Central Valley's climate is often a great surprise to first-time visitors—it's usually cool enough at night to go without air-conditioning, so don't be surprised if many hotels don't have it. *Hotel reviews have been shortened. For full information, visit Fodors.com.*

WHAT IT COSTS IN DOLLARS			
$	$$	$$$	$$$$
Restaurants	under $10	$10–$15	$16–$25	over $25
Hotels	under $75	$75–$150	$151–$250	over $250

Restaurant prices are the average cost of a main course at dinner or, if dinner is not served, at lunch. Hotel prices are the lowest cost of a standard double room in high season.

WEST OF SAN JOSÉ

Believe it or not, as you drive west out of San José, the city's sprawling suburbs and industrial zones do eventually give way to arable land, much of which is occupied by coffee farms. Anchoring the western metro area are snazzy, posh Escazú and getting-snazzier-and-more-posh-all-the-time Santa Ana. Yet, not all has been malled over out here,

CLOSE UP

Eco-Lodges in the Central Valley

You'd never know it driving the highway west from San José past all the shopping malls and car dealerships, but Costa Rica's Central Valley is home to an ample amount of greenery that encompasses country lodges, active volcanoes, a cloud forest, archaeological ruins, and white-water rivers.

Finca Rosa Blanca Coffee Plantation Resort, Heredia. In addition to all the amenities you'd expect from one of the Central Valley's most sumptuous accommodations, you can also take Finca Rosa Blanca's unique sustainability tour for a behind-the-scenes look at what a hotel—in this case, one on a working coffee plantation—can do to be more eco- and community-friendly. What other

tour in Costa Rica lets you take in the workings of the laundry room, the solar panels, and the compost pile?

Rancho Naturalista, Turrialba. Some 430 species of birds live on the property—few lodgings can make such a claim, let alone one so close to the metropolitan area. But the fittingly named Rancho Naturalista near Turrialba has fast become the birding center of the Central Valley.

Xandari Resort & Spa, Alajuela. The 40-acre property in the hills above Alajuela maintains an active program of recycling and uses on-site, organically grown fruits and vegetables. The hotel is also turning back a portion of its coffee plantation to tree cover, which has been set aside as a nature reserve.

4

and both communities remain proud of their histories and traditions. Keep heading west, though, and you'll leave Escazú and Santa Ana's commercialism behind: Grecia, San Ramón, Sarchí, and Atenas are, these days, far more típico Tico communities. Carara National Park, great for birding, is southwest of San José, on the way to the Central Pacific coast.

ESCAZÚ

5 km (3 miles) southwest of San José.

Costa Rica's wealthiest community and the Central Valley's most prestigious address, Escazú (pronounced *es-cah-SOO*) nevertheless mixes glamour with tradition, BMWs with oxcarts, trendy malls with farmers' markets, Louis Vuitton with burlap produce sacks. As you exit the highway and crest the first gentle hill, you might think you made a wrong turn and ended up in Southern California, but farther up you return to small-town Central America. Narrow roads wind their way up the steep slopes, past postage-stamp coffee fields and lengths of shoulder-to-shoulder, modest houses with tidy gardens and the occasional oxcart parked in the yard. Unfortunately, the area's stream of new developments and high-rises has steadily chipped away at the rural landscape—each year you have to climb higher to find the kind of scene that captured the attention of many a Costa Rican painter in the early 20th century. In their place are plenty of fancy homes and condos, especially in the San Antonio and San Rafael neighborhoods. Escazú's

Alajuela
see detail
map

West and North
of San José

0   5 mi
0   5 km

historic church faces a small plaza, surrounded in part by weathered adobe buildings. The town center is several blocks north of the busy road to Santa Ana, which is lined with a growing selection of restaurants, bars, and shops.

During colonial days, Escazú was dubbed the "City of Witches" because many native healers lived in the area. Locals say that Escazú is still Costa Rica's most haunted community, home to witches who will tell your fortune or concoct a love potion for a small fee, but you'd be hard-pressed to spot them in the town's busy commercial district. Try a soccer field instead; the city's soccer team is christened Las Brujas ("the Witches"). You'll see a huge number of witch-on-a-broomstick decals affixed to vehicles here, too. It's the city's official symbol.

GETTING HERE AND AROUND

To drive to Escazú from San José, turn left at the western end of Paseo Colón, which ends at the Parque La Sabana. Take the first right onto the Caldera Highway, and get off the highway at the second exit. The off-ramp curves right, then sharply left; follow it about 1 km (½ mile), sticking to the main road, to El Cruce at the bottom of the hill (marked by the large Physiomed orthopedic clinic). Continue through the traffic light for San Rafael addresses; turn right for the old road to Santa Ana. The trip takes about 20 minutes, much longer during rush hour.

A steady stream of buses for Escazú runs from several stops near, but not inside, the Terminal Coca-Cola in San José (*Avdas. 1–3, Cs. 14–16*), with service from 5 am to 11 pm. ⚠ Be careful: the Coca-Cola neighborhood is a dicey part of downtown San José.

ESSENTIALS

Banks/ATMs BAC San José. ⊠ *200 m south of El Cruce, San Rafael* ☎ *309/2295–9797* ⊕ *www.bac.net.* **Banco de Costa Rica ATM.** ⊠ *125 m west of Municipalidad.* **Banco Nacional.** ⊠ *Southwest side of Parque Central* ☎ *309/2228–0009* ⊕ *www.bncr.fi.cr.*

Medical Assistance Hospital CIMA. ⊠ *12 km (7½ miles) west of downtown San José, next to PriceSmart, just off the hwy. to Santa Ana* ☎ *2208–1000* ⊕ *www.hospitalsanjose.net.*

Pharmacy Farmacia San Miguel. ⊠ *North side of Parque Central* ☎ *2228–2339.*

Post Office Correos. ⊠ *100 m north of church* ⊕ *www.correos.go.cr.*

Taxis Coopetico. ☎ *2224–7979.*

EXPLORING

FAMILY **Butterfly Kingdom.** Butterflies are the "livestock" at this working farm in the heart of Escazú, where caterpillars are raised and then exported in chrysalis form. A tour of the operation takes you through the stages of a butterfly's life. The highlight is the garden where fluttering butterflies surround you. Sunny days fuel the most activity among them; they are quieter if the day is overcast. (The latter conditions make for easier photos.) Bilingual tours in English and Spanish are included in the admission price. ⊠ *Bello Horizonte, 1 km (½ mile) south and 100 m west of Distribuidora Santa Bárbara* ☎ *2288–6667* ⊕ *www.butterflykingdom. net* ⤵ *$12* ⊙ *Tues.–Sat. 10–3:30.*

Iglesia San Miguel Arcángel (*Church of St. Michael the Archangel*). According to tradition, ghosts and witches work their spells, good and bad, over Escazú. The founders of this haunted town fittingly chose the archangel Michael, reputed to have driven Satan from heaven, as their patron saint. The original church on this site dates from 1796, but earthquakes took their toll, as they have on so many historic sites throughout Costa Rica. A complete reconstruction was done in 1962, remaining as true as possible to the original design, but up to current earthquake building codes. The results are still impressive more than five decades later. A statue of St. Michael watches from the left side of the main altar. ⊠ *Parque Central* ☎ *2228–0635* ⊙ *Mon. 8–7, Tues.–Fri. 9–7, Sat. noon–7, Sun. 6 am–8 pm.*

SPORTS AND THE OUTDOORS
HIKING
High in the hills above Escazú is the tiny community of **San Antonio de Escazú,** famous for its annual oxcart festival held the second Sunday of March. The view from here—of nearby San José and distant volcanoes—is impressive by both day and night. If you head higher than San Antonio de Escazú, brace yourself for seemingly vertical roads that wind up into the mountains toward **Pico Blanco,** the highest point in the

Escazú Cordillera, which is a half-day hike to ascend. You can also hike **San Miguel,** one peak east. We recommend you go with an outfitter—far safer than hiking on your own.

Aventuras Picotours. The owner of Aventuras Picotours was the first Costa Rican to reach the summit of Everest, and can lead you on a variety of far less daunting daylong hikes in the hills above town. ⊠ *From the Church of San Antonio de Escazú, 300 m east, 1800 m south, and 50 m east* ☎ *2289–6135* ⊕ *www.picotours.com* ✉ *Tours from $49.*

WHERE TO EAT

$$ ✕ **Barbecue Los Anonos.** For decades, Costa Ricans have flocked to
BARBECUE Los Anonos to enjoy its family-friendly grill fest. The original dining
FAMILY room, a rustic collection of deep booths with wooden benches, has been expanded to add a more elegant space decorated with historic photos. The crowd tends toward families on weekend nights, whereas weekdays are busier during lunch, when business executives come for the economical meals. The best bet is the grilled meat, and there is plenty to choose from, including imported U.S. beef and less expensive Costa Rican cuts. Fresh fish, shrimp, and half a dozen salads round out the choices. ⑤ *Average main: $13* ⊠ *400 m west of Los Anonos Bridge* ☎ *2228–0180* ⊕ *www.restaurantelosanonos.com* ⊘ *Closed Mon.*

$ ✕ **Chez Christophe.** Escazú's very own French-style bistro makes a great
FRENCH place for a breakfast or lunch of sandwiches on baguettes or croissants—the ham or smoked salmon is especially *délicieux.* The pleasant patio has painted murals depicting French food scenes. Even if you don't eat here, stop by for the wonderful selection of French breads and pastries, baked fresh each day. The place closes at 7. ⑤ *Average main: $8* ⊠ *75 m south of Centro Comercial Paco* ☎ *2228–2512* ⊘ *Closed Mon. No dinner.*

$$$$ ✕ **Le Monastère.** This monastery-themed formal restaurant high in the
FRENCH San Rafael hills has a great view of the Central Valley. The dining room is dressed up in antiques, with tables set for a five-course meal; waiters don short friar tunics over their standard black pants and white shirts, which makes the atmosphere too theatrical for some tastes, but the classic French dishes are outstanding. The more casual Cava Grill dining area serves platters of grilled meat. Cantina La Cava, beneath the dining room, has tasty appetizers, live music Thursday to Saturday, and is open into the wee hours. ⑤ *Average main: $26* ⊠ *1½ km (1 mile) southwest of the Paco Shopping Center in San Rafael de Escazú; take old road west to Santa Ana, turn left at Paco and follow signs, always bearing right* ☎ *2228–8515* ⊕ *www.monastere-restaurant.com* ⊘ *Closed Sun. No lunch.*

$$ ✕ **Plaza España.** Generous portions of Spanish tapas and entrées draw
SPANISH diners to this whitewashed adobe house up the hill near San Antonio de Escazú. Wooden-bench tables are distributed along a wraparound porch with views of the Central Valley; inside, tables are arranged in small-to-medium rooms. Presentation isn't the strong suit here: straight-up good food is, as are reasonable prices. Start with a pitcher of sangria and begin sampling; the extensive menu includes dishes such as *tortilla Española* (Spanish omelet). ⑤ *Average main: $14* ⊠ *Del Cruce del*

Barrio El Carmen, 100 m east and 50 m south, San Antonio de Escazú ☎ 2228–1850 🕥 *Closed Mon. No lunch Tues.*

$$$
INDIAN
Fodor'sChoice
★

✕ **Taj Mahal.** This burst of northern Indian flavor is a surprising treat. Richly swathed in warm fuchsias, red ochers, and golds, the mansion's dining area sprawls through a handful of small, intimate rooms and out to a gazebo in the tree-covered backyard. The price-to-portion ratio is a little high, particularly for North Americans used to good, cheap Indian food, but the sharp tandoori dishes, curries, and *biryanis* (seasoned rice dishes) are a welcome vacation from ubiquitous European and American fare. Vegetarians may swoon at the options. Helpful waiters, in black or maroon traditional Punjabi dress, are frank about recommendations. ⑤ *Average main: $18* ⊠ *1 km (½ mile) west of Paco mall on old road to Santa Ana* ☎ 2228–0980 ⊕ *www.thetajmahalrestaurant. com* 🕥 *Closed Mon.*

WHERE TO STAY

$$
HOTEL

⊡ **Beacon Escazú.** Smack-dab in the middle of town, this pleasant place offers a respite from the commotion of central Escazú. **Pros:** friendly, service-oriented staff; feels spacious and airy in spite of downtown location; parking beneath the building. **Cons:** so-so restaurant; on congested street in center of town. ⑤ *Rooms from: $91* ⊠ *150 m west of Parque Central* ☎ 2228–3110, 866/978–6168 *in North America* ⊕ *www. beaconescazucostarica.com* 🗲 *27 rooms* ❘❍❘ *Breakfast.*

$$
B&B/INN

⊡ **Casa de las Tías.** The full range of city services is at your doorstep here, but you're blissfully apart from them at this tranquil bed-and-breakfast at the quiet end of a short road. **Pros:** tranquil, without sacrificing convenience; service goes the extra mile; excellent breakfast. **Cons:** walls could be a little thicker; slightly dated feel. ⑤ *Rooms from: $100* ⊠ *100 m south and 150 m east of El Cruce; turn east just south of Restaurante Carpe Diem* ☎ 2289–5517 ⊕ *www.casadelastias.com* 🗲 *5 rooms, 1 suite* ❘❍❘ *Breakfast.*

$
B&B/INN

⊡ **Costa Verde Inn.** When they need to make a city run, many beach-living expats head straight for this quiet B&B on the outskirts of Escazú, and it's a good example to follow. **Pros:** inviting public areas; excellent value. **Cons:** large student groups in summer; can be difficult to find; pool is for plungers, not swimmers. ⑤ *Rooms from: $65* ⊠ *Escazú* ✥ *From southeast corner of second cemetery (the farthest west), 300 m south* ☎ 2289–9509, 800/773–5013 ⊕ *www.costaverdeinn.com* 🗲 *13 rooms, 3 apartments, 3 studios* ❘❍❘ *Breakfast.*

$$
B&B/INN

⊡ **Posada El Quijote.** Perched on a hill in Escazú's Bello Horizonte neighborhood, with a great view of the city, this B&B strikes the right balance between a small inn and a tasteful private residence. **Pros:** peaceful, friendly place to spend first or last night; excellent staff. **Cons:** need a car to get around; can be difficult to find; standard rooms not as nice. ⑤ *Rooms from: $85* ⊠ *1st street west of Anonos Bridge, 1 km (½ mile) up hill, Bello Horizonte* ☎ 2289–8401 ⊕ *www.quijote.cr* 🗲 *8 rooms, 2 apartments* ❘❍❘ *Breakfast.*

4

Costa Rica's oxcarts are folkloric symbols and a common canvas for local artisans.

NIGHTLIFE

Escazú is the Central Valley's hot spot for nightlife—many San José residents head here for the restaurants, bars, and dance clubs that cater to a young, smartphone-toting crowd. You can't miss the bright lights as you swing into town off the toll highway.

Cantina La Cava. The cellar tavern beneath Le Monastère restaurant is a great place to stop for a drink before dinner, or stay on and while the evening away. You can dance to live music on Friday and Saturday nights. ⊠ *1½ km (1 mile) southwest of Paco Shopping Center in San Rafael de Escazú. Take old road west to Santa Ana, turn left at Paco, and follow signs, always bearing right* ☎ *2228–8515* ⊕ *www.monastere-restaurant.com* ☉ *Mon.–Thurs. 6:30 pm–midnight, Fri. and Sat. 6:30 pm–2 am.*

Henry's Beach Cafe. A popular watering hole with the under-30 set, this spot has televised sports by day, varied music by night, and an island theme of beach paintings and surfboards. Costa Ricans refer to this style of bar as an "American bar," which is fairly accurate. ⊠ *Plaza San Rafael, 200 m north of Centro Comercial Paco, 2nd fl.* ☎ *2289–6250* ⊕ *www.henrysbeachcafe.com* ☉ *Weekdays 3 pm–2 am, weekends noon–2 am.*

Jazz Café Escazú. Music fans chill out here. The boxy club hosts an eclectic live-music lineup similar to that of its popular sister venue in San Pedro and has double the capacity. ⊠ *First exit after the toll booths, next to Confort Suizo, across the hwy. from Hospital Cima* ☎ *2288–4740* ⊕ *www.jazzcafecostarica.com* ☉ *Mon.–Sat. 6 pm–1 am.*

Plaza Itskatzú. A high-end complex, Plaza Itskatzú has a number of restaurants and bars, including the lower-brow (Hooters); chains like Outback Steakhouse; and places for a drink, of which Más T Kila (*2228–1815; www.barmastkila.com*) is a good choice, with an interesting menu of cocktails and 31 varieties of tequila. For live music and DJs, KBaña Classic (*2253–4512, 2253–4565; www.kbanaclassic.com*) is a hot spot. ✉ *Calle Marginal Norte, Carretera a Caldera, 1 km (½ mile) east of Multiplaza* ☎ *2288–1220* ⊕ *www.plazaitskatzucr.com.*

Tintos y Blancos. Although part of the enormous Multiplaza mall, sophisticated wine bar Tintos y Blancos—"reds and whites," as in wine colors—has its own entrance in back. It offers a quality selection of libations, primarily Chilean and Argentine wines, with several French and Italian to round out the choices. ✉ *Multiplaza mall, C. Multiplaza* ☎ *2201–5935* ⊕ *www.tintosyblancos.com* ☉ *Sun.–Thurs. noon–midnight, Fri. and Sat. noon–1 am.*

SHOPPING

Escazú's Saturday-morning farmers' market makes a terrific place to stock up on some fresh fruit and vegetables if you're preparing a do-it-yourself lunch or just want to snack. Vendors start lining the street on the south side of the church around dawn, and things begin to wind down by late morning. If you get the shopping bug and absolutely must visit a mall while on vacation, Escazú is the place to do it. Multiplaza, on the south side of the toll highway, approximately 5 km (3 miles) west of San José, is Costa Rica's most luxurious mall.

Fodor's Choice **Biesanz Woodworks.** Expat artist Barry Biesanz creates unique, world-
★ class items from Costa Rican hardwoods, which are turned (a form of woodworking) on-site. Local artisans also ply their trade here. It's difficult to find, so take a taxi or call for directions from your hotel. ✉ *Bello Horizonte, 800 m south of Escuela Bello Horizonte* ☎ *2289–4337* ⊕ *www.biesanz.com* ☉ *Closed Sun. year-round and Sat. May–Nov.*

Multiplaza. Costa Rica's most upscale mall—think Kenneth Cole, Giorgio Armani, Oscar de la Renta, and many of their Costa Rican counterparts—looms over the highway between Escazú and Santa Ana. ✉ *Caldera Hwy., between Escazú and Santa Ana* ☎ *2201–9097* ⊕ *www.multiplaza.com.*

SANTA ANA

17 km (10 miles) southwest of San José.

Santa Ana's tranquil town center, with its rugged stone church, has changed little through the years, even though condos and shopping malls spread out in all directions. The church, which was built between 1870 and 1880, has a Spanish-tile roof, carved wooden doors, and two pre-Columbian stone spheres flanking its entrance. Its rustic interior—bare wooden pillars and beams and black iron lamps—seems appropriate for an area with a tradition of ranching. Because it's warmer and drier than the towns to the east, Santa Ana is one of the few Central Valley towns that doesn't have a good climate for coffee—it is Costa

Speaking Costa Rican

Spanish in Costa Rica tends to be localized. This is a land where eloquent speech and creative verbal expression are highly valued. For example, here the response to a "thank-you" is the gracious *"Con mucho gusto"* ("With much pleasure") instead of *"De nada"* ("It's nothing"), which is used in much of Latin America. In other cases, informality is preferred: the conventional *Señor* and *Señora*, for example, are eschewed in favor of the more egalitarian *Don* and *Doña*, used before a first name. Even President Luis Guillermo Solís is addressed as "Don Luis Guillermo." *Exercise caution when selecting from the list below, however.* Although young Costa Rican men address their buddies as *maje* (dude), you'll get a withering look if you, a visitor, follow suit.

agarrar de maje to pull someone's leg

birra beer

brete work

cachos shoes

chunche any thingamajig

clavar el pico to fall asleep

con mucho gusto used in response to "thank you" instead of "de nada"

estar de chicha to be angry

estar de goma to have a hangover

harina money

jupa head

macho, macha a person with blond hair, and nothing to do with "masculine"

mae or maje buddy, dude, mate

mamá de Tarzán know-it-all

maría a woman's name; also a taxi meter

matar la culebra to waste time

montón a lot

muy bien, gracias a Dios very well, thank goodness

muy bien, por dicha very well, luckily

paño towel

pelo de gato cat hair; or fine, misty rain that falls in December

peso colón

pinche a tight-fisted person

ponerse hasta la mecha to get drunk

porfa please

pura vida fantastic, great

rojo red; also a 1,000-colón note

si Dios lo quiere God willing

soda an inexpensive local restaurant

torta a big mistake or error

tuanis cool

upe anyone home?

Rica's onion capital, however—and is instead surrounded by pastures and patches of forest; it isn't unusual to see men on horseback here.

GETTING HERE AND AROUND
From San José, turn left at the western end of Paseo Colón, which ends at the Parque La Sabana. Take the first right, and get on the highway. Get off at the sixth exit; bear left at the flashing red lights, winding past roadside stands selling ceramics and vegetables before hitting the town center, about 2 km (1 mile) from the highway. The trip takes

about 25 minutes if there's little traffic. Blue buses to Santa Ana leave from inside San José's Terminal Coca-Cola every eight minutes. ⚠ Be careful: the Coca-Cola area is a dodgy part of downtown San José. To get to places along the toll highway or Piedades, take buses marked "Pista" or "Multiplaza." Those marked "Calle Vieja" leave every 15 minutes and pass through Escazú on the old road to Santa Ana. Buses run from 5 am to 11 pm.

ESSENTIALS

Banks/ATMs Banco de Costa Rica. ✉ *Northwest corner of central park* ☎ *2203–4281* ⊕ *www.bancobcr.com.* **Banco Nacional.** ✉ *100 m south of church* ☎ *2282–2479* ⊕ *www.bncr.fi.cr.*

Medical Assistance Farmacia Sucre. ✉ *25 m south of church* ☎ *2282–1296.*

Post Office Correos. ✉ *Next to Municipalidad* ⊕ *www.correos.go.cr.*

SPORTS AND THE OUTDOORS

GOLF

Valle del Sol. If you can't make it out to one of the country's flashy Pacific golf courses, this public course makes a nice low-key alternative. Your fellow golfers will be well-to-do Costa Ricans and expats who call the western Central Valley—with its California-like climate—home. Valle del Sol mixes it up with a few difficult holes punctuating the straightforward ones. Holes 5, 7, 9, and the exceptionally challenging 10 (par 5) require you to navigate around and between ponds. The dress code calls for collared shirts and blouses, and denim shorts and jeans are prohibited. ✉ *Nearly 2 km (1 mile) west of Davivienda bank* ☎ *2282–9222* ⊕ *www.vallesol.com* 💲 *$67 for 18 holes, $53 after 1:30 pm, $43 after 3:30 pm; $48 for 9 holes. Cart rental: $32 for 18 holes; $23 for 9 holes* 🕐 *Mon. 8–6, Tues.–Sun. 6–6* ⛳ *18 holes, 7000 yards, par 72.*

WHERE TO EAT AND STAY

$$$
ITALIAN

✗**Andiamo Là.** One of the Central Valley's trendiest restaurants stands out with its daily fish and meat specials, including starter carpaccios of salmon, octopus, and beef. The sea bass and jumbo shrimp combination plate comes with a sauce of chopped fresh tomatoes, white wine, and garlic. Surf and turf is pricey, but includes grilled tenderloin and jumbo shrimp with a side of buttery spaghetti and asparagus. Lunch specials are a good value here. Service is as polished as the ample chrome, and there's usually at least one waiter who speaks English. The original restaurant, near San José's east-side Terramall, offers the same menu in a more traditional Italian setting. 💲 *Average main: $19* ✉ *Next to Más x Menos supermarket* ☎ *2282–7879* 🕐 *No dinner Sun.*

$$$
ECLECTIC

✗**Bacchus.** Take a Peruvian chef who trained in France and an Italian owner, and the result is this welcome addition to the local dining scene serving, not surprisingly, a mix of French and Italian dishes. Duck breast in a port sauce, baked mushroom-and-polenta ragout, and a variety of pizzas are among the delights to be found on the menu. Modern art decorates the simple but elegant interior, and outdoor seating is available. An extensive wine list and reasonable prices make it a great pick for dinner. 💲 *Average main: $18* ✉ *200 m east and 100 m north of church* ☎ *2282–5441* 🕐 *Closed. Mon.*

$$$ ⊡ **Hotel Alta Las Palomas.** The view from this hotel perched on a hillside
HOTEL   above Santa Ana is impressive, but so is the building itself with its blend
of colonial and modern style—think archways, hardwoods, and leather.
Pros: classy service; panoramic views; excellent value for the price.
Cons: lower-floor rooms lose out on the view; little to do within walk-
ing distance. ⑤ *Rooms from: $180* ⊠ *2½ km (1½ miles) west of Paco
shopping center, on old road between Santa Ana and Escazú, Alto de
las Palomas* ☎ *2282–4160, 888/388–2582 in North America* ⊕ *www.
thealtahotel.com* ⇨ *18 rooms, 5 suites* ⦿⦿ *Breakfast.*

$$ ⊡ **Hotel Posada Canal Grande.** This small Italian-owned hotel tucked
B&B/INN   into the hills to the west of Santa Ana draws an international clientele
and is a great value. **Pros:** great value; international feel; second-floor
rooms have balconies. **Cons:** spartan bathrooms. ⑤ *Rooms from: $78*
⊠ *Caldera Hwy., 500 m south of Piedades de Santa Ana bus terminal
in Ciudad Colón direction* ☎ *2282–4089* ⊕ *www.hotelcanalgrande.com*
⇨ *12 rooms* ⦿⦿ *Breakfast.*

$$ ⊡ **Hotel Villa Los Candiles.** You'd never expect to find such a quiet, homey
HOTEL   oasis smack-dab in the middle of a suburban business neighborhood,
but here it is. **Pros:** attentive staff; suites have kitchenettes; free Wi-Fi;
pet-friendly. **Cons:** can be difficult to find. ⑤ *Rooms from: $105* ⊠ *350
m east, 25 m south of Más X Menos supermarket* ☎ *2282–8280,
305/433–4031 in North America* ⊕ *www.hotelvillaloscandiles.com*
⊟ *No credit cards* ⇨ *10 rooms, 4 suites* ⦿⦿ *Breakfast.*

SHOPPING

Cerámica Las Palomas. Large glazed pots with ornate decorations that
range from traditional patterns to modern motifs are the specialties
here. Flowerpots and lamps are also common works, and the staff
will happily show you the production process, from raw clay to art.
⊠ *Old road to Santa Ana, opposite Alta Hotel* ☎ *2282–7001* ⊕ *www.
ceramicalaspalomas.webs.com* ⊘ *Closed Sun.*

GRECIA

*26 km (16 miles) northwest of Alajuela, 46 km (29 miles) northwest
of San José.*

The quiet farming community of Grecia—the name means "Greece" in
Spanish—is reputed to be Costa Rica's cleanest town, and some enthu-
siastic civic boosters extend that superlative to all of Latin America,
but the reason most people stop here is to admire its unusual church.
A growing number of expats now call the town home.

GETTING HERE AND AROUND

From San José continue west on the highway past the airport—the
turnoff is on the right—or head into Alajuela and turn left just before
the Alajuela cemetery. Buses leave Calle 20 in San José for Grecia every
30 minutes from 5:30 am to 10 pm. From Alajuela, buses to Grecia/
Ciudad Quesada pick up on the southern edge of town (Calle 4 and
Avenida 10).

ESSENTIALS

Banks/ATMs BAC San José. ✉ *100 m north of central park* ☎ *2295-9696* ⊕ *www.bac.net*. **Banco Nacional**. ✉ *Northwest corner of central park* ☎ *2444-0690* ⊕ *www.bncr.fi.cr.*

EXPLORING

Church of Our Lady of Mercy (*Iglesia de Nuestra Señora de las Mercedes*). The brick-red, Gothic-style church is made of prefabricated iron. It's one of two buildings in the country made from steel frames and iron sheets imported from Belgium in the late 19th century (the other is the metal schoolhouse next to San José's Parque Morazán), when some prominent Costa Ricans decided that metal structures would better withstand the periodic earthquakes that had taken their toll on so much of the country's architecture. The frames were shipped from Antwerp to Limón, then transported by train to Alajuela—from which the metal walls of the church were carried by oxcarts. Locals refer to the building as simply the *Iglesia Metálica* (metal church). The splendid 1886 German pipe organ, regarded as Costa Rica's finest, is worth a look inside. ✉ *Avda. 1, Cs. 1–3* ☎ *2494–1616* ☉ *Daily 8–4.*

SARCHÍ

8 km (5 miles) west of Grecia, 53 km (33 miles) (1½ hrs) northwest of San José.

Fodor's Choice ★ Tranquil Sarchí is Costa Rica's premier center for crafts and carpentry. People drive here from all over the country to shop for furniture, and tour buses regularly descend upon the souvenir shops outside town. The area's most famous products are its brightly painted oxcarts—replicas of those traditionally used to transport coffee. Sarchí, as Costa Rica's consummate day-trip destination, has developed little acceptable lodging of its own. There are plenty of places to stay, however, in the nearby communities (San Ramón, Atenas, and Alajuela).

GETTING HERE AND AROUND

To get to Sarchí from San José, take the highway well past the airport to the turnoff for Naranjo; then veer right just as you enter Naranjo. Direct buses to Sarchí depart from Alajuela (*C. 8 between Avdas. 1 and 3*) every 30 minutes from 6 am to 9 pm; the ride takes 90 minutes.

ESSENTIALS

Bank/ATM Banco Nacional. ✉ *South side of soccer field* ☎ *2454-3044* ⊕ *www.bncr.fi.cr.*

Post Office Correos. ✉ *South side of soccer field* ⊕ *www.correos.go.cr.*

EXPLORING

Souvenirs Costa Rica (*Taller Eloy Alfaro e Hijos*). Costa Rica's only real remaining oxcart factory was founded in 1920, and its carpentry methods have changed little since then. The guiding spirit of founder Eloy Alfaro lives on here, but the business and tradition have passed onto subsequent generations of his family. The two-story wooden building housing the wood shop is surrounded by trees and flowers—mostly orchids—and all the machinery on the ground floor is powered by a waterwheel at the back of the shop. Carts are painted in the back, and although the factory's main product is a genuine oxcart—which sells for about $2,000—there are also some smaller mementos that can easily be shipped home. A cavernous restaurant serves food, buffet style. ⊠ *Sarchí* ⊕ *200 m north of soccer field* ☎ *2454–4131* ⊕ *www. souvenirscostarica.com* ⊘ *Daily 7–5.*

FAMILY **Else Kientzler Botanical Garden** (*Jardín Botánico Else Kientzler*). Some 2,000 plant species, tropical and subtropical, flourish on 17 acres here, and all are well labeled. The German owner named the facility, affiliated with an ornamental-plant exporter, after his late plant-loving mother. About half of the garden's pathways are wheelchair accessible. When the tropical fruit trees are in season, visitors are permitted to pick and eat the fruit. Kids enjoy the maze and playground. ⊠ *400 m north of soccer field* ☎ *2454–2070* ⊕ *www.elsegarden.com* ⊠ *$6* ⊘ *Daily 8–4.*

Fodor's Choice **La Carreta.** The world's largest oxcart, constructed and brightly painted
★ by longtime local factory Souvenirs Costa Rica and enshrined in the *Guinness Book of World Records* can be found in Sarchí's central park. The work—locals refer to it as simply *La Carreta* (the oxcart)—logs in at 18 meters (45 feet) and weighs 2 tons. Since no other country is attached to oxcarts quite like Costa Rica, we don't imagine that record will be broken anytime soon. Oxcarts were used by nineteenth-century coffee farmers to transport the all-important cash crop to the port of Puntarenas on the Pacific coast. Artisans began painting the carts in the early 1900s. Debate continues as to why: the kaleidoscopic designs may have symbolized the points of the compass, or may have echoed the landscape's tropical colors. In any case, the oxcart has become the national symbol. ⊠ *Center of Sarchí, central park.*

WHERE TO EAT

$ ✕ **Restaurante La Finca.** This is a good place to stop for lunch when you
COSTA RICAN need a break from shopping, with a variety of steaks, spicy *chorizos* (sausages), *arroz con pollo* (chicken with rice), and soups—we recommend the maize soup—on the menu. You might not expect it in this mix, but the pizza is pretty good, too. Service is leisurely here—that's a nice way of saying "slow"—and the time is lengthened in proportion to the number of tour buses in town that day. ⑤ *Average main: $9* ⊠ *Down road at turnoff next to Plaza de Artesanía* ☎ *2454–1602* ⊘ *No dinner.*

SHOPPING

Sarchí is the best place in Costa Rica to buy miniature oxcarts, the larger of which are designed to serve as patio bars or end tables and can be broken down for easy transportation or shipped to your home. Another popular item is a locally produced rocking chair with a leather seat and back.

Fodor's Choice **Chaverrí Oxcart Factory** (*Fábrica de Carretas*). In the nicest of the many
★ stores south of town, you can wander through the workshops and see the artisans in action. Despite the name, offerings extend well beyond oxcarts, and Chaverrí is a good place to buy wooden crafts of all kinds. Chaverrí also runs a restaurant next door, Las Carretas, which serves a variety of local food all day until 6 pm and has a good lunch buffet. ⊠ *Main Rd., 2 km (1 mile) south of Sarchí* ☎ *2454–4411.*

Plaza de la Artesanía. Sarchí's answer to a shopping mall gathers a dozen artisan and souvenir shops under one roof. Expect to find oxcarts, the town's signature symbol, and everything else imaginable. If you can't find it here, it probably doesn't exist in Costa Rica. ⊠ *2 km (1 mile) south of Sarchí, Sarchí Sur.*

SAN RAMÓN

23 km (14 miles) west of Sarchí, 59 km (37 miles) (1½ hrs) northwest of San José.

San Ramón hides its real attractions in the countryside to the north, on the road to La Fortuna, where comfortable lodges offer access to private nature preserves. There's not much to see in the town other than its church, but if you happen to be in San Ramón on Friday or Saturday, walk through the bustling farmers' market, La Feria del Agricultor.

FINDING YOUR WAY

No sun to help you get your bearings? Just remember that the entrance to most Catholic churches in Costa Rica faces west, so that the congregation can face east toward Rome. Churches in La Fortuna, and the Central Valley's Orosi and Turrialba are notable exceptions.

GETTING HERE AND AROUND

San Ramón is on the Pan-American Highway west of the exit for Grecia. Buses leave hourly for San Ramón from San José's Terminal de Puntarenas. From Alajuela, buses to San Ramón/Ciudad Quesada pick up on the southern edge of town (Calle 4 and Avenida 10).

ESSENTIALS

Bank/ATM Scotiabank. ⊠ *Pan-American Hwy., entrance to San Ramón* ☎ *2447–9190* ⊕ *www.scotiabankcr.com.*

EXPLORING

Church of San Ramón. Aside from its poets, San Ramón's claim to fame is this massive church, built in a mixture of the Romanesque and Gothic styles. In 1924 an earthquake destroyed the smaller adobe church that once stood here, and the city lost no time in creating a replacement—this great gray concrete structure took a quarter of a century to complete, from 1925 to 1954. To ensure that the second church would be earthquake proof, workers poured the concrete around a steel frame that was designed and forged in Germany (by Krupp). Step past the formidable facade and you'll discover a bright, elegant interior. ⊠ *Across from central park* ☎ *2445–5592* ☉ *Daily 6–11:30 and 1:30–7.*

WHERE TO STAY

$$$$
HOTEL

Villa Blanca. Lovely casitas, each a replica of a traditional adobe farmhouse, are on a working dairy and coffee farm once owned by the late Costa Rican president Rodrigo Carazo and set in the middle of the Los Angeles cloud forest. **Pros:** attentive service; many activities; secluded location; eco-friendly. **Cons:** far from sights; need a car to stay here. ⑤ *Rooms from: $275* ⊠ *20 km (12 miles) north of San Ramón on road to La Fortuna* ☎ *2461–0300, 877/256–8399 in North America* ⊕ *www. villablanca-costarica.com* ⤳ *35 casitas* ⦿ *Breakfast.*

SHOPPING

Feria del Agricultor. An abundance of locally grown fruits, vegetables, flowers, and even livestock is for sale here at San Ramon's farmers' market. The livestock adds to the fun and the atmosphere, and the fresh produce is yummy—it's a great place to buy fresh tortillas, made by hand. ⊠ *800 m west of cathedral* ☺ *Mon.–Sat. 6–noon.*

EN ROUTE

Zarcero. The central park of this small, tidy town 15 km (9 miles) north of Sarchí on the road to Ciudad Quesada looks as if it were designed by Dr. Seuss. Evangelisto Blanco, a local landscape artist, modeled cypress topiaries in fanciful animal shapes—motorcycle-riding monkeys, a lightbulb-eyed elephant—that enliven the park in front of the town church. (An NPR feature on Zarcero dubbed Blanco "Señor Scissorhands.") Soft lighting illuminates the park in the evening. The church interior is covered with elaborate pastel stencil work and detailed religious paintings by the late Misael Solís, a well-known local artist. Sample some cheese if you're in town, too; Zarcero-made cheese is one of Costa Rica's favorites, and it's available in a few shops on the west side of the central park. The town is frequently included as a short stop on many organized tours heading to the northern region of the country. ⊠ *Zarcero.*

ATENAS

42 km (26 miles) west of San José.

By the time you get this far west in the Central Valley, you're likely headed for Costa Rica's famed Central Pacific beaches, but the countryside holds some splendid scenery, from the steep coffee farms around Atenas to the tropical forests of the lowlands. Known for its excellent climate—*National Geographic* once dubbed it the world's best—Atenas ("Athens" in Spanish) is a pleasant, friendly town surrounded by a hilly countryside of coffee and cane fields, cattle ranches, and patches of forest. The small city is off the tourist circuit, which means that here, unlike other highly popular destinations, you'll walk alongside more locals than foreigners and get a more authentic idea of the country. Gazing at the tree-covered peaks and exploring the coffee farms are the main activities in this traditional town. Atenas's center has a concrete church, some well-kept wooden and adobe houses, and a park dominated by royal palms.

Some visitors to Costa Rica prefer using Atenas as their first- and last-night base camp instead of San José, because Atenas is smaller, friendlier, and more tranquil. The international airport is geographically closer to Atenas, but the hilly roads make the ride slightly longer than the trip on San José's express highway.

GETTING HERE AND AROUND

Atenas lies about one hour west of San José on the route to beaches such as Herradura, Jacó, and Manuel Antonio. The older, slower option is to take the Pan-American Highway past the airport and turn right at the overpass with the signs for beach resorts and Zoo Avenue. Turn left from the exit and stay on the main road. Alternately, Atenas has its own exit on Highway 27 that connects San José to Caldera, a quicker route. Buses to Atenas leave hourly throughout the day from the Coca-Cola terminal in San José and arrive at a bus terminal just west of the center of town. One block away is a secondary bus terminal serving communities around Atenas. ⚠ Be careful: the Coca-Cola area is a dicey part of downtown San José.

ESSENTIALS

Banks/ATMs Banco de Costa Rica. ⊠ *Across from west side of church* ☎ *2446–6034* ⊕ *www.bancobcr.com.* **Banco Nacional.** ⊠ *Across from north side of central park* ☎ *2446–5157* ⊕ *www.bncr.fi.cr.*

Hospital Clínica Pública. ⊠ *250 m south, 100 m west of the fire station* ☎ *2446–5522.*

Pharmacy Farmacia Don Juan. ⊠ *West side of Catholic church* ☎ *2446–5055.*

Post Office Correos. ⊠ *50 m east of southeast corner of market* ⊕ *www.correos.go.cr.*

WHERE TO STAY

$
HOTEL
🖵 **Colinas del Sol.** Although it is just a few blocks from the center of Atenas, this pleasant, German-owned lodging feels like it's in the country, with remodeled bungalows arranged throughout wooded grounds. **Pros:** friendly owner and staff; huge pool; pleasant Costa Rican restaurant. **Cons:** can be difficult to find. ⑤ *Rooms from: $69* ⊠ *C. Boquerón, 600 m east of high school gym* ☎ *2446–4244* ⊕ *www.hotelcolinasdelsol. com* ⏎ *15 bungalows* ⊙*Ι Breakfast.*

$$
B&B/INN
🖵 **The Orchid Tree.** Like all Atenas lodgings, this countryside inn makes a convenient first or last night on a Costa Rican vacation, but a devoted group of return visitors frequently opts for extended stays here. **Pros:** huge breakfasts; pleasant common area for socializing with other guests. **Cons:** slightly dark rooms; can be difficult to find. ⑤ *Rooms from: $80* ⊠ *C. Oratorio, Río Grande de Atenas* ☎ *2446–0852, 403/755–2530 in North America* ⊕ *www.orchidtreecostarica.com* ⊟ *No credit cards* ⏎ *4 rooms* ⊙*Ι Breakfast.*

$$
B&B/INN
Fodor'sChoice
★
🖵 **Vista Atenas.** *Vista* means "view" in Spanish, and the name of this comfortable, Belgian-owned lodging perched high on a hillside outside of Atenas fits perfectly, drawing a devoted return clientele. **Pros:** stunning views; attentive service; terrific rates for what's offered. **Cons:** can be difficult to find; steep drive to get here; large, friendly dog on-site so not a place to stay if you dislike canines; standard rooms a bit on the small side. ⑤ *Rooms from: $89* ⊠ *Sabana Larga* ☎ *2446–4272, 209/257–4908 in North America* ⊕ *www.vistaatenas.com* ⏎ *6 rooms, 2 cabins, 1 villa* ⊙*Ι Breakfast.*

CARARA NATIONAL PARK

43 km (27 miles) southwest of Atenas, 85 km (53 miles) southwest of San José.

In the wilderness of Carara National Park and surroundings, you might encounter white-faced capuchin monkeys in the trees or crocodiles lounging on a riverbank. The region is extremely biologically diverse, making it an excellent destination for bird-watchers and other wildlife enthusiasts.

GETTING HERE AND AROUND

Take Highway 27 west of San José beyond Orotina and follow the signs to Jacó and Quepos. The reserve is on the left after you cross Río Tárcoles. From San José, you can hop on a bus to Jacó, Quepos, or Manuel Antonio, and ask to be dropped off near the park entrance, about a two-hour drive. An organized tour is far easier. Jacó is the nearest town and the most logical base for trips into the park. Local travel agencies and tour operators arrange transportation to and guides through the park.

⚠ Cars parked at the trailhead have been broken into. If you don't see a ranger on duty at the Sendero Laguna Meandrica trailhead, avoid leaving anything of value in your vehicle. You may be able to leave your belongings at the main ranger station (several miles south of the trailhead), where you can also buy drinks and souvenirs and use the restroom. Otherwise, visit the park as a day trip from a nearby hotel.

TOURS

Horizontes. The country's premier nature-tour operator can arrange visits to Carara National Park as a day trip from San José or as part of a longer tour. ☎ 2222–2022 ⊕ www.horizontes.com ✐ From $45.

Jaguar Riders. This Jacó-based tour operator can arrange guided tours through the forests of Carara National Park. ✉ Avda. Pastor Díaz, next to Pancho Villa restaurant, Jacó ☎ 2643–0180 ⊕ www.jaguariders.com ✐ From $65.

EXPLORING

Carara National Park (Parque Nacional Carara). Sparse undergrowth here makes wildlife easier to see than in most other parks, although proximity to major population centers means that tour buses arrive regularly in high season, prompting some animals to head deeper into the forest. Come very early or late in the day to avoid the crowds. Bird-watchers can call the day before to arrange admission before the park opens. If you're lucky, you may glimpse armadillos, basilisk lizards, coatis, and any of several monkey species, as well as birds such as blue-crowned motmots, chestnut-mandibled toucans, and trogons. A network of trails takes 15 minutes to four hours to navigate. The park has guides, but you must arrange their services in advance. Camping is not permitted. For more information, see the highlighted listing in this chapter. ✉ East of Costanera, just south of bridge over Río Tárcoles, Orotina ☎ 2637–1080 ✐ $10 ⊙ Daily 7–4.

NORTH OF SAN JOSÉ

As you set out from San José to explore the towns to the north, you first encounter nothing but asphalt, hotels, and malls—not especially scenic. Santo Domingo and San Antonio de Belén blend into the outskirts of San José, and it's only when you get to the heart of these small towns that you feel you've arrived in Central America. Farther north, Alajuela and Heredia are bustling provincial capitals with charismatic central parks. Throughout this area, tucked into the urban scenery and lining volcanic slopes, are fields of that quintessential Costa Rican staple, coffee. North of Alajuela reigns one of the Central Valley's signature sights, the crowd-pleasing Poás Volcano.

SAN ANTONIO DE BELÉN

17 km (10 miles) northwest of San José.

San Antonio de Belén has little to offer visitors but its rural charm and proximity to the international airport. The latter led developers to build several of the San José area's biggest hotels here. The country's sole Mormon temple is also found here, open only to visitors of the faith. The town is a convenient departure point for trips to the western Central Valley, Pacific coast, and northern region. If you stay at any of the big hotel chains here, you likely won't even see the town, just the busy highway between San José and Alajuela.

4

GETTING HERE AND AROUND

From San José, turn right at the west end of Paseo Colón onto the Pan-American Highway (Carretera General Cañas). The San Antonio de Belén exit is at an overpass 6 km (4 miles) west of the Heredia exit, by the Real Cariari Mall. Turn left at the first intersection, cross over the highway, and continue 1 km (½ mile) to the forced right turn, driving 1½ km (1 mile) to the center of town. San Antonio is only 10 minutes from the airport.

ESSENTIALS

Bank/ATM Banco de Costa Rica. ⊠ *50 m north of rear of church* ☎ *2239–1149* ⊕ *www.bancobcr.com.*

Medical Assistance Farmacia Sucre. ⊠ *North side of church* ☎ *2239–3485.*

Post Office Correos. ⊠ *3 blocks west and 25 m north of church* ⊕ *www.correos.go.cr.*

Taxis Asotaxis Belén. ☎ *2293–4712.*

WHERE TO STAY

$$

HOTEL

🖳 **City Express San José Costa Rica.** This comfy Mexican chain with minimalist décor has come to Costa Rica and a stay here puts you just a few miles from Juan Santamaría Airport. **Pros:** bargain rates for what is offered; proximity to airport. **Cons:** sameness of a chain hotel; tricky road access to get here off highway. ⑤ *Rooms from: $79* ⊠ *Autopista General Cañas* ⊹ *Next to McDonald's, Real Cariari shopping center* ☎ *2209-2300, 855/222-8585 in North America* ⊕ *www.cityexpress. com* ⊷ *134 rooms* ⦿*Breakfast.*

$$$

HOTEL

FAMILY

🖳 **Costa Rica Marriott San José.** The stately Marriott offers comprehensive luxury close to the airport, and, despite being a U.S. chain, has many distinctively Costa Rican touches. **Pros:** excellent service; lavish grounds; close to airport. **Cons:** tendency to nickel-and-dime guests; tricky car access from highway. ⑤ *Rooms from: $229* ⊠ *Nearly 1 km (½ mile) west of Bridgestone/Firestone, off Autopista General Cañas* ☎ *2298–0000, 800/236–2427 in North America* ⊕ *www.marriott.com* ⊷ *290 rooms, 10 suites* ⦿*No meals.*

Faith and Folklore in Costa Rica

The Central Valley wears its tradition, both religious and secular, on its collective sleeve. Costa Rica's biggest annual religious festival takes place in Cartago each August 2 and commemorates what tradition holds was a 1635 apparition of the Virgin Mary. It never captured the worldwide attention of Mexico's Guadalupe, France's Lourdes, or Portugal's Fatima, but no matter. The 1 million pilgrims who visit the site on that day alone are testament to its popularity here.

Nearby, at Ujarrás in the Orosi Valley, sit the ruins of the country's first church. Prayers to the Virgin Mary said here are reputed to have staved off pirate attacks—we have no other explanation—and numerous earthquakes. That second one is tougher to explain: this part of the valley has suffered its share of earth tremors throughout history.

Costa Ricans flee to the beach for *Semana Santa,* or Holy Week, in March or April, but the small community of San Joaquín, halfway between Alajuela and Heredia, makes a nice antidote to the beach crowds. The town holds some of the country's most impressive processions reenacting the trial and crucifixion of Jesus.

Turning more pagan, Escazú holds the title of Costa Rica's spirit capital. Witches, mostly benevolent but a few malevolent ones, too, are reputed to populate the community. You'd never know it from all the fast-food restaurants, car dealerships, and shopping malls you see as you pull into town. But old-timers high in the hills have hair-raising stories to tell about those proverbial things that go bump in the night.

Those hills above Escazú also host the annual Día del Boyero, or Oxcart Drivers' Day, in early March. Oxen and carts parade to the church to be blessed by the priest. The blessings must work; oxcarts continue to be a favored mode of work transportation throughout the Central Valley.

$$$ **Doubletree by Hilton Cariari San José.** This low-rise hotel was the metro
HOTEL area's original luxury hotel, and it remains popular for its excellent
FAMILY service and out-of-town location. **Pros:** close to both San José and the
airport; kid-friendly; many amenities. **Cons:** tricky car access; close
to busy highway. ⑤ *Rooms from: $179 ⊠ Autopista General Cañas,
½ km (¼ mile) east of intersection for San Antonio de Belén, Cariari*
☎ *2239–0022, 800/222–8733 in North America* ⊕ *www.hilton.com*
↝ *198 rooms, 24 suites* ⑩ *No meals.*

$$ **El Rodeo.** This quiet hotel bills itself as a "country hotel," though
HOTEL this is more in image than fact—El Rodeo's proximity to the airport
and major business parks is the real draw. **Pros:** proximity to airport;
spacious rooms. **Cons:** generic feel. ⑤ *Rooms from: $89 ⊠ Road to
Santa Ana, 2 km (1 mile) east of Parque Central* ☎ *2293–3909* ⊕ *www.
elrodeohotel.com* ↝ *22 rooms, 7 suites* ⑩ *Breakfast.*

ALAJUELA

20 km (13 miles) northwest of San José.

Because of its proximity to the international airport (5–10 minutes away) many travelers spend their first or last night in or near Alajuela (pronounced *ah-lah-WHAY-lah*), but the beauty of the surrounding countryside persuades some to stay longer. Alajuela is Costa Rica's second-most-populated city, and a mere 30-minute bus ride from the capital, but it has a decidedly provincial air compared with San José. Architecturally, it differs little from the bulk of Costa Rican towns: it's a grid of low-rise structures painted in dull pastel colors. A slightly lower elevation keeps Alajuela a couple of degrees warmer than the capital.

GETTING HERE AND AROUND

To reach Alajuela, head west on the highway past the San Antonio de Belén turnoff and turn right at the airport (watch for the overhead signs). Buses travel between San José (Avenida 2, Calles 12–14, opposite north side of Parque La Merced), the airport, and Alajuela, and run every five minutes from 4:40 am to 10:30 pm. The bus stop in Alajuela is 400 meters west, 25 meters north of the central park (Calle 3 and Avenida 1). Buses leave San José for Zoo Ave from La Merced church (Calle 14 and Avenida 4) daily on the hour from 8 am to noon, returning on the hour from 10 am to 3 pm.

ESSENTIALS

Banks/ATMs BAC San José. ⊠ *100 m north of cathedral* ☎ *2295–9797* ⊕ *www.bac.net.* **Banco de Costa Rica.** ⊠ *50 m west of southwest corner of central park* ☎ *2440–9039* ⊕ *www.bancobcr.com.* **Banco Nacional.** ⊠ *West side of central park* ☎ *2441–0373* ⊕ *www.bncr.fi.cr.*

Hospital Hospital San Rafael. ⊠ *1 km (½ mile) northeast of airport, on main road to Alajuela* ☎ *2436–1001.*

Medical Assistance Farmacia Chavarría. ⊠ *C. 4, Avda. 1–Central* ☎ *2441–1231.*

Post Office Correos. ⊠ *Avda. 5, C. 1* ⊕ *www.correos.go.cr.*

Taxis Cootaxa. ☎ *2442–3030.*

EXPLORING

TOP ATTRACTIONS

Fodor's Choice **Doka Estate.** Considering the amount of coffee you'll drive past in the
★ Central Valley, you might want to devote an hour or so of your vacation to learning about the crop's production. Doka Estate, a working coffee plantation for more than 70 years, offers a comprehensive tour that takes you through the fields, shows you how the fruit is processed and the beans are dried, and lets you sample the local brew. The best time to take this tour is during the October-to-February picking season. Transportation can be arranged from San José, Alajuela, Heredia, Escazú, or San Antonio de Belén. Various add-on packages include breakfast and/or lunch. Doka also features on many area tours in combination with various other Central Valley activities. ⊠ *10 km (6 miles) north of Alajuela's Tribunales de Justicia. Turn left at San Isidro and continue 6 km*

(4 miles), follow signs, San Luis de Sabanilla ☎ 2449–5152, 800/946–3652 in North America ⊕ www.dokaestate.com ☒ $22 ⊘ Tours daily at 9, 10, 11, 1:30, 2:30, and 3:30 (last tour at 2:30 on weekends).

FAMILY **Zoo Ave.** Spread over lush grounds, the zoo has a collection of large cages holding toucans, hawks, parrots, and free-ranging macaws as part of a breeding project for rare and endangered birds, all of which are destined for eventual release. It has 115 bird species, including such rare ones as the quetzal, fiery-billed aracari, several types of eagles, and even ostriches. An impressive mural at the back of the facility shows Costa Rica's 850 bird species painted to scale. Wingless animals include crocodiles, caimans, a boa constrictor, turtles, monkeys, wildcats, and other interesting critters. A botanical garden rounds out the offerings here. Unfortunately, exhibits are labeled in Spanish only. ✉ *La Garita de Alajuela, head west from Alajuela center past cemetery, turn left after stone church in Barrio San José, continue for 2 km (1 mile); or head west on Pan-American Hwy. to Atenas exit, then turn right* ☎ *2433–8989* ⊕ *www.rescateanimalzooave.org* ☒ *$20* ⊘ *Daily 9–5.*

WORTH NOTING

Alajuela Cathedral. The large, neoclassical Alajuela Cathedral has columns topped by interesting capitals decorated with local agricultural motifs, and a striking red metal dome. Construction was completed in 1863. The interior is spacious but rather plain, except for the ornate cupola above the altar. ✉ *C. Central, Avdas. 1–Central* ☎ *2443–2928* ⊘ *Daily 6–6.*

Museo Juan Santamaría *(Juan Santamaría Museum).* The heroic deeds of Juan Santamaría are celebrated in this museum housed in the old jail, on the north side of Parque Central. It's worth a quick look if you have the time; Santamaría's story is an interesting one. A pleasant café inside is a great place to stop for a coffee. Following the lead of the Teatro Nacional in San José, the museum holds a series of weekly concerts called *Música al Mediodía* ("Music at Noon") each Thursday from February to late November. ✉ *Avda. 3, Cs. Central–2* ☎ *2441–4775* ⊕ *www.museojuansantamaria.go.cr* ☒ *Free* ⊘ *Tues.–Sun. 10–5; café Tues.–Sat. 11–5.*

Parque Central. Royal palms and massive mango trees fill the Parque Central—residents frequently refer to the park as the Parque de los Mangos—which also has a lovely fountain imported from Glasgow and concrete benches where locals gather to chat. The futuristic gazebo at the center of the park is a bit of an eyesore and could stand a good coat of paint. Surrounding the plaza is an odd mix of charming old buildings and sterile concrete boxes, including a somewhat incongruous McDonald's. ✉ *C. Central, Avdas. 1–Central.*

Parque Juan Santamaría *(Juan Santamaría Park).* Alajuela was the birthplace of Juan Santamaría, the national hero who lost his life in a battle against the mercenary army of U.S. adventurer William Walker when the latter invaded Costa Rica in 1856. The Parque Juan Santamaría, more a small plaza than a park, has a statue of the young hero. The park gets a little dicey as the sun goes down; confine your visits to daylight hours. ✉ *C. Central and Avda. 2.*

4

Alajuela

SANTA
BÁRBARA

Tribunales
de Justicia ◆

5 ◆
4 ◆
Museo Juan
Santamaría

Alajuela
Cathedral

◆
Parque
Central

Parque Juan
Santamaría

Avenida 9
Avenida 7
Avenida 5
Avenida 3
Avenida 1
Avenida Central
Avenida 2
Avenida 4
Avenida 6
Avenida 8
Avenida 10
Avenida 12

Calle 1
Calle 3
Calle 5
Calle Central
Calle 2
Calle 4
Calle 6
Calle 8
Calle 10
Calle 12

Antonio Arroyo

TO ZOO AVE

Cemetery

Calle El Mesón
Calle Ismael Chavarri

TO
HEREDIA

TO
SAN JOSÉ

8

3

TO SAN ANTONIO
DE BELÉN

123

123

123

125

3

TO
SAN ISIDRO,
POÁS VOLCANO

123

5 **6**

TUETAL
NORTE

3

4

3

ALAJUELA

13C

125

Avenida 3
Avenida 1
Avenida Central

Calle 4
Calle 8
Calle 12

see
inset

153

Aeropuerto Internacional
Juan Santamaría ✈

7

11

3

3

118

TAMBOR

TO
SAN PEDRO

Doka Estate ◆

107

2

118

TO
TACARES,
GRECIA,
SARCHÍ, ARENAL

118

TO
CRUCE MANOLOS,
ATENAS

Zoo Ave ◆

TO
LA GARITA

3

1

2

1

1

KEY
1 Restaurants
(1) Hotels

0 ___ 1 mile
0 ___ 1 km

Restaurants
Bar y Restaurante
El Mirador **3**
Coffee Dreams Café **4**
Delicias de Mi Tierra **1**
Jalapeños Central **5**
La Princesa Marina **2**

Hotels
Hampton Inn & Suites–
San José Airport **8**
Hotel Buena Vista **6**
Hotel La Rosa
de América **1**
Hotel Robledal **7**

Pura Vida Hotel **4**
Siempreverde B&B **5**
Villa San Ignacio **2**
Xandari Resort & Spa **3**

CLOSE UP

A National Hero

When the Costa Ricans drove U.S. invader Walker's army from their country in 1856, they chased his troops to Rivas, Nicaragua. The army of filibusters took refuge in a wooden fort. Juan Santamaría, a poor, 24-year-old drummer with a militia from Alajuela, volunteered to burn it down to drive them out. Legend says that Santamaría ran toward the fort carrying a torch, and that although he was shot repeatedly, he managed to throw it and to burn the fort down.

His bravery wasn't recognized at the time, probably because of his modest origins, but in 1891 a statue depicting a strong and handsome soldier carrying a torch was placed in Alajuela, thus immortalizing Santamaría. The entire account may well be apocryphal; some historians doubt there ever *was* such a person. But don't tell that to the average Tico. Juan Santamaría Day is a national holiday in Costa Rica each April 11 and celebrates the victory at the Battle of Rivas.

EN ROUTE   If you head straight through Alajuela, with the Parque Central on your right, you'll be on the road to Poás Volcano; you should pass the Tribunales de Justicia (the county courthouse) on your right as you leave town. If you turn left upon reaching the Parque Central, and pass the town cemetery on your right, you'll be on the old road to Grecia. About 3 km (2 miles) northwest of town on that road, you'll come upon an old concrete church on the right, which marks your arrival in Barrio San José, a suburban community of Alajuela. A left turn after the church will take you to a lovely rural area called **La Garita**, from which the road continues west to Atenas and the Central Pacific beaches. La Garita is a popular weekend destination for Tico families, who head here for the abundant típico restaurants and *viveros* (greenhouses).

WHERE TO EAT

$$ ✕ **Bar y Restaurante El Mirador.** Perched on a ridge several miles north
ECLECTIC   of town, El Mirador has a sweeping view of the Central Valley that is impressive by day but more beautiful at dusk and after dark, when the basin is filled with twinkling lights. Get a window table in the dining room, or one on the adjacent porch if it isn't too cool. The menu, which includes *lomito* (tenderloin) and *corvina* (sea bass) served with various sauces, and several shrimp and chicken dishes, plays second fiddle to the view; you may want to stop in around sunset for drinks and appetizers instead of dinner. There are at least two other restaurants nearby with similar names and views—this one is on the main road, close to the Buena Vista Hotel. ⑤ *Average main: $13* ⊠ *Road to Poás, 5 km (3 miles) north of Tribunales de Justicia* ☎ *2441–9347.*

$$ ✕ **Coffee Dreams Café.** Breakfasts are tasty and filling at this small café
COSTA RICAN   just north of the cathedral. Gallo pinto leads the early-morning menu, although, in true Costa Rican style, you can order it all day long. Quiches, burgers, and nachos make up the fare the rest of the day. Top things off with a gourmet coffee and scrumptious dessert—bread pudding and mocha cake are particular favorites. Try to snag a table near the back if you're here during weekday rush hour. That'll minimize

traffic noise from the busy street. ⑤ *Average main: $10* ✉ *90 m north of cathedral* ☎ *2430–3970* ☾ *No dinner Sun.*

$$
COSTA RICAN ✕ **Delicias de Mi Tierra.** A string of típico Costa Rican restaurants line this road, and make for popular weekend dining spots for Ticos. The "Delights of My Land" is our favorite. Tasty and traditional Tico favorites are served here: *pozol* (corn-and-pork soup), *casado campesino* (stewed beef with rice, beans, corn, potatoes, and plantains), and *chorreada con natilla* (a corn-bread pancake with sour cream). Long wooden tables and benches are surrounded by cane walls, decorative oxcart wheels, dried gourds, and tropical plants—the kind of theme that's trying so hard to be traditional that it's anything but. Ordering a few *entraditas* (appetizers) is a good way to sample dishes, as is the *parrillada de campo* (country barbecue), a platter with grilled chicken, beef, pork, rice, beans, fried plantains, and salad, or the larger *fiesta de gallos,* a mixed platter of corn tortillas with various fillings. There are also cheap but hearty breakfasts. Get here early for dinner, as closing time is 7 pm. ⑤ *Average main: $11* ✉ *1½ km (1 mile) west of the Barrio San José church* ☎ *2433–8536.*

$$
MEXICAN ✕ **Jalapeños Central.** Tasty, hearty, filling Tex-Mex food and a gregarious owner make this basic downtown joint a great place for lunch or dinner. Everybody seems to know everybody else here—this is a favorite hangout among the area's expat community—and you'll be welcome, too. Fajitas, burritos, enchiladas, and tacos make up the fare, all spiced up or simmered down according to your wishes. The kitchen is always happy to prepare a vegetarian version of any dish, too. ⑤ *Average main: $11* ✉ *150 m north of cathedral* ☎ *2430–4027.*

$$
SEAFOOD ✕ **La Princesa Marina.** This large open-air eatery (part of a small chain), at the intersection of the old Alajuela–Grecia road and the road to La Garita, is popular with Ticos, who pack it on weekends to feast on inexpensive seafood. The selection is vast, with 10 types of fish, shrimp, or octopus ceviche; fish fillets served with various sauces; three sizes of shrimp prepared a dozen ways; whole fried fish; lobster tails; and several *mariscadas* (mixed seafood plates). Pastas, rice dishes, beef, and chicken are some other choices, but the seafood is your best bet. The interior is utilitarian—bare tables, ceiling fans, and dividers of potted plants separating the sections—but you won't feel as if you're in a contrived tourist venue. ⑤ *Average main: $12* ✉ *Barrio San José, north of church* ☎ *2433–7117* ⊕ *www.princesamarina.com.*

WHERE TO STAY

$$
HOTEL ⊡ **Hampton Inn & Suites – San José Airport.** A longtime favorite for first-night and last-night stays, this U.S. chain outlet lets you ease into and out of Costa Rica in familiar surroundings. **Pros:** airport proximity; U.S. amenities; friendly staff. **Cons:** some noise from planes in the evening; sameness of a chain hotel. ⑤ *Rooms from: $121* ✉ *Blvd. del Aeropuerto* ☎ *2436–0000, 800/426–7866 in North America* ⊕ *www.hamptoninn. hilton.com* ⤴ *100 rooms* ⦿ *Breakfast.*

$$
HOTEL
FAMILY ⊡ **Hotel Buena Vista.** Perched high above Alajuela, this hotel's superb staff makes up for the somewhat dated, uninspired interior, and it does have the "good view" it is named for, although most rooms overlook the lawns or pool area. **Pros:** excellent service; family-friendly. **Cons:**

Alajuela Cathedral's painted domed cupola was rebuilt after the 1991 earthquake.

mediocre restaurant; farther from the airport than other options. ⑤ *Rooms from: $139* ✉ *Road to Poás, 6 km (4 miles) north of Alajuela's Tribunales de Justicia* ☎ *2442–8595, 800/506–2304 in North America* ⊕ *www.hotelbuenavistacr.com* ⤳ *11 rooms, 6 suites, 5 cabins* ⦿| *Breakfast.*

$$ 🖵 **Hotel La Rosa de América.** This small hotel tucked off the road to La
HOTEL   Garita is a simple and relaxed place to unwind, with its Canadian own-
FAMILY   ers adding a welcoming energy and a personalized touch to the place.
Pros: great for families; helpful owners; close to a number of restaurants. **Cons:** lacks flair of other options in this price range; it's best to have a car to stay here. ⑤ *Rooms from: $87* ✉ *1 km (½ mile) east of Zoo Ave* ☎ *2433–2741* ⊕ *www.larosadeamerica.com* ⤳ *16 rooms* ⦿| *Breakfast.*

$$ 🖵 **Hotel Robledal.** A *robledal* is an oak grove in Spanish, and ample oak
HOTEL   trees shade the grounds of this quiet oasis not far from the airport. **Pros:** attentive service; good Costa Rican restaurant. **Cons:** can be difficult to find; a couple of the rooms are dark. ⑤ *Rooms from: $88* ✉ *400 m west of Iglesia El Roble* ☎ *2438-3937, 812/962-4386 in North America* ⊕ *www.hotelrobledal.com* ⤳ *15 rooms* ⦿| *Breakfast.*

$$ 🖵 **Pura Vida Hotel.** Extremely well-informed, helpful owners and prox-
B&B/INN   imity to the airport (15 minutes) make this a good place to begin and
end a trip. **Pros:** owners active in the local community; stellar breakfast. **Cons:** large dogs may turn off those with less-than-fuzzy feelings for animals; stairs to climb. ⑤ *Rooms from: $99* ✉ *Tuetal, 2 km (1 mile) north of Tribunales de Justicia; veer left at Y* ☎ *2430–2630* ⊕ *www. puravidahotel.com* ⤳ *2 rooms, 4 bungalows* ⦿| *Breakfast.*

$$ ☲ **Siempreverde B&B.** A night at this isolated bed-and-breakfast in the
B&B/INN   heart of the Doka Estate coffee plantation might be as close as you'll
ever come to feeling like a coffee farmer or to truly getting away from
it all. **Pros:** off-the-beaten-path feel; plenty of tranquility most of the
day. **Cons:** isolated location; tour groups come by for breakfast most
mornings. ⑤ *Rooms from: $85 ⊠ 12 km (7½ miles) northwest of Tri-
bunales de Justicia de Alajuela; turn left at high school ☎ 2449–5562
⊕ www.dokaestate.com ⤳ 7 rooms* ❍❘ *Breakfast.*

$$ ☲ **Villa San Ignacio.** The friendly Villa San Ignacio, with its classy Span-
B&B/INN   ish-style architecture, proves that affordable does not have to equal
FAMILY   generic. **Pros:** spirited environment; great for first or last night; excellent service. **Cons:** roadside rooms can be noisy, opt for garden rooms.
⑤ *Rooms from: $95 ⊠ 2½ km (1½ miles) northwest of the Princ-
esa Marina ☎ 8492–1133 ⊕ www.villasanignacio.com ⤳ 12 rooms*
❍❘ *Breakfast.*

$$$$ ☲ **Xandari Resort & Spa.** The tranquil and colorful Xandari is a strik-
HOTEL   ingly original inn and spa, tailor-made for honeymooners and romantic
Fodor's Choice   getaways. **Pros:** amazing service; ideal setting for romance; guilt-free
★   gourmet delights; eco-friendly, including on-site nature reserve. **Cons:**
some noise from other rooms; should have car to stay here. ⑤ *Rooms
from: $285 ⊠ 5 km (3 miles) north of Tribunales de Justicia; turn left
after small bridge, follow signs ☎ 2443–2020, 866/363–3212 in North
America ⊕ www.xandari.com ⤳ 24 villas* ❍❘ *Breakfast.*

SHOPPING

City Mall. Central America's largest shopping mall weighs in at 330
stores and is most notable for its indoor snow-themed amusement park.
⊠ *Radial Francisco J. Orlich ☎ 4200-5100 ⊕ www.citymall.net.*

Goodlight Books. One of Costa Rica's largest used-book stores stocks
around 9,000 volumes, and a huge number of those are in English. It's
also a great place to hang out for coffee and bakery goods. ⊠ *100 m
north and 300 m west of La Agonía church ☎ 2430–4083 ⊙ Mon.-
Sat. 10:30-6.*

SANTO DOMINGO

*18 km (11 miles) northeast of Escazú, 7 km (4½ miles) northwest of
San José.*

Between Heredia and San José, the pretty town of Santo Domingo de
Heredia, established in the early 19th century, has wide streets and fine
examples of traditional, tile-roof houses, and a monumental church,
the Basílica de Santo Domingo, that stands out as a brilliant white
landmark against the surrounding sea of green coffee farms. There's a
level of tranquility here that belies its proximity to the capital, a mere
30-minute drive away if the traffic gods smile upon you.

GETTING HERE AND AROUND

For the half-hour trip from downtown San José, head north on Calle Central 4 km (2½ miles) to the central park in Tibás; continue 100 meters and
turn left. Follow this road another 2½ km (1¼ miles) to Santo Domingo.

The verdant Central Valley is Costa Rica's breadbasket.

One of the Heredia bus routes leaves from Calle 1, Avenidas 7–9 every three to five minutes and passes through Santo Domingo.

ESSENTIALS

Bank/ATM Banco Nacional. ⊠ *Across from south side of Iglesia El Rosario* ☎ *2244–0439* ⊕ *www.bncr.fi.cr.*

Post Office Correos. ⊠ *Avda. Central, Cs. 2 and 4* ⊕ *www.correos.go.cr.*

EXPLORING

Basílica de Santo Domingo. The splendid, late-19th-century Basílica de Santo Domingo is one of the country's only two basilicas, with two distinctive towers topped with gold domes. It's often a venue for classical-music concerts throughout the year, including the July–August International Music Festival. The building otherwise keeps limited hours, open only for Mass and confessions. ⊠ *East of the soccer field* ☎ *2244–0168* ⊗ *Mon–Wed. and Fri. 6–7 pm, Thurs. 8–9 and 6–7, Sat. 4–7 pm, Sun. 10–noon and 4–7.*

Iglesia del Rosario. This church is older, built in the 1840s, and simpler than the Basílica de Santo Domingo and faces the town's palm-shaded Parque Central. The church keeps limited hours for Mass and confessions. ⊠ *Parque Central* ☎ *2244–0168* ⊗ *Mon.–Wed., Fri., and Sat. 8–9 am; Thurs. 9–4; Sun. 7–8 am.*

FAMILY **INBioparque.** This is Santo Domingo's main attraction, and does an excellent job of not only explaining the country's various ecosystems, but also taking you into them. It's a useful, if expensive, primer before heading out to the hinterlands. You'll wander trails through climate-controlled wetlands and out to tropical dry forest. The forests may not look much different, but your English-speaking guide will explain the subtleties. Along the way, stop at the butterfly farm, insect exhibits, and bromeliad garden. For an extra $3 you can visit the 15 species of snakes housed here in the National Serpentarium. The tour is packed with information—perhaps too much—but if you're visiting Costa Rica for its ecology, it's a worthwhile lesson. An open-air, upscale cafeteria serves typical Costa Rican fare, with a playground within view of terrace tables. The gift shop has a great selection of tagua-nut jewelry and natural-history-themed souvenirs and books. Advance reservations are required for guided tours. ⊠ *Road between Santo Domingo and Heredia, 400 m north and 250 m west of Shell gas station* ☎ *2507–8107* ⊕ *www.inbioparque.com* ✉ *$25* ⊗ *Fri. 8–5 (last admission at 3), weekends 9–5:30 (last admission at 4); tours at 8, 10, and 1 by reservation.*

WHERE TO STAY

$$
HOTEL
☷ **Hotel Bougainvillea.** True to its name, this modern, very comfortable, three-story hotel is awash in bougainvillea on the outside and decorated with an impressive collection of Costa Rican art on the inside. **Pros:** lush and open spaces; good bird-watching; balconies in upper rooms; restaurant on-site. **Cons:** slightly institutional feel in the hallways. ⑤ *Rooms from: $128* ⊠ *2 km (1 mile) east of Santo Domingo de Heredia* ☎ *2244–1414* ⊕ *www.hb.co.cr* ⤴ *77 rooms, 4 suites* ⦿⊙⦿ *Breakfast.*

HEREDIA

4 km (3 miles) north of Santo Domingo, 11 km (6 miles) northwest of San José.

The lively city of Heredia, capital of the important coffee province of the same name, contains a couple of the country's best-preserved colonial structures, along with a contrasting, youthful buzz provided by the National University (UNA) and century-old *colegios* (high schools) scattered around the town. Heredia is nicknamed the City of Flowers (*La Ciudad de Flores* in Spanish), which refers less to the flowers that decorate the city than to a leading founding family named Flores. Flores also refers to beautiful women, for which Heredia is known. (On the topic of names, remember that "h" is always silent in Spanish. Pronounce the small city's name *air-AY-dee-ah*.) Founded in 1706, the city bears witness to how difficult preservation can be in an earthquake-prone country; most of its colonial structures have been destroyed by the tremors and tropical climate—not to mention modernization. Still, the city and neighboring towns retain a certain historic flavor, with old adobe buildings scattered amid the concrete structures. Nearby Barva is also notable for its colonial central square and venerable adobe structures. From Heredia, scenic mountain roads climb northeast, passing through the pleasant, high-altitude coffee towns of San Rafael and San Isidro, each anchored by a notable, Tico-style Gothic church and a pleasant central park.

GETTING HERE AND AROUND

The narrow routes from San José to Heredia are notoriously clogged at almost all times; avoid them during rush hours if possible—and realize that you may encounter traffic jams at other times of the day, too.

Turn right at the west end of Paseo Colón. Follow the Pan-American Highway 2 km (1 mile); take the second exit, just before the highway heads onto an overpass and just after the Hotel Irazú (on the right). To get to the center of Heredia, follow that road for 5½ km (3½ miles), being careful to note which direction traffic in the alternative middle lane is traveling, then turn left at the Universidad Nacional.

Buses run between San José (300 meters east of Hospital San Juan de Dios) and Heredia every 5 to 10 minutes daily (between 5 am and 10 pm). The steady stream of buses leaving from Calle 1, Avenidas 7–9 every three to five minutes passing through Santo Domingo are sometimes a better bet during rush hour, particularly the *directo* buses that start after 3:30 pm; these buses also run from midnight to 3:30 am on the hour. Better still, hop aboard the new, modern train, departing San José from the vintage Atlantic Station, on the north side of the Parque Nacional, and arriving in downtown Heredia 30 minutes later. Trains run every half hour on weekdays from 5:30 to 8 am, then 3:30 to 7:30 pm—geared more toward the needs of workaday commuters than tourists—and the fare is about 95¢. If you're without a car, a taxi is the best way to get to Café Britt or Barva.

ESSENTIALS

Banks/ATMs BAC San José. ✉ *Paseo de las Flores* ☎ *2295-9797* ⊕ *www.bac. net.* **Banco Nacional.** ✉ *25 m south of southwest corner of Parque Central* ☎ *2277-6900* ⊕ *www.bncr.fi.cr.*

Pharmacy Farmacia Chavarria. ✉ *South side of Parque Central* ☎ *2263-4668* ⊕ *www.farmaciachavarria.com.*

Post Office Correos. ✉ *Avda. Central, C. Central-2, northwest corner of Parque Central* ⊕ *www.correos.go.cr.*

EXPLORING

TOP ATTRACTIONS

Fodor's Choice ★ **Café Britt.** The producer of Costa Rica's most popular export-quality coffee gives a lively Classic Coffee Tour highlighting the history of Costa Rica's coffee cultivation through a theatrical presentation that is admittedly a bit hokey. Your "tour guides" are professional actors, and pretty good ones at that, so if you don't mind the song and dance, it's fun. (You might even be called upon to participate.) During the 1½-hour tour, you'll take a short walk through the coffee farm and processing plant, and learn how professional coffee tasters distinguish a fine cup of java. A four-hour Coffee Lovers tour delves into the process at a more expert level. You can also stop in at its Coffee Bar and Factory Store. Although both tours are devoted entirely to the production and history of Costa Rica's most famous agricultural product, Britt is also a purveyor of fine chocolates, cocoas, cookies, macadamia nuts, and coffee liqueurs; you'll see its products for sale in souvenir shops around the country and at the airport as you leave. ✉ *From Heredia, take road to Barva, follow signs* ☎ *2277-1600* ⊕ *www.coffeetour.com* 🖫 *$22 Classic Coffee Tour, $39 with transportation; $30 Coffee Lovers Tour, $47 with transportation* ☉ *Classic Coffee Tour: daily 9, 11, 1:15, and 3:15. Coffee Lovers Tour: 1:15 pm. daily. Coffee shop and store daily 8–5.*

Iglesia de la Inmaculada Concepción (*Church of the Immaculate Conception*). On the east side of the park stands this impressive neoclassical church that locals refer to as simply "La Inmaculada." It was built between 1797 and 1804 to replace an adobe temple dating from the early 1700s and is one of the few structures in Costa Rica remaining from the colonial era. The flat-fronted, whitewashed church has thick stone walls, small windows, and squat buttresses, which have kept it intact through two centuries of earthquakes and tremors. The serene, white interior has two rows of stately, gold-trimmed Ionic columns marching down a long aisle, past 20 lovely stained-glass windows constructed in France. The church is flanked by tidy side gardens, where you can stroll among sculpted trees along concrete paths incised with a floral pattern. The church's soft exterior illumination brightens up the park nightly from 6 pm until midnight. ☒ *Eastern side of Parque Central* 🕾 *2237–0779* ◷ *Daily 6 am–7 pm.*

> **COFFEE CHEAT SHEET**
>
> **café solo:** black
>
> **con azúcar:** with sugar
>
> **con crema:** with cream
>
> **con leche:** with milk
>
> **descafeinado:** decaffeinated (not easy to find here)
>
> **grano entero:** whole beans
>
> **grano molido:** ground
>
> **tostado claro** or **tueste claro:** light roast
>
> **tostado oscuro** or **tueste oscuro:** dark roast

Parque Central. Heredia is centered on tree-studded Parque Central, which gets our vote for the country's loveliest and liveliest central park, surrounded by some notable buildings spanning more than 250 years of history. The park has a large, round, cast-iron fountain imported from England in 1879 and a Victorian bandstand where the municipal band plays on Sunday morning and Thursday night. Families, couples, and old-timers sit on park benches, shaded by fig and towering palm trees, often inhabited by noisy and colorful flocks of crimson-fronted parakeets. Drop into Pops, a national ice-cream chain, at the south side of the park and pick up a cone, then take a seat on a park bench and watch the passing parade. ☒ *C. Central and Avda. Central.*

WORTH NOTING

Casa de la Cultura. Next to the Fortín, the tile-roof building with the handsome wood veranda is Heredia's Casa de la Cultura, which almost always has a free exhibition by local artists. Inside is a very small museum of town history, as well as a handsome inner atrium, with wooden galleries, where concerts are often held. The house was originally the stately home of early-20th-century president Alfredo González Flores (1877–1962). ☒ *Avda. Central and C. Central* 🕾 *2261–4485* ⊕ *casadelaculturaalfredogonzalezflores.blogspot.com* 🖅 *Free* ◷ *Daily 8–8.*

Feria. On Saturday mornings starting at 5, Heredia's open-air *feria,* a lively farmers' market, stretches for almost a kilometer (½ mile) along Avenida 14. Things start to wind down around noon. ☒ *Avda. 14.*

Fortín (*Little Fort*). On the north side of the Parque Central in its own little park stands a strange tower. Built as a military post in the 1870s, it never did see action and now serves as the symbol of the province, one of the few military monuments in this country without an army. The tower is closed to the public. The old brick building next to the Fortín is the Palacio Municipal (Town Hall). ⊠ *C. Central and Avda. Central.*

Mercado Nuevo (*New Market*). Three blocks southeast of the Parque Central is Heredia's covered New Market—that's how everybody refers to it here—officially the Mercado Central, which holds dozens of *sodas* (simple restaurants) along with the usual food stands and vendors supplying the day-to-day needs of the average Costa Rican. While generally safe, the crowded conditions here do invite the occasional pickpocket. Watch your possessions. ⊠ *C. Central and Avda. 6* ⊙ *Mon.–Sat. 7–6.*

Museo de Cultura Popular (*Museum of Popular Culture*). At the edge of a middle-class neighborhood between Heredia and Barva, this museum is housed in a farmhouse with a large veranda built in 1885 using an adobe-like technique called *bahareque*. Run by the National University, the museum is furnished with antiques and surrounded by a garden and a small coffee farm. Just walking around the museum is instructive, but calling ahead to reserve a hands-on cultural tour (such as one on tortilla making) really makes it worth the trip. An open-air restaurant serves bread baked in a clay oven, and fresh tortillas and tamales. ⊠ *From Musmanni bakery in Santa Lucía de Barva, go 100 m north, then turn right for 1 km (½ mile); follow signs* ☎ *2260–1619* ⊕ *www.museo.una. ac.cr* ⊠ *$2* ⊙ *Sun. 10–5, Mon.–Sat. by appointment.*

San Rafael de Heredia. This quiet, tidy, coffee town 2 km (1 mile) northeast of Heredia has a large church notable for its stained-glass windows and bright interior. The road north from the church winds its way up Barva Volcano, ending atop the Monte de la Cruz lookout point. ⊠ *San Rafael de Heredia.*

Sibú Chocolate. Get to know a bean of another kind during a private tasting at the workshop of the country's best artisanal chocolate maker. It starts with an informative talk about the historical and cultural significance of the cacao bean, includes a demonstration of tempering chocolate by hand, and ends, of course, with a sampling of exquisite chocolates made from 100% organic cacao. Tasters can also stay for an elegant lunch ($18) on Sibú's pretty terrace. Reserve 48 hours in advance. ⊠ *Turnoff for San Isidro de Heredia, 1½ km (1 mile) off hwy. to Braulio Carrillo National Park* ☎ *2268–1335* ⊕ *www.sibuchocolate. com* ⊠ *$27, minimum of 4 people* ⊙ *Tours Tues.–Sat. 10 am.*

WHERE TO EAT

$$
ITALIAN

✕ **L'Antica Roma.** More than 40 versions of pizza baked in a wood-burning oven are the main event at this popular, upscale Italian eatery. Every pizza comes with a trio of condiments to spice it up to your taste: homemade hot chili or a garlicky sauce, and grated cheese. Framed black-and-white photos of famous Italians eating spaghetti may inspire you to try one of the decent homemade pastas. There's also an exhaustive menu of meat and chicken cooked Italian style—juicy beef tenderloin substitutes for veal in all the classic Italian veal dishes. Italian wine can be ordered by the glass, carafe, or bottle. Two large-screen TVs with sports add to the happy buzz indoors on busy nights; the tables out on the wrought-iron-enclosed patio lend themselves better to conversation, once rush-hour traffic has subsided. $ *Average main: $10* ⊠ *C. 7 and Avda. 7, across from Hotel Valladolid* ☎ *2262–9073.*

WHERE TO STAY

$$$$
B&B/INN
Fodor's Choice
★

⊡ **Finca Rosa Blanca Coffee Plantation Resort.** Set amid fields of green coffee, this exclusive, hilltop B&B hideaway has a much-deserved reputation as one of the country's sumptuous splurges. **Pros:** eco-consciousness; indulgence with style; service par excellence. **Cons:** some units short on closet and drawer space; overpriced restaurant; hard to find if you are driving your own car. $ *Rooms from: $320* ⊠ *800 m north of Café Britt Distribution Center, Santa Bárbara de Heredia* ☎ *2269–9392, 305/395–3042 in North America* ⊕ *www.fincarosablanca.com* ⟿ *14 suites* ❧*Breakfast.*

$$
HOTEL

⊡ **Hotel Chalet Tirol.** The replica of a cobbled Tirolean town square, complete with fountain and church, may be a bit much, but the cozy, bright, two-story wooden chalets are charming and the Austrian design doesn't seem out of place amid the pines, pastures, and cool air of Volcán Barva's upper slopes. **Pros:** cozy surroundings; most rooms have a fireplace; good restaurant. **Cons:** need a car to stay here; no in-room phones; patchy Wi-Fi. $ *Rooms from: $125* ⊠ *Main road, 10 km (6 miles) north of San Rafael de Heredia, Braulio Carrillo National Park* ☎ *2267–6222* ⊕ *www.hotelchaleteltirol.com* ⟿ *15 suites, 20 chalets* ❧*Breakfast.*

$$
HOTEL

⊡ **Hotel Hojarascas.** The entrance here resembles any other storefront downtown, and you could pass right by without noticing this quiet, family-run gem. **Pros:** good value for what is offered; attentive owner. **Cons:** can hear a bit of noise from the hallway; access can be dificult in your own vehicle because of street congestion. $ *Rooms from: $85* ⊠ *Avda. 8, Cs. 4-6* ☎ *2261-3649* ⊕ *www.hotelhojarascas.com* ⟿ *12 rooms* ❧*Breakfast.*

$$
HOTEL

⊡ **Hotel Valladolid.** The classiest hotel in downtown Heredia, this four-story narrow building first attracted business travelers and visiting professors at the nearby National University, although guests now are just as likely to be vacationers. **Pros:** central location; friendly staff; extensive buffet breakfast with homemade tortillas. **Cons:** limited parking; a few rooms show their age. $ *Rooms from: $86* ⊠ *C. 7 and Avda. 7* ☎ *2260–2905* ⊕ *www.hotelvalladolid.net* ▭ *No credit cards* ⟿ *11 rooms, 1 suite* ❧*Breakfast.*

SHOPPING

Paseo de Las Flores. This airy, pleasant, and huge shopping mall with 320 stores is on the main road south of town. It has a branch of almost every international fashion boutique, as well as a multiplex cinema and a wide choice of cafés and restaurants. ⊠ *2 km (1 mile) south of town on hwy. to San José* ☎ *2261–9898* ⊕ *www.paseodelasflores.com* ⊗ *Mon.–Sat. 10:30–9, Sun. 11–8.*

4

Barva de Heredia. About 3 km (2 miles) due north of Heredia, this colonial town is famous for mask making and for its **Parque Central,** still with the original adobe buildings with Spanish-tile roofs on three sides, and a white-stucco church to the east. The park is filled with whimsical sculptures, including a park bench shaped like an entire seated family, and bizarre masks and clown's heads decorating garbage receptacles. An amphitheater and stage stand ready for the annual mask festival held every August. (A less pleasant part of the August festival is the tradition of smacking one's fellow townspeople with cow or pig bladders—perhaps *not* a good time to visit.) The stout, handsome church with terra-cotta bas-relief flourishes dates from the late 18th century and has a lovely grotto shrine to the Virgin Mary in the church garden. On a clear day you can see verdant Volcán Barva towering to the north. ⊠ *3 km (2 miles) north of Heredia, Barva de Heredia.*

> **VOLCANO-VIEWING ON AN EMPTY STOMACH**
>
> No question: the earlier you get to Poás, the better the views you'll be afforded, especially during the rainy season. If that means skipping breakfast, a number of roadside stands on the way up the volcano sell strawberry jam, *cajeta* (a pale fudge), and rather bland corn crackers called *biscochos* to tide you over until you can have a hearty típico breakfast in the park visitor center's cafeteria.

POÁS VOLCANO NATIONAL PARK

37 km (23 miles) (45 mins) north of Alajuela, 57 km (35 miles) (1 hr) north of San José.

Arenal may be Costa Rica's most famous volcano, but you can peer right into the crater here at Poás—from the vantage point of an observation platform. That gives it an edge in the "cool volcano visit" department.

GETTING HERE AND AROUND

From the Pan-American Highway north of Alajuela, follow the signs for Poás. The road is in relatively good condition. One public bus departs daily at 8 am from San José (Avenida 2, Calles 12–14) and returns at 2 pm. Taxis from San José are around $100 (and around $50 from Alajuela). A slew of tours from San José take in the volcano and combine the morning excursion with an afternoon at La Paz Waterfall Gardens, or tours of Café Britt near Heredia or the Doka Estate near Alajuela.

EXPLORING

La Paz Waterfall Gardens. Five magnificent waterfalls are the main attractions at these gardens on the eastern edge of Volcán Poás National Park, but they are complemented by the beauty of the surrounding cloud forest, an abundance of hummingbirds and other avian species, and the country's biggest butterfly garden. A concrete trail leads down from the visitor center to the multilevel, screened butterfly observatory and continues to gardens where hummingbird feeders attract swarms of these multicolor creatures. Other exhibits are devoted to frogs and snakes. The trail then enters the cloud forest, where it leads to a series of metal stairways that let you descend into a steep gorge to viewing

La Paz Waterfall Gardens attracts 24 different species of hummingbirds and has a huge butterfly garden.

platforms near each of the waterfalls. A free shuttle will transport you from the trail exit back to the main building if you prefer to avoid the hike uphill. Several alternative paths lead from the main trail through the cloud forest and along the river's quieter upper stretch, providing options for hours of exploration—it takes about two hours to hike the entire complex. (Enter by 3 pm to give yourself adequate time.) The complex's Jungle Cat exhibit serves as a rescue center for felines (jaguars, ocelots, and pumas). The visitor center has a gift shop and open-air cafeteria with a great view. The gardens are a stop on many daylong tours from San José that take in the Poás Volcano or area coffee tours. ✉ *6 km (4 miles) north of Vara Blanca* ☎ *2482–2720, 954/727–3997 in North America* ⊕ *www.waterfallgardens.com* ✉ *$40, $54 with lunch, $88 with transportation from San José* ⊘ *Daily 8–5.*

Fodor's Choice
★
Poás Volcano National Park (*Parque Nacional Volcán Poás*). This is widely regarded as Costa Rica's coolest volcano experience. An observation platform lets you peer right inside what is thought to be the largest active volcanic crater in the world. The ride up here is disarming: pleasant farms and lush green cloud forest line the volcano's slopes; friendly fruit and jam vendors along the road beckon you to stop and sample their wares. Only when you get to the bubbling, gurgling, smoking summit do you leave that pastoral scene behind and stare into the crater.

It's wise to step away from the crater and its fumes for fresh air at least once every 10 minutes, and a good place to take that break is the park's bustling visitor center—the country's best—with complete park information, a cafeteria, and a gift shop. *For more information, see the highlighted listing in this chapter.* ✉ *From Alajuela, drive north through town and follow signs* ☎ *2482–2424, 192 national park hotline* 🎫 *$15* ⊘ *Daily 8:30–3:30.*

WHERE TO EAT AND STAY

$$
COSTA RICAN

✕ **Jaulares.** All the cooking here is done with wood, which adds to the rustic ambience of terra-cotta floors, bare wooden beams, and sylvan surroundings. The house specialty, *lomito Jaulares* (Jaulares tenderloin), is a strip of grilled meat served with gallo pinto (rice and beans) and a mild *salsa criollo* (creole sauce); other grilled meats and several fish dishes are also available. Jaulares stays open until midnight on Saturday for live music. ⑤ *Average main: $11* ✉ *2 km (1 mile) north of Laguna de Fraijanes* ☎ *2482–2155* ⊕ *www.jaulares.com* ▭ *No credit cards.*

$
COSTA RICAN

✕ **Restaurante Chubascos.** Dine amid tall pines and colorful flowers on the upper slopes of Poás Volcano, enjoying a small menu of traditional Tico dishes that include platters of *gallos* (homemade tortillas with meat, cheese, or potato fillings) as well as delicious daily specials. The *refrescos* (fresh fruit drinks) are top-drawer, especially the ones made from locally grown *fresas* (strawberries) and *moras* (blackberries) blended with milk. ⑤ *Average main: $9* ✉ *1 km (½ mile) north of Laguna de Fraijanes* ☎ *2482–2280* ⊕ *www.chubascos.co.cr* ⊘ *No dinner Sun.–Fri.*

$$$$
HOTEL

🏨 **Peace Lodge.** These rooms overlooking the misty forests of La Paz Waterfall Gardens seem like something out of the *Lord of the Rings*, with their curved, clay-stucco walls, hardwood floors, stone fireplaces, four-poster beds made of varnished logs, and grottolike bathrooms with private waterfalls. **Pros:** many activities, plus admission to the Waterfall Gardens, included in rates; whimsical furnishings; excellent river trail. **Cons:** pricey; popular with tour groups; sometimes difficult to find space; all but the top floors can be a bit noisy because of creaky stairs. ⑤ *Rooms from: $410* ✉ *6 km (4 miles) north of Vara Blanca* ☎ *2482–2720, 954/727–3997 in North America, 2482–2100 for reservations* ⊕ *www.waterfallgardens.com* ⤴ *16 rooms, 2 villas* ❚◯❙ *No meals.*

$$
B&B/INN
Fodor'sChoice
★

🏨 **Poás Volcano Lodge.** Stylish luxury prevails here: king-size beds, outdoor whirlpool tubs, and luxurious fabrics grace the rooms and many have balconies overlooking the volcano. **Pros:** close to volcano; coffeemakers and electric teakettles in rooms; great breakfasts; beautiful surroundings at a good price. **Cons:** hotel is often fully booked. ⑤ *Rooms from: $145* ✉ *4 km (2½ miles) east of Churrasco restaurant, on road to Vara Blanca, Poás Volcán National Park* ☎ *2482–2194* ⊕ *www.poasvolcanolodge.com* ⤴ *12 rooms* ❚◯❙ *Breakfast.*

SHOPPING

Volcán Poás National Park Visitor Center. The park's visitor center has a well-stocked shop that sells nature-themed T-shirts, cards, and posters. A portion of the profits goes to support conservation projects. ✉ *Poás Volcán National Park* ☎ *2482–2424.*

EAST OF SAN JOSÉ

Cartago, due east of San José, is Costa Rica's oldest city and colonial capital, home to some beautiful old churches, including the country's national shrine, plus other notable historic structures. To the north

East of San José

of Cartago towers massive Irazú Volcano, which is covered with fertile farmland enriched by the volcano's many eruptions and topped by an impressive crater. Southeast of Cartago lies the pastoral Orosi Valley, the cradle of Costa Rican history, and the densely forested Tapantí National Park.

The main attractions near the bustling market town of Turrialba are its namesake volcano, an internationally famous agricultural research center, and the pre-Columbian archaeological ruins of Guayabo. The town lies considerably lower than the rest of the Central Valley, so it enjoys a more moderate climate, a transition between the cooler Central Valley and the sweltering Caribbean coast.

CARTAGO

22 km (14 miles) southeast of San José.

Although most of its structures from the colonial era are gone, Cartago still has some attractive restored buildings, most of them erected after the devastating 1910 earthquake. The city served as the country's first capital until 1823, when the seat of government was moved to the emerging economic center of San José. Today, Cartago is a bustling market town, shopping center, and vibrant student hub. Most visitors see Cartago on their way to or from the Orosi Valley or Turrialba, and there is little reason (or place) to stay the night. The Orosi Valley, a short drive away, has better lodging choices. A couple of interesting sights warrant a half day if you're out this way, however.

GETTING HERE AND AROUND

For the 25-minute drive from San José, drive east on Avenida 2 through San Pedro and Curridabat to the highway entrance, where you have three road options—take the middle one marked Cartago. Shortly before Cartago, a Y intersection marks the beginning of the route up Irazú, with traffic to Cartago veering right.

Buses between San José and Cartago leave every 10 minutes daily (Avenida 10 and Calle 5, 400 meters south of the Teatro Nacional) from 5 am to 6 pm; after 6 the buses leave from Avenida 2 between Calle 1/3, in front of the National Theater. Cartago buses to San José pick up 300 meters west of the Municipal Museum of Cartago (formerly called the Comandancia), from 4:35 am to 11 pm. Buses to Orosi leave Cartago every 15 minutes from 5:15 to 7:30 am, then every 30 minutes until 7 pm, with a bus at 8 and 9 pm, 100 meters east, 25 meters south of the southeast corner of Las Ruinas.

ESSENTIALS

Banks/ATMs BAC San José. ⊠ *100 m south of Ruinas* ☎ *2295–9797* ⊕ *www.bac.net.* **Banco Nacional.** ⊠ *Southeast corner of Las Ruinas* ☎ *2550–1400* ⊕ *www.bncr.fi.cr.*

Hospital Hospital Dr. Max Peralta. ⊠ *200 m south, 150 m west of Las Ruinas* ☎ *2550–1999.*

Hospital Universal. ⊠ *400 m south of Las Ruinas* ☎ *2551-8000* ⊕ *www.hospitaluniversal.com.*

Pharmacy Farmacia Fischel. ⊠ *300 m west of Basílica de Nuestra Señora de los Angeles* ☎ *2552–2430.*

Post Office Correos. ⊠ *Avda. 2, Cs. 15–17.*

Taxis Taxis El Carmen. ☎ *2551–0836.*

EXPLORING

Basílica de Nuestra Señora de los Angeles (*Our Lady of the Angels Basilica*). Cartago's major tourist sight is a hodgepodge of architectural styles from Byzantine to baroque, with a dash of Gothic thrown in. The interior of this 1926 basilica is striking, with a colorful tile floor, intricately painted, faux-finish wood columns, and lots of stained glass. Tradition holds that an apparition of the Virgin Mary in the form of a dark stone occurred here in 1635. This "Black Virgin," or "La Negrita," is Costa Rica's patron saint, and she sits high above the main altar. To the left as you face the altar is a room decorated with amulets given in dedication to the Virgin for her intercession in everything from triumphs over disease to triumphs on the soccer field. The basilica gets mixed reviews. Many deride it, saying that photos actually look more impressive than the real thing. Perhaps that's so, but if you're interested in what makes Costa Rica tick spiritually, a stop here is a must. ⊠ *C. 16, Avdas. 2–4, 7 blocks east of central square* ☎ *2551–0465* ⊙ *Mon.–Sat. 6 am–7 pm, Sun. 6 am–8 pm.*

Bulls dressed in their finest for an oxcart parade in Cartago

Las Ruinas. Churches in one form or another stood at the site of the present-day central park from 1575 to 1841; they kept being knocked down by earthquakes and reconstructed again and again. After a major earthquake in 1841, the citizens of Cartago began work on a new, Romanesque cathedral. But a devastating earthquake in 1910 ended that project, too. Is there a connection between building churches on this spot and the occurrence of earthquakes? No one knows, but townspeople have decided not to tempt fate any longer. The ruins of this unfinished house of worship now stand in a pleasant park, and the interior has been transformed into a lush garden with fountains, a small pond, and flowers planted in the original stone pillar bases. It's a lovely contrast to the adjoining, barren concrete plaza that serves as the city's central park. Among the many legends attributed to the ruins is the gruesome story of the priest who, after falling in love with his sister-in-law, was murdered by his brother. Folks here say his headless ghost still haunts the grounds at night. Although the plaza in front of the ruins is a Wi-Fi hot spot, we recommend not pulling out your laptop or tablet in such a public place—and this has nothing to do with alleged hauntings. Your smartphone should be okay, however. ⊠ *Avda. 2, Cs. 1–2* 🖃 *Free* ⊙ *Weekends 8–4.*

FAMILY
Fodor'sChoice
★

Magmática. Costa Rica forms part of the Pacific Rim's so-called "Ring of Fire." Throughout history, earthquakes have taken their toll on the country, especially the Central Valley. (Fortunately, Costa Rica enforces some of the world's most stringent building codes to mitigate the impact of such disasters.) Guides and exhibits here give a basic Geology 101 lesson in Spanish and English and explain how an earthquake occurs and

CLOSE UP

La Negrita: Costa Rica's Patron Saint

On the night of August 1 and well into the early-morning hours of August 2, the road to Cartago from San José clogs with worshippers, some of whom have traveled from as far away as Nicaragua to celebrate the 1635 appearance of Costa Rica's patron saint, La Negrita (the Black Virgin). The feast day draws an estimated 1 million pilgrims each year, not bad for a country of just 4 million people. At a spring behind the church, people fill bottles with water believed to have curative properties. Miraculous healing powers are attributed to the saint, and devotees have placed thousands of tiny symbolic crutches, ears, eyes, and legs in a room to the left of the altar. Tour buses and school groups, along with shops selling the saint's likeness, make the scene a bit of a circus.

a volcano erupts. Other talks discuss earthquake preparedness, an issue that citizens of this tremor-prone region of the world take to heart. The real attraction is the *Simulador*, an earthquake simulator that mimics the 6.4-magnitude tremor that destroyed much of Cartago on May 4, 1910. The experience is safe—you sit on benches while you shake and rattle—but if you are prone to anxiety attacks or have a heart condition or balance issues, we recommend you not participate. Once your insides have settled down, stop in at the on-site Gallito Pinto restaurant for a yummy Costa Rican lunch. ⊠ *Cartago ✢ 600 m east of El Carmen bridge* ☎ *2552-0304* ⊕ *www.magmatica.cr* ▧ *$15* ☾ *Tues.–Sun. 8–5.*

WHERE TO EAT

Although you can find decent pasta and pizza, haute cuisine just doesn't exist here. Cartago does give you a fine opportunity to eat some *comida típica* (typical food). On just about any street downtown you'll find a soda, and the women in the kitchen will serve you the same style of food they cook at home for their own families. One rule of thumb: the busier, the better—the locals know where to eat well.

$ ✕ **La Puerta del Sol.** A cut above the usual soda, this large, long-estab-
COSTA RICAN   lished restaurant across from the basilica has been feeding pilgrims for six decades. Along with hearty portions of seafood, grilled meats, and typical casados, the restaurant has a popular bar and terrace. ⑤ *Average main: $9* ⊠ *North side of basilica plaza* ☎ *2551–0615.*

IRAZÚ VOLCANO NATIONAL PARK

55 km (35 miles) east of San José.

Costa Rica's highest volcano perches on Central America's "continental divide," offering splendid views of the Caribbean and Pacific coasts from the summit—assuming the skies are clear, that is. But look inside the volcano for the real sight here: Irazú's eerie, chartreuse-color crater lake.

Cartago's Basílica de Nuestra Señora de los Angeles is the focus of the annual pilgrimage to celebrate the appearance of La Negrita, the Black Virgin.

GETTING HERE AND AROUND

From San José, follow directions to Cartago *(above)*. Shortly before the city a Y intersection marks the beginning of the road up Irazú; traffic to Cartago veers right, then left immediately past the first lights. From downtown Cartago, a 45-minute trip, take the road to Irazú at the northeast corner of the basilica. Signs from Cartago lead you to the park.

Buses head to Volcán Irazú from San José (Avenida 2, Calles 1–3) daily at 8 and 8:45 am and return at 12:30 pm. Although public transportation is possible, an organized tour is your best bet. The volcano features as a staple among the offerings of most area tour operators.

Irazú Volcano National Park (*Parque Nacional Volcán Irazú*). Costa Rica's highest volcano, at 3,422 meters (11,260 feet), is one of the most popular with visitors since you can walk right down into the crater. Its presence is a mixed blessing: the ash fertilizes the Central Valley soil, but the volcano has caused considerable destruction through the centuries. ⚠ Do not leave anything of value in your car while you visit the volcano. There have been a lot of thefts in the parking lot here, even though it is supposed to be guarded. Most San José and area tour operators include the volcano among their excursions, and this is the easiest way to visit. *For more information, see the highlighted listing in this chapter.* ⊠ *Volcán Irazú National Park* ☎ *2200–5025* ▣ *$15* ⊙ *Daily 8–4.*

Sanatorio Carlos Durán (*Carlos Durán Sanatorium*). These ruins of a former tuberculosis sanatorium were featured on the TV series *Ghost Hunters International* and have acquired cult status among visitors interested in paranormal phenomena. The complex sits just off the highway on the way to the Irazú Volcano and functioned as Costa Rica's hospital for tuberculosis patients from 1918 to 1973. The institution bears the name of its physician-founder, who also served as the country's president in the late 19th century. The attendant who takes your admission can provide some information, but you're essentially on a self-guided visit here. Most of the alleged spectral sightings are of the nuns who cared for the patients, with a few visitors claiming to see images in their photos they didn't notice when they were snapping pictures. Other visitors don't see anything but claim to hear what they assume are the nuns' voices. We can't promise you'll spot any ghosts here, but don't let that spoil the intrigue. Your greatest risk here is likely natural, rather than supernatural: the outdoor walkways get slippery on rainy days. Tread carefully. ✛ *Prusia de Cartago, 18 km southeast of Irazú volcano, 8 km north of Cartago* ☎ *2240-3016 in San José* ✉ *$3* ☯ *Daily 8–4.*

WHERE TO EAT

$ ✕ **Restaurant 1910.** Decorated with vintage photos of early-20th-century
COSTA RICAN   buildings and landscapes, this upscale restaurant also documents the disastrous 1910 earthquake that rocked this area and all but destroyed the colonial capital of Cartago. The menu is predominantly Costa Rican, with such traditional specialties as *trucha* (trout) and rice with chicken, along with some more-sophisticated dishes, like *corvina* (sea bass) fillet with a coconut liqueur sauce. The Sunday típico buffet is a great introduction to Costa Rican cooking. ⑤ *Average main: $8* ✉ *Road to Parque Nacional Volcán Irazú, 300 m north of Cot–Pacayas turnoff, Volcán Irazú National Park* ☎ *2536–6063* ▭ *No credit cards* ☯ *No dinner Sun.*

THE OROSI VALLEY

45 km (28 miles) southeast of San José.

If you have a day to spend near San José, this idyllic valley makes a classic day trip, passing through coffee plantations shaded by poró trees—their flame-color flowers make a stunning sight during the dry season—oceans of chayote-squash vines, and small towns backed by verdant landscapes, with countless breathtaking views. It's a popular weekend drive for Costa Ricans, but still relatively off the beaten tourist path. The region is one of the few areas in Costa Rica that has remnants (ruins and churches) of the 17th-century Spanish colonial era. Paraíso, the valley's not-so-interesting metropolis, is your first point of access. Heading counterclockwise around the loop road are the area's real gems: Orosi, Tapantí National Park, Cachí, and Ujarrás.

GETTING HERE AND AROUND

A good road makes a loop around the valley and it's easy to take in all the sights along the circle if you have your own vehicle, or if you go on a guided tour—it's a staple of most San José tour operators' offerings. Buses to the town of Orosi leave Cartago every 15 minutes from 5:15 to 7:30 am, then every 30 minutes until 7 pm, with a bus at 8 and 9 pm, 100 meters east and 25 meters south of the southeast corner of Las

Ruinas. Public transportation around the valley is tricky: buses travel clockwise and counterclockwise, but neither route completes the circle.

ESSENTIALS

Banks/ATMs Banco Nacional. ⊠ *200 m south of soccer field, Orosi* ☎ *2533–1390* ⊕ *www.bncr.fi.cr.* **Banco Nacional.** ⊠ *West side of central park, Paraíso* ☎ *2574-7274* ⊕ *www.bncr.fi.cr.*

Pharmacies Farmacia Candelaria. ⊠ *North side of Restaurante Coto, across from soccer field, Orosi* ☎ *2533-1919.* **Farmacia Sucre.** ⊠ *200 m west of central park, Paraíso* ☎ *2574-7286.*

Post Office Correos. ⊠ *100 m north of Municipalidad, Paraíso* ⊕ *www.correos.go.cr.*

EXPLORING

Iglesia de San José de Orosi. The town of Orosi, in the heart of the valley, has but one major sight: this beautifully restored 1743 church, the country's oldest house of worship still in use, and one of the few structures in Costa Rica remaining from the colonial era. Set in a garden, against a green mountainside, it has a classic Spanish-colonial whitewashed facade and bell tower, with a roof made of cane overlaid with terra-cotta barrel tiles. Inside are an antique wooden altar and ancient paintings of the Stations of the Cross and the Virgin of Guadalupe, all brought to Costa Rica from Guatemala. The religious-art museum next door has a small but exquisite collection of furniture and artifacts from the original Franciscan monastery here. A huge, modern new church sits beside the historic one, but happily it's just far enough away not to spoil photos of the picturesque original church. ⊠ *West side of soccer field, Orosi* ☎ *2533–3051* ☷ *Museum $1* ☉ *Church Tues.–Fri. 9–noon and 1–5, weekends 9–noon and 1–7; museum Tues.–Sat. 1–5, Sun. 9–5.*

Iglesia de Ujarrás (*Church of Ujarrás*). The ruins of Costa Rica's first church lie past the Cachí dam near the small hamlet of Ujarrás (*oo-hah-RRASS*). An unlikely Spanish victory over a superior force of invading British pirates was attributed to a stop here to ask for the protection of the Virgin Mary, and a church was constructed in thanksgiving to honor the Virgin of Ujarrás. The entire village was abandoned in 1833 after a series of earthquakes and floods wreaked havoc here, in the lowest point of the Orosi Valley, and the inhabitants resettled at the site that would become the present-day town of Paraíso. Today the impressive, often-photographed ruins sit in a beautifully maintained park with lawns, flower gardens, and a pretty picnic area. A final, scenic 6-km (4-mile) winding drive to Paraíso from Ujarrás completes the road that loops the valley. Visitors fill the site on weekends, but on weekdays you'll likely have the place to yourself. ⊠ *In a small park, 1 km (½ mile) from Restaurante Típico Ujarrás, Orosi* ☎ *2574-8366* ☷ *Free* ☉ *Daily 6–6.*

Jardín Botánico Lankester. The lush gardens of Lankester Botanical Garden, operated by the University of Costa Rica, house one of the world's foremost orchid collections, with more than 1,100 native and introduced species. Bromeliads, heliconias, and aroids also abound in the 7-acre garden, along with 80 species of trees, including rare palms. A Japanese garden has a graceful bridge and a teahouse. The best time to come is February through April, when the most orchids are in bloom.

Iglesia de San José de Orosi is the county's oldest church that is still in use.

The garden's gift shop is one of the few places in Costa Rica to buy orchids that you can take home legally. (They come in small bottles and don't flower for four years, so you'll need some serious patience.) The garden is wheelchair accessible and has excellent restrooms. ⊠ *4 km (2½ miles) east of Cartago at west entrance to Paraíso, Cartago* ☏ *2511-7949* ⊕ *www.jbl.ucr.ac.cr* ⊠ *$10* ⊙ *Daily 8:30–4:30.*

Tapantí National Park (*Parque Nacional Tapantí*). Stretching all the way to the Talamanca Mountains, this reserve encompasses 47 square km (18 square miles) of largely pristine, remote cloud forest, a refuge for more than 400 bird species, including the emerald toucanet, violaceous trogon, and many of the country's hummingbirds. The rangers' office and visitor center are on the right just after the park entrance. You can leave your vehicle at a parking area 1½ km (1 mile) up the road. From here loop trails head off into the woods on both sides. The Oropéndola trail passes a picnic area and several swimming holes with cold, emerald waters. The entrance to La Pava trail begins up a steep forested hillside, about 1½ km (1 mile) from the parking area and leads down a steep hill to the riverbank. If you continue for ½ km (¼ mile) past the trailhead, you arrive at a 91-meter (300-foot) stair trail leading to a lookout. Get an early start—you can enter on foot before 8 am, as long as you pay as you leave. The park clouds over markedly by afternoon and, with between 250 and 300 inches of rain annually, it's renowned as the country's wettest national park; be prepared with a poncho or umbrella.

To get to the park, head south of Orosi; the road becomes a rugged track following the Río Grande de Orosi past coffee plantations, elegant fincas (farmhouses), and seasonal barracks for coffee pickers before it's hemmed in by the steep slopes of thick jungle. At the bottom of the loop road, follow signs for Tapantí National Park. Though it's worth the trip for just an hour or two of exploring, you could easily fill a day in the park. ✉ *14 km (8 miles) south of Orosi, Orosi* ☎ *2206–5615* ✉ *$10* ⊙ *Daily 8–4.*

WHERE TO EAT

$$ ✕ **Bar y Restaurante Coto.** A local institution since 1952, this large rancho

COSTA RICAN restaurant and bar is famous for its huge meat platters—we're talking 1 to 1½ kilos (2¼ to 3½ pounds) of meat—with all the típico side dishes. Or you can dine more daintily on sautéed trout. The interior dining area is actually quite smart, with fresh white tablecloths overlaid with colored cloths, and a view of the lovely Orosi church. ⑤ *Average main: $12* ✉ *Northeast corner of soccer field, Orosi* ☎ *2533–3032* ⊟ *No credit cards.*

$$ ✕ **La Casona del Cafetal.** The valley's most scenic and famous lunch stop

COSTA RICAN sits on a coffee plantation overlooking the Cachí Reservoir. It's firmly on the beaten path, which means frequent visits from tour groups. The spacious indoor dining area has a high barrel-tile roof, but the most sought-after tables are out on the tiled, lakeside portico, draped with flowering vines framing gorgeous lake views. The menu has both Costa Rican staples and sophisticated dishes such as *corvina guarumos* (bass stuffed with mushrooms). Expect a wait on weekends, when diners come from miles around for the gargantuan $25 lunch buffet that ends with delicious, coffee-flavored desserts and the casona's own coffee, made cup by cup in the old-fashioned Costa Rican way. After lunch, take a stroll down the garden path to the lake or check out the souvenir stands in the parking lot. ⑤ *Average main: $14* ✉ *2 km (1 mile) south of Cachí Dam, Orosi* ☎ *2577–1414* ⊕ *www.lacasonadelcafetal. com* ⊙ *No dinner.*

WHERE TO STAY

$$$ ⊞ **Hotel Quelitales.** For quiet, get-away-from-it-all seclusion, this eco-

B&B/INN friendly lodging can't be beat. **Pros:** quiet seclusion; great views; friendly

Fodor's Choice staff; careful attention to sustainability and environment. **Cons:** rough

★ final road to get here; best to have a car to stay here; steep walk to a couple of bungalows. ⑤ *Rooms from: $165* ✉ *3 km (2 miles) east of Cachí, Orosi* ☎ *2577–1919* ⊕ *www.hotelquelitales.com* ➴ *6 bungalows* ⦿*Breakfast.*

$ ⊞ **Kiri Mountain Lodge.** Small and very affordable, this family-run hotel

B&B/INN has easy access to Tapantí park and its own 175-acre private reserve with waterfalls. **Pros:** secluded location; friendly owners; great birding; inexpensive. **Cons:** basic, small rooms; need a car to stay here; can be difficult to get through by phone. ⑤ *Rooms from: $49* ✉ *Turnoff 2 km (1 mile) before Tapantí park entrance, Orosi* ☎ *2533–2272* ⊕ *www. kirilodge.net* ➴ *6 rooms* ⦿*Breakfast.*

$$$ ⊞ **La Casona del Cafetal.** This sophisticated lodging offers dark-wood

B&B/INN queen or king rooms in units scattered around a coffee plantation. **Pros:** amenities such as flat-screen TV and Wi-Fi, which are uncommon out here; attentive service; quiet seclusion. **Cons:** all units, especially standard rooms, are a bit dark; best to have a car to stay here. ⑤ *Rooms* *from: $150 ⊠ 2 km (1 mile) south of Cachí Dam, Orosi ☎ 2577–1414 ⊕ www.lacasonadelcafetal.com ⇨ 7 rooms ᵀᴼᵀ Breakfast.*

$
B&B/INN
🏠 **Orosi Lodge.** Run by a young German couple who have built a warm rapport with the community, the little lodge blends in with Orosi's pretty, old-town architecture: whitewashed walls are trimmed in blue, ceilings are high, and natural wood is used throughout. **Pros:** affordable and pleasant; views from second-floor rooms. **Cons:** no restaurant, just a café. Ⓢ *Rooms from: $62 ⊠ 350 m south, 100 m west of soccer field, Orosi ☎ 2533–3578 ⊕ www.orosilodge.com ⇨ 6 rooms, 1 chalet, 1 house ᵀᴼᵀ No meals.*

SHOPPING

Casa del Soñador (*House of the Dreamer*). Stop in at this unique artisan shop, a picturesque wood cottage embellished with monumental carvings by local wood sculptor Macedonio Quesada, the creator of the House of the Dreamer. Though Macedonio died years ago, his sons Miguel and Hermes are still here, carving interesting, often comical little statues out of coffee roots, which they sell for only $10 to $15. ⊠ *2 km (1 mile) south of Cachí Dam, Orosi ☎ 2577–1186.*

TURRIALBA

58 km (36 miles) east of San José.

The well-to-do agricultural center of Turrialba is a bustling town, with a youthful vibe from the nearby university, a colorful open-air market, and a tree-shaded central park filled with an intriguing collection of large-scale animal sculptures. The region's moist cheese made in nearby Santa Cruz is famous all over Costa Rica. As you begin the descent to Turrialba town, the temperature rises markedly and sugarcane alternates with fields of neat rows of coffee bushes. Turrialba also has a factory you may have heard of: Rawlings makes all the baseballs used in the major leagues. (Unfortunately, it does not offer tours.) Thanks to some spectacular scenery, patches of rain forest in the surrounding countryside, and a handful of upscale nature lodges, ecotourism is increasingly the focus of the town's efforts. Significant numbers of kayakers and rafters also flock here to run the Pacuare and Reventazón rivers. And looming above the town is Volcán Turrialba. Recent eruptions of ash, along with a heavily damaged road, prevent visitors from going to the top. Although volcanic activity keeps you away from the behemoth for safety reasons, don't let that scare you off from visiting other area attractions.

GETTING HERE AND AROUND

There are two ways to reach this area from San José, both of which pass through spectacular landscapes. The more direct route, accessible by heading east through Cartago, continues east through Paraíso, where you turn left at the northeast corner of the central park to pick up the road to Turrialba. Marked by signs, this road leads north to Guayabo National Monument. For the second route, turn off the road between Cartago and the summit of Irazú near the town of Cot, heading toward Pacayas. That narrow route twists along the slopes of Irazú and Turrialba volcanoes, with some stunning scenery—stately pollarded trees lining the road, riotous patches of tropical flowers, and metal-girder bridges across crashing streams.

Direct buses between San José and Turrialba leave hourly from 8 to 8 (slower buses run as early as 5:15 am and as late as 10 pm) from Calle 13, Avenida 6, just west of the downtown court buildings. Direct buses depart from the Turrialba terminal (at the entrance to Turrialba) for San José on the hour from 5 to 5, on the half hour to Cartago, and every two hours to Siquirres.

ESSENTIALS

Banks/ATMs Banco de Costa Rica. ⊠ *Avda. 0 and C. 1* ☎ *2556–0472.* **Banco Nacional.** ⊠ *C. 1 and Avda. Central* ☎ *2556–1211* ⊕ *www.bncr.fi.cr.*

Hospital Hospital Dr. William Allen. ⊠ *Avda. 2, 100 m west of C. 4* ☎ *2558–1304.*

Pharmacy Farmacia San Buenaventura. ⊠ *50 m south of east side of central park* ☎ *2556–0379.*

Post Office Correos. ⊠ *Avda. 8 and C. Central, 200 m north of central park* ⊕ *www.correos.go.cr.*

Taxis Asocut. ⊠ *Turrialba* ☎ *2556–7070.*

EXPLORING

Guayabo National Monument (*Monumento Nacional Guayabo*). On the slopes of Turrialba Volcano lies Costa Rica's most significant and only true archaeological site. Records mentioning the ruins go back to the mid-1800s, but systematic investigations didn't begin until 1968, when a local landowner out walking her dogs discovered what she thought was a tomb. Archaeologists began excavating the site and unearthed the base wall of a chief's house in what eventually turned out to be the ruins of a large community (around 10,000 inhabitants) covering 49 acres, 10 of which have been excavated. The city was abandoned in AD 1400, probably because of disease or war. Guided tours (about two hours) in Spanish or English make the stones come alive, with knowledgeable guides from the U-Suré Guide Association (the name is the indigenous word for house). Starting from the round, thatch-roof reception center, they'll take you through the rain forest to a lookout from which you can see the layout of the excavated circular buildings. Only the raised foundations survive, since the conical houses themselves were built of wood. As you descend into the ruins, notice the well-engineered surface and covered aqueducts leading to a trough of drinking water, which still functions today. Next you'll pass the end of an impressive 8-km (5-mile) paved walkway used to transport the massive building stones; the abstract patterns carved on the stones continue to baffle archaeologists, but some clearly depict jaguars, which were revered as deities. Excavations in 2013 began to unearth an elaborate system of agricultural terraces.

Guayabo has been recognized by the American Society of Civil Engineers as a feat of Latin American civil engineering second only to Machu Picchu. The hillside jungle is captivating, and the trip is further enhanced by bird-watching possibilities: 200 species have been recorded. Facilities at Guayabo are still minimal: there's a souvenir hut opposite the entrance, a pleasant picnic area, and modern restrooms in a replica of a thatched indigenous hut. The access route from the east via Santa Teresita (Lajas) has some rough spots, but you can make it in any car. The alternative Santa Cruz route is a little rougher, but still driveable in a regular car, unless the road is wet—in which case you may need a four-wheel-drive vehicle to get here. ⊠ *Drive through the center of Turrialba to a girdered bridge; take road signed Guayabo National Monument northeast for a total of 16 km (10 miles) (about 25–30 mins' driving); watch for a signed left turnoff, which will take you the final 3 km (2 miles) to the monument. If you've taken the scenic Irazú foothills route to Turrialba, the Santa Cruz route—11 km (7 miles) (about 35 mins' driving)—is an option. Turn left on rough road from Santa Cruz; climb 5 km (3 miles), past the Escuela de Guayabo; turn right at the sign for the monument; the road descends 6 km (4 miles) to the site* ☎ *2559–1220, 8534–1063 to reserve a guide* ⊠ *$5, plus $15 guide fee for 1–3 people, $30 for 4–9 people* ☉ *Daily 8–3:30.*

Turrialba Volcano National Park (*Parque Nacional Volcán Turrialba*). Although you can't drive up to its summit as you can at Poás and Irazú, Volcán Turrialba is an impressive sight from a distance, albeit with some major precautions. The volcano has been increasingly active since early 2010. A series of explosions throughout 2015 and into 2016 occasionally spewed out steam and ash to far reaches of the country and temporarily closed Juan Santamaría International Airport. A heavy content of sulfur dioxide in fumes emanates from the volcano, a phenomenon that has taken its toll on plant and animal life here. △ **If you suffer from a heart or respiratory condition or are pregnant, stay away.** The immediate area, beyond the Volcán Turrialba Lodge (*see Sports and the Outdoors*), remains closed off to residents and visitors at this writing. ⊠ *20 km (12 miles) east of Cot.*

OFF THE BEATEN PATH **Centro Agronómico Tropical de Investigación y Enseñanza** (*Tropical Agricultural Research and Higher Education Center*). A good place for bird-watchers and garden enthusiasts, the center, better known by its Spanish acronym, CATIE, is one of the leading tropical research centers in Latin America, with headquarters here and affiliates in nine other countries. You might catch sight of the yellow-winged northern jacana or the purple gallinule in the lagoon near the main building. The 10-square-km (4-square-mile) property includes landscaped grounds, seed-conservation chambers, greenhouses, orchards, experimental agricultural projects, a large swath of rain forest, labs and offices, and lodging for students and teachers. The most popular attraction is the **Botanical Garden Tour,** a two-hour guided walk to taste, smell, and touch tropical fruits, along with cacao, coffee, and other medicinal and stimulant plants. A favorite stop is the "miracle fruit" tree, whose berries magically make anything sour taste sweet. Reservations are recommended for guided tours, especially on weekends. ⊠ *3 km (2 miles) outside Turrialba, on road to Siquirres* ☎ *2558–2000* ⊕ *www.catie.ac.cr* ⊠ *$12; $25 with guide; $35 for half-day tour* ☉ *Daily 7–4.*

SPORTS AND THE OUTDOORS
MULTI-SPORT OUTFITTERS

Ecoaventuras. This adventure company covers all the stops—horseback riding, mountain biking, kayaking, and rafting—in one- to three-day excursions with pickup from San José area hotels. ⊠ *750 m south of bus terminal* ☎ *2556–7171* ⊕ *www.ecoaventuras.co.cr* ▧ *From $95.*

Explornatura. This downtown company organizes kayaking, horseback riding, mountain biking, and rafting tours, including a family-friendly rafting trip with lots of thrills but fewer chances of spills. ⊠ *40 m west of Hotel Wagelia* ☎ *2556–0111, 866/571–2443 in North America* ⊕ *www.explornatura.com* ▧ *From $75.*

Volcán Turrialba Lodge. Although ascending to the summit of the Turrialba Volcano is not permitted, the lodge can arrange for guided walks and horseback tours of the area, all at a safe distance from the volcano. The lodge itself offers only very rustic accommodation. ⊠ *20 km (12 miles) east of Cot, turn right at Pacayas on road to Volcán Turrialba, 4 km (2½ miles) on dirt road; or from the Turrialba side, follow signs in La Pastora for national park, 14 km (8½ miles) along a patchily paved road; 4WD advised because last 3 km (2 miles) is on rough road* ☎ *2273–4335* ✉ *volturri01@gmail.com* ▧ *From $55.*

WHITE-WATER OUTFITTERS

Costa Rica Ríos. This outfitter specializes in weeklong rafting, kayaking, and canoeing excursions on the Pacuare and Pejibaye rivers, with rafter-to-guide ratios of no more than 5:1. ⊠ *50 m north of central park* ☎ *2556–8664, 888/434–0776 in North America* ⊕ *www.costaricarios. com* ▧ *Excursions from $1,899.*

Ríos Tropicales. Long-established outfitter Ríos Tropicales begins and ends its Pacuare and Reventazón white-water excursions in San José with the option to overnight on the Pacuare. Rafter-to-guide ratios don't exceed 5:1. ⊠ *50 m north of Centro Colón, Paseo Colón* ☎ *2233–6455, 866/722–8273 in North America* ▧ *Excursions from $99.*

Tico's River Adventure. All the standard white-water excursions—the Pacuare and Pejibaye rivers with small groups and a safety kayaker in accompaniment—are available, as well as kayaking classes. ⊠ *1 km (½ mile) north of fire station* ☎ *2556–1231* ⊕ *www.ticoriver.com* ▧ *From $95.*

WHERE TO EAT

$
COSTA RICAN

✗ **La Garza Bar y Restaurante.** With weathered, blond-wood tables and chairs, and big windows with a view out onto the central park, La Garza is a popular meeting spot with a little more atmosphere than most of the eateries in town in spite of its very plain interior. The menu runs the gamut from hamburgers to chicken and has a good seafood selection. Open until 11 pm, this is one of the few places in town for a very late bite to eat. There's a pleasant bar here, too, backed by a Latin sound track or karaoke. ⑤ *Average main: $6* ⊠ *Northwest corner of central park* ☎ *2556–1073.*

$$
COSTA RICAN

✗ **Restaurante La Feria.** A permanent exhibition of local art and the expertise of the owner make this a worthwhile stop. This pleasant, family-style restaurant has the usual midscale Costa Rican fare, ranging from fast food to filet mignon; the house specialty is beef tenderloin topped with a

CLOSE UP

White-Water Thrills

You're struggling to hang on and paddle, you can't hear a thing over the roar, and you were just slammed with a mighty wall of water. Sound like fun? Then you're in the right place. The **Río Pacuare** and the **Río Reventazón** draw rafters and kayakers from all over the world to Turrialba. Right next to Turrialba, the Reventazón has Class II, III, and IV rapids. The Pacuare, farther from Turrialba, has a spectacular 29-km (18-mile) run with a series of Class III and IV rapids. The scenery includes lush canyons where waterfalls plummet into the river and expanses of rain forest.

Nearly every outfitter has day trips, many departing from San José, but some also have multiday trips that include jungle hikes. **Ríos Tropicales** even has its own lodges on the river. Age requirements for children vary by outfitter; **Explornatura** in Turrialba runs a family trip on the gentler Pejibaye River that kids as young as five can enjoy. The typical trip starts with a van ride to the put-in; including a breakfast stop, it usually takes about 2½ hours from hotel to river. After the first half of the run, guides flip one of the rafts over to form a crude lunch table. Then you continue up the river to Siquirres, and pile back in the van for the ride home.

Don't choose your company based merely on price: those with bargain rates are probably skimping somewhere. Good outfitters require you to wear life vests and helmets, have CPR-certified river guides with near-fluent English skills, and have kayakers accompany the rafts in case of emergencies. A 5:1 guest-to-guide ratio is good; 10:1 is not. Local Turrialba companies have better prices and allow you to book a trip at the last minute. Hotels and travel agencies book trips with larger outfitters, who can pick you up from nearly anywhere in the Central Valley. Prices range from about $80 to $120.

People fall out of the raft all the time, and it is usually no big deal. The worst-case scenario is getting trapped underwater in an eddy, or under the raft, but surprisingly, most fatalities—and those are very few—are heart-attack victims, so don't participate if you're high risk. You should also be able to swim. Almost every long-standing company has had a death—it is an unfortunate reality of the business. Don't hesitate to ask about safety records. The vast majority of trips, however, are pure, exhilarating fun.

Spanish-inspired red-wine-and-mushroom sauce. Casados and gallo pinto compete with more-familiar chicken and seafood dishes. Even paella is on the menu (with three hours' notice), and there's home-baked apple pie for dessert. ⑤ *Average main: $11 ⊠ Across from Enersol gas station at western entrance to town* ☎ *2556–5550* ▭ *No credit cards* ☉ *No dinner Tues.*

WHERE TO STAY

$$$
B&B/INN
Fodor's Choice
★

Casa Turire. Lush gardens and manicured lawns surround this gorgeous, hacienda-style luxury hotel overlooking a scenic lake. **Pros:** excellent value; beautiful grounds; attention to sustainable tourism; luxurious suites. **Cons:** small, one-room spa; standard-room bathrooms could use

"For a fun ride, try rafting the Pacuare River in October or November when the water is high." —Photo by Linda137, Fodors.com member

a little upgrading; can be difficult to find. ⑤ *Rooms from: $180* ⊠ *8 km (5 miles) south on Carretera a la Suiza from Turrialba* ☎ *2531–1111, 877/750–6855 in North America* ⊕ *www.hotelcasaturire.com* ➳ *12 rooms, 4 suites* ⦿ *Breakfast.*

$$
B&B/INN
🔲 **Guayabo Lodge.** If fresh mountain air appeals to you, this upscale mountain retreat has comfortable rooms, a first-class restaurant, and spacious, glassed-in sitting areas to enjoy unbeatable volcano and valley views by day and blazing fireplaces by night. **Pros:** cozy and comfortable; high sustainability consciousness; great views. **Cons:** weather can be wet and cool; clouds can obscure the view; can be difficult to get through by phone. ⑤ *Rooms from: $104* ⊠ *2 km (1 mile) west of Santa Cruz de Turrialba* ☎ *2538–8400* ⊕ *www.guayabolodge.co.cr* ➳ *22 rooms, 4 suites* ⦿ *Breakfast.*

$$
HOTEL
FAMILY
🔲 **Hotel Villa Florencia.** This country inn a few miles outside of Turrialba offers peace and quiet, a rural feel, and friendly owners and staff. **Pros:** warm, helpful staff; family-friendly; quiet surroundings. **Cons:** some rooms have dated furnishings; best to have car to stay here; can be difficult to find. ⑤ *Rooms from: $147* ⊠ *La Susanita de Turrialba, 800 m west* ☎ *2557–3536* ⊕ *www.villaflorencia.com* ➳ *20 rooms, 1 suite* ⦿ *Breakfast.*

$$$$
B&B/INN
Fodor'sChoice
★
🔲 **Rancho Naturalista.** Unparalleled bird-watching within a 160-acre private nature reserve with more than 450 recorded species, plus first-class food and comfortable lodging are the reasons nature lovers from all over the world stay here. **Pros:** birder's paradise; hiking trails for guests; warm atmosphere; gourmet meals included. **Cons:** some rooms are a little dated; not a convenient base for day trips; rough final stretch of

road to get here. $ Rooms from: $340 ⊠ 20 km (12 miles) southeast of Turrialba, 1½ km (1 mile) south of Tuís, then up a rough road ☎ 2554–8100, 888/246–8513 in North America, 2554–8101 for reservations ⊕ www.ranchonaturalista.net ⤳ 15 rooms ⍾ All meals.

$ ⛺ **Turrialtico Lodge.** Dramatically positioned on a hill overlooking the
B&B/INN valley east of Turrialba, this Costa Rican–owned rustic wood lodge is a good budget option. **Pros:** rich views at budget prices; coffeemakers in rooms; good opportunity to mingle with Ticos. **Cons:** thin walls in main lodge; less service-oriented than other options. $ Rooms from: $64 ⊠ 8 km (5 miles) east of Turrialba on road to Siquirres ☎ 2538–1111 ⊕ www.turrialtico.com ⤳ 10 rooms, 9 cabins ⍾ Breakfast.

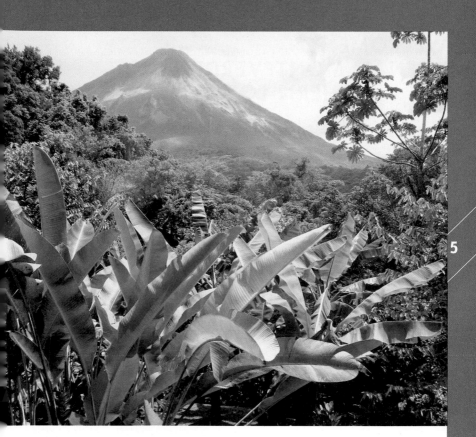

ARENAL, MONTEVERDE, AND THE NORTHERN LOWLANDS

WELCOME TO ARENAL, MONTEVERDE, AND THE NORTHERN LOWLANDS

TOP REASONS TO GO

★ **Soak in a volcano-heated hot spring:** For four decades Arenal was one of the world's most active volcanoes, but it has been in a state of slumber since 2010. It still provides a majestic backdrop from the steamy thermal waters nearby.

★ **Hike to a waterfall:** The reward for a tough hike down to Catarata de la Fortuna is a magnificent waterfall, plummeting nearly 250 feet into a freshwater pool.

★ **Float on a cloud:** Explore Monteverde's misty world on treetop walkways or on exhilarating zip lines up to 100 meters (328 feet) off the ground.

★ **Watch wildlife:** Birds, monkeys, turtles, caiman, and sloths abound in the 25,000-acre Caño Negro National Wildlife Refuge.

★ **Set sail:** Lake Arenal is one of the top windsurfing and kitesurfing spots in the world; winds can reach 50 to 60 mph mid-November through April.

1 Arenal Volcano Area.
Although the volcano is in a passive stage, Arenal remains among the top-10 most visited attractions in Costa Rica. La Fortuna is the closest town to the volcano; the many nearby diversions include hot springs, hanging bridges, white-water rafting, zip lines, waterfalls, and rain-forest tours. Tilarán, west of Lake Arenal, is the place to be if you're a windsurfer or kiteboarder.

2 Monteverde Cloud Forest and Santa Elena.
Home to the rainiest of cloud forests, the Monteverde Cloud Forest area is also the canopy-tour capital of Costa Rica. Hanging bridges, treetop tram tours, and zip lines abound. As if that's not enough, horseback riding, coffee tours, and nature hikes are also available.

5

GETTING ORIENTED

The rich, lush terrain of the Zona Norte (Northern Zone), as it is known locally, runs from the base of the Cordillera Central in the south to the Río San Juan, on the border with Nicaragua in the north. Most visitors begin their visit to Costa Rica in San José, and then head north to La Fortuna. This adventure hub is a base for exploring the Arenal Volcano, La Fortuna Waterfall, and Caño Negro National Wildlife Refuge, and for sportfishing, windsurfing, and kitesurfing at Lake Arenal and rafting on the Sarapiquí River.

3 **Caño Negro National Wildlife Refuge.** In the far north, this wildlife refuge is great for fishing, bird-watching, and communing with nature.

ARENAL VOLCANO

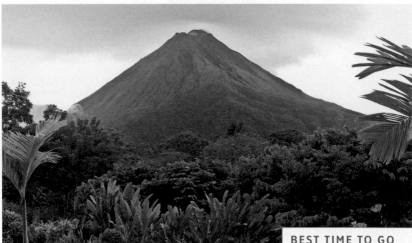

Rising to a height of 1,633 meters (roughly 5,000 feet), Arenal Volcano, Costa Rica's youngest volcano, dominates the region's landscape.

Volcanologists estimate Arenal's age at around 7,000 years, and it was dormant for nearly 500 years until 1968. On July 29, 1968, an earthquake shook the area, and 12 hours later Arenal blew.

Until October 2010, Arenal was in a constant state of activity—thunderous, rumbling eruptions occurred sometimes as frequently as once per hour. Tourists flocked here for the nightly show of rocks spewing skyward. Experts believe the volcano could now remain in a "resting" state for up to 800 years. After heavy rainfall, puffs of steam occasionally rise from the crater, making for an impressive photo of plumes over its cone. Sleeping or not, the lack of lava hasn't dissuaded travelers from seeing the magnificent mound or even hiking its flanks, which offer views of Lake Arenal in the distance. It still remains among the most visited attractions in the country. *(For more information, see the review in this chapter.)*

BEST TIME TO GO

Despite its size, viewing Arenal Volcano can be hit or miss anytime of year. January through April, especially in the early morning, usually means fewer clouds to obscure daytime views. Before the volcano entered a passive stage in 2010, the dry season's clear evenings were the best time to see or hear volcanic activity.

FUN FACT

It's no wonder Arenal Volcano is so photogenic—the conical-shaped supermodel has the third-most-picture-perfect crater in the world. Take aim quickly if you want to get a good shot, as cloud cover makes this natural attraction camera shy.

BEST WAYS TO EXPLORE

BIRD-WATCHING

If you decide to hike the Los Tucanes trail, chances are you'll see at least one of the five species of toucan that have been recorded here: chestnut-billed and keel-billed toucans, the yellow-eared and emerald toucanet, and the collared aracari. You'll never look at a box of Froot Loops the same way after seeing the real thing. Hummingbirds also abound on the volcano's slopes. Look for anything tiny and purple.

HIKING

For intrepid hikers, Las Heliconias trail ($15), which starts at the National Park's reception center, wends through secondary forest and passes by the cooled lava flow from the 1968 eruption. Outside the park, Los Tucanes trail ($10) also leads to the lava fields, but it's more of an uphill hike, beginning near the entrance to the Arenal Observatory Lodge. There's also a steep and arduous 4-hour hike up to Cerro Chatto ($10), a dormant volcano with a lopsided, extinct crater partially filled with water, creating a pretty lake. Arenal Observatory Lodge has a day pass ($32) including 11 km (7 miles) of trails, lunch, and use of swimming pools.

VOLCANIC TIPS

Two words: "from afar." Under no circumstances should you hike the volcano's trails on your own. In rainy season, some trails like Cerro Chato are extremely muddy and treacherous. Pre-2010, lava rocks and volcanic gas occasionally killed trekkers who got too close to the action. The tour operators we recommend know where the danger lies and take appropriate precautions.

Despite the fact that Arenal has entered the "post-eruption era," many visitors still gaze at its majesty from the distance and comfort of several area hotels, restaurants, and hot springs. One of the best spots to view the volcano is from the observation deck at Arenal Observatory Lodge.

TOP REASONS TO GO

All Budgets Welcome
Travelers on tight and even moderate budgets are being priced out of the market in certain regions of Costa Rica. Not so here. You'll find everything from backpackers' digs to luxury hotels in the area around Arenal.

A Perfect Volcano
Arenal's perfect cone, network of hiking trails, and thermal activity that heats neighboring hot springs keep the volcano at the top of the "must-see" list despite the fact that its current dormant phase may last another 800 years.

Sports and Adventure
It might have been the volcano that put Arenal on the map, but it's the area's many recreational activities that keep travelers coming back year after year. From zip lines and hanging bridges to waterfalls and raging rivers, Arenal has more attractions than any other destination in the country.

5

CAÑO NEGRO NATIONAL WILDLIFE REFUGE

Think of a smaller version of Florida's Everglades and you'll have a good picture of the Refugio Nacional de Vida Silvestre Caño Negro.

This lowland rain-forest reserve in the far northern reaches of Costa Rica near the Nicaraguan border covers 98 square km (38 square miles). It looks remote on the map but is easily visited on an organized day tour, especially from La Fortuna. Caño Negro is the core of a UNESCO biosphere called Agua y Paz (Water and Peace), which encompasses more than 2 million acres of wildlife habitat in Costa Rica and Nicaragua.

Caño Negro has suffered severe deforestation over the years, but most of the length of the Río Frío, its principal river, is still lined with trees. The park's vast lake, which floods after seasonal rains, is an excellent place to watch waterfowl. The reserve is home to more than 350 migratory and resident bird species and 310 types of plants. On land, pumas, tapirs, ocelots, cougars, and the always-elusive jaguar are among the more than 160 mammal species that thrive here—consider yourself fortunate if you spot a jaguar. Caimans snap everywhere in the knee-deep marshy waters, too. *(For more information, see the review in this chapter.)*

BEST TIME TO GO

It gets *hot* here, with March and April brutally so, but the January–March dry season is the best time to spot the reserve's migratory bird population. Opportunities abound the rest of the year, too, though. No matter what season, bring sunscreen, water, insect repellent, and a brimmed hat.

FUN FACT

In addition to other bird species, the reserve is the best place to spot the Nicaraguan grackle. This New World blackbird is found only in Nicaragua and northern Costa Rica. It is medium size, with a long, graduated tail and fairly long bill and legs.

BEST WAYS TO EXPLORE

BIRD-WATCHING

This is the best place in the country to see waterbirds. Just sit back in your tour boat and survey the passing parade. You're sure to see anhingas spreading their wings to dry; both glossy and white ibis recognizable by their long curved beaks; roseate spoonbills, often mistaken for flamingos; and the jabiru, king of the storks. Herons and kingfishers lurk on the banks, ready to spear fish, while jacanas, with their huge feet, forage in the water lettuce, looking as though they are actually walking on water. Above the water, watch for gray-color snail kites, which, true to their name, are hunting for snails.

BOAT TOURS

In the dry season you can ride horses, but a visit here chiefly entails a wildlife-spotting boat tour. You could drive up here on your own—roads to the area are in good shape until you approach Los Chiles; then it's 19 km (12 miles) on a gravel road to the park entrance in Caño Negro Town. Once here, you'd need to arrange for boat transportation. You can book the most reputable guides directly through Natural Lodge Caño Negro. Visiting with a tour company out of La Fortuna—it's a two-hour ride each way—is the most common way to see the park, but keep in mind that most Fortuna-based companies tour the perimeter of the reserve rather than the park interior in order to avoid the $5 entrance fee.

CAIMAN TOURS

Famous for its caimans, Caño Negro boasts a sizable population. They're smaller than crocodiles, though—at most 2½ meters (8 feet) long—and they are relatively unthreatening, because they're too small to eat large mammals (such as humans). It's a thrill to see them sunning on a bank or to see their spectacled eyes floating just above the water line.

TOP REASONS TO GO

Bird-Watching
The reserve is one of Costa Rica's lesser-sung bird-watching and wildlife-viewing destinations. Caño Negro is growing in popularity, but, for now, a visit here still feels special.

Fishing
It's not all about wildlife viewing here: Caño Negro is also one of Costa Rica's prime freshwater fishing destinations, with tarpon, snook, and garfish yours for the catch-and-release bragging rights during the September–March season (fishing is prohibited April 1–July 31, and the Garfish ban is March 1–August 31). The two lodges inside the reserve can hook you up.

Great Tours
It's easy to get here from the Arenal area, with tour operators organizing day tours from La Fortuna. If time allows, stay overnight in Caño Negro and reserve a tour through one of the reputable lodges. When selecting a company, make sure the tour actually enters the reserve if you want to make the most of your visit.

Updated by Marlise Kast-Myers

The vast expanse that locals call the Zona Norte (Northern Zone) packs in a larger variety of activities than any other part of the country. You'll find almost everything in this region that Costa Rica has to offer, except beaches, of course.

Spend any amount of time here and you can partake of—take a deep breath—horseback riding, canoeing, kayaking, rafting, rappelling, windsurfing, kitesurfing, wildlife viewing, bird-watching, bungee jumping, shopping, cloud- and rain-forest hiking, swimming, hot-springs soaking, and volcano (albeit now dormant) viewing. The zip-line canopy tour deserves special mention. The activity was invented in Costa Rica and has spread to all corners of the planet, while zipping along cables from platform to platform high in the trees has become Costa Rica's signature adventure activity.

The myriad activities make this, and especially Monteverde, Costa Rica's most kid-friendly region. Young children will "ooh" (and "eee-wwww") at various area animal exhibits devoted to bats, frogs, butterflies, hummingbirds, and snakes. Guided nature hikes abound; shorter treks can be entertaining and cater to younger ones' shorter attention spans. Most sure-footed and confident teenagers can participate in adult activities such as white-water rafting and canopy tours.

A few operators around here will tell you that kids older than eight can participate in canopy tours. Even if their brochures show children happily zipping from platform to platform, the gondola-like trams and hanging bridges are far safer ways for preteens to see the rain-forest canopy.

Most of the activities go on rain or shine, so don't feel you have to avoid a rainy-season visit here. During the wet months, it's almost a given that you'll get a bit damp on your canopy tour, hike, or horseback ride, and most tour operators provide ponchos. But to avoid a thorough soaking, plan activities for the morning. Rains usually begin around 2 pm, like clockwork, from July through December, although they can be more prolonged in September and October. The clearest time of day is normally before 8 am.

PLANNING

WHEN TO GO

HIGH SEASON: MID-DECEMBER TO APRIL

Climate is difficult to pinpoint in this vast region. The Northern Lowlands link the rainier Caribbean in the east to drier Guanacaste in the west. Precipitation generally decreases from east to west. Monteverde is cool, damp, and breezy much of the time, with high winds in January and February. Elsewhere, rain can occur outside the official wet season since the area's low elevation frequently hosts battles between competing weather fronts. Visibility changes daily (and hourly), so your chances of seeing the Arenal volcano crater is more or less the same year-round, though you may have more luck from February to April, the hottest and driest time of the year.

LOW SEASON: JUNE TO MID-NOVEMBER

Throughout the entire region, the warm and humid rainy season normally lasts from June to December. Many places in Arenal and Monteverde are beginning to impose high-season rates in July and August to correspond with prime North American and European vacation times.

We frequently overhear comments such as "I didn't know it would be so rainy in the rain forest." You heard it here first: that's why they call it the rain forest! During the rainy season it's not unusual for it to rain for several days straight, and even during the dry season, brief showers will come up without notice. Be sure to bring a poncho or rain jacket and waterproof footwear.

SHOULDER SEASON: MAY THROUGH JUNE

The wet season just starts to kick in by May, but rarely to a degree that will interfere with your travels. A little precipitation provides a welcome clearing and freshness of the air in the countryside.

PLANNING YOUR TIME

Although not centrally located, the Northern Lowlands can be easily tacked onto stays in other regions of Costa Rica. Fairly decent—decent for Costa Rica, that is—transportation links the region to San José, the Central Valley, and the North Pacific. (Monteverde is the exception, isolated and approached only by rugged roads from all directions.)

If your stay here is limited to two or three days, make La Fortuna or the surrounding Arenal area your base. Don't miss the inactive volcano, a day at the hot springs, or a trip to Caño Negro National Wildlife Refuge.

Most tour operators who have volcano hikes end the day at one of the various thermal springs in the area. The most popular are Baldi, Ecotermales, Springs Resort, and Tabacon, all with cascading pools at varying temperatures and day packages that include lunch or dinner. With waterslides, buffet lines, and busloads of tourists, the larger hot springs can feel a bit like the Disneyland of relaxation. If you plan on spending a good amount of time soaking in the hot springs, opt for staying at a hotel with on-site thermal pools. ■TIP➔ There are free public hot springs past the yellow gate next to Tabacón.

"Half-day" tours to Caño Negro actually take most of a day, from around 7:30 am to 4 pm, and you'll spend about two hours each way in a bus or van.

A week is more than enough time to experience a great deal of this area—especially if you're longing to get out and get moving. Give yourself four days in La Fortuna/Arenal, a great base for exploring the region. Devote the rest of your week to Monteverde Cloud Forest.

GETTING HERE AND AROUND

AIR TRAVEL

Nature Air and SANSA have daily flights from their own airport in San José to La Fortuna (FTN). It's located directly next to the international airport, with a fleet of puddle jumpers and a fast and easy check-in of only 30 minutes before boarding. Most travelers to this region fly into San José's Aeropuerto Internacional Juan Santamaría or Liberia's Daniel Oduber Airport and rent a car. Monteverde and Arenal are equidistant from both. Base your choice of airport on which other areas in Costa Rica you plan to visit in addition to this one.

BUS TRAVEL

Buses in this region are typically large, clean, and fairly comfortable, but often crowded Friday through Sunday. Don't expect air-conditioning. Service tends toward the agonizingly slow: even supposedly express buses marked *directo* (direct) often make numerous stops. Terminal 7-10 in San José serves most of the major towns in this chapter.

CAR TRAVEL

Road access to the northwest is by way of the paved two-lane Pan-American Highway, which starts from the west end of Paseo Colón in San José and runs northwest to Peñas Blancas at the Nicaraguan border. Turn north at Naranjo for La Fortuna; at Lagarto for Monteverde; and at Cañas for Tilarán. This region manages to mix some of the country's smoothest highways with some of its most horrendous roads. The various roads to Monteverde are legendary in the latter regard—but the final destination makes it worth the trip. Four-wheel-drive vehicles are best on the frequently potholed roads. If you don't want to pay for 4WD, at least rent a car with high clearance (many rental agencies insist you take a 4WD vehicle if you mention Monteverde as part of your itinerary). You'll encounter frequent one-lane bridges; if the triangular "CEDA EL PASO" sign faces you, yield to oncoming traffic. Driving in this region can be slow going if you get behind a large truck transporting sugarcane. As the north is prime sugar country, that's quite likely.

It is possible to rent a car in La Fortuna, but for a far better selection, most visitors pick up their rental vehicles in San José or Liberia. GPS units, programmed with Costa Rica's maps, cost about $15 per day and are available at most car-rental agencies. These voice-activated devices are a great way to keep from getting lost, especially since street names don't exist in much of Costa Rica. Vamos Rent-A-Car includes a free cell phone, roof rack, child car seat, cooler, map, and usually a GPS.

HEALTH AND SAFETY

This region is Costa Rica's capital of adventure tourism—it gave birth to the canopy tour—so any risks up here are far more likely to be natural than criminal. Before you set out rafting, zip lining, rappelling, or bungee jumping, be brutally frank with yourself about your abilities, your physical condition, and your fear levels: it's almost impossible to turn back on many excursions once you've started. Even an activity as innocuous as hiking or horseback riding poses a certain amount of risk, and you should never go alone. Nature here is not an amusement park.

Remember also that there is little government oversight of adventure tourism here. Pay close attention during any safety briefings and orientation. Don't be afraid to ask questions, and don't be afraid to walk away if something seems off to you. Look for zip-line tours with built-in brake systems, double cables, and chest harnesses in addition to the normal waist harness. Many companies include GoPro helmet mounts so you can document your canopy adventure hands-free. If you have travel insurance, make sure it covers action sports or adrenaline activities—most standard packages do not cover injuries related to kayaking, horseback riding, zip lining, kitesurfing, or other such sports.

MONEY MATTERS

Outside the centers of Monteverde, La Fortuna, Nuevo Arenal, San Carlos, and Tilarán, ATMs are still few and far between. Stock up on cash when you get a chance.

RESTAURANTS

You'll never go hungry in this region. The north is the country's bread-basket, and the hotels and restaurants out here make use of the bounty to whip up the best in *típico* Costa Rican cuisine. Don't be afraid to ask for tap water; it is safe to drink in all but the most rural areas. Service is generally slow but well worth the wait at most restaurants. Your final bill will include a 13% sales tax and a 10%–12% service charge, though we suggest you tip a little extra.

HOTELS

A few sumptuous resorts hold court in northern Costa Rica, but this region is largely the province of smaller, nature-themed lodgings that invite you to partake of all their eco-activities, and offer good value. Due to the comfortable inland temperatures, most hotels do not have air-conditioning. Also, it's not uncommon for some hotels to request that toilet paper be disposed of in a bin rather than flushed down the toilet, due to local plumbing challenges. Hotel rooms are taxed at the national rate of 13%. *Hotel reviews have been shortened. For full information, visit Fodors.com.*

WHAT IT COSTS IN DOLLARS			
$	$$	$$$	$$$$
Restaurants under $10	$10–$15	$16–$25	over $25
Hotels under $75	$75–$150	$151–$250	over $250

Restaurant prices are the average cost of a main course at dinner or, if dinner is not served, at lunch. Hotel prices are the lowest cost of a standard double room in high season.

CLOSE UP

Eco-Lodges in the Northern Lowlands

The tourist industry up here knows what the region has to offer and is keen to preserve what is green. Hotel owners and tour operators are just as eager to show it off to you with the Certification for Sustainable Tourism Program (CST). Designed to differentiate green businesses of the tourism sector, CST is based on compliance with a sustainable model and is regulated by the Costa Rican National Accreditation Commission on a scale of five levels (or five "leaves") of achievement. Based on the four categories of biological, socio-economic, service, and education, it is globally recognized as the most complete and thorough certification program for sustainable tourism. Since the program was developed in 1998, more than 400 tourism entities have earned the CST certification.

Arco Iris Lodge, Monteverde. Organic foods, active recycling program, biodegradable materials, and involvement in the community make Arco Iris one of our favorite Costa Rican eco-lodges—even if it doesn't call itself that.

Laguna del Lagarto Lodge, Ciudad Quesada. This eco-lodge gives back to its community and has succeeded in bringing employment to a poorer, often forgotten corner of Costa Rica.

Arenal Observatory Lodge, Arenal. This working biological station promotes recycling, water conservation, and low energy use, in addition to employing locals and protecting flora and fauna through its reforestation program.

ARENAL VOLCANO AREA

Whether you come here from San José or Liberia, prepare yourself for some spectacular scenery and curvy roads. Although the roads are well paved, they are quite narrow in places with steep drops and sharp turns. Drive with caution and avoid driving at night. Any discomfort passengers might occasionally experience is more than made up for by the swaths of misty rain forest and dramatic expanses of the Cordillera Central. Schedule at least 3½ hours for the trip from San José.

CIUDAD QUESADA (SAN CARLOS)

55 km (33 miles) northwest of Zarcero.

Highway signs point you to "Ciudad Quesada," but this friendly hub city is simply "San Carlos" in local parlance. Like so many other places in Costa Rica, the landscape is splendid, but what passes for architecture varies from ordinary to downright hideous. San Carlos is where everyone in the region comes to shop, take in a movie, get medical treatment, and generally take care of the necessities. There's also an enormous bus terminal (with a shopping center and multiplex

Arenal Volcano Area and La Fortuna

movie theater) where you can make connections to almost anywhere in the northern half of the country. If you're traveling from San José to points north, your bus will stop here even if it's a so-called express. This lively mountain market town–provincial capital serves a fertile dairy region and is worth a stop for a soak in the soothing thermal waters in the area.

GETTING HERE AND AROUND

Buses from San José leave from Terminal 7-10, located between Avenida 7 and Calle 10. Buses depart on the hour, from 5 am to 7 pm. The trip takes around three hours. The Ciudad Quesada bus terminal is a couple of kilometers from the center of town; taxis wait at the terminal to take you into town. Quesada is just off the Pan-American Highway. Driving from San José or other places in the south is straightforward, as long as you don't get stuck behind a slow-moving truck transporting sugarcane to the Central Valley. Try to get an early start if you're driving yourself; the road between Zarcero and Ciudad Quesada begins to fog over by early afternoon.

ESSENTIALS

Banks/ATMs BAC San José. ⊠ *100 m north and 125 m west of cathedral, Ciudad Quesada* ☎ *2295-9797.* **Banco Nacional.** ⊠ *Across from north side of cathedral, Ciudad Quesada* ☎ *2401-2000.* **Scotiabank.** ⊠ *Across from Mercado de Artesanía, east of the park, Ciudad Quesada* ☎ *2461-9660.*

Medical Assistance Hospital de San Carlos. ⊠ *2 km (1 mile) north of church, Ciudad Quesada* ☎ *2401-1200.*

Post Office Correos. ⊠ *50 meters east of fire station, Ciudad Quesada* ☎ *2460-3399.*

Tourist Information Instituto Costarricense de Turismo. ⊠ *75 m north of Universidad Católica, Ciudad Quesada* ☎ *2461-9102, 866/267-8274 in U.S. and Canada* ⊕ *www.visitcostarica.com.*

EXPLORING

Termales del Bosque. Soak those tired muscles as you watch the birds—for less than you'd pay at most of the other hot springs in the region. You have the option to add breakfast, lunch, or horseback riding to the cost of a basic day pass. ⊠ *Hwy. 140, 7 km (4½ miles) east of Ciudad Quesada, Ciudad Quesada* ☎ *2460-1356* ⊕ *www.termalesdelbosque. com* ⊠ *Hot springs $12; with lunch $23; with breakfast and lunch $28; with lunch and horseback ride $32* ☉ *Daily 8 am–10 pm.*

WHERE TO STAY

$$ 🖫 **Laguna del Lagarto Lodge.** At one of Costa Rica's smaller and more
HOTEL   remote eco-lodges, rustic cabins with single beds are surrounded by a 1,250-acre rain forest near the Nicaraguan border that gives shelter to 390 bird species and counting. **Pros:** birders' paradise; attentive service; great excursions; photography platforms. **Cons:** last 35 km (20 miles) very rough road; rooms lack a/c; Wi-Fi in common areas only; difficult to communicate with property via phone. ⑤ *Rooms from: $75* ⊠ *7 km (4 miles) north of Boca Tapada, 135 km (78 miles) northeast of Ciudad Quesada, Ciudad Quesada* ☎ *2289-8163 in San José* ⊕ *www. lagarto-lodge-costa-rica.com* ⟿ *20 rooms, 18 with bath* ⦿*No meals.*

ARENAL AND LA FORTUNA

50 km (30 miles) (45 mins) northwest of Ciudad Quesada, 17 km (11 miles) east of Arenal Volcano, 190 km (118 miles) (3½ hrs by car; 25 mins by plane) northwest of San José.

As they say, "Location, location, location." Who would think that a small town sitting at the foot of massive Arenal Volcano would attract visitors from around the world? Nobody comes to La Fortuna—an ever-expanding mass of hotels, tour operators, souvenir shops, and *sodas* (small, family-run restaurants)—to see the town itself. Instead, thousands of tourists flock here each year to use it as a hub for visiting the natural wonders that surround it. The volcano, as well as waterfalls, vast nature preserves, great rafting rivers, and an astonishing array of birds are to be found within an hour or less of your hotel. La Fortuna is also the best place to arrange trips to the Caño Negro National Wildlife Refuge.

Canyoneering and waterfall rappelling near the currently inactive Arenal Volcano.

Many people who settled the Northern Lowlands came to the then-isolated region in the 1940s and '50s from other parts of the country to take part in government-sponsored homesteading programs. Thanks to its rich volcanic soil, the agricultural region became one of the most productive in Central America. After the 1968 eruption of Arenal Volcano, La Fortuna was transformed from a tiny, dusty farm town to one of Costa Rica's tourism powerhouses, where visitors converged to see the volcano in action.

As of 2010, the volcano went into a resting phase, which means it is still "active" below the surface, but it's doubtful you'll see more than a puff of steam. Viewing the volcano's peak can be hit or miss, especially during the rainy season (May through November). Locals reckon it is visible about 60 days out of the year. One minute Arenal Volcano looms menacingly over the village; the next minute clouds shroud its cone. Early morning (and sometimes late afternoon), especially in the dry season, is the best time to catch a longer glimpse.

GETTING HERE AND AROUND

Choose from two routes from San José: for a slightly longer but better road, leave the Pan-American Highway at Naranjo, continuing north to Zarcero and Ciudad Quesada. Head northwest at Ciudad Quesada to La Fortuna; or for a curvier but shorter route, continue beyond Naranjo on the Pan-American Highway, turning north at San Ramón, arriving at La Fortuna about 90 minutes after the turnoff. Either route passes through a mountainous section that begins to fog over by afternoon. Get as early a start as possible. Nature Air and SANSA fly daily to La Fortuna (FTN); flights land at an airstrip at the hamlet of El Tanque,

7 km (4 miles) east of town. Van transport ($10 one way) meets each flight to take you into La Fortuna.

Gray Line has daily shuttle bus service between San José, La Fortuna, and Arenal ($50), and Monteverde ($49). Interbus also connects San José with La Fortuna ($52) and Monteverde ($49) daily, with connections from here to a few of the North Pacific beaches. Public buses depart five times daily from San José's Terminal Atlántico Norte. Travel time is four hours. Although billed as an express route, the bus makes many stops.

Desafío Adventures provides a fast, popular, three-hour transfer between Monteverde and La Fortuna via taxi, boat, then another taxi, for $32 each way. It also offers private transfers from San José to La Fortuna for $165 one way. Shared shuttles departing San José daily at 1 pm and 5 pm cost $55 per person.

Taxis in and around La Fortuna are relatively affordable and will take you anywhere; a taxi to the Tabacón resort should run about $18. Get a cab at the stand on the east side of Parque Central.

The string of properties on the highway between La Fortuna and the Tabacón resort has led to a noticeable increase in traffic. It is hardly the proverbial urban jungle, and it is one of the country's prettiest stretches of road, but you should drive with caution. Cars dart in and out of driveways. Visitors congregate along the side of the road (likely sloth-spotting), and drivers gaze up at the volcano that looms over the highway. Keep your eyes on the road.

ESSENTIALS
Banks/ATMs BAC San José. ⊠ *75 m north of gas station, La Fortuna.* **Banco de Costa Rica.** ⊠ *East of central park, in front of the school, La Fortuna* ☎ *2479-9113.* **Banco Nacional.** ⊠ *Central Plaza, 100 m east of Catholic church, La Fortuna* ☎ *2479-9355.*

Bus Contacts Interbus. ⊠ *1 block south of Catholic church, in front Hotel Fas* ☎ *4100-0888 reservations, 2479-7074 La Fortuna office* ⊕ *www.interbusonline.com.*

Medical Clinic Clinica La Fortuna CCSS. ⊠ *300 m east of Parque Central, La Fortuna* ☎ *2479-9142.*

Pharmacy Farmacia Fishel. ⊠ *On the main road, 40 km (25 miles) east of the public park, La Fortuna* ☎ *2479-9778.*

Post Office Correos. ⊠ *Across from north side of church, La Fortuna* ☎ *2479-8070.*

Rental Cars Alamo. ⊠ *100 m west of church, La Fortuna* ☎ *2479-9090* ⊕ *www.alamocostarica.com.* **Mapache.** ⊠ *800 m west of church, La Fortuna* ☎ *2586-6300* ⊕ *www.mapache.com.*

EXPLORING
TOP ATTRACTIONS
Arenal Volcano National Park (*Parque Nacional Volcán Arenal*). Although the volcano is in a resting phase, you might see an occasional plume of smoke. It is still worth visiting the network of three easy trails leading to old lava flows, secondary rain forest, and a lookout point. The park is

home to more than 200 species of birds, as well as monkeys, sloths, coatis, deer, and anteaters. A top trail within the park is Heliconias (0.38 mile), which has a lookout point and connects to Las Coladas Trail (1 mile). You'll see hardened lava streams from 1992 and a 200-year-old ceiba tree on El Ceibo loop (1.43 miles) toward the edge of the park. Outside the national park is the noteworthy Cerro Chatto, an inactive volcano which you can hike from a trailhead near La Fortuna Waterfall or from the Arenal Observatory Lodge. Both trailheads start on private land so expect to pay an entrance fee of up to $10. The challenging, steep, and often muddy Cerro Chatto Trail takes about 3–4 hours to reach the crater lake. Old lava flows are also visible on the popular Los Tucanes Trail that begins near the Arenal Observatory Lodge. Guides are available for hire at the neighboring tour office, Arenal 1968. Bring plenty of water. ⊠ *1½ km (1 mile) from police station, on road to Arenal Observatory Lodge, La Fortuna* ☎ *2460–0620 Regional Office, 2200–4192 Park Administration* 💲 *$15 cash only* ⊙ *Daily 8–4.*

Eco Termales. Open hours at these family-owned hot springs are divided into three 4-hour intervals per day, with only 100 guests entering per segment. This means the six pools and restaurant never get too crowded. Temperatures range from 37° to 41°C (98.6° to 105.8°F), and there is one chilly waterfall to cool you off. Admission includes towel and locker. This is a great alternative to the overcrowded Baldi Hot Springs across the street. ⊠ *3½ km (2 miles) east of the Catholic church, across from Baldi, diagonal from Volcán Look Disco Club, La Fortuna* ☎ *2479–8787* ⊕ *www.ecotermalesfortuna.cr* 💲 *$36; with lunch or dinner $55.*

Grand Spa at Tabacón. Grab a robe and settle into the jungle Jacuzzi while spa valets serve you healthy smoothies. Treatments like the chocolate body wrap and the couples' two-hour massage utilize locally made products and end with champagne and fresh fruit. For a full day of pampering, request the spa package ($150), which includes access to the thermal baths, lunch or dinner, and credit for $100 in spa services. ⊠ *13 km (8 miles) northwest of La Fortuna on hwy. toward Nuevo Arenal, across from Tabacón Resort, La Fortuna* ☎ *2479–2028* ⊕ *www. tabacon.com* 💲 *Hot springs $60; hot springs plus lunch or dinner $85; after 6 pm plus dinner $70; free for Tabacón guests.*

Fodor'sChoice ★ **La Fortuna Waterfall** (*Cataratas de la Fortuna*). A strenuous walk down 500 steps (allow 25 to 40 minutes) is worth the effort to swim in the pool under the waterfall. Wear sturdy shoes or water sandals with traction, and bring snacks and water. You can get to the trailhead from La Fortuna by walking, by horseback, or by taking a taxi (approximately $10). Arranging a tour with an agency in La Fortuna is the easiest option. There are restrooms, free parking, a restaurant, and gift shop. ⊠ *Yellow entrance sign off main road toward volcano, 7 km (4 miles) south of La Fortuna, La Fortuna* ☎ *2479–8338* ⊕ *www. cataratariofortuna.com* 💲 *$11* ⊙ *Daily 8–4.*

Lake Arenal. Costa Rica's largest inland body of water, shimmering Lake Arenal, all 85 square km (33 square miles) of it, lies between rolling green hills and a picture-perfect volcano. Many visitors are surprised to learn it's a man-made lake, created in 1973 when a giant dam was built to provide hydroelectric power for the country. A natural depression was flooded, and a lake was born. Depending on the season, the depth varies between 30 and 60 meters (100–200 feet), with rainbow bass and machaca fish lurking below the surface. When water levels drop, you can see ruins of a cemetery and church jutting from the lake. The almost constant winds from the Caribbean make this area a windsurfing and kiteboarding mecca. Outfitters in La Fortuna, Nuevo Arenal, and Tilarán run fishing, windsurfing, and kiteboarding trips on the lake. Desafío, an operator based in La Fortuna and Monteverde, has a half-day horseback trip between the two towns, with great views of the lake. For the best lake views, reserve a hotel in Nuevo Arenal. ⊠ *15 km (9 miles) southwest of La Fortuna, La Fortuna.*

Mistico Arenal Hanging Bridges. A series of trails and bridges form a loop through the primary rain forest of a 250-acre private reserve, providing great bird-watching and volcano viewing. Sixteen fixed and hanging bridges allow you to see the forest at different levels. Trails are open rain or shine, and there are things to do in both types of weather, including horseback-riding tours that start at 9 am and 1 pm. Shuttle service from La Fortuna and area lodgings can be arranged. ½ ⊠ *2½ km (1½ miles) east of Lake Arenal dam on paved road, La Fortuna* ☎ *2479–8282* ⊕ *www.misticopark.com* ☜ *$24; natural-history tour $36; bird tour $47; night tour $47; horseback riding $50* ⊙ *Daily 7:30–4; early birding tour at 6 am; night tour at 6 pm.*

WORTH NOTING
Church of San Juan Bosco. The town's squat, pale, concrete church, unremarkable on its own, wins Costa Rica's most-photographed-house-of-worship award. The view of the church from across the central park, with the volcano in the background, makes a great photo of the sacred and the menacing. ⊠ *West side of Parque Central, La Fortuna.*

FAMILY **Danaus Ecocenter** (*Ecocentro Danaus*). A small ecotourism project outside town exhibits 60 species of medicinal plants, abundant animal life—including sloths and caimans—and butterfly and orchid gardens. This is a great place to see Costa Rica's famed red poison dart frogs up close. Seven guided tours are offered daily 8 am–3:30 pm, and a two-hour guided evening tour begins at 5:45 and should be reserved in advance. ⊠ *2 km (1 mile) south of La Fortuna, 600 m above the road to Agua Azul, La Fortuna* ☎ *2479–7019* ⊕ *www.ecocentrodanaus.com* ☜ *Evening tour $38; day tour $18 with guide, $13 self-guided* ⊙ *Daily 8–4.*

OFF THE
BEATEN
PATH
Venado Caves (*Cavernas de Venado*). In 1945 a farmer in the mountain hamlet of Venado fell into a hole, and thus discovered these subterranean limestone chambers extending about 2½ km (1½ miles). If you're not claustrophobic, willing to get wet, and don't mind bats—think carefully—this could be the ticket for you. Rubber boots, flashlights, and helmets are provided. If you want to capture the adventure, consider hiring their on-site photographer to follow you through the 10 caves. Most La Fortuna–based tour companies run trips to Venado Caves for about $80. ⊠ *45 mins north of La Fortuna and 20 mins southeast of San Rafael, La Fortuna* ☎ *2478–8008* ⊕ *www.cavernasdelvenadocr. com* ☜ *entrance $22; lunch $8; photographer $20* ⊙ *Daily 8–3.*

SPORTS AND THE OUTDOORS

TOUR OPERATORS

Fodor's Choice **Desafío Adventure Company.** Expert
★ Desafío guides can take you rafting, horseback riding, hiking, rappelling—you name the adventure.

Desafío pioneered rafting trips in this region, and has day trips on the Toro and Sarapiquí rivers (both Class III–IV) for experienced rafters ($89) and half-day rafting on the Balsa River (Class II–III) for less experienced paddlers ($69). Kayaking outings on Lake Arenal ($65) are ideal for beginners, as is a leisurely safari float on the Peñas Blancas ($57). If you're in the mood for something new, Desafío has half-day stand-up-paddling excursions on the lake ($65), and the popular Mambo Combo tour which combines waterfall rappelling and white-water rafting ($159).

If you're interested in getting up to Monteverde from the Arenal–La Fortuna area without taking the grinding four-hour drive, there's an alternative: Desafío Adventures has a five-hour guided horseback trip ($85). The trip involves taxi or van service from La Fortuna to the southern shore of Lake Arenal, and from that trail's end you ride to Monteverde, circumventing poorly maintained trails. A short boat ride across Lake Arenal is included. You leave La Fortuna at 7:15 am and arrive in Monteverde around noon. You can also take the trip in reverse. Desafío will provide a driver to transport your rental vehicle, but you must arrange to include that driver in your rental agreement. Alternatively, you can travel by mountain bike for the same price.
⊠ *Behind church, La Fortuna* ☎ *2479–0020, 855/818–0020 in North America* ⊕ *www.desafiocostarica.com* ☒ *From $57.*

Jacamar Naturalist Tours. The variety of tours here ranges from bird walks and sunset lake cruises to white-water rafting and safari float trips. There are boat trips on Lake Arenal and Caño Negro Lagoon in the morning. ⊠ *Across from Parque Central, south side of Catholic church, La Fortuna* ☎ *2479–9767* ⊕ *www.arenaltours.com* ☒ *From $54.*

Sunset Tours. One of the country's best tour operators pioneered excursions to the Caño Negro National Wildlife Refuge and Venado Caverns. They also offer tours to La Fortuna Waterfall, the volcano, Lake Arenal, and nearby rivers. ⊠ *Across from south side of church, La Fortuna* ☎ *2479–9585, 2479–9800* ⊕ *www.sunsettour.net* ☒ *From $55.*

CANOPY TOURS

Ecoglide Arenal Park. Unlike most zip-line companies, Ecoglide adds an element of safety with their double cables and allows guests to request starting times outside of their regular tour schedule. There are 12 standard zip lines and a Tarzan swing at platform No. 8. For those who want to film while they fly, Ecoglide rents helmets with front camera mounting systems. As with all zip-line tours in Costa Rica, reservations should be made in advance. Set tours start at 7:40, 10, 12:30, and 3.

5

✉ *3 km (2 miles) west of La Fortuna, La Fortuna* ☎ *2479–7120* ⊕ *www.arenalecoglide.com* 🖃 *$55* ⊙ *Daily 7–4.*

Fodor's Choice   **Sky Adventures Arenal Park.** This adventure park on the outskirts of Are-
★   nal Volcano operates two other parks on Lake Arenal and in Monte-
verde. Alpine-style gondolas transport you to the site, from which you
can descend via 3 km (2 miles) of zip lines, hike through the cloud
forest along a series of suspended bridges, or go back the way you
came, on the tram. You'll pass from rain forest into cloud forest, and
can fly above the treetops on Costa Rica's highest zip line. Adrenaline
seekers might opt for biking, rappelling, canyoning, bungee jumping,
or tubing back to base camp. Tours can be mixed and matched for a
full-day adventure. ✉ *26 km (16 miles) west of La Fortuna, El Castillo*
☎ *2479–4100* ⊕ *www.skyadventures.travel* 🖃 *$71 tram and zip lines,*
$61 tram and walk, $44 tram only, $35 walk only, $69 sky river, $55
bike tour ⊙ *Daily 7–5.*

HORSEBACK RIDING

Many outfitters—some nothing more than a guy and a horse—lead riding tours between La Fortuna and Monteverde along treacherous trails.
Some riders have returned with stories of terrified horses barely able to
navigate the way. It's best to stick with Desafío (*see Tour Operators,*
above) or another reputable outfit.

Chaves Tours. Chaves Tours offers three-hour horseback excursions from
La Fortuna to the Fortuna Waterfall. Tours depart daily at 8 am and 1
pm. The ride is appropriate for both novice and experienced riders. ✉ *1*
km (½ mile) west of town center, La Fortuna ☎ *8354–9159, 2479–0606*
⊕ *www.horsebackridingarenal.com* 🖃 *$57.*

RAFTING AND KAYAKING

Desafío and several other La Fortuna operators offer Class III and IV
white-water trips on the Río Toro. The narrow river requires the use
of special, streamlined boats that seat just four passengers and go very
fast. The easier Balsa, Peñas Blancas, Arenal, and San Carlos rivers have
Class II and III rapids and are close enough to town that they can be
worked into half-day excursions.

Canoa Aventura. Canoeing trips with ample wildlife viewing on the Río
Peñas Blancas are a specialty, as are daylong canoe tours of the Caño
Blanco Wildlife Refuge. The three-hour Caño Negro tour takes place
on the Río Frío near the Nicaraguan border where you're sure to see
birds, monkeys, caimans, iguanas, and bats. Tours are appropriate for
beginners, with a selection of easy floats if you're not feeling too adventurous, and instruction is provided, but the folks here can tailor excursions if you're more experienced. ✉ *1 km (½ mile) west of the church,*
La Fortuna ☎ *2479–8200* ⊕ *www.canoa-aventura.com* 🖃 *From $32.*

Flow Trips. Local guides lead rafting excursions on the Sarapiquí River
(Classes II, III, and IV), as well as kayaking trips on Lake Arenal and the
Peñas Blancas River. ✉ *1 km (½ mile) west of La Fortuna, La Fortuna*
☎ *2479–0075* ⊕ *www.flowtrips.com* 🖃 *From $65.*

RAPPELLING

Pure Trek Canyoning. Rappel down three waterfalls and one rock wall ranging in height from 12 to 50 meters (39 to 164 feet). Two guides lead small groups—10 is the maximum size—on a four-hour tour ($101) that departs at 7 am or noon to a private farm near La Fortuna, with plenty of wildlife-watching

opportunities along the way. There is a bit of hiking between waterfalls and long periods of waiting for others in your group, so patience and proper shoes are a must. The excursion includes transportation, all rappelling gear, and a light lunch. ✉ *7 km (4½ miles) west of town center, La Fortuna* ☎ *2479–1313, 866/569–5723 in North America* ⊕ *www.puretrekcanyoning.com* ⌨ *$101.*

WHERE TO EAT

$$$ ✗ **Don Rufino.** Although this is one of the more upscale restaurants in the
ECLECTIC   area, there's no need to dress up here: this is La Fortuna, after all. The
L-shape bar fronting the main street has become a popular expat and tourist hangout, especially when there's live music on the calendar. The user-friendly menu is marked with symbols of chili peppers for spicy dishes, a tomato for vegetarian dishes, and a check mark for those that are highly recommended. Friendly waitstaff might suggest chicken seasoned with chocolate, coffee, and tarragon or forest lasagna made with wild mushrooms, caramelized onions, and ricotta cheese. Their grilled meats are local, organic, and are served with a side of polenta, lentils, and caramelized apples in a balsamic dressing. The tilapia in bacon-and-tomato sauce is also very good. ⑤ *Average main: $16* ✉ *Across from gas station, La Fortuna* ☎ *2479–9997* ⊕ *www.donrufino.com.*

$$ ✗ **El Gran Abuelo.** There's no shortage of steak houses near Arenal, but El
COSTA RICAN   Gran Abuelo pushes to the front of the pack with perfectly grilled steak. Tender and flavorful tri-tip and steak platters can easily feed a small family and are served on huge griddles with sides like garlic-lemon yuca, salad, tortillas, and veggies. Straight from the grill to your table, sizzling entrées are delivered in cast iron skillets with a serious knife to cut into your *carne.* Specials include wine or smoothies, and for non-beef eaters, the ceviche is outstanding. Vegetarians can chose from wood-fired pizzas, pasta dishes, or fresh salads. Hardly anyone leaves without trying the house dessert, a spin on traditional cheesecake made with condensed milk, lime, and cookies. This roadside restaurant is worth the 10-minute drive from La Fortuna. ⑤ *Average main: $12* ✉ *8km from La Fortuna, on road to San Ramon, La Fortuna* ☎ *2479–1749.*

$$ ✗ **La Choza de Laurel.** The smell of rotisserie chicken, porterhouse steak,
COSTA RICAN   and fresh fish bathed in garlic attracts passersby to this open-air restaurant a short walk from the center of town. Wooden picnic tables and a cigar shop storefront replicate an old Costa Rican village, adding a cultural touch to your meal. The menu is overwhelmingly large—as are portions—ranging from pastas and burgers to soups and salads. Stick with local favorites like the black-bean soup with homemade tortillas

5

or the Choza Plate with chicken, rice, beans, chayote, corn, salad, and plantains. For dessert, banana splits are served in half a pineapple so you can eat the bowl. ⑤ *Average main: $12* ✉ *400 m northwest of church, La Fortuna* ☎ *2479–7063* ⊕ *www.lachozadelaurel.com.*

$$$
ITALIAN
Fodor's Choice
★

✕ **Que Rico.** Just below the main road is this lovely Italian-inspired restaurant where wooden tables are draped with red-and-white linens, and soft music and candles add a touch of romance. In typical Costa Rican fashion, the menu is textbook thick, with options ranging from local ceviche and beef carpaccio to caprese salad and tamarind chicken. Stick to the Italian specialties: brick-oven pizza and ravioli are made with a dough that combines five types of flour from Italy and Costa Rica. The Italian sausage pizza has a kick, and the "Volcán" with ham, mushrooms, bacon, and pepperoni is a local favorite. The chef invites kids to make their own pizzas, or they can order from the children's menu. Wine-pairing recommendations are listed next to each item, and there's a "light section" if you're counting calories. Clearly the *bacio perugina* didn't make the cut; these baked pastries are stuffed with Nutella and caramelized almonds and served with vanilla ice cream. ⑤ *Average main: $20* ✉ *6½ km (4 miles) west of church, La Fortuna* ☎ *2479–1020* ⊕ *www.quericoarenal.com.*

$
COSTA RICAN

✕ **Rain Forest Café.** Reasonable prices and excellent quality have made this café a traveler's favorite, with meals ranging from *churrasco* and empanadas to salads and sandwiches. Burritos are perfectly toasted (not overly soft) with homemade tortillas, and of course there's always the typical Costa Rican *casado* (chicken, beef, or fish served with rice, beans, plantains, and salad). The tempting desserts include chocolate pie, carrot cake, flan, and a variety of pastries. For a morning pick-me-up, try the Crazy Monkey smoothie made with banana, milk, cinnamon, and coffee. The free Wi-Fi and books-for-borrow might help you escape from reality, but the wall lined with bagged coffee for sale will remind you where you are. ⑤ *Average main: $8* ✉ *In front of Hotel Las Colinas, 125 m south of the park, La Fortuna* ☎ *2479–7239.*

$$
COSTA RICAN

✕ **Soda y Pizzería La Parada.** La Fortuna's only late-night eatery does a brisk business, and it's a convenient place to grab a quick, cheap meal and stock up on snacks for long bus rides. ("La Parada" refers to the bus stop.) If you have time, try the pizza, pasta, nachos, or grilled fish, but for an on-the-go meal opt for one of the popular burgers, sandwiches, or tacos. There's a buffet, if you'd rather just point and choose. You can defy the hectic atmosphere by ordering a glass of wine (or bottle to go) from their surprisingly impressive selection. The reasonable prices and convenience make this local cafeteria one of the more frenzied spots in town, so look elsewhere if you want some peace with your meal. It's open 6 am–midnight. ⑤ *Average main: $10* ✉ *Across from Parque Central and regional bus stop, La Fortuna* ☎ *2479–9098* ⊕ *www.restaurantelaparada.com.*

WHERE TO STAY

$$$$
RESORT

☷ **Arenal Kioro Suites & Spa.** Other than Observatory Lodge, this is the closest property to Arenal Volcano with rooms boasting hydro-massage Jacuzzis, sitting areas, jaw-dropping views, Juliet balconies, and nearly 700 square feet of space. **Pros:** plentiful breakfast; all rooms face the

RICE AND BEANS

"More tico than *gallo pinto*" is an old saying here, but just how Costa Rican is the country's signature dish? Nicaraguans also claim it, and the rivalry has led to five *Guinness Book of World Records* bids for the largest batch. Costa Rica captured the first title in 2003, only to have Nicaragua top it a mere 12 days later. Costa Rica recaptured the prize in 2005. In 2008 Nicaragua snatched the title back with a 22,000-dish batch of rice and beans. Costa Rica more than doubled that amount at a March 2009 event with a whopping 50,000 servings, a record that still stands. The latest debate on rice and beans is which country cooks up the better batch. Traditionally, Costa Ricans use black beans and add a kick of salsa Lizano with cilantro, while Nicaraguans generally use red kidney beans and top it with pico de gallo. Don't let us get in the middle of this food fight. We'll let you be the judge.

volcano; enormous rooms. **Cons:** dim rooms; no bottled water or ceiling fans in rooms; steep walkways. $ *Rooms from: $295 ⊠ 10 km northeast of La Fortuna, before Tabacon, Arenal ☎ 2479–1700 ⊕ www. hotelarenalkioro.com ⊃ 53 rooms ⊙ Breakfast.*

$$ ⬚ **Arenal Observatory Lodge.** These cozy, comfortable, and simple rooms
HOTEL allow you to sleep as close as anyone should to a volcano—it's a mere 2¾ km (1¾ miles) away, and stellar views and outdoor activities are what the place is all about. **Pros:** best volcano views; secluded location; rate includes breakfast, taxes, and guided hike. **Cons:** rough road to get here; isolated location; no a/c, TV, or phones in rooms; patchy Wi-Fi. $ *Rooms from: $128 ⊠ 5 km from National Park entrance, La Fortuna ☎ 2479–1070 lodge, 2290–7011 in San José, 877/804–7732 in U.S. and Canada ⊕ www.arenalobservatorylodge.com ⊃ 46 rooms, 2 suites ⊙ Breakfast.*

$ ⬚ **Cabinas Los Guayabos.** As one of the best budget options with a vol-
HOTEL cano view, these orange adobe cabins are basic but clean with big windows and private patios, which are great for viewing wildlife and, on clear days, Arenal. **Pros:** good budget value; friendly owners; great volcano views. **Cons:** rustic rooms; breakfast not included; Wi-Fi at reception only; cash only. $ *Rooms from: $65 ⊠ 9 km (5½ miles) west of La Fortuna, La Fortuna ☎ 2479–1444 ⊕ www.cabinaslosguayabos. com ▭ No credit cards ⊃ 9 cabins ⊙ No meals.*

$$$$ ⬚ **Chachagua Rainforest Hotel & Hacienda.** At this working ranch with a
HOTEL brook running through it you can see *caballeros* (cowboys) at work, take a horseback ride into the rain forest, and look for toucans from your room or the deck of your bungalow. **Pros:** children under 11 stay free; free use of fishing and bike gear; nice pool area; good Web-only promotions. **Cons:** 30 minutes from La Fortuna; Wi-Fi signal in reception area only; rough road to hotel. $ *Rooms from: $258 ⊠ 12 km (7 miles) south of La Fortuna, La Fortuna ☎ 2468–1011 ⊕ www. chachaguarainforesthotel.com ⊃ 9 rooms, 10 bungalows ⊙ Breakfast.*

$$ ⬚ **Hotel Kokoro.** Spacious and clean rooms at this hot-springs hotel are
HOTEL like mini log cabins with hardwood floors and sugarcane ceilings—Nos.
FAMILY 16, 17, and 18 even offer views of the volcano. **Pros:** small spa offers

The perfect way to end the day: a nice soak in the hot springs in Arenal Volcano National Park

massages; lovely pool; private hot springs; tour desk with good rates. **Cons:** dim lighting in rooms; restaurant closed in low season; Wi-Fi in common areas only; hot springs open at 2 pm. $ *Rooms from: $120* ⊠ *500 m west of the Quebrada la Palma, La Fortuna* ☎ *2479–1222* ⊕ *www.arenalkokoro.com* ⇆ *29 rooms* ⏐⊙⏐ *Breakfast.*

$$$$ ⚏ **Hotel Royal Corín.** This hotel has a volcano view along with luxury
RESORT perks like a swim-up bar, 5-star cuisine, a swanky lobby, and an impressive spa. **Pros:** on-site hot springs; pleasant hotel-style surroundings; excellent showers; friendly service. **Cons:** some street noise; poor lighting in the rooms; not a lot of local flavor. $ *Rooms from: $290* ⊠ *4 km (2½ miles) west of La Fortuna, La Fortuna* ☎ *2479–2200, 800/659–7826 in North America* ⊕ *www.royalcorin.com* ⇆ *42 rooms, 12 suites* ⏐⊙⏐ *Breakfast.*

$$$ ⚏ **Lost Iguana Resort & Spa.** Despite the relative isolation, travelers flock
HOTEL to this rain-forest resort, largely because each hillside room has a huge picture window and door opening to an individual balcony with volcano views. **Pros:** good breakfast; great volcano views in rain-forest setting; plenty of wildlife; nice spa and gym. **Cons:** removed from sights; small pool; poor lighting in rooms; Wi-Fi in reception area only. $ *Rooms from: $245* ⊠ *Off Hwy. 142, 20 km (12 miles) west of La Fortuna, La Fortuna* ☎ *2479–1557, 2267–6148 in San José* ⊕ *www. lostiguanacr.com* ⇆ *42 rooms* ⏐⊙⏐ *Breakfast.*

$$$$ ⚏ **Nayara Hotel, Spa & Gardens.** Scattered over expansive grounds are
RESORT freestanding casitas, all tastefully decorated with dark-wood furnish-
Fodor's Choice ings and equipped with luxurious touches like indoor-outdoor show-
★ ers, four-post canopy beds, plasma TVs, and whirlpool tubs. **Pros:**

luxurious rooms; attentive staff; early check-in can be arranged; excellent breakfast. Cons: hotel books up early; villas lack volcano views. ⑤ *Rooms from: $285* ✉ *7 km (4½ miles) west of La Fortuna, Arenal* ☎ *2479–1600, 866/311–1197 in North America* ⊕ *www.arenalnayara. com* ⟿ *29 casitas, 21 suites, 16 villas* ¶⦶ *Breakfast.*

$$

HOTEL

🛏 **San Bosco Inn.** In downtown La Fortuna, this inn has clean, bright rooms linked by a long veranda lined with benches and potted plants, and added perks like a large pool, Jacuzzi, in-room Wi-Fi, and communal computers. **Pros:** gated property; good value; close to center of town. **Cons:** some rooms get street noise; boxy design; no bar or restaurant. ⑤ *Rooms from: $88* ✉ *220 m north of gas station, La Fortuna* ☎ *2479–9050, 800/393–0902 in North America* ⊕ *www.hotelsanbosco. com* ⟿ *33 rooms* ¶⦶ *Breakfast.*

$$$$

RESORT

FAMILY

🛏 **The Springs Resort & Spa.** With its own adventure park, hot-springs complex, and activities for all ages, this resort caters to both hotel guests and the outside public with day passes to its massive grounds. **Pros:** stupendous volcano views; hot springs rich in minerals; excellent sushi bar. **Cons:** property has a theme-park feel; rooms are pricey; Wi-Fi signal weak in some areas. ⑤ *Rooms from: $525* ✉ *9 km (5½ miles) west of La Fortuna, then 4 km (2½ miles) north, La Fortuna* ☎ *2401–3313, 954/727–8333 in North America* ⊕ *www.springscostarica.com* ⟿ *43 rooms, 4 villas* ¶⦶ *No meals.*

$$$$

RESORT

🛏 **Tabacón Grand Spa Thermal Resort.** At one of Central America's most relaxing and romantic resorts, it's the hot springs and lovely spa, coupled with attractive rooms (the suites are some of the country's finest) that customarily draw happy guests inland from the ocean. **Pros:** elegant hotel; luxurious hot springs; great volcano views; good restaurant. **Cons:** hot springs can get crowded; breakfast costs $30 if not included in rate; two-night minimum stay. ⑤ *Rooms from: $293* ✉ *13 km (8 miles) northwest of La Fortuna on Hwy. 142, La Fortuna* ☎ *2479–2000, 2519–1999 in San José, 855/822–2266 in North America* ⊕ *www.tabacon.com* ⟿ *74 rooms, 28 suites* ¶⦶ *No meals.*

NIGHTLIFE

People in La Fortuna tend to turn in early, though there are a couple of spots for night owls.

Kazan. Although La Fortuna is not known for its happening nightlife, this central bar is where locals and tourists alike gather to watch the game over a cold beer. They have 2-for-1 cocktails from 5 to 7, free Wi-Fi, and a kitchen serving late-night quick bites. ✉ *North of the park, below Gym Arenal, La Fortuna* ☎ *2479–7561* ⟲ *Open 5–10 pm.*

Lava Lounge. This La Fortuna hot spot has local and imported beers plus plenty of cocktails to get you in the mood for live music, every Wednesday and Saturday from 7 to 10. An unorthodox happy hour is from 9 to 11 am, and you're likely to have desperate-looking dogs under foot, telepathically begging you to take them home. Lava Lounge owner Scott Alan runs a dog rescue at this pooch-friendly establishment. ✉ *25 m west of Catholic church, La Fortuna* ☎ *2479–7365* ⊕ *www. lavaloungecostarica.com.*

NUEVO ARENAL

40 km (25 miles) (1 hr) west of La Fortuna.

Much of the original town of Arenal, at one of the lowest points near Lake Arenal, was destroyed by the volcano's 1968 eruption, and the rest was destroyed in 1973, when Lake Arenal flooded the region. The *nuevo* (new) town was created about 30 km (19 miles) away from the site of the old. It doesn't have much to interest tourists but is about halfway between La Fortuna and Tilarán, making it a good stop for a break, and an even better base, with a few truly lovely lodgings and restaurants nearby.

GETTING HERE AND AROUND

The route from La Fortuna to Nuevo Arenal around the north shore of Lake Arenal has been greatly improved over the years. Watch out for the raccoonlike coatimundis (*pizotes* in Spanish) that scurry along the road. Longtime human feeding has diminished their ability to search for food on their own, and the cookies and potato chips they're frequently fed make matters worse. Public buses run twice daily from La Fortuna to Nuevo Arenal and five times daily from Tilarán. On the main road, at the entrance of town, there's a small shopping area with a pharmacy, post office, and a gas station across the street. The small town has three grocery stores including Super Compro on the main road.

ESSENTIALS

Bank/ATM Banco Nacional. ⊠ *Across from soccer field.*

Pharmacy Farmacia Santa Fé Arenal. ⊠ *next to Super Compro* ☎ *2694–4474.*

Post Office Correos. ⊠ *Across from gas station* ☎ *2694–4310.*

WHERE TO EAT

$$$
ECLECTIC
✕ **Gingerbread.** Ignore the chalkboard menu and let chef Eyal guide you for what might just be the best meal you'll have in Costa Rica. The Israeli native (who trained in New York) is confident in the kitchen, but his boastfulness is not unwarranted, as you'll discover with fresh dishes like filet mignon, shrimp risotto, organic Greek chicken, and blackened tuna. The menu is always changing, with a rotation of hits like lamb curry, palmito artichoke salad, mussels with mushrooms, and tender pork. Portions are large and can be paired with wines from the impressive cellar. Desserts like the macadamia cheesecake are well worth it if you manage to save room. Opt for a table on the patio rather than a booth near the U-shaped bar, unless you like boisterous noise with your meal. Note that the restaurant is open only Tuesday through Saturday from 5 pm to 9 pm and credit cards are not accepted. ⓢ *Average main: $20* ⊠ *Next to Villa Decary* ☎ *2694–0039* ⊕ *www.gingerbreadarenal. com* ⊟ *No credit cards* ☉ *Closed Sun. and Mon. No lunch* ⚲ *Reservations essential.*

$$
ITALIAN
✕ **Los Platillos Voladores.** It might not look like much from the outside, but this Italian restaurant has homemade dishes like tortellini in sage butter, lasagne with bubbly-browned mozzarella, and crispy-thin pizza with folds of prosciutto. Start with a caprese salad and move on to one of the pasta dishes buried beneath a blanket of shaved parmesan. The

paninis make a great meal-to-go on your way to/from the lake. Come hungry or prepare to share since portions are large. The back patio is a quaint spot to enjoy a glass of red. If there's ever been a time to stop calorie-counting, it's now, especially when you sink your teeth into the rich panna cotta. $ *Average main: $10* ✉ *Rt. 142, uphill from German Bakery* ☎ *2694–5005* ☺ *Closed Mon.* ▬ *No credit cards.*

WHERE TO STAY

$$
B&B/INN

▦ **Chalet Nicholas.** Opened in 1992, this rain-forest B&B has old-fashioned charm with three chalet-style bedrooms looking out onto the mystic lake and volcano. **Pros:** attentive owners; great breakfasts; terrific value; birders' paradise. **Cons:** best for dog lovers; need a car to stay here; no children under 10. $ *Rooms from: $90* ✉ *3 km (2 miles) west of Nuevo Arenal* ☎ *2694–4041* ⊕ *www.chaletnicholas.com* ⇆ *3 rooms* ⦿ *Breakfast.*

$$$
HOTEL

▦ **La Mansión Inn Arenal.** Nicely decorated cottages are scattered around 25 acres on Arenal's northeast shore at the point where the volcano begins to disappear from sight, but the lake views (and the sunsets) remain as spectacular as ever. **Pros:** luxurious furnishings; stupendous lake views from private terraces; great pool area. **Cons:** far from sights; need a car to stay here; very slippery path after rain. $ *Rooms from: $230* ✉ *Hwy. 142, 34 km (21 miles) west of La Fortuna* ☎ *8890–3901, 877/660–3830 in North America* ⊕ *www.lamansionarenal.com* ⇆ *12 cottages, 5 suites, 1 villas* ⦿ *Breakfast.*

$$
B&B/INN
Fodor's Choice
★

▦ **Villa Decary.** There's much to recommend at this hillside property, including the large picture windows and balconies overlooking Lake Arenal and the attentive service from the owners. **Pros:** attentive owners; great breakfasts; yoga classes offered. **Cons:** need a car to stay here; minimal road noise; Wi-Fi only reaches lower-level rooms and common areas. $ *Rooms from: $109* ✉ *2 km (1 mile) east of Nuevo Arenal* ☎ *2694–4330, 800/556–0505 in North America* ⊕ *www.villadecary. com* ⇆ *5 rooms, 3 bungalows* ⦿ *Breakfast.*

TILARÁN

22 km (14 miles) (45 mins) southwest of Nuevo Arenal, 62 km (38 miles) (1½ hrs) west of La Fortuna.

A windmill farm in the hills high above Tilarán attests to its being the windiest place in the country, and this lakeside town is used as a base by bronzed windsurfers. For those days when you get "skunked" (the wind fails to blow), horseback riding and mountain biking can keep you busy. A lakeside stroll is a pleasant way to while away a few hours.

GETTING HERE AND AROUND

The road from La Fortuna via Nuevo Arenal is in good shape, with just a few short potholed stretches. Give yourself sufficient time—say, two hours—for the trip, and drive it during daylight hours. Public buses travel to and from La Fortuna twice daily, and from a small terminal at Calle 20 and Avenida 3 in San José five times daily. If you're coming from Monteverde, keep in mind that the first 40 km (24 miles) are unpaved and slow going.

ESSENTIALS

Bank/ATM Banco Nacional. ☒ *South side of Central Plaza* ☎ *2695–5028.*

Post Office Correos. ☒ *Across from Banco de Costa Rica* ☎ *2695–6230.*

SPORTS AND THE OUTDOORS

WINDSURFING AND KITESURFING

Tico Wind. Wind- and kitesurfing equipment is available for rent during the December–May season. The company offers three-hour kitesurfing lessons starting at $225, and a multiday course for $590. A one-hour windsurfing lesson costs $50. You can rent stand-up paddleboards starting at $20 per day. ☒ *Hwy. 142, 15 km (9 miles) north of Tilarán* ☎ *2692–2002* ⊕ *www.ticowind.com* ✉ *From $20.*

Tilawa Windsurf Center. The area's only outfitter open year-round also offers the best selection of windsurfing equipment for rent between May and November, and has lessons year-round. One-hour lessons start at $45, two hours are $75, and three hours $100. ☒ *Lake Arenal Hotel (formerly Hotel Tilawa), Hwy. 142, 8 km (5 miles) north of Tilarán* ☎ *8778–1492* ⊕ *www.costa-rica-windsurf.com* ✉ *From $45.*

WHERE TO STAY

$ ⛱ **Lake Arenal Hotel & Brewery.** This property overlooking Lake Arenal
HOTEL   has large rooms with natural-wood ceilings and some nice perks that include its own on-site microbrewery, a swimming pool, tennis courts, a Jacuzzi, and a skate park. **Pros:** many activities; stupendous lake views; great beers. **Cons:** isolated location; hotel has a bit of a hostel feel; frequent high winds can lead to sleepless nights; rooms look much better on website. ⑤ *Rooms from: $68* ☒ *Hwy. 142, 8 km (5 miles) north of Tilarán, on the way to Nuevo Arenal* ☎ *2695–5050* ⊕ *www. lakearenalhotel.com* ⤳ *21 rooms* ⦿| *Breakfast.*

$$ ⛱ **Mystica Lodge & Retreats.** It's all about healing, yoga, and relaxation at
HOTEL   this Italian-owned lodge, where you can enjoy treetop therapies next to the river or sway in a hammock overlooking Lake Arenal (the property is halfway between Tilarán and Nuevo Arenal). **Pros:** homemade breads at breakfast; hiking trail to stunning ceiba tree; lovely pool; yoga classes. **Cons:** Wi-Fi in common areas only; no closets or a/c; toilet paper cannot be flushed; limited menu at restaurant. ⑤ *Rooms from: $120* ☒ *Hwy. 142, at the turnoff near Plaza del Cafe, 13 km (8 miles) north of Tilarán, Nuevo Arenal* ☎ *2692–1001* ⊕ *www.mysticacostarica.com* ⤳ *6 rooms, 1 villa, 1 house, 1 cabin* ⦿| *Breakfast.*

**▮ EN
ROUTE**
Viento Fresco Waterfalls. On the road from Monteverde, just south of Tilarán, this private farm boasts five cascading waterfalls and swimming holes. The largest plunges 99 meters (328 feet) into a freshwater pool. The site also offers hiking trails, a dairy farm, several caves, changing facilities, and a restaurant serving Costa Rican fare. Horseback riding is also available. ☒ *Tilarán* ⊹ *11 km (6 miles) south of Tilarán near San Miguel* ☎ *2695–3434* ⊕ *www.vientofresco.net* ✉ *$15 waterfalls; $55 horseback riding* ⊗ *Daily 8–5:30.*

MONTEVERDE CLOUD FOREST AND SANTA ELENA

Monteverde is 167 km (104 miles) (3½ hrs) northwest of San José and 110 km (67 miles) (4 hrs) southwest of La Fortuna; Santa Elena is 6 km (4 miles) (30 mins) north of Monteverde and 35 km (22 miles) (2 hrs) southeast of Tilarán.

Monteverde is a rain forest, but you won't be in the tropics—rather in the cool, gray, misty world of the cloud forest. Almost 900 species of epiphytes, including 450 orchids, thrive here; most tree trunks are covered with mosses, bromeliads, ferns, and other plants. Monteverde spans the Continental Divide, extending from about 1,500 meters (4,920 feet) on the Pacific slope and 1,350 meters (4,430 feet) on the Atlantic slope up to the highest peaks of the Tilarán Mountains at around 1,850 meters (6,070 feet). Make Santa Elena your base of operations when visiting this area.

The area's first residents were a handful of Costa Rican families fleeing the rough-and-ready life of nearby gold-mining fields during the 1940s. They were joined in the early 1950s by Quakers, conscientious objectors from Alabama fleeing conscription into the Korean War. A number of things drew them to Costa Rica: just a few years earlier it had abolished its military, and the Monteverde area offered good grazing. The cloud forest that lay above the dairy farms soon attracted the attention of ecologists. Educators and artisans followed, giving Monteverde and its "metropolis," the village of Santa Elena, a certain mystique. These days, Monteverde looks quite a bit different than it did when the first wave of Quakers arrived. New hotels have sprouted up everywhere, traffic grips the center of town, and there's a small shopping center outside of town on the way to the mountain. A glut of rented all-terrain vehicles (ATVs) contributes to the increasing din that disrupts Monteverde's legendary peace and quiet. Some define this as progress while others lament the gradual chipping away at what makes one of Costa Rica's most special areas so special. Reminiscent of a ski town in summer, Monteverde still lets you get away from it all, but you'll have to work harder at it than you used to. In any case, you'll not lack for things to do if seeing nature is a primary reason for your visit. The only way to see the area's reserves, including the Monteverde Cloud Forest, is to hike them.

Note that a casual reference to "Monteverde" generally indicates this entire area, but officially the term applies only to the original Quaker settlement, which is by the dairy-processing plant just down the mountain from the reserve entrance. If you follow road signs exclusively, you'll end up a bit outside the town of Santa Elena.

It takes a little effort to get here, and it can get crowded during high season, but this exceptionally well-protected reserve affords visitors one of the country's best opportunities to view abundant—and stunning—wildlife and colorful high-elevation flora.

CLOSE UP

What Is a Cloud Forest?

Cloud forests are a type of rain forest, but are different from the hot, humid lowland forests with which most people are familiar. First of all, they're cooler. Temperatures in Monteverde Cloud Forest, for example, hover around 18°C (65°F) year-round, and feel colder because of the near-constant cool rain. Cloud forests—also known as montane forests—occur at elevations of around 1,950 to 3,450 meters (6,500 to 11,500 feet). At this altitude, clouds accumulate around mountains and volcanoes, providing regular precipitation as well as shade, which in turn slows evaporation. Moisture is deposited directly onto vegetation,

keeping it lush and green. The trees here, on top of high ridges and near the summits of volcanoes, are transformed by strong, steady winds that sometimes topple them and regularly break off branches. The resulting collection of small, twisted trees and bushes is known as an elfin forest. The conditions in cloud forests create unique habitats that shelter an unusually high proportion of rare species, making conservation vital. Monteverde is Costa Rica's most touristed cloud forest, but not its only one. Other cloud forests are in nearby Santa Elena Reserve, Los Angeles Cloud Forest Reserve near San Ramón, and around San Gerardo de Dota.

DID YOU KNOW?

Monteverde's Quakers, or more officially, the Society of Friends, no longer constitute the majority here these days, but their imprint on the community remains strong. (Don't expect to see anyone dressed like the man on the Quaker Oats box.) Their meetinghouse at Escuela de los Amigos, just south of the Cheese Factory on the road to the reserve, welcomes visitors at meetings of worship, 10:30 am Sunday and 9 am Wednesday. Most of the time is spent in quiet reflection.

GETTING HERE AND AROUND

Getting here means negotiating some of the country's legendarily rough roads, but don't let that deter you from a visit. Years of promises to pave the way up here have collided with politics and scarce funds, but many residents remain just as happy to keep Monteverde out of the reach of tour buses and day-trippers. ("Do we really want this to be a shore excursion for cruise ships?" some residents ask.) A section of Route 606 between Guacimal and Santa Elena was paved in 2016, but other than that, expect about a one-hour bumpy ride. Your own vehicle gives you the greatest flexibility, but a burgeoning number of shuttle-van services connect Monteverde with San José and other tourist destinations throughout the country.

Buses from San José leave twice daily from the Terminal 7-10 (at Calle 10 and Avenida 7), at 6:30 am and 2:30 pm, stopping in the center of Santa Elena and at various locations on the way up the mountain as far as the Cheese Factory. Buses from Santa Elena leave for San José at 6:30 am and 2:30 pm daily. Taxis from Santa Elena are $10–$13. Buses from Tilarán to Santa Elena leave once a day, at 12:30 pm. Desafío Adventure Company offers shared transportation from San José to Monteverde for

$52 (one way). The San José–Monteverde public bus route is notorious for theft; watch your bags, and never let your passport and money out of your sight—or off your person. Never take advice from the street "guides" who meet incoming buses in Monteverde and La Fortuna. They claim to want to help you find accommodations and tours, when in reality they receive kickbacks for sending tourists to less-than-desirable hotels or to unqualified "tour guides."

If you can handle the curvy roads, a windy track leads from Tilarán via Cabeceras to Santa Elena, near the Monteverde Cloud Forest Biological Reserve, doing away with the need to cut across to the Pan-American Highway. You need a 4WD vehicle, and you should inquire locally about the current condition of the road. The views of Nicoya Peninsula, Lake Arenal, and Arenal Volcano reward those willing to bump around a bit. Note, too, that you don't really save much time—on a good day it takes about 2½ hours as opposed to the 3 hours required via Cañas and Río Lagarto on the highway.

By car from the La Fortuna area, it's at least three hours by bumpy road around Lake Arenal; some tour companies provide the trip via minibus and boat (called "Taxi-Boat-Taxi" or "Jeep-Boat-Jeep") for about $30 one way. Gray Line has daily shuttle bus service between San José, La Fortuna, Arenal ($50), and Monteverde ($49). Interbus also connects San José with La Fortuna and Monteverde (each $49) daily, with connections from here to a few of the North Pacific beaches. There will be times you wish you had your own vehicle, but it's surprisingly easy to get around the Monteverde area without a car. Given the state of the roads, you'll be happy to let someone else do the driving. However, if you do arrive by rental car, the road up the mountain from Santa Elena is paved as far as the gas station near the entrance to the Hotel Belmar. Taxis are plentiful; it's easy to call one from your hotel, and restaurants are happy to summon a cab to take you back to your hotel after dinner. Taxis also congregate in front of the church on the main street in Santa Elena. Many tour companies will pick you up from your hotel and bring you back at the end of the day, either free or for a small fee.

ESSENTIALS

Bank/ATM Banco Nacional. ✉ *50 m north of Catholic church, and 50 m east of first corner, next to Orchid Garden, Santa Elena* ☏ *2645–5027.*

Medical Clinic Clinica Monteverde. ✉ *150 m south of soccer field, Santa Elena* ☏ *2645–5076.*

Pharmacy Farmacia Vitosi. ✉ *Across from Chamber of Tourism, Santa Elena* ☏ *2645–5004.*

Post Office Correos. ✉ *50 m south of Herpetarium Adventures Monteverde, Santa Elena* ☏ *2202–2900.*

Tourist Information Chamber of Tourism Monteverde. ✉ *Across from Super Compro supermarket, Santa Elena* ☏ *2645–6565* ⊕ *www.exploremonteverde.com.*

A leisurely stroll across a suspension bridge in Monteverde

EXPLORING

TOP ATTRACTIONS

FAMILY **Butterfly Garden** (*Jardín de Mariposas*). Thirty species of butterflies flit about in four enclosed botanical gardens. Morning visits are best, since the butterflies are most active early in the day. Your entrance ticket (cash only) includes an hour-long guided tour under tin roofs, meaning you won't get wet on rainy days. Be sure to visit the nonprofit gift shop benefiting the local community. ⊠ *Near Monteverde Inn, Monteverde* ✛ *Take right-hand turnoff 4 km (2½ miles) past Santa Elena on road to Monteverde, continue for 2 km (1 mile)* ☎ *2645–5512* ⊕ *www. monteverdebutterflygarden.com* ✉ *$15* ⊘ *Daily 8:30–4.*

Fodor's Choice **Monteverde Cloud Forest Biological Reserve** (*Reserva Biológica Bosque* ★ *Nuboso de Monteverde*). One of Costa Rica's best-kept reserves has 13 km (8 miles) of well-marked trails, lush vegetation, and a cool, damp climate. The collision of moist winds with the Continental Divide here creates a constant mist whose particles provide nutrients for plants growing at the upper layers of the forest. Giant trees are enshrouded in a cascade of orchids, bromeliads, mosses, and ferns, and in those patches where sunlight penetrates, brilliantly colored flowers flourish. The sheer size of everything, especially the leaves of the trees, is striking. No less astounding is the variety: more than 3,000 plant species, 500 species of birds, 500 types of butterflies, and 130 different mammals have so far been cataloged at Monteverde. A damp and exotic mixture of shades, smells, and sounds, the cloud forest is also famous for its population of resplendent quetzals, which can be spotted feeding on the *aguacatillo* (similar to avocado) trees; best viewing times are early mornings from January until September, and especially during the mating season of April and May. Other forest-dwelling inhabitants include hummingbirds and multicolor frogs.

For those who don't have a lucky eye, a short-stay aquarium is in the field station; captive amphibians stay here just a week before being released back into the wild. Although the reserve limits visitors to 250 people at a time, Monteverde is one of the country's most popular destinations. We do hear complaints (and agree with them) that the reserve gets too crowded with visitors at times. Early visitors have the best chance at spotting wildlife in the protected reserve.

Allow a generous slice of time for leisurely hiking to see the forest's flora and fauna; longer hikes are made possible by some strategically placed overnight refuges along the way. At the gift shop you can buy self-guide pamphlets and books; a map is provided when you pay the entrance fee. You can navigate the reserve on your own, but the 2½-hour guided Natural History Walk (7:30 am, 11:30 am, and 1:30 pm) is invaluable for getting the most out of your visit. You may also take advantage of two-hour guided night tours starting each evening at 5:45 (reservations required). The reserve provides transport from area hotels for an extra $6. A guided walking bird-watching tour up to the reserve leaves from the park entrance each morning at 6 for groups of four to six people. Advance reservations are required. ⊠ *10 km (6 miles) south of Santa Elena, Monteverde* ☎ *2645–5122, 2253–3267 in San José* ⊕ *www.reservamonteverde.com* 🖃 *$20 entrance; $37 natural-history walk; $20 night tour; $64 morning bird-watching tour* ☉ *Daily 7–4.*

FAMILY **Monteverde Theme Park** (*Ranario de Monteverde / Frog Pond of Monteverde*). Only in Monteverde would visitors groove to the nightlife at an exhibition of 24 species of frogs, toads, and other amphibians. Bilingual biologist-guides take you through a 45-minute tour of the terrariums in the Frog Pond of Monteverde (Ranario de Monteverde), just outside Santa Elena. For the best show, come around dusk and stay well into the evening, when the critters become more active and much more vocal. (Your ticket entitles you to a second visit the same day, as well as a guided tour.) The complex has a butterfly garden with 30 different species and an insect museum. There's a small frog-and-toad-and-butterfly-theme gift shop and a zip-line tour with nine cables and a Tarzan swing. ⊠ *100 m west of Hotel Poco a Poco, Santa Elena* ☎ *2645–6320* ⊕ *www.monteverdethemepark.com* 🖃 *Frog pond and butterfly garden $14 each; combined ticket $23; zip line $35* ☉ *Frog pond, daily 9–8:30; butterfly garden, daily 9–3; zip line 9–3:30.*

Santa Elena Cloud Forest Reserve (*Reserva Bosque Nuboso Santa Elena*). Several conservation areas near Monteverde are attractive day-trip destinations, especially when the Monteverde Reserve is too busy. The 765-acre Santa Elena Reserve just west of Monteverde is a project of the Santa Elena high school, and has a series of trails of varying length and difficulty that can be walked alone or with a guide on tours that depart daily at 7:30, 9, 11:30, and 1 pm. The 1½-km (1-mile) Youth Challenge trail takes about 45 minutes to negotiate and includes an observation platform with views that extend as far as the Arenal Volcano—that is, if the clouds clear. If you're feeling hardy, try the 5-km (3-mile) Caño Negro trail. There's a shuttle service to the reserve with fixed departures and returns; reservations are required, and the cost is $3 each way. ⊠ *6 km (4 miles) north of Santa Elena, Monteverde* ☎ *2645-5390* ⊕ *www.reservasantaelena.org* ⧉ *$14 entrance; plus $15 for guide services* ⊙ *Daily 7–4.*

WORTH NOTING

FAMILY **Bat Jungle.** Butterflies, frogs, and snakes have their own Monteverde-area exhibits, and bats get equal time with guided tours that provide insight into the life of one of the planet's most misunderstood mammals. Admission includes a 45-minute guided tour through a small exhibit and glass enclosure housing nearly 100 live bats. You can watch them fly, eat, and even give birth. Reservations are recommended. ⊠ *Across from Tramonti Restaurant, Monteverde* ☎ *2645-7701* ⊕ *www. batjungle.com* ⧉ *$13* ⊙ *Daily 9–6.*

FAMILY **Children's Eternal Rain Forest** (*Bosque Eterno de los Niños*). The 54,000-acre rain forest dwarfs the Monteverde and Santa Elena reserves. It began life as a school project in Sweden among children interested in saving a piece of the rain forest, and blossomed into a fund-raising effort among students from 44 countries. The reserve's **Bajo del Tigre trail** makes for a gentle, self-guided 3½-km (2-mile) hike through secondary forest. Along the trail are 27 stations at which to stop and learn about the reserve, many with lessons geared toward kids. A separate guided twilight walk ($22) begins at 5:30 pm and lasts two hours, affording the chance to see the nocturnal side of the cloud forest; reservations are required. Much of the rest of the reserve is not open to the public, but the Monteverde Conservation League offers stays at San Gerardo and Poco Sol, two remote field stations within the forest. The $55 packages include dormitory accommodation and meals. ⊠ *100 m south of CASEM, Monteverde* ☎ *2645-5305* ⊕ *www.acmcr.org* ⧉ *$28 guided day tour; $12 self-guided day tour; $22 guided night tour; transportation from area hotels $4* ⊙ *Daily 8–4.*

Don Juan Coffee Tour. Small groups are the hallmark of these tours that last about two hours and let you see the coffee process from start to finish at the plantation of Don Juan Cruz, one of the original settlers in the area. Transportation can be arranged from all Monteverde-area lodgings. To get a taste without the tour, you can visit their café and gift store next to the post office in Santa Elena. ⊠ *2 km (1 mile) northwest of soccer field, Monteverde* ☎ *2645-7100* ⊕ *www.donjuancoffeetour. com* ⧉ *$35* ⊙ *Tours at 8, 10, 1, 3, and 5:30.*

Fodor's Choice **El Trapiche.** Two-hour tours departing at 10 am and 3 pm guide you
★ from the bean to the cup at this coffee plantation and sugarcane mill where you can sample liquor, java, and other locally made products. The hands-on tour includes a ride on an oxcart and some sweet treats made from homegrown coffee beans, sugarcane, and cacao. ⊠ *Hwy. 606, 2 km (1 mile) northwest of Santa Elena, Santa Elena* ☎ *2645-7650* ⊕ *www.eltrapichetour.com* ⧉ *$32* ⊙ *Tours Mon.–Sat. at 10 and 3, Sun. 3.*

Monteverde and Santa Elena

TO LAS JUNTAS
El Trapiche
TO TÍLARÁN
Santa Elena Cloud Forest Reserve
Selvatura
Don Juan Coffee Tour
Sky Adventures
Cerro Amigo Trail T. V. Tower
Santa Elena Reserve Office
Selvatura Office
Chamber of Tourism
Monteverde Park Office
SANTA ELENA
Original Canopy Tour
Orchid Garden
Herpetarium Adventures
Monteverde
Sendero Tranquilo Reserve
Caballeriza El Rodeo
Monteverde Theme Park
Monteverde Ecological Sanctuary
Tram Monteverde
CERRO PLANO
Monteverde Cloud Forest Biological Reserve
Bat Jungle
MONTEVERDE
La Lechería (Cheese Factory)
Hummingbird Gallery
Butterfly Garden
CASEM
Escuela de Los Amigos
Bajo del Tigre Trailhead
Children's Eternal Rain Forest
Monteverde Coffee Tour
TO PANAMERICAN HIGHWAY
TO LAGARTO, SAN JOSÉ
TO SAN LUIS
0 .5 mile
0 500 meters

KEY
❶ *Restaurants*
① *Hotels*

FAMILY **Herpetarium Adventures Monteverde.** Operated by Sky Adventures, this herpetarium holds more than 50 species of reptiles and amphibians, such as native frogs, toads, turtles, lizards, and snakes in terrariums. Some of the more impressive species are the colorful poison arrow frog, the Jesus Christ lizard, snapping turtles, tarantulas, and the red-eyed tree frog. Animals are most active around 6 pm. Admission includes guided tours in English or Spanish. ⊠ *Across from Plaza Monteverde, Monteverde* ☎ *2645–6002* ⊕ *www.skyadventures.travel/herpetarium* 🖃 *$14* ⊙ *Daily 9–7.*

Monteverde Coffee Tour. Bite your tongue before requesting Costa Rica's ubiquitous Café Britt up here. Export-quality Café Monteverde is the locally grown product, and the tour lets you see the process up close from start to finish, from the area's Turín plantation, 3 km (2 miles) north of Santa Elena where the plants are grown in the shade; transport to the *beneficio,* the processing mill where the beans are washed and dried; and finally to the roaster. Reservations are required, and pickup from area hotels is available. They also operate the Monteverde Coffee Center (coffee shop) in town next to CASEM. ⊠ *Monteverde* ☎ *2645–5550* 🖃 *$30* ⊙ *Tours at 8 am and 1:30 pm.*

Monteverde Ecological Sanctuary. This private, 52-acre wildlife refuge is laced with four trails and houses birds, sloths, agoutis, and coatimundis. You'll also come upon two waterfalls and a coffee plantation. If you can't make it all the way up to the Monteverde Reserve for the day hike, there's a guided, two-hour twilight walk that begins each evening at 5:30. Reservations are required. ⊠ *Turnoff to Jardín de Mariposas, off main road just south of Santa Elena, Monteverde* ☎ *2645–5869* ⊕ *www.santuarioecologico.com* 🖃 *Guided tour $27, self-guided tour $12, twilight walk $25* ⊙ *Daily 7–5.*

Orchid Garden (*Jardín de Orquídeas*). More than 450 species of orchids, one of which is the world's smallest, are on display. Admission includes a 30-minute tour. ⊠ *150 m south of Banco Nacional, Santa Elena* ☎ *2645–5308* ⊕ *www.monteverdeorchidgarden.net* 🖃 *$10* ⊙ *Daily 8–5.*

NEED A
BREAK?
✕ **La Lechería.** Long before tourists flocked up here, dairy farming was the foundation of Monteverde's economy. Quakers still deliver dairy to what is locally referred to as the Cheese Factory, or La Lechería. The factory store sells local cheeses and ice cream. Stop in for a cone. It's open Monday through Saturday 7:30 to 5 and Sunday 8 to 4. If you have more time, take a two-hour tour of the operation Monday through Saturday at 9 or 2. Tours are $12 and wind up with a cheese-sampling session. Reserve in advance. These folks also operate an ice-cream shop across from the Tree House restaurant on the main street in Santa Elena. ⊠ *½ km (¼ mile) south of CASEM, halfway between Santa Elena and Monteverde Reserve, Monteverde* ☎ *2645–7090 tours* ⊕ *www.monteverdecheesefactory.com.*

Bird Country

More than 890 bird species have been identified in Costa Rica, more than in the United States and Canada combined. Consequently, bird-watchers flock here by the thousands. The big attractions tend to be eye-catching species like the keel-billed toucan, but it is the diversity of shape, size, coloration, and behavior that makes bird-watching in Costa Rica so fascinating.

Tropical superstars: Parrots, parakeets, and macaws; toucans and toucanets; and the elusive but legendary resplendent quetzal are a thrill for those of us who don't see them every day.

In supporting roles: Lesser-known but equally impressive species include motmots, with their distinctive racket tails; oropéndolas, which build hanging nests; and an array of hawks, kites, and falcons.

Color me red, blue, yellow . . . : Two of the most striking species are the showy scarlet macaw and the quirky purple gallinule; tanagers, euphonias, manakins, cotingas, and trogons are some of the country's loveliest plumed creatures, but none of them matches the iridescence of the hummingbirds.

Singing in the rain: The relatively inconspicuous clay-color robin is Costa Rica's national bird. It may

look plain, but its song is melodious, and because the males sing almost constantly toward the end of the dry season—the beginning of their mating season—local legend has it that they call the rains.

The big and the small of it: The hummingbird is a mere 6.25 cm (2.5 inches) tall and weighs just over 2 grams (well under an ounce), whereas the jabiru, a long-legged stork, can grow to more than 1.2 meters (4 feet) tall and weigh up to 6.3 kg (14 pounds). Costa Rica hosts 51 members of the hummingbird family, compared with just one species for all of the United States east of the Rocky Mountains.

"Snow birds": If you're here between October and April, don't be surprised if you see some feathered friends from home. When northern birds fly south for the winter, they don't all head to Miami. Seasonal visitors like the Kentucky warbler make up about a quarter of the amazing avian panorama in Costa Rica.

Bird-watching can be done everywhere in the country. And don't let the rainy season deter you: seasonal *lagunas* (lagoons) such as Caño Negro and the swamps of Palo Verde National Park, which disappear during the dry months, are excellent places to see birds.

SPORTS AND THE OUTDOORS

HANGING BRIDGES, TRAMS, AND CANOPY TOURS

FAMILY **Original Canopy Tour.** The first company to offer zip-line tours in Costa Rica has set up 12 platforms in the canopy. Included is an optional Tarzan swing and tree-rappel. Tours last about 2½ hours and begin at 7:30, 10:30, and 2:30. ⊠ *Cerro Plano* 🕾 *2291–4465 in San José for reservations, 305/433–2241 in U.S.* ⊕ *www.canopytour.com* 🖃 *$45.*

FAMILY
Fodor's Choice
★
Selvatura. If your time in Monteverde is limited, consider spending it at Selvatura, a kind of nature-themed adventure park—complete with a canopy tour and hanging bridges—just outside the Santa Elena Reserve. A 100-bird hummingbird garden, an enclosed 20-species *mariposario* (butterfly

> ### ANTS ON PARADE
>
> Tread carefully when you see a tiny green parade on the ground before you. It's a troop of leaf-cutter ants carrying compost material to an underground nest.

garden), a *herpetario* (frog and reptile house), and insect exhibition sit near the visitor center. The only zip-line tour built entirely inside the Monteverde Cloud Forest has 12 lines and 18 platforms, with an optional Tarzan swing at the end to round out the excursion. The Tree Top Walkway takes you to heights ranging from 12 meters (36 feet) up to 60 meters (180 feet) on a 3-km (2-mile) walk. These are some of the longest and strongest bridges in the country and run through the same canopy terrain as the zip-line tour.

You can choose from numerous mix-and-match packages, depending on which activities interest you, or take it all in, with lunch included, for $121. Most visitors get by for much less, given that one day isn't really enough for all there is to do here. ⊠ *Office across from church in town; Selvatura park 7 km (4 miles) northwest of Banco Nacional, Santa Elena ✢ Next to San Gerardo Cloud Forest Reserve ☎ 2645–5929 ⊕ www.selvatura.com ☞ Prices vary, depending on package; zip-line tour $50; Tree Tops Walkway $30 ⊙ Daily 7–4.*

FAMILY
Sky Adventures. Here's a tram/zip line/hanging-bridges entertainment complex all in one. A tram takes you on a mile-long gondola ride through the rain-forest canopy. You can descend via the tram, or along a series of six hanging bridges, at heights of up to 41 meters (138 feet), connected from tree to tree. Your third descent option is 3 km (2 miles) of zip lines through the cloud-forest canopy. Imposing towers, used as support, mar the landscape somewhat. Sky Adventures also operates the herpetarium in town across from Plaza Monteverde. ⊠ *4 km (2½) northeast of town on road toward Santa Elena Reserve, Santa Elena ☎ 2645–6384 office, 2479–4100 park ⊕ www.skyadventures.travel ☞ Full package $83, tram and zip lines $71, tram and bridges $59, tram $44, bridges with guide $35, bridges self-guided $23 ⊙ Daily 7–5.*

FAMILY
Tram Monteverde (*Teleferico Costa Rica*). A two-person aerial tram, or gondola, takes you on an hour-long ride through the rain-forest canopy. You control the speed of your carriage. Alternatively, a 1½-km (1-mile) walk gives you a ground-level perspective. ⊠ *Hwy. 606, 300 m south of the school, just before Ecological Sanctuary, Monteverde ☎ 2645–5960 ☞ $30 ⊙ Daily 8–4.*

HORSEBACK RIDING

The ride from Monteverde to La Fortuna can be dangerous with outfitters that take inexperienced riders along steep trails. Desafío should be your only choice for getting from Monteverde to La Fortuna on horseback. ■ **TIP→ During rainy season (July–December), book horseback trips in the morning since rains usually begin around 2 pm.**

Caballeriza El Rodeo. Escorted 1½-hour horseback-riding tours ($30) with Caballeriza El Rodeo are on a private farm. Excursions are for everyone from beginner to experienced rider. A two-hour sunset tour ($35) begins at 3:30 pm. ⊠ *West entrance of town of Santa Elena, at tollbooth, Santa Elena* ☎ *2645–5764* ✐ *elrodeo@ice.co.cr* ⊕ *www. caballerizaelrodeo.com* 🖃 *$30.*

Desafío Adventures. This long-established company leads horseback tours between Monteverde and Arenal Volcano. You travel by car and boat, with a three-hour horseback ride on a flat trail along the lakeshore. Farms for resting the animals are at each end. This arrangement is infinitely more humane for the horses (and you) than the muddy, treacherous mountain trails used by dozens of other individuals who'll offer to take you to Arenal. ⊠ *Across from Super Compro supermarket, Santa Elena* ☎ *2645–5874, 855/818–0020 in North America* ⊕ *www. monteverdetours.com* 🖃 *$85.*

Sabine's Smiling Horses. Owner Sabine—who speaks English, French, German, and Spanish—offers two-hour treks starting at $45. In addition to the regular waterfall and canyon tours, excursions at full moon are also offered once a month. Pony rides are available for children. ⊠ *1 km (½ mile) west of the cemetery, Santa Elena* ☎ *2645–6894* ⊕ *www. horseback-riding-tour.com* 🖃 *From $45.*

WHERE TO EAT

$$ | MODERN ARGENTINE — ✕ **Café Caburé.** Launched by Argentinean–Bostonian owners who longed for quality chocolate made from local cocoa, this restaurant-bakery-chocolateria is one of only four places in Costa Rica that grinds its own cocoa beans. Start with a meal in the open-air restaurant serving savory empanadas and chipotle wraps with a creamy secret sauce. The homemade cannelloni with spinach, ricotta, and walnuts is a great vegetarian option, and the mole dishes are about as authentic as you can get, since the owner spent years perfecting her culinary skills in Oaxaca, Mexico. The curried chicken and mango salad is a big hit. When it comes to the sweet stuff, the ganache with blackberry sauce and the chocolate-passion-fruit mousse are both decadently delicious, as are the exquisite truffles. Tours of the attached chocolate factory are available daily at 1 and 4 for $15. ⑤ *Average main: $14* ⊠ *Paseo de Stella Tourist Center in Old Monteverde, near the Bat Jungle Tour, Monteverde* ☎ *2645–5020* ⊕ *www.cabure.net* ⊘ *Closed Sun.*

$$$ | COSTA RICAN | **Fodor's**Choice ★ — ✕ **Celajes.** In the wood-polished dining room of Hotel Belmar, this elegant restaurant, whose name means "sunset clouds," is indeed the best place to admire colors in the sky—the views from this lofty perch extend all the way to the coast on clear days. Soft jazz and artisanal cocktails set the tone for the farm-to-table menu, which is focused on organic ingredients sourced locally from the Belmar family ranch. Start with the gorgeous cheese platter or the refreshing grilled-watermelon salad. It's no secret that Costa Rican chicken is remarkably flavorful, but here it's downright divine—stuffed with goat cheese, prosciutto, and spinach, and bathed in a white-wine-and-passion-fruit sauce. The homemade pastas and filet mignon with a coffee glaze are also outstanding.

Although the tiramisu is big enough to share, after one bite you may suddenly become a little selfish. From 4:30 to 5:30, you can swing by for "Tico Time" featuring free appetizers, drink specials, and craft beers from their on-site microbrewery. ⑤ *Average main: $22 ✉ Hotel Belmar, 4 km (2½ miles) north of town, adjacent to Monteverde Cloud Forest Reserve, Monteverde ☎ 2645–5201, 866/978–6424 from U.S. and Canada ⊕ www.hotelbelmar.net.*

$$$
ECLECTIC

✕ **De Lucía.** Cordial Chilean owner José Belmar is the walking, talking (in five languages) menu here, and he's always on hand to chat with guests. The handsome wooden restaurant with red mahogany tables is given a distinct South American flavor by an array of Andean tapestries and ceramics. Entrées include sea bass with garlic sauce and orange chicken served with grilled vegetables and fried plantains. They also boast tasty vegetable lasagna and the best hamburgers in town, which you can wash down with a frosted mug of craft beer. An excellent dessert choice is *tres leches* (three milks), a richer-than-rich cake. ⑤ *Average main: $18 ✉ Turnoff to Jardín de Mariposas, off main road between Santa Elena and Monteverde, Cerro Plano ✛ 125 meters south of public school ☎ 2645–5337 ⊕ www.deluciamonteverde.com.*

$$
MIDDLE EASTERN

✕ **Monteverde Beer House.** Middle Eastern food and craft beer are a rarity in Santa Elena (or anywhere in Costa Rica), but this bold combination has filled a void in the local culinary scene and made this spot a favorite of those seeking a cold brew and hot grub after a drizzly day in Monteverde. An open kitchen keeps things honest, amid a simple setting of cement floors and wood-plank tables. The menu is simply a 10-line card listing kebabs, falafel, hummus, feta salads, pita sandwiches, and such. The hot fries pair nicely with the beer, which includes a chocolate stout. There's occasionally live music on Saturday nights. ⑤ *Average main: $10 ✉ Across from Super Compro, 50 m from Santa Elena bus station, Santa Elena ☎ 2645–6943.*

$$
COSTA RICAN

✕ **Morpho's.** With its rain-forest murals, glass patios, and tree-stump tables, you're never far from nature in this restaurant named for the mesmerizing blue butterflies that flit throughout Costa Rica. Start early with a fresh milk shake, and then return after a hike for the flavorful chicken, pork, beef, or fish dishes, each served with steamed vegetables, parsley potatoes, and creative sauces like pineapple curry, blue cheese, or bay-leaf-and-garlic sauce (a take on chimichurri). Opened in 1996, this Santa Elena staple started out as a vegetarian restaurant, and you'll still find veggie burgers, meatless *casados,* and fresh salads. The top must-try at Morpho's is the peanut-butter pie, prepared daily by the owner's mother. ⑤ *Average main: $15 ✉ 50 m east of Banco Nacional, Santa Elena ☎ 2645–7373 ⊕ www.morphosrestaurant.com.*

$$
BAKERY
FodorsChoice
★

✕ **Orchid Coffee Shop** (*Cafe Las Orquídeas*). It's astonishing the level of culinary perfection that comes out of this A-frame shack. Yes, the menu is enormous, but take your time and let your appetite guide you. The crepes, pancakes, granola, and French toast are all made from scratch. Tomato soup is comforting on a rainy day, and the veggie panini is stuffed with all kinds of organic goodness. Choose from over 25 types of coffee, including the heartwarming "espresso moka" made with hot chocolate, whisky, and mint. The smoothies couldn't be fresher—each one is made with homemade yogurt and local ingredients like pineapple, cucumber, carrot, and basil. With free Wi-Fi, ambient music, and local artwork, the cheerful setting in the center of town is the ideal place to take a break. Save your receipt for a $2 discount on admission to the neighboring Orchid Garden. ⑤ *Average main: $10* ✉ *Next to the Orchid Garden, 150 m south of Banco Nacional, Santa Elena* ☎ *2645–6850.*

$$$
LATIN AMERICAN

✕ **Sofía.** Bilingual waiters in crisp black aprons scurry attentively around the three dining rooms serving a wide variety of dishes. Start with yuca croquettes filled with local provolone, followed by such mouthwatering favorites as shrimp in mango-coconut curry or chicken served with a guava reduction. Other standouts include the sweet-and-sour-fig roasted loin, and the chile relleno. There's also an extensive wine and cocktail selection. ⑤ *Average main: $18* ✉ *Turnoff to Jardín de Mariposas, off main road between Santa Elena and Monteverde, Cerro Plano* ☎ *2645–7017.*

$
CAFÉ

✕ **Stella's Bakery.** This local institution is a good place to get an early-morning fix before heading to the Monteverde Reserve. Pastries, rolls, muffins, natural juices, and coffee are standard breakfast fare, and light sandwiches, soups, and quiches are on offer at lunch. There is also a homemade lasagna if you're in the mood for a hearty meal. ⑤ *Average main: $7* ✉ *Across from CASEM, Monteverde* ☎ *2645–5560.*

$$
ITALIAN

✕ **Tramonti.** Named for a town in southwestern Italy, this glass-walled restaurant is warm and inviting with dangling fairy lights, hardwood floors, candles dripping onto old wine bottles, and chefs tossing dough high overhead beside a wood-fired oven. The *pulpo* (octopus) and beef carpaccios are ultrathin, a perfect accompaniment for the homemade rolls dipped in chili-and-garlic olive oil. Pizzas are served on wooden paddles, and come piled high with toppings like asparagus, mushrooms, ricotta, and Gorgonzola. Calzones, eggplant ravioli, and seafood and meat dishes are served in hearty portions. Service is excellent; takeout is available. ⑤ *Average main: $14* ✉ *3 km from Monteverde Reserve, Across from Bat Jungle, Monteverde* ☎ *2645–6120* ⊕ *www.tramonticr.com.*

$$
ECLECTIC

✕ **Tree House.** It's more about the setting than the food and service at this two-story restaurant built around a 60-year-old ficus tree on Santa Elena's main street. Branches shelter tables from the afternoon mist. The menu mixes pastas and seafood with Costa Rican cuisine; for a taste of everything, try the típico platter. Favorites include tilapia with mushroom sauce and fajitas. The service can be "leisurely" or "slow," depending on your perspective. During the month of December, there's live Latin music 7:30–9:30 pm. ⑤ *Average main: $14* ✉ *Across from Glass Art Studio, Santa Elena* ☎ *2645–5751* ⊕ *www.treehouse.cr.*

WHERE TO STAY

Most hotels in Monteverde don't have air-conditioning or heaters in the rooms, so you might have to crack a window or grab an extra blanket. It also helps to pack accordingly. Since Monteverde caters to wildlife enthusiasts and bird-watchers, most hotels serve breakfast from 6 to 9, with checkout at 10 am. If you're not an early riser, be sure to request a wake-up call so that you don't miss breakfast.

$$
HOTEL

⛨ **Arco Iris Lodge.** You're almost in the center of town, but you'd never know it at this tranquil spot set on 4 acres of birding trails where cozy cabins range from rustic to plush and come with porches. **Pros:** attentive owner and staff; terrific breakfast; ecology-minded place; centrally located. **Cons:** extra charge for breakfast; not all rooms have Wi-Fi; front rooms get some street noise. $ *Rooms from: $91* ⊠ *50 m south of Banco Nacional, Santa Elena* ☎ *2645–5067* ⊕ *www.arcoirislodge. com* ⮑ *20 cabins, 1 house* ⦿ *No meals.*

$$
B&B/INN

⛨ **Casa Batsú.** This charmingly modest B&B is owned and operated by a lovely Costa Rican family that takes pride in every detail, from the homemade breakfasts and manicured gardens to the spotless rooms and warm hospitality. **Pros:** outstanding breakfasts; gracious hosts; excellent value. **Cons:** often books up well in advance; thin walls; cash only. $ *Rooms from: $99* ⊠ *Hwy. 606, 1½ km (1 mile) south of Santa Elena, 100 m northeast from El Tubu Gas Station, Monteverde* ☎ *2645–7004, 303/800–8826 in North America* ⊕ *www.casabatsu.org* ⮑ *3 rooms* ⦿ *Breakfast* ⊟ *No credit cards.*

$$$
HOTEL

⛨ **El Establo Mountain Hotel.** The area's largest, grandest hotel gets high marks for its huge suites, plush decor, a long list of amenities, and many activities. **Pros:** luxurious furnishings; spacious rooms; many activities; great views. **Cons:** massive grounds require shuttle van to navigate; no air-conditioning or heaters; Wi-Fi doesn't reach all rooms; rooms lack artwork, patio furniture, and coffeemakers. $ *Rooms from: $215* ⊠ *3½ km (2 miles) northwest of Monteverde, Monteverde* ☎ *2645–5110* ⊕ *www.hotelelestablo.com* ⮑ *124 rooms, 31 suites* ⦿ *Breakfast.*

$$
HOTEL

⛨ **El Sol.** A charming German–Spanish family tends to guests at this quintessential get-away-from-it-all place just 10 minutes down the mountain from—and a noticeable few degrees warmer than—Santa Elena. **Pros:** great views; whimsically decorated cabins; lovely hosts; same rates year-round. **Cons:** need a car to get here; cash only; Wi-Fi in common areas only; breakfast costs extra. $ *Rooms from: $125* ⊠ *Hwy. 606, 5 km (3 miles) southwest of Santa Elena in La Lindora, Monteverde* ☎ *2645–5838* ⊕ *www.elsolnuestro.com* ⊟ *No credit cards* ⮑ *2 cabins* ⦿ *No meals.*

$$$
HOTEL

⛨ **Fonda Vela.** Steep-roofed chalets have large bedrooms with white-stucco walls, wood floors, and huge windows; some have views of the wooded grounds; others, of the far-off Gulf of Nicoya. **Pros:** secluded location close to reserve; large rooms; indoor pool. **Cons:** far from town; rough road to get here; restaurant closed in low season. $ *Rooms from: $176* ⊠ *1½ km (1 mile) northwest of Monteverde Reserve entrance, Monteverde* ☎ *2645–5125* ⊕ *www.fondavela.com* ⮑ *38 rooms* ⦿ *No meals.*

$$$$
B&B/INN
Fodor's Choice
★

⛨ **Hidden Canopy Treehouses.** Nestled among 13½ acres of rolling hills nearly 3 km (2 miles) from town, five luxury tree houses have wrap-around decks, driftwood headboards, tree-stump nightstands, waterfall showers, and skylight ceilings, ultimately fading the line between nature and decor. **Pros:** great happy hour at sunset; huge film library and board games for guests; exceptional breakfast; rooms have dehumidifiers. **Cons:** two-night minimum stay; patchy Wi-Fi in rooms; no kids under 14; check out at 10 am. $ *Rooms from: $345* ✉ *300 m east of crossroad to Los Nubes, before Sky Adventures Park, Santa Elena* ☎ *2645-5447* ⊕ *www.hiddencanopy.com* ☾ *Closed Sept. 15–Nov. 1* ⇨ *5 tree houses, 2 rooms* ⦿ *Breakfast.*

$$$
HOTEL
Fodor'sChoice
★

⛬ **Hotel Belmar.** Inspired by the owners' years in Austria, two spacious chalets built into a hillside command expansive views of the Gulf of Nicoya and the hilly peninsula and contain elegant, airy, and downright regal rooms—all with balconies, minibars, polished woods, and plush white duvets. **Pros:** excellent restaurant; free in-room coffee delivery; beautifully maintained; eco-friendly. **Cons:** far from town; steep walk if on foot; no TVs; breakfast not included in rate. $ *Rooms from: $189* ✉ *4 km (2½ miles) north of Monteverde, Monteverde* ☎ *2645-5201* ⊕ *www.hotelbelmar.net* ⇨ *22 rooms* ⦿ *No meals.*

$$
HOTEL
FAMILY

⛬ **Los Pinos.** This 18-acre private reserve contains 16 cozy cabins with fully equipped kitchens in which you can prepare meals with produce from the hotel's hydroponic vegetable garden. **Pros:** free vegetables from on-site garden; excellent value; spacious cabins that are good for families or groups. **Cons:** some cabins are slightly dated; no restaurant or meals; steep hike to some cabins. $ *Rooms from: $85* ✉ *200 m east of Cerro Plano School, Montezuma* ☎ *2645-5252* ⊕ *www.lospinos.net* ⇨ *16 cabins* ⦿ *No meals.*

$
HOTEL

⛬ **Monteverde Inn.** Located within Valle Escondido Preserve, basic bedrooms have stunning views of the Gulf of Nicoya as well as hardwood floors, firm beds, and powerful, hot showers—and are a great budget option. **Pros:** good rock-bottom budget value; good views; hearty breakfasts. **Cons:** Spartan rooms; cash only; rough road to hotel. $ *Rooms from: $65* ✉ *100 meters south of Butterfly Garden, Cerro Plano* ☎ *2645-5156* ⊕ *www.valleescondidopreserve.com* ▭ *No credit cards* ⇨ *14 rooms* ⦿ *Breakfast.*

$$$
HOTEL

⛬ **Monteverde Lodge and Gardens.** Reminiscent of a ski lodge, this longtime favorite has extremely comfortable rooms with vaulted ceilings and great views with rates often packaged with a long list of nature activities. **Pros:** rustic luxury; attentive service; private dinners in the butterfly garden; great hiking trails. **Cons:** ground-floor rooms can be noisy; rooms have poor lighting; breakfast ends at 8:30; no TVs might be an issue for some. $ *Rooms from: $188* ✉ *After Hotel Poco a Poco, 500 m to lodge entrance on right, Santa Elena* ☎ *2645-5057, 2257-0766 in San José* ⊕ *www.monteverdelodge.com* ⇨ *24 rooms* ⦿ *Breakfast.*

$$
HOTEL

⛬ **Trapp Family Lodge.** The closest lodge to the Monteverde reserve (but 6 km [4 miles] from the town center) has enormous rooms, with woodpaneled walls and ceilings, marvelously crafted wood furniture, balconies, and lovely views from most. **Pros:** spacious rooms; same rates year-round; closest lodging to reserve entrance. **Cons:** 4 miles from town; rough road to get here; no a/c, fans, or screens on windows; spotty Wi-Fi in rooms. $ *Rooms from: $118* ✉ *Main road from Monteverde Reserve, Monteverde* ☎ *2645-5858* ⊕ *www.trapphotelmonteverde.com* ⇨ *26 rooms* ⦿ *Breakfast.*

SHOPPING

ARTS AND CRAFTS

Cooperativa de Artesanía de Santa Elena y Monteverde (*CASEM*). An artisans' cooperative made up of 85 women and five men sells locally made crafts. The prices are higher than they are at most other places, but the high quality and the knowledge that you are contributing to the livelihood of the community justifies paying a bit more. The attached restaurant serves typical Costa Rican dishes. ⊠ *Next to El Bosque Lodge, Monteverde* ☎ *2645–5190* ☾ *Daily 7:30–5.*

Hummingbird Gallery. Standouts among the books, jewelry, T-shirts, and Costa Rican coffee on display here, are photographs by nature specialists Michael and Patricia Fogden. This is a great place to emulate their efforts: you can capture an image of a hummingbird in action as hundreds flutter around the feeders near the coffee shop. ⊠ *Outside entrance to Monteverde Reserve, Monteverde* ☎ *2645–5030.*

Monteverde Art House. This lovely art gallery offers local paintings, sculptures, photography, pottery, and jewelry. The wooden artwork is amazing, and some of it is displayed inside a unique gazebo. ⊠ *100 m north of Cerro Plano School, Cerro Plano* ☎ *2645–5275* ⊕ *www.monteverdearthouse.com* ☾ *Daily 9–6.*

BOOKSTORES

Librería Chunches. The well-stocked shelves include a good selection of new and used books in English, as well as Spanish-language literature and natural-history guides. They also offer a book exchange. ⊠ *25 m south of Banco Nacional, Santa Elena* ☎ *2645–5147* ☾ *Closed Sun.*

SPECIALTY FOODS

Monteverde Whole Foods Market (*Coopesanta Elena*). This small local store carries organic goods and is the distributor for the area's gourmet Monteverde coffee and accoutrements. ⊠ *Next to CASEM, Monteverde* ☎ *2645–5927.*

NIGHTLIFE

"Wild nightlife" takes on its own peculiar meaning here. You can still get up close with nature after the sun has gone down. Several of the reserves have guided evening walks—advance reservations and separate admission are required—and the Frog Pond of Monteverde, the Herpetarium, and the Bat Jungle keep evening hours. Beyond that, you'll probably while away the evening in a restaurant or your hotel dining room chatting with fellow travelers. Monteverde is an early-to-bed, early-to-rise kind of place—some hotels end breakfast as early as 8:30, so it's best not to oversleep.

CAÑO NEGRO NATIONAL WILDLIFE REFUGE

100 km (60 miles) (2 hrs) north of La Fortuna

If you're seeking a national park experience without the crowds, Caño Negro should be on your list—its excellent birding and wildlife viewing still have an undiscovered feel. Long a favorite among fishing enthusiasts and bird-watchers, this remote area is off the beaten track and may be difficult to get to if your time in Costa Rica is short. You can cross into Nicaragua, via Los Chiles, but there are almost no roads in this part of southern Nicaragua, making access to the rest of the country nearly impossible. The border crossing at Peñas Blancas, near the North Pacific coast, is far more user-friendly.

GETTING HERE AND AROUND

The highway from La Fortuna to Los Chiles, the gateway to the Caño Negro National Wildlife Refuge, is one of the best maintained in the northern lowlands. You can catch public buses in San José at Terminal 7-10 twice a day for a trip of about five hours to Los Chiles, with many stops. Public buses also operate between La Fortuna and Los Chiles. If they have room, many tour companies will allow you to ride along on their shuttles for around $30. If you're not staying way up here, an organized tour of the reserve from La Fortuna is the way most visitors get to and from.

EXPLORING

Fodor'sChoice **Caño Negro National Wildlife Refuge** (*Refugio Nacional de Vida Silves-*
★ *tre Caño Negro*). It's a shame that Caño Negro doesn't grab the same amount of attention in wildlife-viewing circles as other destinations in Costa Rica. Due to the recent saturation of visitors at Tortuguero National Park to the east, however, Caño Negro is starting to gain recognition among bird-watchers and nature lovers for its isolation, diversity, and abundant wildlife. As a feeding ground for both resident and migratory birds, the refuge is home to more than 350 bird species, 310 plants, and at least 160 species of mammals. The reserve is a splendid place to watch waterfowl and resident exotic animals, including cougars, jaguars, and several species of monkeys. It's also one of the best places to see a basilisk, more commonly known as the "Jesus Christ Lizard" because of its ability to run on water. Comprising the vast wetland sanctuary is a web of channels and lagoons ideal for exploring by boat, and even more so by canoe to reach remote lowlands, swamps, and seasonal floodplains. If you're not staying at one of the two lodges up here, the refuge is easily visited as a day trip from La Fortuna. It's important to note that most Arenal-area tour operators do not actually enter the refuge (to avoid paying the $5 per person entrance fee). Tour companies often claim that the areas surrounding the park are equally spectacular, but this is not the case. Although you're likely to see wildlife on the outskirts, you won't see a fraction of what you might encounter inside the park, which lacks the parade of tour boats disturbing the habitat. For the best tour of the refuge, book through resident guide Jimmy Gutierrez at Natural Lodge Caño Negro. There are no public facilities in the park, which consists

5

mostly of wetlands fed by the Frio River and best explored only by boat. Bring a camera, binoculars, and plenty of bug spray. *For more information, see highlighted listing in this chapter.* ✉ *Off Hwy. 35, 180 km (112 miles) north of La Fortuna* ☎ *2460–0620, 2471–1309* ⊕ *www.sinac.go.cr* ✉ *$5; fishing license $30* ⊙ *Daily 7–4.*

Natural Lodge Caño Negro. Unlike most La Fortuna–based tour operators visiting the area, Natural Lodge Caño Negro offers excursions that actually take place inside the reserve rather than along its outskirts. Resident guide Jimmy Gutierrez is an expert on local wildlife and can arrange motorized boat tours or excursions by canoe to reach remote areas not accessible by motorboat. A two-hour wetlands tour departs at 8 am or 2 pm and costs $40; a three-hour tour starting at 8 am includes lunch and costs $65. Sportfishing, day hikes, and night tours are also available. Rates do not include the $5 park entrance fee. ✉ *250 m west of the school* ☎ *2471–1426, 8352–6555* ⊕ *www. canonegrolodge.com* ✉ *From $40.*

◾ DID YOU KNOW?

Now you see it, now you don't: Caño Negro's lake forms during the rainy season when the Río Frío floods its banks. By February, dry conditions begin to shrink the lake, and by April, all that's left are a few spotty lagoons.

WHERE TO STAY

$$
HOTEL

⊡ Hotel de Campo. Under the shade of tropical fruit trees, white bungalows of high-quality wood each contain two bright, sparkling rooms with terra-cotta tile floors and front patios that open onto a central swimming pool. **Pros:** secluded location; close to reserve; tons of wildlife. **Cons:** need a car to get here and road is very rough; food slightly overpriced; small pool. ⑤ *Rooms from: $95* ✉ *Caño Negro village, 100 m past grocery* ☎ *2471–1012* ⊕ *www.hoteldecampo.com* ⤴ *17 rooms* ⦿ *Breakfast.*

$$
HOTEL

⊡ Natural Lodge Caño Negro. It might come as a surprise to find such attractive and comfortable rooms, with nice appointments and high ceilings, in so remote a place, but the lack of pretense and laid-back atmosphere fit right into the surroundings on the east side of the reserve. **Pros:** secluded location; close to reserve; excellent boat tour; great for bird-watching. **Cons:** need a car to get here; no Wi-Fi in the rooms; rough and bumpy road. ⑤ *Rooms from: $125* ✉ *Caño Negro village, 250 m west of the school* ☎ *2471–1426, 8352–6555* ⊕ *www. canonegrolodge.com* ⤴ *42 rooms* ⦿ *Breakfast.*

GUANACASTE AND THE NICOYA PENINSULA

WELCOME TO GUANACASTE AND THE NICOYA PENINSULA

TOP REASONS TO GO

★ **Beaches:** White sand, black sand, palm-fringed strands, beaches for swimming, partying, surfing, and sunbathing—the sheer variety of Guanacaste's beaches can't be beat.

★ **Big wind:** From November to May, the trade winds whip across Northern Guanacaste with a velocity and consistency that make the Bahía Salinas a world-class windsurfing and kitesurfing destination.

★ **Endangered nature:** Guanacaste's varied national parks protect some of Central America's last remaining patches of tropical dry forest, a distinctive ecosystem where you might spot magpie jays or howler monkeys in the branches of a gumbo-limbo tree.

★ **Scuba diving:** Forget the pretty tropical fish. Sharks, rays, sea turtles, and moray eels are the large-scale attractions for divers here.

★ **Surfing:** Offshore winds, warm water, and hollow barrels make for epic waves at more than a dozen Guanacaste beaches.

1 Far Northern Guanacaste. Dry, hot Far Northern Guanacaste is traditionally ranching country, but it does include the impressive wildernesses of Santa Rosa and Rincón de la Vieja national parks, the latter of which holds one of Costa Rica's most active volcanoes. Liberia, the capital of Guanacaste Province, is the closest town to Costa Rica's second-largest airport. Farther to the north is Bahía Salinas, second only to Lake Arenal for wind- and kitesurfing.

2 Guanacaste Pacific Coast. The number and variety of beaches along the northern border of the Nicoya Peninsula, from the Papagayo Peninsula to Tamarindo and down to Playa Junquillal, make it a top beach destination. Each beach has its specialty, be it surfing, fishing, diving, or just plain relaxing. Hotels and restaurants are in generous supply.

3 The Nicoya Peninsula. Lively beach towns dot the coast of the Nicoya Peninsula from Nosara down to Playa Tambor, at the southern tip. In the south, communities are small and quiet, with a funky, European vibe. National parks Palo Verde and Barra Honda are the main attractions in the interior of the peninsula. The former is a prime bird-watching park; the latter has caves and waterfalls to explore.

GETTING ORIENTED

Guanacaste Province—a vast swath of land in northwestern Costa Rica—is bordered by the Pacific Ocean to the west and the looming Cordillera de Guanacaste volcanic mountain range to the east. To the south is the Nicoya Peninsula, with almost continuous beaches along more than 100 km (62 miles) of Pacific coastline. Some roads are unpaved, especially those to the national parks and those connecting less developed beaches, so the best way to get around is in a 4WD vehicle. Take a plane, bus, or shuttle van to Liberia and pick up your rental car there.

6

RINCÓN DE LA VIEJA NATIONAL PARK

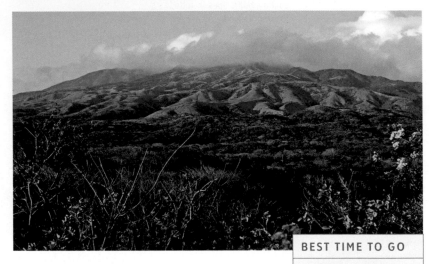

Rincón de la Vieja National Park is Costa Rica's mini-Yellowstone, with volcanic hot springs and bubbling mud pools, refreshing waterfalls, and cool forest trails. Often shrouded in clouds, the currently active volcano dominates the landscape northwest of Liberia, rising above the sunbaked plains.

It has two windswept peaks, Santa María, 1,916 meters (6,323 feet) high on the east slope, and Rincón de la Vieja at 1,895 meters (6,254 feet) on the west. The latter slope has an active crater that hardy hikers can climb to when the trail is open. It's usually closed in the wet season, and when the crater is too active. Fumaroles on its lower slope constantly let off steam. Las Pailas entrance has the most accessible trails, including an easy loop trail that wends past all the interesting volcanic features and a waterfall that flows from August to November. When the volcano is very active, the entire park is closed to visitors, so check with lodges or tour operators before you go. *(For more information, see the review in this chapter.)*

BEST TIME TO GO

Good times to visit are January through May, during the dry season. December and January can be very windy, but that means temperatures stay cooler for hiking. May to November—the green season—is when the fumaroles and boiling mud pots are most active, but the crater is often covered in clouds so it's not the best time to hike to the top. During wet season, trails are slippery and muddy, and can get crowded during school break (from mid-December through February). If you're planning a long hike, get here early since the park officially closes at 3 pm but you can still exit up until 5 pm. The park is closed Monday all year.

BEST WAYS TO EXPLORE

BIRD-WATCHING

Wherever you walk in this park, you are bound to hear the three-note song of the long-tailed manakin. It sounds something like "Toledo," and that's what the locals call this bird. Along with their lavish, long tail feathers, the males are famous for their cooperative courting dance: two pals leap back and forth over each other, but only the senior male gets any girl who falls for this act. The hard-to-spot rock wren lives closer to the top of the volcano. Birding is excellent most of the year here except for December and January when the weather is dry but often too windy to distinguish between a fluttering leaf or a flittering bird. Outside of birds, this park hosts the largest population of the guaria orchid, Costa Rica's national flower.

HIKING

The only way to explore the park trails is on foot, along well-marked paths that range from easy loops to longer, more demanding climbs. The ranger station at Las Pailas entrance provides maps of the park trails and restrooms before you set off. The easiest hike is Las Pailas loop, which starts just past the ranger station; it takes about two hours to hike. If you want to venture farther afield, follow the signs for La Cangreja trail. After passing through dense, cool forest, you'll emerge through an avenue of giant agave plants into an open, windy meadow. Your reward is the cool waterfall and swimming hole at the end of the trail. There are also warm springs in the rocks surrounding the pool, so you can alternate between warm and cool water in this natural spa.

ON HORSEBACK

Saddle up to explore the lower slopes of the volcano, just outside the park borders. Local ranches and lodges organize daylong trail rides to waterfalls and sulfur springs. Your nose will tell you when you are approaching the springs—it's not the picnic lunch gone bad, it's the distinctive rotten-egg smell of sulfur.

TOP REASONS TO GO

Wildlife
Here you can find more than 300 species of birds, plus mammals such as white-tailed deer, coyotes, howler and capuchin monkeys, armadillos, and the occasional harlequin snake (not poisonous).

6

Climbing to the Crater
The hike to the crater summit is the most demanding but also the most dramatic. The trail climbs 8 km (5 miles) through shaded forest, then up a sunbaked, treeless slope to the windswept crater, where temperatures plummet. Be sure to check in at the ranger station before attempting this hike; the trail may be closed when the volcano is dangerously active.

Geological Wonders
Three-kilometer (2-mile) Las Pailas loop trail showcases the park's famous geothermal features. Along the trail you'll see fumaroles with steam hissing out of ground vents, a *volcancito* (baby volcano), and boiling mud fields named after pots (*pailas*) used for boiling down sugarcane.

SANTA ROSA NATIONAL PARK

Renowned for its wildlife, Santa Rosa National Park, part of the larger Guanacaste Conservation Area, protects the largest swath of extant lowland dry forest in Central America, about 91,000 acres. *Dry* is the operative word here, with less than 1,500 millimeters (59 inches) of rainfall a year in some parts of the park.

If you station yourself near watering holes in the dry season—January to April—you may spot deer, coyotes, coatis, and armadillos. The park also has the world's only fully protected nesting beach for olive ridley sea turtles. Treetop inhabitants include spider, capuchin, and howler monkeys, as well as hundreds of bird species. The deciduous forest here includes giant kapok, guanacaste, and mahogany trees, as well as calabash, acacia, and gumbo-limbo trees with their distinctive peeling bark. The park is also of historical significance to Costa Rica because it was here, in 1856, that an army of Costa Rican volunteers decisively defeated an invading force of mercenaries led by an American adventurer named William Walker. *(For more information, see the review in this chapter.)*

BEST TIME TO GO

Dry season is the best time to visit if you want to see wildlife. The vegetation is sparse, making for easy observation. It's also the best time to drive to the park's beaches. Be aware: it can get very hot and very dry, so take plenty of water if you plan on hiking. In the rainy season, trails can become mud baths, excluding the Indio Desnudo Trail, which is fine year-round.

FUN FACT

Moving from sparse, sunlit secondary forest into the park's shady primary forest areas, you can experience an instant temperature drop of as much as 5C° (9F°). Temperatures seldom fall below a pleasant 20°C (68°F), but you still might want to wear layers.

BEST WAYS TO EXPLORE

GETTING AROUND

Only the first 12 km (7 miles) of the park's roads are accessible by vehicles. The rest of the park's 20 km (12 miles) of hiking trails have been significantly improved. It's easy to drive to La Casona headquarters along a paved road and pick up a short loop hiking trail, but beyond that point you need a 4WD vehicle. During the rainy season, the roads beyond La Casona are often impassable even to 4WD vehicles. Get an early start for any hikes to take advantage of cooler temperatures.

A HISTORICAL TOUR

Costa Rica doesn't have many historical sites—relics of its colonial past have mostly been destroyed by earthquakes and volcanic eruptions. So La Casona, the symbolic birthplace of Costa Rica's nationhood, is a particularly revered site. Most Costa Ricans come to Santa Rosa on a historical pilgrimage. Imagine the nation's horror when the place was burned to the ground in a fire purposely set in 2001 by disgruntled poachers who had been fined by park rangers. The government, schoolchildren, and private businesses came to the rescue, raising the money to restore the historic hacienda and replace the exhibits of antique farm tools and historical photos.

TURTLE-WATCHING

Thousands of olive ridley sea turtles emerge from the sea every year, from July to December, to dig nests and deposit eggs on the park's protected beaches at Playa Nancite and Playa Naranjo. Pacific green sea turtles and the huge leatherbacks also clamber ashore, but in much smaller numbers. If you're a hardy outdoors type, you can hike the 12 km (8 miles) to Playa Naranjo and pitch your tent near the beach. Unlike most other turtle-nesting beaches with organized tours, this is a natural spectacle you'll get to witness far from any crowds. Playa Nancite is a totally protected beach and thus off-limits to tourists.

TOP REASONS TO GO

Explore the Forest

The short (about 1-km [½-mile]) La Casona nature-trail loop, which starts from the park headquarters, is a great way to get a sampling of dry tropical forest and to spot wildlife. Look for signs leading to the *Indio Desnudo* (Naked Indian) path, named after the local word for gumbo-limbo trees.

Serious Surfing

Off Playa Naranjo lies the famous Witch's Rock, a towering rock formation famous for its surfing breaks. If you're interested in checking it out but don't feel like walking for miles, take a boat from Playas del Coco, Playa Hermosa, or Playa Tamarindo.

Wildlife-Watching

Wildlife is easy to spot here thanks to the low-density foliage of this tropical dry forest. Scan the treetops and keep an eye out for spider, white-faced capuchin, and howler monkeys. If you're lucky you might even spot an ocelot.

6

PALO VERDE NATIONAL PARK

One of the best wildlife- and bird-watching parks in the country, Palo Verde extends over 198 square km (76 square miles) of dry deciduous forest, bordered on the west by the wide Tempisque River.

With fairly flat terrain and less density than a rain forest, wildlife is often easier to spot here. Frequent sightings include monkeys, coatis, peccaries, lizards, and snakes. Keep an eye out for the harlequin snake. It's nonpoisonous but its coloring mimics the deadly coral snake.

The park contains seasonal wetlands at the end of the rainy season that provide a temporary home for migratory and resident aquatic birds, including herons, wood storks, jabirus, and flamingo-like roseate spoonbills. Crocodiles can be spotted in the waters of the Tempisque River year-round, and storks nest on islands at the mouth of the river where it empties into the Gulf of Nicoya. Trails are well marked, but the weather here can be very hot and windy. Mosquitoes, especially in the marshy areas, are rampant during the wet season (May–December). *(For more information, see the review in this chapter.)*

BEST TIME TO GO

The best time of year to visit is at the beginning of the dry season, especially in January and February, when the seasonal wetlands are shrinking and birds and wildlife are concentrated around smaller ponds. During the month of April, the wetlands are completely dry. Set off early in the morning or after 3 in the afternoon, when the heat is less intense.

FUN FACT

The park is named after the lacy, light-green palo verde bush, also known as the Jerusalem thorn. Even when it loses its leaves, this tree can still photosynthesize through its trunk, so it can withstand the droughts common to this area.

BEST WAYS TO EXPLORE

BIRD-WATCHING

The greatest number of wildlife species you're likely to see here are birds, close to 300 recorded species. Many of them are aquatic birds drawn to the park's vast marshes and seasonal wetlands. The most sought-after aquatic bird is the jabiru stork, a huge white bird with a red neck and long black bill. You may well spot it soaring overhead—it's hard to miss. Palo Verde and surrounding areas are the most important breeding sites for this species.

PARK STRATEGIES

Unlike many of the other national parks, you can drive 7 km (4½ miles) of fairly rough road from the park entrance to the OTS research station, where most of the trailheads begin. From that point, the best way to see the park is on foot. Plan to spend a couple of nights in the dormitory-style park lodge so that you can get an early-morning start. You'll want to start early because this is a very, very hot area. Hike open areas in the cooler mornings and then choose shaded forest trails for hikes later in the day. Make sure you have a good sun hat, too.

RIVER CRUISE

A river does run through the park, so a delightful and less strenuous wildlife-viewing option is to cruise down the Tempisque River on a chartered boat with a guide who'll do the spotting for you. Without a boat, you are limited to observing the marshy areas and riverbanks from a long distance. Be sure the boat you choose has a bilingual naturalist on board who knows the English names of birds and animals. River cruises are by reservation only, which can be arranged through the OTS research station.

TOP REASONS TO GO

Birds, Birds, Birds
Even if you're not used to looking at birds, you'll be impressed by the waves of migratory waterbirds that use this park as a way station on their routes. Think of the 2001 documentary *Winged Migration* and you'll have an idea of the number of birds that flock here.

Lots of Wild Animals
Hiking the forest trails is hot work, especially in the dry season. But the wildlife viewing here makes it worthwhile. Watch for monkeys, peccaries, spiny tailed iguanas, and coatis. Take plenty of water with you wherever you walk, and use insect repellent or wear long sleeves and pants.

Outdoor Adventures
The Organization for Tropical Studies has a number of activities to choose from, including guided nature walks, mountain biking, boat tours, and even an occasional nighttime tour. The park service offers bunk-bed lodging without air-conditioning.

6

Updated
by Marlise
Kast-Myers

Reliably sunny, dry weather brings planeloads of sun-starved Northerners to the North Pacific area of Costa Rica every winter, and a windswept coastline makes Guanacaste and the Nicoya Peninsula popular with surfers eager to relive the legendary "Endless Summer" of the sport's early years.

Ever since the 1966 cult-classic film put Costa Rica on the map, surfers and travelers alike have flocked to the beaches where waves peel, hammocks sway, and monkeys and iguanas clamber in treetops. It's easy to understand why many who come to visit return year after year or even devise a plan to stay; Guanacaste and the Nicoya Peninsula cast their spell the moment you enter the rain forest or hit the coast. From the luxury resorts and cattle ranches in Northern Guanacaste to the surf towns and fishing villages in the Nicoya Peninsula, the region serves up everything from high-rise resorts to utter isolation with a side of sustainable living. An abundance of marine life and stellar diving spots also lure fishers and underwater aficionados. Add in some stunningly scenic national parks and a range of thrilling outdoor adventures, and you have all the ingredients that make this region an all-around top spot to experience Costa Rica's charms. Although most tourists head here for the dry "high" season, it's even more beautiful—and cheaper, cooler, and less crowded—in the "green" or low season, April to December.

PLANNING

WHEN TO GO
HIGH SEASON: MID-DECEMBER TO APRIL
This is the driest region of the country, with only 165 centimeters (65 inches) of average annual rainfall. It's also the hottest region, with average temperatures around 30°C to 35°C (86°F to 95°F) in high season. It's no wonder that winter-weary Northerners come here for guaranteed sunshine and heat. The beaches and trails can get packed during these drier months, especially mid-December to February, when school is out in Costa Rica. January can be quite breezy, especially along the coast, thanks to the annual Papagayo winds. February through April are the

driest months: skies are clear, but the heat is intense and the landscape is brown and parched. Fishing and scuba diving are at their best during this period, though.

LOW SEASON: MAY THROUGH OCTOBER

Major downpours are pretty much guaranteed every afternoon during the rainy season, which brings lower prices, fewer crowds, and a lush green landscape. But mornings are usually fresh and clear. Unpaved beach roads can become quite muddy, making travel difficult and some roads impassable.

SHOULDER SEASON: NOVEMBER TO MID-DECEMBER

This is the best time to visit, when the rains have abated, the landscape is lush, and the evening air is cool. Hotels and restaurants are prepped for the impending tourist influx, and staff are fresh and eager to please. Except for the popular U.S. Thanksgiving week, you can usually get a deal. High-season rates begin mid-December.

PLANNING YOUR TIME

Visiting this region for 10 days to two weeks will introduce you to its wonders and give you a real taste of the North Pacific. Schedule plenty of beach time for lounging, sunbathing, surfing, diving, and snorkeling. Logistically, you also need to take into consideration slow travel over bumpy roads. A beach like Tamarindo with lots of restaurants and nightlife can keep you entertained for a week or more, whereas a more solitary beach might merit only a couple of days. Also plan to visit some protected areas to enjoy canopy tours, wildlife viewing, and hiking. Outdoorsy types should consider spending a few days around Rincón de la Vieja National Park for its amazing hiking, bird-watching, and horseback riding. Other parks to consider are Palo Verde National Park, Santa Rosa National Park, and Barra Honda National Park. Many North Pacific beaches are just a few hours' drive from the Arenal Volcano area, so the region can be combined with the Northern Lowlands.

GETTING HERE AND AROUND

AIR TRAVEL

Aeropuerto Internacional Daniel Oduber Quirós (LIR) in Liberia is an international gateway to the coast, with a large, air-conditioned terminal. Tamarindo, Nosara, Playa Sámara, and Punta Islita also have small airstrips. Flying from San José to these airports is the best way to get here if you are already in the country. If your primary destination lies in Guanacaste or Nicoya, make sure you investigate the possibility of flying directly into Liberia instead of San José, which saves some serious hours on the road.

Alaska Airlines has direct service between Los Angeles and Costa Rica's two international airports in San José and Liberia. SANSA and Nature Air have scheduled flights between San José and Liberia, as well as destinations on the Nicoya Peninsula. Don't forget to factor in the exit tax, $29 by air and $7 by land, payable in U.S. dollars, colones, or credit card. Some airlines include this fee in the ticket price.

BUS TRAVEL

You can ride in a comfortable, air-conditioned minibus with Gray Line, connecting San José, Liberia, Playa Flamingo, Playa Conchal, Playa Potrero, Playa Brasilito, Playa Hermosa, Playas del Coco, Ocotal, Tamarindo, Rincón de la Vieja, and Playa Langosta. The Gray Line bus from San José to Liberia and Tamarindo begins picking up passengers from hotels daily around 8:45 am. The return bus leaves the Tamarindo and Flamingo areas around 8:40 am and 4 pm. Interbus has door-to-door minivan shuttle service from San José to all the major beach hotels (in Papagayo, Flamingo, Tamarindo, Coco, Ocotal, Nicoya, and Sámara). Fares range from $42 to $57 per person. Reserve 48 hours in advance to guarantee a seat.

Bus Contacts Gray Line. ☎ 2220–2126 ⊕ www.graylinecostarica.com. **Interbus.** ☎ 4100–0888 ⊕ www.interbusonline.com.

CAR TRAVEL

Most unpaved roads here alternate between being extremely muddy and treacherous during the rainy season and being extremely dusty during the dry season. That said, it can be a real adventure exploring the coastline if you have a 4WD or a hired driver with a good, sturdy car. The major artery in this region is the Pan-American Highway (CA 1), which heads northwest from San José to Liberia, then due north to the Nicaraguan border. It's fairly well maintained, but the convoys of trucks and buses often create heavy traffic and there are few passing opportunities. Construction to widen the highway south of Liberia began in 2012, creating sporadic delays. To skip the hours of frustrating driving, consider flying into Liberia, whose airport provides easy access to the region. Local hotels and tour companies can help you arrange for ground transportation in many cases. In Guanacaste, it's usually safe to take *pirata* (pirate, or unofficial) taxis, but always negotiate the price before getting into the cab, or ask your hotel to call a reputable driver.

The northwest is accessed via the paved two-lane Pan-American Highway (CA 1), which begins at the top of Paseo Colón in San José. Take the Friendship Bridge (aka Río Tempisque Bridge) across the Tempisque River to get to the Pacific beaches south of Liberia. Once you get off the main highway, dust, mud, potholes, and other factors come into play, depending on which beach you visit. The roads to Playa Flamingo, Playa Conchal, Playa Brasilito, Tamarindo, Playa Grande, Playa Sámara, Playas del Coco, Hermosa, and Ocotal are paved all the way; every other destination may require some dirt-road maneuvering.

FERRY TRAVEL

If you're headed to the southern Nicoya peninsula (Curú, Tambor, Montezuma, Malpaís, or Santa Teresa), the ferry ride from Puntarenas to Paquera across the Gulf of Nicoya is not only the fastest route, it's also the most scenic, with great views of the mountainous coast and islands.

RESTAURANTS

Seafood and fresh fish are tops here, followed by fast food—pizza, tacos, barbecue—to satisfy the hordes of hungry surfers and beachgoers. But there are many sophisticated restaurants, too, offering Asian-fusion,

Italian, French, and international cuisine, especially in the tourist-heavy beach towns of Hermosa, Flamingo, Tamarindo, Nosara, and Sámara. ■TIP→ Many restaurants, especially tourist-oriented ones with dollar-denominated menus, do not include the 13% national sales tax plus mandatory 10–12% service. By law, menus are required to show the total price including tax, but many owners flout this law. Be sure to ask if taxes are included; otherwise you may be surprised by a bill that's 25% higher than you expected.

HOTELS

A wide range of lodging options awaits you here, so choose wisely. If your goal is to take leisurely swims and lounge quietly on the beach with a cocktail in hand, then avoid the beaches that are renowned for surfing waves. Expensive resorts like the Four Seasons are generally well balanced with budget hotels that charge less than $75 per night. Wherever you stay, be sure to factor in the 13% sales tax. As in all of Costa Rica, the places we recommend most highly are the small owner-operated hotels and bed-and-breakfasts that blend in with unspoiled nature and offer one-on-one attention from the staff and owners. Most hotels will be able to connect you with local tour operators and knowledgeable staff members who can help show you the best aspects of each destination, whether it's a local park with howler monkeys, a great family-run restaurant on the beach, or a thrilling canopy tour. *Hotel reviews have been shortened. For full information, visit Fodors.com.*

WHAT IT COSTS IN DOLLARS			
$	**$$**	**$$$**	**$$$$**
Restaurants	under $10	$10–$15	$16–$25	over $25
Hotels	under $75	$75–$150	$151–$250	over $250

Restaurant prices are the average cost of a main course at dinner or, if dinner is not served, at lunch. Hotel prices are the lowest cost of a standard double room in high season.

TOURS

Horizontes Nature Tours. With a focus on nature and adventure, Horizontes has independent, private tours with your own guide and driver as well as small-group tours. Customized tours are available for bird-watchers, families, couples, yogis, and beachgoers. ☎2222–2022, 888/786–8748 toll-free in U.S. ⊕ *www.horizontes.com* ✉ *From $920.*

FAR NORTHERN GUANACASTE

North of Liberia, all the way to the Nicaraguan border, a towering volcanic mountain range looms over vast plains that end at a windy coastline dotted with pristine beaches. This is Far Northern Guanacaste, one of the lesser-traveled but vastly rewarding parts of Costa Rica. Liberia, the capital of Guanacaste Province, is the closest town to Costa Rica's second-largest airport. You'll most likely pass through it on your way to the beaches southwest of the city or to the nearby national parks of Guanacaste, Santa Rosa, or Rincón de la Vieja. This

Eco-Lodges of the Nicoya Peninsula

On the mainland, sweeping plains bordered by volcanoes hold remnants of Central America's tropical dry forest. On the Pacific-edged Nicoya Peninsula, conservationists try to protect turtle-nesting beaches from the encroachments of ever-grander resort hotels and vacation houses. Some exemplary resorts are proving that conservation, sustainability, and comfort can go hand in hand.

Harmony Hotel, Nosara. This hotel has earned five leaves in sustainability with its use of biodegradable cleaning products and toiletries, solar-heated hot water, and conscientious recycling policies.

Hotel Lagarta Lodge, Nosara. On a 90-acre private reserve, the quaint Hotel Lagarta Lodge minimizes its environmental impact by keeping a sharp eye on its water and energy consumption.

Hotel Punta Islita, Punta Islita. The ultra-luxurious Hotel Punta Islita is a top performer in the technical categories of water management, energy conservation, and waste disposal.

last park is home to Volcán Rincón de la Vieja, an active volcano that spews out fumes on a regular basis.

Northwest of Rincón de la Vieja, on the coast, Parque Nacional Santa Rosa (Santa Rosa National Park) is a former cattle ranch where Costa Ricans defeated the invading mercenary army of American William Walker in 1856. As part of the larger Guanacaste Conservation Area, Santa Rosa protects the country's largest remnant of tropical dry forest, as well as an important nesting beach for olive ridley sea turtles, which lay their eggs in the sand between July and November. Closer still to the Nicaraguan border is the town of La Cruz, overlooking the lovely Golfo de Santa Elena, and the remote, windswept beaches of Bahía Salinas.

LA CRUZ

40 km (25 miles) northwest of Liberia.

North of Santa Rosa National Park on the west side of the highway is the turnoff to La Cruz, a scruffy, bustling little town. Noteworthy for the stunning views of Bahía Salinas from its bluff, La Cruz is also close to the nearby windswept beaches on the south shore of Bahía Salinas, in the hamlet of Jobo, and in the Golfo de Santa Elena. Visit the area sooner rather than later; in 2015, Dreams Las Mareas opened its doors, and now other hotels and real estate projects are following suit with initial phases of development.

The Nicaraguan border lies just north of La Cruz at Peñas Blancas.
■TIP➜ **Travelers may be stopped at two checkpoints south of La Cruz for passport and cursory vehicle inspection. Police vigilance is heightened in the region.**

GETTING HERE AND AROUND

La Cruz is a straight shot, one hour's trip north of Liberia on the well-maintained Pan-American Highway. Buses leave Liberia for La Cruz, or you can flag down a bus that says "La Cruz" on its windshield anywhere along the highway north of Liberia.

ESSENTIALS

Banks/ATMs Banco Nacional. ✉ *Pan-American Hwy. across from police station* ☎ *2679–9389.* **Banco Popular.** ✉ *75 m east of northeast corner of central park* ☎ *2679–9352.*

Pharmacy Farmacia La Cruz. ✉ *1 block north of central park* ☎ *2679–8048.*

Post Office Correo. ✉ *50 m south of the park.*

WHERE TO STAY

$
B&B/INN
Fodor's Choice
★

Cañas Castilla. Swiss expats Guido and Agi spent their first years in Costa Rica living off the land without running water or electricity, but today their little paradise is a full-fledged farm with cows, horses, chickens, and rustic cabins for overnight guests. **Pros:** friendly owners; nature abounds; all rooms are wheelchair accessible; delicious food. **Cons:** patchy Wi-Fi in common areas only; no phones; muddy in rainy season; extra charge for a/c. **$** *Rooms from: $56* ✉ *Approx. 5 km (3 miles) north from La Cruz* ✛ *Turn off the hwy. to the right into Sonzapote*

Crossing into Nicaragua at Peñas Blancas

CLOSE UP

BORDER CROSSING AND TRANSPORTATION

Costa Rica and Nicaragua share a busy border crossing at Peñas Blancas, 18 km (11 miles) north of La Cruz along a paved highway. ■TIP➜ Rental vehicles may not leave Costa Rica. Central Line, Tica Bus, and Transnica bus companies (⇨ *see Bus Travel in Travel Smart Costa Rica*) travel direct between San José and Managua via this route. You can also take a Tralapa bus to the border from other points in Costa Rica. You'll make your crossing, then catch a Nicaraguan bus or taxi to Rivas, 35 km (22 miles) farther, which is the regional hub for buses departing to other parts of Nicaragua. The fee to cross the border is $7 (paid on the Nicaraguan side), plus a $2 surcharge if you cross from noon to 2 pm or on weekends. Nicaraguan shuttle taxis transport people between the border posts. The crossing is open daily 6 am to 10 pm, but only until 8 pm on Sunday; get there with time to spare or you *will* be stranded.

Returning to Costa Rica is basically the same process in reverse; you are charged a $1 municipal tax and $2 exit tax to leave Nicaragua by land. Banks on both sides of the border change their own currency and U.S. dollars. Colones are not accepted or exchanged in Nicaragua; likewise for Nicaraguan córdobas in Costa Rica. Overland border-crossing procedures can be confusing if you don't speak Spanish, but attendants on the cross-border buses can help shepherd you through the formalities. The phone number for Costa Rican immigration in Peñas Blancas is ☎ 2677–0053.

STAYING IN NICARAGUA

The colonial city of Granada, the twin volcanoes of the island of Ometepe, the surfing town of Popoyo, and the lively beach town of San Juan del Sur are the draws in southern Nicaragua. If you plan on staying in Granada, hip and sceney Tribal Hotel ⊕ *www.tribal-hotel.com* is the place to be; in Popoyo, Soma Surf Resort ⊕ *www.surfresortnicaragua.com* has chic accommodations, great food, and surf lessons.

---

after the school. Follow the signs 2 km east to Finca Cañas Castilla. ☎ *8381–4030 cell* ⊕ *www.canas-castilla.com* ⤳ *6 rooms* ⦿ *No meals.*

$$
B&B/INN
⛺ **Tierra Madre.** Located 25 km (15½ miles) northeast of La Cruz, this remote estate is made up of four hillside bungalows with volcano views and a backdrop of Lake Nicaragua. **Pros:** excellent farm-to-table meals; three swimming pools; unique activities. **Cons:** Wi-Fi in common areas only; long muddy road; might be too rustic for some. ⑤ *Rooms from: $120* ⊠ *25 km northeast of La Cruz, 5 km from nearest village of Los Andes, La Cruz* ☎ *506/8705–4249* ⊕ *www.tierramadre.co.cr* ⤳ *4 bungalows* ⦿ *Breakfast.*

BAHÍA SALINAS

15 km (9 miles) west of La Cruz.

The large windswept bay at the very top of Costa Rica's Pacific coast is the second-windiest area in the country, after Lake Arenal, making it great for windsurfers and kitesurfers, as well as beachgoers looking for breezy, uncrowded, pristine beaches. It also happens to be the sunniest and driest side of Costa Rica. Strong onshore breezes blow from November to May, when only experienced riders are out on the waves and the water grows steadily cooler. The south (bay) side has the strongest winds, and choppy, colder water from January to May.

In July and August the wind is more appropriate for beginner kitesurfers and windsurfers, whereas any time of year you can enjoy the area's diving and beaches. On the sheltered Golfo de Santa Elena, to the west, are two beaches that rank among the most beautiful in all of Costa Rica: Playa Rajada and Playa Jobo, although Dreams Las Mareas Resort has claimed ground at Jobo Bay. Other beaches lining the bay are Playa Copal, Playa Papaturro, and Playa Pochotes. There are plans to build a community of luxury condos along Santa Elena Peninsula by 2019. Still, it's a far cry from the overdeveloped beaches of Guanacaste's gold coast farther to the south. Just offshore is Isla Bolaños, a national wildlife refuge with white-sand beaches and turquoise water. This famous nesting spot for birds can only be seen from afar between April and November, as landing here is not allowed.

GETTING HERE AND AROUND

From Liberia, drive 45 minutes toward La Cruz, the last town before the Peñas Blancas border crossing. From a high point in La Cruz, the road to Salinas descends both in altitude and condition. Turn left toward Bahía Salinas, the only road leading to the beaches. Signs direct you to Puerto Soley where the road splits shortly thereafter and heads right to El Jobo. Playa Copal is about 13 km (8 miles) along the same road from La Cruz. The first few kilometers of the beach road are paved, but expect a bumpy ride most of the way.

BEACHES

Playa Copal. Playa Copal is a narrow, dark-beige beach that wouldn't be worth visiting except for the fact that it is one of the main venues for kitesurfing. Winds are often gusty but consistent November to May, which is why several kite schools have set up shop nearby. Food and drink are available at nearby Ecoplaya Hotel, but we don't recommend staying there. A couple of kilometers to the east is Playa Papaturro, another windy beach where you'll find simple accommodations and a kitesurfing school at Blue Dream Hotel. **Amenities:** food and drink. **Best for:** solitude. ⊠ *About 2 km (1 mile) east of the branch road that leads to Ecoplaya.*

Playa Jobo. Dominated by the massive Dreams Las Mareas Resort, Playa Jobo is still one of the most beautiful beaches in the area. Cradled within the sheltered cove is fine brown sand and calm water, making this beach safe for swimming. Motorized water sports are not allowed, so despite the resort's size, the bay remains relatively quiet. A few sailboats are anchored offshore. Playa Jobo is fringed with acacia trees that have sharp thorns, and there are rocks jetting on either side of the cove where many people begin a snorkel adventure (beware of sea urchins and jellyfish). This beach is a refuge to turtles and manta rays, which you might see in the shallow, clear waters. Windy days are frequent, so watch for blowing sand. At high tide, the beach is narrow. This, combined with the slight slope to the shore, has most people sunbathing by the pool or lounging in the grassy area between the sand and the resort. Although all beaches in Costa Rica are public, this strand is difficult to reach unless you're staying at Dreams Resort. Your other options are to approach by boat or access from around the cove. **Amenities:** food and drink. **Best for:** snorkeling; sunset; swimming. ⊠ *Dreams Las Mareas Resort, 3-km (2-mile) walk or drive west from Ecoplaya Beach Resort.*

Playa Rajada. Gorgeous, horseshoe-shaped Playa Rajada is a wide sweep of almost-white, fine-grain sand. Shallow, warm waters make it perfect for swimming, and an interesting rock formation at the north end invites snorkelers. It's also a favorite beach for watching sunsets. **Amenities:** none. **Best for:** snorkeling; sunset; swimming. ⊠ *5 km (3 miles) west of Ecoplaya Beach Resort or 3 km (2 miles) north of the town of El Jobo.*

SPORTS AND THE OUTDOORS

Inshore fishing is quite good in the bay during windy months, when snapper, roosterfish, wahoo, and other fighters abound. Scuba divers might also encounter big fish from December to May, though visibility can be poor then. From May to December the snorkeling is good around the rocky points and Isla Bolaños.

TOUR OPERATORS

Ecoplaya Beach Resort. Local adventure tours organized by this resort hotel include boating to Isla Bolaños (a tiny island that is a refuge for such seabirds as the brown pelican), inshore fishing, hiking, and snorkeling and windsurfing, as well as farther-afield adventure tours to Santa Rosa National Park, Palo Verde National Park, Hacienda Guachipelín, and the historic city of Granada, in nearby Nicaragua. ⊠ *La Coyotera Beach, 15 km (10 miles) west of La Cruz on a rough dirt road* ☎ *2676–1010* ⊕ *www.ecoplaya.com* ⤢ *Day tours $150; boat tour to Isla Bolanos $30.*

KITESURFING AND WINDSURFING

Blue Dream Kitesurfing School. Ideally situated near windy Playa Papaturro (11 km [7 miles] west of La Cruz, turn left at sign for Papaturro), this kitesurfing school is run by Nicola Bertoldi, a multilingual instructor with lots of experience; private lessons cost $45 per hour. Nine hours of beginner's kitesurfing private lessons cost $360, including equipment. But the best deals are all-inclusive packages starting at $499 that include five days of lessons, lodging, and meals at the school's Blue Dream Hotel, on a ridge with ocean views. Check their website for wind conditions and closure dates, as the school often shuts down once the breezes stop. ⊠ *60 m east Playa Papaturro entrance* ☎ *8826–5221, 2676–1042* ⊕ *www.bluedreamhotel.com.*

Cometa Copal Kitesurfing. Cometa Copal Kitesurfing school on Playa Copal (10 km [6 miles] west of La Cruz), is run by American Bob Selfridge, who rents equipment and provides kitesurfing lessons for $40 per hour. Beginner courses with nine hours of private instruction cost $400. ⊠ *Playa Cometa* ☎ *8553–7664* ⊕ *www.kitesurfingincostarica. com* ⤢ *From $40.*

WHERE TO STAY

$ 🖵 **Blue Dream Hotel.** Catering predominantly to kitesurfers, this breezy
HOTEL property on a steep hillside is one of the more affordable lodging options
FAMILY in Bahía Salinas, with suites, bungalows, rooms, and dorms just minutes
from the water. **Pros:** very affordable; kitesurfing lessons; water views;
discounts for longer stays. **Cons:** steep climb to top rooms; not much
to do outside of kitesurfing; stray animals and neglected grounds; only
the suite is recommended. ⑤ *Rooms from: $49 ✉ 60 m west of Playa
Papaturro entrance* ☎ *8826–5221, 2676–1042* ⊕ *www.bluedreamhotel.
com* ⟿ *1 suite, 4 bungalows, 10 rooms, 1 dorm* ⦿l *No meals.*

$$$$ 🖵 **Dreams Las Mareas Costa Rica.** As the first all-inclusive luxury resort in
RESORT the Bahía Salinas area and the first hotel in Guanacaste to feature swim-
FAMILY up rooms, Dreams Las Mareas stands out from the AI pack with no hid-
Fodor'sChoice den charges, no restaurant reservations, no towel cards, and no plastic
★ wrist bands. **Pros:** lovely swim-up rooms; calm beach; wine, tequila, coffee tastings included; designated kids' pool. **Cons:** isolated on a bumpy
road; steep, vast grounds require a lot of walking; patios and bathrooms
lack privacy. ⑤ *Rooms from: $340 ✉ Playa Jobo, west of Bahia Salinas*
☎ *2690–2400, 866/237–3267 in U.S.* ⊕ *www.dreamsresorts.com/las-
mareas* ⟿ *447 rooms* ⦿l *All-inclusive.*

PLAYA BAHÍA JUNQUILLAL

*26 km (16 miles) northwest of
Santa Rosa National Park entrance.*

This 2½-km (1½-mile), tree-fringed
beach is as close as you can get to
a white-sand beach in this part of
Guanacaste. Not to be confused
with the Playa Junquillal on the
western coast of the Nicoya Peninsula (that's farther south), this
beach is part of the Guanacaste
Conservation Area, and is a wildlife
refuge to the north of Santa Rosa.

GETTING HERE AND AROUND

From the Pan-American Highway,
take the road signed for Cuajiniquil, 43 km (26 miles) northwest
of Liberia and 8 km (5 miles) north
of Santa Rosa National Park. Follow the paved road 14 km (8 miles)
to the beach turnoff, along a dirt
road for another 4 km (2½ miles).
From the Bahía Salinas area, take
the scenic dirt road (4WD recommended); then follow the road near
Puerto Soley (signed for Cuajiniquil) 7 km (4½ miles) to the beach
entrance. It's about 30 minutes from the Pan-American turnoff and one
hour from Bahía Salinas.

**THIEVES ON THE
BEACHES**

Guanacaste's idyllic landscapes
and friendly people belie an
ever-present threat of theft. Sadly,
Costa Rica's thieves manage
to ruin a lot of vacations by
absconding with backpacks,
cameras, wallets, and passports,
the last of which necessitates
a trip to San José. Keep your
valuables in your hotel safe—
preferably the safe in the hotel
office—and don't ever leave
anything in an unattended
car, even while checking into
your hotel. Hotel parking lots
are popular spots for local
kleptomaniacs, as are beaches.

6

BEACHES

Bahía Junquillal (*Junquillal Bay Wildlife Refuge*). The warm, calm water makes this one of the best swimming beaches on the Golfo de Santa Elena. Stay for the day or camp out in the well-kept, shaded camping area with cold-water showers, bathrooms, grills, and picnic tables ($15 per person onetime park entrance for foreigners, plus $19 per person per night to camp). Compared to other camping areas in Costa Rica, prices are steep since this is part of the Junquillal Bay Wildlife Refuge. You can snorkel if you bring your own gear. **Amenities:** showers; toilets. **Best for:** solitude; swimming; fishing. ⊠ *18 km (11 miles) west of Pan-American Hwy., Cuajiniquil turnoff* ⊕ *www.acguanacaste.ac.cr* ⌨ *$15.*

WHERE TO STAY

$$
B&B/INN
🔲 **Santa Elena Lodge.** This simple family-run lodge with cozy rooms on the outskirts of Cuajiniquil provides the closest accommodations to both Playa Bahía Junquillal and Santa Rosa National Park, making it a good option for nature lovers and anyone who wants to stray from the vacationing crowds. **Pros:** friendly owners; near beach and park; clean and comfortable rooms. **Cons:** little English spoken; basic accommodations. ⑤ *Rooms from: $80* ⊠ *10 km (6 miles) west of Pan-American Hwy., 4 km (2.5 miles) east of Junquillal, Cuajiniquil* 📷 *2679–1038* ⊕ *www.santaelenalodge.com* ⌨ *8 rooms* ⦿ *Breakfast.*

SANTA ROSA NATIONAL PARK

35 km (22 miles) northwest of Liberia.

Santa Rosa National Park blends forest and pristine beaches overlooking the famed surf spot Witch's Rock. North of Liberia, the park is less frequented than other national parks in Costa Rica due to the difficult terrain (especially in rainy season) and the remote location far off the beaten path. The country's first national park, it still has an untouched beauty that is evident from the chirping birds among the treetops to the white-tailed deer drinking from watering holes. There are several campsites where travelers can soak in the sounds of Santa Rosa's symphony, comprised of howler monkeys, coyotes, bats, and the occasional jaguar. The best time to experience the typical dry-forest vegetation and wildlife is during dry season when leaves are sparse and roads are accessible.

GETTING HERE AND AROUND

The turnoff for Santa Rosa National Park from the Pan-American Highway is well marked, about 30 minutes outside of Liberia. From Liberia you can hop on a bus heading north to La Cruz and get off at the park entrance, but you'll have to hike 7 km (4½ miles) in the hot sun to the La Casona park headquarters from there. La Posada del Tope arranges shuttle vans from Liberia to the park entrance for $20 per person round-trip.

EXPLORING

Santa Rosa National Park (*Parque Nacional Santa Rosa*). Thanks to sparse foliage, it's not difficult to spot wildlife within Santa Rosa's tropical dry forest, especially if you're with an experienced guide. There are impressive flora and fauna, and even on a half-day visit you might see monkeys, birds, deer, and coatis hiding in the dry-forest vegetation. Santa Rosa's wealth of natural beauty is due in part to its remoteness—it isn't as busy as some of Costa Rica's other parks. Most trails are easily accessible and relatively flat.

To get deep into the park, you must have a 4WD, and many roads are impassable in rainy season. The park headquarters, a historic ranch house and museum called La Casona, and a nearby camping area are 7 km (4½ miles) from the Pan-American Highway via a paved road.

> ## WALKER'S LAST STAND
>
> Santa Rosa Park was the site of the 1856 triumph over American invader William Walker in the famous Battle of Santa Rosa—one of the few historic military sites in this army-less country. The rambling colonial-style ranch house called **La Casona** was the last stand of a ragged force of ill-equipped Costa Ricans who routed the superior mercenary army of the notorious Walker. Disgruntled poachers burned La Casona to the ground in 2001, but it has since been rebuilt.

From park headquarters it's 11 km (7 miles) to **Playa Naranjo,** where the famed Witch's Rock surf break is located (surfers get there by boat). The road here is very rough (4WD only). **Playa Nancite**—the site of one of the world's few completely protected olive ridley turtle *arribada,* or mass nesting (accessible primarily to biologists and students; permit required)—is an additional 5 km (3 miles) by footpath north of Playa Naranjo. A permit can be obtained from the Ecotourism Office in the administrative center. The most impressive coastal views are from the Mirador Valle Naranjo and Mirador Tierras Emergidas. For bird-watching, follow the Los Platos trail about 5 km (3 miles) past the administrative center on the way to the coast. It is best to visit the park with a guide, since some areas are poorly marked, and you're more likely to see wildlife you would have missed otherwise. ✉ *Km 269, Pan-American Hwy. 35 km (22 miles) north of Liberia* ☎ *2666–5051* ⊕ *www.acguanacaste.ac.cr* 🎫 *$15 park entrance; $4 camping* ☉ *Daily 8–4.*

EXPLORING

Guanacaste National Park. The 325-square-km (125-square-mile) Parque Nacional Guanacaste, bordering the east side of the Pan-American Highway 30 km (18 miles) north of Liberia, was created to preserve rain forests around Cacao Volcano (1,633 meters [5,443 feet]) and Orosí Volcano (1,464 meters [4,879 feet]), which are seasonally inhabited by migrant wildlife from Santa Rosa National Park. The connecting border of these two national parks serves as a biological corridor for birds resettling between cloud, rain, and dry forests. Popular with researchers, the park isn't quite ready for tourism yet. There are very few facilities and no well-marked trails; if you want to hike, it's best to hire a professional guide. In rainy season, roads are impassable; a 4WD vehicle is required year-round. Established under Dr. Daniel Janzen, the park is part of the Guanacaste Conservation Area, a mosaic of interdependent protected areas, parks, and refuges; the goal is to accommodate the migratory patterns of animals, from jaguars to tapirs. Much of the park's territory is cattle pasture, which is regenerating into new forest faster than predicted. Today the park has howler and capuchin monkeys, collared peccaries, white-tailed deer, pumas, sloths, coatis, bats, and more than 5,000 species of butterflies and moths. Among the 300 different birds are parakeets, hawks, cuckoos, and magpie-jays. ⊠ *35 km (22 mi) north of Liberia* ⊹ *Adjacent to Santa Rosa National Park* 🖼 *$15* ⊗ *8–4.*

SPORTS AND THE OUTDOORS
HIKING
Several trails to the beaches lead off the road before it becomes impassable to vehicles. The hike to Playa Naranjo (11 km [7 miles] west of La Casona) requires good physical condition and lots of water. You can get a map of the trails at the park entrance.

Casona nature-trail loop (*Sendero Indio Desnudo*). The short (about 1-km [½-mile]) Casona nature-trail loop from the park headquarters is worth taking to get a brief sampling of the woods. Look for the "Indio Desnudo," or "Naked Indian," path, named after the local word for gumbo-limbo trees. This is one of the few trails that doesn't get overly muddy, even after a heavy rain in wet season. Carry plenty of water and insect repellent. ⊠ *Santa Rosa National Park.*

SURFING
Witch's Rock (*Pena Bruja*). Witch's Rock towers offshore over a near-perfect beach break off Playa Naranjo in Santa Rosa National Park. The massive boulder once howled and whistled, causing passersby to believe the rock was haunted by a witch. In reality, it was only the offshore winds billowing between the water and stone that made the eerie sound. Years of erosion have silenced the howling, but the boulder, and the name, remain. If you are interested in surfing Witch's Rock, take a boat tour from Playas del Coco, Playa Hermosa, or Playa Tamarindo, to the south. Tropic Surf offers surf trips to Witch's Rock from its shop at Four Seasons Resort Peninsula Papagayo. ⊠ *Santa Rosa National Park.*

WHERE TO STAY
There are basic, dormitory-style lodgings and a camping area ($4) near the park's administrative center; you can also camp within Santa Rosa National Park at the very basic and remote campsites at the beaches of Naranjo and Murcielago. No more than 20 people can camp within the park at a time. Call the park headquarters (☎ 2666–5051) for information. Most people visit the park on day trips from Liberia, or nearby Cuajiniquil.

RINCÓN DE LA VIEJA NATIONAL PARK

25 km (15 miles) northeast of Liberia.

Wildlife, rivers, waterfalls, and mud baths are just the tip of the volcano when it comes to the natural wonders of Rincón de la Vieja National Park. Dominating the scenery east of the Pan-American Highway just north of bustling Liberia, the national park's 34,800 acres are home to two peaks, the most impressive being Rincón de la Vieja at 1,895 meters

(6,254 feet), which is often enveloped in clouds. Expect to see monkeys, sloths, and birds in a single day's exploration. For lodging, take your pick from working ranches, river lodges, rustic B&Bs, and garden villas; just be sure to rent a 4WD vehicle to reach the more remote properties, especially in rainy season. To get a taste of the area, there are plenty of activities that blend nature and adventure, like horseback riding, river rafting, zip lining, and hiking on a network of trails that set off from the Santa María ranger station and wind past hot springs, mud baths, and waterfalls. Lathering up with the volcanic mud softens the skin and detoxifies the body, and it makes for a fun photo op.

GETTING HERE AND AROUND
There are two park entrances on the volcano's southern slope: the less traveled one at Hacienda Santa María on the road leading northeast from Liberia (one hour), where there is camping available; and the one at Las Pailas, past Curubandé off the Pan-American Highway. To get to Las Pailas entrance from Liberia, take the first entrance road 5 km (3 miles) northwest of Liberia off the Pan-American Highway. The turnoff is easy to miss—follow signs for Hacienda Guachipelín or the town of Curubandé. It's a 17-km (10½-mile) road, paved until the final stretch beyond Hacienda Guachipelín. Non-hotel guests must pay a small toll (about $1.50) to access the private road to the park entrance. The Santa María entrance is 25 km (15 miles) northeast of Liberia along the Colonia Blanca route, which follows the course of the Río Liberia. The turnoff from the Pan-American Highway to the hotels on the western slope of the volcano is 12 km (7 miles) northwest of Liberia, turning right at the road signed for Cañas Dulces. A 4WD vehicle is recommended for all these slow and bone-rattling rides.

ESSENTIALS
Shuttle La Posada del Tope Tours. ⊠ *C. Real between Avdas. 2 and 4, 150 m south of cathedral entrance, Downtown* ☎ 2666–3876.

EXPLORING
Fodor's Choice **Rincón de la Vieja National Park** (*Parque Nacional Volcán Rincón de la* ★ *Vieja*). It might be a trek to get here, but Rincón de la Vieja National Park doesn't disappoint with its multitude of natural wonders from hot springs and mud baths to refreshing waterfalls and a smoldering volcano. Dominating 140 square km (54 square miles) of the volcano's upper slopes, this tropical rain forest is usually blanketed in clouds, with a short dry transition between January and April. The park has two peaks: Santa María and the barren Rincón de la Vieja. The latter has an active crater, leading park authorities to close some trails, especially during wet season (check the status before you visit).

The wildlife here is diverse, with birds, deer, coyotes, monkeys, and armadillos. There are two main entrances: Santa María and Las Pailas; the latter is the most common place to enter the park and is closest to the trails (there's a $1.50 charge for private road use). The park does not have guides; we recommend the nature guides at Eco Explorer and Tours Your Way. Many of the attractions people visit in Rincón de la Vieja are accessible without actually entering the park, since the ranches that border it also hold significant forest and geothermal sites. (⇨ *For more information, see the highlighted listing in this chapter.)* ✉ *Rincón de la Vieja National Park* ☎ *2666-5051* ⌚ *$15* ◷ *Tues.–Sun. 7–5; last entry at 3 pm.*

SPORTS AND THE OUTDOORS

TOUR OPERATORS

Buena Vista Lodge & Adventure. An hour's drive west of the park, this lodge lies on a large ranch where visitors enjoy horseback riding, waterfall hikes, a canopy tour, hanging bridges, a 425-meter (1,394-foot, long, not steep) waterslide through the forest, and hot springs. Tours are $15 to $50 per person; a combination tour that lasts six to seven hours costs $90, including lunch. ✉ *Western slope of volcano, 10 km (6 miles) north of Cañas Dulces* ✛ *Near Borinquen Resort* ☎ *2690-1414 in Liberia* ⊕ *www.buenavistalodgecr.com* ⌚ *From $15.*

Eco Explorer. Ranked among the top guides in Costa Rica, Carlos Luis Jiménez of Eco Explorer offers birding, nature, and adventure tours to national parks in the Liberia and Papagayo areas. Day tours to Rincón de la Vieja, Santa Rosa, and Palo Verde must be reserved 48 hours in advance; they begin at 5:30 or 7:30 am and last until 3 or 5 pm, depending on the package. ✉ *Rincón de la Vieja National Park* ☎ *8927–9630* ⊕ *www.ecoexplorercr.com* ⌚ *From $100.*

Fodor's Choice **Hacienda Guachipelín Adventure Tours.** This experienced outfitter has the
★ most exciting tours in the area, including horseback riding, river tubing, hot springs and mud baths, guided waterfall hikes, and hikes on the slopes of the national park volcano (from $25 to $62). The popular canyon tour includes rock climbing, rappelling, zip lines, suspension bridges, and a Tarzan swing. A one-day, all-you-can-do adventure pass, including lunch, is a great deal at $85. ✉ *Road to Rincón de la Vieja National Park* ☎ *2666–8075, 888/730–3840 toll-free in U.S.* ⊕ *www. guachipelin.com* ⌚ *From $25.*

Sensoria. If you want to experience the area's natural attractions without all the adrenaline-pumping activities, Sensoria has peaceful jungle trails, waterfalls, pools, and an observation tower. The entrance fee includes lunch and a guided 3-hour hike during which you'll visit vibrant blue waterfalls, hot springs, and natural pools. Bring a change of clothes, bug spray, and water shoes. The hiking tour begins daily at 9:30 am. Tours are by reservation only and no children under 6 are allowed. ✉ *Rincón de la Vieja National Park* ✛ *From Pan-American Highway, turn right towards Quebrada Grande. Turn left towards Dos Ríos. Left at high school and continue towards Buenos Aires de Upala. Turn right at sign for "AyA". Follow signs for Sensoria and continue 3.7 km to entrance.* ☎ *506/2288-6229* ⊕ *www.sensoria.cr* ⌚ *$110.*

Tours Your Way. Playas del Coco–based Mainor Lara Bustos guides tours to Rincón de la Vieja or Palo Verde for $115, including transportation, entrance fees, lunch, and snacks. ✉ *Rincón de la Vieja National Park* ☎ *8820–1829* ⊕ *www.tours-your-way.com.*

CANOPY TOURS

Buena Vista Lodge & Adventure. The zip-line canopy tour ($40) here has 10 cables that are up to 27 meters (90 feet) off the ground and up to 135 meters (450 feet) long. For an additional $10, the Extreme Canopy Adventure Tour follows a slightly different route and includes the

Tarzan Swing (a 150-foot free fall). ✉ *Western slope of volcano, 10 km (6 miles) north of Cañas Dulces ✛ Near Borinquen Resort ⊕ www. buenavistalodgecr.com ✉ From $40.*

Rincón de la Vieja Canopy. This combined adventure tour at Rincón de la Vieja Mountain Lodge includes zip lining, rappelling, horseback riding, kayaking, hot springs, mud baths, and a buffet lunch. ✉ *21 km (12 miles) northeast of Pan-American Hwy.; 5 km (3 miles) north of Hacienda Guachipelín; 2 km (1 mile) south of Las Pailas park entrance, at Rincón de la Vieja Mountain Lodge ☎ 2200–0238 ⊕ www. hotelrincondelaviejacr.com ✉ From $85.*

HIKING

Nearly all the lodges and outfitters in the area offer guided hikes through the park to the fumaroles, hot springs, waterfalls, and (when possible) to the summit or the edge of the active crater.

If you're doing a self-guided hike, stop for trail maps and hiking information at the park stations at both entrance gates. To give yourself enough time to complete the longer hikes, make sure you start out between 7 and 9 am.

Loop through the park. A less strenuous option than the trail to the summit is the fascinating 3-km (2-mile) loop through the park, which takes about two hours to complete, starting at Las Pailas entrance. Along the well-marked trail you'll see fumaroles exuding steam, a *volcáncito* (little volcano), and Las Pailas, the boiling mud fields named after pots used for boiling down sugarcane. From the mud pots, a spur trail leads 5 km (3 miles) to a series of hot springs. If you tread softly in the nearby forest, you may spot animals such as howler, capuchin, and spider monkeys, as well as raccoon-like coatis looking for handouts. Remember the cardinal rule of wildlife encounters: don't feed the animals. ✉ *Rincón de la Vieja National Park.*

La Cangreja Waterfall loop. A popular hike out of Las Pailas is the four-hour, 10-km (6-mile) La Cangreja Waterfall loop, passing through beautiful primary forests and windswept savannas. The *catarata* (waterfall) has a cool swimming hole below; the surrounding rocks have pockets of hot springs. Check with park rangers to make sure this trail is open. ✉ *Rincón de la Vieja National Park.*

Trail to the summit. The 8-km (5-mile) trail to the summit heads up into the forest from Las Pailas park entrance, then emerges onto a windy, exposed shale slope that's slippery and hard going, and has poor visibility owing to clouds and mist. It's a trip for serious hikers, best done in the dry season with preparation for cold weather at the top. The trail has been closed since 2014 due to volcanic activity, but may reopen in the future. Check with park rangers to make sure the trail is open when you visit. ✉ *Rincón de la Vieja National Park.*

HORSEBACK RIDING

Borinquen Mountain Resort & Spa. A day package here ($80) begins with a horseback ride and a 90-minute canopy tour, followed by lunch and free time to soak in the hotel's hot springs and relax in the natural steam bath. ✉ *12 km (7½ miles) northwest of Liberia on the Pan-American*

6

Hwy., then 23 km (14 miles) north on the dirt road that passes Cañas Dulces ☎ *2690–1900* ⊕ *www.borinquenresort.com* ✉ *From $80.*

Buena Vista Lodge & Adventure. This lodge and tour operator has horseback trips to hot springs and waterfalls ($40). If not everyone in your party is a horse lover, tractor transport ($35) is available to the hot springs as well. ✉ *Western slope of volcano, 10 km (6 miles) north of Cañas Dulces* ✦ *Near Borinquen Resort* ⊕ *www.buenavistalodgecr. com* ✉ *From $40.*

Hacienda Guachipelín. This is the premier working ranch in the area, with more than 100 well-bred and well-trained horses, and miles of trails to three waterfalls, tropical dry forest, and hot springs. Horseback tours range from $25 to $35. The Hacienda also offers a cowboy-for-a-day tour ($50) that includes harnessing your horse, rounding up cattle, and milking a cow. ✉ *Hacienda Guachipelín* ☎ *2690–2900, 888/730–3840 toll-free in U.S. or Canada* ⊕ *www.guachipelin.com* ✉ *From $25.*

WHERE TO STAY

$$
RESORT
FAMILY
Fodor's Choice
★

Blue River Resort. Named for the blue river that flows nearby, this property on the volcano's northern slope is worth the trek to experience the resort's hot springs, adventure tours, and spacious rustic cabins with terrace-hammocks. **Pros:** family-friendly; great activities; nearby waterfalls. **Cons:** rough, unpaved road; limited, somewhat pricey menu; Wi-Fi in common areas only. $ *Rooms from: $150* ✉ *600 m west of Rio Celeste Bridge, Dos Rios* ☎ *2206–5000, 2206–5506, 954/688–3646 in U.S.* ⊕ *www.blueriverresort.com* ⏎ *25 rooms* ⊚ *Breakfast; Some meals.*

$$$
RESORT

Borinquen Mountain Resort & Spa. The spacious villas and bungalows on this 570-acre ranch are the most upscale—and expensive—accommodations in the area, but the room rate includes access to their hot springs, mud baths, and a Costa Rican breakfast. **Pros:** attractive, well-equipped bungalows; peaceful environment; lots of outdoor activities. **Cons:** far from park entrance; 12-km (7½-mile) unpaved road; Wi-Fi only in restaurant and reception areas; occasional sound of ATVs, golf carts, and leaf blowers. $ *Rooms from: $194* ✉ *13 km (8 miles) northwest of Liberia on Pan-American Hwy., then 19 km (12 miles) north on the dirt road toward Cañas Dulces* ☎ *2690–1900* ⊕ *www.borinquenresort. com* ⏎ *16 villas, 17 bungalows, 6 junior suites* ⊚ *Breakfast.*

$$
HOTEL
FAMILY

Hacienda Guachipelín. One of the best values in the Rincón area for hair-raising adventure and nature tours, this hotel also gets top billing for its comfortable rooms, excellent restaurant, and friendly service. **Pros:** near park entrance; lots of activities; excellent value; home-cooked Costa Rican cuisine. **Cons:** caters to large groups and day visitors; some rooms are near horse stables; $50 fee for check-out after 12 pm. $ *Rooms from: $120* ✉ *17 km (10 miles) northeast of the Pan-American Hwy., on road to Las Pailas park entrance* ☎ *2666–8075, 888/730–3840 toll-free in U.S.* ⊕ *www.guachipelin.com* ⏎ *64 rooms, 2 suites* ⊚ *Breakfast.*

$
HOTEL

Rancho Curubandé Lodge. Convenient to both Rincón de la Vieja (20 km [12 miles]) and Santa Rosa National Park (30 km [18 miles]), these very affordable, two-bedroom villas and standard rooms are part of a working farm owned by a Costa Rican family. **Pros:** easy access to

DID YOU KNOW?

In the geothermal areas around Rincón de la Vieja, you'll find mud pots (pools of bubbling mud), fumaroles (holes that emit steam and gases), and hot springs.

highway to Santa Rosa National Park; very affordable, family-friendly bungalows. **Cons:** some highway noise; half-hour uphill climb to Rincón de la Vieja National Park (8 km [5 miles] are unpaved); small, boxy rooms. $ *Rooms from: $65* ⊠ *600 m off Pan-American Hwy. on road to Las Pailas* ✢ *From hwy., follow blue signs to lodge and Rincon de la Vieja. Turn right and continue 600 m to lodge on right* ☎ *2665–0375* ⊕ *www.rancho-curubande.com* ⮌ *16 rooms, 2 villas* ⦿| *Breakfast.*

LIBERIA

214 km (133 miles) (4–5 hrs) northwest of San José.

Once a dusty cattle-market town, Liberia has galloped toward modernization, becoming the commercial, as well as the administrative, capital of Guanacaste. There are still a few vestiges of its colonial past on quieter side streets. But Liberia has virtually become one big shopping mall, complete with fast-food restaurants—dueling McDonald's and Burger King face off at the entrance to town—and a multiplex theater. Walk a couple of blocks south of the main street along Calle Real, though, and you can still find some of the whitewashed adobe houses for which Liberia was nicknamed the "White City," as well as some grand town houses that recall the city's glory days. A few have been restored and are now hotels and cafés. Liberia today is essentially a good place to have a meal and make a bank stop at any one of a dozen banks, including Scotiabank, Citibank, and HSBC. Liberia can also serve as a base for day trips to Santa Rosa and Rincón de la Vieja national parks. Keep in mind that Liberia is the hottest city in Costa Rica, getting up to 115°F (46°C) in April. The drive from San José takes between four and five hours, so it makes sense to fly directly into Liberia if you're going only to the North Pacific. It's easy to rent a car near the airport.

GETTING HERE AND AROUND

From San José, follow the Pan-American Highway west past the Puntarenas exit, then north past Cañas to Liberia. The road is paved but is under construction in places. It's a heavily traveled truck and bus route, and there are miles and miles where it is impossible to pass, but many drivers try, making this a dangerous road. South of Liberia, the road is being widened, so expect delays. Hourly direct buses leave San José for Liberia each day, and there are half a dozen daily flights, so it might be worth busing or flying to Liberia and renting a car from here. International flights into Liberia are available through Alaska Airlines, American, Delta, JetBlue, Southwest, Sun Country, and United.

The *avenidas* (avenues) officially run east–west, whereas the *calles* (streets) run north–south. Liberia is not too big to walk easily, but there are always taxis lined up around the pleasant central park.

ESSENTIALS

Bank/ATM Banco de Costa Rica. ⊠ *C. Central at Avda. 1, Diagonally across from central park* ☎ *2666–9002.*

Hospital Liberia Hospital (*San Rafael Arcangel Medical Center*). ⊠ *North end of town* ✢ *100 m east, 25 m south from Ascención Esquivel School* ☎ *2666–1717.*

Liberia

LIBERIA

Stadium (Estadio)
La Agonia Church (Iglesia La Agonía)
Cemeterio General
Calle 9
Calle 7
Calle 5
Calle 3
Calle 1
Calle Central
Calle 2
Calle 4
Calle 6
Calle 10
Calle 12
Cathedral (Catedral)
Parque Central
Plaza
Bus Station
Bus Terminal
Calle Real
PAN-AMERICAN HWY.
TO AIRPORT

Bagaces
Llanos de Cortés
CR1
Hda. Las Ciruelas
Pijije
Salto
PAN-AMERICAN HWY.
Fincc Guaria

TO RINCON DE LA VIEJA NATIONAL PARK
Colorado
Cerececeda
R. Liberia
Avda Central (Avda. 0)
CR1
Liberia see inset
Capulín
Santa Ana
Juanilama
Hda. San Rafael
Hda. El Real
R. Colorado

Daniel Oduber International Airport
Guardia
Comunidad
Angeles
Palmira

KEY
🍴 Restaurants
① Hotels

Restaurants ▶
Café Liberia **3**
The Green House **2**
Restaurante Café Europa ...**1**
Restaurante Casa Vieja **4**

Hotels ▶
Hilton Garden Inn
Liberia Airport **2**
Hotel Liberia **1**

6

Pharmacy Farmacia Lux. ✉ *Avda. 25 de Julio, in front of Super Compro, 100 m west of the park* ☎ *2666–0061.*

Post Office Correo. ✉ *300 m west of hwy., 200 m north of Avda. Central* ✛ *Near Banco Nacional* ☎ *506/2666–1649.*

Rental Cars Alamo. ✉ *2 km (1 mile) northeast of Liberia airport* ☎ *2668–1111, 800/522–9696 in U.S.* **Budget.** ✉ *1 km (½ mile) east of Liberia airport* ☎ *2668–1118.* **Economy.** ✉ *5 km (3 miles) east of Liberia airport* ☎ *2666–2816.* **Enterprise.** ✉ *2 km (1 mile) northeast of Liberia airport* ☎ *506/ 2668–1111* ⊕ *www.enterprise.com.* **Hertz.** ✉ *Pan-American Hwy., 1 km (½ mile) northeast of the airport* ☎ *2668–1179.* **Vamos Rent-A-Car.** ✉ *5 km (3 miles) east of Liberia Airport on Hwy. 21* ☎ *2665–7650, 950–8426 from U.S* ⊕ *www.vamosrentacar.com.*

EN ROUTE

Yes, that is a life-size dinosaur standing beside the highway 20 minutes north of Puntarenas. It is one of 26 lifelike models of extinct and endangered animals arranged along a 1½-km (1-mile) forest trail at Parque MegaFauna Monteverde (*Pan-American Hwy.,* ☎ *2638–8193*). Along with the spectacular models outdoors, an impressive insect museum can be explored for a $5 ($3 for kids) entrance fee. The park is open daily 8 am to 5 pm. If you're just passing, you can still stop and take a photo of your kids in front of the baby dinosaur hatching out of a giant egg.

WHERE TO EAT

$$$
FRENCH
Fodor's Choice
★

✕ Café Liberia. Step back 150 years into one of Liberia's grandest mansions, complete with an original ceiling painting of cupids, doves, and garlands of flowers. This restored house, with two magnificent dining rooms and a courtyard garden, is home to an upscale café and restaurant. Creative takes on tropical ingredients, all with a French twist, make this the most sophisticated restaurant in town. Loyal customers drive over an hour for the incredibly fresh ceviche with mango and cilantro. Don't miss the Wagyu beef burger, the chicken pesto sandwich, or the mahimahi with chimichurri. Herbs are grown on-site, juices are 100% natural, and the organic coffee is perhaps the best you'll taste in Costa Rica. Save room for any of the fabulous desserts, like the classic cheesecake, lemon pie, or the molten chocolate lava cake made with Belgian chocolate. ⓢ *Average main: $16* ✉ *C. Real Antigua, 125 m south of central park* ☎ *2665–1660* ⊕ *www.sdevenelle4.wix.com/cafe-liberia* ☾ *Closed Sun. No lunch Mon.*

$$$
ECLECTIC

✕ The Green House. This modern glass building seems almost out of place on the road connecting Liberia to the coast. Filling a void in healthy cuisine, the restaurant serves wraps, salads, sushi, and sandwiches such as organic chicken with fresh basil. Vegetarians have plenty of options, including veggie skewers, orzo salad, spring rolls, asparagus soup, or a portobello sandwich. The bruschetta, tacos, and burgers are particularly delicious, while the seafood dishes are hit or miss. The prices are much higher than what you'll find in central Liberia, but it's a good stop for a quick bite. ⓢ *Average main: $20* ✉ *Hwy. 21, on road to airport in front of Pájaro Azul, 2 km (1 mile) from Liberia intersection* ☎ *2665–5037, 2665–8901* ⊕ *www.thegreenhousecostarica.com* ☾ *Closed Sun.*

$$$ ✕ **Restaurante Café Europa** (*Panaderia Alemana*). The aroma of baking
GERMAN bread is irresistible as you pass this German bakery, just south of the
FAMILY Liberia airport, whose baked goods are delivered all over the peninsula.
The display case is filled with tempting strudels, Bundt cakes, and flaky
fruit pastries. The cheesecakes and cinnamon rolls are so soft and moist,
you might lose your fork. There is also a full-fledged restaurant, serv-
ing everything from wood-fired pizzas to fish sandwiches. The menu is
huge, and so are portions, making this the ideal place to come pre- or
post-flight. The German owner has made sure that Deutsche classics
hit the table, including bratwurst with sauerkraut, pork schnitzel, and
hearty dark breads. The restaurant also has a gluten-free menu, a beer
garden, and playground. It's open daily from 5 am to 9 pm. ⑤ *Aver-
age main: $16* ✉ *5 km (3 miles) west of Liberia airport* ☎ *2668–1081*
⊕ *www.panaleman.com.*

$$ ✕ **Restaurante Casa Vieja.** Appropriately named, this century-old house
ITALIAN will take you back in time to an era when dining rooms were inti-
mate settings and secret family recipes ruled the kitchen. Soft music
and friendly service set the tone for the homemade pastas and wood-
fired pizzas, rolled thin and served crispy. The gnocchi pomodoro will
sweep your taste buds off to Italy, and the vegetarian pizza will have
you ditching rice and beans for the rest of your trip. Ask about the
daily specials like salmon in cream sauce with grilled zucchini or baby
prawns wrapped in phyllo and topped with chipotle aioli. Settle your
meal with a zesty chilled shot of limoncello, a sweet *digestivo* before you
sink your teeth into chocolate soufflé with amaretto gelato. ⑤ *Average
main: $12* ✉ *Ave Central, between Calle 5 and 7* ⊹ *50 m east of casino*
☎ *506/6105–5026* ⊙ *Closed Wed.*

WHERE TO STAY

$$$ ⛉ **Hilton Garden Inn Liberia Airport.** Comfortable and convenient, espe-
HOTEL cially if you're catching an early-morning flight or you need a break
from driving before heading south to the beach, this five-story contem-
porary Hilton has all the mod cons, including Wi-Fi, HDTVs, micro-
waves, and fridges. **Pros:** kids under 12 stay free; excellent amenities;
free shuttle to and from airport; good restaurant. **Cons:** no shaded
parking area; breakfast not included; some airplane noise. ⑤ *Rooms
from: $169* ✉ *Across from Liberia International Airport on main hwy.*
☎ *2690–8888* ⊕ *www.liberiaairport.hgi.com* ⇄ *169 rooms, including
8 handicapped-access rooms, 8 suites* ⧓ *No meals.*

$ ⛉ **Hotel Liberia.** Built in 1918, this colonial-style B&B is screaming with
HOTEL potential, and although it's not quite there (they have dorm rooms
in the back), the historical building and central courtyard make this
budget property a good option when passing through. **Pros:** beautiful
courtyard; great rates; centrally located; historical icon. **Cons:** no air-
conditioning; some street noise; attracts a hostel crowd; needs restora-
tion. ⑤ *Rooms from: $40* ✉ *C. Real, 75 m south of the central park*
☎ *2666–0161* ⊕ *www.hotelliberiacr.com* ⇄ *21 rooms* ⧓ *No meals.*

GUANACASTE PACIFIC COAST

Strung along the southern coast of Guanacaste are sparkling sand beaches lined with hotels and resorts in every price category. As recently as the 1970s, fishing and cattle ranching were the area's mainstays. Development has barreled ahead full speed, though, turning laid-back fishing villages into beach towns with sophisticated restaurants, hotels, shops, and nightlife. Development has also brought congestion, noise, construction chaos, water pollution and shortages, and higher prices. If resort life and the party scene are not your style, there are still some blissfully tranquil beaches just beyond the paved roads.

PAPAGAYO PENINSULA

47 km (29 miles) west of Liberia.

The Papagayo Peninsula, a crooked finger of land cradling the west side of Bahía Culebra (Snake Bay), enjoys guaranteed sun from January to April, making it a prime site for all-inclusive hotels catering to snowbirds escaping Northern winters. Five large hotels are already situated around Papagayo Bay, and others are slated to be built here, all part of a government-sponsored development program modeled after Cancún. Just before the entrance to Andaz Resort is the impressive Marina Papagayo, where luxury yachts and sailboats dock. Although the hotels are reminiscent of their Caribbean counterparts, the beaches are distinctly Costa Rican, with brown sand and aquamarine water that grows cool from January to April. Isolation is the name of the game here, which means that getting out of the man-made "paradise" to explore anything off-property often entails a pricey tour.

High season here coincides with dry season, when the heat is intense and the landscape becomes brown and brittle. In the rainy season (August to December), the landscape is greener and lusher. The sparkling water and spectacular sunsets are beautiful year-round.

GETTING HERE AND AROUND

All hotels here have airport pickup. To get to the Four Seasons from the Liberia airport (the hotel refuses to put up directional signs in order to protect its privacy), drive 10 km (6 miles) south of Guardia, over the Río Tempisque Bridge, then take the turn on the right signed for Andaz Peninsula Papagayo Resort. Follow this road about 20 km (12 miles) to its end at the entrance to the resort. For Casa Conde Hotel, El Mangroove, and Secrets Papagayo, take the road toward Playa Panama.

BEACHES

Playa Panama. On the southern end of Culebra Bay, this calm beach with black sand stretches 2 km (1¼ miles), and is frequented by guests staying at nearby El Mangroove resort and Casa Conde Beachfront Hotel. Devoid of rocks and waves, the water is virtually flat, making this a popular spot for stand-up paddleboarding, kayaking, and swimming. There's a wooden shack next to El Mangroove offering overpriced water activities and equipment. Local vendors stand beachside, selling everything from sarongs to snow cones. With a minimum of six people, you can organize a snorkeling tour on a boat to the outer bay. There isn't much shade on the sand, but a grassy area between the resorts and the beach is lined with swaying palms and mesquite trees. A path meanders from one end of the bay to the other, meaning you can stroll without getting too much sun. There's guarded parking ($1 tip) between the two hotels. **Amenities:** food and drink; water sports. **Best for:** kayaking; swimming; walking. ✉ *Playa Panama, at Culebra Bay, In front of El Mangroove.*

SPORTS AND THE OUTDOORS

CANOPY TOUR

Witch's Rock Canopy Tour. Taking advantage of one of the few remaining patches of dry tropical forest on the Papagayo Peninsula, Witch's Rock Canopy Tour gives you your money's worth: 24 platforms, with a thrilling 450-meter (1,485-foot) cable zip between two of them; three hanging bridges; a waterfall in rainy season; and hiking trails. The 1½-hour tour is $75 per person; transportation from area hotels is extra. ✉ *On road to Four Seasons Resort, 17 km (10 miles) west of DYI Center on main hwy. from Liberia* ☎ *2696–7101, 2696–7103* ⊕ *www. witchsrockcanopy.com* 💲 *From $75.*

GOLF

Four Seasons Golf Course at Peninsula Papagayo. Teeing off from one of the highest points on the Peninsula, this 18-hole, par-72 championship course is designed by Arnold Palmer and has breathtaking views on every play. Surrounded by ocean and forest, you're likely to encounter howler and white-faced monkeys during your game. Several holes are perched on cliffs backed by ocean, like hole 17 with spectacular views from both the tee and the green. Increasing the challenge are tough drops from the tees and small greens. Signature hole 6 demands skill; it's a long 446-yard par 4 with a tee shot that plays 200 feet downhill to a valley. In addition to the award-winning course, there's a driving range, a sand-bunker practice area, putting and chipping greens, and a pro shop. Tee times are offered from 7 am to 4 pm. ✉ *Four Seasons Resort Costa Rica* ✛ *26 km north of Liberia, follow signs to Andaz Resort* ☎ *2696–0000* ⊕ *www.fourseasons.com/costarica* 💲 *$230* 🏌 *18 holes, 6800 yards, par 72* ☞ *Closed Mon.*

SURFING

Tropic Surf. No one mixes surfing and luxury better than this highly professional outfitter, offering lessons ($110) and half-day excursions ($350) to Witch's Rock and Ollies Point aboard their fleet of boats. Their quiver is top-notch, ranging from shortboards to stand-up paddleboards. Trained instructors are on hand for all levels, delivering water and sunscreen while you surf. In addition to their location at Four Seasons Resort Peninsula Papagayo, they have over 20 destinations worldwide. ✉ *Four Seasons Peninsula Papagayo* ☎ *+61/7/5455–4129 Australia office* ⊕ *www.tropicsurf.net* 💲 *From $110.*

WHERE TO EAT AND STAY

$$$

INTERNATIONAL

✗**Makoko.** Experience culinary magic at El Mangroove's trendy poolside restaurant, where guests can dine with a glimpse of the ocean or head indoors to the more formal dining room enclosed in glass. Most ingredients are locally grown and nearly every item on the menu is

6

organic, including the grass-fed beef. Start with red-snapper carpaccio with grapefruit and fennel, or the seared scallops with caramelized cauliflower. Signature entrées include roasted sea bass with shiitake mushrooms, and the remarkably tender Worcestershire-glazed short ribs slow-cooked for 24 hours and served with apple-jalapeño puree. Portions are small, which means you may have room for the chocolate cheesecake. The mosquitoes are enough to ruin your meal so wear long pants or dine indoors. $ *Average main: $22* ⊠ *At intersection near Hilton Resort, Golfo de Papagayo* ☎ *4701–0000* ⊕ *www.elmangroove. net* ◐ *No lunch.*

$$$$
RESORT

⚏ **Andaz Peninsula Papagayo.** Earth tones and natural details prevail in this Hyatt property created by architect Ronald Zürcher, who utilized indigenous woods, sugarcane, and bamboo in the design of the rooms, each contemporary and bright with ocean views. **Pros:** friendly staff; free Kids' Club; design reflects natural surroundings. **Cons:** pricey meals; rooms have dim lighting; small and rocky beach; inconsistent service. $ *Rooms from: $800* ⊠ *Peninsula Papagayo, next to Four Seasons Resort* ☎ *2690–1234* ⊕ *www.andazpapagayo.com* ⇗ *132 rooms, 21 suites* ❘⚬❘ *No meals.*

$$$$
HOTEL
FAMILY

⚏ **Casa Conde Beachfront Hotel.** Spread over verdant grounds just behind relatively pristine Playa Panama, this all-inclusive property has an excellent location with bay views, balmy breezes, and a huge swimming pool. **Pros:** spacious rooms; immaculate grounds; close to beach; new rooms added in 2014. **Cons:** early check-ins cost $25/pp; rooms near pool can be noisy; no activities. $ *Rooms from: $310* ⊠ *Playa Panama, 3 km (2 miles) north of Playa Hermosa* ☎ *2586–7300 San José office, 2672–1008* ⊕ *www.grupocasaconde.com* ⇗ *50 rooms* ❘⚬❘ *All-inclusive.*

$$$$
HOTEL

⚏ **El Mangroove.** Barefoot luxury abounds at this hip boutique hotel where an airy courtyard leads to a 45-meter pool lined with beach bungalows and modern rooms. **Pros:** 24-hour room service; nice gym and spa; gorgeous rain showers; all-inclusive plan available. **Cons:** poolside cabana costs $150 per day; only two rooms have ocean views; mosquitoes in common areas; staff lacks attention to detail. $ *Rooms from: $320* ⊠ *Bahia Papagayo, at Playa Panama, at intersection before Hilton Resort, Golfo de Papagayo* ☎ *4701–0000* ⊕ *www.elmangroove. net* ⇗ *85 rooms* ❘⚬❘ *No meals.*

$$$$
RESORT
Fodor's Choice
★

⚏ **Four Seasons Resort Costa Rica.** After a $35 million property enhancement, the Four Seasons has secured its reputation as one of the most luxurious hotels in Costa Rica with newly decorated rooms, a remodeled lobby, spa, and restaurants, and the addition of several luxury retail boutiques. **Pros:** impeccable service; lovely beach; surf trips to Witch's Rock. **Cons:** breakfast not included; 30 minutes from main road; expensive; except for Caracol Steakhouse, food can be disappointing considering the price. $ *Rooms from: $1,100* ⊠ *25 km (15 miles) west of Guardia, Follow signs to Andaz Resort and continue to end of road* ☎ *2696–0000, 800/332–3442 in U.S and Canada* ⊕ *www. fourseasons.com/costarica* ⚹ *$230 for 18 holes* ⇗ *120 rooms, 23 suites, 16 villas* ❘⚬❘ *No meals.*

Guanacaste Pacific
Coast and the
Northern
Nicoya Peninsula

PLAYA HERMOSA

27 km (17 miles) southwest of Liberia airport.

Beautiful Playa Hermosa, once a laid-back fishing community, has grown exponentially with condominiums and villas covering the scrubby hills overlooking the wide, curved beach. Warm, swimmable water, prime dive sites, choice fishing grounds, and sunset views of the Papagayo Peninsula are all reasons why Canadian and American expatriates are buying condos here. In the early morning, though, Playa Hermosa is still the kind of place where the beach is the town's main thoroughfare, filled with joggers, people walking their dogs, and families out for a stroll. Not to be confused with the mainland surfers' beach of the same name south of Jacó, this Playa Hermosa has long been occupied by small hotels, restaurants, and homes along the length of the beach, so the newer hotel behemoths and other developments are forced to set up shop off the beach or up on the surrounding hillsides.

GETTING HERE AND AROUND

Heading south from Liberia along Highway 21, take the turnoff in Comunidad signed for Playa Hermosa and Playas del Coco. Playa Hermosa is about 15 km (9 miles) northwest. The paved road forks after the small town of Sardinal, the right fork heading into Hermosa and the left leading to Playas del Coco. Local directions usually refer to the first and second entrance roads to the beach, the first entrance being the southern one. There is no through beachfront road, so you have to approach the beach from either of these two roads. Transportes La Pampa buses leave from Liberia for Playa Hermosa daily starting at 4:30, 4:40, 4:50 am (to get workers to their hotel jobs), then at 7:30 and 11:30 am and 1, 3:30, and 5:30 pm. The trip takes about 1½ hours. A taxi from Playa Hermosa to Playas del Coco costs about $15 and takes about 15 minutes.

ESSENTIALS
Playa Hermosa has a large supermarket, Luperón, on the main road, between the first and second beach entrances, open daily 7 am to 8:30 pm, where you can stock up on just about everything you need—food, wine, liquor, toiletries, even fresh-baked French and ciabatta bread.

BEACHES
Playa Hermosa. Not to be confused with the surfers' beach near Jacó by the same name, Playa Hermosa's 2-km-long (1-mile-long) crescent of dark gray volcanic sand attracts heat, making the early morning or late afternoon the best time to visit (with the latter providing spectacular sunsets). The beach fronts a line of shade trees, so there's a welcome respite from the heat of the sun. The crystal-clear water—it's a Blue Flag beach—is usually calm, with no strong currents and with comfortable temperatures of 23°C to 27°C (74°F to 80°F). For offshore diving, there's an average visibility of 6 meters (20 feet), and rock reefs that attract large schools of fish, sea turtles, sharks, manta rays, and moray eels. Sea views are as picturesque as they get, with bobbing fishing boats, jagged profiles of coastline, rocky outcroppings, and at night the twinkling lights of the Four Seasons Resort across the bay. At the beach's north end, low tide creates wide, rock-lined tidal pools. Food and drinks are available at Hotel El Velero. **Amenities:** food and drink; water sports. **Best for:** swimming; walking. ⊠ *Playa Hermosa.*

SPORTS AND THE OUTDOORS
BOATING AND FISHING
The fishing at Playa Hermosa is mostly close to the shores, and yields edible fish like dorado (mahimahi), snapper, amberjack, tuna, and wahoo. Roosterfish, marlin, and sailfish are all catch-and-release. Some local restaurants are happy to cook your catch for you. You can rent a boat or snorkel with **North Pacific Tours.** Most Hermosa-based snorkeling companies head to nearby spots where you may see turtles, eagle rays, eels, parrot fish, snapper, puffer fish, and angle fish. Start out early when waters are calm.

Charlie's Adventure. Operating out of the Hotel Condovac, Occidental Allegro, and Occidental Grand, this tour company organizes ATV tours, fishing trips, diving excursions, as well as the seven-hour Aqua Combo boat tours of Hermosa Bay, which includes snorkeling, bottom fishing, and a beach barbecue lunch ($90, including drinks). There's also a sunset boat tour. ⊠ *Hotel Condovac, north end of beach* ☎ *2672–0275* ⊕ *www.charliesadventure.com* ⊠ *From $50.*

Hotel El Velero. This beachfront hotel has a 38-foot sailing yacht for five-hour sunset cruises ($75 per person). Daytime tours include snorkeling and a picnic lunch with soft drinks ($85 per person). ✉ *100 m north of Aqua Sport* ☎ *2672–1017* ⊕ *www.costaricahotel.net* ✎ *From $75.*

North Pacific Tours. Based in Playa Hermosa, this reliable outfitter has private and customized charters for fishing, surfing, and snorkeling tours aboard a 28-foot center-console panga. They run various fishing tours in the area, starting at $400 for a half-day excursion. ✉ *Playa Hermosa* ☎ *506/8398–8129* ⊕ *www.northpacifictours.com* ✎ *From $60.*

WHERE TO EAT
A few of Playa Hermosa's best restaurants are at hotels.

$$$
PERUVIAN

✕ **Aqua Sport.** There's not much "aqua sport" going on at this Peruvian beachfront restaurant, unless you count drinking margaritas in a hammock. It's the kind of place you drop by on day one, and find yourself coming back to for the remainder of your vacation—blame the setting of Adirondack chairs lining the beach combined with fresh fish like grilled snapper served with shoestring fries. There are seven types of ceviche and a seafood soup that is good enough to make you miss the sunset between bites. For something absolutely non-Costa Rican, try the Peruvian Causa, a spicy potato-layered dish with tuna, octopus, or shrimp. You can also order familiar favorites like tacos, burgers, and surf and turf. Service is slow and prices are high, but there's live music (Saturdays) and tables in the sand. ⑤ *Average main: $17* ✉ *Second entrance to Playa Hermosa, at the beach* ☎ *506/2672–0151.*

$$$
TAPAS

✕ **Ginger Restaurant Bar.** This tapas restaurant, featuring Asian and Mediterranean flavors, is in a modernistic glass-and-steel tree house that's cantilevered on the side of a hill and includes a spacious deck. Delectable appetizer-size offerings include seared pepper-crusted tuna atop pickled ginger slaw, or pan-fried sea bass fillets with a divine ginger-and-mandarin-orange butter sauce. Not to be missed are Ginger's crispy shoestring fries, served with roasted garlic mayo. Portions are small, but layers of condiments and garnishes make them surprisingly satisfying. The fun thing to do is order several dishes and share. The varied wine list includes Old and New World wines by the glass, and specialty martinis and tropical cocktails go well with the tapas. For dessert, warm chocolate lava cake is rich enough to share, but only with someone you truly love. Be aware that the menu prices do not include tax and service (another 23%). It's open 5 to 10 pm. ⑤ *Average main: $18* ✉ *Main hwy., south of Hotel Condovac* ☎ *2672–0041* ⊕ *www.gingercostarica.com* ⊘ *Closed Mon. No lunch.*

$$$$
SEAFOOD
Fodor'sChoice
★

✕ **Mario's Cuisine.** A set four-course dinner, by reservation only, served at 8 pm sharp, in the home of prodigy-chef Mario Rivera, makes this underground supper club one of the most memorable restaurants on the coast. On the open brick patio, guests share a communal table adorned with tea-light candles and fresh flowers. Come with an open mind as the chef and his charming wife Ericka serve beautifully prepared dishes made from Mario's daily spearfishing catch. You're likely to try yellowfin tuna with passion-fruit sauce, needlefish marinated in fresh herbs, or parrot fish and roasted tomatoes topped with lobster bisque. Everything is made from scratch, and they will gladly accommodate vegetarians or those with gluten-free diets. The $65 set menu includes two appetizers, an entrée, and dessert like the creamy raspberry-wine gelato. Since

6

there's no drinks menu, plan to bring your own wine. A 50% deposit is required before dining. Once you fall in love with the adorable hosts, set aside a day for their cooking class, spearfishing tour, or Spanish lessons available upon request. ⑤ *Average main: $65* ✉ *1st entrance to the beach, 300 m from the main road* ☎ *5705–1645, 8741–3376* ⚱ *Reservations essential.*

WHERE TO STAY

$$ 🔆 **Hotel & Villas Huetares.** The best bargain in town, this long-established

HOTEL   family hotel offers two-bedroom garden villas surrounding a central

FAMILY   pool, as well as a two-story annex with 16 spacious rooms. **Pros:** close to beach; good kitchens; beautiful grounds and pool. **Cons:** lots of noise from kids, especially on weekends; no hot water; weak Wi-Fi signal. ⑤ *Rooms from: $92* ✉ *2nd entrance road to Playa Hermosa, 100 m (1 block) in from the main hwy.* ☎ *2672–0052* ⊕ *www.villahuetares.com* 🛏 *16 rooms, 24 villas* ⦿ *Breakfast.*

$$ 🔆 **Hotel El Velero.** This laid-back hotel is right on the beach, and, though

HOTEL   nothing fancy, it has comfortable rooms and is an excellent option if

FAMILY   you're watching your expenses. **Pros:** on the beach; affordable; friendly; informal. **Cons:** tiny pool; most rooms lack views; some rooms are dark and boxy; neighboring disco can be noisy on weekends. ⑤ *Rooms from: $99* ✉ *2nd entrance to Playa Hermosa, on beach road* ☎ *2672–0036* ⊕ *www.costaricahotel.net* 🛏 *22 rooms* ⦿ *No meals.*

$$ 🔆 **Hotel La Finisterra.** From its perch high above the southern end of

HOTEL   Playa Hermosa, this small hotel commands the best view of the beach and bay, along with the best terrace for watching sunsets. **Pros:** good food; very friendly staff; great views. **Cons:** steep climb up from beach; small pool; breakfast included in high season only. ⑤ *Rooms from: $140* ✉ *1st entrance to Playa Hermosa, left before Hotel Playa Hermosa, 250 m up hill* ☎ *2672–0227* ⊕ *www.lafinisterrahotel.com* 🛏 *11 rooms* ⦿ *Breakfast.*

$$$ 🔆 **Hotel Playa Hermosa Bosque del Mar.** This beachfront hotel on the

HOTEL   southern end of Playa Hermosa features luxurious rooms and suites

Fodor'sChoice   on a beautiful, spacious property shaded by century-old, vine-draped

★   trees. **Pros:** superb garden and beachfront location; all-inclusive meal plan available; beautiful restaurant; all rooms have terraces. **Cons:** some rooms near the pool are dark; mosquitoes; expensive for the area. ⑤ *Rooms from: $226* ✉ *End of 1st entrance to Playa Hermosa* ☎ *2672–0046* ⊕ *www.hotelplayahermosa.com* 🛏 *20 junior suites, 12 deluxe suites, 1 penthouse suite* ⦿ *No meals.*

$$ 🔆 **Villa del Sueño.** Although the handsome garden restaurant is the main

HOTEL   attraction at this elegant hotel, the spacious rooms and well-equipped villas are quite comfortable, too, and the hotel is about a block from the beach. **Pros:** excellent restaurant; good value; standard and superior rooms remodeled in 2015. **Cons:** not on the beach; can be noisy when there's live music; breakfast not included in high season. ⑤ *Rooms from: $115* ✉ *1st entrance to Playa Hermosa, 500 m west of main hwy.* ☎ *2672–0026* ⊕ *www.villadelsueno.com* 🛏 *14 rooms, 27 villas, 3 2-bedroom villas* ⦿ *No meals.*

NIGHTLIFE

Hotel El Velero. This lively beachfront hotel hosts beach barbecues on Wednesday and Saturday nights, and Taco Tuesday (half-off tacos). The crowd is thirtyish and up. ⊠ *2nd entrance to Playa Hermosa, then 100 m north of Aqua Sport on beach road* ☎ *2672–1017* ⊕ *www. costaricahotel.net.*

Villa del Sueño. In high season, Villa del Sueño hosts live music on Tuesday, Friday, and Sunday nights, as well as occasional concerts featuring top national bands and performers. ⊠ *1st entrance to Playa Hermosa, 500 m west of main hwy.* ☎ *2672–0026* ⊕ *www.villadelsueno.com.*

SHOPPING

La Gran Nicoya. You can get any souvenir you could possibly want at this lively emporium. There's also a restaurant, a coffee tour, and the occasional folklore show. Last-minute shoppers can stop in on their way to nearby Liberia airport. It's open 8 to 6 daily, except Good Friday. ⊠ *25 m south of Guardia soccer field, on main hwy. south of Liberia airport, before turnoff to Hermosa, Hermosa* ☎ *2667–0062.*

Villa del Sueño. The small but upscale gift shop at Villa del Sueño has colorful and flattering beach cover-ups, designed and made locally. They also sell a few souvenirs and snacks. ⊠ *1st entrance to Playa Hermosa, 500 m west of main hwy.* ☎ *2672–0026.*

6

PLAYAS DEL COCO

25 km (16 miles) southwest of Liberia airport; 10 km (6 miles) south of Playa Hermosa.

Messy, noisy, colorful, and interesting, Playas del Coco has the best souvenir shopping, the most dive shops, and the liveliest nightlife and barhopping on this part of the coast. It's still a working fishing port, with a port captain's office, a fish market, and an ice factory for keeping the catch of the day fresh—not for cooling margaritas, although many are enjoyed here. The beach has a beautiful boardwalk with palm trees, benches, and even cold showers. An explosion of condominium and villa projects has brought new money to the community, along with new commercial development, including the upscale Pacifico Village shopping center at the entrance to town. This center boasts a flagship AutoMercado, the country's top grocery chain, as well as a bank, pharmacy, restaurants, fast-food chains, a UPS office, and a few clothing boutiques. Fresh seafood, myriad souvenir shops, and plenty of bars have always drawn tourists here, but Playas del Coco also has a high concentration of tour operators offering diving, fishing, and surfing excursions at remote breaks such as Ollie's Point and Witch's Rock. Because Coco is mere minutes from Playa Hermosa, however, you can just as easily enjoy those sports while staying at that more pleasant beach. If you like to shop and party, and want some local color, Coco's slightly raucous ambience can be appealing.

GETTING HERE AND AROUND

The easy drive from the Liberia airport to Playas del Coco takes about 30 minutes. The paved highway turns into a grand, divided boulevard as you enter town; it ends at the beach. If you don't have a car, the best way to get here from Playa Hermosa is in a taxi, for about $20 each way.

ESSENTIALS

Banks/ATMs BAC San Jose. ⊠ *At Pacifico Village, next to AutoMercado.*
Banco Nacional. ⊠ *Main street, at entrance to town.*

Hospital Public Health Clinic (*Ebais La Costa Coco Clinic*). ⊠ *Next to La Puerta del Sol hotel* ☎ *2670–0987* ⊕ *www.cocoebais.com.*

Pharmacy Fischel Pharmacy. ⊠ *Pacifico Village, next to AutoMercado* ☎ *800/347–2435.*

Post Office Correo. ⊠ *At entrance to town on main road* ✛ *100 m south of Hotel Flor de Itabo.*

SPORTS AND THE OUTDOORS

BOATING

Marlin Del Rey. With operations in Tamarindo, Playa Flamingo, and Playas del Coco, Marlin Del Rey offers sailing tours on their 65-foot catamaran complete with a water slide and inflatable boat. Trips will take you to deserted white-sand beaches and include snorkeling, lunch, and an open bar. Sunset tours depart at 1:30 pm and cost $85 per person. ⊠ *Main Street* ☎ *506/2653–1212, 877/827–8275 in U.S.* ⊕ *www. marlindelrey.com* ☒ *$85.*

DIVING AND SNORKELING

Half a dozen dive shops populate this small town. The standard price for a two-tank dive is $85; Catalina Island dives are $115. This coast doesn't have the coral reefs or the clear visibility of the Caribbean coast, but it does have a lot of plankton (hence the lower visibility) that feeds legions of fish, some of them really, really big. Manta rays and sharks (white-tipped, nurse, and bull varieties) are among the stars of the undersea show. It takes about 20 to 45 minutes to reach most dive sites.

Deep Blue Diving Adventures. This organization has daily scuba-diving trips to the top dive spots in the Papagayo Gulf, as well as Catalina and Murciélagos islands (Bat Islands). ⊠ *Corner of Chorrera and Cangrejo* ☎ *2670–1004* ⊕ *www.deepblue-diving.com* ☒ *From $85.*

Fodor's Choice ★ **Rich Coast Diving.** This longtime operator has enthusiastic guides and is the only PADI five-star CDC facility with the Green Star Award in Costa Rica. It offers daily fun dives, PADI courses, and snorkeling trips. ⊠ *Main street, near intersection with road to Playa Ocotal, near Medical Center* ☎ *2670–0176* ⊕ *www.richcoastdiving.com* ☒ *From $80.*

Sirenas Diving Costa Rica. With nearly 20 years of experience, this dive operation has a full range of scuba activities, from beginner training to open-water PADI certification and dive master courses. Multi-tank dives are organized at more than 20 sites. Guides and trainers are very good, and their safety standards have the DAN (Divers Alert Network) seal of approval. Prices range from $100 for two-tank morning dives to $495 and up for the PADI open-water certification course. Courses are offered from their PADI dive boat in Playas del Coco, and there's no physical office, so reservations are essential. ⊠ *Playas del Coco* ☎ *8813–7882, 8387–4710* ⊕ *www.sirenasdivingcostarica.com* ✉ *From $100.*

Summer Salt Dive Center. This longstanding small dive center is great for beginners. They focus on safety and fun in diving and snorkeling, and also offer whale-watching and water tours of the Gulf of Papagayo. ⊠ *Main street, 100 m south of the park* ☎ *2670–0308* ⊕ *www.summersalt.com* ✉ *From $70.*

FISHING

Fishing charter boats go out 24 to 64 km (15 to 40 miles) seeking yellowfin tuna, mahimahi, grouper, and red snapper close in, and sailfish, marlin, and roosterfish offshore (beyond 64 km [40 miles]).

GOLF

Vista Ridge Golf & Country Club. Formerly Papagayo Golf & Country Club, this 18-hole, par-72 course is affordable and just 10 minutes from Playas del Coco. You can play the whole course for $100, including a golf cart and a cooler with ice and water, but don't expect the Four Seasons. The greens are small and slow once the afternoon winds kick in, with some challenging holes toward the back tees. Long drives through the rainforest mean you'll encounter plenty of wildlife and ocean views while you play. Signature hole 18 (par 3) drives 171 yards directly through the towering trees. The first tee time is at 7:30, and the last is at 1:30 pm. There's a country club, driving range, putting green, swimming pool, and a Sunday tournament that starts at 8 am ($60, includes breakfast). ⊠ *10 km (6 miles) southeast of Playas del Coco, Libertad* ☎ *2697–0169* ⊕ *www.vistaridgecr.com* ✉ *$100 for 18 holes* 🏌 *18 holes, 6028 yards, par 72* ⊘ *Closed Fri.*

SURFING

Witch's Rock and Ollie's Point. These legendary surfing spots are no more than an hour's boat ride away from Playas del Coco off the coast of Santa Rosa National Park. You can surf as long as you pay the $15 park entrance fee.

You can sign up for a surfing trip with any beach-town tour operator, but local authorities allow excursions to Witch's Rock and Ollie's Point to originate only from the main dock at Playas del Coco, in boats owned by local boat owners, in order to curb overcrowding and undue environmental stress. The 40-minute boat trip to Witch's Rock costs about $250, or $350 to surf both Witch's Rock and Ollie's Point, which is located an additional 20 minutes north. For those prices, your boat captain will spend the day waiting aboard while you surf. Luxury surf excursions to both breaks are also available through Tropic Surf, based at The Four Seasons Resort on Peninsula Papagayo. ⊠ *Playas del Coco.*

WHERE TO EAT

$$$
ECLECTIC

✕ **Citron.** It might not be beachfront, but this snazzy restaurant has an upscale vibe with hardwood floors, white brick walls, and a wine bar shaking up divine watermelon martinis. For more ambience, grab a table on the outside deck where dishes like salmon risotto, poached sea bass, and shrimp sautéed in coconut milk are served. For something from the land, try the caramelized pork in a honey-and-lime sauce or

THE ECOLOGICAL BLUE FLAG

The tourist industry here estimates that three-quarters of visitors to Costa Rica make a beach excursion. With that in mind, the national water utility, Acueductos y Alcantarillados (AyA), in conjunction with the Instituto Costarricense de Turismo, evaluates and ranks water and environmental quality in coastal communities. Those that achieve at least a 90% score are awarded a Bandera Azul Ecológica (Ecological Blue Flag) to fly as a symbol of excellence. The program, modeled on one begun in Spain in 1986, awards flags as prizes for communities. Participants are required to form a Blue Flag committee, a move that brings together diverse sectors of an area's population, many of which otherwise fiercely compete for tourist dollars. The program has prompted communities to put resources into improving environmental quality of life for themselves and for their guests.

Blue Flag locales receive year-round inspections of water quality—both ocean and drinking water—trash cleanup, waste management, security, signage, and environmental education. (Winners dare not rest on their laurels: a few know the shame of having their flags yanked.) In 2002, the competition was opened to inland communities; recent years have seen eco-friendly schools, businesses, and institutions recognized—even an exceptionally green auto mechanic shop in San José flies a flag.

Blue flags fly proudly in the following locations:

Central Valley: CATIE, Heredia, San Rafael de Heredia.

Arenal, Monteverde, and the Northern Lowlands: La Fortuna, Monteverde Cloud Forest Reserve.

Guanacaste and the Nicoya Peninsula: Playa Bahía Junquillal, Bahía Salinas (Playa Copal, Playa Jobo, Playa Rajada), Curú National Wildlife Refuge, Isla Tortuga, Nosara (Playa Garza, Playa Guiones, Playa Pelada), Ostional, Playa Avellanas, Playa Conchal, Playa Grande, Playa Hermosa, Playa Junquillal, Playa Langosta, Playa Ocotal, Playa Pan de Azúcar, Playa Panamá, Playa Potrero, Playa Sámara, Playa Tambor, Punta Islita, Puntarenas, Santa Teresa.

Manuel Antonio and the Central Pacific Coast: Caldera, Isla del Coco, Jacó, Malpaís, Manuel Antonio (Playa Manuel Antonio, Playa Espadilla Norte, Playa Espadilla Sur), Playa Bejuco.

The Osa Peninsula and the South Pacific: Ballena National Marine Park, Barú, Cabo Matapalo, Carate, Las Cruces Biological Station, Playa Dominical, Playa Nicuesa, Playa Pavones, Playa Zancudo, Puerto Jiménez (Playa Blanca), San Gerardo de Rivas.

Tortuguero and the Caribbean Coast: Cahuita (Playa Blanca, Playa Negra, Puerto Vargas), EARTH, Gandoca-Manzanillo Wildlife Refuge, Puerto Viejo de Talamanca (Playa Chiquita, Playa Cocles, Playa Negra, Punta Uva), Tortuguero.

the heavily requested Dijon beef tenderloin. Don't skip dessert—try the Bailey's panna cotta with passion-fruit coulis. $ *Average main: $17* ⊠ *Pacifico Retail Village, Suite C #10, Rte. 151* ☎ *2670–0942* ⊕ *www. citroncoco.com* ☾ *Closed Sun. No lunch.*

$$$ ✕ **Garden 248 Gastropub.** Look for the string of paper lanterns over a
INTERNATIONAL   white-pebble patio and you'll know you've arrived at this cool spot famous for creative cuisine and local microbrews. The tiny kitchen delivers miraculous freshness, and whips up one-of-a-kind dishes like deviled eggs filled with bacon and shrimp, avocado-mango-seafood soup, and sea bass tiradito in a plantain shell. You can't go wrong with the spring rolls, beef sliders, tuna steak, or German sausage. No matter how many times you've had chips and guacamole, chances are this gastropub will take the prize with its homemade yuca-and-plantain chips. There's indoor and outdoor dining, but for some reason, the beer just tastes better in the garden on one of the funky couches made from recycled wooden pallets. $ *Average main: $20* ⊠ *200 m south of Luperon Supermarket, 200 m south of Pacífico Plaza* ☎ *8573–4412* ☾ *Closed Sun.*

$$ ✕ **The Lookout.** As if the breathtaking view high in the hills above Playas
SEAFOOD   del Coco weren't enough, the innovative menu at one of the few oyster
Fodor'sChoice   bars in Costa Rica takes it a step further. Aside from oysters prepared
★   raw, charbroiled, steamed, or fried, there are also sandwiches and sushi. More creative dishes include avocado fries with chipotle dip, lobster grilled cheese, Korcan beef tacos, and the ahi tuna sticky rice bowl. The Monkey Head Brewing Company, an on-site microbrewery (which you can tour) produces 17 beers on tap. The cocktails are divine, like the kiwitini or watermelon mojito. Come for happy hour from 3 to 5, and stay until the sun goes down. If you've got your heart set on oysters, come on Tuesday or Thursday when they're delivered fresh; otherwise they run out quickly. Reservations are recommended during sunset hours. $ *Average main: $10* ⊠ *Rooftop of Hotel Chantel, up the hill in Vista Marina* ☎ *8755–7246* ⊕ *www.thelookoutcoco.com* ☾ *Closed Mon. Closed Mon.–Wed in Oct. No lunch.*

WHERE TO STAY

$$ ⊡ **Hotel Chantel.** On a hilltop, this boutique hotel has vibrant Mediter-
HOTEL   ranean-style rooms, apartments, and a luxurious two-bedroom pent-house—all with ocean views. **Pros:** breathtaking views; great rates; amazing rooftop restaurant. **Cons:** not child-friendly (no children under 10); small pool; 5-minute drive to Coco Beach and 10 minutes to Ocotal Beach. $ *Rooms from: $89* ⊠ *Playas del Coco* ✛ *At entrance to Playas del Coco, turn left at anchor, follow signs to hotel.* ☎ *506/2670–0389* ⊕ *www.hotelchantel.com* ⇝ *11 rooms* ⦶ *Breakfast.*

$$ ⊡ **La Puerta del Sol.** Facing a formal garden with sculpted shrubs and a
HOTEL   lovely pool, this tranquil enclosure just two blocks from the beach has airy, Mediterranean-style guest rooms splashed with tropical colors. **Pros:** intimate; comfortable; some rooms renovated in 2015. **Cons:** a few cats prowling the garden; hard beds; restaurant open for breakfast only; rooms lack charm. $ *Rooms from: $100* ⊠ *180 m to right (north) off main road to town* ☎ *2670–0195* ⊕ *www.lapuertadelsolcostarica. com* ⇝ *8 rooms, 1 suite, 1 apartment* ⦶ *Breakfast.*

6

$$$$
HOTEL
Fodor's Choice
★

📷 **Villa Buena Onda.** Tucked away in the quiet hills of Playas del Coco, this "good vibe" hotel delivers luxury, service, and elegance. **Pros:** impeccable service; organic meals; perfect for couples. **Cons:** usually full; only top-floor rooms have ocean views; not family-friendly (no kids under 16). ⑤ *Rooms from: $434 ⊠ At entrance to Coco, turn left before old anchor, stay right (straight) at the fork, left before bridge, continue to top of hill, villa is on the left ☎ 4031–7707, 800/414–0159 in U.S. or Canada ⊕ www.villabuenaonda.com ⤴ 7 rooms; 1 suite ⍭ All meals.*

NIGHTLIFE
Coconutz. Local expats meet up at this popular sports bar and grill. It's usually packed during happy hour (3 to 7), which features a DJ. They also have pool tables, TVs for *Monday Night Football*, a full range of bar food, and live music on Friday and Saturday. Wednesday night is movie night with all-you-can-eat pizza and pasta, and Tuesday features karaoke at 7:30. There's also free Wi-Fi, but don't expect to be able to focus on work over the noise. ⊠ *Main road, across from El Coco Casino* ☎ *2670–1982 ⊕ www.coconutz-costarica.com.*

Lizard Lounge. At this popular lounge there's Mexican food and dancing every night on a big dance floor. The reggae, techno, and rap beats appeal to a very young crowd. Happy hour is 11 to 7 and there's free Wi-Fi. Ladies drink free on Wednesday and Friday nights. ⊠ *Main road, west of Hotel Coco Beach and Casino* ☎ *2670–0307.*

SHOPPING
Souvenir stalls and shops line the main drag near the entrance to the beach.

Galería & Souvenirs Sussy. If you're looking for something in particular and you can't find it at this cluttered emporium, chances are they don't make it in Costa Rica. Along with a huge selection of interesting notebooks and albums made of botanical materials, the place also sells locally made shell belts. Next door is their clothing store selling beachwear, sandals, bags, and hats. ⊠ *Main street, on right before beach* ☎ *2670–0569.*

PLAYA OCOTAL

3 km (2 miles) south of Playas del Coco.

Just a few minutes south of Playas del Coco, this beach couldn't be more different than its rapidly developing neighbor. Quiet and serene, there is little commercial development, aside from a couple of beachfront restaurants. A large resort hotel dominates the beach, and private condominium complexes and luxurious villas pile up on the steep hills overlooking the ocean.

GETTING HERE AND AROUND
The drive is 10 minutes from Playas del Coco on a paved road to the gated entrance of Playa Ocotal. The road winds through a heavily populated Tico residential area, so be on the lookout, especially at night, for bicyclists without lights, children, dogs, cows, and horses on the road. There are no buses from Playas del Coco to Ocotal, but it's about $6 by taxi.

EXPLORING

The Monkey Farm. Despite the name, you're likely to see more goats, ducks, chickens, pigs, and other farm animals than you are monkeys. At this volunteer-run operation, animals are rescued, rehabilitated, and released back into the wild. At any given time, you might see reptiles, raccoons, and (usually) a monkey or two that are being treated for injuries. Keep in mind this is not a zoo, nor is it a tourist trap, meaning that animals roam free and the sanctuary survives on a donation basis. The sustainable farm has an impressive aquaponics setup and offers horseback-riding tours—$45 per hour in the jungle or $60 per two hours on the beach. The road to the farm is rough, especially during rainy season, so a 4WD is advised. ⊠ *On road from Playas del Coco to Ocotal, 1/2 mile from Playa Ocotal* ☎ *8853–0165* ⊕ *www.themonkeyfarm.org* ✉ *Donation suggested* ☉ *Daily 8–4.*

BEACHES

Playa Ocotal. One of the most dramatic beaches in the country, this serene crescent of black-sand beach ringed by rocky cliffs contrasts nicely with the sparkling, clean turquoise water. It's only ½ km (¼ mile) long, but the views stretch for miles and include nearby offshore islands and the jagged profile of the Santa Elena Peninsula 34 km (21 miles) away. This is prime fishing, diving, and relaxing territory. Right at the entrance to the Gulf of Papagayo, it's a good place for sportfishing enthusiasts to hole up between excursions. There's good diving at Las Corridas, just 1 km (½ mile) away, and excellent snorkeling in nearby coves and islands, as well as around the rocks at the east end of the beach. **Amenities:** food and drink. **Best for:** snorkeling. ⊠ *10-min drive south of Playas del Coco.*

WHERE TO EAT AND STAY

$$$
COSTA RICAN
✗ **Picante.** It's hot and it's tropical, and, as the name warns (*picante* means "spicy"), some of the dishes here make your taste buds tingle. The menu spices up (literally) local fish and tropical fruits in dishes like grilled mahimahi with orange chipotle sauce. If you can't face a whole red snapper, try the excellent fish tacos made with fresh snapper. There's also a milder kids' menu. The large terrace restaurant is poolside and faces a gorgeous beach, but it is backed by the cookie-cutter condominium development at Bahía Pez Vela. The long road here is worth it for the delicious coconut cream pie and cheesecake for dessert. ⑤ *Average main: $16* ⊠ *At Bahia Pez Vela Resort, 1½ km (1 mile) south of Ocotal* ☎ *2670–0901* ⊕ *www.bahiapezvela.com.*

$$$
B&B/INN
☷ **Hotel Villa Casa Blanca.** If you want to be close to Playas del Coco but still have some solitude, you can't beat this Victorian-style bed-and-breakfast enveloped in a hillside bower of tropical plantings. **Pros:** romantic; quiet location; use of outdoor kitchen. **Cons:** smallish, aging rooms; noisy parrots; chilly pool. ⑤ *Rooms from: $155* ⊠ *Near Father Rooster, 150 m from the beach* ☎ *2670–0448* ⊕ *www.villacasablancahotel.com/* ➽ *10 rooms, 4 suites* ⎰⎱*Breakfast.*

DID YOU KNOW?

Magnificent beaches and a dramatically sculpted shoreline are southern Guanacaste's trademarks. Here you'll find no shortage of wildlife-watching opportunities. Be sure to check out the tide pools that form on the rocky headlands at each end of Playa Ocotal.

NIGHTLIFE

Father Rooster. The best place to enjoy a quiet sunset margarita—or make that a rooster-rita—is at this laid-back bar and restaurant on the beach. You can relax on the wooden deck, or at the tables right on the sand, and enjoy a romantic dinner featuring fresh fish and Tex-Mex favorites. Portions here are huge and there's free Wi-Fi, a pool table, a big-screen TV, and occasional live music to keep you entertained. It's open 11 to 10, though it does close for private parties so you may want to call ahead. Guests from the Four Seasons often anchor here for a drink before sailing back to Peninsula Papagayo. ⊠ *100 m west of El Ocotal Beach Resort, 3 km (2 miles) south of Playas del Coco* ☎ *2670–1246* ⊕ *www.fatherrooster.com.*

PLAYA PAN DE AZÚCAR

8 km (5 miles) north of Flamingo Beach.

Playa Pan de Azúcar literally means "Sugar Bread Beach," though most locals call it simply Playa Azúcar (Sugar Beach). With only two built-up properties, the entire stretch of beach feels practically deserted and very private, qualities that can be hard to find in this area. Sweet, indeed.

GETTING HERE AND AROUND

Getting to the beach area of Playa Pan de Azúcar is a snap since the road is paved and well marked. From Liberia Airport, head toward the Belén intersection. Turn right toward Huacas, following the signs to Flamingo and Potrero. After passing through Brasilito, veer right toward Potrero and Playa Pan de Azúcar. Don't be lured by the "short-cut" that passes through the mountains from Sardinal to Flamingo. It might actually take longer, and you'll need a 4WD vehicle and a GPS if you want to drive (dry season only) this 16-km (11-mile) route that locals call the "Monkey Trail." The first part of the road is graded, but rapidly deteriorates as it travels over river crossings, through jungle, and down rocky terrain. Even some Ticos get lost on this route, so if you take it, keep asking for directions along the way. The only buses to Playa Pan de Azúcar are from Playa Flamingo for $6 or from the Santa Cruz terminal, departing five times daily for $4; a taxi from Playa Flamingo costs about $20.

BEACHES

Playa Pan de Azúcar. A seemingly endless stretch of soft, light-colored sand, this Blue Flag beach is the idyllic paradise people picture in their tropical dreams. There is only one property on the entire beach, the Hotel Sugar Beach, offering parking, restrooms, and a restaurant open to the public except during private events. The north end of the beach has some good snorkeling when the sea is calm—usually around low tide—and swimming out from the middle of the beach is relatively safe. Watch out for a few rocks on both sides of the cove, and if the swell is big, children and weak swimmers shouldn't go in past their waist. This beach is frequented by Ticos on weekends, but it is still relatively peaceful compared to neighboring beaches. Playa Penca, a short walk south along the beach, can be a good swimming beach as well. A large part of the attraction here is the forest that hems the beach, where you may see howler monkeys, black iguanas, magpie jays, trogons, and dozens of other bird species. **Amenities:** parking (free); food and drink; toilets. **Best for:** solitude; swimming. ⊠ *Playa Pan de Azúcar.*

SPORTS AND THE OUTDOORS
Most of the operators who work out of Flamingo can pick up guests at the Hotel Sugar Beach for diving, sportfishing, sailing, horseback riding, and other excursions.

WHERE TO STAY

$$$

RESORT

Fodor's Choice

★

Hotel Sugar Beach. The theme of this secluded, ultra-comfortable hotel with a shimmering infinity pool and thin, curving beach is harmony with nature, but it's the friendly staff and outstanding service that keep this property ahead of the pack. **Pros:** yoga classes; natural setting; kids under 12 stay free; warm and friendly staff. **Cons:** waves and rocks can make the ocean dangerous for kids; small pool; Wi-Fi in common areas only. ⑤ *Rooms from: $158* ⊠ *8 km (5 miles) north of Playa Flamingo* ☎ *2654–4242* ⊕ *www.sugar-beach.com* ⇆ *14 rooms, 10 suites, 2 houses* ⦿ *Breakfast.*

PLAYA POTRERO

4 km (2½ miles) north of Flamingo.

A typical small town with a school, church, and supermarket arranged around a soccer field, Potrero is not very scenic. The main attraction is the long beach on the curve of Flamingo Bay and the smattering of small hotels and restaurants lining the road to town.

GETTING HERE AND AROUND
Just before crossing the bridge at the entrance to Flamingo, take the right fork signed for Playa Potrero. The road follows the shoreline. Local buses run from Flamingo to Potrero, but it's so close that you're better off taking a taxi.

ESSENTIALS
An ATM is available at the Flor de Pacifico center near Ristorante Marco Polo, on the east side of Potrero. For groceries, there's Super Wendy across from Hotel Isolina and a small convenience store called Super Potrero next to Bar Las Brisas.

BEACHES
Playa Potrero. Stretching 4 km (2½ miles), this relatively undeveloped wide, brown-sand beach, across Potrero Bay from built-up Flamingo, catches ocean breezes and spectacular sunsets, which you can watch while bobbing in the warm, swimmable water. The pelican-patrolled beach is anchored at one end by the small Tico community of Potrero and at the other end by the Flamingo skyline. Although large houses and condominium developments have sprung up on any hill with a view, at beach level there is only one unimposing hotel and some low-lying private houses set well back from the beach; beachgoers never feel hemmed in or crowded, thanks to the local folks who keep the beach clean and deserving of Blue Flag status. The best area for swimming is midway between Flamingo and Potrero town, near the Bahía del Sol Hotel. The best beach view and breezes are from a bar stool at Bar

Las Brisas. About 10 km (6 miles) offshore lie the Catalina Islands, a barrier-island draw for divers and snorkelers; dive boats based in Flamingo can get there in 10 minutes. **Amenities:** food and drink. **Best for:** sunset; swimming; walking. ⊠ *Potrero.*

SPORTS AND THE OUTDOORS

DIVING

Catalina Islands. The Catalina Islands are a major destination for dive operations based all along the coast. These barrier islands are remarkable for their diversity and appeal to different levels of divers. On one side, the islands have 6- to 9-meter (20- to 30-foot) drops, great for beginners. The other side has deeper drops of 18 to 24 meters (60 to 80 feet), better suited to more experienced divers. Among the 25 dive sites, the top are **Dirty Rock, Elephant Rock, Big Catalina,** and **Cupcake.** From January to March, when the water is colder, you are almost guaranteed manta ray sightings at these spots. Cownose and devil rays are also spotted here in large schools, as well as bull and white-tipped sharks, several types of eels, and an array of reef fish. Dive operators from Playa Hermosa south to Tamarindo offer trips to these islands. Reserve through your hotel, or directly through a dive shop. The islands are a 30-minute boat trip from Potrero Bay. ⊠ *Potrero.*

6

WHERE TO EAT

$$ ✕ **The Beach House.** On the road connecting Potrero and Flamingo, this
AMERICAN   beachfront restaurant welcomes travelers with cheerful decor and witty signs like "Trespassers will be *offered a*shot." Water laps just a few feet from your table, and there's a pier out back, making this a popular lunch spot after a catamaran cruise. The menu is heavy on American classics like hamburgers, chicken sandwiches, BLTs, and fried shrimp. The tasty sangrias and margaritas are sure to keep you dazed during sunset. If you hook it, they'll cook it with a side of fries for $10. Like many restaurants in Costa Rica, service is slow, but worth the wait. Kids eat free on Wednesday. The Beach House is easy to spot by the rainbow-colored picket fence; parking is limited so prepare to walk. ⑤ *Average main: $15* ⊠ *800 m north of Banco Nacional, Potrero* ✛ *north end of Playa Flamingo on way to Potrero* ☎ *2654–6203* ⊕ *www. beachhouseplayaflamingo.com.*

$$ ✕ **Ristorante Marco Polo.** Marco Polo, the main restaurant at the Tuscan-
ITALIAN   style Villagio Flor de Pacífico mega-development of red-roof villas east of Potrero, serves proper al dente pasta with homemade sauces and a dozen different wood-fired pizzas. Crusts are thin and crispy and salads are organic and fresh. They also serve more substantial dishes such as grilled tuna, fresh lobster and shrimp, and tenderloin with a béarnaise sauce. Save room for the tiramisu, of course. The pool beside the dining area is open to restaurant guests, meaning you can tan before you dine. ⑤ *Average main: $12* ⊠ *Playa Potrero Villagio Flor, 1 km (½ mile) east of Potrero, Potrero* ☎ *2654–4905, 8517–6413* ⊕ *www. ristorantemarcopolo.com* ☯ *Closed Mon.*

$$ ✕ **The Shack.** The Shack successfully blends a Tico menu with Gringo
AMERICAN   favorites. It's a popular spot with expats who come for the cold beers, chimichangas, burgers, and *pura vida* vibe. Grab a seat under the tin roof and try the fresh fish-and-chips, heaping nachos, cheeseburgers,

or the famous chili dogs. Start the day with their sweet breakfast menu of macadamia banana pancakes, plum-cinnamon French toast, chocolate-chip waffles, or fresh smoothies. Thursdays draw a crowd with open-mic night or live music. The Shack gimlet with cucumber and basil packs a powerful punch. ⑤ *Average main: $10* ⊠ *200 m west of El Castillo, Potrero* ☎ *2654–6038* ⊘ *Closed Mon.*

WHERE TO STAY

$$$ ⚏ **Bahía del Sol.** Snagging the best spot on the beach, Bahía del Sol has
RESORT   a gorgeous, beachfront pool and comfortable rooms built around a
FAMILY   garden of tropical shrubs and towering trees. **Pros:** on the beach; lovely
Fodor'sChoice grounds; excellent restaurant; friendly, first-rate service. **Cons:** front
★   terraces are not very private; hotel closed during October. ⑤ *Rooms from: $189* ⊠ *South end of Potrero Beach, Potrero* ☎ *2654–4671* ⊕ *www.bahiadelsolhotel.com* ⊘ *Closed Oct.* ↻ *13 rooms, 15 suites* ⯄ *Breakfast.*

$$ ⚏ **Hotel Isolina.** This small hotel complex, a little island (*isolina*) of palm
HOTEL   trees shading two pools, has basic and clean rooms with some of the best rates in the area, making it popular with Costa Rican families seeking a weekend getaway. **Pros:** all rooms face the pool; affordable; secure parking; clean rooms. **Cons:** loud a/c; breakfast not included for rooms with kitchenettes; dated rooms need upgrades; Wi-Fi near reception only. ⑤ *Rooms from: $102* ⊠ *100 m north of Restaurant La Perla, on beach road, Potrero* ☎ *2654–4333* ⊕ *www.isolinabeach.com* ↻ *9 standard rooms, 22 equipped rooms, 3 2-bedroom villas* ⯄ *Breakfast.*

NIGHTLIFE

Bar La Perla. It's *Cheers* in a beachtown where everyone knows your name, even if you're a tourist. Expats come for the microbrews, the satellite TV tuned to football, a game of Ping-Pong or pool, and the live music. Although the bar brings the people in, it's the food that keeps them there—braised oxtail, pork ribs, tuna poke, and burgers seem to justify another round. If you stay long enough, you'll find that the sweet homemade cheesecake goes surprising well with a bitter IPA. ⊠ *Calle Principal and Ave Tres, near The Shack, Potrero* ☎ *2654–4500.*

PLAYA FLAMINGO

80 km (50 miles) southwest of Liberia.

One of the first northern beaches to experience overdevelopment—a fact immortalized in the concrete towers that straggle up the hill above the bay—Flamingo still has some hidden charms. It's perhaps most famous for its large sportfishing fleet, though they're moored out in the bay waiting for the government to grant a new concession to update and operate the marina here. Working girls are lured to Flamingo by the boatloads of single-for-the-week fishermen. This adds a faintly salacious whiff to some local nightspots.

GETTING HERE AND AROUND

To get to Playa Flamingo from Liberia, drive 45 km (28 miles) south to Belén and then 35 km (22 miles) west on a good, paved road. The trip takes just over an hour. If you're coming from the Playas del Coco and Ocotal area, you can take a 16-km (10-mile) shortcut, called the Monkey Trail, starting near Sardinal and emerging at Potrero. It's then 4 km (2½ miles) south to Flamingo. Attempt this only in dry season, with a GPS, and in a 4WD, since there are a few river crossings. The drive from San José takes 4½ hours, and costs about $230 per five-passenger van. You can also take a van from Liberia, a 50-minute scenic drive for around $80 per van. Ecotrans has transportation between Liberia airport and Playa Flamingo for $25 per person. (⇨ *See Bus Travel in Travel Smart Costa Rica.*)

Ecotrans. ⊠ *Flamingo* ☎ *506/2654–4852, 954/353–6737 in U.S.* ⊕ *www.ecotranscostarica.com.*

ESSENTIALS

Bank/ATM Banco de Costa Rica. ⊠ *Main road leading to Playa Flamingo, at the intersection of the road to Playa Potrero, Flamingo* ✢ *Across from Hotel Flamingo Marina Resort* ☎ *2654–4984.*

Pharmacy Farmacia Playa Flamingo. ⊠ *La Plaza Flamingo, beside Marie's Restaurant at entrance to town, Flamingo* ☎ *2654–5524.*

BEACHES

Playa Flamingo. Hidden away to the southwest of the town, Flamingo Beach is picture-perfect, with almost-white sand sloping into a relatively calm sea, and buttonwood trees separating it from the road. This beach is great for swimming, with a fine-sand bottom and no strong currents, though there are a few submerged rocks in front of the Flamingo Beach Resort, so you should swim a bit farther south. There's sometimes a bit of surf—if the waves are big, keep your eye on little paddlers. There is minimal shade along the beach's 1-km-long (½-mile-long) stretch, and few services except at Coco Loco restaurant on the south end. Otherwise, the closest restaurants are in the beach resort and the adjacent town. To find the beach, go straight as you enter town, and instead of going up the hill, turn left after the Flamingo Beach Resort. **Amenities:** food and drink. **Best for:** swimming; walking. ⊠ *Southwest of town, in front of Flamingo Beach Resort, Flamingo.*

SPORTS AND THE OUTDOORS

BOATING

Lazy Lizard Catamaran Sailing Adventures. Laze away a morning or afternoon sailing or sunbathing on either a 34-foot or 38-foot catamaran. You can swim or snorkel during the four-hour tour, starting at 8:30 am (minimum of eight people) and 2 pm. Included in the $85 price (per person) is snorkeling equipment, kayaks, drinks, and food. ⊠ *Flamingo Marina, Flamingo* ☎ *2654–5900* ⊕ *www.lazylizardsailing.com* ⌦ *From $85.*

DIVING AND SNORKELING

Flamingo offers the quickest access to the Catalina Islands, visible from its beach, where big schools of fish, manta rays, and other sea creatures gather. Coastal reefs to the north are visited on day trips that combine snorkeling with time on undeveloped beaches. Most diving excursions to Catalina Islands depart from Potrero Bay.

The reclusive zebra moray eel likes to hide its entire body in rock or coral holes.

Aquacenter Diving. Based in the Flamingo Marina Resort, this dive shop runs two-tank dives at the Catalina Islands ($100, including gear rental) and snorkeling trips ($65, including equipment), as well as offering a full range of PADI certification courses. ✉ *Flamingo Marina Resort, Flamingo* ☎ *8877–7420* ⊕ *www.aquacenterdiving.com* ✉ *From $65.*

FISHING

Although the marina is still closed while officials consider bids to rebuild it, there are plenty of sportfishing boats bobbing in Flamingo Bay. Larger boats have moved to moorings in the Papagayo Marina near the Andaz Resort. In December the wind picks up and many of the smaller, 31-foot-and-under boats head to calmer water farther south. But the wind brings cold water and abundant baitfish, which attract marlin (blue, black, and striped), Pacific sailfish, yellowfin tuna, wahoo, mahimahi, grouper, and red snapper. January to April is consequently prime catch-and-release season for billfish.

WHERE TO EAT

$$$

ITALIAN

✗ **Angelina's.** Guanacaste-inspired and locally sourced, the cuisine here pays tribute to the owner's Italian roots. This restaurant is one of the area's more upscale places to dine, with marble tables, parchment lamps, and driftwood-integrated decor under an open-air patio. Homemade pizzas, like the thin-crust Playa Blanca with wild mushrooms and truffle-scented béchamel, are the draw for most diners. Fresh-from-the-sea dishes include mahimahi with mango salsa or lobster tail served with homemade black pasta. There are vegan and gluten-free options, and $4 cocktails from 4 to 6. The wine list is extensive and microbrews are on tap. It's worth saving room for the flourless chocolate cake with coffee reduction and homemade ice cream. $ Average main: $18 ⊠ Plaza Commercial, 2nd fl., Flamingo ☎ 2654–4839 ⊕ www. angelinasplayaflamingo.com ⊙ No lunch.

$$
SEAFOOD ✕ **Coco Loco.** The "crazy coconut" is one of the few places where you can dine with your toes in the sand while watching the sunset without anything separating you from the water. Service is slow, so plan to stay awhile and enjoy the view with their signature coconut cocktail. Start with the fried calamari or mixed ceviche, and move on to mains like the blackened swordfish wrap, the sesame-crusted yellowfin tuna taco, or the slow-cooked ribs with pineapple barbecue sauce. Although not on the menu, they usually have a whole lobster for $20. Entrées come with a choice of coleslaw, fruit, fries, or rice and beans, and can be prepared Caribbean style with coconut milk. If you haven't already overdosed on coconut, try the homemade coconut sorbet. Sunset diners should come with mosquito spray since those little buggers love naked feet in the sand. $ Average main: $10 ⊠ On Playa Flamingo, 650 m south of Flamingo Beach Resort, Flamingo ☎ 2654–6242 ⊕ www. cocolococostarica.com.

$$
SEAFOOD ✕ **Marie's Restaurant.** A Flamingo institution serving beachgoers and locals for more than three decades, this popular restaurant has an array of sandwiches and salads, as well as reliably fresh seafood in large portions at reasonable prices. Settle in at one of the wooden tables beneath the ceiling fans and massive thatched roof for a traditional Costa Rican ceviche, avocado stuffed with shrimp, or heart of palm and *pejivalle* (palm fruit). The main fare includes whole fried red snapper, shrimp and fish kebabs, and a delicious *plato de mariscos* (shrimp, lobster, and fish served with garlic butter, potatoes, and salad). For a lighter meal, you can't beat the scrumptious fish tacos. Save room for Marie's signature banana-chocolate bread pudding. At breakfast, try the unusual papaya pancakes, French toast made with cream cheese and jam, or eggs Benedict. There's free Wi-Fi for customers and live music three times a month (call ahead for schedule). $ Average main: $15 ⊠ Plaza commercial center; near north end of beach, Flamingo ☎ 2654–4136 ⊕ www.mariesrestaurantcostarica.com.

WHERE TO STAY

$$
RESORT
FAMILY 🏨 **Flamingo Beach Resort.** This three-story resort has a prime location overlooking beautiful Flamingo Beach, along with a huge swimming pool and every water sport that kids of any age could want. **Pros:** beachfront; big pool; all-inclusive meal plans available. **Cons:** noisy with kids during vacation times; plastic all-inclusive wristbands are uncomfortable; patchy Wi-Fi. $ Rooms from: $129 ⊠ Hotel entrance on left past Marie's Restaurant, Flamingo ☎ 2654–4444, 2283–8063 in San José, 877/856–5519 toll-free in U.S. ⊕ www.resortflamingobeach. com ⤴ 112 rooms, 8 suites ⊙ All-inclusive; Breakfast.

6

$$ ⊞ **Hotel Guanacaste Lodge.** On the outskirts of Flamingo, a short drive
HOTEL   from the beach, this Tico-run lodge offers basic accommodations for
a fraction of what the town's big hotels charge. **Pros:** affordable; nice
pool; large rooms. **Cons:** unattractive from the outside; no in-room
phones or safes; simple furnishings with few amenities; rooms lack
character. ⑤ *Rooms from: $100 ⊠ 200 m south of the Potrero-Fla-
mingo crossroads, Flamingo ☎ 2654–4494 ⊕ www.guanacastelodge.
com ⤳ 10 rooms |⊙| Breakfast.*

NIGHTLIFE

Mariner Inn Bar. This often boisterous bar, thick with testosterone, is the
place to be if you enjoy socializing with fishermen trading fish tales.
There's free Wi-Fi and a communal computer for use for $2 per hour.
⊠ *Bottom of hill, entering Flamingo, Flamingo ☎ 2654–4081 ⊕ www.
marinerinn.com.*

BRASILITO AND PLAYA CONCHAL

8 km (5 miles) south of Flamingo.

A small, scruffy fishing village just 1 km (½ mile) north of Playa Con-
chal, Brasilito has a jumble of houses huddled around its main square,
which doubles as the soccer field. It's cluttered, noisy, and totally Tico—
a lively contrast to the controlled sophistication of the gated Playa Con-
chal resort and residential development less than a mile south. Fishing
boats moor just off a wide beach, and there's a range of seafood restau-
rants, from inexpensive *marisquerías* to a few notable establishments
taking pride in organic and locally sourced ingredients.

GETTING HERE AND AROUND

The drive south to Brasilito from Flamingo is 10 minutes on a paved
highway. Brasilito is just 1 km (½ mile) north of the entrance to the mas-
sive Westin Golf Resort & Spa and private Reserva Conchal housing
development, which blocks the main road access to Playa Conchal. To
reach Playa Conchal without driving through the guard-posted resort,
turn left at the end of the town square in Brasilito and follow the dirt
road across a stretch of beach and over a steep hill; the beach stretch
is impassable at high tide. Buses run from Flamingo to Brasilito three
times daily, at 7:30 and 11:30 am and 2:30 pm. A taxi from Flamingo
is about $10.

ESSENTIALS

The closest bank and ATM are in Flamingo.

Pharmacy Farmacia El Cruce. ⊠ *Crossroads at Huacas, Playa Conchal*
☎ *2653–8787.*

BEACHES

Playa Brasilito. Fishing boats moor just off this wide beach, about 3 km
(2 miles) long with golden sand flecked with pebbles and a few rocks.
The surf is a little stronger here than at Flamingo Beach, but the shal-
low, sandy bottom keeps it swimmable. There is one hotel almost on
the beach, the quirky Hotel Brasilito with an attached restaurant called
The Spot. The sea is cleaner off nearby Playa Conchal, which is also

more attractive. **Amenities:** food and drink. **Best for:** snorkeling; walking. ⌧ *Playa Brasilito, Playa Conchal.*

Playa Conchal. Named for the bits of broken shells that cover its base of fine white sand (the Spanish word for shell is *concha*), lovely Playa Conchal is an idyllic strand sloping steeply into aquamarine water and lined with trees. As its Blue Flag attests, it's clean and invites safe swimming. Although it's dominated by the sprawling Westin Playa Conchal, you don't need to stay at that all-inclusive resort to enjoy Conchal, since it's a short beach walk south from Brasilito. There are beach chairs and somewhat pushy vendors outside the resort (the $20 per hour massages are worth considering), but the southern part of the beach is often deserted. The point that defines Conchal's northern end is hemmed by a lava-rock reef that is a popular snorkeling area—locals rent equipment on the beach. Waves can be powerful at times, so keep an eye on little ones. Despite the availability of shell jewelry, remember that shell collecting is not officially permitted on Costa Rican beaches. **Amenities:** food and drink. **Best for:** snorkeling; swimming; walking. ⌧ *Playa Conchal.*

SPORTS AND THE OUTDOORS
GOLF
Reserva Conchal Golf Course. One of the best golf courses in the country, this 18-hole, par-71 course designed by Robert Trent Jones Jr. is perfectly maintained and reserved for guests of the Westin Golf Resort & Spa, who can try out their swing for $150, cart included; renting clubs costs an extra $40. The well-laid-out course has wide fairways and beautiful views including a couple of holes overlooking the water. Holes 16, 17, and 18 pose a challenge, with downhill tee shots and a drive that lands close to the water. Allow extra time to observe the wildlife, including howler monkeys, lizards, coatis, and birds. ⌧ *The Westin Resort & Spa, Playa Conchal, entrance, less than 1 km (½ mile) south of Brasilito, Playa Conchal* ☎ *2654–3500* ⊕ *www.reservaconchal.com* 🏷 *$150 for 18 holes* 🏌 *18 holes, 6956 yards, par 71.*

WHERE TO EAT
$$
ECLECTIC ✕ **Papaya.** Grab a table in the second-floor lounge overlooking the pool while the kitchen cooks up fresh seafood delivered daily by local fisherman. Try the coconut shrimp to start and follow it up with sesame-crusted tuna or Thai curry. Vegetarians will finally get their chance to gloat, thanks to dishes like veggie BLTs with soy bacon and falafel burritos. There are also delicious salads with shredded papaya and tangy dressings, as well as local *casados* to remind you that you're in Costa Rica. Wash it all down with an unparalleled passion-fruit mojito. The breakfast specials are a bargain. There's live music on Tuesday nights. Dinner is by reservation only. ⑤ *Average main: $15* ⌧ *Conchal Hotel, 200 m south of the bridge, Brasilito* ☎ *2654–9125* ⊕ *www.conchalcr. com* ☉ *Closed Wed.* ⌧ *Reservations essential.*

$$
FRENCH ✕ **Septimo Cielo.** Every gourmet dish at this French restaurant is suited to the tastes of an epicure. Taking you to "Seventh Heaven" are starters like the pumpkin soup with scallops and pancetta, followed by beautifully presented entrées like duck and beef tenderloin served with baby

vegetables and roasted potatoes. The Thai linguine, curried tuna, and chicken with risotto leave no doubt that Chef Kevin Ribault is internationally recognized for a reason. The setting suggests "fine dining" romance—white curtains, black linens, and fairy lights. The extensive wine list and oversized white dishes adorned with dollops, dribbles, and sprinkles of flavors *might* even make you dress up for the occasion. ⑤ *Average main: $12* ✉ *300 m east from Brasilito soccer field, Brasilito* ✛ *400 m from Playa Brasilito, road to Playa Flamingo* ☎ *2654–5670* ▭ *No credit cards.*

WHERE TO STAY

$$
HOTEL
Fodor's Choice
★

⚏ **Conchal Hotel.** It may not be on the beach, but this quaint 13-room boutique hotel is certainly a diamond in the rough in rustic Brasilito, with breezy rooms framing an attractive pool-centered courtyard and a second-story restaurant luring travelers from afar with wholesome cuisine. **Pros:** B&B feel; outstanding restaurant; friendly owners. **Cons:** some street noise; 15-minute walk to the beach; hotel often full. ⑤ *Rooms from: $99* ✉ *200 m south of the bridge, Brasilito* ☎ *2654– 9125, 347/298–9356 in U.S.* ⊕ *www.conchalcr.com* ⟲ *13 rooms* ⦿| *Breakfast.*

$
HOTEL

⚏ **Hotel Brasilito.** Budget travelers who don't need amenities will love this rustic, two-story, wooden hotel's affordable price and seafront location, if not its no-frills but adequate A-frame rooms. **Pros:** inexpensive; beachfront; good restaurant. **Cons:** boxy rooms, some without TVs, a/c, or phones; can be noisy; rooms need upgrading. ⑤ *Rooms from: $74* ✉ *Between soccer field and beach, Brasilito* ☎ *2654–4237* ⊕ *www. brasilito.com* ⟲ *18 rooms* ⦿| *No meals.*

$$$$
RESORT
FAMILY

⚏ **The Westin Golf Resort & Spa, Playa Conchal.** So vast that guests ride around in biodiesel shuttles, this all-inclusive Starwood property is set on 2,400 acres with nearly every vacation wish granted, from lagoon-style pools and a picture-perfect beach to eight restaurants and a championship golf course. **Pros:** saltwater pools; surrounding wildlife; beach access; abundant activities. **Cons:** no food and drink service on the beach; only three rooms have ocean views; easy to get lost; most restaurants require reservations. ⑤ *Rooms from: $400* ✉ *Entrance less than 1 km (½ mile) south of Brasilito, Playa Conchal* ☎ *2654–3500* ⊕ *www.starwoodhotels.com/westin* ⟲ *282 junior suites, 84 Royal Beach rooms, 38 Royal Beach suites* ⦿| *All-inclusive.*

PLAYA GRANDE

21 km (13 miles) north of Tamarindo.

Down the (long, paved) road from Tamarindo, but only five minutes by boat across a tidal estuary, lies beautiful, pristine Playa Grande. By day, it's one of the best surfing beaches in the country, and by night it's a nesting beach for the giant leatherback sea turtle. The beach has thus far escaped the overdevelopment of nearby Tamarindo, and is consequently lined with thick vegetation instead of hotels and strip malls. But Playa Grande isn't immune to development; developers have sold hundreds of lots, and there are at least 75 finished houses. The ongoing battle to protect the beach continues. The good thing is that the homes are 200 meters from the beach, thanks to a legislated buffer zone and a decree that no lights can be visible from the beach, to avoid disturbing the turtles. A few hotels and restaurants make this a pleasant, tranquil alternative to Tamarindo. And if you want to go shopping or barhopping, Tamarindo is only a boat ride away.

GETTING HERE AND AROUND

The road from Tamarindo is paved for the duration of the 30-minute drive. The gated community of Palm Beach Estates, where most hotels are, is about 2 km (1 mile) south of the main Playa Grande entrance on a potholed dirt road. Alternatively, you can take a small boat across the Tamarindo Estuary for about $3 per person and walk 30 minutes along the beach to the main surf break. A lesser-known break is just a 10-minute walk; boats travel (8–4:30) between the guide kiosk at the north end of Tamarindo and either Villa Baulas or Hotel Bula Bula in Playa Grande. Otherwise, a taxi from Tamarindo to Playa Grande will cost about $30 one way.

EXPLORING

Nesting giant leatherback turtles. Playa Grande used to host the world's largest visitation of nesting giant leatherback turtles, but the number of turtles has fallen drastically in the past 20 years, from a high of 1,504 in 1989 to less than 40 currently. This loss is due to long-line commercial fishing boats that trap turtles in their nets, causing the turtles to drown, along with poaching of turtle eggs and loss of habitat. The beach is still strictly off-limits from 6 pm to 6 am from October 20 to February 15, during the peak nesting season. You can visit only as part of a guided tour with a park ranger, from the headquarters for Parque Nacional Marino Las Baulas (Leatherback Marine National Park), 100 meters east of Hotel Las Tortugas. If you are extremely lucky, spotters will find a nesting turtle. At their signal, you'll walk down the beach as silently as you can, where in the darkness you'll witness the remarkable sight of a 500-pound creature digging a hole in the sand large enough to deposit up to 100 golf-ball-size eggs. About 60 days later, the sight of hundreds of hatchlings scrambling toward open water in the early morning is equally impressive. Turtle-watching takes place around high tide, which can be shortly after sunset, or in the early morning. Plan on spending one to six hours at the ranger station waiting for a turtle to come up, during which you can watch a video on the turtles in English (the guides speak mostly Spanish). You are only charged if a turtle sighting is confirmed. Visitation is limited to 60 people per night (in groups of 15 max) and unregistered visitors are not allowed. Reservations should be made one week in advance either by phone or at Las Baulas National Park headquarters at Playa Grande. ✉ *100 m east of main beach entrance* ☎ *2653–0470* 🎫 *$25, includes guided tour* ◷ *Oct. 20–Feb. 15 by reservation made between 8 am and 5 pm.*

BEACHES

Playa Grande. In addition to being a paradise for surfers and sunbathers, the narrow woodsy patch that lines this wide, pristine Blue Flag beach holds howler monkeys and an array of birds, and the mangrove estuary on the north end of the beach has crocodiles. Be aware that the surf is a

Costa Rica's shores are visited by the green turtle, the olive ridley (above), the hawksbill, the loggerhead, and the leatherback turtle.

little heavy for safe swimming and there's an abundance of mosquitoes during the rainy months, especially near the estuary, so bring plenty of repellent. The beach's shores and waters are protected within Parque Nacional Marino Las Baulas. Admission is free during daylight hours but off-limits at night during the turtle-nesting season (October 20 to February 15), when tourists come on guided turtle tours, hoping to catch the increasingly rare sight of a leatherback turtle building a nest and depositing eggs. The beach gained protected status in part because a surfer who arrived here more than 30 years ago was so upset by the widespread turtle-egg poaching that he adopted a conservationist's agenda. Louis Wilson, owner of Las Tortugas Hotel, spearheaded a campaign to protect the nesting *baulas* (leatherback turtles) that eventually resulted in the creation of the national park. When walking on the beach, be sure to avoid the dry sand above the high tide line where turtles lay their eggs. **Amenities:** food and drink. **Best for:** surfing; walking. ⊠ *Playa Grande*.

SPORTS AND THE OUTDOORS
■ TIP➜ Unless you are a strong swimmer attached to a surfboard, don't go in any deeper than your waist here. There is calmer water for snorkeling about a 30-minute walk north of Las Tortugas, at a black-sand beach called Playa Carbón.

TOUR OPERATORS
All the area hotels can arrange guided boat tours of the estuary for around $25 per person. You may see crocodiles, monkeys, herons, kingfishers, and an array of other birdlife; go either early in the morning or late in the afternoon, and bring insect repellent.

Estuary Tours. Two-hour canoe tours of the nearby Tamarindo Estuary ($30 canoe, $20 guide) set off at 6 am with local naturalist guide Jonathan. Kids under eight years old are free. Hotel Las Tortugas can arrange the tour for you. ⊠ *Playa Grande* ☎ *8534–8664* ⌁ *From $30.*

SURFING

Playa Grande is renowned for having one of the most consistent surf breaks in the country. Only experienced surfers should attempt riding this beach break, which often features big barrels and offshore winds. The waves are best at high tide, especially around a full moon.

Hotel Bula Bula. You can rent both long- and shortboards for $15 to $25 a day at this surfer-friendly hotel. ⊠ *Palm Beach Estates, 2 km (1 mile) east of Playa Grande* ☎ *2653–0975* ⊕ *www.hotelbulabula.com.*

Hotel Las Tortugas. The hotel rents boards for $15 to $20 a day and offers surfing lessons at their beachfront Caribbean-style snack bar. ⊠ *Playa Grande* ☎ *2653–0423* ⊕ *www.lastortugashotel.com.*

YOGA

Yoga at RipJack Inn. RipJack Inn has its own yoga shala where classes are held daily at 8:30 am or 4 pm. The cost is $15 and yoga mats are provided. ⊠ *100 m south of Hotel Las Tortugas, at RipJack Inn* ☎ *2653–1636* ⊕ *www.ripjackinn.com* ⌁ *$15.*

WHERE TO EAT

$$$

INTERNATIONAL

✕ **Restaurant Cantarana.** You can usually count on creative, au courant dinners at this upscale, pricey second-story restaurant in the trees. The menu changes depending on availability of local ingredients, but there's usually seafood and daring dishes like stingray, sesame-crusted tuna, octopus salad, and shrimp brochette with coconut sauce. The rabbit is superb. For something more familiar, try the handmade pizzas. There are several vegetarian, lactose-free, and gluten-free options on the menu. For dessert, there's a creamy passion-fruit custard. Presentation is always beautiful, and the service is efficient and friendly. $ *Average main: $20* ⊠ *Hotel Cantarana, Palm Beach Estates, 2 km (1 mile) east of park headquarters* ☎ *2653–0486* ⊕ *www.hotel-cantarana.com* ☾ *Closed Sept. and Oct. No lunch.*

$$$

SEAFOOD

✕ **Upstairs at the RipJack.** There are rooms for rent and a yoga school downstairs, but most people come to chow down at this casual place a block from the beach, or party at the extensive bar, which occupies about a third of the restaurant. Portions are large so pace yourself, especially if you order the popular barbecue ribs with mashed potatoes. On the seafood side, you can count on teriyaki tuna, grilled mahi, and coconut-crusted sea bass. The salads are topped with healthy ingredients like chickpeas, avocado, and quinoa. The chalkboard menu features the daily specials, your best bet for what's in season. Prices are on the high side but you can arrive early for half-priced cocktails from 4 to 6; the spicy jalapeño margarita packs a punch. There is also Sunday brunch in high season. $ *Average main: $18* ⊠ *RipJack Inn, 100 m south of park headquarters* ☎ *2653–0480* ⊕ *www.ripjackinn.com.*

WHERE TO STAY

$$ ▢ **Hotel Bula Bula.** At the eastern edge of the estuary in the Palm Beach
HOTEL   Estates gated community, this pleasant hotel—the name means "Happy
Happy"—has its own landing for ferrying guests and restaurant patrons
the 1 km (½ mile) to and from Tamarindo. **Pros:** friendly; good restaurant; lots of amenities. **Cons:** rooms small for price; 10-minute walk
from beach; mosquitoes. ⑤ *Rooms from: $135 ✉ Palm Beach Estates,
3 km (2 miles) east of Playa Grande ☎ 2653–0975, 877/658–2880 in
U.S. ⊕ www.hotelbulabula.com ⤳ 10 rooms �‖ Breakfast.*

$$ ▢ **Hotel Las Tortugas.** With a prime location on the beach, this place is
B&B/INN   perfect for surfers, nature lovers, and sun worshippers with a range of
budgets. **Pros:** on the beach; friendly owners; good value. **Cons:** busy
location; spotty service at times; rooms lack amenities. ⑤ *Rooms from:
$95 ✉ Entrance to Las Baulas Marine National Park, 33 km (20 miles)
north of Tamarindo ☎ 2653–0423 ⊕ www.lastortugashotel.com ⤳ 11
rooms, 1 suite, 8 dorms, 17 apartments �‖ No meals.*

TAMARINDO

82 km (51 miles) southwest of Liberia.

Once a funky beach town full of surfers and local fishermen, Tamarindo is now a pricey, hyped-up hive of commercial development and real estate speculation, happily accompanied by a dizzying variety of shops, bars, and hotels, and probably the best selection of restaurants of any beach town on the Pacific coast. There's a shopping center at the entrance to town with an upscale AutoMercado supermarket and a Scotiabank branch and ATM. On the downside, the congested two-lane beach road through Tamarindo comes to a halt at times throughout the day, especially when delivery trucks stop in front of shops and restaurants, while drivers inch past the flashing hazards and distracted pedestrians. Strip malls, billboards, and high-rise condominiums clutter the rest of the main street and obscure views of the still-magnificent beach. Beyond the chaos of Diria Grand Boulevard (the commercial center), the main road bends toward Playa Langosta and gains some composure and tranquility (other than the potholes).

Tamarindo serves as a popular base for surfing at the nearby Playas Grande, Langosta, Avellanas, and Negra. There are plenty of outdoor options in addition to surfing, among them diving, sportfishing, wildlife-watching, and canopy tours. You can also play 18 rounds at the nearby Hacienda Pinilla golf course, or simply stroll the beach and sunbathe. Some low-life elements are making security an issue, especially with car break-ins that occur minutes after you leave your vehicle. Most upscale hotels and inns have their own security and gated parking. Once you're on the beach, almost all the negatives disappear (just keep an eye on your belongings).

GETTING HERE AND AROUND

Both Nature Air and SANSA fly to Tamarindo from San José. By car from Liberia, travel south on the highway to the turnoff for Belén, then head west and turn left at the Huacas crossroads to Tamarindo, passing through the small village of Villareal. The drive from Liberia to

Tamarindo takes just over one hour. There are no direct bus connections between Playa Grande or Playa Avellanas and Tamarindo. A taxi or a shuttle van is the way to go from nearby towns if you don't have wheels. **Tamarindo Shuttle.** The Tamarindo Shuttle ferries passengers between the various beaches in a comfortable van and will also pick you up at the Liberia airport, $20 per person, minimum of two; evening flights require a minimum of three passengers. Shared shuttles from San José cost $50 per person. ⊠ *Tamarindo* ☎ *2653–4444, 2653–2626* ⊕ *www. tamarindoshuttle.com.*

ESSENTIALS
Bank/ATM Banco Nacional. ⊠ *Across from Arco Iris Hotel* ☎ *2653–0366.*

Pharmacy Farmacia Tamarindo. ⊠ *Main road into town, diagonally across from Best Western Tamarindo Villas* ☎ *2653–0210.*

Post Office Correo. ⊠ *Across from airport on main road between Villareal and Tamarindo* ☎ *2653–0676.*

Rental Cars Alamo. ⊠ *Diagonal to Hotel El Diriá, main road* ☎ *2653–0727.* **Budget.** ⊠ *Hotel Zullymar, main road* ☎ *2653–0756.* **Economy.** ⊠ *Main road entering Tamarindo, across from Witch's Rock Surf Camp* ☎ *2653–0728.* **Hertz.** ⊠ *100 m east of Hotel Pasatiempo* ☎ *2653–1358.*

BEACHES
Playa Tamarindo. Wide and flat, the sand here is packed hard enough for easy walking and jogging, but swimming and surfing have become questionable since the town lost its Blue Flag clean-beach status (because of overdevelopment and the total absence of water treatment). The water quality is especially poor during the rainy months, when you'll want to do your swimming and surfing at nearby Playa Langosta or Playa Grande. Despite this, surfing is still the main attraction here, and there's a young crowd that parties hard after a day riding the waves. Witch's Rock Surf Shop has showers, toilets, surfboard rental, a swimming pool, and a restaurant where you can watch the surfers over a cold beer. Strong currents at the north end of the beach get a lot of swimmers into trouble, especially when they try to cross the estuary without a surfboard. There's street parking and a public dirt lot in front of El Vaquero Brewpub. **Amenities:** food and drink; toilets; showers; parking. **Best for:** partiers; surfing; walking. ⊠ *Tamarindo.*

SPORTS AND THE OUTDOORS
BOATING
Rocky Isla El Capitán, just offshore, is a close-in kayaking destination, full of sand-dollar shells. Exploring the tidal estuaries north and south of town is best done in a kayak at high tide, when you can travel farther up the temporary rivers. Arrange kayaking trips through your hotel.

FAMILY **Blue Dolphin Sailing.** Set sail on a 40-foot catamaran for an afternoon of sunning, snorkeling, and kayaking aboard the *Blue Dolphin.* The boat departs at 1 pm from the beach in front of El Pescador Restaurant and returns around sunset. It's $85 ($42 for kids under 12) per person, including appetizers and open bar. During high season there's also a morning tour, from 8 am to noon, $70 (half price for kids under 12)

Tamarindo and Playa Langosta

TO LIBERIA, AIRPORT, PLAYA AVELLANAS →

Pacific Ocean

Playa Grande

ACOTAM
Boats to Playa Grande

Isla Capitán

0   500 M
0   1,000 ft

Playa Tamarindo

TAMARINDO

Calle Central

Corona

Av. Central

Atardecer

Calle Cardinal

Guarumo

Playa Langosta

PLAYA LANGOSTA

KEY
❶ *Restaurants*
① *Hotels*

including snorkel gear and fishing poles. ✉ *Tamarindo* ☎ *8842–3204* ⊕ *www.bluedolphinsailing.com* ✉ *From $70.*

Iguana Surf. This longtime surf shop, with an office across from the beach, organizes guided 2½-hour kayak tours of the Tamarindo Estuary and offers a full roster of local tours, including snorkeling. ✉ *Across from the beach, 100 m north of El Diriá Hotel* ☎ *2653–0613* ⊕ *www. iguanasurf.net* ✉ *From $50.*

Marlin del Rey Sailing Tours. This custom-built, 66-foot catamaran, with a large, comfortable main saloon, takes you on a day tour ($75, minimum 15 people) that includes snorkeling, an open bar, lunch, and snacks. It leaves at 8 am. The sunset tour departs at 1:30 pm ($85, no minimum), with time to snorkel, walk along a deserted beach, and enjoy the open bar and a gourmet feast, complete with homemade chocolate-chip cookies. ✉ *Plaza Esmeralda, next to Subway* ☎ *2653–1212, 877/827–8275 in U.S.* ⊕ *www.marlindelrey.com* ✉ *From $75.*

FISHING

Rhino Charger Sportfishing. With over 30 years of sportfishing experience, this U.S.-owned and -operated company has a well-maintained 34-foot Island Hopper, the only boat in the Tamarindo fleet equipped with a fly bridge. There are always two English-speaking crew members onboard, with enough room for up to seven anglers per trip. Charters cost $750 for a half day and $1,100 for a full day. Rates include fishing gear, snacks, and beverages. ✉ *Tamarindo Bay, boat departs from El Pescador* ☎ *506/8310–0003 cell, 772/905–2941 in U.S.* ⊕ *www. rhinocharger.com* ✉ *From $750.*

SURFING

FAMILY **Iguana Surf.** Right across from the beach, this popular surf shop rents surfboards ($20 per day) and boogie boards and offers group lessons four times a day ($45, for ages three and up), as well as private lessons ($80). It's open 8 to 6 daily. ✉ *Across from the beach, 100 m north of El Diriá Hotel* ☎ *2653–0613* ⊕ *www.iguanasurf.net* ✉ *From $45.*

Witch's Rock Surf Camp. This hip, popular hotel, restaurant, and surf school is surfer central in Tamarindo, with a large surf shop and all the latest gear and board rentals. Surf lessons ($85) include all-day board rental, in-water training, and a surf seminar, such as a shaping tutorial with Robert August of *Endless Summer* fame. They also offer courses for intermediate and advanced surfers. If you're just looking to rent a board, this is the place as they have the most solid quiver in town. It's right on the beach just steps from the best surf breaks. ✉ *North end of beach, main road in Tamarindo, across from Economy Rent a Car* ☎ *2653–1238, 888/318–7873 toll-free in U.S. and Canada* ⊕ *www. witchsrocksurfcamp.com* ✉ *From $85.*

TURTLE-WATCHING TOURS

ACOTAM. ACOTAM, a local conservation association, conducts turtle-viewing tours in Marino Las Baulas National Park with local guides for $35, including park entrance fee. The group picks you up at your hotel and briefs you at their headquarters on the estuary that separates Tamarindo and Playa Grande. An open boat then takes you across the estuary, where you wait at the park station until a turtle has been spotted.

With so few leatherback turtles nesting, you are more likely to see green sea turtles instead. The turtle-nesting season runs from mid-October to mid-February. They also offer covered-boat mangrove tours along the Tamarindo River year-round for $25 per person (minimum two). ✉ *Tamarindo* ☎ *2653–1687* ✒ *guiaslocalestama@gmail.com* 💲 *From $25.*

WHERE TO EAT

$$$$

BARBECUE

FAMILY

✕ **Black Stallion Surf Saloon.** This "Costa Rican cowboy saloon with a surfer twist" is a full-day experience that starts with zip lining, horseback riding, and ATV tours, and ends with a BBQ feast of smoked meats like ribs, pork, chorizo, ranch chicken, and grilled vegetables. You can mix and match activities or skip right to the fiesta at 7 pm, featuring a Guanacaste-inspired menu made with ingredients from their working ranch. Homegrown bananas, mangoes, and citrus are used to infuse cocktails and make dressings and sauces for the farm-to-table dishes. Every Friday, the menu switches from meats to seafood with barbecued shrimp, corvina, mahimahi, and lobster delivered fresh from local fishermen. Even vegetarians rave about the endless options of all-you-can-eat grilled fruits, vegetables, and salads. The rustic ranch dining room is intimate and memorable, and the remote location just outside of Tamarindo means you're likely to get a spectacular star show. ⑤ *Average main: $45* ✉ *The Black Stallion Hills Ranch, 10 min drive from Tamarindo* ☎ *8869–9765* ⊕ *www.blackstallionhills.com* ⚓ *Reservations essential* ⏱ *Dinner at 7 pm.*

$$$

ECLECTIC

✕ **Dragonfly Bar & Grill.** Paper lanterns suspended over wooden tables and polished concrete floors bring rustic elegance to this A-frame restaurant supported by tree-trunk columns. The place has been a favorite for years and remains trendy. For starters, try the beet salad with blue cheese and candied walnuts or the tuna tartare with avocado and mango. Expect entrées like seared yellowfin tuna with wasabi aioli, filet mignon with caramelized onions and chimichurri, or homemade squid ink pasta with mussels, shrimp, and mahimahi in a garlic rosé sauce. Adding to the dining experience are refreshing cocktails, live music (Wednesdays 7–9 pm), and a delightful passion-fruit cheesecake and fried ice cream. ⑤ *Average main: $17* ✉ *100 m past turnoff for Langosta Beach road, then left 50 m, behind the Hotel Pasatiempo, past La Baula Pizza* ☎ *2653–1506* ⊕ *www.dragonflybarandgrill.com* ⊙ *Closed Sun. and Sept. 15–Nov 15. No lunch.*

$$$

SEAFOOD

✕ **El Coconut.** With a red, black, and dark-wood interior, this high-gloss restaurant with giant pre-Columbian stone sculptures is one of Tamarindo's more upscale restaurants open for lunch. Seafood is the main event, with the catch of the day—usually mahimahi—served half a dozen ways; or instead try the tenderloin with a choice of sauces, or classic surf and turf. The innovative jumbo shrimp or lobster in a pineapple, raisin, and ginger sauce is delicious; other sauces for fish include a traditional Norwegian *sandefjords smor* (a creamy butter sauce with lime). Service is smooth and more formal than at most beach restaurants, and there are more than 1,000 bottles housed in the temperate wine cellar. The overpriced menu means you're likely to get a table during high season without a reservation. There's live music some Friday nights. ⑤ *Average main: $25* ✉ *Main street, 150 m south of Tamarindo Vista Villas,* *across from Witch's Rock Surf Camp* ☎ *2653–0086* ⊕ *www.elcoconut-tamarindo.com* ☾ *Closed Mon.*

$$$ ✗**Nogui's.** Pleasing a loyal legion of local fans since 1974, Nogui's offers
SEAFOOD   a hearty Costa Rican menu and an ocean view. It is one of Tamarindo's
best options for lunch, with a good selection of sandwiches, huge salads,
and excellent fish tacos at reasonable prices. At dinner they offer a full
seafood menu and various meat dishes. The recipes and presentation
are nothing fancy, but the seafood is fresh and, instead of the ubiq-
uitous rice and beans on the side, Nogui's has a puree of *tiquisque,* a
potato-like tuber. The homemade pies are legendary, notably the coco-
nut cream and apple pie à la mode, and it's open at 6 am for breakfast.
The signature margarita is made with tamarind fruit. On the downside,
the waitresses here often seem sullen and put out. ⑤ *Average main: $16*
✉ *South side of Tamarindo Circle, on beach* ☎ *2653–0029* ⊕ *www.
noguistamarindo.com* ☾ *Closed Wed. and Oct.*

$$$ ✗**Pangas Beach Club.** You can't get any closer to the water than at this
FRENCH FUSION   outdoor beach garden, where rustic tables are shaded by enormous ficus
FAMILY   trees draped with wicker lamps. Dig your toes into the raked sand or
Fodor's Choice   grab a table in the two-story restaurant where the chef blends classic
★   French cuisine with Costa Rican flavors. The menu highlights fresh
seafood with fruit reductions and organic meats seared on hot lava
stones. It's one of the few places in Tamarindo serving lamb, and 100%
of the ingredients are local. For something light, try the tropical goat
cheese salad with mango chutney or the yellowfin tuna tower topped
with mango and avocado. There's a Sunday brunch from 9 to 3 and
daily happy hour from 5 to 7. For a dash of entertainment with your
meal, come on Wednesday night from 7 to 9 pm or Sunday afternoon
from 11:30 to 1 pm when there's live music. Better yet, start early with
the coconut French toast and stay all day nursing a tamarind margarita
or star-fruit colada. Bring the kids—there's an on-site nanny hired to
watch children free of charge. ⑤ *Average main: $25* ✉ *500 m southwest
of Automercado* ☎ *2653–0024* ⊕ *www.lasmareas.com.*

$$ ✗**Pizzeria La Baula.** Wildly popular, this casually chic, alfresco pizzeria
PIZZA   on a quiet side street has plenty of cars parked outside most nights,
FAMILY   particularly Sunday when all the Tamarindo locals seem to meet and
greet here. Families are especially fond of La Baula—the Costa Rican
name for the leatherback turtle—because of its reasonable prices, noisy
buzz, and adjacent playground and picnic-like dining area, which keeps
expanding to accommodate the crowds. There's also a softly lighted din-
ing area for more-romantic dinners. Everyone enjoys the consistently
delicious thin-crust pizzas. The prosciutto, arugula, and Parmesan pizza
is perfect. If you're not a fan of pizza, there's little other choice on the
menu. They also serve Italian wine by the glass and a tasty little tira-
misu, followed by a glass of limoncello or sambuca. ⑤ *Average main:
$15* ✉ *Next door to Dragonfly Bar & Grill, 100 m north of Hotel
Pasatiempo; behind Banco Nacional* ☎ *2653–1450* ☾ *No lunch.*

$$$ ✗**Seasons by Shlomy.** At this intimate, poolside restaurant in the casually
MEDITERRANEAN   chic Hotel Arco Iris, innovative chef Shlomy Koren, Israeli-born and
Fodor's Choice   Cordon Bleu–trained, transforms fresh local ingredients into sophisti-
★   cated Mediterranean-fusion dishes you would pay a small fortune for

A group of local musicians rocking out in Tamarindo

on the Riviera. The luring smell of sautéed garlic teases the senses for what's ahead: salty soft focaccia, lobster and leek terrine, portobellos on polenta, and black miso fish on eggplant and white beans. Vegan dishes are plentiful, like the cauliflower with tahini and scallions, or the green risotto with basil, leeks, and mushrooms. The pan-seared snapper served over artichoke and spinach is beautifully moist, and sashimi comes doused in ginger-flavored, sizzling sesame oil. Richness prevails in the white chocolate mousse with strawberries. Service is swift and attentive and the occasional live jazz adds to the pleasant atmosphere. ⑤ *Average main: $18* ✉ *Hotel Arco Iris, uphill from turnoff to Langosta beach road* ☎ *8368–6983* ⊕ *www.seasonstamarindo.com* ▭ *No credit cards* ☯ *Closed Sun. and mid-Sept.–mid-Oct. No lunch* ☞ *Cash only.*

$$ ✕ **Sprout.** This little seedling has sprouted into one of the most successful
CAFÉ restaurants in Tamarindo. Finicky eaters will find favor in the simple but spot-on menu that features fresh, local, and organic ingredients. Grab a table and a clipboard menu highlighting sandwiches, salads, and smoothies blended with fruits and vegetables so delightful that you'll forget they're good for you. Sink your teeth into top picks like the blackened mahimahi sandwich with mango-habanero mayo on toasted ciabatta or the piled-high hamburger on homemade brioche. The dressings, dips, and sauces, like pesto aioli on the grilled veggie wrap and jalapeño-cilantro aioli on the smoked pork sliders, are finger-licking good (literally). Perfect for an after-surf lunch are the Baja-style fish tacos with lime wedges and salsa cups. There's free Wi-Fi and plenty of shade if you need a break from the beach. ⑤ *Average main: $10* ✉ *Entrance to Tamarindo* ✛ *Across from Witch's Rock Surf Camp* ☎ *2653–2374* ☯ *Closed Sun.*

WHERE TO STAY

$$ ⸬ **Hotel Arco Iris.** Beautiful bungalows dot the grounds of this chic com-
HOTEL pound, half a block off one of Tamarindo's main drags. **Pros:** transpor-
tation service and concierge; boutique feel; great restaurant; good value.
Cons: not a lot of privacy in bungalows; no water views; small pool.
⑤ *Rooms from: $125* ✉ *Follow signs past turnoff to Playa Langosta
and go up hill to right* ☎ *140/2653–0330* ⊕ *www.hotelarcoiris.com* ➳ *5
bungalows, 8 rooms* ⦿| *Breakfast.*

$$ ⸬ **Hotel Luna Llena.** Looking a little like a cheerful Fellini film set of a fan-
HOTEL tasy tropical village, this collection of bright yellow, conical bungalows
FAMILY is fun and affordable. **Pros:** secluded; lush grounds; cheerful decor; nice
Costa Rican breakfast. **Cons:** several blocks away from beach; some
common areas smell of smoke; lots of kids; resident cats and dogs might
be bothersome to some. ⑤ *Rooms from: $90* ✉ *From road to Playa
Langosta, 1st left (uphill)* ☎ *2653–0082* ⊕ *www.hotellunallena.com*
➳ *7 rooms, 7 bungalows* ⦿| *Breakfast.*

$$ ⸬ **Hotel Pasatiempo.** A longtime local hangout, this pretty collection of
HOTEL bungalows is clean, comfortable, and well priced, making this laid-
FAMILY back spot a great option for moderate budgets and families. **Pros:**
affordable; gorgeous pool and garden; 10% discount when booking
directly through hotel. **Cons:** seven-minute walk to beach; rooms close
to the bar can be noisy; some mosquitoes. ⑤ *Rooms from: $94* ✉ *100
m southeast of high-rise Pacific Park condo at turnoff for Playa Lan-
gosta Rd.* ☎ *2653–0096, 2653–4701* ⊕ *www.hotelpasatiempo.com*
➳ *22 rooms* ⦿| *Breakfast.*

$$$$ ⸬ **Las Mareas.** If space, privacy, luxury, and location are your priorities,
RENTAL then these 2,800-square-foot villas are your best option, with Bali-
nese decor and all the comforts of home. **Pros:** ideal for large groups;
five-minute walk to central Tamarindo; high-end amenities. **Cons:** no
meals; one-week minimum stay during holidays; maid service every
other day. ⑤ *Rooms from: $550* ✉ *Across from Las Pangas Beach Club,
at entrance to Tamarindo* ☎ *2653–1561, 8832–5773* ⊕ *www.lasmareas.
com* ➳ *6 villas* ⦿| *No meals.*

$$ ⸬ **Tamarindo Bay Boutique Hotel.** Opened in 2014, this boutique hotel
HOTEL built from recycled materials is inspired by the owners' travels to South-
Fodor'sChoice east Asia and has nine contemporary rooms overlooking a pool-cen-
★ tered courtyard. **Pros:** outstanding breakfasts; huge rooms; immaculate
and peaceful property; UV-treated pool. **Cons:** no ocean views; ground-
floor rooms get some noise from above; no kids under 18. ⑤ *Rooms
from: $110* ✉ *100 m south of Banco Nacional, next to Hotel Arco
Iris* ☎ *2653–2692, 8706–9470* ⊕ *www.tamarindobayhotel.com* ➳ *9
rooms* ⦿| *Breakfast.*

NIGHTLIFE

Tamarindo is one of the few places outside San José and Jaco where the
nightlife really jumps. Although party-hearty hot spots come and go
with the tides, Tamarindo does have some perennially popular nightspots, along with a couple of low-key options.

Aqua Discoteque. With an oceanview patio, this trendy disco is open
Monday, Friday, and Saturday nights, from about 10 pm, with changing

DJs and live bands. There's a mechanical bull and music typical of any hip club you might find in the States. There are free drinks for ladies every Monday night, and an open bar from 9 to 12 on Saturday night. ⊠ *Above Iguana Surf* 🖃 *$5 cover.*

Crazy Monkey Bar. Popular with the surfing crowd, Crazy Monkey Bar features live salsa music, a fire show, and DJs that attract locals who really know how to move—and a crowd of appreciative onlookers. Friday night is ladies' night. ⊠ *At Best Western Tamarindo Vista Villas, Main road entering Tamarindo* ✛ *Across from Witch's Rock Surf Camp* ☎ *2653–0114* 🖃 *$5 cover.*

El Vaquero Bar. After a sunset surf session, pull up a bar stool in the sand and enjoy a craft beer made at the neighboring Volcano Brewing Company. Happy hour is from 5 to 7, and there's live music Saturday and Sunday nights. If you've worked up an appetite, try the chicken wings, jalapeño poppers, hamburgers, and nachos. This is the best place to watch the surfers over a cold one. ⊠ *In front of Economy Rental Car, next to Witch's Rock Surf Camp* ☎ *2653–1238* ⊕ *www. witchsrocksurfcamp.com/el-vaquero-brewpub.*

Sharky's. This is the biggest, most popular sports bar in town, with huge TV screens showing up to six games at once. After the game, both floors play extremely loud music for dancing. Karaoke is on Tuesday, Ladies' Night is Saturday, and beer pong is on Sunday, which you may or may not want to avoid. If sports aren't your thing, the bar food is amazingly good. The action starts at 11:30 am and goes to 2:30 am. ⊠ *Ave. Central, Across from Plaza Tamarindo* ☎ *2653–4705* ⊕ *www.sharkysbars.com.*

SHOPPING

Most stores lining the main road along Diria Grand Boulevard sell the same souvenirs. It's hard to leave town without at least one sarong or T-shirt in your suitcase. There are a few upscale clothing and jewelry shops worth a visit.

Amo La Vida. One of the most intriguing shops in town, this eclectic emporium has exquisite local jewelry handmade in Tamarindo, plus exotic home-decorating items from Morocco and Egypt, including atmospheric wall sconces and accent lamps. ⊠ *Diria Grand Boulevard, Main street, beside El Diriá Hotel* ☎ *2653–1507.*

Azul Profundo Boutique. The theme of this Tamarindo boutique is "Don't worry, be hippy" with a collection of upscale beachwear and jewelry ranging from tie-dye sundresses and OM pendants to pura vida earrings and wool belts. They also have beach bags, hats, and bikinis. There's an emphasis on yoga jewelry, meaning you can find inner peace in style. ⊠ *Local #1 Centro Comercial Plaza* ☎ *2653–0395* ⊕ *www. azulprofundoboutique.com.*

PLAYA LANGOSTA

2 km (1 mile) south of Tamarindo.

A chic bedroom community of Tamarindo, just five minutes away by car, Playa Langosta is tranquil and elegant. It has not totally escaped development, but most of the low-rise buildings on the northern half are tucked behind the mangrove trees, so you can enjoy an unsullied dramatic beachscape, with surf crashing against rocky outcroppings. A few high-rise condominiums have invaded the area, but they are mostly set back. Past Playa Langosta Beach Club are a handful of hotels and B&Bs that outshine properties in neighboring Tamarindo.

GETTING HERE AND AROUND

In 2016, the dirt road from Tamarindo to Playa Langosta was still being paved. A few side roads are still dirt, so to keep down the dust, the road is periodically spread with an industrial molasses mixture, which accounts for the stickiness and the lovely sweet smell. You can walk along the beach, at low tide, all the way from Tamarindo Beach, but be careful not to get caught on the headland rocks as the tide comes in. Most hotels offer pickup in Tamarindo for car-free visitors. Or you can take a taxi.

BEACHES

Playa Langosta. This Blue Flag beach is actually two beaches: To the north is an upscale, residential area where every foot of beachfront has been built up; the beach here is rather narrow, since the coast is lined with rocks, and the light-gray sand is coarse. To the south, the beach is a pristine, protected annex of Marino Las Baulas National Park, where the occasional leatherback turtle nests at night and beachcombers and surfers roam by day. The dividing point is the San Francisco Estuary, the mouth of which is a knee-high wade at low tide, and a deep river with dangerous currents around high tide. The beach here is wider and less rocky, and it's where surfers find the best surf breaks. If you walk up the river at low tide, you may see snowy egrets, baby blue herons, tail-bobbing spotted sandpipers, and, if your eyes are sharp, tiny white-lored gnatcatchers, endemic to these parts. The rockier parts of the beach are excellent for spotting seabirds, including American oystercatchers. Amenities are available at Playa Langosta Beach Club. **Amenities:** food and drink; toilets. **Best for:** surfing; sunset; walking. ⊠ *Playa Langosta.*

SPORTS AND THE OUTDOORS

Tour operators in Tamarindo, just a few miles north, offer activities in the Playa Langosta area.

WHERE TO EAT

$$$ × **Playa Langosta Beach Club.** This beach club–restaurant–lounge–jazz
FRENCH club is the most romantic and sophisticated dining spot on the beach. By
Fodor'sChoice day, you can lounge by the pool or surf between bites of ceviche, panini,
★ burgers, or mussels with fries. By night, you'll find tables set with white linens and candles arranged under swaying palms around two glowing pools, while the sound of waves breaking on the beach blends with the very cool soft jazz (live on Friday). Start with a lobster and mango salad or a flaky pastry nest filled with goat cheese and spinach. Move on to a divine fillet of sole bathed in a velvety, peppery champagne-cream sauce. The ahi tuna is almost too beautiful to eat, topped with arugula and caviar on a tower of thin and crispy potatoes. There's a good wine list and light, refreshing Argentinian wines by the glass. For dessert, try the crepe suzette flambée. Come back the next day to work off your meal at the attached fitness center or yoga studio. ⑤ *Average main: $25*

⊠ *Langosta Beach road, 200 m north of Capitán Suizo* ☎ *2653–1127* ⊕ *www.langostabeachclub.com* ☞ *Beach club day pass $25.*

WHERE TO STAY

$$$
HOTEL

☷ **Casa Cook.** With just a few rooms on the quiet, southern end of Tamarindo beach, this friendly, family-run beachfront place is one of Tamarindo's most peaceful lodging options. **Pros:** intimate and beachfront; 24-hour security; friendly; major discounts July–October. **Cons:** often full; not a lot of privacy in casita. Ⓢ *Rooms from: $230* ⊠ *Road into Playa Langosta, 100 m before Hotel Capitán Suizo* ☎ *2653–0125* ⊕ *www. casacook.net* ⌦ *2 cabinas, 1 casita, 1 apartment, 1 house* ⦿*No meals.*

$$$$
HOTEL
Fodor's Choice
★

☷ **Hotel Capitán Suizo.** Nature, tranquility, luxury, and an unbeatably beautiful beach setting make this environmentally conscious boutique hotel the most elegant choice in town. **Pros:** secluded beachfront hotel; excellent restaurant; lovely gardens and pool; high sustainability rating. **Cons:** not all rooms are beachfront; pricey; no TVs (a con for some guests). Ⓢ *Rooms from: $295* ⊠ *Right side of Playa Langosta road, halfway between Tamarindo and Langosta* ☎ *2653–0075* ⊕ *www. hotelcapitansuizo.com* ⌦ *22 rooms, 8 bungalows, 2 beachfront suites, 2 beachfront garden rooms, 1 4-bedroom suite* ⦿ *Breakfast* ☞ *Usually closed for maintenance between Sept. and Oct.*

$$$
B&B/INN

☷ **Sueño del Mar.** The name of this beachfront bed-and-breakfast means "Dream of the Sea," and the front gate opens into a dreamy world of intimate gardens, patios, and hand-painted tiles. **Pros:** intimate; well appointed; friendly service; great beachfront; no kids under 12. **Cons:** tiny pool; lack of privacy in small rooms; pricey. Ⓢ *Rooms from: $210* ⊠ *130 m south of Capitán Suizo, veer right for 45 m, then right again for about 90 m to entrance gate, across from back of Cala Luna Hotel* ☎ *2653–0284* ⊕ *www.sueno-del-mar.com* ⌦ *3 rooms, 1 suite, 2 casitas* ⦿ *Breakfast.*

NIGHTLIFE

Hotel Capitán Suizo. For a pleasant Wednesday or Friday evening, try barbecue on the beach at the Hotel Capitán Suizo, starting at 6:30 with a cocktail, then on to a lavish barbecue buffet and live folk music and dancing ($40 with reduced rates for kids; reserve in advance). Available December to May only. ⊠ *Hotel Capitan Suizo, right side of road, past Playa Langosta Beach Club* ☎ *2653–0075* ⊕ *www.hotelcapitansuizo. com* ▥ *Dinner show $40.*

Jazz at Playa Langosta Beach Club. Sink into a comfortable chair at this chic poolside lounge on Playa Langosta to watch the sunset over the Pacific and listen to jazz under the stars, Fridays 7 to 9 pm. ⊠ *200 m north of Hotel Capitán Suizo, road between Tamarindo and Playa Langosta.*

PLAYA AVELLANAS

17 km (11 miles) south of Tamarindo.

Traditionally a far cry from its northern neighbor's boom of real estate development, Avellanas has seen Tamarindo escapees slowly encroaching on it for years, building private houses and a smattering of small hotels. The 2008 opening of the massive gated community of Hacienda

Pinilla—complete with a JW Marriott and golf course—marked the beginning of major development. As you bump along the dusty, rough beach road, most of the cars you pass have surfboards on top. But non-surfers are welcome, as Avellanas (pronounced ah-vey- *ya*-nas) is a lovely spot for anyone who just likes sea and sand.

GETTING HERE AND AROUND

You have to drive inland from Tamarindo to Villa Real, where you turn right for the 13-km (8-mile) trip down a bumpy road to reach Playa Avellanas. It takes about 20 minutes. There are rivers to cross in rainy season, when you may want to drive via Paraíso and Playa Negra. All of the roads in the gated community of Hacienda Pinilla are paved.

Tamarindo Shuttle. If you're without a car, take the Tamarindo Shuttle van. They have private transport to Playa Avellanas for $50 or to the JW Marriott at Hacienda Pinilla for $35. ☎ 2653–4444 ⊕ *www. tamarindoshuttle.com.*

BEACHES

Playa Avellanas. This beach's main claims to fame are surfing and hanging around at Lola's, a very cool beach restaurant-bar. Wide and sandy at the main access point, the beach itself is beautiful, with a line of palms and beach almonds for shade. Rocky outcroppings and a small river mouth mark its southern end, and a mangrove swamp lies behind its northern half. Its Blue Flag designation means the water is clean, but you shouldn't go in deeper than your waist when the waves are big, because of rip currents. That's when the surfers take over. Jellyfish can be a problem, so you might want to wear a rashguard. Unfortunately, security is an issue here, as at most Costa Rican beaches; posted signs warn visitors not to leave anything of value in parked cars or unattended on the beach. There is guarded parking at the beach entrance near Lola's; be sure to have small bills to tip the attendant when you leave. If you are staying in the gated resort community of Hacienda Pinilla, it is better to park in the private lot and enter from its beach club. **Amenities:** food and drink; parking (free). **Best for:** surfing; walking. ⊠ *Playa Avellanas.*

SPORTS AND THE OUTDOORS
GOLF

Hacienda Pinilla Golf Course. Mike Young, who has designed some of the best golf courses in the southern United States, designed the par-72 championship course at Hacienda Pinilla. It has ocean views and breezes, and plenty of birds populate the surrounding trees. Not as busy as some of the other courses in Guanacaste, the fairways are wide with long par 4s and challenging holes at 15 and 9. The latter, a par 4, shoots over a few bunkers to an elevated green. Non-hotel guests pay $150 for 18 holes in high season, including carts and range balls. Club rental is $50 more. ⊠ *In Hacienda Pinilla gated community, next to JW Marriott, 10 km (6 miles) south of Tamarindo via Villa Real, Tamarindo* ☎ *2681–4500* ⊕ *www.haciendapinilla.com* 🖃 *$150 for 18 holes* ⚑ *18 holes, 7200 yards, par 72.*

SURFING

Locals claim there are eight breaks here when the swell is big, which means Avellanas doesn't suffer the kind of overcrowding the breaks at Playas Negra and Langosta often do. Tamarindo-based surf schools can arrange day trips here.

Cabinas Las Olas. You can rent boards at Cabinas Las Olas for $15 a day. ⊠ *Main road, on right* ☎ *2652–9315.*

WHERE TO EAT

$ ✕ **Beach Box.** On the dirt road to Playa Avellanas, just before you hit the

MEXICAN FUSION   water, is the appropriately named Beach Box—a breakfast joint serving fresh-squeezed juices and fat breakfast burritos wrapped in parchment paper and served in wicker baskets. It's no more than a shipping container kitchen attached to a bamboo-shaded patio. Despite the simple setting, there's no skimping on ingredients, with soft flour or corn tortillas packed with organic chicken, spicy beef, or shredded pork. Vegans will enjoy the fried plantain slices, black-bean dips, homemade salsas, ripe avocados, and tomatoes roasted on an open grill. And the tortilla chips (made from scratch) make it impossible to eat just one. This glorified taco stand is popular with Marriott guests who walk down the beach for hearty breakfasts costing less than the tip they'd leave back at the resort. ⑤ *Average main: $7* ⊠ *150 m east of main parking lot in Avellanas, Avellanas* ☎ *2653–2258* ☉ *Closed Wed. and Sept. 15–Nov. 15. No dinner* ☞ *Cash only* ☐ *No credit cards.*

$$ ✕ **Lola's.** In deference to Lolita, the owners' pet pig (the original Lola

VEGETARIAN   used to freely roam the beach and enjoy the surf), the menu at this hip beach café is heavily vegetarian. It has exactly the kind of ambience one comes to Costa Rica for, with tables scattered along the beach amid palm and almond trees, hammocks swinging in the wind, palm fronds rustling, and surfers riding the glistening waves in front. Seating, or more precisely, lolling, is on reclining, African-style hardwood chairs, or at shaded tables. Along with fresh-fruit smoothies, ultra-thin vegetarian pizzas, and veggie soy burgers, the menu includes organic chicken and "responsible fish" (fish caught in nets that don't also trap turtles). Seared ahi tuna with sun-dried tomatoes and olive tapenade served on ciabatta bread is a winner, as are the ceviche, fish-and-chips, pesto pasta, and assorted salads. Mahi tacos are the latest addition to the menu, served with rice and beans. You can arrange in advance for private beach dinners (minimum 10 people) by candlelight. Operating hours are 10 to 5, but you can order fruit smoothies between 8 and 10 am. ⑤ *Average main: $11* ⊠ *At main entrance to Playa Avellanas* ☎ *2652–9097* ☉ *Closed Mon. No dinner.*

WHERE TO STAY

$$ ☵ **Cabinas Las Olas.** Frequented mainly by surfers, this is a good option

B&B/INN   for anyone seeking easy beach access, relative solitude, and comfortable,

FAMILY   if not fancy, lodging. **Pros:** near beach; surf shop with board rental and lessons; secluded. **Cons:** mosquitoes a problem in rainy season; simple rooms; patchy Wi-Fi. ⑤ *Rooms from: $90* ⊠ *1 km (½ mile) before Avellanas, on right* ☎ *2652–9315* ⊕ *www.cabinaslasolas.co.cr* ☉ *Closed Oct.* ⇋ *10 rooms* ⧆| *Breakfast.*

$$$$
RESORT

JW Marriott Guanacaste Resort & Spa. In the gated community of Hacienda Pinilla, this luxury resort is centered around a 25,000-square-foot infinity pool that merges with a short stretch of beach in the west, making every sunset a major event. **Pros:** luxurious; largest infinity pool in Central America; equestrian center. **Cons:** very pricey; service is slow and not up to JW standards; beach is rocky; ground-level rooms facing walkways get outside noise. $ *Rooms from: $500* ⊠ *In Hacienda Pinilla Beach resort and residential community* ⊕ *www.marriott.com/sjojw* ☏ *289 rooms, 21 suites* ⏐○⏐ *No meals.*

> ### A SURF CLASSIC
>
> Americans—surfer Americans, at least—got their first look at Playa Negra in 1994's *The Endless Summer II*, a film by legendary surf documentarian Bruce Brown.

$$$$
HOTEL
Fodor's Choice
★

Los Altos de Eros Luxury Inn & Spa. This intimate adults-only inn is the place to be for honeymooning couples with enough money left over after the wedding to pamper themselves, or for stressed-out high achievers in need of some serious relaxation therapy. **Pros:** secluded location; excellent service; peaceful; outstanding spa. **Cons:** scheduled mealtimes; often full; no kids under 18; difficult to find. $ *Rooms from: $295* ⊠ *Cañafistula, 14 km (8½ miles) southeast of Tamarindo, Avellanas* ☎ *8850–4203* ⊕ *www.losaltosdeeros.com* ☏ *5 rooms, 1 suite* ⏐○⏐ *Some meals.*

PLAYA NEGRA

3 km (2 miles) south of Playa Avellanas.

Surfer culture is apparent here in the wave of beach-shack surfer camps along the road that leads to the rocky strand of beach. But Playa Negra is growing up fast, with some interesting cafés and restaurants popping up to cater to beachgoers and residents of an upscale residential development called Rancho Playa Negra.

GETTING HERE AND AROUND

From Playa Avellanas, continue south 10 minutes on the rough beach road to Playa Negra. If it's rainy season and the road is too rough, you can approach along a slightly more civilized route from Santa Cruz. Drive 27 km (16½ miles) west, via Veintisiete de Abril, to Paraíso, then follow signs for Playa Negra for 4 km (2½ miles). Taxis are the easiest way to get around if you don't have a car; they cost about $40 from Tamarindo.

BEACHES

Playa Negra. Contrary to the name, the beach is not black, but rather beige with dark streaks. This is primarily a surfer's beach, so it's not great for swimming because it tends to have fast hollow waves and is lined with rocks. There is one calm, short stretch of clear sand to the south of the Playa Negra Hotel, and at low tide a large tidal pool forms there. The spindly buttonwood trees that edge the beach provide sparse shade. The dirt road to Playa Negra is bumpy and muddy during rainy season so drive with caution. Food and drink are served at Playa Negra Hotel's *palapa* restaurant on the beach. **Amenities:** food and drink; parking (free). **Best for:** surfing; walking. ⊠ *Playa Negra.*

6

SPORTS AND THE OUTDOORS

SURFING

Surfing cognoscenti dig the waves here, which are almost all rights, with beautifully shaped barrels. It's a spectacular, but treacherous, rock-reef break for experienced surfers only. There's also a small beach break to the south of the rocks where neophytes can cut their teeth. Both breaks can be ridden from mid- to high tide.

Hotel Playa Negra. The point break is right in front of the only beachfront hotel, which can arrange surfing classes ($40 per hour for a private lesson), and rents boards ($20 per day). ✉ *4 km (2½ miles) northwest of Paraíso on dirt road, then follow signs carefully at forks in road; or 10 mins south of Playa Avellanas on rough beach road* ☏ *2652–9298* ⊕ *www.playanegra.com* ⊠ *From $40.*

WHERE TO EAT

$$ ✗ **Café Playa Negra.** The stylish creation of Peruvian artist Andrea Raffo,
PERUVIAN this hacienda-like hall showcases her art, with squares of stained glass built into the walls, and a small gallery next door displaying handmade works. Andrea matches her passion for art with a talent for food, featuring such Peruvian specialties as ceviche and *causa,* cold mashed potatoes studded with shrimp and tuna chunks. The menu also includes mahimahi prepared five different ways, and a few familiar favorites like hamburgers and BLTs. Desserts are homemade and delicious, and the pisco sour cocktail is not to be missed. Saturdays feature two-for-one mojitos and sushi. Take note of the operating hours: breakfast is from 7 to 10, lunch from noon to 4, and dinner from 5 to 9. There's also a separate art gallery and free Wi-Fi. Ⓢ *Average main: $12* ⊠ *Main street* ☏ *2652–9351* ⊕ *www.cafeplayanegra.com* ⊗ *Closed Tues. and Oct.*

$$ ✗ **Kon Tiki.** A favorite local hangout, this rustic pizzeria has an outdoor
ITALIAN clay oven and an open kitchen. There are 14 types of pizza, like the house special with goat cheese, pesto, and caramelized onions. They also serve salads and gluten-free pizzas, as well as barbecued meats from the pizza oven (with 24 hours' notice). If you can't find a pizza that sounds good, you can build your own from a list of toppings. As the area's top local hangout, the place gets packed, so plan to enjoy some sangria while you wait for your food and bill. Ⓢ *Average main: $14* ⊠ *700 m after the soccer field at Los Pargos* ☏ *2652–9117* ⊕ *www. kontikiplayanegra.com* ⊗ *No lunch.*

$$$ ✗ **Restaurant Deevena.** An unexpected outpost of divine French cuisine,
FRENCH FUSION this oasis of elegance overlooks a sparkling blue pool edged by lush
Fodor'sChoice palms, while lounge chairs shaded by orange umbrellas tempt diners
★ to stay overnight (six stylish rooms are available). Lunch and dinner feature lots of local seafood, produce, and goat cheese from the chef's nearby farm. Try the fresh grouper fillet bathed in lemon-herb-butter sauce, or the seared ahi tuna with ginger-carrot purée. Vegetarians can feast on ravioli stuffed with wild mushrooms, sage, and sun-dried tomatoes. Desserts include classic French options—fruit crepes, crème brûlée—as well as chocolate lava cake with raspberry compote. The service here is exemplary. You can order wonderful wines by the glass or bottle—a rare opportunity in these remote parts. While waiting for your meal to arrive, ask to view the photo album of the chef's famous

clients. $ *Average main: $17* ⊠ *25 m off main road that runs through Playa Negra; watch for Villa Deevena sign* ☎ *2653–2328* ⊕ *www. villadeevena.com* ⊙ *Closed Mon. and Sept. and Oct.*

WHERE TO STAY

$$$
HOTEL
⊡ **Hotel Playa Negra.** Pastel-colored, round cabinas are sprinkled across sunny lawns strewn with tropical plants at this gorgeous oceanfront place with a huge round pool. **Pros:** in front of reef break; friendly; comfortable accommodation; family suites available. **Cons:** not a great swimming beach; rocky road to hotel; some rooms lack a/c. $ *Rooms from: $160* ⊠ *4 km (2½ miles) northwest of Paraíso on dirt road (watch signs for Playa Negra), then follow signs carefully at forks in road; or 10 mins south of Playa Avellanas on beach road* ☎ *2652–9134* ⊕ *www. playanegra.com* ⊙ *Restaurant closed Sept.–Nov. 1* ⟿ *10 bungalows, 7 bungalow suites* †⊙† *No meals.*

$$
HOTEL
⊡ **Villa Deevena.** Although most travelers visit this out-of-the-way spot for its famed French restaurant by the same name, Deevena is equally gaining renown for its hospitable staff and elegant rooms that surround a pool. **Pros:** excellent restaurant; saltwater pool; family-run business. **Cons:** outdoor showers attract bugs; not on the beach; breakfast not included. $ *Rooms from: $110* ⊠ *25 m off main road that runs through Playa Negra; watch for Villa Deevena sign* ☎ *2653–2328* ⊕ *www. villadeevena.com* ⊙ *Closed Sept. and Oct.* ⟿ *6 rooms* †⊙† *No meals.*

6

PLAYA JUNQUILLAL

4 km (2½ miles) south of Paraíso, 34 km (22 miles) southwest of Santa Cruz.

Seekers of oceanfront tranquility need look no further than Junquillal (pronounced hoon-key- *yall*), a beach town as far away from the crowd as you can get on a decent road. A surprisingly cosmopolitan mélange of expats has settled in this out-of-the-way area. There's a supermarket at the entrance to an upscale housing development, but Junquillal is still barely on the tourist map; consequently its few hotels offer some of the best deals on the North Pacific coast. Avoid visiting between September and November when hotels close, beaches are empty, and Junquillal virtually turns into a ghost town.

GETTING HERE AND AROUND

In rainy season, the 4-km-long (2½-mile-long) beach road from Playa Negra to Playa Junquillal is sometimes not passable. The alternative is driving down from Santa Cruz one hour on a road that's paved most of the way. The Castillos bus company runs a bus to Junquillal from the central market in Santa Cruz four times a day (at 5 and 10 am, and 2:30 and 5:30 pm); the trip takes about 40 minutes. A taxi from Santa Cruz or Tamarindo costs about $50; from the Liberia airport, $95 to $100.

ESSENTIALS

The closest town for most services is Santa Cruz, 34 km (22 miles) northeast.

Hospital Clínica. ⊠ *16 km (10 miles) northeast of Playa Junquillal, Veintisiete de Abril* ☎ *2658-0127.*

BEACHES

FAMILY **Playa Junquillal.** This wide swath of light-brown sand stretches over 3 km (2 miles), with coconut palms lining much of it and hardly a building in sight. Two species of sea turtle nest here, and a group of young people collect and protect their eggs, releasing the baby turtles after sunset. The surf is a little strong, so watch children carefully. There's a kids' playground right at the beach, and a funky little restaurant with concrete tables amid the palms. At low tide, it's a perfect beach for taking long, romantic strolls or for exploring active tide pools. Surfers head here to ride the beach break near Junquillal's northern end, since it rarely gets crowded. **Amenities:** food and drink. **Best for:** surfing; walking. ⊠ *Playa Junquillal.*

> **DID YOU KNOW?**
>
> Guanacaste was a political monkey-in-the-middle for centuries, bouncing between Spain, Nicaragua, and independence. In 1858, Guanacastecans finally voted to annex themselves to Costa Rica, an event celebrated every July 25 with a national holiday.

WHERE TO STAY

$
HOTEL
FAMILY
Fodor's Choice
★

Guacamaya Lodge. Spread across a breezy hill with expansive views above the treetops of the surrounding forest and the sea, the Guacamaya is a real find, with affordable, spacious cabinas surrounding a generous-size pool, lawn, and tropical plants. **Pros:** excellent value; clean; friendly. **Cons:** hilly 5-minute walk to the beach; meals and taxes not included in rate. ⑤ *Rooms from: $65* ⊠ *275 m east of Playa Junquillal* ☎ *2658-8431* ⊕ *www.guacamayalodge.com* ☾ *Closed Sept. and Oct.* ➟ *6 bungalows, 4 studios, 2 2-bedroom villas* ⦿ *No meals.*

$$
HOTEL

Hotel Iguanazul. On a bluff overlooking lava rocks replete with tide pools, and beyond them the sea, this hotel offers eco-friendly rooms on the shores of pristine Playa Blanca. **Pros:** in-house doctor lives on-site; beachfront; peaceful isolation. **Cons:** rough road to get here; breakfast not included in rate; no refunds. ⑤ *Rooms from: $120* ⊠ *Playa Blanca, North end of Playa Junquillal* ☎ *2658-8124* ⊕ *www.hoteliguanazul.com* ➟ *24 rooms* ⦿ *No meals.*

$$
B&B/INN

Mundo Milo Eco Lodge. This hidden eco-lodge with a kidney-shaped pool is made up of five bungalows themed after Africa, Persia, and Mexico. **Pros:** 300 meters from the beach; great value; delicious food at restaurant. **Cons:** no children under age five; closed in September and October; bumpy road. ⑤ *Rooms from: $77* ⊠ *C. Mundo Milo, 300 m from the beach* ☎ *2658-7010* ⊕ *www.mundomilo.com* ➥ *No credit cards* ☾ *Closed Sept. and Oct.* ➟ *5 rooms, 1 house* ⦿ *Breakfast.*

THE NICOYA PENINSULA

Updated by Dorothy MacKinnon

South of Tamarindo, you'll find the interesting anomaly of a trendy restaurant or upscale hotel plunked at the end of a tortuous dirt road. The key to enjoying the Nicoya Peninsula is to pick your spot—happening beach town or off-the-beaten-path seclusion.

The parks and wildlife refuges in and around the Río Tempisque are prime places to hike, explore caves, and spot birds and other wildlife. And there's a small smattering of culture, too, in the town of Nicoya, with its colonial-era church, and in Guaitil, with pottery made in the pre-Columbian Chorotega tradition. The town of Nicoya is the commercial and political hub of the northern Nicoya Peninsula. By road, Nicoya provides the best access to Sámara, Nosara, and points south and north, and is linked by a smooth, well-paved road to the northern Nicoya beach towns.

The southern tip of the Nicoya Peninsula is one of Costa Rica's less developed regions, where some of the country's most gorgeous beaches, rain forests, waterfalls, and tidal pools lie at the end of some of its worst roads. Within the region are quiet, well-preserved parks where you can explore pristine forests or travel by boat or sea kayak to idyllic islands for bird-watching or snorkeling. Other outdoor options include horseback riding, gliding through the treetops on a canopy tour, or surfing on some of the country's most consistent waves. In the laid-back beach towns of Montezuma, Santa Teresa, and Malpaís, an international cast of surfers, nature lovers, yoga enthusiasts, holistic new-agers, and expatriate massage therapists live out their dreams in paradise.

NOSARA

28 km (17 miles) southwest of Nicoya.

One of the last beach communities for people who want to get away from it all, Nosara's attractions are the wild stretches of side-by-side beaches called Pelada and Guiones, with surfing waves and miles of sand on which to stroll, and the tropical dry forest that covers much of the hinterland. Regulations here limit development to low-rise buildings 180 meters (600 feet) from the beach, where they are, thankfully, screened by trees. Americans and Europeans, with a large Swiss contingent, are building at an increasingly rapid pace. There still appears to be an aesthetic sense here that is totally lacking in Tamarindo, despite a plethora of trendy juice bars, fast-food taco stands, and souvenir stalls cropping up at the beach entrances. Offsetting the fast-food wave are the two organic farmer's markets in town, Sunday 9 to 2 and Tuesday starting at 8 am, in the Esquinas Skate Park next to the police station. Hotel owners and community members are participating in a reforestation project along the beachfront to create a lusher biological corridor and the results are beautifully evident already. The town of Nosara itself is inland and not very attractive, but it does have essential services, as well as the airplane landing strip. Almost all the tourist action is at the beaches.

For years, most travelers headed here for the surf. The wide range of surf schools and waves varying from beginner to expert levels make Nosara one of the best places to learn to surf. Along with surfing, the Nosara Yoga Institute, which offers instructor training and daily classes for all levels, is a major draw for health-conscious visitors. Healthy-food options, spas, and exercise classes abound. You'll see lots of yoga practitioners on the beaches around sunrise and sunset.

Bird-watchers and other nature enthusiasts can explore the tropical dry forest on hiking trails, on horseback, or by floating up the tree-lined Nosara River in a kayak, guide boat, or paddleboard. The last leg of the access road to Nosara, from either direction, is still abysmal, and the labyrinth of woodsy roads around the beaches and hard-to-read signs make it easy to get lost, which is why most hotels here provide local maps for their guests. Don't get in your car without one—especially at night. For local news and tourist information, pick up a free copy of the excellent monthly, bilingual newspaper *The Voice of Guanacaste* (⊕ *www.vozdeguanacaste.com*).

GETTING HERE AND AROUND

From Nicoya, drive south, almost to Sámara, but take the very first road sign for Nosara, 1 km (½ mile) south of the big gas station before Sámara. This high road is rough for about 8 km (5 miles), but there are bridges over all the river crossings. When you join up with the beach road near Garza, you still have a very bumpy 10 km (6 miles) to go. The roads into Nosara are in really bad shape, so a 4WD vehicle is definitely recommended. Budget about one hour for the trip from Nicoya. On the bright side, the main road above the beaches has finally been paved, cutting down on the choking dust in dry season. But all the dirt side roads to the beaches are still either dustbowls or mired in mud. The more remote the area, the more likely that someone will stop to help you change a tire or tow you out of a river. Usually, Good Samaritans won't accept any payment and are more trustworthy than those who offer to "help" in the States.

You can also fly directly to the town of Nosara on daily scheduled SANSA and Nature Air flights, or take an air-conditioned shuttle van from San José. Major rent-a-car companies have offices in Playa Guiones.

ESSENTIALS

Banks/ATMs Banco de Costa Rica. ⊠ *Next to Servicentro Nosara gas station, main road* ☎ *2682–5232.* **Banco Popular.** ⊠ *Main St., next door to Café de Paris, Playa Guiones* ☎ *2682–0011.*

Hospital Centro Médico Nosara. ⊠ *next door to Mandala shop, 100 m west of Café de Paris, on road to Playa Guiones* ☎ *2682–1212.*

Pharmacy Farmacia Nosara. ⊠ *In town, on right side of airstrip* ☎ *2682–5149.*

Post Office Correo. ⊠ *Next to soccer field in town* ☎ *No phone.*

Rental Cars Alamo/National. ⊠ *Playa Guiones road* ☎ *2682–0300.* **Economy.** ⊠ *Below Marlin Bill's Restaurant, at intersection of main road and Playa Guiones road* ☎ *2682–1146.*

Taxi Abel's Taxi. ☎ *8812–8470.*

EXPLORING

Ostional National Wildlife Refuge (*Refugio Nacional de Fauna Silvestre Ostional*). This wildlife refuge protects one of Costa Rica's major nesting beaches for olive ridley turtles. Locals have formed an association to run the reserve on a cooperative basis, and during the first 36 hours of the *arribadas* (mass nesting) they are allowed to harvest the eggs, on the premise that eggs laid during this time would likely be destroyed by subsequent waves of mother turtles. Though turtles nest here year-round,

Beginning surfers love Sámara's almost placid water and its undeveloped palm-fringed beach.

the largest arribadas, with thousands of turtles nesting over the course of several nights, occur from July to December; smaller arribadas take place between January and May. They usually occur around high tide, the week of a new moon. People in Nosara can tell you when an arribada has begun. To avoid overcrowding on the beach, visitors must join a guide-led tour of the nesting and hatching areas for $10 per person. Stop at the kiosk at the entrance to the beach to arrange a tour, or at the Association of Guides office, 25 meters south of the beach entrance on the main road, next to Cabinas Ostional. A new bridge over the Río Montaña has made access easier from Nosara. ⊠ 7 km (4½ miles) north of Nosara ☎ 2682–0428 ⤢ $10.

BEACHES

Fodor's Choice
★

Playa Guiones. This beach is one of the natural wonders of Costa Rica: a wide expanse of light-brown sand, sandwiched between rolling surf and green seagrape vines starting at the high-tide mark and backed by rejuvenating secondary forest. With some of the most consistent surf on the Pacific coast, Playa Guiones attracts a lot of surfboard-toting visitors, but the always-breezy beach is also a haven for sun lovers, beachcombers, and anyone who wants to connect with nature. The only building in sight is the bizarre Hotel Nosara, which was originally the only choice for lodging in town but is now a rambling private residence complete with an unfinished onion-dome tower. Otherwise, this glorious Blue Flag beach has 7 km (4½ miles) of hard-packed sand, great for jogging, riding bikes, and saluting the sun. Because there's a 3-meter (10-foot) tide, the beach is expansive at low tide but rather narrow at high tide, when waves usually create strong currents that can make the sea dangerous for nonsurfers. Most hotels post tide charts. Guiones is at the south end of the Nosara agglomeration, with three public accesses. The easiest one to find is about 300 meters past the Harmony Hotel, beyond the parked ATVs and souvenir stalls. **Amenities:** shade. **Best for:** surfing, walking. ⊠ *Playa Guiones.*

Playa Pelada. North along the shore, Playa Guiones segues seamlessly into crescent-shape Playa Pelada, where the water is a little calmer and just as clean, also designated a Blue Flag beach. There are tide pools to explore and a blowhole that sends water shooting up when the surf is big. Lots of trees provide shade. This is the locals' favorite vantage point for watching sunsets—great photo ops, with beached fishing boats adding color and interest to the foreground. Olga's Beach Club bar is nothing fancy, but it's a good place for a cool beer and fried red snapper. More upscale and romantic are the cushioned settees in front of La Luna Bar & Grill, on a slight rise overlooking the beach. **Amenities:** food and drink. **Best for:** sunset; surfing; swimming. ⊠ *Playa Pelada.*

SPORTS AND THE OUTDOORS
TOUR OPERATORS
Experience Nosara. For in-depth insights into the natural world, join a bilingual naturalist on a three-hour kayak tour along the Río Nosara ($70 per person), or on a leisurely hike to a hidden waterfall with swimming holes ($65, including lunch). Out on the ocean, the company offers surfing and two-hour stand-up paddleboard lessons and 2½- to 3-hour tours ($100); plus a five-hour snorkeling tour at Playa Juanillo, including a picnic lunch ($75, minimum four people). ⊠ *Nosara* ☎ *8705–2010* ⊕ *www.experience-nosara.com.*

Harbor Reef Surf Resort. This long-established hotel has an excellent tour desk that can arrange fishing, surfing, nature tours, and river expeditions. It can also arrange educational visits to the Refuge for Wildlife, which specializes in rescued howler monkeys. ⊠ *Follow signs from Café de Paris turnoff, Playa Guiones* ☎ *2682–0059, 2682–1000* ⊕ *www. harborreef.com.*

BIRD-WATCHING
Experience Nosara. Bilingual naturalist Allan Azofeifa leads serious birders on bird-watching tours, with an early-morning expedition on foot in the Nosara Biological Reserve or a kayak paddle up river to catch sight of some of the 270 species recorded here ($70, minimum two people). ⊠ *Nosara* ☎ *8705–2010* ⊕ *www.experience-nosara.com.*

FAMILY **River Safari.** Glide up the Nosara and Montaña rivers in a flat-bottom boat with an almost noiseless electric motor. Wading herons, egrets, roseate spoonbills, ospreys, and kingfishers are common sights. The German-born naturalist guide also knows where crocodiles hunker down in mud caves along the riverbank. Trips are $38 per person. ⊠ *Boat moored at bottom of hill leading up to Hotel Lagarta Lodge* ☎ *2682–0610* ⊕ *www.riversafari.de.*

FISHING
Fishing Nosara. This outfit can hook you up with local English-speaking captains who can take you fishing for 2½ hours, a half day, or full day, on boats ranging from 6 to 10 meters (20 to 31 feet). Rates start at

$200 for 2½ hours and top out at $900 for a full day on the largest, best-equipped boat. The shop sells rods, lures, fishing shirts, hats, and souvenir t-shirts. ✉ *In Paradise Rentals office on main road to Playa Guiones, Playa Guiones* ☎ *2682–0606* ⊕ *www.fishingnosara.com.*

HORSEBACK RIDING

FAMILY **Boca Nosara Tours.** German equestrienne Beate Klossek and husband Hans Werner take small groups of up to eight people on 2½-hour horseback nature tours through the jungle and along the beach ($50 to $70 per person, according to group size). They can also take a group of up to 12, with one guide for every four riders. Horses are well mannered and well treated. There are smaller saddles for kids, from six years old and up. ATV tours, starting from $70, are also offered, along with two-hour kayak tours ($70). You can rent a kayak ($30 for two hours) and paddle on your own. Kids under 12 are half price. ✉ *150 m below Hotel Lagarta Lodge, at mouth of Nosara River* ☎ *2682–0280* ⊕ *www.bocanosaratours.com.*

SURFING

Nosara has been called the best place in the world to learn how to surf, so if you've always wanted to try it, this is the place. Surf shops and surf schools are proliferating to satisfy the growing demand. Guiones is the perfect beginners' beach, with no rocks to worry about. Local surf instructors say that the waves here are so consistent that there's no week throughout the year when you won't be able to surf. Every year, the Costa Rica National Surfing Circuit comes here for surf trials.

Coconut Harry's Surf Shop. This Nosara surfing institution on the main road has a store full of surfing gear, along with a new taco bar. Most of the surfing action has shifted to a convenient beach location 100 meters from the main Playa Guiones beach entrance. You'll find board rentals ($15 to $20 per day), gear, lessons ($45 for 1½ hours, board included, for a group of three; a private lesson is $70), and board storage. ✉ *Main road, across from Café de Paris* ☎ *2682–0574 Main road shop, 8602–1852 beach location* ⊕ *www.coconutharrys.com.*

Corky Carroll's Surf School. Named after a renowned veteran American surfer, this school has its own hotel for surfing students, with prebooked lodging and lessons packages. It also offers one-on-one 60-minute lessons ($60) including board rental for the day and a cold beer at the end of the session, in the school's rancho where you can watch a video of the morning lessons, including your own. ✉ *Near Casa Romántica, off Playa Guiones road* ☎ *2682–0384* ⊕ *www.surfschool.net.*

Safari Surf School. This popular beachfront school, owned by a veteran surfer from Hawaii, is certified by the International Surfing Association. There are special packages for women, as well as a kids' surf camp. Most students come on package deals that include transportation and lodging at the school's brand-new, Olas Verdes surfer lodge, with 17 spacious suites, an alfresco restaurant, and a swimming pool. A short trail through the woods leads straight to the beach and surfing breaks. You can also pay as you learn, $55 for a 1½-hour group lesson or $75 for a private lesson, surfboard included. ✉ *Olas Verdes, Guiones beach* *road, 300 m. south of Harbor Reef Hotel, Playa Guiones* ☎ *2682–0113* ⊕ *www.safarisurfschool.com.*

YOGA

Harmony Hotel Healing Center. Close to Playa Guiones, the Harmony Hotel holds yoga classes daily for $15 a session. It also has a wide selection of New Age therapeutic massages and a full range of herbal spa services. ⊠ *Playa Guiones road,* ✢ *near beach entrance* ☎ *2682–4114* ⊕ *www.harmonynosara.com.*

Fodor'sChoice **The Nosara Yoga Institute.** This reputable, internationally known insti-
★ tute focuses on teacher certification, but also offers a variety of daily 75-minute yoga classes to the public ($15, cash only; mats included), including Vinyasa, Relax and Renew, and Core Flow, starting at 8:30 am till 5:30 pm. There's also a candlelight session. You can pre-book weeklong workshops and retreats throughout the year. ⊠ *Southeast end of town, on main road to Sámara* ☎ *2682–0071, 866/439–4704 in U.S.* ⊕ *www.nosarayoga.com.*

WHERE TO EAT

$$ ✕ **Café de Paris.** Vestiges of the original Swiss-French owners linger on
ECLECTIC at this bakery and alfresco eatery, open for breakfast and lunch. In
FAMILY addition to hearty sandwiches, the café serves burgers and salads. It's a good place to cool off, and perk up, with a *café frappé,* espresso blended with bananas and ice cream. The adjoining bakery is great for take-out beach picnics, with French-style bread and an array of pastries and tarts, including chocolate mousse. There's free Wi-Fi. ⑤ *Average main: $12* ⊠ *Main road, at Playa Guiones entrance* ☎ *2682–1036* ⊘ *Cafe closed Sun. No dinner.*

$$ ✕ **El Chivo.** It's a daily fiesta at this wildly popular new Mexican res-
MEXICAN taurant named for the "goat" of Mexican legend. A large garden area
FAMILY planted with tables is illuminated by strings of colorful lights. Square, blue-and-white wooden tables and chairs fill a thatched-roof rancho next to a long, rustic, cantina-style bar. All the Mexican favorites are here—in generous portions—with some intriguing and sophisticated additions. Kids' menu dishes come with healthy carrot and celery sticks. Bocas to accompany the many tequila-based cocktails include breaded-and-fried jalapeño peppers stuffed with cream cheese; or grilled sweet corn with chipotle cream and cheese. Pitchers of sangria, local craft beers, and imported Mexican beers are on tap. Families tend to populate the garden while surfers and grown-ups gravitate to the bar area. Save room for pots of cayenne-accented chocolate cream, or share a plate of cinnamon-and-sugar-sprinkled churros. Kids will love it here, and so will their parents. ⑤ *Average main: $15* ⊠ *road to Playa Pelada* ☎ *2682–0887* ⊕ *www.elchivo.co.*

$$ ✕ **Il Peperoni.** Head to this spot for the biggest pizzas in town in a large,
ITALIAN roofed-over garden near Playa Pelada. The house pizza is thin-crust
FAMILY with carrots, broccoli, olives, red peppers, onions, mushrooms, ham, and pepperoni. If you like it hot, dribble on some of the house specialty: red-hot, flavored oil. You can watch your pizza being dressed, then slotted into a wood-fired, freestanding brick oven, or choose from a full menu of salads, pasta, grilled fish, seafood, and meat, all Italian-style.

It's cheerful and hearty—no one leaves here still hungry. In high season there's sometimes live music at dinner. $ *Average main: $15* ⊠ *Across from Condominios Las Flores, road to Playa Pelada* ☏ *2682–0545.*

$$$
MEDITERRANEAN
FAMILY

✗ **La Luna Bar & Grill.** Sunrise to sunset, this casually chic restaurant overlooking Playa Pelada is the most scenic place to have breakfast, lunch, cocktails, or dinner. Tables spill out of the interior onto a wide, covered terrace and onto the sand. The menu is mostly Mediterranean, ranging from Moroccan-spiced or Limoncello-marinated fish of the day, to beef or fish carpaccio and brick-fired pizzas. At sunset, you can cozy up in a settee on the sand with a cocktail, and share a Mediterranean platter of dips, including harissa-hot hummus served with fluffy pita. Breakfast, starting at 7 am, ranges from typical Costa Rican to full English, with eggs, bacon, sausage, baked beans, grilled mushrooms, and tomatoes. Vegetarians can opt for toast topped with avocado and goat cheese. For a sweet finish, try the Nutella and banana "pizza" with vanilla ice cream. Some outdoor, picnic-style tables make this restaurant family-friendly during the day, while the terrace tables are more romantic at night. $ *Average main: $16* ⊠ *Playa Pelada* ✛ *overlooking the beach* ☏ *2682–0122.*

$$
MEDITERRANEAN

✗ **Le Bistrot at Giardino Tropicale.** Famous for its wood-oven pizzas, this breezy, all-wood restaurant with tree-trunk pillars is set amidst trees above the hotel of the same name. Lunch is the best deal in town, with pork, chicken, or fish casados elegantly presented with *patacones* (plantain fritters), a mound of white rice, a ramekin of red beans, and a mixed salad with creamy vinaigrette, all for $6. Dinners focus on grilled, stewed, and sauced meats including buffalo and lamb dishes, a rarity in these parts. Desserts are not to be missed—a passion-fruit crème brûlée is crunchy on top, smooth and tart below, and comes with a spoonful of strawberry coulis. The two-chocolate mousse, and a moist chocolate *moelleux* (cake) will make chocolate fans happy. The wine list features affordable French wines. Service is friendly and the chefs enjoy describing what's on the menu. $ *Average main: $14* ⊠ *Giardino Tropicale Hotel, main road, 100 meters west of road to Playa Guiones* ☏ *2682–0258* ⊙ *Closed Mon.*

$$
AMERICAN
FAMILY

✗ **Marlin Bill's.** Feeling carnivorous? Sink your teeth into a 22-ounce bone-in, rib-eye steak or 16-ounce pork chops in American-size portions at this open-air restaurant with a great sunset view. Lighter choices include grilled fish and salads, eggplant parmigiana, homemade spinach-and-ricotta ravioli in marinara sauce, and delicious "dorado fingers"—battered fish-fillet strips served with tartar sauce. Margaritas and rum-based drinks flow, and beer drinkers can try Libertas, a Costa Rican craft beer, on draft. Homemade desserts include key lime pie. The decor is decidedly nautical, with fish-themed art on the walls. Fishing and real-estate talk over beer and chicken wings keeps the U-shape bar abuzz. This is the go-to place for traditional holiday meals—turkey with all the trimmings and pumpkin pie—and also for Monday-night football and televised soccer games. There's free Wi-Fi, and the cheerful waitresses speak English. $ *Average main: $14* ⊠ *Hilltop above main road, near Coconut Harry's Surf Shop* ☏ *2682–0458* ⊙ *Closed Sun.*

$ ✕ **Robin's Cafe & Ice Cream.** Robin's is famous for homemade ice cream
VEGETARIAN   in an array of tempting flavors—the Mayan Chocolate is a standout—
FAMILY   along with refreshing tropical-fruit sorbets. This casual patio café also
serves breakfast all day and full meals with a focus on wholesome foods,
including vegetarian and raw-food dishes. Overstuffed veggie quesadillas will appeal to all tastes, along with pad thai rolls and yummy vegan
veggie burgers. Locals line up to buy the dense, fudgy brownies when
they come out of the oven. Gluten-free brownies and cookies are also
on offer. ⑤ *Average main: $9* ⊠ *Road to Playa Guiones, 25 m west of
Banco Popular* ☎ *2682–0617* ⊟ *No credit cards* ⊙ *No dinner.*

$$$ ✕ **Tibidabo.** The decor here is minimalist—polished gray concrete floor,
CATALAN   modern tables and chairs, stainless-steel overhead fans—but the food is
a cornucopia of classic Catalonian tapas and imported Iberian special-
ties. Even the simplest *tapa* is expertly executed here: the *montadito
de tortilla* is a tender omelet encasing tiny potatoes and caramelized
onions, atop a crush of fresh tomatoes spread across slices of toasted
homemade bread. Simple but perfect. Aficionados of Iberian ham will
recognize the best—and most expensive—acorn-fed pork on offer.
Paired with a glass of Spanish *verdejo* or *tempranillo*, the tapas menu
makes a satisfying light lunch or dinner. For a heartier meal, paella for
two has to be ordered in advance, by e-mail. For dessert, the crema
Catalana is as it should be: crunchy on top, creamy inside, and not too
sweet. There's a kid's menu of chicken or fried eggs with fries, but after
the sun goes down, this restaurant and cocktail bar is too sophisticated
for restless youngsters. ⑤ *Average main: $17* ⊠ *Road to Playa Guiones*
✛ *200 meters north of The Harmony Hotel* ☎ *2682–0837* ✍ *tibida-
bonosara@gmail.com* ⊙ *Sun., Sept., Oct.*

WHERE TO STAY

$$ ⊡ **Casa Romántica Hotel.** Calm, tranquil, and close to the beach, this
B&B/INN   hotel's name ("Romantic House") says it all: the Spanish colonial–
style house has an upstairs veranda and a graceful arcade with views
of a crystal-blue kidney-shape pool surrounded by a glorious tropical
garden. **Pros:** very close to beach; good restaurant; good value. **Cons:**
rooms comfortable but not spectacular; usually quiet but children can
make the pool area noisy at times. ⑤ *Rooms from: $110* ⊠ *200 m
southwest of Gilded Iguana* ☎ *2682–0272* ⊕ *www.casa-romantica.net*
⤵ *12 rooms, 1 house* ⏀ *Breakfast.*

$$ ⊡ **Giardino Tropicale Hotel.** In lush gardens shaded by large trees, you'll
B&B/INN   find comfortable deluxe rooms and smaller, simpler cabinas with fresh
FAMILY   linens and rocking chairs on the porches, centered on a sparkling
17-meter (56-foot), salt-filtered swimming pool. **Pros:** good value; envi-
ronmentally friendly; laptop-size safety boxes. **Cons:** road noise; extra
charge for air-conditioning; short walk to beach. ⑤ *Rooms from: $95*
⊠ *Main street, past entrance to Playa Guiones* ☎ *2682–4000* ⊕ *www.
giardinotropicale.com* ⤵ *4 cabinas, 2 with kitchens; 4 deluxe rooms
w. kitchenettes, 1 suite with full kitchen, 1 two-story rancho with full
kitchen* ⏀ *No meals.*

$ ⊡ **The Gilded Iguana.** This lively hotel-bar-restaurant has been a Nosara
B&B/INN   fixture for more than 25 years with six large, air-conditioned rooms
FAMILY   and a small, kidney-shaped pool with a waterfall and pool bar. **Pros:**

very economical rooms; laid-back; lively bar. **Cons:** spotty service; can be noisy; cheaper rooms don't have air-conditioning. ⑤ *Rooms from: $65* ✉ *Playa Guiones* ☎ *2682-0259* ⊕ *www.thegildediguana.com* ⋘ *10 rooms, 2 suites* ⏐⊙⏐ *No meals.*

$$
B&B/INN
⌂ **Harbor Reef Surf Resort.** It's easy to lose yourself in the junglelike gardens of this comfortable surfer hotel, where rooms and suites cater to surfers of every age, with plenty of space for boards and gear inside. **Pros:** attractive grounds; near beach and surf breaks; good restaurant. **Cons:** bland rooms; very small pools. ⑤ *Rooms from: $120* ✉ *Follow signs from Café de Paris turnoff toward Playa Guiones* ☎ *2682-1000* ⊕ *www.harborreef.com* ⋘ *16 rooms for two to four people; 4 family suites, 2 with kitchens; 2 six-person suites with kitchen; 1 two-bedroom house with kitchen* ⏐⊙⏐ *Breakfast.*

$$$$
B&B/INN
Fodor'sChoice
★
⌂ **The Harmony Hotel.** This ultracool, holistic retreat gets top marks for both comfort and sustainability, thanks to American owners who are surfers of an age where comfort, quiet, and thinking ecologically are more appealing than partying. **Pros:** on beach; excellent food; aromatic, eco-friendly toiletries and natural repellent; one free yoga class per guest per stay. **Cons:** pricey; not overly kid-friendly but babies welcome; standard rooms are smallish. ⑤ *Rooms from: $330* ✉ *From Café de Paris, take road almost all the way to Playa Guiones, look for sign leading to tree-shaded parking lot on right* ☎ *2682-4114, 2682-1073* ⊕ *www.harmonynosara.com* ⋘ *10 rooms, 13 1-bedroom bungalows, 1 2-bedroom suite* ⏐⊙⏐ *Breakfast.*

$$$
B&B/INN
Fodor'sChoice
★
⌂ **Hotel Lagarta Lodge.** A birders' and nature lovers' Valhalla, this magnificent nature lodge on a promontory has amazing views of the forest, river, and coast north of Nosara. **Pros:** amazing views and grounds; close to nature; sustainable; all-new suites. **Cons:** not on the beach; some steps to rooms; steep, rough road to get here. ⑤ *Rooms from: $200* ✉ *Top of hill at north end of Nosara* ☎ *2682-0035* ⊕ *www. lagarta.com* ⋘ *8 jungle rooms; 12 larger suites* ⏐⊙⏐ *No meals.*

$$$
B&B/INN
Fodor'sChoice
★
⌂ **Luna Azul.** Sequestered in the green hills above Playa Ostional, 5 miles north of Nosara, tranquil, tasteful Luna Azul is full of clever design and healthful attributes, surrounded by a private nature reserve abounding with birds and wildlife. **Pros:** isolated in a picturesque environment; good restaurant; luxurious rooms; excellent breakfast; free Wi-Fi. **Cons:** getting here involves some rough roads; restaurant prices do not include tax and service. ⑤ *Rooms from: $170* ✉ *1 km (½ mile) north of Ostional, 8 km (5 miles) north of Nosara* ☎ *8821-0075, 2682-1400* ⊕ *www.hotellunaazul.com* ⋘ *3 bungalows, 2 2-room duplex bungalows* ⏐⊙⏐ *Breakfast.*

NIGHTLIFE

The Gilded Iguana. Live acoustic music on Sunday nights draws a big crowd. ✉ *Playa Guiones* ☎ *2682-0259.*

Kaya Sol. There's always plenty of surfing talk at Kaya Sol, a friendly, laid-back bar near the beach with a pool table, tree-trunk tables, and a light, inexpensive menu. ✉ *Playa Guiones* ☎ *2682-0080.*

Olga's Beach Club. Sunset is the main event in the evening on Playa Pelada, and both locals and tourists gather to watch it here at this beach shack and bar with the best view. Olga's also serves an excellent fried whole red snapper. ✉ *End of the road to Playa Pelada.*

Restaurante La Luna. Sip an exotic tropical cocktail or munch on hummus and pita bread while watching the sun set at this lovely Mediterranean restaurant, which has settees and rattan chairs set out on the sand, as well as seats in the chic new indoor lounge and restaurant. ✉ *Beachfront, Playa Pelada* ☎ *2682–0122.*

Tropicana Discobar. The popular Tropicana is where the Latin dance action is on Friday and Saturday nights, from 9:30 pm to 2:30 am, for locals who love to dance and visitors who want to salsa, too. ✉ *Downtown Nosara, beside the soccer field* ☎ *2682–0140.*

SHOPPING

Arte Guay. This is the place to find the largest selection of local crafts and every imaginable souvenir, plus beachwear and sun hats. ✉ *Just past Café de Paris on road to Playa Guiones, right-hand side* ☎ *2682–1406.*

Coconut Harry's Surf Shop. Along with surfing wear and gear, this funky, jam-packed shop has an interesting selection of jewelry and bottled hot sauces that will spice up the local *comida típica* (typical fare). From 11 to 5, you can also grab a fresh, hot taco from the shop's new taco bar. ✉ *Main road, across from Café de Paris* ☎ *2682–0574.*

Mandala. Yoga fans will swoon over the pretty yoga tops here, made of feather-light, Peruvian pima cotton. There are also yoga pants and cool beachwear of the shop's own design. There's a selection of Birkenstock sandals, too. An array of aromatherapy potions makes the shop a pleasant place to be, along with the air-conditioning. Look for the large Buddha posed in front of the shop; open 9 to 5 daily. ✉ *Playa Guiones road ✛ beside Alamo car rental.*

The Silver Tree. This elegant jewelry store is a cut above the usual souvenir shop, with beautiful handmade pieces from local artists as well as sophisticated resort wear. There are also unusual, high-quality handcrafted gifts, art, and one-of-a-kind curios, locally made and from around the world. ✉ *2nd fl. in minimall beside Café de Paris, on Playa Guiones road* ☎ *2682–1422.*

SPAS

Tica Massage and Studio Guiones. Relaxing massages, facials, and salt glows in a jungle setting ($65 per hour) are available by appointment at Tica Massage. Under the same management and in the same location, Studio Guiones offers a full schedule of Pilates and yoga classes, as well as surfers' stretch sessions and core workouts. Dance and movement classes in this studio include a kids-in-motion class; check the website for exercise and dance class schedules. ✉ *Heart of Guiones Wellness Center, across from Harmony Hotel, Playa Guiones* ☎ *2682–0096* ⊕ *www.ticamassage.com; www.studioguiones.com.*

SÁMARA

36 km (23 miles) southwest of Nicoya, 26 km (16 miles) south of Nosara.

Sámara has miles of palm-shaded beach, safe swimming water, and an abundance of budget accommodations and seafront restaurants, making it especially popular with budget travelers, both Tico and foreign. This can be a lively place on weekends, with beach bars and handicraft vendors setting up on the main drag. A sandy roadway with the occasional car runs alongside the coconut palms and Indian almond trees that line the beach, so be sure to look both ways when you move between the surf and the town. Like nearby Nosara, Sámara is becoming more nature- and health-conscious. There's a weekly farmers' market featuring organic produce (Tuesday, 8 to 11 am), along with goat and cow cheeses, *kombucha* (a probiotic brewed tea), artisanal breads, local honey, salsas, and jellies. Friday, from 2 to 5:30 pm, there's another market selling mostly baked goods and handicrafts.

GETTING HERE AND AROUND

The drive from Nicoya to Sámara is one of the most scenic in Costa Rica, passing through rolling hills and green vistas before descending to the wide, south-facing bay hemmed by palm-lined sand. The road is paved all the way and takes about an hour. ■TIP➔ Potholes are spreading, so drivers need to keep their eyes on the road instead of the beautiful views. A rough beach road from Nosara is passable in dry season (it's more direct, but takes just as long); do not attempt this road when it rains. To get from Nosara to Sámara via the paved road, drive south 5 km (3 miles) past Garza. At the T in the road, ignore the road toward Sámara (the beach road) and take the road to the left, toward Nicoya. This will take you uphill to merge with the main Nicoya–Sámara highway. Sámara-bound buses leave Nicoya from a stop 300 meters east of the central park. They depart almost hourly from 5 am to 3 pm (there's no bus at 7 am) and then at 4:30, 6:30, 8, and 9:45 pm. For the latest bus schedule, look online at ⊕ *www.samarabeach. com*. There's also a direct Tracopa–Alfaro bus from San José daily at noon and, in high season only, at 5 pm (☏ *2221–4214*); the trip takes about five hours and costs $9.

ESSENTIALS

Banks/ATMs Banco de Costa Rica. ✉ *North side of soccer field, Downtown* ☏ *2656–2112.* **Banco Nacional.** ✉ *50 m west of Catholic church* ☏ *2656–0089.*

Hospital Clinica. ✉ *1 km (½ mile) west of Sámara in Cangreja* ☏ *2656–0166.*

Pharmacy Farmacia Sámara. ✉ *next door to Miniplaza Patio Colonial, main road at entrance to Sámara.*

Post Office Correo. ✉ *Beside church, across from soccer field.*

Rental Cars Alamo. ✉ *Main road into town, beside Hotel Giada* ☏ *2656–0958.*

6

BEACHES

Playa Sámara. This is the perfect hangout beach, with plenty of shade, bars, and seafront restaurants to take refuge in from the sun. Its wide sweep of light-gray sand is framed by two forest-covered hills jutting out at either end. The waves break out on a reef that lines the entrance of the cove several hundred yards offshore, which keeps the water calm enough for safe swimming without rip currents and leaves enough surf to have fun in. The reef holds plenty of marine attractions for diving and snorkeling excursions. Isla Chora, at the south end of the bay, provides a sheltered area that is especially popular for kayakers and snorkelers—it even has a tiny beach at lower tides. After years of hard work to clean up the beach, Sámara Beach now sports a Blue Flag. Those seeking solitude should head to the beach's western or eastern ends. **Amenities:** food and drink; water sports. **Best for:** snorkeling; surfing; swimming.

SPORTS AND THE OUTDOORS
TOUR OPERATORS

Sámara is known more for gentle water sports such as snorkeling, kayaking, and paddleboarding than for surfing, although the calmer waters provide a good place for beginners, so surf schools have multiplied fast. There are also two high-flying adventures here: a zip-line tour and ultralight flights and flying lessons. ATV tours, tearing along dirt roads, are popular with travelers who are particularly fond of dust, or mud, according to the season. For a quieter, closer contact with nature, there's a new guided hike in a private forest reserve. For information on area activities, visit the informative ⊕ www.samarainfocenter.com or drop into their office at the entrance to Lo Que Hay Taquería, on the beach road. You'll find brochures, maps, and friendly advice.

Carrillo Adventures. Horseback riding, river and sea kayaking, dolphin-watching, fishing, snorkeling, and trips to Palo Verde, Arenal, and Monteverde national parks can all be booked here. This long-established, local tour company also provides daily shuttle service to the Liberia airport at 8:30 am ($50 per person, minimum two people) and to Tamarindo for the same price. ✉ across from Hotel Giada on main road to beach ☎ 2656–0606 ⊕ www.carrilloadventures.com 🖆 From $35.

Samara Adventure Company. This tour operator offers an array of local tours, including kayaking, dolphin-watching, and mountain-bike tours, as well as paddleboarding and tours in Monteverde and Arenal national parks. It also arranges transportation by private shuttle to other parts of the country. ✉ Main street, beside Hotel Giada ☎ 2656–0920 ⊕ www.SamaraAdventures.com 🖆 From $50.

Sámara Trails. Take a 2½-hour hike ($40; under 12, $30) with a bilingual naturalist guide through a mango plantation and into a private reserve to experience the dry tropical forest and its denizens—howler monkeys, trogons, and mot-mots, among them. There's a daily morning tour at 7 am, or earlier if you want to see more birds; and another at 3 pm. Transportation from Sámara is included; book at Sámara Adventure Tours in town. ✉ Werner Sauter Biological Reserve ✛ 3 km (2 mi) northeast of Sámara ☎ 2656–0920, 800/726–8120 toll-free from U.S.

CANOPY TOURS

FAMILY **Wing Nuts Canopy Tour.** Named after a famous surfer, this three-hour, 10-platform zip-line tour ($60) flies through a patch of tropical forest just south of town, with ocean views from some of the platforms. It's small but just right for younger or timid children, and they have special tot-size harnesses for kids as young as three years old. Canopy tours take off at 8, 9, noon, and 1 pm; reserve by phone. Kids (up to 12) pay $45. ⊠ *In hills above Sámara, office 1 km (½ mile) east of downtown Sámara* ☎ *2656–0153* ⊕ *www.wingnutscanopy.com.*

DIVING AND SNORKELING

The reef offshore is the best place to snorkel. Kayakers also paddle out to Isla Chora to snorkel on the leeward side of the island.

KAYAKING

Samara Adventure Company and Carrillo Adventures organize kayaking tours, on both ocean and river, in plastic sit-on-top kayaks.

C&C Surf School. This established surf school also runs three-hour, guided kayak snorkeling tours on the Río Tigre and out to Isla Chora and the nearby reef ($40, including gear and a fruit snack). ⊠ *On beach next to Tree House Inn* ☎ *5006–0369* ⊕ *www.cncsurfschool.com.*

Ticos Surf School. This beachfront surf school also has stand-up paddleboards and kayaks to rent. Kayaking tours through the mangroves or on the ocean are $40 per person; 1½-hour paddleboard lessons ($40) include an extra hour of practice time. ⊠ *On the beach* ☎ *8705–2304* ⊕ *www.ticossurf.com.*

SURFING

The surf is relatively gentle at Sámara, so it's a good place for beginners. The challenging waves for more experienced surfers are farther south, at Playa Camaronal, which has both left and right breaks.

C&C Surf School. The most experienced beachfront surf school offers lessons from beginner up ($60 per 90-minute private lesson, including five-day board rental; $40 for two or more beginners) with certified instructors, and a huge selection of boards for rent ($4 per hour; $10 per day or $15 for 24 hours). ⊠ *On beach in center of town* ☎ *5006–0369* ⊕ *www.cncsurfschool.com.*

ULTRALIGHT FLIGHTS

Sámara Ultralight Tours. Take off for a thrilling ride over Sámara from the beach near Flying Crocodile Lodge or a larger runway 10 minutes from town, on an ultralight flight ($110 cash for 20-minute tour, $150 for 30 minutes). Pilot Jörg also gives flying lessons. ⊠ *Playa Buena Vista, 6 km (4 miles) northwest of Sámara* ☎ *8330–3923.*

WHERE TO EAT

$$$ ✕ **El Lagarto Steakhouse and Seafood.** If surf and turf is on your must-eat
BARBECUE list, El Lagarto serves up fresh, local seafood and high-quality meat from lean Brahman cattle, grilled to perfection on a massive, open-air, wood-fired barbecue. Sink your teeth into juicy tenderloin, lamb chops, mahimahi, prawns, tuna, mussels, chicken breast stuffed with mushrooms and cheese, portobello mushrooms, or a whole grilled lobster. You won't find any barbecue sauce here; everything is simply brushed

with extra-virgin olive oil and seasoned with a bit of garlic, salt, and pepper to complement the flavor of the food. Dinners include grilled vegetables and potatoes; a salad is à la carte. There's also a kids' menu, an ample wine list, and an extensive cocktail selection, not to mention banana splits. The restaurant is open for dinner only, though it opens at 3 pm for cocktails. Tax and service are not included on the menu prices, so expect to pay 25% more than advertised. ⑤ *Average main: $18* ⌧ *200 m west and 150 m south of Banco Nacional* ☎ *2656–0750* ⊕ *www.ellagartobbq.com* ⊘ *No lunch.*

$$$
ITALIAN
Fodor'sChoice
★

✕ **Gusto Beach Creativo.** A romantic setting, ocean breezes, and a creative, Italian menu make this the most popular restaurant in Sámara. By day, rustic wooden tables are shaded by white sails strung between palms; by night, diners bask in the glow of white globe lamps and light-festooned trees. You can sit under a covered area or out on the sand. The soundtrack is cool and hip, and the food is good, too. From tuna tartare to spaghetti *alle vongole*, this kitchen is first class. Along with Italian wines by the glass, you can sip a glass of Prosecco straight or add peach, orange, or strawberry juice to make a champagne cocktail worthy of the Italian Riviera. Save room for the standout panna cotta desserts. Gusto starts the morning at 8:30 with great espresso and croissants; the rest of the day, there are salads, burgers, Italian fries sprinkled with parmesan and pepper, and, of course, pizzas. Service is efficient and executed with style. It's cash-only and menu prices do not include the obligatory 25% tax and service. ⑤ *Average main: $16* ⌧ *Beach road, center of town* ▭ *No credit cards.*

$$
ITALIAN
Fodor'sChoice
★

✕ **Mama Gui.** Elegant design aligns with ultra-sophisticated Italian cuisine at this exciting new restaurant. Italian recipes infused with tropical flavors make up the menu, like the tender corvina (sea bass) tartare, blended with pineapple, coriander, almonds, lime, ginger, sweet red peppers, tomatoes, scallions, and pear, or the giant grilled shrimp, marinated in limoncello liqueur. Old World ingredients include the best of Italian cheeses, truffle oil, artisanal pastas, and balsamic vinegar. Desserts are prepared fresh each day. Dove-gray walls are enlivened by blue-and-white striped fabrics and elegant tropical-bird wallpaper in the air-conditioned interior. The attentive chef makes frequent appearances in the dining room and on the small outdoor terrace and his enthusiasm in contagious. Service is polished and smooth. The restaurant is small and cash-only, open for dinner from 5 to 11 daily. ⑤ *Average main: 14* ⌧ *250 meters west of Catholic Church, before narrow bridge* ☎ *2656–2347* ⊘ *Wed. in low season, Sept. to Nov.* ⚭ *Reservations essential* ▭ *No credit cards.*

$$
ITALIAN
FAMILY

✕ **Mare de Vino.** An ample selection of good Italian food, including 14 versions of crispy pizzas, 19 pastas, generous salads, and a lengthy Italian wine list (available by the glass, too), makes this sidewalk trattoria, formerly called Pizza & Pasta a Go-Go, a good spot for lunch or dinner. Tuna carpaccio is a lighter option, or try the *insalata caprese* with fresh basil. There's also a selection of local Tico dishes and seafood. Unlike the checkered tablecloths you'd find elsewhere, here you have glass tabletops showcasing shells, or plain wooden tables by the pool. Save room for a delicious Tico-Italian version of tiramisu or a mint-chocolate panna cotta. ⑤ *Average main: $14* ⊠ *Hotel Giada lobby, main road, 150 m north of beach* ☎ *2656–0132.*

$$$
COSTA RICAN
✗ **Tabanuco Beachfront Restaurante & Bar.** Right on the beach, this lively nightspot also has an elegant terrace restaurant that's romantically torch-lighted at night. Come for fresh ceviche and grilled whole fish and seafood, Tico-style, as well as curried chicken and grilled meat dishes. It's open from 11 am to 10 pm, with lots of shade under massive trees and cool breezes off the ocean. Afternoons, you can sit on pastel-colored beach chairs at tables with umbrellas, right on the sand. ⑤ *Average main: $18* ⊠ *On the beach, 30 m west of main beach entrance* ☎ *2656–1056* ☉ *Closed Sun.*

WHERE TO STAY

$$
B&B/INN
🖭 **Hotel Belvedere.** After a day on the beach, it's refreshing to retreat to this small hotel buried in a dense, cool garden on a breezy hill overlooking Sámara. **Pros:** affordable; clean; quiet. **Cons:** 10-minute walk down to beach and a bit longer climbing back up the hill. ⑤ *Rooms from: $80* ⊠ *Entering Sámara, go 100 m left at the first cross street* ☎ *2656–0213* ⊕ *www.belvederesamara.net* ⇱ *20 rooms, 2 apartments* ⦿ *No meals.*

$
B&B/INN
🖭 **Hotel Casa del Mar.** Facing the beach, this small, pleasant, well-tended hotel is one of Sámara's best values. **Pros:** helpful staff; easy on the wallet; free Wi-Fi. **Cons:** close, but not right on the beach; no swimming pool; some noise from road; some rooms share a bathroom. ⑤ *Rooms from: $50* ⊠ *Main beach strip, 45 m east of school* ☎ *2656–0264* ⊕ *www.casadelmarsamara.net* ⇱ *17 rooms, including 6 with shared bathroom* ⦿ *Breakfast.*

$$
B&B/INN
🖭 **Hotel Giada.** This eco-conscious hotel in the heart of town has two small swimming pools surrounded by greenery and brilliant bougainvillea. **Pros:** affordable; friendly; hair dryers in rooms. **Cons:** not right on the beach; smallish rooms; street noise can affect some rooms. ⑤ *Rooms from: $90* ⊠ *Main strip, 250 m north of beach* ☎ *2656–0132* ⊕ *www. hotelgiada.net* ⇱ *24 rooms* ⦿ *Breakfast.*

$$
B&B/INN
🖭 **Sámara Tree House Inn.** One of the few hotels right on the beach, this small inn has lofty, breezy bungalows up at palm-tree level, perfect for folks who love the open air and looking down on the beach action. **Pros:** right on the beach; small and cozy. **Cons:** neighboring bars and restaurants can be noisy; very small pool. ⑤ *Rooms from: $135* ⊠ *Beach road, across from supermarket* ☎ *2656–0733* ⊕ *www.samaratreehouse.com* ⇱ *4 tree houses, 2 rooms* ⦿ *Breakfast.*

$$$
RENTAL
🖭 **Villas Kalimba.** You may never want to leave this tranquil oasis of luxury villas hidden behind scrolled white-and-orange walls, where the architecture is Mexican but the style is all Italian. **Pros:** spacious villas; all the comforts of home; lovely garden. **Cons:** not right on beach; some noise from beach road. ⑤ *Rooms from: $160* ⊠ *200 m east of Sámara Police Station, along beach road* ☎ *2656–0929* ⊕ *www. villaskalimba.com* ⇱ *1 one-bedroom villa; 5 two-bedroom villas, 4 casas* ⦿ *No meals.*

$$$
RESORT
FAMILY
🖭 **Villas Playa Sámara.** Families come back to this property year after year for good reason: there's lots to do, the villas are spacious and practical, and the beach setting is fabulous. **Pros:** great location; spacious villas; ample grounds; excellent sportfishing nearby. **Cons:** no phones

6

Idyllic Playa Carrillo is perfect for swimming, snorkeling, or just sunning.

in rooms; 15-minute walk along the beach to Sámara center. $ *Rooms from: $199* ✉ *Off main road to Playa Carrillo, 2 km (1¼ mile) south of town* ☎ *2656–1111 Hotel, 4052–4646 for reservations* ⊕ *www.villasplayasamara.com* ⬎ *59 villas, 16 deluxe rooms* ⏐⊙⏐ *No meals.*

NIGHTLIFE

La Vela Latina Beach Bar. This is the best spot around for grown-up soft music and cocktails on the beach at sunset, especially with two-for-one drinks from 5 to 7 pm. Tables and chairs spill out onto the sand, under palms and almond trees strung with ropes of lights. The soundtrack is more jazzy than rap-driven. You can order sushi and Thai dishes along with your cocktails. It's a good late-night option for nightcaps, since it's open until midnight. ✉ *Across from Villas Kalimba, on beach* ☎ *2656–2286.*

Lo Que Hay Bar & Taquería. Live music plays some nights at this friendly bar right on the beach. It's open until midnight and so is the kitchen if you're hungry for a late-night taco. There's also a large flat-screen TV and free Wi-Fi. If you stayed up all night, this place also serves breakfast starting at 7 am. ✉ *Beach road, across from Sámara Organics Market Café* ☎ *2656–0811.*

Micro Bar. This tiny *boîte* of a bar is the coolest place in town, with an Escher-inspired tile floor and hip lighting. Bellying up to the bar is a pleasure; in fact, practically the entire space is given over to a handsome bar with an old-fashioned bar rail to lean on. A cool soundtrack accompanies your beer tasting. You can try a sample of any of the 24 Costa Rican craft microbrews on tap for $1. Once you find your favorite, a

12-ounce cold brew costs around $4. A few high tables spill out onto the street, surrounded by groups of happy beer drinkers. ⊠ *Beach road, across from Sámara Tree House Inn* ☏ *8539–1805.*

Tabanuco. This beachfront restaurant and bar is a little more upscale than most and attracts a slightly older, well-heeled crowd. The action heats up on the dance floor after 10 pm, with a high-tech sound-and-light system; live music includes reggae Friday nights and Ladies' Night, with free shots, on Thursday. Happy hour offers two-for-one cocktails or local beer. ⊠ *On the beach* ☉ *Closed Sun.*

SHOPPING

Souvenir stands are set up along the main street and the entrance to the beach, along with the inevitable handmade-jewelry stalls. Most shops here have pretty much the same beachwear and souvenirs for sale.

CoCo Tales. Delicate coconut carvings and sophisticated, one-of-a-kind jewelry made with polished amber, turquoise, and orange-toned spondylus shells are the specialty of Carlos, a skilled local artisan. You'll find him in his workshop, 9 to 7:30 daily, on Sámara's main street into town. Carlos and his wife Simon also make lovely papier-mâché globe lamps, along with a range of coconut-oil soaps and lotions. ⊠ *In front of Cabinas Arenas, main street into town* ☏ *8807–7056.*

Dragonfly Galería. Weird, wacky, and wonderful, this arts-and-crafts gallery sells local art and carvings, plus shell, feather, and bead jewelry. Leonardo, the owner, also paints temporary henna tattoos. He opens the shop daily at 4:21 pm. Just follow the trail off the main road through the trees decorated with fantastical glowing lamps. ⊠ *Across the street from Century 21 office, main road leading to beach* ☏ *2656–0964.*

Sámara Organics Market. More than a market for a wide range of gluten-free and organic foods, this spacious, pleasant shop sells imported olive oils and other gastronomic treats, rare in these parts. There's also a large selection of artisan-made clothes, toys and *objets d'art.* You can sit in one of the lounge chairs here and sip an espresso, a just-pressed exotic fruit drink, or a healthy, organic potion. Vegetable dips and spreads are packaged to go, along with organic brownies, cookies, and cakes. ⊠ *On beach road, across from Sporting Club Gusto Beach* ⊕ *www.samaraorganics.com.*

PLAYA CARRILLO

7 km (4½ miles) southeast of Sámara.

With its long, reef-protected, crescent beach backed by an elegant line of swaying coconut palms and sheltering cliffs, Playa Carrillo (interchangeably called Puerto Carrillo) is a candidate for the most picturesque beach in Costa Rica. A smooth, paved boulevard runs along the beach, with sparkling turquoise waters on the sea side and a hedge of scarlet bougainvillea on the land side. The main landmark here is the Hotel Guanamar, high above the south end of the beach. Unfortunately, the former private fishing club and previously grand hotel has been bought and sold so often that its charm has faded. But its bar still has the best view. A massive new hotel, called Nammbú, with dozens of villas, is being built on the hill overlooking the beach on the south side, so Playa Carrillo may be more populated in future.

GETTING HERE AND AROUND
It's an easy 15-minute drive south on the smooth, paved road from Sámara. If you're not staying at a hotel in Carrillo, you'll have to park your car either in a sunbaked concrete lot halfway along the beach or on the grassy median at the south end of the beach. You can also take a taxi from Sámara or hop on the local bus.

ESSENTIALS
Sámara is the closest town for banks and other services.

EXPLORING

FAMILY **La Selva Wild Animal Refuge & Zoo.** This modest collection of mostly rescued small animals offers a great chance to see them up close in chest-high corrals under the shade of trees and shrubs. The Italian owners are a little eccentric, and the place is not terribly well kept. There are plenty of usually hard-to-see nocturnal animals, so the best time to visit is just before sunset, when the roly-poly armadillos and big-eyed kinkajous are starting to stir. There are also skunks, spotted pacas, raccoons, bats, and scarier species like boas, poison dart frogs, caimans, and crocodiles. A bromeliad and orchid collection is artistically arranged around the zoo. If you come early in the day, the best time to see the day animals in action, your ticket is also good for a return early-evening visit. It's pricey, but the ticket price helps to buy food for the animals. Every Tuesday and Friday is crocodile feeding time at 5 pm. ⊠ *Look for signed road on left, just after crossing bridge at south end of beach* ☎ *2656–2236* ☜ *$20* ☉ *Daily 8–7; last admission 6:30 pm.*

BEACHES

Fodor's Choice **Playa Carrillo.** Unmarred by a single building at beach level, this pic-
★ ture-perfect, white strand is ideal for swimming, snorkeling, strolling, and lounging—just remember not to sit under a loaded coconut palm. Signs posted by the municipality announce that the only entry "fee" is: make no fires, and take your garbage away with you. There are some concrete tables and benches, but they get snapped up quickly. This is a popular beach with locals, and it gets quite busy on weekends. The only commercial activity is a hand-wheeled cart selling fruit ices. **Warning:** Recently, some crocodiles have been hanging out at the river mouths at both ends of the beach, so keep a lookout and only wade or swim in the middle of the beach. **Amenities:** none. **Best for:** snorkeling; swimming; walking. ⊠ *Playa Carrillo.*

SPORTS AND THE OUTDOORS
FISHING
From January to April, the boats moored off the beach take anglers on fishing expeditions for catch-and-release marlin and sail fishing, as well as good-eating dorado, yellowfin tuna, and wahoo.

Kingfisher. Captain Rick Ruhlow, a U.S. Coast Guard–licensed skipper with over 20 years' experience fishing Costa Rican waters, takes up to five anglers out on *Kingfisher,* a fully equipped 31-foot Palm Beach fishing boat; it's the only boat that stays full-time in Carrillo from

November to September. A full day's fishing offshore costs $1,250; inshore $850. ⊠ *Playa Carrillo* ☏ *8834–7125, 2656–0091* ⊕ *www. costaricabillfishing.com.*

WHERE TO EAT

$$$
ARGENTINE
FAMILY

✕ **El Colibrí Steakhouse.** Tired of fish? Sink your chops into steak—rib eye, New York, or T-bone—grilled on an open fire and served Argentine-style with garlicky chimichurri sauce at this family-run, pleasant rancho restaurant. Other specialties include grilled chorizo sausages or Milanesa, the classic Argentine breaded steak, served with french fries. Wash it down with a glass or bottle of Argentine *vino tinto*. There's salad, chicken, and, yes, fish when available, but people come here mainly because of the meat. Six air-conditioned cabinas, four with kitchens, face a small pool next to the restaurant. There's free transportation from Sámara for a party of four or more. A new branch of the restaurant has opened in Nosara. $ *Average main: $16* ⊠ *From main beach road, turn left at soccer field, then left again* ☏ *2656–0656* ⊕ *www.cabinaselcolibri.com* ☾ *Closed Mon. and all of Oct. No lunch.*

PUNTA ISLITA

6

16 km (11 miles) south of Playa Carrillo in dry season, 30 km (21 miles) south of Carrillo by alternative mountain route in rainy season.

Punta Islita is named for a tiny tuft of land that becomes an island at high tide. It's synonymous in Costa Rica with Hotel Punta Islita, one of the country's most exclusive, luxurious, and gorgeous resorts, popular with honeymooners and romantics of any age. Just about everything in Punta Islita—from outdoor activities to food—revolves around, and is available through, this resort. Just uphill from the beach, the small village of Punta Islita is an artistic work in progress, thanks to a community art project led by a few renowned Costa Rican artists who have turned almost all the buildings into galleries, workshops, or works of art in themselves.

GETTING HERE AND AROUND

Thanks to a new bridge over the Río Oro, it's a quick, 30-minute trip south of Playa Carrillo. A 4WD vehicle is recommended since the dirt road on the other side of the bridge is hilly and rough. Most well-heeled guests fly into the hotel's private airstrip.

BEACHES

Fodor'sChoice
★

Punta Islita. The curved beach here is rocky but good for walking, especially at low tide when tidal pools form in the volcanic rock. Sunsets are gorgeous, but despite its Blue Flag designation, this is not a great swimming beach. Be sure to take a stroll through the small village up from the beach, which is a memorable experience. Outdoor activities, food, and drinks are all available through the beachside resort. **Amenities:** food and drink. **Best for:** sunset; walking. ⊠ *Punta Islita.*

EXPLORING

Fodor'sChoice
★

Museo Islita. More than 10 years in the making, this open-air contemporary art museum—the only one in the country— is a treasure trove of art displayed in a gallery and throughout the entire village. Supported by

Hotel Punta Islita, visiting resident artists have inspired local villagers to create colorful murals and mosaics ornamenting public spaces and buildings, even beautifying the recycling center and trees in the village plaza. The museum building showcases one-of-a-kind textile prints, folk-art paintings on wood, jewelry, and *objets* made from recycled materials, all for sale. Stop in at the museum to buy a colorful walking-tour map ($2), with details and photos of the village art, and to watch a local artist at work. ⊠ *Punta Islita.*

WHERE TO STAY

$$$
RESORT
Fodor's Choice
★

🏨 **Hotel Punta Islita.** Overlooking the ocean from a forested ridge, this secluded and sublime hotel is luxury incarnate, with villas, casitas, suites, and spacious rooms sprinkled around the bougainvillea-bedecked hillside. **Pros:** gorgeous views; ultraluxurious rooms; top-notch service. **Cons:** isolated; distant, rocky beach; very pricey; steep paths to and from restaurant and beach club, but there is a shuttle van. ⑤ *Rooms from: $215* ⊠ *16 km (11 miles) south of Playa Carrillo* ☎ *2231–6122 in San José, 2656–2020 hotel, 866/446–4053 toll-free in U.S.* ⊕ *www.hotelpuntaislita.com* ⟳ *16 rooms, 8 suites, 8 casitas, 24 villas* ⦿⦿ *Breakfast.*

PALO VERDE NATIONAL PARK

52 km (32 miles) south of Liberia.

Definitely not most people's idea of a lush, tropical jungle, Palo Verde National Park's deciduous forest is hot, but also very dry and an ideal habitat for easy-to-spot monkeys, deer, peccaries, and lizards. Seasonal wetlands the size of lakes attract waterfowl by the thousands, as well as the photographers who come to shoot the grand avian spectacle.

GETTING HERE AND AROUND

To get to Palo Verde from Liberia, drive south along the Pan-American Highway to Bagaces, then turn right at the small, easy-to-miss sign for Palo Verde, along a rough dirt road for 28 km (17 miles). Count on an hour to drive the distance from the main highway to the park entrance; it's a very bumpy road. You'll have to pay the $12 park entrance fee to get to the Organization for Tropical Studies station. The OTS station is about 7 km (4½ miles) beyond the park entrance; the park headquarters is less than 1 km (½ mile) farther. The gatekeeper takes lunch from noon to 1 pm. The drive from Liberia should take a total of about 1½ hours.

EXPLORING

Las Pumas Rescue Shelter (*Centro de Rescate Las Pumas*). Sad but true, one of the few places left in the country where you are guaranteed to see large wild cats, including a jaguar, is this animal rescue center. The small enclosures also hold jaguarundis, pumas, margays, and ocelots. The shelter houses other species, including otters, grissons, white-faced and spider monkeys, and scarlet macaws, all native to the area. Some animals and birds are rehabilitated and released into the wild. The larger cats are probably here for life, as it's dangerous for them to be released. Donations to the nonprofit foundation, founded in 2003 by a Swiss conservationist, are welcomed. ⊠ *4½ km (3 miles) north* *of Cañas on main hwy.* ☎2669–6044, 2669–6019 *for reservations* ⊕*www.centrorescatelaspumas.org* ✉*$5* ⊘ *Dec.-May and July-Aug., daily 8–5; Sept.-Nov., daily 8–4.*

Llanos de Cortés. Just 3 km (2 miles) north of the Palo Verde road at Bagaces, take the dirt road signed for Llanos de Cortés to get to this hidden waterfall less than 2 km (1 mile) off the highway. About ½ km (¼ mile) along the dirt road you'll see on your right a large rock with "Cataratas" scrawled on it. Follow this bumpy road about 1.3 km (0.8 mile) to its end and then clamber down a steep path to the pool at the bottom of a spectacular, wide, 15-meter (50-foot) waterfall. This is a great place for a picnic; avoid weekends if you can when it's often crowded and noisy. Don't leave anything of value in your car. ⊠ *Off Pan-American Hwy., Bagaces.*

Fodor's Choice
★

Palo Verde National Park (*Parque Nacional Palo Verde*). Since this dry deciduous forest is less dense than a rain forest, it's much easier to spot the fauna along the hiking trails, including white-tailed deer, coatis, collared peccaries, and monkeys. This park's 198 square km (76 square miles) of terrain is fairly flat—the maximum elevation is 268 meters (879 feet). The west boundary of the park is bordered by the Río Tempisque, where crocodiles ply the waters year-round. The park also holds Costa Rica's highest concentration of waterfowl, the most common the black-bellied whistling duck and the blue-winged teal, with close to 30,000 during dry season. Although not as common, other waterfowl spotted here are the fulvous whistling duck, the glossy ibis, the pinnated bittern, the least bittern, the snail kite, and the very rare masked duck. Other birds endemic to the northwest, which you may find in the park's dry-forest habitat, are streaked-back orioles, banded wrens, and black-headed trogons. In the wet season, from September through March, the river and the park's vast seasonal wetlands host huge numbers of migratory and resident aquatic birds, including herons, wood storks, jabirus (giant storks), and elegant, flamingo-like roseate spoonbills. There is a raised platform near the Organization for Tropical Studies (OTS) research station, about 8 km (5 miles) past the park entrance, with a panoramic view over a marsh filled with ducks and jacanas. A narrow metal ladder leads to the top of the old tower, big enough for just two people at the top. For a good look at hundreds of waterfowl, there's also a long boardwalk jutting out over the wetlands. It's almost always hot and humid in these lowlands—March is the hottest month—so be prepared with water, a hat, and insect repellent. Hostel-type lodging in rustic dormitory facilities with bunk beds and shared bathrooms ($13), and family-style meals for overnight guests only ($7 breakfast; $9 for lunch or dinner) can be arranged through the park headquarters. ⇨ *For more information, see the highlighted listing in this chapter.* ⊠ *29 km (18 miles) southwest of Bagaces* ☎2206–5965 ✉*$12* ⊘ *Daily 8–dusk; entrance gates open 8–noon and 1–4.*

6

SPORTS AND THE OUTDOORS
TOUR OPERATORS
Organization for Tropical Studies. This nonprofit, scientific consortium of universities offers overnight packages with a guided walk, excellent family-style meals, and lodging in very basic, no-frills rooms with bunk beds, overhead fans, and private bathrooms ($93 per person). Although the accommodations are spartan, staying here is the only way to set off on a 6 am birding tour (the park gates don't open till 8). The biological research station overlooks the Palo Verde wetlands, and expert naturalist guides can arrange a boat tour ($45 plus guide fee) along wetlands lining both sides of the Tempisque River, as well as long hikes on the park trails. Call at least a day ahead to arrange the boat tour. Bring binoculars and cameras. Guides can direct you to a perennial nest where jabirus are in residence with their chicks, January through February. Guests still have to pay the $12 entrance fee per person to the national park. ⊠ *7 km (4½ miles) past park entrance* ☎ *2524–0607* ⊕ *www.ots.ac.cr.*

BIRD-WATCHING
The best bird-watching in Palo Verde is on the wetlands in front of the Organization for Tropical Studies' biological station. The OTS has expert guides who can help you see and identify the varied birds in the area ($80 private tour; $48 per person for two or more), but if you have good binoculars and a bird book, you can identify plenty of species on your own. A boat excursion to Isla Pájaros south of the Río Tempisque is particularly interesting for birders. Toward the end of rainy season this 6-acre island near Puerto Moreno is an exciting place to see hundreds of nesting wood storks, cormorants, and anhingas. You can get close enough to see chicks being fed in nests. ■TIP➔ The best time to go is very early in the morning, to avoid heat and to guarantee the most bird sightings.

Aventuras Arenal. This adventure-tour company specializes in ecological tours and has guides with good eyes who usually know the English names for birds. The boat chugs slowly up the Río Tempisque ($45, including juice and lunch) and departs from the dock at Bebedero or Puerto Humo. You can also arrange to have the boat tour start from the dock in Palo Verde National Park and hire a guide ($57 per person, minimum two people) from the OTS Research Station in the park. ⊠ *Palo Verde National Park* ☎ *2479–9133* ⊕ *www.aventurasarenal.com.*

RIVER RAFTING
FAMILY **Ríos Tropicales.** Two-hour floating trips down the Río Corobicí are great for bird- and monkey-watching and are safe and gentle enough for kids ages five and older. This experienced, national rafting company also offers more adventurous Class II and III rafting trips on the Río Tenorio. The floating trips cost $65 including lunch (ground transportation within the local area is $30 extra); rafting trips are $105 per person, $30 extra for transport. ⊠ *Km 193, Pan-American Hwy., Cañas* ☎ *2233–6455* ⊕ *www.riostropicales.com.*

FAMILY **Safaris Corobicí.** This small, local company specializes in three-hour float trips down the Río Corobicí ($40; $52 with lunch) that put in (and end) near its office location, near Km 192 on the Pan-American Highway. It also offers an early-morning bird-watching float tour ($52 with lunch) and a half-day float, with lunch in its Cocobolo restaurant afterward ($65). Boats are launched from 7 to 3:30 daily. There are also gentle float trips that connect with the Tenorio River ($60 including lunch). The office is right at the entrance to Las Pumas Rescue Shelter. ⊠ *Km 192 on main hwy. to Liberia, 4½ km (3 miles) north of Cañas, Cañas* ☎ *2669–6191* ⊕ *www.nicoya.com.*

WHERE TO EAT AND STAY

$$$
BARBECUE
FAMILY
Fodor's Choice
★

✕ **Tres Hermanas Bar-B-Q & Grill.** You can't miss the giant white Brahman bull and the King Kong–size howler monkey at the turnoff from the Pan-American Highway, heading for the bridge to Nicoya. Kitschy roadside statues don't always signal good food, but this is home to the country's best barbecued pork and beef, slow-roasted for 16 to 18 hours over a wood fire and served with dynamite BBQ sauce. Sides go beyond coleslaw or fries to include lentils stewed with bacon and onions, or fried yucca. If you've been tempted to try Costa Rican–style *chicharrones*, try them here—served with refried beans, local cheese, tortilla chips, and salsa. Beyond barbecue, there are imported beef steaks, plus a filet mignon smothered in mushroom sauce. If you can persuade any non-carnivore to enter the premises, the menu also has salads and fish. A playground keeps small children occupied while parents dig in. And there's a Pops ice-cream parlor attached to the restaurant. ■ TIP→ The Tres Hermanas restrooms are the poshest and cleanest on the long stretch of highway between Puntarenas and Liberia. ⑤ *Average main: $16* ⊠ *Pan-American Hwy., in Limonal, at turnoff for Puente La Amistad and Nicoya* ☎ *2662–8584* ⊕ *www.bbqtreshermanas.com.*

$
B&B/INN

⌂ **La Ensenada Lodge.** Part of a national wildlife refuge, this is the most comfortable and affordable base for bird-watching, crocodile spotting, and nature appreciation on this side of the Río Tempisque. **Pros:** wildlife; interesting setting; good value. **Cons:** very simple rooms; large tour groups at times; no air-conditioning. ⑤ *Rooms from: $66* ⊠ *Take the signed turnoff at Km 155 of the Pan-America Hwy. and drive along a gravel road, about 13 km (8 miles) southwest to the lodge* ☎ *2289–6655 office in San Jose, 2661–4090 lodge* ⊕ *www.laensenada.net* ⊟ *No credit cards* ↻ *25 cabin rooms* ⧖ *No meals.*

$$$$
ALL-INCLUSIVE

⌂ **Rancho Humo Estancia.** The most comfortable way to experience the birds and wildlife of the Tempisque wetlands is to roost at this new eco-boutique hotel, a luxurious version of a traditional hacienda, set in a private reserve directly across from Palo Verde National Park. **Pros:** wetlands setting; incredible bird-watching; most luxurious hotel in the area. **Cons:** meager portions at meals; dusty gravel road for 26 km (16 miles). ⑤ *Rooms from: $500* ⊠ *Pozo de Agua, Nicoya* ✛ *26 km (17 miles) north of Quebrada Honda, on the east side of the Puente de la Amistad* ☎ *2698–1197* ⊕ *www.ranchohumo.com* ↻ *3 rooms, 5 junior suites, 2 family suites* ⧖ *All meals.*

BARRA HONDA NATIONAL PARK

100 km (62 miles) south of Liberia, 13 km (8 miles) west of Río Tempisque Bridge.

You can't miss this park's massive peak, once thought to be a volcano. Within that mountain, however, is an intricate network of caves to be explored, and hiking trails on its slopes lead to scenic cascades and views over the Gulf of Nicoya.

THE FIRST GUANACASTECOS

The Chorotega tribe first settled the Guanacaste area and grew corn and fished. Chief Nicoya was the Chorotegan leader who greeted the conquistadors in 1523 and bequeathed his name to the town and peninsula.

GETTING HERE AND AROUND

From the Río Tempisque Bridge, drive west along a paved highway. Then follow a dirt road (signed off the highway) for 10 km (6 miles) to the park entrance. If you don't have a car, there is a bus that departs from the town of Nicoya at 7:30 am, Monday through Saturday. You can also take a taxi from Nicoya to the park entrance or go with one of many tour companies in beach towns on the Nicoya Peninsula.

EXPLORING

FAMILY **Barra Honda National Park** (*Parque Nacional Barra Honda*). A mecca for speleologists, the caves beneath the 390-meter (1,184-foot) **Barra Honda Peak** were created millions of years ago by erosion after the ridge emerged from the sea. You can explore the resulting calcium carbonate formations on a guided tour, and perhaps catch sight of some of the abundant underground animal life, including bats, birds, blindfish, salamanders, and snails. The caves are spread around almost 23 square km (9 square miles), but many of them remain unexplored.

Every day starting at 8 am, local guides take groups rappelling 18 meters (58 feet) down into **Terciopelo Cave**, which shelters unusual formations shaped (they say) like fried eggs, popcorn, and shark's teeth. You must wear a harness with a rope attached for safety. The tour costs $29 per person (minimum of two) including equipment rental, guide, and entrance fee. Kids under 10 are not allowed into this cave, but they can visit the kid-size La Cuevita cavern ($5), which also has interesting stalagmites. Both cave visits include interpretive nature hikes. The caves are not open during the wet season (September–November), for fear of flooding.

Those with a fear of heights, or claustrophobia, may want to skip the cave tour, but Barra Honda still has plenty to offer, thanks to its extensive forests and abundant wildlife. You can climb the 3-km (2-mile) Los Laureles trail (the same trail that leads to the Terciopelo cave) to Barra Honda's summit, where you'll have sweeping views over the surrounding countryside and islet-filled Gulf of Nicoya. Wildlife you may spot on Barra Honda's trails include howler and white-faced monkeys, skunks, coatis, deer, parakeets, hawks, dozens of other bird species, and iguanas. It's a good idea to hire a local guide from the **Asociación de Guias Ecologistas**. The park has camping facilities ($2 per night), and the ranger station, open 8 am to dusk, has potable water and restrooms. There are also a couple of basic cabins to rent ($30). ✉ *13 km (8 miles) west of Río Tempisque Bridge* ☎ *2659–1551* 🖅 *$12* ⊙ *Daily 8 am–dusk.*

NICOYA

27 km (15 miles) west of the Río Tempisque Bridge.

Once a quaint provincial town, Guanacaste's former colonial capital is now a bustling, modernized shopping center, thanks to the bridge over the Río Tempisque that brings tourists headed for the nearby beaches. But there are still a few historical remnants around the central park. A noticeable Chinese population, descendants of 19th-century railroad workers, has given Nicoya numerous Chinese restaurants. The town has supermarkets, 24-hour service stations, and ATMs that take international cards.

GETTING HERE AND AROUND

The town of Nicoya is 40 minutes west of the Río Tempisque Bridge on a paved road. If you're running out of gas, oil, or tire pressure, the Servicentro Nicoyano on the north side of Nicoya, on the main road, is open 24 hours.

CHOROTEGAN POTTERY

In the country village of Guaitil, 24 km (15 miles) north of Nicoya, artists—most of them women—have revived a vanishing tradition by producing clay pottery handmade in the manner of pre-Columbian Chorotegans. The town square is a soccer field, and almost every house facing it has a pottery shop out front and a round, wood-fired kiln in back. Pottery designs range from imitation Mexican to inspired Cubist abstractions. Prices range from $12 to $300, depending on size; most are around $30. Pieces do crack easily, so pack them carefully.

ESSENTIALS

Banks/ATMs Banco de Costa Rica. ✉ *West side of central park* ☎ *2685-5110.*

Hospital Hospital de L'Anexion. ✉ *Main road into town from hwy.* ☎ *2685-8400.*

Pharmacy Farmacia y Clinica Medica Nicoyana. ✉ *Main street, near Restaurante Nicoya* ☎ *2685-5138.*

Post Office Correo. ✉ *Southwest corner of park.*

EXPLORING

Church of San Blas. Nicoya's last remaining colonial landmark is the impressive, whitewashed, mission-style Church of San Blas. Originally built in 1644, the church was reconstructed after the first church was leveled by an 1831 earthquake. The spare interior is made grand by seven pairs of soaring carved-wood columns. Inside are folk-art wood carvings of the Stations of the Cross arrayed around the stark white walls, a small collection of 18th-century bronze mission bells, and some antique wooden saints. Arched doorways frame verdant views of park greenery and distant mountains. A recent earthquake damaged the church and it is currently under repair, but should be open to visitors by January 2017. ⊠ *North side of central park* ☎ *No phone* 🌐 *By donation* ⊙ *Erratic hrs.*

WHERE TO EAT AND STAY

$$
CHINESE
✕ **Restaurante Nicoya.** Nicoya has a few Chinese restaurants, but this one stands out for being the most central and atmospheric, with hanging lanterns, a colorful collection of international flags, and an enormous menu with 85 Asian dishes. The sea bass sautéed with fresh pineapple, chayote, and red peppers is excellent. ⑤ *Average main: $10* ⊠ *Main road, 70 m south of Coopeallianza Bldg.* ☎ *2685–5113.*

$
HOTEL
🏨 **Hotel Río Tempisque.** There aren't many reasons to stay overnight in Nicoya, but if you get stuck here, this lush garden hotel is the best option. **Pros:** quiet; convenient; affordable. **Cons:** simple; not memorable; very busy in January. ⑤ *Rooms from: $66* ⊠ *Hwy. north to Santa Cruz, outside Nicoya* ☎ *2686–6650* ⇴ *106 rooms* ⦿ *No meals.*

PUNTARENAS

82 km (50 miles) west of San José.

This town is not on the Nicoya Peninsula, but rather on Costa Rica's mainland. It is best known as a cruise-ship port and launching pad for ferries heading southeast to the coast of the Nicoya Peninsula and for cruises sailing out on the Gulf of Nicoya. Puntarenas is also a major fishing port with a lively fish market. The town's reputation suffers from the unimpressive parts you see from your car as you roll through town on the way to the ferry dock. But the town has a lot of character off the main drag, thanks to its illustrious past as an affluent port town and principal vacation spot for San José's wealthy, who arrived by train in the last century. Once the port was moved and roads opened to other beaches, Puntarenas's economy crashed, but it's making a comeback. Sitting on a narrow spit of sand—*punta de arenas* literally means "point of sand"—that protrudes into the Gulf of Nicoya, the town boasts a beautifully groomed, wide beach with views of the Nicoya Peninsula and spectacular sunsets, along with a public swimming pool, the San Lucas Beach Club, and a marine-life museum. Ticos arrive by bus and car to enjoy the beach and stroll the Paseo de los Turistas, a beachfront promenade lined with tree-shaded concrete benches and seafood restaurants. Crowds of locals, called *porteños,* cruise by on bicycles, the town's most popular form of transport. Pick up a map with a guided walking tour of the town's sites from the tourist office across from the cruise-ship dock.

GETTING HERE AND AROUND

The drive from San José to Puntarenas takes just over one hour. From San José, take the new toll Highway 27 to the port of Caldera, then swing north toward Puntarenas. From here it's another 15 minutes to the ferry dock. Buses run every hour, from 6 am to 7 pm, from the Empresarios Unidos bus terminal in San José (Avenida 12, Calle 16) to Puntarenas. The trip takes two hours and 20 minutes. If you travel to Puntarenas by public bus, take a taxi to the ferry dock.

The Southern
Nicoya Peninsula

Ferries shuttle passengers between Puntarenas and Paquera on the Nicoya Peninsula, where they board buses bound for Cóbano, Montezuma, and Malpaís/Santa Teresa.

ESSENTIALS

Banks/ATMs Banco de Costa Rica (BCR). ✉ *100 m west of municipal market.* **Banco Nacional.** ✉ *300 m west of municipal market* ☎ *2661-0233.*

Ferry Travel Coonatramar. ☎ *2661-1069* ⊕ *www.coonatramar.com.* **Naviera Tambor.** ☎ *2661-2084* ⊕ *www.navieratambor.com.*

Hospital Hospital Monseñor Sanabria. ✉ *8 km (5 miles) east of Puntarenas* ☎ *2630-8000.*

Pharmacy Don Gerardo Farmacia. ✉ *2 blocks north of bus station, across from Mutual de Alajuela bank* ☎ *2661-4963.*

Post Office Correos. ✉ *Avda. 3 west of Ca. Central, across from Banco Nacional.*

Tourist Information ICT Tourist Office. ✉ *Plaza El Pacifico, Paseo de Los Turistas, in front of Muelle de Cruceros, Ground floor, on the plaza* ☎ *2661-2980.*

EXPLORING

FAMILY **Parque Marino del Pacifico.** To get an idea of what's swimming *under* the Gulf of Nicoya, visit this modest aquarium and marine park. You'll see crocodiles, pelicans, sea turtles and representatives of the deep, including small sharks. Exhibits are both indoors and outdoors and there's a playground for kids to let off steam. ⊠ *500 m east of the cruise-ship dock, on the Paseo de Los Turistas* ☎ *2661–5272* ⊕ *www. parquemarino.org* 🖅 *$10* ⊙ *Tues.–Sun. 9–5.*

WHERE TO EAT AND STAY

$$ ✕ **Casa Almendro.** The best perch along the Paseo de los Turistas is a
SEAFOOD table on the breezy veranda of this updated seafood and grill restaurant with a beach view. The menu is modern, with starters like salads, ceviches, and huge disks of *patacones* (fried, squashed platanos), served with frijoles and shredded beef. Along with the classic fish fillet grilled with butter and fresh garlic, there's a spicier option with a jalapeño and fresh tomato sauce, as well as tuna in teriyaki sauce and grilled salmon. Grilled beef and BBQ pork ribs will satisfy meat eaters. There's a choice of South American, Italian, and Spanish wines. Save room for *flan de coco*, dense and creamy with toasted coconut and caramel sauce. This place has polished service, with friendly, attentive waiters. ⑤ *Average main: $15* ⊠ *Paseo de los Turistas, at Ca. 21* ⊹ *just west of Hotel Tioga* ☎ *2661–0901.*

$$$ ✕ **Gugas.** In a quiet rancho surrounded by huge *tabacón* plants and
GERMAN cooled by ceiling fans, Gugas serves up local fish and seafood, but is also notable for its German recipes. The German owner receives high praise from locals for his gypsy-style schnitzel, using slow-cooked pork tenderloin, and for grilled German sausages, as well as local fish and seafood dishes. There's a long bar to perch at, and it's just one block north of the cruise-ship dock and the bustle of the Paseo de los Turistas. ⑤ *Average main: $18* ⊠ *From the cruise-ship dock on Paseo de Los Turistas, 100 m due north* ☎ *2661–0707* ⊙ *Closed Mon. (unless there is a cruise ship in port).*

$$ 🕮 **Hotel Las Brisas.** Right on the beach, this white, three-story building
HOTEL with Greek columns is centered around a pool deck that features stun-
FAMILY ning sunset views over the Nicoya Peninsula. **Pros:** unbeatable gulf views; good restaurant; very close to ferry dock. **Cons:** can be noisy when families gather around the pool. ⑤ *Rooms from: $139* ⊠ *West end of Paseo de los Turistas* ☎ *2661–4040* ⊕ *www.lasbrisashotelcr.com* ⤴ *26 rooms* ⦿l *Breakfast.*

$$ 🕮 **Hotel Tioga.** This grande dame of Puntarenas hotels facing the beach
HOTEL is showing its age, but it still evokes the bygone era of the 1950s when
FAMILY Puntarenas was the major destination on the Central Pacific coast. **Pros:** full of 1950s character; close to beach and restaurants; pleasant, sunny pool. **Cons:** a little timeworn; smallish rooms around the pool; busy on weekends. ⑤ *Rooms from: $88* ⊠ *Paseo de los Turistas, 8 blocks west of cruise-ship dock* ☎ *2661–0271* ⊕ *www.hoteltioga.com* ⤴ *52 rooms* ⦿l *Breakfast.*

CURÚ NATIONAL WILDLIFE REFUGE

7 km (4½ miles) south of Paquera, 1½ to 2 hrs southwest of Puntarenas by ferry.

With miles of trails through forest and mangrove swamp, this uncrowded, private refuge is most famous for its pristine beach, perfectly sited for swimming, snorkeling, and easy kayaking to nearby Tortuga Island. The land was once owned by the Pacific Lumber Company, which logged the area's rosewood, cedar, and mahogany trees. Thanks to its protected status, the area is now home to more than 230 species of birds, 78 species of mammals, and 500 species of plants.

GETTING HERE AND AROUND

From the town of Paquera it's a short drive to Curú National Wildlife Refuge. You can also take a bus bound for Cóbano; just ask the driver to drop you off at the entrance to the refugio.

FAMILY **Curú National Wildlife Refuge** (*Refugio Nacional de Vida Silvestre Curú*). Established by former farmer and logger-turned-conservationist Frederico Schutt in 1933, this 106-hectare (262-acre) refuge is named after the indigenous word for the spiky-barked *pochote* trees that flourish here. The reserve is home to hordes of phantom crabs on the beach, howler and white-faced capuchin monkeys in the trees, red brocket deer grazing in open fields, and plenty of hummingbirds, kingfishers, woodpeckers, trogons, and manakins (including the bird-watcher's coveted long-tailed manakin). The refuge, classified as a Blue Flag project, is working on building an artificial reef. Visitors can stay in very basic beachfront cabins with solar power ($30 per person, including entrance fee); meals are $10 each. Call ahead to arrange for lodging or horseback rides ($15 for one hour; $25 for three-hour tour). Kayaking tours and early-morning bird-watching walks are organized by Turismo Curú. The entrance fee to the reserve is $12. ⊠ *7 km (4½ miles) south of Paquera on road to Cóbano, left side of road, Paquera* ☎ *2641–0100* ⊕ *www.curuwildliferefuge.com* ⊠ *$12* ⊙ *Daily 7–4.*

Paquera. If you take the ferry from Puntarenas to the southern tip of the Nicoya Peninsula, you'll arrive at a ferry dock 5 km (3 miles) north of the small community of Paquera. You can pick up supplies at the supermarkets, fill up your tank on the way to the beach, and grab a quick bite to eat at a pizza joint en route. The 5 pm ferry from Puntarenas is the last ferry that connects to the public bus services to Montezuma, Malpaís, and Santa Teresa. ⊠ *Puntarenas.*

SPORTS AND THE OUTDOORS

TOUR OPERATORS

Seascape Kayak Tours. From November to May, experienced Canadian guide Bruce Smith leads half- and full-day kayak excursions in Ballena Bay, leaving from Curú and Playa Tambor ($85 to $165, minimum two people). Smith also leads three- and five-day kayaking tours. ⊠ *Curú National Wildlife Refuge, Paquera* ☎ *8314–8605* ⊕ *www.seascapekayaktours.com* ⊠ *From $85.*

Turismo Curú. Guided 90-minute nature walks of the Curú Wildlife Refuge are a specialty of this tour operator ($15 plus $12 admission to refuge). The company also offers inexpensive kayaking trips to nearby Isla Tortuga, including snorkeling; a half-day tour is $67, full day is $127, including lunch and the refuge admission fee. You can rent kayaks by the hour ($10 single, $15 double). All tours require a minimum of two people. For large groups, there is boat transportation from Puntarenas directly to Curú. The tour operator has an office in Paquera and a dive shop on-site at the refuge, with tanks, tours, and diving lessons. A two-tank dive, including boat to Isla Tortuga, gear, and cool drinks is $102 for certified divers; a Discovery tour for non-certified divers is also $102, including 30 minutes of instruction and one tank. ⊠ *Main road, across from Esso station, Paquera* ☎ *2641–0004, 2641–0688* ⊕ *www.turismocuru.com* ⊠ *$12.*

EN ROUTE

Cóbano. Paquera is the closest city to Tambor, but if you're headed to Montezuma or Malpaís, you'll pass through Cóbano, 12 km (7½ miles) southwest of Tambor. The town has a supermarket, two gas stations, and a large Banco Nacional with the area's only consistently reliable ATM. (Montezuma and Malpaís/Santa Teresa now have cash machines, but they frequently run out of money.) If you're hungry, stop in at El Artesano del Gusto Artisanal ☎ *(8309–3799)* for a slice of hot quiche or coffee and croissant, on the main road through Cóbano, across from the Gollo appliance store. ⊠ *Cóbano.*

PLAYA TAMBOR AREA

27 km (17 miles) south of Paquera.

Much of the vast Bahía Ballena shoreline is taken up by a massive all-inclusive hotel and an adjoining private residential development and golf course. But to the south, near the actual village of Tambor, visitors can explore the barely developed Playa Tambor, a beautiful flat beach with nothing more than a volleyball net, a few concrete tables set under shade trees, and one beach shack serving pizza. This beach was never developed as much as Montezuma or Malpaís, making it a better destination for those who want to get away from the crowds. It can serve as a convenient base for fishing excursions, bird-watching, horseback-riding trips, and day trips to Curú National Wildlife Refuge and Isla Tortuga.

GETTING HERE AND AROUND

You can fly directly to Tambor (TMU) from San José on SANSA and Nature Air. Taxis meet every flight and can take you to a nearby hotel ($15), to Montezuma ($50), or to Malpaís ($60).

SPORTS AND THE OUTDOORS

Unlike other beach towns, tiny Tambor doesn't have tour operators on every corner or rental shops of any kind—not even for a basic bike. The receptionist at your hotel can set up tours of the area's diverse natural attractions.

FISHING

In the open sea off the Gulf of Nicoya, sailfish, marlin, tuna, mahimahi, and wahoo are in abundance from November to March. Local fishermen in small boats are your best guides to finding fish in the gulf, including

Isla Tortuga, just off the coast near Curú National Wildlife Refuge

snapper, sea bass, and jacks, almost year-round. Prices for fishing range from $375 for half-day trips to $900 for full-day excursions.

Dive Academy Ballena Blanca. This PADI-certified dive outfit operates fishing tours aboard 26-foot Apex boats. Inshore half-day costs $375 to $450; offshore whole day is $900. Dive excursions include trips to three wrecks nearby and a cave dive that offers a chance to see a white-tipped reef shark. A two-tank dive, including equipment and transfers from hotel to boat, costs $100 to $125, depending on dive location. ⊠ *Los Delfines center, next door to Tambor airport, Tambor* ☎ *2683–0015, 8729–3167* ⊕ *www.diving-costa-rica.com.*

HIKING

An easy and quick excursion from Tambor is the 1-km (½-mile) hike south of town to the secluded beach of Palo de Jesús. From the town's dock, follow the road south until it becomes a shady trail that winds its way over rocks and sand around Punta Piedra Amarilla. The trees along the way resound with squawks of parakeets and the throaty utterings of male howler monkeys.

HORSEBACK RIDING

The Tango Mar Resort has its own stables and offers horseback tours that can take you down trails through the rain forest or down to the beach to see an array of wildlife. Set off early in the morning or late in the afternoon, when it is cooler and you are more likely to see birds and animals. Tours range from $40 for a two-hour ride on hotel property to $60 for a longer ride to Montezuma, along the beach.

WHERE TO STAY

$$$
B&B/INN
⊡ **Tambor Tropical.** Centered on the scenic sweep of placid Bahía Tambor with its warm, shallow water, intimate Tambor Tropical offers "beds with a view" in spacious suites, along with sportfishing, horseback riding, bird-watching, and just lolling in a hammock by the pretty, blue-tile pool. **Pros:** spacious suites; tranquil, beautiful setting; easy access. **Cons:** no air-conditioning in two suites; no kids under 16; Continental, not full breakfast, included. Ⓢ *Rooms from: $232* ⊠ *From Tambor main street, turn left at beach, Tambor* ☎ *2683–0011, 866/890–2537 in U.S.* ⊕ *www.tambortropical.com* ↪ *12 suites* ⦿ *Breakfast.*

$$$
RESORT
FAMILY
Fodor's Choice
★
⊡ **Tango Mar Resort.** Set on stunning, palm-fringed Playa Quizales and backed by 15 acres of exuberant gardens and a 9-hole executive golf course, this comfortable, contemporary resort has a wide range of luxurious lodging options that appeal to families and couples of every age, including honeymooners. **Pros:** gorgeous setting; friendly service and attention to detail; lots of activity options. **Cons:** quiet evenings; large groups on occasion; stairs to climb to villas and some rooms. Ⓢ *Rooms from: $195* ⊠ *Playa Quizales, 3 km (2 miles) south of Tambor, Tambor* ☎ *2683–0001, 800/297–4420 in North America* ⊕ *www. tangomar.com* ↪ *18 rooms, 6 deluxe beachfront rooms, 17 suites, 2 villas* ⦿ *Breakfast.*

ISLA TORTUGA

90 mins by boat from Puntarenas.

Soft white sand and casually leaning palms fringe this island of tropical dry forest off the southern coast of the Nicoya Peninsula. Sounds heavenly? It would be if there weren't quite so many people. Tours from Jacó, Herradura, San José, Puntarenas, and Montezuma take boatfuls of visitors to drink from coconuts and snorkel around a large rock. On the boat ride from Playa Tambor or Montezuma you might spot passing dolphins. Though state owned, the island is leased and inhabited by a Costa Rican family. It makes for an easy day trip out to sea, costing $20 to $109, depending on the duration and departure point.

GETTING HERE AND AROUND

Every tour operator in Playa Tambor and Montezuma offers trips to Isla Tortuga, one of the area's biggest attractions, or you can kayak from the nearby Curú National Wildlife Refuge. Admission to the island is $7 (included in tour prices).

BEACHES

FAMILY
Isla Tortuga. This idyllic, unpopulated island has a white-sand beach fronting clear turquoise water, where you'll see a good number of colorful fish, though in the company of many tourists, arriving in many boats of all sizes. A 40-minute hiking trail (small fee) wanders past monkey ladders, strangler figs, bromeliads, orchids, and the fruit-bearing *guanábana* (soursop) and *marañón* (cashew) trees up to a lookout point with amazing vistas. **Amenities:** water sports, toilets, lockers, food and drinks. **Best for:** snorkeling; swimming. ⊠ *Isla Tortuga* ◪ *$7.*

SPORTS AND THE OUTDOORS
KAYAKING

FAMILY **Calypso Cruises Island Tours.** This company pioneered excursions in the
Fodor'sChoice Gulf of Nicoya in 1975 with tours aboard a luxury catamaran yacht
★ to Isla Tortuga. You can depart from San José, Manuel Antonio, or
anywhere in between. A typical itinerary includes a Tico breakfast en
route to the port, snorkeling, banana boat rides, and five hours on the
island, with a first-class lunch served with chilled white wine—all for
about $150. If you're in Puntarenas, the Calypso Cruises dock has an
air-conditioned, elegant restaurant, the Shrimp Shack, serving excellent lunches. ⊠ *Isla Tortuga* ☎ *2256–2727, 855/855–1975 in North
America* ⊕ *www.calypsocruises.com* ✉ *From $150.*

FAMILY **Turismo Curú.** This tour operator arranges motorboat tours to the island,
leaving from Curú Wildlife Refuge at 9 am and spending one hour on
a less-frequented beach on one of the Morteros Islands, and two hours
on the beach at Tortuga, plus snorkeling ($52 per person, including
snorkeling gear, lunch, and entrance fee to Curú). Tortuga Island is
only 3 km (2 miles) off the beach of Curú, so experienced kayakers can
paddle there, accompanied by a security boat ($77 per person, fruit and
snacks included). You can also take a boat tour to Tortuga and spend an
hour kayaking around the island ($55). ⊠ *Main road, across from Esso
station, Paquera* ☎ *2641–0004* ⊕ *www.turismocuru.com* ✉ *From $52.*

6

MONTEZUMA

*7 km (4½ miles) southeast of Cóbano, 45 km (28 miles) south of
Paquera, 18 km (11 miles) south of Tambor.*

Beautifully positioned on a sandy bay, Montezuma is hemmed in by a
precipitous wooded shoreline that has prevented the overdevelopment
that has affected so many other beach towns. Its small, funky town center is a pastel cluster of New Age health-food cafés, trendy beachwear
shops, jaunty tour kiosks, lively open-air bars and restaurants and, at
last count, three ice-cream shops, two selling Italian gelato. Most hotels
are clustered in or around the town's center, but the best ones are on the
coast to the north and south, where the loudest revelers are the howler
monkeys in the nearby forest. The beaches north of town, especially
Playa Grande, are lovely.

Montezuma has been on the international vagabond circuit for years,
attracting backpackers and alternative-lifestyle types. Yoga is a main
attraction, with a wide range of classes, and the town is becoming more
of a cultural draw, with a low-key film festival of shorts and documen-
taries, and an occasional poetry festival. At night, the center of town
often fills up with tattooed travelers and artisans who entertain each
other and passersby. When college students are on break, the place can
be a zoo. People used to jokingly refer to the town as Monte *fuma,*
with *fuma* meaning "smoke" in Spanish—get it?—but, for better or
for worse, Montezuma is being tamed and becoming more civilized
and attractive, with plenty of grown-up lodging and dining options to
choose from.

North and south of the town center have always been quiet, and the attractions here include swaths of tropical dry forest, waterfalls, and beautiful virgin beaches that stretch across one national park and two nature preserves. One especially good walk (about two hours) or horseback ride leads to a small waterfall called El Chorro that pours into the sea, where there is a small tidal pool at lower tides.

GETTING HERE AND AROUND

Most people get here via the ferry from Puntarenas to Paquera, which is an hour's drive from Montezuma, with a bumpy dirt-road stretch from Cóbano to Montezuma. The quickest way to get here, however, is to fly to nearby Tambor. One of the taxis waiting at the airstrip will take you to Montezuma for $50, about a 1½-hour drive. There are also one-hour water taxis ($40) that travel every morning between Jacó and Montezuma, departing from Montezuma at 9:30 am and Jacó at 10:45 am. There are no banks in town; the closest bank is in Cóbano. There is an ATM on the beach road in Montezuma, but it's not the most secure or reliable place to withdraw money.

ESSENTIALS

Bank/ATM Banco Nacional. ⊠ *Main road, Cóbano* ☏ *2212–1000.*

SPORTS AND THE OUTDOORS

In Montezuma it seems that every other storefront is occupied by a tour operator. In spite of the multitude of signs advertising "Tourist Information," none are officially sanctioned by the Costa Rican tourist office.

TOUR OPERATORS

Cocozuma Traveller. Montezuma's oldest and most experienced tour company offers horseback riding to a beachfront waterfall ($40), a full-day snorkeling trip to Isla Tortuga with lunch ($50), and various sportfishing options ($250–$800). ⊠ *Main road, next to El Sano Banano* ☏ *2642–1011* ⊕ *www.cocozumacr.com* ⛱ *From $40.*

Zuma Tours. If you want to get out on the water, this reliable agency organizes snorkeling tours to Tortuga Island, sportfishing trips from three to eight hours, and surf lessons. They also offer ATV rentals and transport by shuttle van, and taxi boats ($40) between Jacó and Montezuma. ⊠ *Main street, south of El Sano Banano Hotel* ☏ *2642–0024* ⊕ *www.zumatours.net* ⛱ *From $45.*

HIKING

Hiking is one of the best ways to explore Montezuma's natural treasures, including beaches, lush coastline, jungles, and waterfalls. There are plenty of options around town or in nearby parks and reserves. Just over a bridge, 10 minutes south of town, a slippery path patrolled by howler monkeys leads upstream to two waterfalls and a fun swimming hole. If you value your life, don't jump or dive from the waterfalls. Guides from any tour operator in town can escort you, but save your money. This one you can do on your own. The path is very crowded on weekends, especially in January and around Easter.

El Chorro. To reach the beachfront waterfall called El Chorro, head left from the main beach access and hike about two hours to the north of town along the sand and through the woods behind the rocky points.

The trip takes you across seven adjacent beaches, on one of which there is a small store where you can buy soft drinks. Bring water and good sunblock. El Chorro can also be reached on a horseback tour organized by any of the local tour operators. ⊠ *Montezuma.*

J.C.'s Journeys. In pursuit of nature, bilingual, certified guide Juan Carlos Aguirre leads three-hour bird-watching tours starting at 5:30 am ($60 per person, minimum two people) including breakfast; and two-hour nocturnal tours, complete with a night-vision scope to help you spot creatures along a forest stream ($30 per person, minimum of two). You can also hire Juan Carlos for a private birding tour. ⊠ *Montezuma* ☎ *8975–8832* ⊕ *www.jcsjourneys.com.*

WHERE TO EAT

$$$
ECLECTIC

✗ **Cocolores.** Follow the glow of multicolor lanterns to this dinner-only, open-air eatery within sight and sound of the ocean. The simple wooden tables are on a patio bordered with gardens or, during the drier months, practically on the beach. The Italian and Argentine owners serve an eclectic menu ranging from shrimp curry to squid in spicy puttanesca sauce to tenderloin with porcini mushrooms. The restaurant usually opens just in time for sunset, at 4:30. ⑤ *Average main: $16* ⊠ *Behind Hotel Pargo Feliz, on beach road* ☎ *2642–0348* ⊟ *No credit cards* ⊙ *Closed Mon. and last 2 wks of Oct. No lunch.*

$$
VEGETARIAN

✗ **El Sano Banano Restaurant.** Montezuma's first natural-food restaurant is named after the chewy dried bananas made by the owners, who also own the upscale Ylang Ylang resort on the beach. This popular eatery serves the best vegetarian fare in town, including scrambled tofu for breakfast and excellent wraps, salads, fajitas, and spring rolls, with plenty of vegan and gluten-free options. On the sidewalk terrace, which is the best people-watching spot in town, you can enjoy a delicious Mocha Chiller, made with frozen yogurt, or a fruit smoothie made with local coconut milk. The homemade cakes and pies are scrumptious. The standout is the Chocolate Volcano, a mountain of ice cream atop cake, with a lava of chocolate sauce. For vegans, there's a non-dairy chocolate mousse. A shaded garden terrace behind the restaurant is cool and pleasant, but bring mosquito repellent. A battalion of ceiling fans keeps the air moving in the spacious dining room decorated with murals of tropical beach scenes. ⑤ *Average main: $12* ⊠ *Main road* ☎ *2642–0944* ⊕ *www.ylangylangbeachresort.com.*

$
ITALIAN

✗ **Ice Dream.** Literally, the coolest place in town is this blissfully air-conditioned ice-cream parlor with an array of refreshing Italian gelato flavors, cool fruit smoothies, and milk shakes. It's airy and bright with large windows looking onto the main street and an outdoor terrace, if you want to be part of the street scene. Lavazza coffee is served, along with homemade Italian savories, including toasted panini and bruschetta. This is the only air-conditioned space in town, so it makes a welcome retreat from the heat. ⑤ *Average main: $6* ⊠ *Southeast corner of main street and beach road* ☎ *2642–0160* ⊟ *No credit cards.*

$$$
ITALIAN
Fodor's Choice
★

✗ **Playa de los Artistas.** Arty driftwood tables and sculpted chairs scattered along the rocky beach and an inventive Mediterranean menu have made this one of the most scenic, as well as one of the best, restaurants in the country for more than 20 years. The decor is funky

6

with "found" art and hanging lamps, and every guest gets a warm welcome from the chef's gracious wife, Daniela, and a bevy of notably gorgeous, multilingual waitresses. The restaurant is most spectacular at night, when flickering lanterns combine with crashing surf to create a dramatic and romantic dinner experience. The eclectic menu changes daily and features local seafood, lamb, beef, and even duck. Daily pasta specials focus on seafood. The homemade ravioli stuffed with interesting combinations of seafood and vegetables is always a winner. Portions are plentiful and artistically presented on huge platters. On weekends, Italian owner-chef Nicola fires up the barbecue and wood-fired pizza oven. Don't pass up the velvety, dark-chocolate tart if it's on the dessert menu. The restaurant is sometimes open Saturday night, on the chef's whim; call ahead to find out. ⑤ *Average main: $20 ✉ 275 m south of town, near Los Mangos Hotel ☎ 2642–0920 ☯ Closed Sun. No lunch weekdays, no dinner Sat.*

$$$
VEGETARIAN
Fodor'sChoice
★

✕ **Ylang Ylang Restaurant.** One of Montezuma's most scenic and sophisticated restaurants, Ylang Ylang is nestled between the beach and the jungle, offering views of waves crashing against the rocks. The lunch menu lists a selection of sushi, salads, wraps, and sandwiches with various vegan, gluten-free, and raw dishes. The ocean view and elegant terrace setting make it worth the 10-minute walk down the beach. At night, the restaurant turns on the romance with flickering candles and an inventive dinner menu that ranges from Thai-style teriyaki tuna steak to penne in seafood sauce. Whatever you choose, you'll want to save room for desserts, such as the tiramisu espresso crepe. At night, they can provide transportation from town if you make a reservation. ⑤ *Average main: $18 ✉ On beach, ½ km (¼ mile) north of town, at Ylang Ylang Beach Resort ☎ 2642–0636 ⊕ www.ylangylangbeachresort.com.*

WHERE TO STAY

$$
B&B/INN

🏨 **El Sano Banano Village Café Suites.** If quiet and cool is what you are seeking, these comfortable, tastefully decorated rooms above the popular restaurant of the same name are air-conditioned and soundproofed—and they are a bargain. **Pros:** budget-friendly; Ylang Ylang Beach Resort privileges; excellent restaurant. **Cons:** most guest rooms lack windows; can feel a little claustrophobic. ⑤ *Rooms from: $75 ✉ Main road ☎ 2642–0636 ⊕ www.ylangylangbeachresort.com/ sanobananohotel/ ➹ 12 rooms ⑩ Breakfast.*

$$
B&B/INN
Fodor'sChoice
★

🏨 **Hotel Amor de Mar.** This chic and charming small hotel on a grassy lawn between the rocky shoreline and the entrance to Montezuma's most popular waterfall hike is the perfect place to spend a romantic weekend. **Pros:** beautiful property; friendly staff; artistic design elements. **Cons:** most of the rooms are small; some noise and commotion from nearby parking lot for waterfall; steps to upper rooms. ⑤ *Rooms from: $90 ✉ South of town, past bridge ☎ 2642–0262 ⊕ www.amordemar.com ➹ 9 rooms, 2 beach villas ⑩ No meals.*

$$
HOTEL

🏨 **Hotel El Jardín.** Spread across a hill a few blocks from the beach, this hotel has recently refreshed rooms and villas with ocean, pool, and garden views. **Pros:** central location; good value. **Cons:** a few rooms catch a bit of noise from bars in town; steep paths to climb. ⑤ *Rooms from:*

$80 ✉ West end of main road ☎ 2642–0074 ⊕ www.hoteleljardin.com ⏚ 14 rooms, 2 villas ⏚ No meals.

$$
HOTEL

⏚ **Hotel Los Mangos.** The rhythmic sounds of the nearby ocean make these affordable octagonal wood bungalows spread across a shady, green mango grove the perfect place to practice yoga or just relax. **Pros:** great pool; lots of wildlife; yoga. **Cons:** road noise; could use updating; slightly uphill concrete paths to cabins. *$ Rooms from: $75 ✉ Near entrance to waterfall trail, ½ km (¼ mile) south of town ☎ 2642–0384 ⊕ www.hotellosmangos.com ⏚ 10 rooms, 6 with private bath; 9 bungalows ⏚ No meals.*

$$
HOTEL
FAMILY

⏚ **Luz de Mono.** About 50 meters (160 feet) from the beach, this hotel has comfortable, tastefully decorated rooms amidst a lush, almost junglelike garden. **Pros:** secluded feel although in center of town; lots of shade in huge garden; conveniently located. **Cons:** some steeper inclines to reach villas. *$ Rooms from: $85 ✉ End of the main road, across from beach entrance ☎ 2642–0090 ⊕ www.luzdemono.com ⏚ 12 rooms, 6 villas ⏚ Breakfast.*

$$$
RESORT
Fodor's Choice
★

⏚ **Ylang Ylang Beach Resort.** Secluded and serene, this gorgeous tropical resort with a holistic slant sits in an exuberant garden, nestled between the sea and a lush forest. **Pros:** gorgeous, natural setting; great restaurant; excellent service. **Cons:** ocean-view tent cabins offer limited privacy; 15-minute walk to town along beach. *$ Rooms from: $180 ✉ 700 m north of school in Montezuma ☎ 2642–0636, 888/795–8494 in North America ⊕ www.ylangylangbeachresort.com ⏚ 8 bungalows, 1 treetop tent cabin, 3 suites, 3 standard rooms, 6 ocean-view tents ⏚ Some meals.*

NIGHTLIFE

Montezuma's nightlife is focused on a handful of bars where locals and foreigners mix, a refreshing change from larger beach towns where the clientele tends to be more segregated. A few venues boasting live music have recently appeared on the scene, including El Sano Banano and Ylang Ylang Beach Resort, where guest musicians and bands perform. Street-side artisans selling their creations often animate the area with drumming and dancing that draws passersby to stop and shake their hips, too.

Cafe Restaurant Organico. Every Monday is open mike at this Italian-owned hot spot. The fun gets started around 7:30 and goes late into the night if enough performers show up. Cool down with a bowl of excellent, chili-spiced, chocolate Italian gelato while you watch the show. *✉ Across from Cocolores, on the beach road ☎ 2642–1322.*

Chico's Bar. Music blasts from the dark, uninviting entrance, but farther back is a brighter, spacious deck with pool tables and dancing. Directly behind is an open-air beach bar with a more laid-back atmosphere and a breezy ocean view. *✉ On beach road, where main street through Montezuma ends ☎ No phone.*

Restaurante Moctezuma. You can't get any closer to the beach than at this breezy, casual bar, which serves the cheapest beers in town. At night, candles and moonlight illuminate the tables in the sand. *✉ 1st fl, Hotel Moctezuma.*

SHOPPING

Beachwear, banana paper, wooden crafts, and indigenous pottery are some of what you find in colorful shops in the town's center. During the dry season, traveling artisans from around the world unfold their street-side tables just before the sun begins to set; candles light up the handmade leather-and-seed jewelry, dream catchers, and knit tops.

Deep Forest Aquamarine. Among the many craft and souvenir stands and shops in town, this artisans' cooperative stands out for fabulous mosaic-tiled mirrors, original jewelry, carved-wood bird mobiles, pottery, and charming, painted wooden porcupines with colored toothpicks for spines. It's open 9 to 9 daily in high season. ⊠ *beside El Sano Banano Restaurant, main street* ☎ *8848–0146.*

Galeria La Floresta. Visit this outdoor gallery to see a display of fantastical, stunning lamps and sconces made from driftwood, bamboo, and shells. Swiss artist Claudia Bassaeur makes unique and beautiful lamp shades with marbled, handmade paper imported from Santa Fe, New Mexico. She also makes extraordinary jewelry, using found "treasure." Call ahead to make an appointment. The gallery is on the main road in Cabuya, on the way to Cabo Blanco Absolute Nature Reserve. ⊠ *7 km south of Montezuma on road to Cabuya* ✢ *200 meters past Hotel Celaje* ☎ *2642–1211, 8836–6876.*

CABO BLANCO ABSOLUTE NATURE PRESERVE

10 km (6 miles) southwest of Montezuma, about 11 km (7 miles) south of Malpaís.

True to its name, this reserve at the southernmost tip of the Nicoya Peninsula is absolutely natural, and very hot. Challenging hiking trails lead through humid, evergreen forest, brimming with wildlife, to a magnificent beach with a view of a nearby island, home to hundreds of sea birds.

GETTING HERE AND AROUND

The road to the reserve from Montezuma is usually passable and well graded in the dry season. It's also scenic, with rows of huge, spiky pochote trees and one massive ficus tree with its own historical plaque. En route, a narrow bridge crosses the wide Río Lajas, where you can cool off in the shallow, clear water of this river, which runs over flat rocks, *lajas* in Spanish. The road from Malpaís is much rougher and a 4WD is recommended, especially in the rainy season. From Montezuma or Malpaís, take the road signed to Cabuya. Taxis can take you to or from Montezuma for $15 one way—that's always the easiest option—but buses to Cabuya also leave from Montezuma daily at 8 am, 10 am, 2 pm, 4 pm, and 6 pm.

EXPLORING

Fodor'sChoice ★ **Cabo Blanco Absolute Nature Preserve** (*Reserva Natural Absoluta Cabo Blanco*). Conquistadors named this area Cabo Blanco on account of its white earth and cliffs, but it was a more benevolent pair of foreigners—Swede Nicolas Wessberg and his Danish wife, Karen Mogensen, arriving here in the 1950s—who made it a preserve. Appalled by the first clear-cut in the Cabo Blanco area in 1960, the pioneering couple launched an international appeal to save the forest. In time their efforts led not only to the creation of the 12-square-km (4½-square-mile) reserve but also to the founding of Costa Rica's national park service, the National Conservation Areas System (SINAC). Wessberg was murdered on the Osa Peninsula in 1975 while researching the area's potential as a national park. A reserve just outside Montezuma was named in his honor. A reserve has also been created to honor his wife, who dedicated her life to conservation after her husband's death.

Informative natural-history captions dot the trails in the Cabo Blanco forest. Look for the sapodilla trees, which produce a white latex used to make gum; you can often see V-shape scars where the trees have been cut to allow the latex to run into containers placed at the base. Wessberg cataloged a full array of animals here: porcupine, hog-nosed skunk, spotted skunk, gray fox, anteater, cougar, and jaguar. Resident birds include brown pelicans, white-throated magpies, toucans, cattle egrets, green herons, parrots, and blue-crowned motmots. A fairly strenuous 10-km (6¼-mile) round-trip hike, which takes about two hours in each direction, follows a trail from the reserve entrance to **Playa Cabo Blanco.** The beach is magnificent, with hundreds of pelicans flying in formation and paddling in the calm waters offshore—you can wade right in and join them. Off the tip of the cape is the 698-square-meter (7,511-square-foot) **Isla Cabo Blanco,** with pelicans, frigate birds, brown boobies, and an abandoned lighthouse. As a strict reserve, Cabo Blanco is open only five days a week. It has new restrooms (in honor of the park's 50th anniversary in 2013), picnic tables at the entrance, and a visitor center with information panels on park history and biological diversity, but no other tourist facilities, and overnight camping is not permitted. Most visitors come with their own guide. This is one of the hottest parks in the country, so be sure to bring lots of water with you. ⚠ **An official sign at the entrance warns people with cardiovascular problems NOT to walk the strenuous trail to Cabo Blanco beach.** ✉ *10 km (6 miles) southwest of Montezuma via Cabuya, Montezuma* ☎ *2642–0093, 2642–0312* 💲 *$12* 🕐 *Wed.–Sun. 8–4.*

6

WHERE TO EAT

$ ✕ **Panadería y Café Cabuya.** The best place to stop before or after a
BAKERY visit to Cabo Blanco is this pleasant terrace café with perhaps the best baked goods in the area. Your eyes will pop when you see the bakery display. Huge, moist brownies and crunchy oatmeal cookies will see you through a Cabo Blanco hike. After a trek through the park, have a slice from one of the giant cakes, topped with meringue and cherries, washed down with espresso or iced coffee. On the savory side, there are pita sandwiches, salads, and seafood dishes, including grilled mahimahi or roosterfish with a tomato, garlic, and red pepper sauce. Fruit smoothies and batidas (milk shakes) make a refreshing end to a hike or a sunning session in the nearby Río Lajas. It's open 6:30 to 8 pm. 💲 *Average main: $9* ✉ *center of Cabuya, on road to Cabo Blanco Absolute Nature Reserve, Montezuma* ✛ *8 km (5 miles) south of Montezuma* ☎ *2642–1184* 🚫 *No credit cards.*

MALPAÍS AND SANTA TERESA

12 km (7½ miles) southwest of Cóbano, 52 km (33 miles) south of Paquera.

Once frequented mostly by die-hard surfers in search of some of the country's largest waves and by naturalists en route to the nearby Cabo Blanco Absolute Nature Preserve, this area is now a 10-km (6-mile) stretch of hotels, restaurants, and shopping centers strung along a mostly dirt road that is choking with dust in the dry season and awash in mud the rest of the year. Despite the congestion, the string of beaches and consistent surf still draw a multitude of surfers. Health-oriented spas, organic restaurants, and yoga classes are also attracting a very international, young crowd, from Europe, Australia, and North America.

Coming from Cóbano, the road alternates between paved and dirt sections until it reaches an intersection, known locally as El Cruce, marked by a cluster of shopping centers, banks, restaurants, and hotel signs. To the left is the partially paved route to relatively tranquil Malpaís, and to the right is the road to Santa Teresa, which has a few paved sections but is mostly a rutted, narrow, dirt road clogged with trucks, ATVs, bicycles, and pedestrians. Playa Carmen, straight ahead, is the area's best place for surfing, though swimmers will want to be careful of rip currents. Malpaís and Santa Teresa are so close that locals disagree on where one begins and the other ends. You could travel up the road parallel to the ocean that connects them and not realize you've moved from one town to the other.

GETTING HERE AND AROUND

From Paquera it's an hour's drive to Malpaís via Cóbano. After Cóbano, the road is partially paved. There are some bumpy dirt sections, which can become quite muddy in the rainy season, so a 4WD vehicle is your best bet. There is a direct bus from San José, leaving at 6 am and 2 pm to Santa Teresa, crossing with the ferry from Puntarenas (Transportes Hermanos Rodríguez, ☎ *2642–0219*). The trip takes about six hours and costs about $15, including ferry fare. Taxis waiting at Tambor's airstrip will take up to four people to Malpaís for $45–$50.

Tropical Tours Shuttles. Tropical Tours can set you up with a shuttle to San José ($50), about 5½ hours, using vans and the Puntarenas to Paquera ferry. It also has shuttles to the Liberia airport ($55) and to popular beach towns Tamarindo ($50) and Sámara ($50). ⊠ *50 m north of El Cruce, Malpaís* ☎ *2640–1900* ⊕ *www.tropicaltourshuttles.com.*

ESSENTIALS

Bank/ATM Banco Nacional. ⊠ *Centro Comercial Playa Carmen, at the cross-roads, Malpaís* ☎ *2640–0640.*

Medical Center Lifeguard Urgent Medical Centre. ⊠ *At the crossroads, around the corner from BCR bank, Malpaís* ☎ *2220–0911.*

Pharmacy Farmacia Amiga. ⊠ *Centro Comercial Playa Carmen, at the cross-roads, Malpaís* ☎ *2640–0463.*

Taxi Taxi. ⊠ *Malpaís* ☎ *8360–8166.*

BEACHES

Playa Carmen. This Blue Flag beach, sometimes referred to as El Carmen, is just a stone's throw from the commercial development along the beach road, so it tends to attract more people. There's a parking lot and palm trees for shade. The waves offer excellent surfing for all levels, with dozens of beach breaks scattered along the wide, sandy strand. The sea grows rough and dirty during the May-to-December rainy season, with frequent swells that sometimes make it impossible to get out on a surfboard. Swimmers need to be careful of rip currents. Lifeguards are on duty year-round on weekends, from 9 am to sunset; more days during holiday periods. **Amenities:** food and drink. **Best for:** surfing, sun bathing. ⊠ *Playa Carmen, Santa Teresa.*

Playa Malpaís. South of the bustle of Playas Carmen and Santa Teresa, this Blue Flag beach is quieter and rockier, with interesting volcanic formations. The tougher surfing here was the original attraction that drew surfers from around the world, with a challenging break over a rock platform. Swimming is not advised but the dramatic scenery is unbeatable. **Amenities:** food and lodging at Ritmo Tropical, Blue Jay Lodge, on far side of beach road, not right on the beach. **Best for:** surfing, sunsets. ⊠ *Malpais, Malpaís.*

Playa Santa Teresa. Playa Carmen seamlessly segues into Playa Santa Teresa, about 1 km (½ mile) to the north. This flat, sandy Blue Flag beach is edged by forest and punctuated with rocky sections and tide pools at low tide. It's usually a calmer option for surfers, but swimmers need to take care, especially since there are no lifeguards here. The farther north you go, the less crowded the beach is. **Amenities:** beachfront hotels include Tropico Latino, Latitude 10, Florblanca and Pranamar; Rancho Itauna provides food and entertainment facing the beach. **Best for:** surfing, sunbathing, walking. ⊠ *Santa Teresa, Santa Teresa.*

SPORTS AND THE OUTDOORS

TOUR OPERATORS

Olingo Ecotours. You'll see and learn more at Cabo Blanco or Curú nature reserves in the company of a private naturalist guide from this outfit. Half-day wildlife tours, 7 am to 1 pm, are $100 per person, minimum two people; $75 for three or more, transportation included. Bird-watching tours, 6 to 10 am or 3 to 6 pm, are $105 per person (minimum two) or $80 (three or more), transportation included. Out on the water, surf lessons are $60 for a private lesson, $50 per person (two or more) for two hours. ⊠ *Malpaís* ☎ *2640–0888, 8399–0696* ⊕ *www.olingosurfandnaturetours.com* 🖢 *From $50.*

Tropical Tours. This outfitter can set you up with a horseback-riding jaunt ($40), or a day trip to Isla Tortuga ($70). ⊠ *50 m north of El Cruce, Malpaís* ☎ *2640–1900* ⊕ *www.tropicaltourshuttles.com* 🖢 *From $40.*

CANOPY TOURS

Canopy Malpais del Pacifico. The only canopy tour in the area has an 11-platform adventure with ocean views that takes about an hour and a half ($45). Transportation to the zip line, near the entrance of Cabo Blanco Absolute Nature Reserve, is $5 round-trip. You can walk, glide, or rappel through 60 acres of forest and hike some forest trails.

6

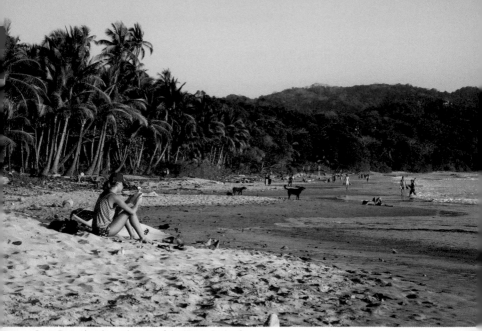
Santa Teresa beach, southern tip of the Nicoya Peninsula

Bring binoculars to spot birds and other wildlife. ⊠ *Near entrance to Cabo Blanco Absolute Nature Reserve, Malpaís* ☎ *2640–0360* ⊕ *www. canopymalpais.com* ✉ *From $45.*

SURFING

From November to May, the Malpaís area has some of Costa Rica's most consistent surf, as well as clear skies and winds that create idyllic conditions.

Kina Surf Shop. This shop stands out among the dozens of surf shops scattered along the beach road for its surfing expertise and wide range of boards and accessories. If you're a first-time surfer, they can fit you with the correct board from their stock of more than 60 different shapes and sizes. Surf lessons for all levels cost $60 (minimum two people) for about two hours, including board for the rest of the day and a rash guard. ⊠ *Plaza Solar, in front of Brunelas, main street, Santa Teresa* ☎ *2640–0627* ⊕ *www.kinasurfcostarica.com* ✉ *From $60.*

WHERE TO EAT

$$$ ✕ **Koji's Restaurant.** North of Santa Teresa, this trendy sushi place off
SUSHI a dusty dirt road is currently the most popular restaurant in the area. About 30 wood tables are scattered around a gravel-bottomed, Zenlike garden, with palm trees and a stand of bamboo. The decor is mainly votive candles, flaming torches, and tin-can hanging lamps. So why the stampede to eat here? Fabulous sushi, sashimi, and tempura carefully crafted by a charismatic Japanese chef named, of course, Koji. On the daily blackboard menu, all the usual hand rolls and wraps are on

offer, expertly made and artistically presented. One of the most popular dishes on the menu is the Koji roll: a double dose of shrimp and shrimp tempura, with avocado, cucumber, spicy tuna, and a "special" sauce. There's also tempura shrimp, beef tenderloin, and ginger-pork main dishes. Vegetarians can order spring rolls and steamed vegetables with quinoa, but it hardly seems worth it to make the trip here unless you are going to chow down on fish and seafood. To wash it down, there are coconut-milk fruit shakes, sake, Costa Rican craft beer, and notably expensive wine. Cash only. ⑤ *Average main: $18* ✉ *200 m north of Pranamar, near Playa Hermosa, Santa Teresa* ☎ *2640–0815* ⊘ *Closed Mon. No lunch* ⚱ *Reservations essential.*

> ## BATTLE OF THE BAKERIES
>
> The morning line at **The Bakery** in Playa Carmen attests to its popularity. This self-advertised "artisan bakery" delivers sweet buns along with an all-day "Ultimate breakfast" of eggs, chopped salad, focaccia, brownie, fresh OJ, and coffee or tea. But if you hanker after an authentic, flaky French croissant, head for **Marianne's Panadería/ Pastelería Francesca**, where you can enjoy a true Continental breakfast on a quiet terrace. At Italian-flavored **Ginger Cafe**, you can start the day with espresso and a Nutella-filled croissant, or a ham and cheese brioche bun.

6

$$$ ╳ **Nectar.** Savor the experience of
SEAFOOD the Florblanca Resort's fabulous garden setting at this poolside alfresco
Fodor's Choice restaurant. Fresh seafood is the specialty here, with inventive daily spe-
★ cials that focus on the day's catch prepared with Asian and Mediterranean flavors. On the meat side, there's a lamb burger, dressed with sundried tomato pesto, feta cheese, and sage-speckled aioli. The emphasis is on organic and local produce. After 3:30, the dedicated sushi chef produces such treats as panko-crusted prawn roll with ahi tuna, mango, and avocado. Come for lunch and enjoy the calming sea view peeking through the tropical foliage, or come for a special-occasion, candlelit dinner backed by the sound of the surf. It's pricey, but worth the splurge if you crave a sophisticated scene. ⑤ *Average main: $25* ✉ *Resort Florblanca, 2 km (1 mile) north of soccer field, Malpaís* ☎ *2640–0232* ⚱ *Reservations essential.*

$ ╳ **Product C Playa Carmen.** For the freshest, tastiest, and most affordable
SEAFOOD seafood in town, make a bee-line to this fish market and restaurant with
Fodor's Choice the most entertaining chefs in town. A trio of cheerful Canadian expats
★ shucks, slices, grills, and prepares fresh local oysters, sashimi, grilled fish fillets doused in ginger and sesame dressing, savory fishcakes, and refreshing ceviche. The velvety, flavorful fish pâté is addictive, while the "candied" tuna with a pineapple glaze, served carpaccio-style, is a revelation. Take a seat at the counter inside and enjoy the buzz and banter in the open kitchen, or sit at an umbrella-shaded table under palms in the courtyard. Don't leave Malpaís without ordering at least one of their spicy-sauced fish tacos, served with paper-thin slices of cabbage, parsley, and onions. There are other restaurants in the Central Valley with the Product C name, but this is the true original. ⑤ *Average main:*

*$8 ⊠ Centro Commercial Playa Carmen, at the Cruce, Santa Teresa
⚓ behind Farmacía Amiga ☎ 2640–1026 ⊙ Closed Sun. No dinner.*

$$
MODERN ITALIAN

✗ Restaurante Al Chile Viola. Sit yourself down amidst a sea of chili-pepper-red tabletops, chandeliers, hangings, and funky objets d'art for an Italian meal like you have never tasted before. Chef Emiliano from Florence will challenge your taste buds with imaginative dishes using authentic Italian ingredients, while his lovely wife, Luz, works her Tica charm in the dining room. The exciting menu includes traditional homemade pastas—beef lasagne, eggplant parmigiana, osso buco à la Romana, and seafood such as sea bass rolled around grilled vegetables. But the chef outdoes himself with an unusual, standout dish of Bulls Balls Ravioli—yes, tasty testes finely minced with spices, stuffed into pasta purses, and served with a creamy prosciutto sauce. For dessert, Emiliano makes a killer dark-chocolate mousse sprinkled with sea-salt crystals, or try the signature frozen coffee made with local Cafe Tica liqueur. During high season (December to May), there's live music three times a week. Ⓢ *Average main: $14 ⊠ 200 m north of Super La Hacienda, on main road, Santa Teresa ☎ 2640–0433 ⊙ Closed Sun. and Oct. No lunch.*

WHERE TO STAY

$
B&B/INN

⊞ Blue Jay Lodge. Perched along a forested mountainside, these wooden cabins feel like tree houses; you'll hear howler monkeys and an array of birdsong from your bed. **Pros:** natural setting; good value; nice respite from lowland heat and dust, since road in front is paved. **Cons:** steep terrain; most bungalows don't have air-conditioning. Ⓢ *Rooms from: $73 ⊠ From El Cruce, 800 m south toward Malpaís, Santa Teresa ☎ 2640–0089 ⊕ www.bluejaylodgecostarica.com ↝ 14 cabins* ¶⊙ *Breakfast.*

$$$$
RESORT
Fodor's Choice
★

⊞ Florblanca. Named for the white flowers of the frangipani trees growing between the restaurant and the beach, this ultraluxurious resort is dedicated to relaxation and rejuvenation. **Pros:** gorgeous villas and grounds; friendly; great yoga classes; no kids under six. **Cons:** very expensive; on rocky stretch of beach; insects sometimes a problem. Ⓢ *Rooms from: $400 ⊠ 2 km (1 mile) north of soccer field, Santa Teresa ☎ 2640–0232, 800/685–1031 toll-free in North America ⊕ www.florblanca.com ↝ 10 villas, 1 surf house, 4 bungalows* ¶⊙ *No meals.*

$$
HOTEL
FAMILY

⊞ Hotel Tropico Latino. This beachfront hotel has everything—a spectacular beach with major surf break; a trendy restaurant with ocean views; a round, palm-fringed pool; bungalows and rooms sprinkled throughout a mature garden; twice-daily yoga sessions on the beach; and a full-service spa. **Pros:** great location on beach; large pool; lush gardens. **Cons:** cheaper rooms are dark and close to dusty, noisy road; not quiet—more of a buzz with lots of people coming and going. Ⓢ *Rooms from: $145 ⊠ 700 m north of the crossroads, Santa Teresa ☎ 2640–0062 ⊕ www.hoteltropicolatino.com ↝ 8 bungalows, 1 2-bedroom house, 1 equipped studio, 21 rooms* ¶⊙ *No meals.*

$$$$
B&B/INN
Fodor's Choice
★

Latitude 10°. Totally removed from the crowd, this exclusive and exquisite, intimate beach resort is for well-heeled couples who want to enjoy the action of the Santa Teresa beach scene without actually staying in it. **Pros:** serene and private; outstanding service; direct beach access. **Cons:** very quiet; away from the Santa Teresa beach scene. ⑤ *Rooms from: $330* ⊠ *Just north of Florblanca, on main road, Santa Teresa* ☎ *2640–0396, 8309–2943 rates and reservations* ⊕ *www. latitude10resort.com* ⇨ *5 villas, 1 guest room* ⦿ *Breakfast.*

$$$
B&B/INN

Pranamar Oceanfront Villas & Yoga Retreat. You don't have to be on a yoga retreat to appreciate this nirvana of design, artistry, and natural beauty in a serene setting. **Pros:** gorgeous garden and beach setting; excellent restaurant; warm, friendly service. **Cons:** noisy children may not suit the serenity here; bumpy dirt road to get here. ⑤ *Rooms from: $250* ⊠ *Playa Hermosa, Santa Teresa* ✚ *5 km north of the Cruce in Playa Carmen* ☎ *2640–0852* ⊕ *www.pranamarvillas.com* ⇨ *5 bungalows, 4 two-story villas, 1 two-story house* ⦿ *Breakfast.*

$$
HOTEL
FAMILY

Ritmo Tropical. Tranquil, comfortable, and nicely priced, this small hotel and spa a short walk from the beach is consistently the best deal in Malpaís. **Pros:** very clean rooms; economical; lively restaurant; quiet. **Cons:** a bit of a walk to town, but on a paved road. ⑤ *Rooms from: $90* ⊠ *100 m south of El Cruce on road toward Malpaís, Malpaís* ☎ *2640–0174* ⊕ *hotelritmotropical.com* ⇨ *8 bungalows, 2 rooms, studio for four with kitchen* ⦿ *No meals.*

SHOPPING

Boutique Jungle Avenue. In the Centro Commercial Playa Carmen, this small store sells funky beachwear, as well as versatile skirts and tops, made by local designers. ⊠ *Centro Comercial Playa Carmen, at the Cruce, Playa Carmen, Sant Teresa* ☎ *2640–0817.*

Del Monserrat Custom Jewelry Studio. For a truly unique souvenir, have designer Esteban del Monserrat create a custom ring, necklace, or pair of earrings with natural gem stones. The ready-made designs by this well-traveled jewelry maker are stunning, using chunky, beaten silver reminiscent of sunken Spanish treasure. ⊠ *Centro Commercial Playa Carmen, at the Cruce, Santa Teresa.*

Pranamar. At the far-north end of Santa Teresa, the gift shop in this yoga-centered retreat sells exquisite jewelry from Bali, Guatemala, and local Costa Rican artisans. Delicate filigree silver armlets, headbands, and bracelets made with freshwater pearls, abalone, amethyst, and other semiprecious stones add some soulful bling. ⊠ *Pranamar Oceanfront Villas & Yoga Retreat, north end of Playa Santa Teresa, Malpaís* ☎ *2640–0852* ⊕ *www.pranamarvillas.com.*

NIGHTLIFE

La Lora Amarilla. In the middle of Santa Teresa, this huge disco bar with both live music and DJs attracts locals and the international tourist crowd who want to dance. Tuesday is reggae night; Wednesday and Friday feature Latin beats; and Saturday and Sunday there's live music and karaoke. ⊠ *On main road, across from Chiropractic Clinic, Playa Santa Teresa, Santa Teresa* ☎ *2640–0132.*

6

Ranchos Itauna. This beachfront restaurant-lounge in Santa Teresa is a fixture on the nightlife scene, with "Sunset Sessions" Tuesday to Sunday, featuring international live and DJ music, from 4 to 11 pm. Bonfires and torch-fire shows add to the excitement. The crowd is a mix of locals and tourists. ⊠ *100 m north of Super Costa, Santa Teresa* ☎ *2640–0095* ⊕ *www.ranchos-itauna.com.*

MANUEL ANTONIO AND THE CENTRAL PACIFIC COAST

WELCOME TO MANUEL ANTONIO AND THE CENTRAL PACIFIC COAST

TOP REASONS TO GO

★ **Adventure sports:** Snorkel among colorful fish, get muddy on mountain adventures, and zip through treetops near Jacó and Manuel Antonio.

★ **Fishing:** Deep-sea fishing at Quepos, Jacó, or Herradura gives a chance to hook a sailfish, marlin, wahoo, or yellowfin tuna.

★ **Nature and wildlife:** Explore the seaside forest and see sloths, iguanas, agoutis, monkeys, and 350 species of birds at Manuel Antonio National Park.

★ **Sunsets:** Whether you view it from the beach or while sipping hilltop cocktails in Manuel Antonio, this region has some of the country's best venues for watching the sunset.

★ **Surfing:** This is Costa Rica's surf central. Jacó, Playa Hermosa, Esterillos, and Manuel Antonio beckon surfers, from beginners to pros.

1 Central Pacific Coast. From Tárcoles, the highway along the coast connects the lively surf towns of Jacó and Playa Hermosa to several quiet beach communities dotting the South Pacific. This is the place to surf, do a multitude of activities, party, and laze on the beach.

2 Manuel Antonio Area. Boutique hotels and sustainable resorts cradle the steep cliffs of this coastal town, where white-sand coves border the wildlife-rich Manuel Antonio National Park.

> 369

GETTING ORIENTED

Most of the Central Pacific is mountainous, and beach towns are backed by forested peaks. Humid evergreen forests, oil-palm plantations, and cattle pastures blanket the land. The coastal highway connects all towns from Tárcoles to the southern Pacific. The hub town of Jacó makes a good base for visiting surrounding beaches and wildlife areas. Farther south are neighboring Quepos and Manuel Antonio, Costa Rica's most popular destination, followed by smaller towns barely touched by tourism.

7

MANUEL ANTONIO NATIONAL PARK

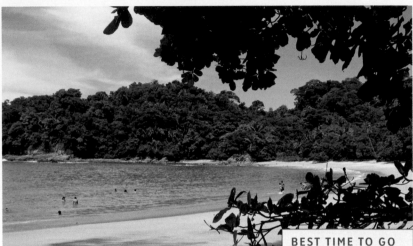

At only 7 square km (3 square miles), Manuel Antonio National Park—Costa Rica's smallest park—has impressive natural attractions: wildlife, rain forest, white-sand beaches, and rocky coves with abundant marine life.

The forest is dominated by massive ficus, silk-cotton trees, black-and-white Guapinols, and Panama trees as well as guacimo colorado, bully tree, cedar, and cenizaro. It's home to both two- and three-toed sloths, green and black iguanas, agoutis (similar to the guinea pig, but with longer legs), raccoons, coatis, three species of monkeys, and more than 350 species of birds.

The well-maintained trails are short, mostly paved—and heavily traveled. Make no mistake about it: this is no undiscovered wilderness. In fact, Manuel Antonio is Costa Rica's most visited attraction. There are 5 km (3 miles) of coastline, and it's one of the few parks where you can combine nature walks with swimming off idyllic beaches. There's no commercial beach development, so the beaches are picture-perfect. *(For more information see the review in this chapter.)*

BEST TIME TO GO

Visit any day and any month but October, when it's very wet. Although it rains in September, you're likely to have the park to yourself and showers usually don't kick in until early afternoon. May through November is less crowded, while December through April has the most trail traffic. Come early, ideally between 7 and 8 am, because park rangers allow only 800 people inside at a time. Keep in mind that the park is closed on Monday.

FUN FACT

The park's territory is too small to support all of its monkeys, so forested corridors and suspended bridges have been built to allow the monkeys to come and go.

BEST WAYS TO EXPLORE

HIKING

Don your hiking shoes and set off on Sloth Trail, the main route that leads to Manuel Antonio beach. The coral reef here makes it a good spot for snorkeling. A second trail leads to Playa Espadilla Sur. These two stunning beaches lie on either side of a *tombolo*, a sandy strip that connects the mainland to rocky Punta Catedral, which used to be an island thousands of years ago. Farther east, where fewer visitors venture, Playa Escondido is rocky and secluded. Trails from the entrance to Punta Catedral and Playa Escondido are in excellent shape. Trails farther east are progressively rougher due to the steep terrain. Sturdy walking sandals are good enough for most of the trails, but light hiking boots or closed shoes will help you avoid nasty encounters with biting ants.

WILDLIFE-WATCHING

Manuel Antonio is famous for its monkeys, especially the noisy white-faced monkeys that pester tourists at the beach. A troop of rare squirrel monkeys also lives here, one of the few places in the country where you can still find them. These tiny monkeys—*mono titi* in Spanish—are an endangered species. Catching sight of them is a real wildlife coup. The smallest of Costa Rica's four monkey species, these little guys have squirrel-like bushy tails, but they only use them for balance—they can't swing from them.

Watch, too, for less active creatures, such as the more-or-less stationary sloth, especially along the park's Sloth Trail. They sleep much of the day, curled up high in the trees. Look for clumps of green and brown and watch carefully to see if they move.

You'll see many more animals and birds with a guide than without one. You can hire an official guide at the park entrance. If you're interested in seeing birds, be sure to hire a guide that is carrying a scope for close-up views.

TOP REASONS TO GO

Beaches

There are gorgeous beaches with no commercial clutter or noise, but you need to bring your own snorkeling gear, snacks, and drinks. Only sandwiches, fruit, and nonalcoholic beverages are allowed in the park. There are toilet facilities and cold-water, open-air showers.

Monkeys

Along with the ubiquitous capuchin monkeys performing for visitors on the beaches, you'll also find howler monkeys (*congos*) draped over tree branches in the forest, and more rarely, the endangered squirrel monkey.

Pelicans

Just off Playa Espadilla, you can swim out to some rocks and tread water while pelicans dive for fish.

Views

For a fabulous coastal view, take the path that leads up to Punta Catedral's rocky hill, draped with thick jungle. You'll pass a lookout point with a view out at the Pacific and the park's islets. Be sure to explore the paved Sendero El Mirador (Look Out Point Trail), one of the best trails in the park.

7

Updated
by Marlise
Kast-Myers

The Central Pacific region of Costa Rica is a long swath of gorgeous land, encompassing sublime coastline dotted with national parks and palm-lined beaches, and inland stretches of ranches, coffee plantations, small villages, and forested mountains. There's a reason this is a popular place to visit: the region has a lot of *pura vida* to offer.

If you're a first-timer to Costa Rica, this region is all about Manuel Antonio and the acclaimed national park of the same name. (Manuel Antonio and the Arenal Volcano in the Northern Lowlands make the classic "get your feet wet" visit to Costa Rica.) For Costa Ricans, the Central Pacific often means Jacó, the closest beach town to San José, and an odd mix of burgeoning condo developments, nightclubs, hotels, and surf shops. But you need not limit yourself to these two anchors: Herradura, Playas Hermosa, Esterillos, and Bejuco along this stretch of coast offer a little more solitude, although development is slowly creeping up here, too.

The region is easily accessible by way of the San José–Caldera Highway CR27, which connects to the Southern Coastal Highway CR34.

PLANNING

WHEN TO GO
HIGH SEASON: DECEMBER TO APRIL
Dry season means high season here. Your payback for braving the crowds is nearly ideal weather. Expect warm, sunny days and pleasant evenings. If, however, you're not big on heat, March and April may feel stiflingly hot. Lots of visitors push hotel prices up and crowd the beaches, especially on dry-season weekends. Weekdays offer a slight respite from the crowds. During Holy Week and the last week of December, rooms are even harder to come by. If you're in the area during high season and want to visit one of the parks, especially Manuel Antonio, get an early start and arrive by 7 am.

LOW SEASON: SEPTEMBER TO NOVEMBER

This is the wettest of the rainy season, when showers become frequent and prolonged. The landmass and wind patterns that cause hurricane activity off the Caribbean coast create significant rain in the Central Pacific. Nature-themed activities usually go on rain or shine, but beach-lazing plans may well go awry. Keep in mind that some smaller hotels and restaurants actually close for several weeks during low season.

SHOULDER SEASON: MAY TO AUGUST

The rains begin in mid-May, but the first half of the wet season sees warm, mostly sunny days with lighter afternoon showers. It's easy to plan around them, and the precipitation keeps everything lush and green. Mid-year school vacations fall in early July, with Costa Rican families flocking to the beach, especially Jacó and Manuel Antonio.

PLANNING YOUR TIME

A week gives you enough time to visit several beaches on the central coast, and still explore the wildlife of Manuel Antonio National Park. Adventure seekers might want to set aside a day for a surf lesson, forest hike, or canopy tour. The perfect balance is three days in scenic Manuel Antonio, two days at a secluded beach near Tárcoles or Playa Bejuco, and a couple of days for surfing and action close to bustling Jacó.

GETTING HERE AND AROUND

AIR TRAVEL

The 20-minute flight between San José and Quepos, on Nature Air or SANSA, can save you the three-hour drive and costs just under $90 one way. From San José, both airlines have four daily flights to Quepos departing between 8 and 3. Flights from San José to Tambor, on Nature Air or SANSA, take 30 minutes—a fraction of the time it takes to drive to Puntarenas and ferry over.

BUS TRAVEL

Public buses to and within this entire region are punctual and economical, and local shuttles from San José can drop you off at your hotel's doorstep. Public buses leave San José almost hourly between 6 am and 7:30 pm and take four hours to reach Quepos. From here you have to take local transportation to your hotel in Manuel Antonio. Gray Line and Interbus are more direct, with hotel pickup in San José and Quepos or Manuel Antonio. Both companies offer a morning and afternoon trip for around $52 one way.

Bus Contacts Gray Line. ☎ *2220–2126, 800/719–3905 toll-free from U.S and Canada* ⊕ *www.graylinecostarica.com.* **Interbus.** ☎ *4100–0888* ⊕ *www. interbusonline.com.*

CAR TRAVEL

Highway 27 connects San José to the Pacific port of Caldera, near Puntarenas. This 77-km (46-mile) toll road eliminates a winding drive through the mountains and puts the coast just one hour from the capital. Costa Ricans call the modern road the *Carretera a Caldera* (Caldera Highway). Before the coast, an exit to the two-lane paved coastal highway, or *Costanera*, leads southeast to Tárcoles, Herradura, Jacó, Hermosa, Esterillos, Bejuco, and Quepos. An asphalt road winds its way over the hill between Quepos and Manuel Antonio National Park—plan on about 1½ hours to drive to Jacó and 2½ hours to Quepos.

TOURS

King Tours. A roster of tours includes trips to renowned attractions like Manuel Antonio National Park, as well as crocodile boat adventures, deep-sea and coastal fishing trips, horseback rides, and canopy tours. The company can also book tours to destinations elsewhere in the country, such as Poás and Arenal volcanoes, Monteverde Cloud Forest, and Isla Tortuga. ✉ *Main road into Playa Herradura, in front of Los Sueños, Playa Herradura* ☎ *2643–2441, 800/213–7091 in North America* ⊕ *www.kingtours.com* ✉ *From $85.*

Rios Tropicales. High-quality adventure tours include hiking, biking, kayaking, and white-water rafting trips on rivers near Manuel Antonio. Their Quepos franchise, H20 Adventures, organizes day excursions on the Naranjo and Savegre rivers. ✉ *Central Colon Bldg., San José* ☎ *2233–6455, 866/722–8273 in North America* ⊕ *www.riostropicales. com* ✉ *$70–$99.*

Team CRT. The many services include a variety of Central Pacific tours, such as a canopy tour near Manuel Antonio, kayaking, and rafting. They also provide car rentals, private drivers, shuttle vans, and a 4WD off-the-beaten-path "adventure" transfer between San José and Manuel Antonio. ☎ *2508–5000, 888/236–4447 in North America* ⊕ *www.costarica4u.com* ✉ *Kayaking $69; canopy tour $75; rafting and national park tour $98.*

BIRD-WATCHING GUIDES

Costa Rica Gateway. Since 1993, expert birders (and brothers) Kevin and Steven Easley have been organizing comprehensive and customized bird-watching tours. They know where the birding hot spots are, as well as all the best birding places to stay and how to capture the birds on film. ✉ *Alajuela* ☎ *2433–8278, 888/246–8513 in U.S.* ⊕ *www. costaricagateway.com* ✉ *Tours start at $110.*

Costa Rica Living and Birding. Guide Patrick O'Donnell is not only knowledgeable but also particularly good at helping new birders see the birds. He offers custom birding tours, mostly day trips from the San José area. For up-to-date birding news, check out his informative blog. ✉ *Santa Barbara de Heredia* ☎ *8402–7321, 716/778–2091 in U.S.* ⊕ *birdingcraft.com/wordpress* ✉ *From $110.*

RESTAURANTS

You'll find the liveliest dining mix in the country outside San José here, especially in Manuel Antonio. The crowd of international visitors has brought international restaurants ranging from Japanese to Italian, but, as you'd expect in a coastal region, seafood still reigns here. For traditional Costa Rican cuisine, your best bet is a roadside *soda* where locals gather for their daily *casado* (rice, beans, plantains, and an entrée of chicken, beef, or fish). Your final bill will include a 15% sales tax and a 10–12% service charge.

HOTELS

The Central Pacific has a good mix of high-quality resorts, eco-lodges, rental villas, boutique hotels, and *cabinas* (usually low-cost, freestanding cabins with more amenities than a standard room). You'll also find some of the country's priciest lodgings. As a rule, prices drop 20% to 30% during the rainy season. Hotel rooms are taxed at the national rate of 13%. Reserve as far in advance as possible during the busy dry season, especially on weekends. Near Manuel Antonio National Park, the cliff-side hotels with ocean views are the more activity-rich, attractive, and expensive places to stay. *Hotel reviews have been shortened. For full information, visit Fodors.com.*

WHAT IT COSTS IN DOLLARS			
	$	$$	$$$	$$$$
Restaurants	under $10	$10–$15	$16–$25	over $25
Hotels	under $75	$75–$150	$151–$250	over $250

Restaurant prices are the average cost of a main course at dinner or, if dinner is not served, at lunch. Hotel prices are the lowest cost of a standard double room in high season.

THE CENTRAL PACIFIC COAST

7

From Tárcoles to Quepos along Costa Rica's Pacific coast, you'll find patches of undeveloped jungle, small surf towns, and some of the country's most accessible beaches. The proximity of these strands to San José leads Costa Ricans and foreigners alike to pop down for quick weekend beach vacations. Surfers have good reason to head for the consistent waves of Playas Jacó and Hermosa, and anglers and golfers should consider Playa Herradura for its golf courses and ocean access. You might find Herradura and Jacó overrated and overdeveloped, but the latter is a good option if you're looking for shopping, surfing, and nightlife.

TÁRCOLES

90 km (54 miles) southwest of San José.

Crocodile boat tours on the Río Tárcoles are this small town's claim to fame. You don't actually have to drive to Tárcoles to do the tour, operators can pick you up in Herradura or Jacó. Budget (or time-conscious) travelers may want to simply stop near Río Tárcoles bridge where dozens of crocodiles gather on the banks. It's easy to snap a few photos from the top of the bridge, but be sure to lock your car and watch for oncoming traffic and Tourist Police, who make this a regular ticketing location for speedy drivers. The muddy river has gained a reputation as the country's dirtiest, thanks to San José's inadequate sewage system, but it amazingly remains an impressive refuge for wildlife. A huge diversity of birds results from a combination of transitional forest and the river, which houses crocodiles, herons, storks, spoonbills, and other waterbirds. This is also one of the few areas in the country where you can see scarlet macaws, which you may spot on a boat tour or while hiking in a private reserve nearby. If you have the time, drive 12 km (8 miles) south of the Río Tárcoles bridge and take a dip in the pools of Catarata Manantial de Agua Viva. As the highest waterfall in Costa Rica, these freshwater cascades are located 4 km (2½ miles) past Hotel Villa Lapas.

GETTING HERE AND AROUND

By car, head west from San José on Highway 27 to Orotina and follow the signs to Herradura, Jacó, and Quepos. After crossing the bridge over the Río Tárcoles, look for the entrance to the town of Tárcoles on the right. On the left is the dirt road that leads to the Hotel Villa Lapas and the waterfall reserve. Any bus traveling to Jacó can drop you off at the entrance to Tárcoles. Let the driver know in advance.

SPORTS AND THE OUTDOORS

BOAT TOURS

On the two-hour riverboat tours through the mangrove forest and Tárcoles River, you might see massive crocodiles, Jesus lizards, iguanas, and some of roughly 50 colorful bird species, including the roseate spoonbill and boat-billed heron. Tours reach the river's mouth, providing nice sea views, especially at sunset. ■**TIP→ Around noon is the best time to spot crocs sunbathing; bird enthusiasts prefer afternoon rides to catch scarlet macaws. During the rainy season (May to November), the river may grow too rough for boats in the afternoon.**

Crocodile Man Tour. Small scars on the hands of the two brothers who run the company are the result of the tour's most original (and optional) attraction: feeding fish to the crocs. The boats are small enough to slide up alongside the mangroves for a closer look. Transportation is provided from nearby beaches, but not from San José. Daily tours take place every two hours from 8 to 4. ⊠ *Main road into Tárcoles* 🕾 *2637–0771* ⊕ *www.crocodilemantour.com* 🖃 *$30* ⊙ *Daily 7–4.*

DIVING

Okeanos Aggressor. Eight- and 10-day dive safaris to Cocos Island operate year-round. ⊠ *Tárcoles* 🕾 *800/348–2628 in U.S.* ⊕ *www.aggressor. com* 🖃 *From $4,000.*

Undersea Hunter. The boat operates 10-day dive trips to Cocos Island year-round and is part of a fleet that also includes *Argo* and *Sea Hunter.* ⊠ *Tárcoles* 🕾 *2228–6613 in San José, 800/203–2120 in North America* ⊕ *www.underseahunter.com* 🖃 *From $5,945.*

HIKING

Catarata Manantial de Agua Viva. This is Costa Rica's tallest waterfall, cascading 600 feet into freshwater pools where you can cool off after a strenuous 3-km (2-mile) hike to the river basin. This trek is not suitable for children, the elderly, or those with health conditions. Wear proper shoes as rocks can be sharp and slippery. ⊠ *On dirt road 4 km (2½ miles) past Hotel Villa Lapas* 🕾 *8831–2980* 🖃 *$20* ⊙ *Daily 7–4.*

Sky Way. Hotel Villa Lapas manages this suspension-bridge nature walk, consisting of five bridges spread out over a 2½-km (1½-mile) old-growth-forest nature trail. You can do the trail with a guide ($40), and will most likely see scarlet macaws, yellow-billed cotinga, and the

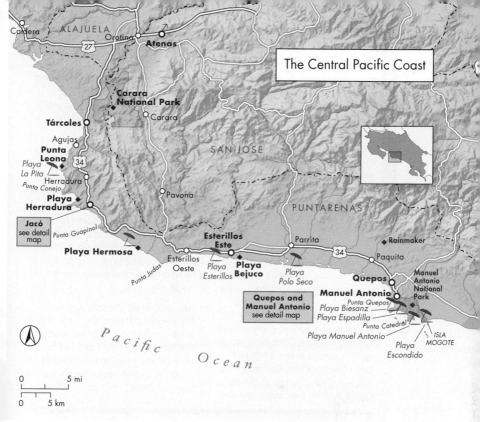

The Central Pacific Coast

Pacific Ocean

| 0 | 5 mi |
| 0 | 5 km |

black-hooded antshrike. A shuttle picks you up at the hotel. ✉ *Hotel Villa Lapas, Off Costanera, after bridge over Río Tárcoles* 🕾 *2637–0232* ⊕ *www.villalapas.com* ✈ *Sky Way $20; Guided Tours $40.*

WHERE TO EAT

$$ ✗ **Steve n' Lisa's.** A convenient location, free Wi-Fi, and good food
ECLECTIC make this roadside restaurant, just south of the entrance to Tárcoles, a popular pit stop for those traveling between San José and the Central Pacific beaches. The menu includes breakfast, lunch, and dinner with entrées that range from hamburgers and pasta to pizza and a pricey surf and turf. The seafood soup and fried chicken are popular with locals. This restaurant is on the main road to Jacó, so plan to hear the sound of semis while you dig into your rice and beans. ⑤ *Average main: $12* ✉ *On Costanera Sur, north of gas station near Río La Pita* 🕾 *2637–0665.*

WHERE TO STAY

$$ 🏨 **Hotel Villa Lapas.** Within a tranquil rain-forest preserve, the stucco
RESORT rooms here are nothing special, but are a great escape for nature lov-
FAMILY ers with their white tile floors, hardwood ceilings, and large baths.
Pros: surrounded by forest; lots of activities; birds; kid-friendly.
Cons: rooms sometimes musty; property is a bit tired looking; often busy with tour groups; patchy Wi-Fi. ⑤ *Rooms from: $150* ✉ *Off*

CLOSE UP

Diving the Deep at Cocos Island

Rated one of the top diving destinations in the world, Isla del Coco is uninhabited and remote, and its waters are teeming with marine life. It's no place for beginners, but serious divers enjoy 30-meter (100-foot) visibility and the underwater equivalent of a big-game park. Scalloped hammerheads, white-tipped reef sharks, Galápagos sharks, bottlenose dolphins, billfish, and manta rays mix with huge schools of brilliantly colored fish.

Encompassing about 22½ square km (9 square miles), Isla del Coco is one of the largest uninhabited islands on Earth. Its isolation has led to the evolution of dozens of endemic plant and animal species. The rocky topography is draped in rain forest and cloud forest and includes more than 200 waterfalls. Because of Isla del Coco's distance from shore (484 km

[300 miles]) and its craggy topography, few visitors to Costa Rica—and even fewer Costa Ricans—have set foot on the island.

Costa Rica annexed Coco in 1869, and it became a national park in 1978. Today only extremely high-priced specialty-cruise ships, park rangers, volunteers, and scientists visit this place. The dry season (November to May) brings calmer seas and is the best time to see silky sharks. During the rainy season large schools of hammerheads can be seen, but the ocean is rougher.

Two companies, *Okeanos Aggressor* and *Undersea Hunter*, offer regular 8- to 10-day dive cruises to Isla del Coco that include three days of travel time on the open ocean and cost roughly $5,000 to $6,000, depending on the boat and dates.

EN ROUTE

Costanera, 3 km (2 miles) after bridge over Río Tárcoles, turn left on dirt road for 600 m ☎ 2637-0232 ⊕ www.villalapas.com ⤳ 67 rooms ⏏ All meals; Breakfast.

Even if you choose to bypass Tárcoles and its crocodile tours, you can still get a peek at the huge reptiles as they lounge on the riverbanks: on the Costanera, pull over just after crossing the Río Tárcoles bridge and walk back onto it. Bring binoculars if you have them. ■TIP➔ Be sure to watch for traffic and lock your car—vehicles have been broken into here.

PUNTA LEONA

13 km (8 miles) south of Tárcoles.

Past Tárcoles, the first sizable beach town of the Central Pacific coast is Playa Herradura. In between, the road passes tiny Playa La Pita, then heads inland where it crosses the entrance to Punta Leona, a vast hotel and residential complex. The road then winds its way up a steep hill, atop which is the entrance to the luxury hotel Villa Caletas. On the other side of that ridge is the bay and beach of Herradura.

BEACHES

Playa La Pita. About a kilometer (½ mile) south after the entrance to Tárcoles, the Costanera passes this small beach that provides your first glimpse of the Pacific if you're coming down from San José or the Central Valley. The beach is rocky, and its proximity to the crocodile-infested Río Tárcoles makes the water murky and dangerous for swimming, but it's a nice spot to stop and admire the ocean and birds. **Amenities:** food and drink. **Best for:** walking; sunsets. ⊠ *Tárcoles.*

WHERE TO EAT AND STAY

$$$$
ECLECTIC
✕ **Mirador Restaurant.** White tablecloths, glass walls, and yellow-and-blue-checkered curtains contribute to the sophisticated but not overly stuffy atmosphere of this hotel dining room. Expensive prix-fixe meals include your choice of appetizer, main dish, and dessert. Appetizers range from the traditional escargots to a shrimp-and-lobster bisque. The entrées include beef tenderloin with chimichurri, jumbo shrimp sautéed with white wine and passion fruit, and roasted duck with truffle oil. A covered terrace below the restaurant is popular for sunset viewing over a cocktail, and offers a tapas menu that is much less expensive than choices in the main restaurant. The extensive wine list includes several blends from the region. $ *Average main: $50* ⊠ *Villa Caletas hotel, off coastal hwy., 3 km (2 miles) south of Punta Leona, Tárcoles* ☎ *2630–3000* ⊕ *www.hotelvillacaletas.com/mirador* ⊘ *No lunch.*

$$$
RESORT
Fodor's Choice
★
⌂ **Villa Caletas.** Perched 1,200 feet above the sea on a promontory south of Punta Leona, the elegant rooms sequestered in the jungle have jaw-dropping views of the surrounding foliage and sea below. **Pros:** gorgeous views; secluded setting; on-site spa; green practices. **Cons:** some rooms are musty; lots of stairs; 20-minute drive to nearest beach; pricey food and drinks. $ *Rooms from: $220* ⊠ *Off coastal hwy., 3 km (2 miles) south of Punta Leona, on right, Tárcoles* ☎ *2630–3000, 2257–3653 in San José* ⊕ *www.hotelvillacaletas.com* ⇥ *10 rooms, 31 suites, 11 villas* ⦿ *No meals.*

PLAYA HERRADURA

20 km (12 miles) south of Tárcoles.

Just north of bustling Jacó, this small beach town, named for its horseshoe-shaped bay, is made up of hotels, a golf course, and a marina. Once a sleepy fishing village, it has transformed into one of the country's fastest-developing areas. The entrance to town is marked by a shopping complex complete with fast-food chains and a surf shop. A paved road connecting the coastal highway to the beach dead-ends at the sand where three seafood shacks line the shores; the best is the more upscale El Pelicano. Golfers and sportfishing fans alike are drawn to the pristine beauty of Playa Herradura, and the placid waters tend to keep surfers farther down the coast, where waves are abundant.

GETTING HERE AND AROUND

By car, head 20 minutes straight down the Pacific Highway. The town's entrance is on the right-hand side, where a long paved road leads to the beach. Follow the signs to the Marriott.

BEACHES

Playa Herradura. If sportfishing, boating, and golfing are your priorities, this is a good option. If you're looking for nature, seclusion, a beautiful beach, or a bargain, keep driving. Rocky Playa Herradura is a poor representative of Costa Rica's breathtaking beaches, although its tranquil waters make it considerably safer for swimming and stand-up paddleboarding than most central and southern Pacific beaches. It gets its name from the Spanish word for "horseshoe," referring to the shape of the deep bay in which it lies. Playa Herradura's safety factor, coupled with the fact that it's the closest beach to San José, has turned it into a popular weekend getaway for *Josefinos,* who compete for shade beneath the sparse palms and Indian almond trees that line the beach. On the north end is Los Sueños, which includes a large marina, shopping center, hundreds of condos, a golf course, and a massive Marriott hotel. This is the sportfishing capital of Costa Rica, so expect plenty of boats anchored offshore. The rough black sand makes the water look somewhat dark and dirty at times. **Amenities:** food and drink (at hotels); toilets (at marina). **Best for:** swimming; water sports. ⊠ *Near Los Suenos Marriott, 4 km (2½ miles) north of Jacó.*

SPORTS AND THE OUTDOORS

Few activities are available directly in Playa Herradura, but that doesn't mean you have to settle for less. Most of the area's diverse outfitters can pick you up at your hotel for activities near Jacó and Playa Hermosa. Your hotel's reception desk is often a good source of information.

Costa Rica Dreams. One of the area's oldest and most reputable sportfishing outfitters offers trips to fishing grounds just an hour offshore in calm waters. As the only authorized charter operator in Los Suenos, tours leave the marina at 7 am and return at 4 pm. Sunset cruises and boat trips to Tortuga Island are also available. ⊠ *Los Sueños Marina, at charter dock at Playa Herradura* ☎ *2637–8516, 337/205–0665 in North America* ⊕ *www.costaricadreams.com* ☒ *From $1,350.*

La Iguana Golf Club. Designed by Ted Robinson, this course at Los Sueños Marriott is cradled between rain forest and ocean, allowing you to play alongside local wildlife like macaws, iguanas, and monkeys (known to steal the ball when you're not looking). The championship course is long, narrow, and well manicured, and there's a putting green, driving range, and PGA-qualified golf instructors. Overlooking the 18th hole is a restaurant where you can take a break and admire the scenery. Marriott members get a discount on the green fees, otherwise expect a pricey game of golf and expensive restaurant and pro shop. ⊠ *Los Sueños Marriott, 1 km (½ mile) west of Herradura entrance, Herradura* ☎ *2630–9151* ⊕ *www.golflaiguana.com* ☒ *$150 for 18 holes* ↑ *18 holes, 6698 yards, par 72.*

WHERE TO EAT AND STAY

$$$

SEAFOOD

✕ **Restaurante El Pelícano.** It may not look like much at first glance, but this open-air restaurant across the street from the beach serves some dishes you'd be hard-pressed to find in other casual beach-town places. The interior is limited to green-tile floors, thin wooden columns, turquoise tablecloths, and soft candlelight. Request one of the outdoor tables under the bamboo dome. Starters include fish croquettes in a lemon sauce, green peppers stuffed with shrimp and mushrooms, and clams au gratin. Grilled tuna in a mango sauce, sea bass in a heart-of-palm sauce, lobster, and tenderloin are a few of the main dishes. The most "formal" option on the beachfront, this lovely restaurant has been in operation since 1983. ⓢ *Average main: $20* ✉ *Turn left at end of main road into Playa Herradura* ☏ *2637–8910* ⊕ *elpelicanorestaurante.com.*

$$$$
RESORT
FAMILY
⌗ **Los Sueños Marriott Ocean and Golf Resort.** This mammoth multimillion-dollar resort in a palatial colonial-style building has a gorgeous view of Herradura Bay and combines modern amenities with traditional Central American decorative motifs, such as barrel-tile roofing and hand-painted tiles. **Pros:** good base for excursions; kids' club; swimming pool the size of a soccer field. **Cons:** expensive; so-so rooms and service; beach can be dirty; no Jacuzzi. ⓢ *Rooms from: $319* ✉ *1 km (½ mile) west of road to Jacó from San José, follow signs at entrance of road to Playa Herradura* ☏ *2630–9000, 888/236–2427 in North America, 2298–0000 in San José* ⊕ *www.marriott.com* ⇆ *191 rooms, 10 suites* ⏍ *Breakfast.*

JACÓ

7 km (4 miles) south of Playa Herradura, 114 km (70 miles) southwest of San José.

Its proximity to San José has made Jacó the most developed beach town in Costa Rica. Nature lovers and solitude seekers should skip this rather seedy place, which is known mostly for its nightlife, surf scene, and prostitution. More than 80 hotels and cabinas back its long, gray-sand beach, and the mix of restaurants, shops, and bars lining Avenida Pastor Díaz (the town's main drag) give it a cluttered appearance devoid of any greenery. Any real Costa Rican-ness evaporated years ago; U.S. chain hotels, casinos, restaurants, and a new shopping center have invaded the area, and you can pretty much find anything you need, from law offices and dental clinics to tattoo parlors and appliance stores. In recent years, several expats have opened a handful of cheerful cafés, restaurants, and hotels on side streets, offering a splash of color to the grungy town. Jacó does provide everything in terms of tours and outdoor activities, and makes a convenient hub for exploring neighboring beaches and attractions. Theft can be a problem here; watch your things like a hawk.

GETTING HERE AND AROUND

The drive from San José takes less than two hours; take Highway 27 west of San José beyond Orotina, and then take the exit to Jacó and Quepos. The exit, on the right after Herradura, is well marked. There's a gas station at the second entrance to town close to Club del Mar. Buses leave from San José's Terminal 7-10 station seven times daily, with an extra run on weekends.

ESSENTIALS

Banks/ATMs BAC San José. ⊠ *Centro Comercial Il Galeone* ☎ *2295–9797.*
Banco Nacional. ⊠ *Avda. Pastor Díaz* ☎ *2643–3621* ⊕ *www.bncr.fi.cr.*

Hospital Clínica Jacó. ⊠ *In front of Plaza de Deportes* ☎ *2643–1767.*

Pharmacies Farmacia Jacó. ⊠ *Plaza El Jardin, Avda. Pastor Diaz, across from Mas X Menos supermarket* ☎ *2643–3205.* **Farmacia La Economica.** ⊠ *Avda. Pastor Diaz, across from Banco Nacional* ☎ *2643–6544.*

Post Office Correos. ⊠ *Avda. Pastor Diaz, across from the municipality and Transit Police.*

Rental Cars Alamo. ⊠ *Avda. Pastor Díaz, 50 m south of Subway* ☎ *2643–1752* ⊕ *www.alamocostarica.com.* **Budget.** ⊠ *Avda. Pastor Díaz, 200 m south of Hotel Tangeri* ☎ *2643–2665* ⊕ *www.budget.co.cr.* **Economy.** ⊠ *Avda. Pastor Díaz, 100 m south of Best Western* ☎ *2643–1098* ⊕ *www.economyrentacar.com.* **Hertz.** ⊠ *Beside Hotel Tangerí, in front of Kentucky Fried Chicken* ☎ *2221–1818* ⊕ *www.hertz.com.*

Taxis Taxi services. ⊠ *Jacó* ☎ *2643–2020, 2643–2121, 2643–3030.*

BEACHES

Playa Jacó. This long, palm-lined beach west of town is a pleasant enough spot in the morning but can burn the soles of your feet on a sunny afternoon. Though the gray sand and beachside construction make this spot less attractive than most other Costa Rican beaches, it's a good place to soak up the sun or enjoy a sunset. The beach is popular with surfers for the consistency of its waves, but when the surf is up, swimmers should beware of dangerous rip currents. Smaller waves make this beach ideal for surf lessons or longboarders. Bigger waves are found 5 km (3 miles) south at Playa Hermosa. During the rainy months the ocean here is not very clean. The stretch near Jacó Laguna Resort is less crowded and their Tiki Bar is a great spot to grab a cocktail at sunset. **Amenities:** food and drink; toilets (at local restaurants and hotels). **Best for:** sunsets; surfing. ⊠ *Jacó.*

SPORTS AND THE OUTDOORS

TOUR OPERATORS

You don't have to physically step into any tour office, because everyone from a reception desk attendant to a boutique salesperson can book you a local adventure. Almost every tour can pick you up at your hotel's doorstep. ■TIP➔ Keep in mind that part of your price tag includes the salesperson's commission, so if you hear higher or lower prices from two different people, it's likely a reflection of a shift in the commission. You can try negotiating a better deal directly from the outfitter.

Gray Line Costa Rica. Specializing in transportation services, Gray Line also arranges day trips from Jacó to Arenal and Poás volcanoes, Manuel Antonio National Park, Sarchí, Isla Tortuga, and raft trips on the Savegre River. ⊠ *Best Western Jacó Beach Resort* ☎ *2220–2126 in San José, 800/719–3905 in U.S.* ⊕ *www.graylinecostarica. com* ⊠ *Sightseeing from $59; rafting from $99.*

CANOPY TOURS

Fodor's Choice ★ **Rainforest Adventures.** A modified ski lift offers easy access to the tropical transitional forest, with eight-seat gondolas that float through the treetops within a 222-acre private nature reserve. The company has guided tours that explain aspects of the local ecology, sustainability

> ### RIPTIDES
>
> Riptides (or rip currents), common in Jacó and Manuel Antonio's Playa Espadilla, are dangerous and have led to many deaths over the years. If you get caught in one, don't panic and don't try to swim against it as paddling to shore will simply expend your energy. Riptides are generally less than 100 feet wide, so simply swim parallel to shore until you feel the power dissipate. Once you are out of the current, swim back to the beach. The best policy is not to go in deeper than your waist when the waves loom large, and never swim alone.

programs, as well as a variety of eco-adventures. There is also a small serpentarium, a butterfly garden, a bat sanctuary, and a medicinal plant garden. A "Tranopy" tour combines the tram with a 10-cable zip-line tour. A top attraction is a 164-foot waterfall climbing tour that includes zip lines, forest trekking, and a free fall. The International Ecotourism Society named Rainforest Adventures one of the most sustainable theme parks in the world. It is also considered to be one of the safest due to their double cables, chest harnesses, platform railings, certified guides, braking system, and high-tech equipment inspected annually. ⊠ *3 km (2 miles) west of Jacó* ☎ *2257–5961, 866/759–8726 in North America* ⊕ *www.rainforestadventure.com* ⊠ *From $20.*

HORSEBACK RIDING

■**TIP→** When selecting a horseback-riding company, make sure the horses look healthy, cared for, and well fed, since some local outfitters place profits over the welfare of the horses.

Discovery Horseback Tours. A British couple runs these 2½-hour trail rides on healthy horses. You'll spend some time in the rain forest and also stop at a small waterfall where you can take a dip. Another tour takes you on a sunset ride on the beach. An alternate tour runs three hours and takes in a small village and butterfly farm. For experienced riders only, the "Trail Less Traveled" is a 2½-hour challenging ride through rivers and rain forest. Tours start at 8:30 and 2:30 weekdays, 8:30 only on Saturday. ⊠ *Jacó* ☎ *2643–7151* ⊕ *www.horseridecostarica.com* ⊠ *From $75; cash only.*

KAYAKING AND CANOEING

Kayak Jacó. Looking for waters calmer than those at Jacó Beach? Kayak Jacó takes you to Playa Agujas for sea-kayaking tours and Hawaiian-style outrigger canoe trips. The half-day tours include snorkeling (conditions permitting) at secluded beaches. A 2½-hour night tour starts at sunset and ends with s'mores and a bonfire on the beach. ⊠ *Playa Agujas* ☎ *2643–1233* ⊕ *www.kayakjaco.com* ✉ *From $70. Transportation to/from your hotel $20.*

SURFING

Jacó has several beach breaks, all of which are best around high tide. Surfboard-toting tourists abound in Jacó, but you don't need to be an expert to enjoy the surf, as waves are often small enough for beginners, especially around low tide. Abundant surf shops rent boards and give lessons, usually closer to the south end of the beach where most surf schools set up camp. Prices range from $50 to $60 for two hours and usually include a board and transportation. If you plan to spend more than a week surfing, it might be cheaper to buy a used board and sell it back at the standard half price before you leave. Otherwise, you'll be paying airline transportation fees around $150 (one way), and most likely your board will arrive damaged despite your bubble-wrapping efforts. For rental, Jacó has plenty of surf shops with solid quivers, with cheaper boards starting at $10 an hour. If you don't have much experience, don't go out when the waves are really big—Jacó sometimes gets very powerful swells, which result in dangerous rip currents. During the rainy season, waves are more consistent than in the dry months, when Jacó sometimes lacks surf.

Dominical Surf Lessons. Owned and operated by Costa Rican Surf Champion Debbie Zec, this Jaco-based surf school holds lessons at several local breaks and can take surfers to nearby Playa Dominical between Quepos and Uvita. Their standard ratio is two students per instructor, and they offer two-hour beginner courses. Rates include equipment and drinking water. ⊠ *Jacó* ☎ *8927–3450* ⊕ *www.dominicalsurflessons. com* ✉ *From $54.*

School of the World. This unique language school offers one-day workshops in everything from photography and salsa dancing to yoga and stand-up paddleboarding, but they specialize in Spanish and surfing lessons. ⊠ *Off Avda. Pastor Díaz, 300 m east of POPS* ⊹ *Turn left after Condominiums Nasua, 50 m on the left* ☎ *2643–2462, 305/517–7689 in U.S.* ⊕ *www.schooloftheworld.org* ✉ *From $35.*

Tortuga Surf School. Private surf lessons with Tortuga include board rental, water, fruit, and ISA-certified instructors (International Surfing Association). They also offer five- and seven-day Surf and Stay camps that combine lodging, lessons, and local excursions. ⊠ *Hotel Perico Azul, C. Santana and Avda. Pastor Diaz* ☎ *2643–3348* ⊕ *www. tortugasurfcamp.com* ✉ *From $50, cash only.*

SWIMMING

The big waves and dangerous rip currents that make surfing so popular here can make swimming dangerous. Lifeguards are on duty only at specific spots, and only sporadically. If the ocean is rough, stay on the beach—dozens of swimmers have drowned here over the years.

When the ocean is calm, especially around low tide, you can swim just about anywhere along Jacó Beach. The sea is always calmer near the beach's northern and southern ends, but the ocean bottom is littered

CLOSE UP

Surf Slang

Barrel: The area created when a wave breaks onto itself in a curl, creating a surfable tube that's the surfer's nirvana. Also called the "green room."

Drop in: To stand up and drop down the face of a wave. Also used when one surfer cuts another off: "Hey, don't drop in on that guy!"

Duck dive: A maneuver where the surfer first pushes his or her board underwater and then dives with it, ducking under waves that have already broken or are about to break. It's difficult with a longboard (see Turtle roll).

Goofy foot: Having a right-foot-forward stance on the surfboard. The opposite is known as "regular."

Close out: When a wave or a section of a wave breaks all at once, rather than breaking steadily in one

direction. A frustrating situation for surfers, giving them nowhere to go as the wave comes crashing down.

Ding: A hole, dent, crack, or other damage to a board.

Grom: A young surfer, usually under 15, who "rips" or "kills it" (is amazing).

Kook: Someone (usually a beginner) trying to pass as a surfer.

Outside: The area farther out from where waves are most regularly breaking. Surfers line up here to catch waves.

Stick: A surfboard.

Turtle roll: A maneuver where the surfer rolls over on the surfboard, going underwater and holding the board upside down. Used by longboarders and beginners to keep from being swept back toward shore by breaking waves.

with rocks there, as it is in front of the small rivers that flow into the sea near the middle of this beach.

WHERE TO EAT

$$
ECLECTIC
✕**Graffiti Restro Cafe and Wine Bar.** The gritty-gourmet concept of this Jacó hot spot plays with the senses, starting with an interior that blends graffiti with soft candlelight and funk music. The menu features fresh, locally grown ingredients, which go into dishes like cacao-and-coffee-rubbed beef tenderloin and a tuna-tartare tower that melts in your mouth. For something with a kick, try the snook seasoned with five Caribbean spices and topped with caramel soy. If you've dined elsewhere, drop by this understated spot to listen to live music on Wednesday and Friday. Sample a signature martini with lemongrass and ginger or cucumber and basil, and indulge in one of the extraordinary desserts like chocolate cheesecake or peanut-butter-and-banana flambé. $ *Average main: $15* ✉ *Pacific Center No. 23, Avda. Pastor Díaz, across from Hotel Tangeri* ☎ *2643–1708* ⊕ *www.graffiticr.com* ۞ *Closed Sun. No lunch.*

$$
CAFÉ
✕**Green Room.** Bordered by a white picket fence, this charming café serves meals prepared with organic ingredients delivered daily by local farmers. A tin roof draped in silk, concrete floors, wooden tables, and local art offer a cheerful escape from the grime of Avenida Pastor Diaz.

CLOSE UP

Tips for a First-time Surfer

If you're a first-timer, there are a few things you need to know before getting in the water.

Pick your beach carefully. Sámara is a good choice, as is Jacó or Tamarindo. You want beach breaks and small, gentle waves with some white wash to push you to shore. Make sure to ask about riptides.

Expect introductory lessons to cover the basics. You'll learn how to lie on the board, paddle out, pass the incoming waves, and how to pop up on your board. If you're a natural, you'll be able to hop up and stay standing in the white wash of the wave after it breaks.

Have realistic expectations. Even if you have experience in other board sports, like snowboarding or skateboarding, don't expect to be surfing on the face of the wave or tucking into barrels on your first day. It literally takes years before you can reach that level.

Choose the right gear. If you're a beginner, start on a longboard, preferably made of foam (aka, "soft top surfboard"). Be sure to wear a rashguard or a wet suit to help protect your chest and stomach from getting scraped or stung by jellyfish. Hydrate, and apply sunscreen.

The ever-changing chalkboard menu usually features home-ground burgers with fresh-baked buns or seared ahi on buckwheat noodles with roasted vegetables. Breakfasts are hearty, ranging from banana pancakes to eggs Florentine. Salads are topped with fresh strawberries, and cocktails are made with natural fruit juice—try the lemon basil margarita. You're likely to hear Jack Johnson on the stereo by day and live acoustic by night. ⑤ *Average main: $10* ⊠ *Corner of Avda. Pastor Diaz and C. Cocal* ☎ *2643–4425.*

$$
\$\$ \qquad ✕ **Side Street Bisto.** By the creators of Graffiti Restro, this laid-back bistro
$$

\$\$
BISTRO
Fodor's Choice
★

✕ **Side Street Bisto.** By the creators of Graffiti Restro, this laid-back bistro dishes up fresh salads, baked goods, nano brews, and gourmet sandwiches on artisanal brick-oven breads. It takes two hands to keep the portobello sandwich together, which is oozing with baby Swiss, caramelized onion, and organic spinach. Beautifully seared with a soy glaze, the tuna steak sandwich is topped with wasabi aioli and guacamole. Sides range from quinoa salad and fruit skewers to homemade potato chips and thick-cut fries. Garden cocktails are muddled with all sorts of goodness like honey, pear, lime, sage, rosemary, and basil. The breezy green spaces under Jacó's oldest tree give the place a casual, airy feel indicative of the surf lifestyle. On Sunday mornings there's free yoga at 9 followed by bottomless mimosas with brunch, and live reggae at 1. Be sure to check out the Nano Brew Closet where they make their hand-crafted beers. On your way out, grab one of the gigantic cookies with dark chunks of chocolate. ⑤ *Average main: $11* ⊠ *C. Copacabana, 250 m south of Best Western, 20 m west of Bar Isaga* ☎ *2643–2724* ⊙ *No dinner Mon.–Thurs.*

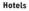

Hotels ▼

Nightlife ▼

Restaurants ▼

Shopping ▼

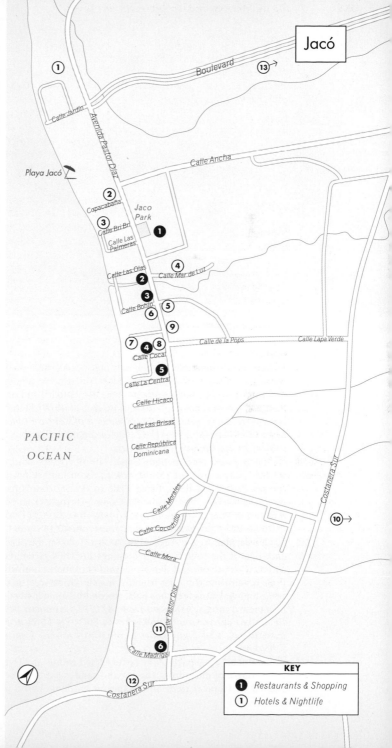

Jacó

Boulevard

Calle Jardín

Calle Ancha

Playa Jacó

Copacabana

Jaco Park

Calle Bri Bri

Calle Las Palmeras

Calle Las Otas

Calle Mar de Luz

Calle Bohío

Calle de la Pops

Calle Lapa Verde

Calle Cocal

Calle La Central

Calle Hicaco

Calle Las Brisas

Calle República Dominicana

PACIFIC OCEAN

Calle Morales

Calle Cocodrillo

Calle Mora

Avenida Pastor Díaz

Costanera Sur

Calle Pastor Díaz

Calle Madrigal

Costanera Sur

KEY

1 *Restaurants & Shopping*

① *Hotels & Nightlife*

A beautiful heron perched near the beach at Jacó.

WHERE TO STAY

$$
HOTEL
FAMILY

Apartotel Flamboyant. Though nothing special, these small beachfront rooms and apartments, many with kitchenettes, are a good deal. **Pros:** beachfront; good value; secure parking; all standard and superior rooms have a/c. **Cons:** very simple rooms; no meals; no Wi-Fi in rooms; rocky beach. $ *Rooms from: $97 ✉ 100 m west of Centro Comercial Il Galeone* ☎ *2643–3146, 2643–1732* ⊕ *www.apartotelflamboyant.com* ⤴ *8 rooms, 14 apartments* ⵔ *No meals.*

$$
HOTEL

Canciones del Mar Boutique Hotel. The poetically named "Songs of the Sea" is tranquil and intimate, with rooms and suites that overlook the sea or lush gardens. **Pros:** close to ocean; rooms have kitchens; wheelchair-access room available. **Cons:** basic breakfast; property needs renovation; some dark rooms. $ *Rooms from: $140 ✉ End of C. Bri Bri* ☎ *2643–3273* ⊕ *www.cancionesdelmar.com* ⤴ *16 suites* ⵔ *Breakfast.*

$$$
RESORT

Club del Mar. At the second entrance to Jacó on the beach's southern end, one of the town's better lodgings includes green-and-cream-hue rooms with private teak balconies and extremely comfortable condos. **Pros:** beachfront; tranquil; friendly; lush grounds; tasteful design. **Cons:** some highway noise reaches back to condos; some insects; no bathtubs in standard rooms. $ *Rooms from: $211 ✉ Costanera, 300 m south of El Arroyo gas station* ☎ *2643–3194, 866/978–5669 in North America* ⊕ *www.clubdelmarcostarica.com* ⤴ *10 rooms, 1 suite, 22 condos* ⵔ *No meals.*

$$$
HOTEL

DoceLunas. The spacious, teak-furnished rooms at "Twelve Moons" are a couple of miles from the sea and sand, set amid 5 acres of lawns shaded by tropical trees and luxuriant gardens with a mountainous green backdrop. **Pros:** more secluded than other Jacó lodgings; terrific restaurant; two rooms for mobility-impaired guests; beautiful grounds. **Cons:** 10-minute walk to beach; some rooms are rather dark; Wi-Fi in common areas only. ⑤ *Rooms from: $186* ⊠ *On coastal hwy. from San José, pass the 1st entrance to Jacó; take dirt road on left with signs for Docelunas at main entrance to Quebrada Seca* ☎ *2643–2211* ⊕ *www. docelunas.com* ⏎ *12 rooms, 8 suites* ❍| *Breakfast.*

$$

HOTEL

FAMILY

⌕ **Hotel Mar de Luz.** A few blocks from the beach, this family-focused property boasts three swimming pools, equipped kitchens, and comfortable rooms of varying size and style. **Pros:** attentive owner; solar-powered property; close to the beach; good breakfasts. **Cons:** some rooms are musty with lukewarm water; bathrooms need renovation; thin walls. ⑤ *Rooms from: $130* ⊠ *C. Mar de Luz, behind Subway, east of Avda. Pastor Díaz* ☎ *2643–3000* ⊕ *www.mardeluz.com* ⏎ *27 rooms, 2 suites* ❍| *Breakfast.*

$$$

HOTEL

FAMILY

Fodor'sChoice

★

⌕ **Hotel Pumilio.** A peaceful retreat just five minutes outside bustling Jacó, this all-suites hotel is surrounded by lush rain forest and has tastefully decorated rooms with fully equipped kitchens and patios overlooking the pool, mountains, and gardens. **Pros:** quiet location; beautiful and clean rooms; good online promotions; excellent staff. **Cons:** far from beach; restaurant serves breakfast only; $8 taxi ride into town; very firm beds. ⑤ *Rooms from: $200* ⊠ *From Herradura's stoplight 2 km (1 mile) on Rte. 34 south, 1 km (½ mile) to the left* ☎ *2643–5678, 800/410–8018 in U.S.* ⊕ *www.hotelpumilio.com* ⏎ *10 rooms* ❍| *Breakfast.*

$$$

HOTEL

⌕ **Jacó Laguna Resort.** On the quiet southern end of Jacó beach, this property is clean and comfortable and just far enough from town to offer a peaceful night of sleep. **Pros:** in low season, guests are generously upgraded; great Tiki Bar; ideal location. **Cons:** hallway noise; poor lighting in rooms; weak Wi-Fi signal in some rooms; mattresses lack support. ⑤ *Rooms from: $175* ⊠ *Corner of C. Madrigal and Avda. Pastor Díaz* ☎ *2643–3362, 215/942–5135 in U.S.* ⊕ *www.jacolagunaresort. com* ⏎ *26 rooms* ❍| *Breakfast.*

NIGHTLIFE

Whereas other beach towns may have a bar or two, Jacó has an avenue full of them, with enough variety for many different tastes. After-dinner spots range from restaurants perfect for a quiet drink to loud bars with pool tables and dance clubs. You can even try your luck at one of the town's casinos.

BARS

La Perla. The large corner bar and wooden chairs and tables are great for a laid-back cocktail, people-watching, and tropical feel. They have two-for-one mojitos and margaritas all day, every day. ⊠ *Corner of Avda. Pastor Díaz and C. Bohío, across from Orange Pub* ☎ *2643–3326.*

Le Loft. This chic club is popular with locals and surfers who like to party until the sun comes up. Plan to stand in line behind a velvet rope for a while, unless you have an "in" with the bouncer. Above all, dress to impress. ⊠ *Red bldg. across from Los Amigos and Pops, 2nd fl.* ☎ *8834–0065* ▣ *$10; free for women* ☾ *Closed Mon.*

Los Amigos. Sports fans can get their fix at this lively restaurant and bar with nine plasma TVs, two projectors, and six satellite feeds hosting every sporting event imaginable. Cold air conditioning, cheap eats, and draft beers make this one of the most popular spots in town. ⊠ *Corner of Avda. Pastor Diaz and C. Pops* ☎ *2643–2961* ⊕ *www.losamigosjaco.com.*

Orange Pub. This is a good choice for a cocktail, after-dinner drinks, or a late-night meal. It has a big bar in back, pool tables, and DJs and dancing on weekends. ⊠ *Avda. Pastor Díaz, north of Il Galeone mall, across from C. Bohio* ☎ *2643–3387* ⊙ *Closed Tues., Wed., and Sun.*

CASINOS

Croc's Casino. Only in Jacó would you find a mini Las Vegas, with a casino of slot machines, table games, sexy dealers, and free cocktails for gamblers. There's always a game on the big screen and country music playing poolside. For those who've had one too many rounds, you can stay the night at the massive Croc's resort, which is comfortable but devoid of Costa Rican character. ⊠ *Jacó* ✛ *Take second entrance into Jaco at the Maxi Pali store. Follow the "T", turn right, casino is ½ mile down on the left, oceanfront* ☎ *800/809–5503 in U.S. or Canada, 2643–1180* ⊕ *www.crocscasinoresort.com.*

LIVE MUSIC

Side Street Bistro. This colorful bistro has live music several days of the week and handcrafted brews made in house. Drop by on Sundays at 1 for brunch and reggae. ⊠ *C. Copacabana, 250 m south of Best Western, 20 m west of Bar Isaga* ☎ *2643–2724.*

SHOPPING

Souvenir shops with mostly the same mass-produced merchandise are crowded one after the other along the main street in the center of town. Most of the goods, like wooden crafts and seed jewelry, are run-of-the-mill souvenir fare, but a few shops have more unusual items. If you plan on buying any surf-related products, this is your place, as even surf wax is hard to come by once you leave Jacó. Construction is underway on Jaco Walk, a massive shopping center slated to host retail stores, restaurants, entertainment venues, cultural exhibits, and business offices all in one open space. Several shops and restaurants opened in late 2016, and the full complex is expected to be finished by 2020.

CRAFTS

Cocobolo. Named for the tropical hardwood of the Cocobolo tree, this large shop is jam-packed with wooden handicrafts hanging from the ceiling, walls, and shelves. It's much of what you find in other stores, but with more tasteful items and a richer variety. In addition to wood carvings, they sell clothing, hammocks, jewelry, and locally made crafts. ⊠ *Avda. Pastor Díaz, 300 m north of Banco Nactional, next to Jass Surf Shop* ☎ *2643–3486.*

FOOD AND CANDY

Costa Rica Coffee Experience (*Fruity Monkey Poop*). For locally grown coffee and reasonably priced artisan crafts, this place offers the best shopping in Jacó. They serve marvelous iced coffees, natural iced teas, and fresh-roasted coffee. Be sure to try a sample of their chocolate, pineapple licorice, and "Fruity Monkey Poop" (actually just candied nuts). ⊠ *Avda. Pastor Díaz, across from Banco Nacional & Mas x Menos market* ☎ *2643–6197.*

SPORTING GOODS

Cartón. Cartón sells new and used boards and shapes for some of Costa Rica's top surfers. It's not only the shape, but also the artwork that makes Cartón's boards so extraordinary. Boards can be shipped internationally for around $80. Their two-hour surf lessons are held just past the surf shop at Madrigal Beach. ⊠ *C. Madrigal, near the gas station* ☎ *2643–3762* ⊕ *www.cartonsurfboards.com.*

Jass Surf Shop. As Jacó's first surf shop, this well-stocked store has a good variety of surf gear at decent prices. They sell new and used surfboards and stand-up paddleboards, and will buy back your board at the end of your trip for half the purchase price. Two-hour surf lessons cost $45. ⊠ *Avda. Pastor Diaz, next to La Perla, 200 m north of Banco Nacional* ☎ *2643–3850* ⊕ *www.jasssurfshop.com.*

PLAYA HERMOSA

5 km (3 miles) south of Jacó, 113 km (70 miles) southwest of San José.

On the other side of the rocky ridge that forms the southern edge of Jacó Beach is Playa Hermosa, a swath of dark-gray sand and driftwood stretching southeast as far as the eye can see, with consistent waves for surfers. For nonsurfers, outdoor options include horseback and canopy tours in the nearby forested hills, but all of these can be done from other beaches. As for the town itself, there's really not much, which is part of the attraction for travelers who want to escape Jacó's crowds and concrete towers. Most of the restaurants, bars, and hotels have cropped up one after the other on a thin stretch separating the highway and the beach. From June to December, olive ridley turtles nest on the beach at night, especially when there's not much moonlight. ■TIP→ Note: there is a second Playa Hermosa on the Guanacaste Pacific coast.

GETTING HERE AND AROUND

If you have a car, take the coastal highway 5 km (3 miles) past Jacó. You'll see the cluster of businesses on the right. If you don't have your own transportation, take a taxi from Jacó or a local bus toward Quepos.

BEACHES

Playa Hermosa. Despite its name, "Beautiful Beach" is hardly spectacular. The southern half of the wide beach lacks palm trees or other shade-providing greenery; its sand is scorching hot in the afternoon; and frequent rip currents make it unsafe to swim when there are waves. But board riders find beauty in its consistent, hollow surf breaks. Beginner surfers should stick to Jacó since waves here are powerful and punchy, and will close out on big days. The beach's northern end is popular because it often has waves when other spots are flat, and the ocean is cleaner than at Jacó, except after heavy rains when there is floating debris. There is also plenty of forest covering the hills, and scarlet macaws sometimes gather in the Indian almond trees near the end of the beach. Amenities are all at the Backyard Bar. **Amenities:** food and drink; showers; toilets. **Best for:** sunsets; surfing. ⊠ *Playa Hermosa.*

7

SPORTS AND THE OUTDOORS

You can arrange activities throughout the Central Pacific from Playa Hermosa. Most tour operators and outfitters include transportation in their prices. *For more options, see Sports and the Outdoors in Jacó, above, or consult your hotel's reception.*

NATURE AND WILDLIFE TOURS

Chiclets Canopy Tour. Guided daily tours (7 and 9 am; 1 and 3:30 pm) take you through the rain-forest

> ### NOT THAT PLAYA HERMOSA
>
> "¡Ojo!" as they say. Watch out: Costa Rica has two Playa Hermosas. Don't confuse this one with the larger, more developed beach of the same name on the Guanacaste Pacific coast. Each has its fans, but the Central Pacific's Playa Hermosa is better known to Costa Ricans and to surfers.

canopy to 15 platforms and a suspension bridge. Cables strung between platforms perched high in a dozen trees have views of tropical foliage, wildlife, and the nearby coast. ⊠ *West of Costanera, ½ km (¼ mile) north of Hermosa* ☎ *2643–1880* ✉ *Tour $60.*

Playa Hermosa Turtle Tours. Raúl Fernández takes small groups to look for nesting sea turtles on Playa Hermosa between July and December, as part of a project to collect the eggs and raise them in a hatchery. The best months to spot nesting turtles are September–November. Tour times vary depending on the tide; he can provide transportation from hotels in Jacó. ⊠ *Playa Hermosa* ☎ *8817–0385* ✉ *Tour $45.*

SURFING

Most people who bed down at Playa Hermosa are here for the same reason—the waves that break just a shell's toss away. There are half a dozen breaks scattered along the beach's northern end, and the surf is always best around high tide. Hermosa's conditions change rapidly depending on the tides, wind, and swell activity. Because it is a beach break, though, the waves here often close out, especially when the surf is more than 8 feet. If you don't have much experience, don't go out when the waves are really big—Hermosa sometimes gets very powerful swells, which result in dangerous rip currents. If you're a beginner, don't go out at all. Surf instructors in Hermosa take their students to Jacó, an easier place to learn the sport. If you need to rent a board, some hotels have their own quiver and will allow you to rent by the hour ($10).

Nika Surfboards. For all your surfing needs, Nika has ding repair, surf lessons, and boards for rent or sale. ⊠ *Costanera, 4 km (2½ miles) south of Hermosa on road to Esterillos* ☎ *2643–2871* ⊕ *www.nikasurfboards. com* ✉ *2-hour lessons $50.*

WHERE TO EAT AND STAY

$$ ✕ **The Backyard Bar.** Playa Hermosa's original nightlife spot has two
ECLECTIC seating areas, each with its own bar. Television sets on the wraparound bar in the front room show sports matches and surf videos. A wooden deck in back overlooking the beach is great for lunch and sunset, mostly because of the pleasant sea breezes and view of the surfers. The usual bar food—Tex-Mex standards and burgers—is complemented by fresh seafood, including ceviche, grilled tuna, lobster, and jumbo shrimp. It's

popular especially on Friday and Saturday, when there's a surf contest at 4 pm and live music at 6 pm. $ *Average main: $11* ⊠ *Costanera, southern end of town, next to The Backyard Hotel* ☎ 2643-7011 ⊕ *www.backyardhotel.com.*

$$
HOTEL
The Backyard Hotel. Surfers are the main clientele in these nice rooms with high ceilings, clay-tile floors, and sliding-glass doors that open onto semiprivate balconies and terraces, most of which have good views of Playa Hermosa. **Pros:** steps from the surf; gated parking; friendly staff. **Cons:** noise from bar next door; bland breakfast; thin sheets and towels; pricey food. $ *Rooms from: $133* ⊠ *Costanera, southern end of town* ☎ 2643-7011 ⊕ *www.backyardhotel.com* ↝ *6 rooms, 2 suites* ❙◎❙ *Breakfast.*

$$
HOTEL
Casa Mia. Hidden from public view behind high walls and a large fortress-style wooden door, intimate Casa Mia (formerly Casa Pura Vida) is one of the best places to stay in Playa Hermosa. **Pros:** well maintained; communal kitchen; beachfront; excellent value. **Cons:** not all rooms have ocean views; no meals; 50% non-refundable deposit; beach has strong undertow. $ *Rooms from: $85* ⊠ *Costanera, 200 m south of soccer field* ☎ 2643-3490 ⊕ *casamiacostarica.com* ↝ *7 rooms, 1 apartment* ❙◎❙ *No meals.*

$$
B&B/INN
Surf Inn. Right in front of Hermosa's beach break, a mural of tall palms and peeling waves marks the entrance to this well-priced inn which offers small apartments and studios. **Pros:** surfers' paradise; decent rates; kitchens in rooms; almost half price in low season. **Cons:** noise from neighboring bar; studios are dark; no meals; two-night minimum stay on weekends and holidays. $ *Rooms from: $120* ⊠ *Costanera, next to Backyard Hotel, 200 m south of soccer field* ⊕ *www.surfinnhermosa.com* ↝ *4 studios, 2 apartments* ❙◎❙ *No meals.*

ESTERILLOS ESTE

20 km (12 miles) southeast of Playa Hermosa, 3 km (2 miles) northwest of Playa Bejuco.

Just 20 minutes southeast of Jacó, Playa Esterillos is divided into three sections; Este (East), Central, and Oeste (West). While Esterillos Oeste and Central are inhabited by locals, the undeveloped area of Esterillos Este is where you'll find several boutique hotels capitalizing on the seclusion and beachfront location. Head-high waves break year-round, making it one of the most consistent surf spots in Costa Rica. At low tide, the dark stretch of sand is unbelievably wide, inviting beachcombers for a leisurely stroll. Almond trees and swaying palms frame the shoreline, and you can walk for miles without seeing another soul. If you want to get away from it all, the isolation and "best-kept secret" feel make Esterillos Este the perfect escape.

GETTING HERE AND AROUND
From Playa Hermosa, head 20 km (12 miles) south on the coastal highway (Costanera). Pass Esterillos Oeste and Esterillos Central before turning right onto the dirt road labeled Esterillos Este. Continue ½ km (¼ mile) to the beach road and follow the signs in either direction to your hotel.

ESSENTIALS

The nearest medical facilities are at the hospital in Parrita, 15 minutes south on the coastal highway. Construction is underway for a shopping center outside of Esterillos Este past Playa Bejuco: a grocery store, gym, and several shops are open, and other services including an ATM are in the works. Supplies are also available at the Mini Super in Playa Bejuco or at the Super Sol in Esterillos Oeste. Other services can be found north in Jacó or south in Parrita.

BEACHES

Playa Esterillos. Serious surfers from Jacó and Playa Hermosa head to Playa Esterillos to ditch the crowds when waves are pumping. This isolated beach break dishes up hollow barrels, and gets more swell than neighboring surf spots. It works best at high tide with a south or southwest swell direction, but beginners will want to stay clear of the pounding waves. Lessons ($60) and board rental ($20) can be organized through Encantada Ocean Cottages, but if you're a novice surfer, it's best to stick to the inside whitewash with supervision. At low tide, this dark beach looks like a chocolate field, perfect for beachcombing or an afternoon stroll. You can walk for miles without seeing another set of prints in the sand. Other than a couple sodas in Esterillos Oeste, there are no beach amenities, and those within local hotels are exclusively for guests. Just offshore in Esterillos Oeste is a mermaid statue that you can walk to at low tide. If you drive here, don't leave any valuables in the car. **Amenities:** parking (roadside; free). **Best for:** solitude; surfing. ⊠ *Playa Esterillos, Costanera Sur, 20 mins south of Playa Jacó, Esterillos Este.*

SPORTS AND THE OUTDOORS

HORSEBACK RIDING

The Riding Adventure. Beach riding is the specialty here. Trips set out from a cattle ranch 20 minutes south of Jacó and include a stop at a waterfall for swimming or trail walking. Tours take place twice daily and include an optional lunch for an additional $10. Transportation from your hotel can be arranged for $10, or you can start at the meeting point for beach tours next to Monterey Del Mar Hotel in Esterillos Este. ⊠ *Monterey Del Mar Hotel, Esterillos Este* 🕿 *8834–8687, 8733–1972* ⊕ *www.theridingadventure.com* 🖅 *From $65* ⊙ *Tours Wed.–Mon. at 8 am and 2:30 pm.*

WHERE TO STAY

$$$$ · HOTEL · 🖫 **Alma Del Pacifico Beach Hotel & Spa.** Combining Costa Rica's vibrant architecture with modern design, this tranquil property offers spacious rooms and colorful beach bungalows with indoor-outdoor rain showers and private gardens. **Pros:** promotions on website; spacious rooms; creative and colorful design; very private. **Cons:** wild beach; hard mattresses; simple breakfast; far from town. ⑤ *Rooms from: $305* ⊠ *3 km (2 miles) north of Playa Bejuco, next to Encantada Cottages, Esterillos Este* 🕿 *2778–7070, 303/459–7939 in North America* ⊕ *www. almadelpacifico.com* 🖙 *20 rooms* ⑩ *Breakfast.*

$$
HOTEL
FAMILY
Fodor's Choice
★

Encantada Ocean Cottages. Framing a blue-tiled pool are freestanding cottages with thoughtful and creative touches like luxurious bedding atop artsy bed frames (made from repurposed pallets), colorful throws, polished cement floors, and lofts with twin beds. **Pros:** peaceful location; surf lessons and board rental available and daily yoga classes; comfy beds; 24-hour security. **Cons:** neighbor's barking dog next to beachfront suite; often full; no shower curtains. ⑤ *Rooms from: $135* ✉ *Next to Alma Del Pacifico Beach Hotel, Esterillos Este* ☎ *2778–7048, 855/580–0006 in North America* ⊕ *www.encantadacostarica.com* ⇆ *6 cottages, 1 villa* ⁜ *Breakfast.*

PLAYA BEJUCO

27 km (16 miles) south of Playa Hermosa, 32 km (19 miles) south of Jacó.

Serious surfers wanting to escape the crowds at Jacó and Playa Hermosa, or anyone simply seeking to stray from the beaten path, need drive only 20 minutes south to Playa Bejuco's relatively deserted, palm-lined beach. One could stroll for an hour along the light-gray swath of sand and rarely encounter a soul. Several vacation homes and two small hotels sit behind the first part of the beach, and behind them is a large mangrove forest where you might see macaws or white-faced monkeys. Most locals survive on farming and fishing, meaning this area is relatively undeveloped other than the occasional soda serving up rice and beans.

GETTING HERE AND AROUND
If you have a car, take coastal Highway 27 km (16 miles) south past Playa Hermosa to the turnoff for Playa Bejuco, which is 1 km (½ mile) west of the highway. If you don't have a car, take a taxi from Jacó, or local bus toward Quepos.

BEACHES
Playa Bejuco. The surf here is as big and consistent as at Playa Hermosa, but with a fraction of the surfers. As at Hermosa, dangerous rip currents develop, so swimmers should go in no deeper than their waist when the waves are big. Aside from surfing and beachcombing, there is little to do here, which makes it a good place for people wanting to do nothing at all. Like most surrounding beaches, Bejuco has dark brown sand with the occasional palm tree offering shade on the shore. The mosquitoes can be quite fearsome during the rainy months. Amenities are at neighboring Delfín Beach Resort and Hotel Playa Bejuco. **Amenities:** food and drink; toilets. **Best for:** solitude; surfing. ✉ *35 km (22 miles) north of Manuel Antonio and 30 km (19 miles) south of Jacó.*

SPORTS AND THE OUTDOORS
SURFING
There are various beach breaks scattered along Playa Bejuco. Waves tend to close out at this exposed break when the swell is big, but then you can try the mouth of the estuary, 1 km (½ mile) south of the hotels. Waves have an A-frame shape that work best early morning at mid-tide. Once the wind kicks in, the waves get sloppy and wild. Bejuco

7

is a do-it-yourself beach, without surf schools or decent board rentals nearby, and because the waves break so close to shore, it's not a good spot for beginners. Encantada Ocean Cottages in neighboring Esterillos Este has a few surfboards for desperate surfers traveling without their own gear.

WHERE TO STAY

$$
HOTEL
🕎 **Delfín Beachfront Resort.** Expect swan towels and plastic flowers at this comfortable but slightly dated hotel, best known for its proximity to good surf and fresh fish. **Pros:** beachfront; clean rooms; great views. **Cons:** cramped bathrooms; beach has rip currents; hard mattresses; pool is often dirty. ⑤ *Rooms from: $140* ⊠ *Take road into Playa Bejuco, turn left at beach, hotel is 300 m on left* ☎ *2779–4245* ⊕ *www. delfinbeachresort.com* ⇆ *14 rooms* ⊙*Breakfast.*

$$
HOTEL
FAMILY
🕎 **Hotel Playa Bejuco.** In exchange for being 250 feet away from the beach, you get spacious, well-equipped rooms with views of the pool and gardens rather than surf and sand. **Pros:** big pool; decent restaurant; spacious rooms. **Cons:** not on the beach; nearby beach has rip currents; slightly dated rooms. ⑤ *Rooms from: $126* ⊠ *Road to Playa Bejuco, on left after the bridge, just before the beach* ☎ *2779–2000* ⊕*www. hotelplayabejuco.com* ⇆ *20 rooms* ⊙*Breakfast.*

MANUEL ANTONIO AREA

South of the beach communities and surf stops along the Central Pacific coast are the towns of Quepos and Manuel Antonio, as well as the popular Manuel Antonio National Park. Unless you're stocking up on supplies or making a bank run, it's better to bypass Quepos, a former banana port and now a somewhat run-down fishing town. Most travelers head straight to Manuel Antonio, where boutique hotels and luxury resorts are perched on beachside cliffs or frame the national park. Between surf lessons, canopy tours, exploring the national park, and relaxing on the beach, it's easy to fall in love with this quaint town where the jungle meets the shore. Equally impressive is the town's reputation for sustainability practices, from green hotels to organic cuisine. Although some consider Manuel Antonio overdeveloped, nobody can deny its spectacular natural beauty.

QUEPOS

23 km (14 miles) south of Parrita, 174 km (108 miles) southwest of San José.

This hot and dusty town is the gateway to Manuel Antonio, and also serves as the area's hub for banks, supermarkets, and other services. Because nearby Manuel Antonio is so much more attractive, there is little reason to stay here, but many people stop for dinner, for a night on the town, or to go sportfishing. Quepos's name stems from the indigenous tribe that inhabited the area until the Spanish conquest wiped them out. For centuries the town of Quepos barely existed, until the 1930s, when the United Fruit Company built a banana port and populated the area with workers from other parts of Central America. The town

CLOSE UP

Eco-Lodges in Manuel Antonio

An ecological transition zone between the dry forests of the North Pacific and the rain forests of the South Pacific, the Central Pacific is home to animals and plants of both regions. It is one of the easiest places to get a good look at the American crocodile, many of which gather near the bridge over the Tárcoles River. At Manuel Antonio National Park, you can see wildlife and enjoy an ocean swim at the same time. Just outside the park are a handful of luxury resorts that have earned four and five leaves in sustainability, a remarkable achievement considering the stringent guidelines of the CST Certification System.

Arenas del Mar Beachfront and Nature Resort, Manuel Antonio. This luxury hotel has an impressive eco-pedigree. It is the brainchild of Teri and Glenn Jampol, owners of Finca Rosa Blanca in the Central Valley, one of the first lodges in the country to achieve five-leaf sustainability status. The first most obvious eco-aspect guests encounter is the reception center in a forest clearing, where you leave your car

behind and ride an electric golf cart to the main open-air lobby. Other green practices include ionization systems for the swimming pools, biodegradable cleaning products, solar-heated water, a recycling program, and a black-water treatment system. A behind-the-scenes sustainability tour is free to hotel guests.

Hotel Sí Como No, Manuel Antonio. From its meticulous recycling policy and energetic reduction of waste and energy consumption to its innovative conservation programs, Sí Como No has led the way in sustainable tourism. Perched on a hillside in the center of developed Manuel Antonio, this luxury hotel is not a classic eco-lodge, but owner Jim Damalas has worked hard to minimize the hotel's environmental impact. The most notable contribution to local ecotourism is the hotel's nearby Butterfly Garden and a 20-acre wildlife refuge. The hotel is a member of the Green Hotels of Costa Rica and has attained the five leaves for sustainability.

7

thrived for nearly two decades, until Panama disease decimated the banana plantations in the late 1940s. The fruit company then switched to less lucrative African oil palms, and the area declined. Only since the 1980s have tourism revenues lifted the town out of its slump, a renaissance owed to the beauty of the nearby beaches and nature reserves. Forests around Quepos were destroyed nearly a century ago, but the massive Talamanca Mountain Range, some 10 km (6 miles) to the east, holds one of the largest expanses of wilderness in Central America.

GETTING HERE AND AROUND

The drive from San José to Quepos is under three hours. Follow the directions for Jacó and continue south another 40 minutes. Buses from San José's Tracopa bus station (Avenida 5 and Calle 14/16) drop you off in downtown Quepos. SANSA and Nature Air run multiple flights per day, 20 minutes one way, between San José and Quepos (XQP), as well as direct flights between Quepos and Palmar Sur in the Southern Pacific and La Fortuna in the Northern Lowlands.

ESSENTIALS

Banks/ATMs BAC San José. ⊠ *Avda. Central* ☎ *2777-0781.* **Banco Nacional.** ⊠ *50 m west and 100 m north of bus station* ☎ *2777-0113.*

Medical Assistance Ambulance. ☎ *911.* **Farmacia La Económica.** ⊠ *Main road, in front of the market at La Galeria Comercial* ☎ *2777-2130.* **Hospital de Quepos.** ⊠ *4 km (2½ miles) on road to Dominical, 1 km west of the airport* ☎ *2774-9510.*

Post Office Correos. ⊠ *C. Central, next to soccer field.*

Rental Cars Alamo. ⊠ *Downtown, 50 m south of Korean school* ☎ *2242-7733, 800/462-5266 in U.S.* **Hertz.** ⊠ *75 m south of the Catholic church* ☎ *2777-3365, 888/437-8927 in North America.*

Taxis Taxi services. ☎ *2777-3080, 2777-1207.*

Tourist Information Instituto Costarricense de Turismo. ⊠ *25 m east of the docks* ☎ *2777-4217, 866/267-8274 in North America* ⊕ *www.visitcostarica.com.*

EXPLORING

OFF THE BEATEN PATH

Rainforest Spices (*Villa Vanilla*). Thirty minutes east of Quepos, this spice plantation produces vanilla, cinnamon, cocoa, pepper, allspice, turmeric, and a variety of exotic fruits, essential oils, and medicinal plants. Half-day tours include a visit to the harvesting warehouse, a walk through the fields, and a tasting of Ceylon cinnamon and chocolate gourmet treats prepared by the in-house pastry chef. If you get hooked on the vanilla-bean cheesecake, the cardamom ice cream, or the cinnamon tea, you can stock up on organic spices at the shop on your way out. Tastings and transportation from the Quepos/Manuel Antonio area are included in the tour price. ⊠ *16 km (10 miles) east of Quepos* ✛ *Take paved road toward hospital and airport, at gas station intersection, continue east on the gravel road. After 6 km, pass through Naranjito and continue 1 km to "Y" intersection. Stay left, continue 5 km to Villa Vanilla on left.* ☎ *2779-1155, 8839-2721* ⊕ *www. rainforestspices.com* ⊟ *$50 cash only* ☉ *Tours Mon.–Fri. at 9 am and 1 pm, Sat. at 1 pm. Closed Sun.*

Rainmaker Conservation Project. This private nature reserve is spread over Fila Chota, a lower ridge of the Talamanca Range 22 km (13 miles) northeast of Quepos, and protects more than 1,500 acres of lush and precipitous forest, with river-walk or canopy-bridge routes to follow in the lower section. The reserve is home to many of Costa Rica's endangered species, and you may spot birds here that you won't find in Manuel Antonio. You are likely to see scarlet macaws and toucans, due to a re-population of the species in the Quepos Biological Corridor. Their long-time resident sloth "Charlie Rainmaker" helps educate guests about rain-forest conservation. The reserve encompasses five ecozones and represents 75% of the species found in Costa Rica. It isn't as good a place to see animals as the national park, but Rainmaker's forest is different—lusher and more precipitous—and the view from its bridges is impressive. Guided tours are available from Manuel Antonio, or you can stop and take a self-guided tour on your way to or from Quepos. The park also offers an early-morning bird-watching tour and a night reptiles-and-amphibians hike. The restaurant serves lunch ($8) and there's an on-site microbrewery that utilizes Rainmaker's mountain waters. It's best to visit Rainmaker in the morning, since—true to its name—it often pours in the afternoon. ⊠ *22 km (13 miles) northeast of Quepos* ☎ *8588–2586, 540/349–9848 in U.S., 8960–3836 park cell* ⊕ *www.rainmakercostarica.org* ▦ *$20; $30 for guided tours* � *Daily 7:30–4:30.*

SPORTS AND THE OUTDOORS

There's a tour operator or travel agency on every block in Quepos that can sell you any of about a dozen tours, but some outfitters give discounts if you book directly through them. The dry season is the best time to explore the area's rain forests. If you're here during the rains, do tours first thing in the morning.

CANOPY TOURS

FAMILY

Fodor's Choice

★

Canopy Safari. There are many zip-line tours in the area that take you flying through the treetops, but Canopy Safari has earned a reputation for long and fast-paced rides. The company's privately owned forest is about a 30-minute car ride from Quepos, and the tour includes gliding down 10 zip lines, a Tarzan swing, two rappel lines, and a visit to the on-site butterfly garden and serpentarium. Tours take place at 7 and 10 and include either breakfast or lunch. ⊠ *Office downtown, next to the Poder Judicial* ☎ *2777–0100, 888/765–8475 in North America* ⊕ *www. canopysafari.com* ▦ *Tour $85.*

FISHING

Quepos is one of the best points of departure for deep-sea fishing in southwestern Costa Rica. The best months for hooking a marlin are from October to February and in May and June, whereas sailfish are abundant from November to May, and are caught year-round. From May to October you're more likely to catch yellowfin tuna, roosterfish, mahimahi, and snapper. Sailfish and marlin are always catch-and-release.

Bluefin Tours. A fleet of 26-, 28-, and 33-foot boats is used for catch-and-release sportfishing, conventional fishing, and fly-fishing. ⊠ *Downtown, next to Adobe Rent-A-Car and across from the soccer field* ☎ *2777–0000* ▦ *Full-day charters $845–$1,350.*

Costa Mar Fishing. The largest fleet in Quepos has eight boats ranging from 26 to 60 feet, and consequently has a wide range of rates. ⊠ *Entrance to Quepos, next to Café Milagro* ☎ *2777–0593* ⊕ *www. costamarfishing.com* ▦ *Full-day charters from $750.*

KAYAKING AND RAFTING

Iguana Tours. Guides show off the area's natural beauty on white-water rafting trips on the Naranjo (Class III–IV) and Savegre (Class II–III) rivers and kayak adventures at sea or in a mangrove estuary. They also offer bird-watching, horseback riding, dolphin-watch catamaran trips, and canopy tours. ⊠ *Downtown Quepos, across from soccer field* ☎ *2777–2052* ⊕ *www.iguanatours.com* ▦ *From $59.*

SNORKELING AND DIVING

Oceans Unlimited. This is one of the few diving companies in the area that has an on-site training pool. They offer all-day diving excursions to Caño Island, local dives, and PADI-certification courses; rental

7

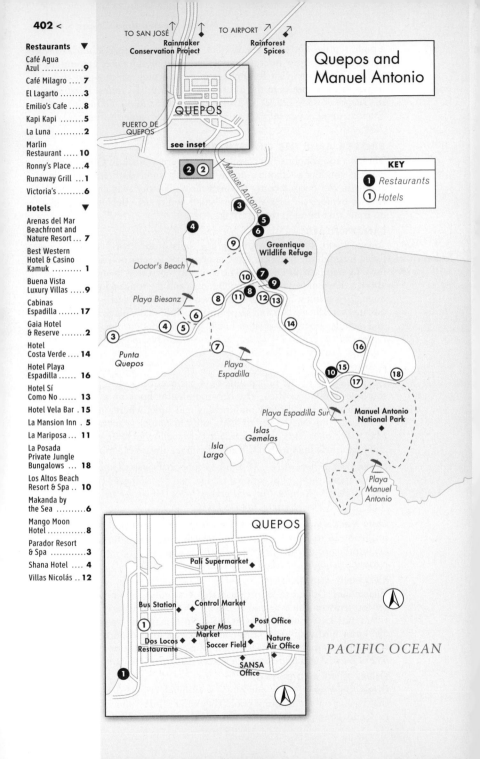

Quepos and
Manuel Antonio

KEY
① Restaurants
① Hotels

QUEPOS

PACIFIC OCEAN

Local guides lead hikes in the hills outside of Quepos.

equipment is included. ✉ *Marina Pez Vela* ☎ *2777–3171* ⊕ *www.* *scubadivingcostarica.com* ✉ *From $99; Caño Island day trip $170.*

WHERE TO EAT AND STAY

$$$
SEAFOOD
✕ **Runaway Grill.** This favorite with sportfishermen ("You hook 'em, we cook 'em"), is the town's best place for seafood, serving everything from shrimp scampi to fresh tuna with mushrooms to bouillabaisse and paella. You can also get hearty burgers or a handful of Mexican dishes, and there's a kids' menu. You won't find any billfish (like marlin or swordfish) on the menu, owing to the restaurant's conservation policy, but the back wall is covered with pictures of them—and their proud reelers. Weathered fishing caps hang from the bar's ceiling. Their location, overlooking the marina, offers the best view in town. For those who want to make the most of happy hour, ask about their free marina shuttle service. ⑤ *Average main: $20* ✉ *Marina Pez Vela* ☎ *2519–9095* ⊕ *www.runawaygrill.com.*

$$
HOTEL
▦ **Best Western Hotel & Casino Kamuk.** The downtown's best and priciest accommodations (though they pale in comparison to Manuel Antonio properties) have all the perks and ho-hum blandness of a chain hotel, and only two rooms have sea views (marred by power lines). **Pros:** reassurance of chain name; decent value given cleanliness; good service. **Cons:** small rooms; far from beach; some street noise; foot traffic from casino open until 4 am. ⑤ *Rooms from: $80* ✉ *Downtown, 100 m after last bridge into Quepos* ☎ *2777–0811, 800/780-7234 in North America* ⊕ *www.kamuk.co.cr* ⇥ *44 rooms* ⚇ *Breakfast.*

NIGHTLIFE
Dos Locos. Older American expats often congregate day and night to people-watch or, on Wednesday at 7 pm and Saturday at noon, to listen to live music. ⊠ *Avda. Central at C. Central, near bus station* ☎ *2777–1526* ☉ *Closes at 7 pm Sun.*

MANUEL ANTONIO

3 km (2 miles) south of Quepos, 179 km (111 miles) southwest of San José.

You need merely reach the top of the forested ridge on which many of Manuel Antonio's hotels are perched to understand why it is one of Costa Rica's most popular destinations. That sweeping view of beaches, jungle, and shimmering Pacific dotted with rocky islets confirms its reputation. Unlike the tropical forests in other parts of the country, Manuel Antonio's humid tropical forest remains green year-round. The town itself is spread out across a hilly and curving 5-km (3-mile) road that originates in Quepos and dead-ends at the entrance to Manuel Antonio National Park. Along this main road, near the top of the hill, or on Punta Quepos are the area's most luxurious hotels and fine-dining restaurants, surrounded by rain forest with amazing views of the beaches and offshore islands. The only problem with staying in one of those hotels is that you'll need to drive or take public transportation to and from the main beach and national park, about 10 minutes away. More hotel and restaurant options are available at the bottom of the hill, within walking distance of the beach, but they lack the sweeping view.

GETTING HERE AND AROUND
Manuel Antonio is a 15-minute drive over the hill from Quepos and 25 minutes from the Quepos airport. Between SANSA and Nature Air, there are eight flights per day linking San José and Quepos (XQP)—flying time is 20 minutes—as well as direct flights between Quepos and La Fortuna in the Northern Plains and Palmar Sur in the Southern Pacific. Buses depart from San José's Tracopa bus station (Avenida 5, Calle 14/16) for Manuel Antonio four times a day, at 6 am, noon, and 6 and 7:30 pm, traveling the opposite direction at 6 and 9:30 am, noon, and 5 pm. They pick up and drop off passengers in front of hotels on the main Quepos–Manuel Antonio road. Shuttle services Gray Line and Interbus offer hotel-to-hotel service to and from San José, Jacó, Monteverde, Arenal, and major North Pacific beaches. The trip from San José takes about 2½ hours by car or 3½ hours by bus. A local public bus makes the 20-minute trip from Quepos to Manuel Antonio every half hour from 7 to 7, then hourly until 10 pm.

ESSENTIALS
Bank/ATM Banco Promérica. ⊠ *Main road, at top of hill, between Economy Rent a Car and Cafe Milagro* ☎ *2777–5101.*

Rental Cars Economy. ⊠ *Next to Banco Promerica, across from Salsipuedes* ☎ *2777–5353.*

Taxis Taxi services. ☎ *2777–3080, 2777–1207.*

EXPLORING

FAMILY **Greentique Wildlife Refuge.** This park (previously named Manuel Antonio Nature Park and Fincas Naturales Wildlife Refuge) is operated by Hotel Sí Como No. A former teak plantation has been reforested to allow native trees to spring back among the not-so-native ones. A footpath winds through part of the 20-acre tropical forest, and naturalist guides do a good job of explaining the local ecology and identifying birds. The reserve is home to three kinds of monkeys, as well as iguanas, motmots, toucans, tanagers, and seed-chomping rodents called agoutis. Two-hour guided walks are given throughout the day, plus a nighttime jungle trek that departs at 5:30 pm. The quickest and least expensive tour is an hourly walk through exhibits on 12 species of butterflies. Unfortunately, you can't explore the reserve at your own pace. ⊠ *Main road Km 4; entrance across from Sí Como No Hotel,* ☏ *2777–0850* ⊕ *www. sicomono.com* ⊠ *Guided tours $15–$39* ⊗ *Daily 8–4.*

FAMILY **Manuel Antonio National Park** (*Parque Nacional Manuel Antonio*). Costa
Fodor'sChoice Rica's smallest park packs in an assortment of natural attractions, from
★ wildlife sheltered by rain forest to rocky coves teeming with marine life. Meandering trails framed by guácimo colorado, mangrove, and silk-cotton trees serve as refuge to sloths, iguanas, agoutis, coatis, raccoons, monkeys, and birds. This is one of the country's best places to see squirrel monkeys and white-faced capuchin monkeys. The great diversity of wildlife is easily spotted from the well-maintained trails, and, because the animals are so used to humans, you're likely to see them up close, especially near groups of tourists eating lunch at the beach. Security guards now inspect bags at the park entrance as new restrictions only allow visitors to bring fruit, sandwiches, and non-alcoholic beverages. The mass-amounts of junk food stolen and consumed by wildlife has led to serious health problems for the animals. As tempting as it may be, do not feed the wildlife.

Just beyond the entrance, the park's main trail leads to Manuel Antonio Beach, with white sand and submerged volcanic rock great for snorkeling. A second trail winds through the rain forest and spills onto Playa Espadilla Sur, the park's longest beach, which is often less crowded due to rough waters.

Farther east, Playa Escondido (Hidden Beach) is rocky and secluded, but not open to the public due to safety precautions; however, you can view it from afar.

Despite its size, Manuel Antonio is Costa Rica's most-visited national park before Poás Volcano. A few tips to make the most of a visit:

Park entrance tickets are sold exclusively at Coopealianza offices in Quepos and Manuel Antonio, one of which is located 50 meters before the park entrance. Tickets are valid for one year from date of purchase, for a single visit. Hire a private guide with ICT certification issued by the Costa Rica Tourism Board.

Arrive as early as possible—between 7 and 8 am is the best time to see animals (and it's cooler, too).

Beware of manzanillo trees (indicated by warning signs)—their leaves, bark, and apple-like fruit secrete a gooey substance that irritates the skin.

⚠ It's common for non-certified guides to approach tourists and offer their services. Even if you ask to see identification, they might only show a Costa Rican ID or a driver's licence. Make sure that you only hire a guide that has a badge reading "ICT" with a valid expiration date. Non-certified guides often charge as much as ICT-approved guides, but tours only last an hour to 90 minutes (as opposed to three hours), and you won't see a fraction of the wildlife you might with an experienced guide.

⇨ *For more information, see the highlighted listing in this chapter.* ✉ *Manuel Antonio* ☎ *2777–5185* ▣ *$16* ⊙ *Tues.–Sun. 7–4.*

BEACHES

When the surf is up, riptides are a dangerous problem on Playa Espadilla, Manuel Antonio's main beach, which runs parallel to the road near the park's entrance. ■TIP→ Never leave your valuables unattended while you're swimming.

Playa Biesanz. For a less turbulent swim and smaller crowds than at other Manuel Antonio beaches, head to this quiet beach within a sheltered cove. There are a few tide pools near a cluster of rocks and, during low tide, you can see fragments of turtle traps dating back to AD 900, when the area was inhabited by Quepoa Indians. You can rent snorkeling gear for $10 and kayaks for $30. Prepare to pay $1–$2 to the unofficial parking attendant who monitors cars on the road. Bring your own food, drinks, and bug spray since there are no amenities and a few mosquitoes on the jungle trail. You're likely to see monkeys and butterflies on the trail connecting the road to the sand. **Amenities:** none **Best for:** snorkeling; solitude. ✉ *Near Hotel Parador.*

Playa Espadilla. As the road approaches Manuel Antonio National Park, it skirts the lovely, forest-lined beach of Playa Espadilla, which stretches for more than 2 km (1 mile) north from the rocky crag that marks the park's border to the base of the ridge that holds most of the hotels. One of the most popular beaches in Costa Rica, it fills up with sunbathers, surfers, volleyball players, strand strollers, and sand-castle architects on dry-season weekends and holidays. For most of the year, it is surprisingly quiet, especially at the northern end below Arenas del Mar. Even on the busiest days it is long enough to provide an escape from the crowd, which tends to gather around the restaurants and lounge chairs near its southern end. Though many people often swim and surf here, beware of rough seas and deadly rip currents. There are usually lifeguards on duty closest to the park. If you plan on surfing on the north end, beware of the rocks lurking just below the break closest to the cliffs. You can access this isolated section of Playa Espadilla by way of a 1-km (½-mile) dirt road near Arenas del Mar. There's free parking on the sand, accessible by four-wheel-drive vehicles only. **Amenities:** food and drink. **Best for:** surfing; walking. ✉ *Manuel Antonio.*

Playa Manuel Antonio. The town's safest swimming area is sheltered Playa Manuel Antonio, the second beach in the national park. Its white sand makes it attractive for lounging around, and the warm, clean water is good for snorkeling. There are plenty of palm trees where you can find shade on this wide stretch of sand, and just outside the park are vendors selling fresh coconut water and lychees. Keep watch over your food as raccoons and monkeys are known to steal lunches while people are swimming. Huge mounds of lava rock shelter this cove on both sides of the rugged coastline. Several shacks just outside the park rent beach chairs for about $15 a day. Beaches inside the national park do not have lifeguards or food vendors, unlike those near the entrance. **Amenities:** parking; showers; toilets. **Best for:** snorkeling; swimming; walking. ✉ *6 km (4 miles) south of Quepos; near park entrance.*

> ## IN THE THICK OF IT
>
> There's more rain forest on private land than in Manuel Antonio National Park, which means it's not unusual to see many of the animals the park is famous for from the balcony of your hotel room or from your breakfast table. It also means that local landowners play an important role in conserving the area's flora and fauna.

SPORTS AND THE OUTDOORS

TOUR OPERATORS

Manuel Antonio's list of outdoor activities is almost endless. Tours generally range from $40 to $100 per person and can be booked through your hotel's reception desk or directly through the outfitter. During the rainy season, some outdoor options might lose their appeal, but clouds usually let loose in the afternoon, so take advantage of sunny mornings. Most nature-themed activities go on rain or shine.

Jade Tours. The certified and knowledgeable guides at Jade Tours will turn your park trek into an entertaining biology class, as they point out camouflaged wildlife in the treetops. Their team has over a decade of experience and will help you snap all those picture-perfect images of Costa Rica's flora and fauna through their high-powered scope. Included in the rate are transportation, park entrance, and snacks. ✉ *in Manuel Antonio* ☎ *2777–0932, 8632–8760* ⊕ *www.costaricajadetours. com* ✉ *$50.*

Fodor's Choice **Johan Chaves Nature and Birding Tours.** Raised in Manuel Antonio, Johan
★ Chaves provides three-hour guided tours of the national park that start bright and early at 7:30. Johan's true passion for wildlife and nature make him one of the most sought-after guides in the region, so reserve (by email) well in advance. In addition to being an expert birder, he is extremely knowledgeable about animal behavior and Costa Rica's history. He has a talent for keeping children intrigued on the trail and for spotting wildlife around every turn. Bring water, sunscreen, walking shoes, bug spray, a camera, and swimsuit if you plan to linger at the beach following the tour. The fee includes park entrance and transportation to and from your hotel. ✉ *Manuel Antonio* ☎ *2779–1189, 8850–4419 cell* ✏ *johanchaves@yahoo.com.mx* ⊕ *www.johanchaves. weebly.com* ✉ *$46 cash only.*

CANOPY TOURS

El Santuario Canopy Adventure Tour. Just 20 minutes from Manuel Antonio National Park, this canopy tour boasts the longest single zip line in Central America, extending nearly 1½ km (1 mile) over the treetops. Tours include 14 platforms, 3 towers, 6 bridges, 3 nature walks, and

7

You can hike to white-sand beaches in Manuel Antonio National Park—just one of the reasons it is so popular.

1 double-belay rappel. The company has double anchored zip lines with built-in braking systems. Transportation and lunch are included in the tour fee. ⊠ *Manuel Antonio* ☎ *2777–6908, 877/914–0002 in U.S.* ⊕ *www.elsantuariocanopyadventure.com* ✉ *Tour $75.*

Tití Canopy Tour. You'll find a relatively slow-paced zip-line tour here, a rarity in Costa Rica, through a forest reserve that is contiguous with the national park. Also available is a night zip-line tour, lighting your way by headlamp. Guides go above and beyond to make you feel comfortable and safe and will help you spot animals. ⊠ *Costanera Hwy., 150 m south of Quepos Hospital* ☎ *2777–3130* ⊕ *www.titicanopytour.com* ✉ *$70; night tour $80.*

HIKING
Highly visited Manuel Antonio National Park is the obvious place to go, but you can also gain a rich appreciation of the local forests' greenery and wildlife in private reserves like Greentique Wildlife Refuge and Rainmaker. ■TIP➜ Bring binoculars!

HORSEBACK RIDING
Brisas del Nara. This outfitter takes riders of all ages and levels through the protected Cerro Nara mountain zone, 32 km (20 miles) from Manuel Antonio, and ends with a swim in a natural pool at the foot of a 300-foot waterfall. Full-day tours include three hours on horseback, with breakfast and lunch included; the ride on the half-day tour lasts two hours. For those who want a little less trot in their tour, they have a safari-truck option that visits many of the same attractions. ⊠ *Manuel Antonio* ☎ *2779–1235* ⊕ *www.horsebacktour.com* ✉ *From $65.*

KAYAKING

Iguana Tours. Half-day sea-kayaking trips to the islands of Manuel Antonio National Park require some experience when the seas are high. On a mellower paddle through the mangrove estuary of Isla Damas you might see monkeys, sloths, and various birds. ✉ *Downtown Quepos, across from Catholic church, Quepos* ☏ *2777–2052* ⊕ *www. iguanatours.com* ✉ *From $65.*

SURFING

Local Surf School. At the isolated section of Playa Espadilla near Arenas Del Mar Resort, this surf school has bilingual instructors and a decent quiver of long and short boards. Several of the surf instructors are certified lifeguards. Showers, drinking water, beach security, and one-on-one training make this a good option. ✉ *Playa Espadilla near Arenas Del Mar Resort* ☏ *8486–6401, 6061–3019* ✉ *Lessons from $50; rentals from $10.*

Manuel Antonio Surf School (*MASS*). Beginner surfers are in good hands with this reputable surf school that guarantees every student will get up on a wave by the end of the session. They teach the mechanics of surfing, wave theory, and offer lessons for all levels at several breaks in Manuel Antonio, Playitas, Isla Damas, and Dominical. Three-hour group lesson fees include transportation, gear, snacks, and certified instruction. Half-day tours to Damas Island include lunch. If just one lesson isn't enough, they have a surf retreat five minutes outside Dominical. Solo surfers traveling without boards can rent from their solid quiver. ✉ *Calle Principal, across from Pajaro Azul* ☏ *2777–4842* ⊕ *www.manuelantoniosurfschool.com* ✉ *Lessons from $65, tours from $100, rentals from $25.*

WHITE-WATER RAFTING

The three white-water rivers in this area have limited seasons, when the rains from August to October raise them to their perfect peak. The **Naranjo River** offers a short but exciting run, with Class III to V calling for some experience (April–December only). The **Parrita River** provides a relatively mellow (Class II to III) white-water route, but it's only navigable in two-person inflatable duckies. The **Savegre River** has two navigable stretches—a Class II to III lower section that's a mellow trip perfect for neophytes, and a more rambunctious upper section of Class III to IV. It flows past patches of rain forest that are usually navigable year-round, and it's also good for fly-fishing.

Amigos del Rio (*ADR*). Catering to all levels of adrenaline junkies, Amigos del Rio has six-hour rafting trips on the Savegre River (Class III rapids), four-hour trips on the Naranjo River (Class III and IV), and five-hour trips on the El Chorro section of the Naranjo River (Class IV and V). Included in the rate are breakfast, lunch, transportation, equipment, and bilingual guides. Tours depart at 7 and 11:30 am daily. The Naranjo River tour runs May to December, El Chorro runs from January to April, and Savegre trip is available year-round. ✉ *2 km (1 mile) on main road to Manuel Antonio National Park, 100 m past Hotel Gaia* ☏ *2777–0082, 877/393–3332 in North America* ⊕ *www. amigosdelrio.net* ✉ *From $70.*

H2O Adventures. The Manuel Antonio franchise for Ríos Tropicales, the biggest rafting outfitter in the country, runs kayaking excursions and rafting trips on the Naranjo River, departing daily at 8 and 1. For something less turbulent, they have a rafting trip down the Savegre River at 8 and 11. Transportation and lunch are included. ⊠ *250 m east from Catholic church, Quepos* ☎ *2777–4092, 888/532–3298 in U.S.* ⊕ *www.h2ocr.com* ⊠ *From $70.*

WHERE TO EAT

$$$ ✕ **Cafe Agua Azul.** Follow your nose to this simple second-floor room
SEAFOOD offering breathtaking views by day and a deliciously inventive selection of seafood by night. The lunch menu is strong on salads and sandwiches, but the dinner options include some of the best entrées in town. In addition to nightly fish and pasta specials, they offer such inventive delicacies as seared tuna over a tequila-and-lime cucumber salad, calamari sautéed with capers and olives, and coconut-crusted mahimahi. The blackened fish sandwich and grilled burger with fries hit the spot after a day at the beach. $ *Average main: $18* ⊠ *Main road, above the Villas del Parque office, 2nd fl.* ☎ *2777–5280* ⊕ *www.cafeaguaazul.com* ⊗ *Closed Wed. and Oct.*

$$$ ✕ **Café Milagro** (*El Patio de Café Milagro*). In 1993, university students
CAFÉ Adrienne Pellizzari and Lance Byron first came to Manuel Antonio on a summer vacation, but it was their quest for good coffee and cuisine that made them stay. In the end, they created their own *milagro* (miracle) blend, making this cozy café the only place in town that serves its own fresh-roasted coffee. The eclectic menu is heavy on vegetarian and organic dishes, like chilled avocado soup, mango chayote salad, and grilled vegetables with quinoa. They also serve roasted pork with sautéed papaya and dorado with a Caribbean salsa. The breakfast burritos, baked goods, and inventive selection of sandwiches make this a top breakfast and lunch spot. Tables in the front dining room overlook the road, but there's also seating in the back garden. They have craft beers on tap, and there's live music Monday through Saturday from 7 pm to 9 pm. The attached store and their small coffee roaster in Quepos sell bags of their award-winning coffee to take home. $ *Average main: $17* ⊠ *Main road to park, across from Los Altos* ☎ *2777–0794* ⊕ *www.cafemilagro.com.*

$$$$ ✕ **El Lagarto.** Meat lovers can get their fix at this local grill, where siz-
STEAKHOUSE zling cuts are seared on a wood-fire grill and served on chopping blocks. Anyone with a fondness for woodwork will appreciate the floors inlaid with tree stumps and the tabletops made from driftwood. A palapa bar serves powerful margaritas and daiquiris, but it's the grass-fed beef from neighboring La Fortuna that you'll want to try. Other specialties include whole red snapper, pork ribs, or lamb (with 24-hour notice). All mains include a baked potato, tomato, and grilled zucchini. Vegetarians can opt for the portobello mushrooms smothered in garlic and cheese, served in a cast-iron skillet. There's a second location in Samara. $ *Average main: $35* ⊠ *200 m north of the soccer field* ☎ *2777–6932* ⊕ *www.ellagartobbq.com* ⊗ *No lunch.*

$$ ✕ **Emilio's Café.** Sweeping views, organic cuisine, and a bohemian vibe
MEDITERRANEAN are what you'll get at this popular café where soft jazz sets the stage

for all kinds of good eats. Breakfast offerings include eggs Benedict, waffles, or delectable French toast—fluffy on the inside and crunchy on the outside. At lunch or dinner, try the sesame-crusted tuna, falafel pita, or one of the vegetable sandwiches served with homemade pesto or salsa picante. If you're looking for a sweet treat, try the passion-fruit pie or peanut-butter cake with fresh fruit juice, frozen mint lemonade, or a frothy cappuccino. Vegetarians and gluten-free eaters have plenty to choose from, as does anyone obsessed with chocolate. They often host live-music events on weekends during high season. ⓢ *Average main: $12* ✉ *40 m before Hotel Mariposa* ☎ *2777–6807* ☾ *Closed Tues.*

$$$
ASIAN FUSION
✕ **Kapi Kapi.** Low lighting, ocher walls, dark hardwood, and potted palms provide Manuel Antonio's best ambience for dinner, despite the lack of an ocean view. The name is a greeting in the indigenous Maleku language, but the menu is a cosmopolitan invention and includes such un-Costa Rican starters as goat cheese salad, and "seafood cigars"— a mix of fresh tuna, shrimp, and mahimahi deep-fried in an egg-roll wrapper and served on a cabbage salad. The main courses include Asian-inspired dishes like prawns with a tamarind-coconut-rum glaze and macadamia-encrusted mahimahi with a plum chili sauce. Be sure to order the chocolate soufflé in advance, otherwise you'll be stuck listening to the table next to you rave about its perfection. ⓢ *Average main: $24* ✉ *East side of main road, across from Pacífico Colonial condos* ☎ *2777–5049* ⊕ *www.restaurantekapikapi.com* ☾ *Closed Oct. No lunch.*

$$$
INTERNATIONAL
Fodor's Choice
★
✕ **La Luna.** It's hard to know what's more impressive—the view or the cuisine at this restaurant without walls, where the sun melts into the Pacific and La Luna (the moon) takes center stage. Innovative starters range from Gorgonzola-and-tomato tarts to honey-garlic calamari. For something tender and moist, try the Parmesan chicken, the plantain-coconut mahimahi, or the ginger-and-panko-crusted tuna. The five-course tasting and wine pairing ($75) is a bargain considering the fine blends that are served. Portions tend to be on the small side, but the service is outstanding. Happy hour, from 4 to 6, includes discounted tapas and cocktails. If you want to learn the secrets of the young prodigy chef, reserve a spot in the cooking class. ⓢ *Average main: $22* ✉ *Gaia Hotel, Km 2.7 Carretera Quepos* ☎ *2777–9797* ⊕ *www.gaiahr.com.*

$$$
COSTA RICAN
✕ **Marlin Restaurant.** The outdoor tables are pretty much always full, owing to a location on Manuel Antonio's busiest corner, across the street from the beach near the National Park entrance. This is a convenient place to grab breakfast after an early-morning hike—maybe banana pancakes or a *típico*, with eggs and *gallo pinto* (black beans and rice). The lunch and dinner menu ranges from the ubiquitous *arroz con pollo* (rice with chicken) to tenderloin with french fries, and jumbo shrimp in garlic and lemon butter. The fresh mahimahi and tuna are always a good bet. Daily happy hour is 4:30–6:30, featuring 2-for-1 cocktails. ⓢ *Average main: $20* ✉ *Main road, south of the hill, on corner across from bus stop and beach* ☎ *2777–1134.*

$$
COSTA RICAN
✕ **Ronny's Place.** A spectacular sunset view comes with friendly, attentive service and a small but tempting menu that includes such typical Tico dishes as *sopa negra* (black-bean soup), ceviche, shrimp and fish

on a skewer, and filet mignon wrapped with bacon and topped with a mushroom sauce. The red snapper is excellent, as are the coconut-breaded jumbo shrimp. This is the best place in town to soak in the view—especially when accompanied by a glass of their famous white wine–and–vodka sangria. Ronny's is somewhat secluded up a long dirt road that crosses a green valley on a narrow ridge in front of the sea. If you come after dark, you might be disappointed, since the ocean view is the true star of the show. ⑤ *Average main: $15* ⊠ *1 km (½ mile) west of main road, down dirt road across from Amigos del Río* ☎ *2777–5120* ⊕ *www.ronnysplace.com* ⊙ *Closed Oct 1–15.*

$$$ ✕ **Victoria's.** If the sound of live music by Rafa Mora (Costa Rica's lead-
ITALIAN   ing classical guitarist) isn't enough to lure your senses, then the smell of brick-oven pizza surely will be. Thin and crispy top picks include New York style with pepperoni, sausage, and ham, or pesto-chicken pizza with toasted walnuts and caramelized onions. Staying true to Italian cuisine are the homemade meatballs, advertised as "to die for, but not recommended on first dates." The tuna chipotle and filet mignon are hearty dishes and come with a side of roasted potatoes and vegetables. There's a children's menu, and a touch of Southern hospitality, espe-cially when owner Mark Dalton makes his way from table to table (he's originally from South Carolina). If the lights dim, it just means someone ordered the banana flambé, a dessert and show worth saving room for. Live music is performed Sunday through Thursday from 6 to close. ⑤ *Average main: $24* ⊠ *Across from Pacifico Colonial Condo-miniums; next to Kapi Kapi* ☎ *2777–5143* ⊕ *www.victoriasgourmet. com* ⊙ *No lunch.*

WHERE TO STAY

$$$$ 🖾 **Arenas del Mar Beachfront and Nature Resort.** On hillsides sloping down
RESORT   to two pristine, almost-deserted beaches, chic and elegant rooms are decorated with gorgeous natural fabrics and flamboyant local art and have huge private terraces with comfortable outdoor seating. **Pros:** best of both worlds: luxury and eco-consciousness; best beach access in Manuel Antonio; wonderful bird-watching and wildlife viewing; beach with surf lessons and lifeguard. **Cons:** very steep paths and stairs; humidity can leave bathrooms somewhat musty; pricey. ⑤ *Rooms from: $380* ⊠ *El Parador road at far west end of Playa Espadilla* ☎ *2777–2777, 888/240–0280 in U.S.* ⊕ *www.arenasdelmar.com* ⛵ *38 rooms, 10 suites* ⦿*|Breakfast.*

$$$ 🖾 **Buena Vista Luxury Villas** (*Tulemar Bungalows and Villas*). Tucked
HOTEL   inside the peaceful 33-acre gated Tulemar Gardens, circular glass villas
Fodor'sChoice   perched on jungle hillsides are connected by paved trails that meander
★   past three swimming pools and spill onto the beach. **Pros:** accommodat-ing staff; exceptional design; within private gated reserve surrounded by wildlife. **Cons:** some units don't have ocean views; not wheelchair acces-sible; condo-hotel means some services are lacking. ⑤ *Rooms from: $185* ⊠ *Tulemar Gardens, next to Los Altos Beach Resort* ☎ *2777–0580, 866/569–6241 in North America* ⊕ *www.buenavistaluxuryvillas. com* ⛵ *35 units* ⦿*|No meals.*

$$ **⚇ Cabinas Espadilla.** These quiet cabinas open onto porches overlooking a
HOTEL tropical garden and a wide lawn, shaded by palm trees, and with a large
FAMILY pool. Pros: good value; short walk from beach and national park; nice
grounds. Cons: mediocre rooms; street noise in some units; Wi-Fi does
not reach all rooms. $ *Rooms from: $131* ✉ *On road beside Marlin Restaurant* ☎ *2777–2113* ⊕ *www.espadilla.com* ⇆ *16 cabinas* ⦿ *Breakfast.*

$$$$ **⚇ Gaia Hotel & Reserve.** On 13 acres of private reserve, this boutique
HOTEL hotel is contemporary and very chic, with rooms rendered in slate,
FAMILY hardwood, and rattan with Italian fittings. Pros: outstanding service;
free shuttle to beach and town; best spa in Manuel Antonio; free movie
and book library; 24-hour room service. Cons: awkward high step
into the tub; rooftop pools are shallow and impractical; 3 km (2 miles)
from the beach; must walk through the restaurant to reach reception.
$ *Rooms from: $290* ✉ *Km 2.7 Carretera Quepos, near Plaza Yara, in
Manuel Antonio* ☎ *2777–9797, 800/226–2515 in U.S.* ⊕ *www.gaiahr.
com* ⇆ *16 rooms, 3 suites, 2 villas* ⦿ *Breakfast.*

$$ **⚇ Hotel Costa Verde.** Their motto, "still more monkeys than people"
RESORT is not an understatement, as you're likely to see howler and white-
FAMILY faced monkeys on the forest trails surrounding these varied accommodations. Pros: great ocean views; wildlife; daily yoga; efficiencies a
good value. Cons: most efficiencies suffer road noise; 1½ km (1 mile)
from the beach; service inconsistent; breakfast not included. $ *Rooms
from: $135* ✉ *Road to national park, on south side of hill, on left*
☎ *2777–0584, 866/854–7958 in North America* ⊕ *www.costaverde.
com* ⇆ *70 rooms* ⦿ *No meals.*

$$$ **⚇ Hotel Playa Espadilla.** Simple but spacious mint-green and cream rooms
HOTEL are a short walk from the beach and are surrounded by green lawns bor-
FAMILY dered on two sides by the tall trees of Manuel Antonio National Park.
Pros: surrounded by forest; close to beach and national park; guests
can use amenities at sister property Cabinas Espadilla. Cons: service
inconsistent; showers often lack hot water; basic rooms. $ *Rooms from:
$200* ✉ *150 m on side road from Marlin Restaurant, 1st left, 300 m
before park entrance* ☎ *2777–0903* ⊕ *www.espadilla.com* ⇆ *16 rooms*
⦿ *Breakfast.*

$$$ **⚇ Hotel Sí Como No.** This sustainable resort with its own wildlife ref-
RESORT uge sits atop one of the most idyllic hillsides in Manuel Antonio. Pros:
FAMILY neighboring wildlife refuge; nice views; environmentally sustainable;
good restaurants. Cons: 3 km (2 miles) from beach; standard rooms
overpriced; a few suites too close to road. $ *Rooms from: $250* ✉ *Road
to the park, just after Villas Nicolás, right-hand side* ☎ *2777–0777,
888/742–6667 in North America* ⊕ *www.sicomono.com* ⊗ *Closed Oct
1–15* ⇆ *39 rooms, 19 suites* ⦿ *Breakfast.*

$$ **⚇ Hotel Vela Bar.** In 2015, a full renovation and new management trans-
HOTEL formed what had been a run-down property into Manuel Antonio's
best budget secret with delightful rooms overlooking a central pool,
just minutes from Playa Espadilla and the national park. Pros: clean
rooms; walking distance to national park and beach; renovated in 2015.
Cons: skimpy breakfast; tiny pool; no children under 12. $ *Rooms
from: $140* ✉ *Up road from Marlin Restaurant, on left* ☎ *2777–0413*
⊕ *www.velabar.com* ⇆ *16 rooms* ⦿ *Breakfast.*

7

The Pacific coast is backed by mangrove, rain, transitional, and tropical dry forests.

$$$$
B&B/INN

🛏 **La Mansion Inn.** White silk curtains, black onyx flooring, and classical music welcome you to the reception area of this boutique hotel, where rooms have ocean views, white tile floors, balconies, and a mixed bag of styles. **Pros:** excellent views; unique bar; free shuttle to Manuel Antonio National Park. **Cons:** steep driveway with limited parking; hodgepodge of styles; no children under 12. ⑤ *Rooms from: $280* ✉ *1 km (½ mile) west of La Mariposa, next to Hotel Makanda, in Manuel Antonio* ☎ *2777–3489, 800/360–2071 in U.S.* ⊕ *www.lamansioninn. com* ⇆ *24 rooms* ⦿| *Breakfast.*

$$$
RESORT

🛏 **La Mariposa.** The best view in town—a sweeping panorama of verdant hills, the aquamarine ocean, and offshore islands—is the claim to fame for this array of spacious rooms tucked between the jungle and gardens ablaze with colorful flowers. **Pros:** gorgeous views; free shuttle to the beach; website often has last-minute specials; large bathrooms. **Cons:** 2 km (1 mile) from beach; some ocean-view balconies lack privacy; sections of hotel slightly dated. ⑤ *Rooms from: $215* ✉ *West of main road, right after Barba Roja, across from Mango Moon Hotel* ☎ *2777–0355, 800/572–6440 in U.S.* ⊕ *www.lamariposa.com* ⇆ *62 rooms* ⦿| *Breakfast.*

$$
RESORT
Fodor's Choice
★

🛏 **La Posada Private Jungle Bungalows.** This cluster of distinctive A-frame bungalows, nestled on the edge of the national park and also just a short walk from the beach, is as close as you'll get to sleeping in the park. **Pros:** good value; near beach and park; movie library; friendly staff. **Cons:** chaotic outside the hotel during park hours; small pool; rooms slightly dated. ⑤ *Rooms from: $135* ✉ *250 m up side road from Marlin Restaurant, at park entrance* ☎ *2777–1446* ⊕ *www.laposadajungle.com* ⇆ *4 bungalows, 2 apartments, 1 villa, 1 house* ⦿| *Breakfast.*

$$$$ ⊞ **Los Altos Beach Resort & Spa.** These three- and four-bedroom Balinese-
RESORT   inspired luxury condo suites boast 2,500 square feet of living space with
FAMILY   industrial kitchens, slate floors, granite counters, rich hardwoods, and
rattan furnishings. **Pros:** great views; cooking classes available; ideal for
families; enormous rooms. **Cons:** higher-level suites cost more; $150
charge per room over two guests; only high-rise in Manuel Antonio,
a bit of an eyesore. ⑤ *Rooms from: $375 ⊠ Km 4 on road to Manuel
Antonio National Park, across from Café Milagro, in Manuel Antonio
☎ 2777–8888, 888/803–1332 in U.S. ⊕ www.thepreserveatlosaltos.
com ⥹ 28 condos* ⦿ *Breakfast.*

$$$$ ⊞ **Makanda by the Sea.** These bright, spacious, white-and-cream villas
RESORT   are among the area's most tasteful (and expensive) accommodations,
and the hypnotic views of the jungle-framed Pacific Ocean make this
secluded rain-forest retreat worth every penny. **Pros:** tranquil; rooms
remodeled in 2015; ocean views; stocked kitchens. **Cons:** 15-minute
hike to the beach; no children under 16; spotty Wi-Fi; slippery steps.
⑤ *Rooms from: $315 ⊠ 1 km (½ mile) west of La Mariposa ☎ 2777–
0442, 888/625–2632 in North America ⊕ www.makanda.com ⥹ 7
villas, 4 studios* ⦿ *Breakfast.*

$$ ⊞ **Mango Moon Hotel.** The rooms vary in size and amenities, but the
HOTEL   intimate atmosphere and hospitable staff make you feel as if you're
staying with a friend rather than at a hotel. **Pros:** nice view; tranquil
area; friendly staff. **Cons:** thin curtains and weak a/c; not much pri-
vacy; some rooms dark and dated; no Wi-Fi in rooms. ⑤ *Rooms from:
$150 ⊠ Between La Mariposa and Makanda ☎ 2777–5323 ⊕ www.
mangomoonhotel.com ⥹ 10 rooms* ⦿ *Breakfast.*

$$$$ ⊞ **Parador Resort & Spa.** Terra-cotta floors, steamer trunks, marble stat-
RESORT   ues, bronzed knights, and elaborate antiques create a high-end Spanish
colonial style at this beachfront resort perched on the end of a secluded
peninsula. **Pros:** outstanding service; tranquil location; free shuttle to
national park. **Cons:** pricey food; 15-minute drive to Manuel Antonio
National Park; not ideal setting for kids. ⑤ *Rooms from: $325 ⊠ End of
peninsula at Biesanz Beach, in Manuel Antonio ☎ 2777–1414 ⊕ www.
hotelparador.com ⥹ 92 rooms, 30 suites* ⦿ *Breakfast.*

$$$$ ⊞ **Shana Hotel.** Everything—walls, furniture, paintwork, staff uni-
RESORT   forms—is blindingly white, in striking contrast to the lush greens of
the hillside grounds, and the service is some of the best in Manuel
Antonio. **Pros:** attentive service; relaxing spa; sleek design. **Cons:** not
oceanfront; weak Wi-Fi signal in some rooms; steep driveway. ⑤ *Rooms
from: $260 ⊠ Road to Quepos, 300 m downhill from La Mansión
Inn ☎ 2777–7373 ⊕ www.shanahotel.com ⥹ 40 rooms* ⦿ *Breakfast.*

$$$ ⊞ **Villas Nicolás.** On a hillside about 3 km (2 miles) from the beach,
HOTEL   terraced, Mediterranean-style, privately owned (and rented) villas
have impressive views and offer one and two bedrooms, kitchens, and
(in most) large balconies with hammocks. **Pros:** good location; most
rooms have great views; grounds are well maintained. **Cons:** some units
need updating; fee to use beach towels; a bit of hike to the beach; no
TVs. ⑤ *Rooms from: $170 ⊠ Road to park, across from Hotel Byb-
los ☎ 2777–0481 ⊕ www.villasnicolas.com ⥹ 19 rooms* ⦿ *Breakfast.*

7

NIGHTLIFE
BARS
Barba Roja. As one of Manuel Antonio's first restaurants, this is still one of the best places to go for sunset cocktail hour and local beers on tap. ⊠ *Main road, 100 m before Cafe Milagro* ☏ *2777–0331* ⊕ *www. barbarojarestaurant.com* ⊘ *Closed Mon.*

Billfish Bar. With large-screen TVs and pool tables, Manuel Antonio's consummate sports bar fills up on game nights. Ladies' Nights are on Monday and Friday, and there are free Latin dance lessons on Thursday. You can also try your luck in the casino. ⊠ *Byblos Hotel, main road, across from Villas Nicolas* ☏ *2777–0411, 888/929–2567 in U.S.* ⊕ *www.bybloshotelcostarica.com* ⊘ *Closed Wed.*

Salsipuedes Tapas Bar. This colorful tapas bar hidden behind tropical foliage is a great sunset venue. It's one of the few places you can enjoy a quiet drink, except on Monday and Friday when they have live music (December–June). ⊠ *Main road, north of Barba Roja, in front of Banco Promérica* ☏ *2777–5019* ⊘ *Closed Tues.*

DANCE CLUBS
Karma Lounge. Considered the gay-friendly lounge bar of Manuel Antonio, this club has dancing, live DJs, and happy hour from 8 to 10. ⊠ *Below Victoria's Restaurant, next to Kapi Kapi* ☏ *2777–7230* ⊡ *$4* ⊘ *Closed Mon.*

MUSIC CLUBS
Victoria's. This upscale Italian restaurant is also a popular nightspot, with classical guitarist Rafa Mora performing most evenings. ⊠ *Main road, across from Pacifico Colonial Condominiums, next to Kapi Kapi* ☏ *2777–5143* ⊕ *www.victoriasgourmet.com.*

SHOPPING
There's no shortage of shopping in this town. The beach near the entrance to the park is lined with a sea of vendors who sell T-shirts, hats, and colorful beach wraps. More-authentic handicrafts are sold at night by artisans positioned along the sidewalk in central Manuel Antonio.

Regalame. This appealing art gallery is a showplace for paintings, drawings, pottery, woodwork, and jewelry by area artists. ⊠ *Next to Sí Como No Hotel* ☏ *2777–0777* ⊕ *www.regalameart.com.*

THE OSA PENINSULA AND THE SOUTH PACIFIC

WELCOME TO THE OSA PENINSULA AND THE SOUTH PACIFIC

TOP REASONS TO GO

★ **Bird-watching:** Spot beauties such as the scarlet macaw and resplendent quetzal.

★ **Enormous Corcovado National Park:** The last refuge of endangered jaguars and tapirs.

★ **Kayaking:** Head to the Golfo Dulce or along the jungly channels of the Sierpe or Colorado rivers.

★ **Mountain hikes:** Hiking paths here range from easy daytime treks around luxurious lodges to Costa Rica's toughest: 3,820-meter (12,532-foot) Cerro Chirripó.

★ **Wild places to stay:** Relax in the country's top eco-lodges, rustic thatch-roof beach bungalows, and cozy mountain cabins.

1 The Central Highlands. The main road climbs more than 2,134 meters (7,000 feet) over mountains and above the clouds of the Central Highlands before descending into the huge Valle de El General agricultural region. Highlights are fabulous mountain lodges, world-class bird-watching, and high-altitude hikes.

2 Valle de El General Region. This prosperous region, centered around the bustling market town of San Isidro de El General, is the gateway to Chirripó National Park, home of the country's highest peak.

3 Dominical and Ballena National Marine Park. The coast has miles of beaches peppered with small beach communities, including Dominical, a lively surfer haven, and Ojochal, a French-accented enclave. Ballena National Marine Park offers 10 km (6 miles) of pristine beaches and a chance to watch dolphins and the migrating whales for which the park is named.

4 The Golfo Dulce. The eastern Golfo Dulce draws anglers and kayakers to Golfito, nature lovers to eco-lodges accessible only by boat, beachcombers to slow-paced Zancudo, and serious surfers to Pavones.

Map labels:
División · San Gerardo de Rivas · Mt. Chirripó · Cerro Chirripó National Park · CR2 · San Isidro de El General · Mercedes · 18 · 22 · SAN JOSÉ · Juntas · VALLE DE EL GENERAL · CR2 · Dominical · Pejibaye · 244 · Uvita · Ballena National Marine Park · Punta Mala · 18 · Palmar Norte · Sierpe · Sierpe R. · Drake · Rincón · OSA PENINSULA · San Pedrillo · Corcovado National Park · Pacific Ocean · Sirena

GETTING ORIENTED

The most remote part of Costa Rica, the South Pacific encompasses the southern half of Puntarenas Province and La Amistad International Biosphere. The region descends from mountainous forests just an hour south of San José to the humid Golfo Dulce and the richly forested Osa Peninsula, six to eight hours from the capital by car.

8

0   10 mi
0   10 km

LIMÓN

CORDILLERA DE TALAMANCA

La Amistad National Park

Cabagra

Buenos Aires

Brujo

Terraba

Helechales

Paso Real

Alturas

Jabillo

237

PUNTARENAS

Union

San Vito

Chacarita

16   **PANAMA**

245

Piedras Blancas National Park

CR2   Río Claro

Ciudad Neily

Golfo Dulce

4   Golfito

14

Zancudo

Paso Canoas

Puerto Jiménez

Laurel

5

Conte

adrigal

El Higo

Pavones

Carate

Banco

Cabo Matapolo

Punto Banco

5 The Osa Peninsula. The wild Osa Peninsula consists almost entirely of Corcovado National Park, 1,156 square km (445 square miles) of primary and secondary rain forest straight out of a David Attenborough nature documentary.

CHIRRIPÓ NATIONAL PARK

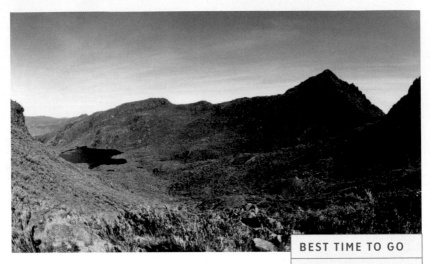

Chirripó National Park is all about hiking. The ascent up Mt. Chirripó, the highest mountain in Costa Rica, is the most popular, challenging, and exclusive hike in the country.

From the trailhead to the peak, you gain more than 2,438 meters (8,000 feet) of elevation, climbing through shaded highland forest, then out into the wide-open, windswept wilds of the *páramo*, scrubby moorland similar to the high Andes. It's a 48-km (30-mile) round-trip, and you need at least three days to climb to the base, explore the summits, and descend. The modern but chilly stone hostel is the only available accommodation, with small rooms of four bunks each, shared bathrooms, and a no-frills restaurant. A generator and solar panels provide some electricity, but the hostel is still bare-bones rustic. Trails from the hostel lead to the top of Chirripó and the nearby peak of Terbi, as well as half a dozen other peaks and glacier lakes. A new hiking route starts from the small pueblo of San Jerónimo, 40 km (25 mi) southwest of San Gerardo. It's a shorter trail, at 14.5 km (9 ½ mi) each way, with spectacular views on the way up to Crestones. *(For more information see the review in this chapter.)*

BEST TIME TO GO

Between sometimes freezing temperatures and more than 381 centimeters (150 inches) of rain a year, timing is of the essence here. The best months are in the dry season, January to May. The park is open all year, but during much of October, and all of November and December, the trails are often too wet and slippery to hike safely.

FUN FACT

A climb up Chirripó is a rite of passage for many young Costa Ricans, who celebrate their graduation from high school or college with a group expedition.

BEST WAYS TO EXPLORE

HIKING

There's no getting around it: the only way to explore this park is on foot. And the only way is up. It's a tough climb to Mt. Chirripó's base camp—6 to 10 hours from the official park entrance, depending on your physical condition—so most hikers head out of San Gerardo de Rivas before the first light of day. You can hire porters to lug your gear up and down for you, so at least you can travel relatively light.

People who live in Costa Rica train seriously for this hike, so be sure you are in good enough shape to make the climb. Smart hikers also factor in a couple of days in the San Gerardo de Rivas area to acclimate to the high altitude before setting out. The hike down is no picnic, either: your knees and ankles will be stretched to their limits. But it's an adventure every step of the way—and the bragging rights are worth it.

MOUNTAIN HIGHS

The base-camp hostel at Los Crestones is at 11,152 feet above sea level, so you still have some hiking ahead of you if you want to summit the surrounding peaks. Take your pick: Chirripó at 12,532 feet; Ventisqueros at 12,467 feet; Cerro Terbi at 12,336; and, for the fainter of heart, Mt. Uran at 11,811 feet. Mountain hikers who collect "peaks" can add all four mountaintops to their list.

BIRD-WATCHING

Although your eyes will mostly be on the scenery, there are some highland species of birds that thrive in this chilly mountain air. Watch for the volcano junco, a sparrowlike bird with a pink beak and a yellow eye ring. Only two humming-birds venture up this high—the fiery-throated hummingbird, which lives up to its name; and the volcano hummingbird, which is the country's smallest bird. If you see a raptor soaring above, chances are it's a red-tailed hawk.

TOP REASONS TO GO

You Did It!
The sheer sense of accomplishment at completing this tough hike is the number one reason to take on this challenge. You need to be in very good shape.

Ocean Views
On rare, perfectly clear days, the top of Chirripó is one of the few places in the country where you can see both the Pacific and Atlantic oceans.

Top of the World
The exhilaration of sitting on top of the world, with only sky, mountain peaks, and heath as far as the eye can see, motivates most visitors to withstand the physical challenges and the spartan conditions in the hostel.

Unique Environment
A climb up Chirripó gives visitors a unique chance to experience extreme changes in habitat, from pastureland through rain forest and oak forest to bleak, scrubby páramo (a high-elevation ecosystem). As the habitat changes, so does the endemic wildlife, which thins out near the top, along with the air.

8

BALLENA NATIONAL MARINE PARK

Great snorkeling, whale-watching, and beach-combing draw visitors and locals to Ballena National Marine Park, which protects four relatively tranquil beaches as well as a mangrove estuary, a remnant coral reef, and a vast swath of ocean.

Playa Uvita, fronting the small town of Bahía Ballena, is the longest, widest, and most visited beach, and the embarkation point for snorkeling, fishing, and whale-watching tours. Restaurants and cabinas line the nearby main street of the town. Playa Colonia, the most easily accessible beach, has safe swimming and a view of rocky islands. Playa Ballena, south of Playa Colonia, is a lovely strand backed by lush vegetation. Finally, tiny Playa Piñuela is the prettiest of the park beaches, in a deep cove that serves as the local port. It's also the narrowest beach, with a pebbled slope down to the sand. Along with the tropical fish you'll see while snorkeling, you may be lucky enough to see humpback whales and dolphins. *(For more information, see the review in this chapter.)*

BEST TIME TO GO

December to April is the best time for guaranteed sunny beach weather, as well as for sightings of humpback whales with their young. The whales also roam these waters in late July through late October. Bottlenose dolphins abound in March and April. Avoid Easter week and weekends in December to February, when locals camp in the park by the hundreds.

FUN FACT

Playa Uvita features a *tombolo*, a long swath of sand connecting a former island to the coast. At low tide, the exposed brown sandbar resembles a whale's tail.

BEST WAYS TO EXPLORE

BEACHCOMBING
The park's beaches are ideal to explore on foot, especially Playa Uvita, which has the longest and widest stretch of sand. Visitors and locals flock here in the late afternoon to catch spectacular sunsets. Don't forget your camera! At low tide, you can walk out onto the Whale's Tail sandbar. During the day, you'll see moving shells everywhere—hermit crabs of every size are constantly scuttling around. Although it all looks idyllic—and it mostly is—don't leave valuables unattended on the beach.

CAMPING
If you brought a tent, pitch it here. Camping on the beach is allowed at Playas Ballena, Colonia, and Piñuela. You can't beat the price, as camping is included in the park admission. Every beach has *sanitarios* (basic toilets) and cold-water showers. But bring your own drinking water. Costa Ricans are avid—and often noisy—campers, so try to avoid busy weekends and school holidays.

IN AND ON THE WATER
Swimming here is relatively safe, but check with the park ranger or your hotel about the best swimming spots. Watch for the *banda amarilla* (yellow ribbon) signs that indicate dangerous currents. Or just watch where the locals are frolicking in the water. Get a little farther out in the water on a fishing charter and try your hand at reeling in mahimahi, tuna, and mackerel. Whale- and dolphin-watching excursions are also a fun option—bottlenose dolphins are most often spotted, but humpback whales, especially mothers with babes, are the stars of the show. If you want to be the captain of your boat, sea kayaks are a popular way to explore the park's mangroves and river estuaries. Playa Ventanas, just south of the park's official border, has tidal rock caves you can kayak through. You can also paddle out to close-in islets and look for brown boobies, the tropical seabirds that nest here.

TOP REASONS TO GO

Alone Time
If solitude is what you're after, the park's beaches are relatively uncrowded, except on weekends and school holidays when locals come to camp and relax. Neither Playa Colonia nor Playa Piñuela sees a lot of traffic, so you can have them virtually to yourself almost anytime. There have been some nighttime drug-trafficking problems on these beaches, so don't hang out after dark.

Beaches
Miles of wide, sandy beach backed by palm trees and distant green mountain ridges make this one of the most scenic and accessible coastlines in the country. Playa Uvita and Playa Ballena, with their warm, swimmable waters and soft sand, attract the most beachgoers.

Whales and Dolphins
Catching sight of a mother humpback whale with her young swimming alongside is a thrill you won't soon forget. And watching dolphins cavorting around your excursion boat is the best entertainment on water.

8

CORCOVADO NATIONAL PARK

For those who crave untamed wilderness, Corcovado National Park is the experience of a lifetime. Covering one-third of the Osa Peninsula, the park is blanketed primarily by rain forest and holds Central America's largest remaining tract of lowland Pacific rain forest.

The remoteness of Corcovado and the difficult access to its interior make it one of the country's most pristine parks—barely disturbed by human presence—where massive, vine-tangled primary-forest trees tower over the trails and birds and wildlife abound. Your chances of spotting endangered species are better here than anywhere else in the country, although it still takes a combination of luck and determination. The rarest and most sought-after sightings are the jaguar and Baird's tapir. Corcovado also has the largest population of scarlet macaws in the country. Bordering the park are some of Costa Rica's most luxurious eco-friendly jungle lodges and retreats. *(For more information, see the review in this chapter.)*

BEST TIME TO GO

Dry season, January to May, is the best time to visit, but it's also the most popular. With only a limited number of camping spots available, it's crucial to reserve well in advance if you want to stay overnight in the park. New rules require that you are accompanied by a certified guide. June through August will be wetter, but may also be a little cooler. The long-distance trails are virtually impassable from September to December, when most visitors arrive in boats.

STAY ON TRAILS

Warning signs to stay on the trails should be heeded: in 2007, the Minister of Tourism got lost and wandered around in a daze for three days after following a baby tapir off the trail and being attacked by its mother.

BEST WAYS TO EXPLORE

BIRD-WATCHING AND WILDLIFE

The holy grail of wildlife spotting here is a jaguar or a Baird's tapir. You may be one of the lucky few to see one of these rare, elusive animals. In the meantime, you can content yourself with coatis, peccaries, and agoutis on the ground and, in the trees, some endemic species of birds you will see only in this part of the country: Baird's trogon, riverside wren, and black-cheeked ant-tanager, to name a few.

GETTING HERE AND AROUND

The easiest way to visit the park is on a guided day trip by boat, organized by a lodge or tour company in Drake Bay, Sierpe, or Uvita. The well-heeled can fly in on an expensive charter plane to the Sirena airfield. But no matter how you arrive, the only way to explore is on foot. There are no roads, only hiking trails. If you have a backpack, strong legs, a certified guide, and a reservation for a tent site you can enter the park on foot at three staffed ranger stations and spend up to five days deep in the wilds.

HIKING

There are two main hiking routes to Corcovado. When you're planning your itinerary, keep in mind that the hike between any two ranger stations takes at least a day. The hike from La Leona to Sirena is about 16 km (10 miles) and requires crossing a wide river mouth and a stretch of beach best negotiated at low tide. Some people plan this hike before dawn to avoid the blistering sun. The 10-km (6 1/4-mile) route from Los Patos to Sirena is the coolest trail, through forest all the way.

TOP REASONS TO GO

Flora and Fauna
The sheer diversity of flora and fauna and the chance to see wildlife completely in the wild are the main draws here. The number of cataloged species, to date, includes 500 trees (49 of them in peril of extinction), 150 orchids, 375 birds, 124 mammals (11 on the endangered list; 55 are bats), 123 butterflies, 71 reptiles, 46 amphibians, and more than 8,000 insects.

Off the Beaten Track
Day visitors get to taste the thrill of being completely off the beaten track, in an untamed natural world. But for campers at La Sirena and San Pedrillo stations, the chance to spend days roaming miles of trails without hearing a single man-made sound is a rare treat.

Test Your Limits
The physical challenges of hiking in high humidity and living very basically, along with the psychological challenge of being completely out of touch with "the real world," can be rewarding.

8

Updated
by Dorothy
MacKinnon

Visitors go south to heed the call of the wild. The jewels in the South Pacific crown are the idyllic Golfo Dulce and the wild Osa Peninsula, brimming with wildlife and natural adventures. There is no place like it, especially when you travel off the grid, far from the sounds of modern civilization. With miles of undulating Pacific coastline, there is rarely a crowded beach. Up in the highlands, the hiking and bird-watching are unsurpassed.

The South Pacific encompasses everything south of San José, down to the border with Panama, and all the territory west of the Talamanca Mountains, sloping down to the Pacific coast. Adventures abound in this rugged region. On land, hiking, bird-watching, horseback riding, and wildlife viewing are the main activities, along with some thrilling tree-climbing, zip-lining, and waterfall-rappelling opportunities. On the water, there's surfing, snorkeling, diving, fishing, sea kayaking, and whale- and dolphin-watching, as well as swimming and beachcombing.

What makes many of these activities special is that, given the wildness of the locations, the focus is more on nature than on entertainment. No matter what you're doing, you'll come across interesting flora and fauna and natural phenomena. Another key to what sets this area apart is the large number of trained naturalist guides. Most eco-lodges have resident guides who know not only where to find the birds and wildlife, but also how to interpret the hidden workings of the natural world around you.

The hiking in the south is simply spectacular, so don't leave home without your hiking boots. The most challenging hike in the country is Chirripó Mountain, a 6- to 10-hour haul up to the national-park hostel, a base camp for exploring surrounding peaks. Dramatic but less challenging hikes include the well-maintained, wide trails in the cool high-altitude forests of the Savegre Valley; the dramatic Coastal Path south of Drake; and forest trails to waterfalls and swimming holes in the Golfo Dulce, Osa Peninsula, and around Dominical.

PLANNING

WHEN TO GO

PEAK SEASON: JANUARY TO APRIL

The dry season has the most reliably sunny weather. But be aware that the climate swings wildly in the south, from bracing mountain air to steamy coastal humidity. In the mountains it's normally around 24°C (75°F) during the day and 10°C (50°F) at night. Temperatures can fall close to freezing on the upper slopes of Cerro de la Muerte and elsewhere, so be sure to pack warm layers. Temperatures in coastal areas are usually 24°C–32°C (76°F–90°F), but it's the humidity that does you in.

OFF-SEASON: SEPTEMBER TO DECEMBER

The rainy season can be very wet indeed, especially September through November. The wet season is longest in the Osa Peninsula, where showers usually last through January. Roads sometimes flood and many lodges close in the rainiest months (October and November). Elsewhere during the long rainy season, mornings tend to be brilliant and sunny, with refreshing rain starting in mid-afternoon. Many lodges offer discounted "green season" rates. Often, there is a two- or three-week period of dry weather with brilliant sunshine in late June into July, a mini-summer called *el veranillo*.

SHOULDER SEASON: EARLY DECEMBER AND APRIL TO MAY

Early December, when the landscape is lush and green after months of rain and crowds of tourists have yet to arrive, can be delightful in most of the Southern Zone. April into May is another good time to visit, when crowds have thinned out and the rains are just starting to freshen up the landscape

PLANNING YOUR TIME

You need at least a week to truly experience any part of the Osa Peninsula. Even if you fly, ground transportation to your lodge may be painfully slow, so plan two days for travel alone. It's best to choose one base and take day trips from there. In three weeks, you can experience the entire region, including mountains, beaches, and the Osa Peninsula.

If you are driving south, keep in mind that Cerro de la Muerte is often covered with fog in the afternoon, so plan to cross the mountains in the morning. This mountain road has been much improved, but it's safer—not to mention more scenic—to drive it in dry, clear weather. More and more visitors take the coastal highway these days, but they miss out on the dramatic mountain vistas.

Don't try to cover too much ground on a set schedule. It is simply impossible to overestimate how long it takes to drive a certain route or make transportation connections in this part of the country, especially during rainy season when flooding and landslides can close roads and bad weather can delay flights. But remember, getting there is part of the adventure.

8

GETTING HERE AND AROUND
AIR TRAVEL

SANSA and Nature Air have direct flights to Drake Bay, Palmar Sur, and Puerto Jiménez. SANSA flies Cessna planes and has the most flights to Golfito, including a daily flight to San Isidro de El General. Nature Air flies DeHavilland aircraft with larger windows that are great for sightseeing. The company prides itself on its sustainability, claiming to be the world's first carbon-neutral airline.

Alfa Romeo Aero Taxi, at the Puerto Jiménez airport (really more of an airstrip), flies small charter planes to Carate, Tiskita, and Corcovado National Park's airstrip at La Sirena. The one-way price to Corcovado is $390 for up to five people.

Airline Contact Alfa Romeo Aero Taxi. ⊠ *Puerto Jiménez Airport* ☎ *2735–5178* ✆ *aerocorcovado@racsa.co.cr.*

BUS TRAVEL

Bus fares from San José average about $10, depending on distance and number of stops. The best way to get around the region's roads is by bus—let someone else do the driving. Bus fares are cheap, and you'll meet the locals. But the going is generally slow, departures are often very early in the morning, and schedules change so frequently that you'll want to confirm the day before you travel.

Based in Dominical, Monkey Ride has shuttle-van services in each direction between San José and the Dominical/Uvita/Ojochal area starting at $44 per person.

Bus Contact Monkey Ride. ⊠ *Pueblo del Río, main street, Dominical* ☎ *2787–0454, 8651–9090* ⊕ *www.monkeyridecr.com.*

CAR TRAVEL

Owing to the often dismal state of the roads (deteriorated bridges and potholes galore) and hazardous driving conditions (flooded rivers), we don't recommend driving in the southern reaches of the South Pacific, especially in rainy season. If you decide to drive, make sure your vehicle has 4WD, high clearance, and a spare tire. Give yourself lots of daylight time to get to where you are going (the sun sets around 5:30). You can also fly to Golfito or the Osa Peninsula and rent a 4WD vehicle. The Southern Zone was the very last part of Costa Rica to be settled and the first road from San José to San Isidro wasn't begun until the 1950s.

HEALTH AND SAFETY

You are more likely to suffer from dehydration than any other health issue. Carry plenty of water wherever you go, wear a hat, and use sturdy hiking boots and long pants when hiking trails where biting insects may strike or the occasional snake might be sleeping in the sun. Do not leave any valuables in your car or your room—always put them in the safe provided by your hotel or lodge.

MONEY MATTERS

ATMs are sprouting up everywhere in the Southern Zone. The places you won't find a bank are remote communities, for example the beaches south of Golfito on the mainland, or in Drake Bay and lodges south of Puerto Jiménez.

RESTAURANTS

Count on finding lots of fresh fish and tropical fruits on the menu, whether at a roadside *soda* (casual eatery) serving *comida típica* (typical food) or a sophisticated restaurant in Dominical or Ojochal. Up in the mountains, don't miss out on eating fresh, farmed trout. The food at most remote eco-lodges is excellent.

HOTELS

Expect reasonable comfort in unbelievably wild settings. Most accommodations are in small hotels, lodges, and cabins run by hands-on owners, many of them foreigners who fell in love with the country during a vacation here and stayed. Generally speaking, the farther south and more remote the lodge, the more expensive it is. Bad roads (causing supply problems) and lack of electricity and communications make hotel-keeping costly, especially in the Osa Peninsula and Golfo Dulce, where a fresh egg can cost up to a dollar. When comparing per-person prices, take into account that most of these places include meals, transport, guides, and unique locations.

The country's premier eco-lodges are almost all in the Southern Zone, ranging from simple tents to sophisticated lodges. But keep in mind that if you yearn to be close to nature, you have to be prepared for encounters of the natural kind in your shower or bedroom. Keep a flashlight handy for nighttime trips to the bathroom and always wear shoes. *Hotel reviews have been shortened. For full information, visit Fodors.com.*

WHAT IT COSTS IN DOLLARS				
	$	**$$**	**$$$**	**$$$$**
Restaurants	under $10	$10–$15	$16–$25	over $25
Hotels	under $75	$75–$150	$151–$250	over $250

Restaurant prices are the average cost of a main course at dinner or, if dinner is not served, at lunch. Hotel prices are the lowest cost of a standard double room in high season.

TOURS

Costa Rica Expeditions. This is the most experienced ecotourist outfit in Costa Rica, specializing in customizing countrywide nature tours and led by expert, bilingual, local naturalist guides. ☏ *2521–6099* ⊕ *www.costaricaexpeditions.com.*

Horizontes Nature Tours. This expert ecotourist company arranges small-group and custom tours with naturalist guides and ornithologists, including nature-photography tours. ☏ *2222–2022, 888/786–8748 toll-free in the U.S.* ⊕ *www.horizontes.com.*

TRAVELING WITH KIDS

The Southern Zone is like Outward Bound for families, where kids and parents can face challenges—such as no TVs or video games!—and have fun together. Plunge the family into real-life adventures with added educational value. You might inspire a future herpetologist or marine biologist among your progeny.

Eco-Lodges in the South Pacific

The South Pacific Zone is Costa Rica's last frontier, with a wealth of protected biodiversity. It's also the cradle of the country's ecotourism, including some of the world's best eco-lodges.

Casa Corcovado Jungle Lodge, Drake Bay. This jungle lodge, bordering Corcovado National Park, gets top eco-marks for its energy-saving solar and microhydroelectric systems, and its recycling and waste-management leadership in the area. The lodge financed the building of a recycling center in Sierpe, and all the area's glass and aluminum is now recycled. The owner is a founding member of the conservationist Corcovado Foundation.

Lapa Ríos, Cabo Matapalo. The premier eco-lodge in Costa Rica, Lapa Ríos protects 1,000 acres of forest in its private preserve edging Corcovado National Park. The lodge provides direct employment to more than 45 area families. Lapa Ríos was the first area lodge to offer a free sustainability tour, highlighting innovative eco-friendly practices.

Playa Nicuesa Rainforest Lodge, Golfito. From its initial construction to its daily operations, this Golfo Dulce lodge, accessible only by boat, has been committed to sustainability. Solar power, an organic septic system, composting, and a chemical-free garden attest to the owners' eco-credentials.

Go horseback riding to waterfalls and swimming holes. Steal into the night with infrared flashlights to scout out frogs and other fascinating, nocturnal creepy-crawlies. Paddle a kayak in a calm gulf where dolphins play. Rappel down a waterfall, climb inside a hollow tree, or zip line through the canopy.

The more remote areas of the south are ideal for kids ages seven and up. Babies and all their paraphernalia are hard to handle here, and toddlers are tough to keep off the ground where biting insects and snakes live.

VISITOR INFORMATION

There aren't many official tourist offices in the south. The Dominical Information Center is a great source for everything from bus schedules to maps to tour arrangements. There is also a hard-to-find, official government tourist office in Río Claro, en route to Golfito. Always ask for recommendations from your hosts. Lodge and hotel owners know their turf and they want happy guests, so they are unlikely to steer you astray.

THE CENTRAL HIGHLANDS

Famous for spectacular mountain vistas, high-altitude coffee farms, cloud-forest eco-lodges, and challenging mountain hikes, the Central Highlands of Cerro de la Muerte are less than an hour south of San José, climbing up the Pan-American Highway.

ZONA DE LOS SANTOS

Santa María de Dota is 65 km (40 miles) south of San José.

Empalme, at Km 51 of the Pan-American Highway, marks the turnoff for Santa María de Dota, the first of the picturesque coffee-growing towns, named after saints, that dot this mountainous area known as the Zona de Los Santos (Zone of the Saints). The route itself is about 24 km (15 miles) long.

GETTING HERE AND AROUND

From San José, drive southeast on the paved Pan-American Highway, heading toward Cartago, then follow the signs south for San Isidro de El General. The two-lane road climbs steeply, and there are almost no safe places to pass heavy trucks and slow vehicles, but the views are worth it. Make an early start, because the road is often enveloped in mist and rain in the afternoon. It typically takes about 90 minutes to reach Km 51, where you turn right at Empalme to reach Santa María de Dota, 14 km (8½ miles) along a wide, curving, paved road.

EXPLORING

Ruta de Los Santos (*Route of the Saints*). The scenic road that winds through the high-altitude valleys from Empalme to San Pablo de León is appropriately called the Ruta de Los Santos—the towns it passes are named after saints. It's nicely paved to facilitate shipping the coffee produced in the region. On the 30-minute drive from Empalme to San Pablo de León Cortés, you travel through misty valleys ringed by precipitous mountain slopes terraced with lush, green coffee plants. The 24-km (15-mile) route also captures the essence of a fast-disappearing traditional Tico way of life built around agriculture. Stately churches anchor bustling towns full of prosperous, neat houses with pretty gardens and vintage 1970s Toyota Land Cruiser trucks.

8

WHERE TO EAT AND STAY

$ ✕ **Café de Los Santos.** This pretty café, within sight of the town's majestic
CAFÉ   church in San Marcos de Tarrazú, showcases the area's high-altitude *arabica* Tarrazú coffee, the "celestial drink" for which this zone is famous. There are more than 30 specialty coffee drinks, plus homemade sweet and savory pastries. While waiting for your coffee to brew, check out the vintage photos of oxcarts and coffee harvests lining the walls. ⑤ *Average main: $5 ✉ 6 km (4 miles) west of Santa María de Dota, 200 m east of church, San Marcos de Tarrazú* ☎ *2546–7881* ☾ *Closed Sun.*

$ ✕ **Mutute Café Boutique Tarrazú.** A giant, colorful *chorreador*, the tradi-
COSTA RICAN   tional wooden stand for making coffee with a sock-like filter, marks the spot for this tiny but sophisticated café, a showplace for the award-winning, high-altitude coffee from Monte Copey in the nearby Tarrazú coffee region. The café's slogan is: Life is too short to drink cheap coffee. If you agree, watch Barrista Monserrath Navarros expertly concoct flavorful espresso and cappuccino, complete with artistic swirls in the milk foam. Homemade sweets and savories accompany coffee and natural fruit drinks, and you can buy handsomely packaged ground coffee to take home. The café is right on the highway, with easy parking. ⑤ *Average main: $5 ✉ Empalme, Km. 51 Pan-American Hwy.* ☎ *2571–2323* ⊟ *No credit cards.*

$$ 🛏 **El Toucanet Lodge.** For serenity and mountain greenery, you can't beat
B&B/INN this family-run lodge with panoramic views and the opportunity to see
FAMILY hummingbirds and other highland species from the dining terrace. **Pros:**
fresh mountain air; tranquility; affordable; good birding. **Cons:** simple
furnishings; limited menu; some steps to climb to cabins. ⑤ *Rooms
from: $88* ⊠ *Rt. 315, 7 km (4½ miles) east of Santa María de Dota,
Copey* ☎ *2541–3045* ⊕ *www.eltoucanet.com* ۞ *Closed Sept. and Oct.*
↪ *6 rooms, 2 junior suites* ❐ *Breakfast.*

SHOPPING

Coopedota Santa Maria. The best place to buy local coffee is where 800
farmers bring their raw coffee beans to be roasted and packed into jute
bags. This is the first carbon-neutral coffee producer in the world. You
can buy three dozen different coffee beverages and export-quality coffee
at the café shop for about $8 per pound. Choose between light or dark
roast and *en grano* (whole bean) or *molido* (ground). A variety of tours
are offered ($22 to $36), covering everything from processing to tasting
to the cooperative's innovative recycling. The classic two-hour Coffee
Experience tour ($22), which reveals the process from bean to bag, is
offered weekdays 7–3, and weekends by appointment. Check out the
website for details of tours or email coffee-experience@coopedota.com
to make reservations. ⊠ *C. Central, Santa María de Dota* ☎ *2541–2828
for coffee tour, 2541–0102 café* ⊕ *www.coopedota.com* ۞ *Mon.–Sat.
8–6, Sun. 12–6.*

SAN GERARDO DE DOTA

*89 km (55 miles) southeast of San José, 52 km (32 miles) south of Santa
María de Dota.*

Cloud forests, invigorating mountain air, well-maintained hiking trails,
and excellent bird-watching make San Gerardo de Dota one of Costa
Rica's premier nature destinations. The tiny hamlet is in the narrow
Savegre River valley, 9 km (5½ miles) down a twisting, partially paved
track that descends abruptly to the west from the Pan-American High-
way. The peaceful surroundings look more like the Rocky Mountains
than Central America, but hike down the waterfall trail and the veg-
etation quickly turns tropical again. Beyond hiking and bird-watching,
activities include horseback riding and zip lining.

GETTING HERE AND AROUND

The drive from San José takes about three hours, and from Santa María
de Dota about an hour. At Km 80 on the Pan-American Highway, turn
down the dirt road signed "San Gerardo de Dota." It's a harrowing,
twisting road with signs warning drivers to gear down and go slow.
Some newly paved sections help ease the steepest curves. Tourist vans
often stop along the road when the guides spot birds; grab your bin-
oculars and discreetly join them!

SPORTS AND THE OUTDOORS

BIRD-WATCHING

Although you can see many birds from your cabin porch and viewing platform, most bird-watching requires hiking, some of it along steep paths made extra challenging by the high altitude (from 7,000 to 10,000 feet above sea level). Come fit and armed with binoculars and layers of warm clothing. The early mornings are brisk up here, but you'll warm up quickly with the sun and the exertion of walking.

Fodor's Choice ★ **Savegre Hotel, Natural Reserve & Spa.** With the best bird guides in the area, including veteran birder Marino Chacon ($90 for a half day), this hotel organizes the best highland birding and hiking tours in the oak forests and surrounding mountains. Two observation and photography shelters perched on a hillside garden overlooking a bird-friendly orchard are in the works, complete with battery-charging facilities for cameras and computers. ⊠ *Savegre Hotel, Natural Reserve & Spa, off Pan-American Hwy.* ☎ *2740–1028* ⊕ *www.savegre.com.*

THE RESPLENDENT QUETZAL

The forest around San Gerardo de Dota is renowned for resplendent quetzals, considered by many to be the most beautiful bird in the Western world. Male quetzals in full breeding plumage have metallic green feathers, crimson stomachs, helmetlike crests, and extravagantly long tail feathers. Ask guides or hotel staff about quetzal hangouts; early morning during the March-to-May nesting season is the best time to spot them but an ongoing program to plant *aguacatillo* trees, the birds' favorite food source, means they are seen most of the year.

HIKING

Some of the best hiking in the country is in this valley.

Río Savegre Trail. The most scenic and interesting trail in the area is the one that begins at the Savegre Hotel, Natural Reserve & Spa and follows the Río Savegre to a spectacular waterfall. To get to the trailhead, follow the main road past the hotel to a fork, where you veer left, cross a bridge, and head over the hill to a pasture that narrows to a footpath. Although it is only 2 km (1¼ miles) each way and there are some steps to help you negotiate the steepest parts, the hike can be slippery, especially near the bottom, and takes about two hours. Do not attempt to swim in the pool below the waterfall. The current is very swift and dangerous. ⊠ *Savegre Hotel, Natural Reserve & Spa, off Pan-American Hwy.* ⊕ *www.savegre.com* ⊠ *Free.*

Savegre Hotel, Natural Reserve & Spa. This world-renowned, bird-watching hotel runs a daylong, guided, natural-history hike (about $165 for up to eight people, including transportation) that starts with a drive up to the páramo (high-altitude ecosystem) of Cerro de la Muerte. The trail begins at the cluster of communication towers and descends through the forest into the valley. Miles of prime bird-watching and hiking trails wind through the private forest reserve. Night temperatures on the slopes of Cerro de la Muerte can approach freezing. Pack accordingly for cold

8

mornings. ✉ *Savegre Hotel, Natural Reserve & Spa, off the Pan-American Hwy.* ☎ *2740–1028* ⊕ *www.savegre.com* ⊠ *$165 for up to 8 hikers.*

WHERE TO EAT

$ ✕ **Kahawa.** Perched on the boulder-strewn bank of the rushing Savegre River, this handsome, blond-wood-and-stone rancho specializes in serving up fresh trout in a myriad of delicious ways. There's pasta with smoked trout, trout fillet with coconut sauce, trout tacos, morsels of fried trout with tartar sauce, and the signature sandwich: smoked trout with cream cheese, capers, tomato, and lettuce on a bun. Local beer, fruit smoothies, and cinnamon-spiced tamarindo juice wash it all down. The coffee—Kahawa means coffee in Swahili—is excellent, as are the homemade desserts. Riverside tables are perfect for bird-watching, so bring your binoculars. Come early if you want dinner; it's open daily 7:30 to 6. ⑤ *Average main: $$8* ✉ *San Gerardo de Dota* ✛ *from the Pan-American Hwy. at Km 80, about 8 km down the steep road to San Gerardo de Dota* ☎ *2740–1081* ⊙ *No dinner* ⊟ *No credit cards.*

COSTA RICAN

WHERE TO STAY

$ ⌂ **Cabañas y Senderos Las Cataratas.** One of the best deals—and fresh-trout meals—in the valley is at this family-run restaurant and bed-and-breakfast with simple cabins, set beside a series of scenic trout ponds in gardens filled with flowers and hummingbirds. **Pros:** excellent fresh trout; authentic Tico culture; tranquil. **Cons:** very steep driveway, 4X4 required; call ahead on weekdays to make sure someone is there. ⑤ *Rooms from: $65* ✉ *3 km (2 miles) from main hwy., along road to San Gerardo de Dota* ☎ *2740–1064, 2740–1065* ⤴ *4 cabins* ⦿ *Breakfast; All meals.*

B&B/INN

$$$ ⌂ **Dantica Lodge and Gallery.** High style at high altitude, this avant-garde lodge clinging to the side of a mountain has unbeatable valley views, great bird-watching, luxury accommodations, a sophisticated restaurant, and the top ecological sustainability rating. **Pros:** stylish casitas; gorgeous natural setting with miles of trails; excellent restaurant. **Cons:** steep access along narrow trails to forest casitas; some casitas close to road. ⑤ *Rooms from: $195* ✉ *Road to San Gerardo de Dota, 4 km (2 miles) west of Pan-American Hwy.* ☎ *2740–1067* ⊕ *www.dantica.com* ⤴ *7 casitas, 1 deluxe suite, 1 master suite, 2 2-bedroom bungalows* ⦿ *Breakfast.*

B&B/INN
FAMILY
Fodor'sChoice
★

$$$ ⌂ **Paraíso Quetzal Lodge.** Nestled in a cloud forest just minutes off the main highway, this rustic but comfortable lodge is, indeed, a paradise for resplendent quetzals and for those who want to spot this sought-after bird and other highland birds, including hordes of hummingbirds. **Pros:** scenic views; pristine cloud forest; amazing hikes and bird-watching. **Cons:** very simple food; steep paths to some cabins; very cold nights. ⑤ *Rooms from: $184* ✉ *Km 70 Pan-American Hwy., Cerro de la Muerte* ☎ *2200–0241, 8810–0234* ⊕ *www.quetzalsparadise.com* ⤴ *10 bungalows, 4 superior bungalows* ⦿ *Some meals.*

B&B/INN

$$ ⌂ **Savegre Hotel, Natural Reserve & Spa.** Famous for its miles of bird-watching trails and its expert guides, this once-rustic lodge now has cabin suites with handsome wood furnishings, crackling fireplaces, and deep bathtubs, plus a full-service, riverside spa. **Pros:** great trails;

B&B/INN
Fodor'sChoice
★

A male white-throated mountain-gem hummingbird in a defense posture. Río Savegre, San Gerardo de Dota.

amazing, abundant birdlife; excellent guides. **Cons:** steep trails and high altitude may tax some visitors; most meals are served buffet style; be prepared for very cold nights. ⑤ *Rooms from: $126* ✉ *San Gerardo de Dota* ✛ *At Km. 80 of Pan-American Hwy. take very steep road for 9 km (5 1/2 miles) to hotel entrance, a bridge over the Río Savegre* ☎ *2740– 1028* ⊕ *www.savegre.com* ᐳ *21 rooms, 29 cabin suites* ⦿ *Breakfast.*

$$
Trogón Lodge. Set in a riotous garden filled with fuchsias, hydrangeas, and hummingbirds, Trogón Lodge is more a picturesque hideaway than a hiking-heavy destination. **Pros:** lush garden; convivial public area; small but excellent gift shop. **Cons:** steep, short trails that end at road; limited outdoor privacy except in honeymoon suite. ⑤ *Rooms from: $134* ✉ *San Gerardo de Dota* ✛ *At Km. 80 on Pan-American Hwy., follow very steep, partially paved road down 7½ km (4½ miles)* ☎ *2740– 1051 lodge, 2293–8181293–8181 (reservations) for reservations only* ⊕ *www.grupomawamba.com* ᐳ *22 rooms, 1 suite* ⦿ *Breakfast.*

B&B/INN

VALLE DE EL GENERAL REGION

The Valle de El General (The General's Valley) area encompasses vast expanses of highland wilderness on the upper slopes of the Talamanca mountains and the high-altitude páramo of Chirripó National Park, as well as prosperous agricultural communities amid vast, sunbaked fields of pineapple and sugarcane. It is bounded to the north and west by the central highlands of the massive Cordillera de Talamanca and to the south by La Amistad International Park. The valley is named for the

Río de El General, one of the many rivers that rise in the Talamancas and run down through the valley, making it ideal for farming.

SAN ISIDRO DE EL GENERAL

54 km (34 miles) south of San Gerardo de Dota.

Although San Isidro de El General has no major attractions, the bustling market town is a good place to have lunch, get cash at one of the many ATMs, or fill your tank—the main highway into town is lined with service stations, some operating 24 hours. Advice to map readers: there are other San Isidros in Costa Rica, but this is the only San Isidro de El General. Just to confuse matters more, this town also goes by the name Peréz Zeledón. The town is the jumping-off point for hiking the scenic highlands around San Gerardo de Rivas, and climbing the country's highest peak, Chirripó. There's also excellent bird-watching in nearby nature reserves, including the original homestead, now a museum, of famed ornithologist Alexander Skutch.

GETTING HERE AND AROUND

The Pan-American Highway takes you straight into San Isidro de El General. It's 129 km (80 miles) south of San José and about 1½ hours' drive south of the San Gerardo de Dota highway exit. Truck traffic can be heavy and painfully slow. For folks in a hurry, there's a daily 35-minute SANSA flight from San José to the San Isidro airstrip, leaving San José at 7:55 am and returning at 8:40 am. Buses to Dominical leave from the San Isidro de El General bus terminal, southeast of the cathedral, near the Pan-American Highway. Buses bound for San Gerardo de Rivas, the starting point of the trail into Chirripó National Park, depart from San Isidro de El General at 5:30 am from the central park and at 2 pm from a stop at the central market.

ESSENTIALS

Banks/ATMs ATH Coopealianza. ⊠ *South side of central park beside Hotel Chirripó, San Isidro de el General.* **Banco Nacional.** ⊠ *North side of central park, San Isidro de el General* ☎ *2212–2000.*

Hospital Hospital Escalante Pradilla. ⊠ *Off main street, east of municipal stadium, San Isidro de el General* ☎ *2771–3122.*

Pharmacy Farmacia Santa Marta. ⊠ *Northwest of central park, across from cultural center, San Isidro de el General* ☎ *2771–4506.*

Post Office Correo. ⊠ *South side of park, San Isidro de el General.*

Visitor Information Selva Mar. ⊠ *South of central park, San Isidro de el General* ☎ *2771–4582* ⊕ *www.selvamar.com.*

EXPLORING

FAMILY **Centro Biológico Las Quebradas** (*Las Quebradas Biological Center*). In a lush valley 7 km (4½ miles) northeast of San Isidro de El General, this community-managed nature reserve protects 1,853 acres of dense forest in which elegant tree ferns grow in the shadows of massive trees, and colorful tanagers and euphonias flit about the foliage. Five km (3 miles) of trails wind uphill through the forest and along the Río

The Central Highlands and Valle De El General Region

Quebradas, which supplies water to San Isidro de El General and sur-rounding communities. There's also an easily accessible sensory garden, with plants to smell and taste, and a butterfly garden. To get here from the Pan-American Highway, head 7 km (4½ miles) northeast at the sign for Las Quebradas. The reserve is 2 km (1 mile) north of town on an unpaved road. ⊠ *Off Pan-American Hwy., 7 km (4½ miles) northeast of San Isidro de El General, Las Quebradas* ☎ *2771–4131* 💲 *$4* ☉ *Tues.–Sun. 8–4.*

Los Cusingos Bird Sanctuary. Here you'll find birding trails and the house of the late Dr. Alexander Skutch, the region's preeminent ornithologist and coauthor of *A Guide to the Birds of Costa Rica,* the birders' bible. His 190-acre estate, an island of forest amid a sea of new farms and housing developments, is now run by the nonprofit Centro Científico Tropical (Tropical Science Center), which has improved 2 km (1 mile) of trails and maintains the simple house where Dr. Skutch lived—without electricity—from 1941 until his death in 2004, just a week shy of his 100th birthday. Room by room, the moldy books, piles of jour-nals, vintage typewriter, and humble bedrooms and kitchen speak to Skutch's lifelong philosophy of simplicity. Among the 200 or so bird species that still visit the property are *cusingos* or fiery-billed aracaris—colorful, small members of the toucan family, for which the property is named—and mixed tanager flocks. The sanctuary is a half-hour's drive southeast of San Isidro de El General in the town of Quizarrá. Just show up, or call ahead if you want a guided tour. ⊠ *15 km (10 miles) southeast of San Isidro de El General, Quizarrá ⊹ south on Panamerican Hwy, cross bridge over Río General and watch for small, blue Riserva Biologica sign on left, take that turn, through town of Peñas Blancas, past cemetery and watch for sign on right for Quizzará* ☎ *2200–5472* ⊕ *costarica.com/attractions/los-cusingos-bird-sanctuary* ⊠ *$13* ☉ *Mon.–Sat. 7–4, Sun. 7–1.*

SPORTS AND THE OUTDOORS
TOUR OPERATOR
Selva Mar. The most experienced Southern Zone tour operator, Selva Mar organizes nature, horseback, waterfall, and birding tours, as well as boat transportation to remote Osa lodges. ⊠ *South of southeast corner of central park, San Isidro de el General* ☎ *2771–4582* ⊕ *www. selvamar.com* ⊠ *From $110.*

BIRD-WATCHING
Tropical Feathers. Run by an expert birder with over 15 years of experience, Tropical Feathers offers multiday bird-watching packages and arranges customized tours, including wildlife-photography tours, in the San Isidro de El General and Dominical area and points south. Half-day birding tours start at $60 per group; full day, $100; transportation extra, if needed. Check the website for excellent photos and bird lore. ⊠ *San Isidro de el General* ☎ *8382–1148* ⊕ *www.costaricabirdingtours.com.*

HIKING
The major tourist draw is climbing Mt. Chirripó (the highest peak is 3,820 meters or about 12,532 feet) in Chirripó National Park. There is a limit of 52 hikers in the park on any one day. A new system is in place to make reservations easier and hiking safer, with tour packages that include lodging before the hike, porters, guides, and accommodation in the park hut. *See Hotel de Montaña El Pelícano for details.* Alternatively, opt for a different hike in the surrounding area.

WHERE TO EAT
$ **✕ El Potro Bar & Restaurant.** You can't miss this roadside restaurant on
COSTA RICAN   the steep climb north from Perez Zeledon—just look for the sign of the rearing horse (*el potro*). From the large, covered terrace, you can sit and gaze at the valley view and, if you're lucky, spot some wildlife in the trees below. The menu is Costa Rican, straightforward and simple, but well executed. The seafood soup is a meal in itself, chock-full of mollusks in a flavorful tomato broth. Nachos, quesadillas, and fried calamari go well with the cocktails and local beers. There are also heartier meals with chicken and grilled meats. It's cheerful, inexpensive, and the servers are attentive and friendly. $ *Average main: $9* ⊠ *1 km north of the Gasotica service station in San Isidro de El General, Pan-American Highway, San Isidro de el General* ☎ *2772–2430.*

$ **✕ El Trapiche de Nayo.** The panoramic valley view is worth a stop at
COSTA RICAN   this rustic roadside restaurant that serves the kind of food Ticos eat at
FAMILY   *turnos* (village fund-raising festivals), including hard-to-find *sopa de mondongo* (tripe soup). Easier to stomach are the *gallos,* thick tortillas

cooked on a wood stove, which you stuff with cooked hearts of palm, root vegetables, or chicken in salsa. Some Saturdays, raw sugarcane is pressed in an antique mill and boiled in huge iron cauldrons to make smooth *sobado,* a molasses-flavored fudge. Service is leisurely, to say the least, but the restrooms have been upgraded, so it's a decent pit stop. Come early for dinner: it's open 7 am to 8 pm daily. $ Average main: $8 ⊠ *Pan-American Hwy., 6 km (4 miles) north of San Isidro de El General, San Isidro de el General* ☎ *2771–7267* ⊟ *No credit cards.*

$ ✕ **Kafe de la Casa.** This is as hip as it gets in downtown San Isidro
COSTA RICAN de El General. Along with excellent cappuccino and homemade muffins, you can enjoy breakfast here all day long, in a funky, retro-rustic atmosphere combining '50s diner and Tico country. There's also a full menu of meat and chicken dishes. Sample them all in the Bandeja de la Casa, a monster plate of cheese fingers, chicken or beef fajitas, *platano* (plantain), refried beans, and tortillas. Healthier options include yogurt smoothies and omelets. This is the place to find out what's happening culturally around town and perhaps chance upon an art exhibit, an acoustic concert, or a poetry reading in the café. On weekdays, it stays open until 7 pm. $ *Average main: $8* ⊠ *C. 4 at Avda. 3, just behind the Musoc bus station, San Isidro de el General* ☎ *2770–4816* ⊗ *Closed Sun. No dinner Sat.*

$ ✕ **Restaurante Bazooka's.** The slogan here is "American as apple pie," and
DINER there is indeed apple pie à la mode, as well as all-day breakfast and a selection of hearty burgers, triple-decker sandwiches, and meal-size salads at this popular roadside diner. Don't skip the chunky fries—they are worth the calories. Pancakes, waffles, and ice-cream sundaes will satisfy your sweet tooth. Hungrier eaters can chow down on hearty servings of barbecue ribs or various cuts of steak, accompanied by reasonably priced Spanish wines. There are Tico touches, too, with local fish and shrimp with rice and *tres leches* cake, the classic Tico dessert. The $5 lunch specials are an excellent value and there is free Wi-Fi. Tables are spread through different rooms of the cheerfully updated wooden hacienda, all of them pleasant, with lots of natural light. There is also a shaded terrace if you want to get away form the TVs. If you're in a hurry, everything is available to go. The eatery is on the main highway, so you don't have to negotiate San Isidro de El General's sometimes confusing one-way streets. Just look for the big pink Bazooka's sign at the northern entrance to town. $ *Average main: $8* ⊠ *Pan-American Hwy., next door to Beto Solis gas station, San Isidro de el General* ☎ *2771–2050* ⊕ *www.bazookasrestaurant.com.*

$ ✕ **Restaurant La Georgina.** Since 1947, this large cafeteria in a white clap-
COSTA RICAN board building has been the traditional roadside stop for busloads of travelers crossing the highlands of Cerro de la Muerte. There are comfortable restrooms, and the bright eating area has blond-wood tables and chairs. Grab a tray and choose from a steam table of Costa Rican specialties—beef in salsa, cheesy tortillas, grilled sweet platanos stuffed with cheese, and homemade muffins and sweet rolls. Or just order a hot chocolate and take a seat at the counter along the back wall and enjoy the main attraction: a row of hummingbird feeders abuzz with birds, notably fiery-throated hummingbirds. Make sure you wear a

8

jacket or sweater—the altitude here is over 3,000 meters (10,000 feet) and it gets chilly. It's open 6–6 daily. ⑤ *Average main: $6* ✉ *Km 95 on the Pan-American Hwy., San Isidro* ☎ *2200–4313.*

WHERE TO STAY

$$$$
RESORT

⊡ **Hacienda Alta Gracia.** Breathtakingly luxurious, this ambitious resort high above the lush valley of the General River is aimed at well-heeled equestrians, with a stable of 48 beautiful horses to groom and ride, capacious casitas, a sybaritic spa, and sophisticated dining. **Pros:** exceptionally luxurious spa; gorgeous gardens; excellent breakfast included, along with free international calls; attentive, personal service. **Cons:** long walks to casitas or you can wait for an electric cart to ferry you to and fro; more suited to couples and teens than young children; need to be tech-savvy to operate all the devices. ⑤ *Rooms from: $350* ✉ *Santa Teresa de Cajón de Perez Zeledón, San Isidro de el General* ✛ *20 km (13 mi) south of San Isidro de El General on the Pan-American Hwy., then left onto Cajón road about 10 km (6 mi)* ☎ *2105–3080 hotel, 855–452–6326 toll-free* ⊕ *aubergeresorts.com* ⟲ *20 suites, 30 casitas with one or two bedrooms* ⦿*I Breakfast.*

$
HOTEL

⊡ **Hotel Los Crestones.** Flowering hedges make this pleasant and affordable motel feel homey, even though it's near the sometimes-noisy stadium (the quietest rooms are numbers 18 to 21). **Pros:** affordable prices; pleasant rooms; secure parking and easy wheelchair access. **Cons:** noisy rooms at the front; a few cheaper rooms lack air-conditioning. ⑤ *Rooms from: $65* ✉ *Road to Dominical, southwest side of stadium, San Isidro de el General* ☎ *2770–1200* ⊕ *www.hotelloscrestones.com* ⟲ *27 rooms* ⦿*I No meals.*

$$
HOTEL
FAMILY

⊡ **Hotel Zima.** Within walking distance of the main bus station, this Best Western hotel has pleasant bungalows arranged in an attractively landscaped row, leading to a swimming pool and a terrace restaurant with a barbecue. **Pros:** close to bus station and restaurants; nice beds and furniture; safe parking. **Cons:** not a scenic location, just off main highway; smallish rooms. ⑤ *Rooms from: $108* ✉ *Half a block east of Pan-American Hwy., across from MUSOC bus terminal, San Isidro de el General* ☎ *2770–1114* ⊕ *www.hotelzima.net* ⟲ *28 rooms* ⦿*I Breakfast.*

SAN GERARDO DE RIVAS

20 km (12½ miles) northeast of San Isidro.

Chirripó National Park is the main reason to venture to San Gerardo de Rivas, but if you aren't up for the physically challenging adventure of hiking up Chirripó it's still a wildly scenic place, reminiscent of the Himalayas, to spend a day or two. Spread over steep terrain at the end of the narrow valley of the boulder-strewn Río Chirripó, San Gerardo de Rivas has cool mountain air, excellent bird-watching, invigorating hiking trails, and ethereal views.

GETTING HERE AND AROUND

The good news is that most of the winding road from San Isidro de El General to San Gerardo de Rivas is now paved. There are still a few gravel patches and some steep, narrow stretches, however, so a 4WD is still recommended. Buses run twice a day from San Isidro.

EXPLORING

FAMILY **Cloudbridge Private Nature Reserve.** This private nature reserve staffed by volunteers and a senior biologist has an easy trail to a waterfall, plus almost 12 km (8 miles) of river and ridge trails, including one trail that utilizes 4 km (2½ miles) of the Chirripó National Park trail. It's a pleasant alternative for hikers who aren't up to the challenge of Chirripó or haven't reserved a spot far in advance. There's also an art gallery featuring nature paintings by artist Linda Moskalyk, and accommodations in four fully equipped houses (starting at $60). Volunteers often occupy the simple rental cabins, so check the website for availability. There's no admission fee to hike in the reserve but donations are requested. ⊠ *2½ km (1 mile) northeast of San Gerardo de Rivas* ⊕ *www.cloudbridge. org* ⊠ *By donation* ☾ *Daily sunrise–sunset.*

WHERE TO STAY

$ ⊡ **Hotel de Montaña El Pelícano.** On a precipitous ridge south of town, this
B&B/INN modest lodge built of wood is an affordable and comfortable launching pad for a hike up Chirripó, or a pleasant spot to relax and breathe in fresh mountain air and scenery. **Pros:** official Chirripó hike operator; one-of-a-kind museum; affordable. **Cons:** smallish rooms in main lodge; very steep drive to hotel. Ⓢ *Rooms from: $60* ⊠ *Main road, south of Chirripó National Park office* ☎ *2742–5050* ⊕ *www.hotelpelicano.net* ⤶ *8 rooms, 4 cabins, 1 apartment* ✦○✦ *Breakfast.*

$$$$ ⊡ **Monte Azul.** Set in a private nature reserve bordering the rushing Chir-
B&B/INN rripó River, this sleek and chic boutique hotel is an artistic triumph, both
Fodor'sChoice inside and out, with luxurious accommodations and sophisticated cui-
★ sine unmatched in the area. **Pros:** gorgeous natural setting and gardens; stunning design aesthetic; excellent food (included in room rate). **Cons:** pricey. Ⓢ *Rooms from: $498* ⊠ *Off main road, 5 km (3 miles) south of San Gerardo de Rivas, Chimirol* ☎ *2742–5222* ⊕ *www.monteazulcr. com* ☾ *Closed Sept. and Oct.* ⤶ *4 bungalows* ✦○✦ *All meals.*

SHOPPING

Fodor'sChoice **Samaritan Xocolata.** The sign says "Fine, Organic Artisan Chocolate,"
★ but all you need to know is that this chocolate is delicious. You can buy chocolate to go, including turtle-shaped chocolates filled with caramel and nuts, bonbons filled with ginger citrus or pistachio with Himalayan pink salt, beautifully gift-wrapped 70% dark chocolate, or truffles (including vegan-friendly rosemary-walnut and non-dairy mixed-berry, so no one has any dietary excuse to resist). You can sit down at a patio table and sip thick, hot chocolate or try a cup of spicy cacao tea. If you're in the area for a while, you can book a 2½-hour chocolate workshop held Tuesdays and Saturdays, to learn how it's made ($25, minimum of two people; two days notice required). ⊠ *Canaan de Rivas on main road to Chirripó, 75 m north of Catholic church and soccer field* ✛ *2½ km (1 mile) south of San Gerardo de Rivas* ☎ *8820–7095* ⊕ *www.samaritanxocolata.com.*

8

CHIRRIPÓ NATIONAL PARK

Park entrance is a 4-km (2-mile) hike uphill from San Gerardo de Rivas.
Chirripó National Park is the ultimate challenge for serious local and visiting hikers. But the rewards are worth it—from the visitors' hut you can summit surrounding peaks and, on a clear day, see both the Atlantic and Pacific oceans. It does, however, require top fitness and advance planning, since the number of hikers is limited each day, in order to preserve the sensitive ecosystems hikers traverse.

San Gerardo de Rivas National Parks Service. You are required to report to the San Gerardo de Rivas National Parks Service before you start, usually the day before your climb, since you need to start hiking long before the office opens at 8 am. It's open until noon, and then 1 to 4 pm, Monday through Friday. All hikers must first reserve a hiking spot with SINAC, the national park organization, by phone or Internet, and pay the park fee ($18 per day) by bank transfer within three days. Bookings open up three months in advance. (⊕ www.sinac.go.cr ☎ from outside Costa Rica: 506-2742-5348). To arrange accommodation at the summit hut, along with food and porters for the hike, hikers with paid park reservations in place can then contact Consorcio Aguas Eternas, a consortium of local lodges, guides, and porters, working in partnership with SINAC. They will e-mail a complete set of options and prices, in Spanish only (infochirriposervicios@gmail.com ☎ 506/2742-5097). For the new guided hiking trail from San Jerónimo, contact ATURENA, the local hiking authority. (info@sanjeronimochirripo.com ☎ 8374-3443). ✉ *Main street* ☎ *2742–5083.*

EXPLORING

Chirripó National Park (*Parque Nacional Chirripó*). The main attraction of this national park is Mt. Chirripó, the highest mountain in Costa Rica and a mecca for both hikers and serious summiteers. It's a 48-km (30-mile) round-trip hike, with an elevation gain of 2,100 meters (6,890 feet) to reach the hostel, and another 340 meters (1,000 feet) to reach the summit. You need to be very fit and acclimatize before setting out. The round-trip usually takes three days—one day to climb to the hostel, one day to explore the surrounding summits, and one day to descend.

With the number of hikers limited to 52 per day on the San Gerardo route, and only 15 hikers per week from the new San Jerónimo trail, it's becoming an ever-more exclusive experience to hike here. Lodging at the summit hut is set at $35 per night. Though the hostel is slightly more comfortable than it used to be, keep in mind that it is still fairly basic, with bunk beds and no hot water for showers. It's chilly at the top, so be sure to pack lots of layers. The maximum stay at the hostel is three days, two nights. Lodging and food service in the simple restaurant are arranged by Consorcio Aguas Eternas, which also can provide all the gear you need, from pillows, towels, and sleeping bags to porters to haul them. Depending on which of the various meal packages and local lodging before and after the hike you choose, prices for a hike start at about $250 per person. Porter fees are set at about $4 per kilo, and charged each way. The easiest way to arrange a hike is through one of the hotels that belong to the consortium, such as Hotel de Montaña El Pelícano, which can arrange all the details, from park reservation to lodging, food, and gear. ⇨ *For more information, see the highlighted listing in this chapter.* ✉ *Consorcio Aguas Eternas, main street, south side of soccer field, San Gerardo de Rivas* ☎ *2742–5200, 2742–5097* ✎ *infochirriposervicios@gmail. com* ✉ *$18 per day park fee; $36 (plus 13% tax) per day for lodging in park, plus food* ☉ *Closed 2 wks in Nov.*

DID YOU KNOW?

Although it takes the fittest hikers at least four hours to get to the base camp of Chirripó, hundreds of competitors from around the world converge on tiny San Gerardo de Rivas every February to run a 34-km (22-mile) race up and down Chirripó. A local family of hardy brothers shares the record time: three hours and 15 minutes!

SPORTS AND THE OUTDOORS

Hikes and other activities in the park are arranged by the **Consorcio Aguas Eternas** (☎ *2742–5097* or ⊕ *infochirriposervicios@gmail.com*), a new consortium that provides guides, porters, provisions, and gear, as well as lodging for Chirripó hikes.

SAN VITO

110 km (68 miles) southeast of San Isidro, 61 km (38 miles) northeast of Golfito.

Except for the tropical greenery, the rolling hills around the bustling hilltop town of San Vito could be mistaken for a Tuscan landscape. The town actually owes its 1952 founding to 200 Italian families who converted forest into coffee, fruit, and cattle farms. A remnant of the Italian flavor lingers on in the statue dedicated to the *pioneros* standing proudly in the middle of town. San Vito today is a bustling agricultural market town, the center of the Coto Brus coffee region. Many coffee pickers are from the Guaymí indigenous group, who live in a large reserve nearby and also over the border in Panama. They're easy to recognize by the women's colorfully embroidered, long cotton dresses.

8

GETTING HERE AND AROUND

If you are driving south from San Isidro, your best route is along the wide, smooth Pan-American Highway via Buenos Aires to Paso Real, about 70 km (43 miles). Then take the scenic high road to San Vito, 40 km (25 miles) farther along. This road is paved and it's the most direct and prettiest route. Another route, which many buses take, is via Ciudad Neily, about 35 km (22 miles) northeast of Golfito, and then 24 km (15 miles) of winding steep road up to San Vito, at almost 1,000 meters (3,280 feet) above sea level. There are direct buses from San José four times a day, and buses from San Isidro twice a day.

Gesneriaceae flowers at the Wilson Botanical Garden in San Vito

ESSENTIALS

Most of the banks in town have cash machines that accept foreign cards.

Banks/ATMs ATH Coopealianza. ⊠ *Center of town, 200 m east of the Catholic church and north of hospital* ☏ *2773–3763.* **Banco Nacional.** ⊠ *Across from south side of central park* ☏ *2212–2000.*

Hospital Hospital San Vito. ⊠ *South of town, on road to Wilson Botanical Garden* ☏ *2773–3103.*

Pharmacy Farmacia Assisi. ⊠ *Center of town, main street* ☏ *2773–3281.*

Post Office Correo. ⊠ *Far north end of town, beside police station.*

EXPLORING

La Amistad National Park (*Parque Nacional La Amistad*). At more than 1,980 square km (765 square miles), La Amistad is by far the largest park in Costa Rica. However, it's a mere portion of the vast La Amistad Biosphere Reserve that stretches into western Panama. Altitudes range from 1,000 meters (3,280 feet) to 3,500 meters (11,480 feet). There are miles of rugged, densely forested trails and plenty of wildlife (two-thirds of the country's vertebrate species live here), but because access is extremely difficult, it's not worth visiting the park unless you plan to spend several days, making this a trip only for experienced hikers. To get to the official park entrance at Altamira (4WD essential), drive 31 km (20 miles) west from San Vito along the road to Paso Real. Turn right at the park sign at Guacimo (also known as Las Tablas), near two small roadside restaurants. Then drive about 20 km (13 miles) uphill on a rough road, very muddy in rainy season. The last couple of kilometers are on foot.

ASOPROLA, a local tourism cooperative, organizes package tours (*www.actuarcostarica.com*) that include guided hikes and lodging at a rustic lodge near the Altamira park entrance, with both private and dormitory rooms with hot-water showers ($12), as well as an organic restaurant run by a local women's cooperative. You can also arrange a homestay with a local family. The alternative is rustic campsites for $6 per person. Reserve space about a week in advance. Check the website for exact directions, since very few maps show these roads or Altamira de Biolley. ⊠ *Altamira de Biolley, 31 km (20 miles) west of San Vito, then 20 km (13 miles) uphill* ☏ *2200–5355 national park* 🎫 *$10 per day* ☉ *Daily sunrise–sunset.*

Fodor's Choice
★

Wilson Botanical Garden. A must-see for gardeners and bird-watchers, the world-renowned Wilson Botanical Garden is enchanting even for those who are neither. Paths through the extensive grounds are lined with exotic plants and shaded by avenues of palm trees and 15-meter-high (50-foot-high) bamboo stalks. In 1961, U.S. landscapers Robert and Catherine Wilson bought 30 acres of coffee plantation and started planting tropical species, including palms, orchids, bromeliads, and heliconias. Today the property extends over 635 acres, and the gardens hold around 2,000 native and more than 3,000 exotic species. The palm collection—more than 700 species—is the second largest in the world. Fantastically shaped and colored bromeliads, which usually live in the tops of trees, have been brought down to the ground in impressive mass plantings, providing one of many photo opportunities.

The garden was transferred to the Organization for Tropical Studies in 1973, and in 1983 it became part of Amistad Biosphere Reserve. Under the name Las Cruces Biological Station, Wilson functions mainly as a research and educational center, so there is a constant supply of expert botanists and biologists to take visitors on natural-history tours in the garden and the adjoining forest trails. Birders can hike to the new canopy tower in the forest, funded by the local San Vito Birding Club, to get up to eye level with birds in the treetops. Twice a month, members of the San Vito Bird Club lead free birding tours of the garden, complete with binoculars and field guides to share. Check *www.sanvitobirdclub.org* for the bird-walk schedule. If you spend a night at the garden lodge, you have the garden all to yourself in the late afternoon and early morning, when wildlife is most active. Guests also have access to the Río Java trail, where monkeys abound. ⊠ *Road to Ciudad Neily, 6 km (4 miles) south of San Vito* ☏ *2773–4004* ⊕ *www.esintro.co.cr/lascruces_general_info.shtml* 🎫 *$8 garden; tour $25 for one to three people; $35 for four to six people.* ☉ *Daily 7–5; reception closes for lunch noon–1.*

WHERE TO EAT AND STAY

$$
ITALIAN
FAMILY

✕ **Pizzería Liliana.** Treat yourself to authentic pizza made from all-natural ingredients at the classiest restaurant in town, or dig into the macaroni *sanviteña* style: with white sauce, ham, and mushrooms. The classics are here as well, and they're all homemade—lasagna, cannelloni, and ravioli—as well as hearty chicken and meat dishes. If you can't decide between pasta or meat, try the *plato mixto*: a half-portion of lasagna along with a quarter chicken and fries or salad. The authentic vinaigrette is a welcome change from more acidic Tico salad dressings. In true Italian fashion, the friendly, family-run restaurant can be noisy, but it's a happy buzz. For a more romantic dinner, ask for a table on the pretty garden terrace. It's open from 10:30 am until 10 every evening, making it one of the few places in town where you can eat late. Ⓢ *Average main: $10 ⊠ West of central square, up short hill* ☎ *2773–3080.*

$$ ⊡ **Casa Botania B&B.** Book a comfortable room with a sweeping view of

B&B/INN   forest and mountains at this delightful, small hilltop B&B, owned by

FAMILY   a charming young Belgian–Costa Rican couple. **Pros:** affordable rates; great views; amiable hosts; gourmet vegetarian food. **Cons:** close to road but not much traffic noise at night; big, but friendly dog. Ⓢ *Rooms from: $75 ⊠ Road to Wilson Botanical Garden, 5 km (3 miles) south of San Vito* ☎ *2773–4217, 8711–3008* ⊕ *www.casabotaniabedandbreakfast. com* ⤳ *4 bungalows, 1 two-bedroom house* ⏐◉⏐ *Breakfast.*

$$ ⊡ **Cascata del Bosco Hotel, Restaurant & Bar.** Just 200 meters from the

B&B/INN   entrance to Wilson Botanical Garden, this collection of four totally private, round bungalows, set amid gardens and forest teeming with birds, is designed for nature-lovers. **Pros:** close to Wilson Botanical Garden; attractive cabins; affordable. **Cons:** no phones in rooms. Ⓢ *Rooms from: $85 ⊠ 200 m from entrance to Wilson Botanical Garden, Las Cruces* ☎ *2773–3208* ⊕ *www.cascatadelbosco.com* ⤳ *4 cabins* ⏐◉⏐ *Breakfast.*

$$$ ⊡ **La Amistad Ecolodge.** This comfortable Alpine-style lodge offers a rare

B&B/INN   opportunity to explore La Amistad Park, which borders this 25,000-acre family estate, most of which is primary forest studded with rivers and spectacular waterfalls. **Pros:** unequaled hiking trails; scenic waterfalls. **Cons:** rough access road. Ⓢ *Rooms from: $226 ⊠ 32 km (20 miles) east of San Vito along a rough, rocky road* ☎ *8380–1255 lodge, 2228–0405 reservations office* ⊕ *www.haciendalaamistad.com* ⤳ *8 rooms, 4 junior suites* ⏐◉⏐ *All meals.*

$$$ ⊡ **Wilson Botanical Garden.** The best features of the dozen comfortable

B&B/INN   rooms here, in three modern buildings built of glass, steel, and wood,

Fodor's Choice   are the private balconies cantilevered over a forested ravine, perfect for

★   bird-watching. **Pros:** unparalleled setting with 24-hour access to botanical garden and nature trails; excellent birding and wildlife viewing. **Cons:** family-style meals are served strictly on schedule so be ready to sit at the table when the dinner bell rings. Ⓢ *Rooms from: $180 ⊠ Las Cruces Biological Station, road to Ciudad Neily, 6 km (4 miles) south of San Vito* ☎ *2524–0607 Organization for Tropical Studies office in San José, 2773–4004 Wilson Botanical Garden reception* ⊕ *www. tropicalstudies.org/lascruces* ⤳ *12 rooms* ⏐◉⏐ *All meals.*

SHOPPING

Finca Cántaros. In a vintage farmhouse between San Vito and Wilson Botanical Garden, Finca Cántaros sells crafts by indigenous artisans from near and far, including charming calabash gourds painted by Maleku artists, and colorful *molas* (appliqué work) made by Kuna women from the San Blas Islands in Panama. The owner's own mixed-media prints celebrate tropical nature with watercolor, colored pencil, and hand-carved rubber blocks used as printing stamps. You can also find a great selection of colorful, high-glaze ceramics from San José artists, as well as Sibú artisanal chocolates. Profits help support the adjacent free lending library. Behind the shop lies a 7-hectare (17.3-acre) private nature reserve ($6 adults; discounts for children) where you can walk the bird-filled forest trails around a lake and explore an indigenous archaeological site. ⊠ *Linda Vista, Road to Ciudad Neily, 3 km (2 miles) south of San Vito* ☏ *2773–3760* ⊕ *www.fincacantaros. com* ⊗ *Daily 6:30–5.*

EN ROUTE

San Vito to Ciudad Neily. The 33-km (21-mile), recently paved road from San Vito to Ciudad Neily is twisting and spectacular, with views over the Coto Colorado plain to the Golfo Dulce and Osa Peninsula beyond. You can stop halfway at **Mirador La Torre** to enjoy excellent fruit *naturales* (fruit juice), and the view, from their counter stools. Watch out for some tricky curves where there are no guardrails. ⊠ *San Vito.*

San Vito to Paso Real. The paved, scenic road from San Vito to Paso Real travels along a high ridge with sweeping valley views on either side. Halfway between Boca Limon and Las Vueltas, stop to enjoy a *refresco* and the views at open-air **Restaurante La Carreta.** As the road descends, the wide valley of El General River opens up before you, planted with miles of spiky pineapples and tall sugarcane. Few passing opportunities require a lot of patience, especially in the valley if you find yourself caught in a slow-moving convoy of trucks hauling pineapple and sugarcane. ⊠ *San Vito.*

DOMINICAL AND BALLENA NATIONAL MARINE PARK

On the other side of a mountain ridge, just a scenic hour-long drive west of San Isidro de El General, you reach the sunny southern Pacific coast, with its miles of beaches for surfing, strolling, kayaking, and snorkeling. Ballena National Marine Park alone encompasses almost 10 km (6 miles) of protected beaches. Scattered along the coast are small communities with increasing numbers of international residents and interesting restaurants and lodging options.

8

DOMINICAL

34 km (21 miles) southwest of San Isidro, 40 km (25 miles) south of Quepos.

Sleepy fishing village–turned–surfer town, Dominical is undergoing a lively makeover, with a newly paved beach road, new restaurants and shops, a farmer's market on Friday mornings, and an artisans' fiesta with live music the first Saturday night of the month. As more and more luxury villas pop up all over the hillsides above the beaches, new wealth is boosting the economy. It's still a major surfing destination, attracting surfers of all ages, with a lively restaurant and nightlife scene. Favorite local hangouts come and go, so don't hesitate to try something new.

Dominical's real magic lies beyond the town, in the surrounding terrestrial and marine wonders: the rain forest grows right up to the beach in some places, and the ocean offers world-class surfing.

Much of the lush forest that covers the steep hillsides above the beaches is protected within private nature reserves. Several of these reserves, such as Hacienda Barú, protect significant tracts of the rain forest.

GETTING HERE AND AROUND

The paved road west over the mountains and down to Dominical is scenic at its best and fog-shrouded at its worst. There are lots of curves and a few dicey landslide areas, so take your time and enjoy the scenery along the hour-long drive from San Isidro de El General. From Quepos, the paved Costanera Highway makes for an easy half-hour drive to Dominical, although you do have to contend with huge transport trucks barreling along. Buses from San Isidro de El General leave six times a day, three times a day from Quepos. If you want to avoid driving altogether, Monkey Ride has air-conditioned vans with room for six to eight passengers that make trips to and from San José (starting at $44).

ESSENTIALS

Bank/ATM Banco de Costa Rica. ⊠ *Plaza Pacífica* ☎ *2787–0381.*

Rental Cars Solid Car Rental. ⊠ *Villas Río Mar reception area, river road* ✛ *1 km (1/2 mile) west of Dominical, along river road* ☎ *2787–0111* ⊕ *www.solidcarrental.com.*

Tour Companies Costa Rica Dive and Surf. ⊠ *Main street, across from Sundancer Hotel* ☎ *8319–5392, 2787–0362* ⊕ *www.costaricadiveandsurf. com.* **Dominical Surf Adventures.** ⊠ *Main street, across from Pueblo del Río* ☎ *8897–9540, 2787–0431* ⊕ *www.dominicalsurfadventures.com.*

Pineapple Kayak Tours. Catering to kayakers of all ages and skill levels, this outift takes you paddling through the Ventanas caves, the Hatillo mangroves, along the Dominical coast, and up and down the Río Barú. Tours start at $55 per person. ⊠ *Main street* ✛ *beside police station* ☎ *8873–3283* ✍ *negodominicalcr@yahoo.com* ⊕ *www. pineapplekayaktours.com.*

Visitor Information Dominical Information. ⊠ *Pueblo del Río, main street* ☎ *2787–0454* ⊕ *www.dominicalinformation.com.*

EXPLORING

FAMILY
Fodor'sChoice
★

Hacienda Barú. This leading ecotourism and conservation wildlife refuge offers spectacular bird-watching and excellent naturalist-led hikes, as well as a turtle-protection project and nature-education program in the local school. You can stay at the cabins and poolside rooms or on platform tents in the jungle, or just come for the day to walk the forest and mangrove trails ($8 self-guided trails), zip through the canopy on cables, climb trees, or stake out birds on an observation platform (tours from $25). ⊠ *Costanera Hwy. 3 km (2 miles) north of Dominical* ☎ *2787–0003* ⊕ *www.haciendabaru.com* ☞ *$8, tours $25–$125* ☼ *Daily 7 am–dusk.*

FAMILY
Fodor'sChoice
★

Nauyaca Waterfalls. This massive double cascade, the longer one tumbling down 45 meters (150 feet), is one of the most spectacular sights in Costa Rica. The falls—also known as Barú River Falls—are on private property, so the only way to reach them is to take a horseback tour. ⊠ *Hwy. to San*

Isidro de El General, 10 km (7 miles) northeast of Dominical ✉ info@ cataratasnauyaca.com ⊕ www.cataratasnauyaca.com.

FAMILY **Parque Reptilandia.** With more than 300 specimens, this impressive collection includes snakes, lizards, frogs, turtles, and other reptilian creatures, housed in visitor-friendly terrariums and large enclosures. Stars of the exhibit are a Komodo dragon, Gila monsters, a very large anaconda, and a 150-pound African spur-thighed tortoise that likes to be petted. Kids love the maternity ward showcasing newborn snakes. More mature snakes live under a retractable roof that lets in sun and rain. Although snakes are generally more active in sunlight, this is still a great rainy-day activity. Guided night tours can also be arranged to watch nocturnal animals. If you're not squeamish, snake-feeding day is Friday, spread out from 10 am to 3 pm. ✉ *Road to San Isidro, 11 km (7 miles) east of Dominical* ☎ 2787–0343 ⊕ *www.crreptiles.com* ✉ *$12* ⊗ *Daily 9–4:30.*

FAMILY **Pozo Azul.** Hidden in a forest about 5 km (3 miles) south of town, this waterfall is considerably smaller than Nauyaca Waterfalls. Off the main highway, head up the road toward Bella Vista lodge and take the first road to the right, past the new school and through a stream; follow the road straight uphill for about 300 meters to where the road widens. If the stream is too high to cross, go back to the highway and drive south to the next left turn, where there's a bus stop, and go through a small village, over the new bridge, then turn right up the mountain for 300 meters. You can park here and climb down the steps to the river on the right, where there is a lovely swimming hole at the base of a waterfall, often populated by local kids when school is out. Pay strict attention to the posted sign that warns not to leave anything of value in your parked car. Avoid holiday times and weekends, when there are often large crowds. ✉ *Dominical.*

BEACHES

Playa Dominical. Long, flat, and rarely crowded, Playa Dominical is good for beachcombing among all the flotsam and jetsam that the surf washes up onto the brown sand. There's shade and parking under palm trees along the new brick-paved road that parallels the beach. The water is relatively clean and local businesses make sure things look tidy. Photo opportunities abound here, with buff surfers riding the waves and vendors' clotheslines of colorful sarongs flapping in the sea breeze. Tortilla Flats restaurant is practically on the beach. Huge waves and dangerous rip currents make it primarily a surfing beach. In high season, flags mark off a relatively safe area for swimming, under the watchful gaze of a professional lifeguard. **Amenities:** food and drink; lifeguards; parking (free). **Best for:** surfing; walking. ✉ *Dominical.*

Playa Dominicalito. About 1 km (½ mile) south of Playa Dominical, this wide beach is usually calmer and more suited to boogie boarding and beginner surfers. There are hidden rocks near the shore, so the best time to swim is at low tide. This is one of the best walking beaches, with lots of shade under tall palms and beach almond trees. The sun sets behind a huge rocky outcropping topped with tiny palm trees, an ideal shot for photographers. There is an unofficial campground running

Nauyaca waterfalls is a three-tiered waterfall and well worth the visit.

parallel to the beach, which is popular with locals, especially during Easter, Christmas, and school holidays. **Amenities:** parking (free). **Best for:** sunset; walking. ⊠ *Dominical.*

SPORTS AND THE OUTDOORS
FISHING
Angling options range from expensive sportfishing charters to a trip in a small boat to catch red snapper and snook for supper. The five most common fish species here, in the order in which you are likely to catch them, are sailfish, dorado, yellowfin tuna, wahoo, and marlin.

Captain Isidro. Go fishing for wahoo and roosterfish the Tico way in a *panga,* a locally made, roofed-over boat, with a bilingual captain. Casual fishers can try their luck inshore for $70 an hour; more serious fishers can try for tuna and dorado around Caño Island, for $800 for the day or $450 for half a day. ⊠ *Dominical* ☎ *2787–0341.*

Las Rocas Marea Alta Sportfishing. Cast off with Captain George or Captain Allan on a 24-foot, center-console sportfishing boat equipped with outriggers. Inshore fishing costs $90 per hour, with a minimum of three hours, while a whole day offshore is $850 for up to four anglers, with lunch, drinks, and snacks. If you want to try your luck close in, you can dip a rod from a 15-foot panga, a traditional fishing boat, for $200 for a half day. The boats are also available for snorkeling tours and for whale- and dolphin-watching. ⊠ *Km 146 on Costanera Hwy., south of Hotel Roca Verde* ☎ *2787–0480, 8606–5118.*

HORSEBACK RIDING

FAMILY **Don Lulo.** Horseback-riding tours to Nauyaca Waterfalls depart Monday to Saturday at 8 am from Don Lulo's stables. The tour ($70) includes a light breakfast and lunch at the family homestead near the falls. You can swim in the cool pool beneath the falls, so bring a bathing suit and sunscreen. There is a river to cross, but otherwise the 12-km (7½-mile) ride is easy. Be sure to reserve a day in advance. In rainy season, raincoats are provided. ⊠ *Road to San Isidro, 10 km (6 miles) northeast of Dominical* ☎ *2787–0541, 2787–0542* ⊕ *www.cataratasnauyaca.com.*

SURFING

The surfing is great in Dominical, thanks to the runoff from the Barú River mouth, which constantly changes the ocean bottom and creates well-shaped waves big enough to keep intermediate and advanced surfers challenged. The best surfing is near the river mouth, and the best time is two hours before or after high tide, to avoid the notorious riptides.

Dominical Surf Adventures. One-on-one, two-hour surfing lessons are $60; group lessons are $50 per person. All lessons include transportation, surfboard, rash guard, fruit, and soft drinks. Board rental starts at $10 per day. ⊠ *Main street, across from Pueblo del Río* ☎ *2787–0431, 8897–9540* ⊕ *www.dominicalsurfadventures.com.*

WHERE TO EAT

$ ✕ **Cafe Mono Congo.** Pull up a counter stool or sit at a table on the riv-
VEGETARIAN erside terrace at this friendly café with creative vegetarian and gluten-free dishes. For breakfast, try a hearty Tico Bowl chock-full of brown rice and pinto beans, topped by a mini-omelet with red peppers, spring onions, local cheeses, tomato, avocado, and plantains—with chipotle sauce on the side. A lighter option is smashed avocados on a toasted bagel with goat cheese sprinkled with pink salt. Vegetable lasagne or burritos are a bargain at $6. Desserts are not only gluten-free, they are addictive: Chocolate Papaya Pie combines dark chocolate with papaya to make a rich mousse filling for a date, almond, and coconut crust. Organic juices, shakes, kombuchas, and herbal teas are on tap, as are a wide selection of local and imported Californian craft beers. It's open 6:30 am to 9 pm daily. ⑤ *Average main: $6* ⊠ *Pueblo del Río, main street* ☎ *8485–5523* ▭ *No credit cards.*

$ ✕ **El Pescado Loco.** Beer-battered onion rings, fresh hand-cut fries, and
SEAFOOD fried pickles have taken Dominical by storm at this casual, alfresco kiosk in the recently renovated Pueblo del Río complex on the riverfront. The fish tacos are outstanding—crispy beer-battered fish fillets accompanied by avocado slices, red cabbage, and a spicy sauce are folded into a thin, soft tortilla. You can substitute fried shrimp or go vegetarian with black beans and vegetables or spicy tofu. The tortillas even come in a gluten-free version. Ultra-healthy grilled fish and vegetables are also on the menu, along with less healthy but delicious classic fish-and-chips. Beer, sodas, and fruit smoothies wash it all down. Seating is at wooden benches and tables—or hammocks for the really laid-back—on a covered wood patio. ⑤ *Average main: $8* ⊠ *Pueblo del Río, main street* ☎ *2787–4073* ▭ *No credit cards.*

$$
COSTA RICAN
✗ **La Parcela.** Picture a dream location: a high headland jutting out into the sea with vistas up and down the coast. Throw in a breeze-swept terrace, polished service, and some fine seaside cuisine. Shrimp and lobster dishes, if pricey, are excellent. A perfect light lunch, and less expensive, is the beer-battered fish with crunchy carrot and cabbage salad, served with guacamole. Reasonably priced appetizers include ceviche, fried calamari, and clams in white-wine sauce. Desserts here are rich—mud pie and a delectable chocolate cake à la mode—and substantial enough to share. If you're just passing through Dominical, this is a good place for a cold beer and an appetizer, or a *naturale*, a tall glass of freshly whipped fruit juice. Sunsets here are spectacular. There is some controversy about this restaurant's eco-sensitive location, so call ahead to make sure it's still up and running. ⑤ *Average main: $15 ⊠ 4 km (2½ miles) south of Dominical, off Costanera Hwy.* ☎ *2787–0016* ⊕ *www. laparcelacr.com.*

$$
VEGETARIAN
✗ **Maracatù.** Who says vegetarian food has to be boring? From spicy pad thai with tofu to crunchy falafel served with brown rice and organic salad, this restaurant can make vegetarians ecstatic and even the most committed carnivore happy. The tacos are delicious and priced right for budget-conscious beachgoers. The eclectic decor reflects the global reach of the kitchen: Moroccan stained-glass lamps, bamboo furniture, and cushions covered in East Indian fabrics. There's free Wi-Fi, a soothing world-music sound track every night, and noisier live or DJ music occasionally. ⑤ *Average main: $12 ⊠ Main street, across from soccer field* ☎ *2787–0091* ⊕ *www.maracatucostarica.com* ☾ *No lunch.*

$$$$
STEAKHOUSE
✗ **Patron's Bar & Grill.** Amid all the organic and vegetarian focus on food in this health-conscious town, meat lovers can enjoy sinking their teeth into U.S.D.A. imported T-bone, porterhouse, and filet mignon steaks at this upscale lounge and restaurant. Lamb crusted with herbs, and BBQ pork ribs round out the meat selections. Expect to pay a high premium for the imported steaks—up to $45. Easier on the budget (and digestion) are the local fish dishes prepared in interesting ways, like mahi-mahi wrapped in banana leaf with shrimp and cheddar cheese. There are plenty of salads for the non-carnivores—including classic Greek or a walnut-and-strawberry salad with blue cheese—and vegetarian lasagne. The place has a clubby, masculine feel, as befits a steak house. It's also open for breakfast and lunch. ⑤ *Average main: 26 ⊠ Main street ⊹ beside football field, in former San Clemente premises* ☎ *2787–8010* ⊕ *www.patronscostarica.com.*

$$$
ECLECTIC
✗ **¿Por Qué No?** If you are looking for the most romantic restaurant in Dominical, this pretty, garden-terrace spot sparkling with fairy lights is it, with a view of sky and sea, close enough to hear waves crashing on the rocks below. The menu is sophisticated, with dishes like red snapper in an almond crust with baby potatoes, and a salad of feta and watermelon. Wood-fired pizzas feature wildly exotic ingredients, at a price. The accompanying wine choices are mostly South American. If your budget is modest, check out the new aperitif bar on the restaurant's oceanside deck built around a beach almond tree whose leafy canopy supplies a natural roof. It's the ideal place to watch a Pacific sunset (it's open 3 to 7 pm). The restaurant is open for breakfast as well. ⑤ *Average*

main: $16 ✉ Costa Paraiso Hotel, off Costanera Hwy. ⊹2 km (1½ miles) south of Dominical ☎2787–0340 ⊕www.costa-paraiso.com ⊗ Closed Monday ⚖ Reservations essential.

$$ ✕ **Restaurante Charter.** Is that a plane that just crash-landed in the jungle? It's hard to miss Charter Restaurant's Boeing 727 as you approach Dominical from San Isidro de El General. Kids of all ages will delight in stopping here if only to get close to a real plane (minus the engine), transported here, piece by piece, by the aircraft-enthusiast owner. The gimmick is irresistible, the food in the rancho restaurant next to the plane beats any airplane food, and the portions are huge. There are succulent grilled pork ribs and spiced-up tenderloin tips flambéed in brandy and sherry. For lunch there's the Plane Burger, with bacon, chili peppers, lettuce, and tomato. Fish and seafood are fresh and the excellent pastas include a standout penne à la vodka. If the kids tire of checking out the plane, there's also a swimming pool to keep them amused while grown-ups enjoy lunch. Cocktails are a bargain, at only $6. Dinners are candlelit and romantic—a little like dining on the set of the TV show *Lost*. ⑤ *Average main: $11* ✉ *1½ km (1 mile) northeast of Dominical, on road from San Isidro de El General* ☎506/2787–0172.

ECLECTIC
FAMILY

$ ✕ **Restaurant Su Raza.** Among the handful of sodas in town serving typical Costa Rican food, this one is notable for its affordably priced whole fish and hearty portions of seafood served on a breezy veranda. Stick to the *desayuno típico* for breakfast, with traditional rice and beans and eggs, starting at 7 am. The omelets are great, but they come with limp french fries, the bane of Tico restaurants. There's a big TV screen to keep you company while you eat. ⑤ *Average main: $8* ✉ *Main street* ☎2787–0105 ▭ *No credit cards.*

COSTA RICAN

$$ ✕ **Sushi.** With a view over the Barú estuary, this breezy, open-air Japanese restaurant serves up local seafood in all the usual rolls and sashimi, with some tropical twists. Try the Tico Roll, with spicy shrimp, avocado, cucumber, and mango, wrapped in sweet plantain. Or dig into the Ahi Poke salad, with cubes of raw tuna marinated in sesame oil, chili, and soy sauce, atop a Hawaiian salad sprinkled with peanuts or almonds. There's imported Sapporo beer, along with hot and cold sake or hot green tea to drink. Dark bamboo furniture, Japanese lanterns, and colored globes set the modern, minimalist scene, while a smooth, jazzy music mix sets a cool mood. You can perch on a stool at the counter to watch the sushi chefs at work. ⑤ *Average main: $11* ✉ *Pueblo del Rio, Main street* ☎8826–7946 ⊗ *No dinner Friday, no lunch Saturday.*

JAPANESE

$$ ✕ **Tortilla Flats.** A perennially popular surfer hangout, this casual, breezy place has the advantage of being right across from Dominical Beach, which you can spy through a fringe of palm trees. Surf videos play on big screens, and there's free Wi-Fi. Popular items on the menu are the fresh-baked baguette sandwiches stuffed with interesting combinations. Try the grilled chicken, avocado, tomato, and mozzarella sandwich. Light eaters can opt for half a sandwich. Fresh-fish specials, notably the fish tacos, and typical Mexican fare round out the casual menu. There are excellent margaritas and flavored daiquiris, downed at the huge U-shape bar. Live bands or a DJ play from the stage, usually

SOUTHWESTERN

8

on Wednesday, Friday, or Saturday nights. The restaurant is open for breakfast, too. 💲 *Average main: $12* ⊠ *Across from Dominical Beach* ☎ *2787–0033* ⊟ *No credit cards.*

WHERE TO STAY

Lodgings in the lowlands of Dominical and the area a little to the north tend to be hot and muggy and not as comfortable as the more luxurious, private, and breezy places up in the hills above Dominicalito, to the south.

$$
RENTAL
FAMILY

🖵 **Coconut Grove Oceanfront Cottages.** Right on the beach, this well-maintained cluster of cabins and beach houses set in a gorgeous garden is ideal for couples or families who want to fend for themselves. **Pros:** best location in town: right on beach; close to cool ocean breezes; friendly owners; free Wi-Fi. **Cons:** furnishings are simple and a little tired; guests must love animals. 💲 *Rooms from: $85* ⊠ *Dominicalito Beach, Costanera Hwy. at Km 147, 3 km (2 miles) south of Dominical* ☎ *2787–0130* ⊕ *www.coconutgrovecr.com* ⊟ *No credit cards* ⇋ *3 cabins, 2 beach houses* ⦿ *No meals.*

$$
B&B/INN

🖵 **Cuna del Angel Hotel and Spa.** This elegant hotel is a heavenly spot for those who like to indulge themselves, with a small spa, an excellent restaurant, and exceptional service. **Pros:** delightful decor; excellent restaurant; friendly service in hotel and spa. **Cons:** ground-level rooms lack privacy; water pressure is sometimes low; steep steps to Jungle Rooms and restaurant. 💲 *Rooms from: $126* ⊠ *Costanera Hwy., Puertocito, 9 km (5 miles) south of Dominical* ☎ *2787–4343* ⊕ *www.cunadelangel. com* ⇋ *22 rooms* ⦿ *Breakfast.*

$$
B&B/INN
FAMILY
Fodor's Choice
★

🖵 **Hacienda Barú National Wildlife Refuge and Ecolodge.** This wildly family-friendly, comfortable eco-lodge makes a great base for exploring vast tracts of surrounding forest, both primary and secondary, plus mangroves, and a beach with nesting turtles. **Pros:** prime wildlife viewing; excellent guides; great value. **Cons:** older cabins are not fancy; no air-conditioning but rooms and cabins are well ventilated with ceiling and wall fans. 💲 *Rooms from: $85* ⊠ *Off Costanera Hwy., 3 km (2 miles) north Dominical* ☎ *2787–0003* ⊕ *www.haciendabaru.com* ⇋ *6 cabins, 6 guest rooms* ⦿ *Breakfast.*

$
B&B/INN

🖵 **Pacific Edge.** Unbeatable views and affordable prices set these private, spacious wood cabins apart, literally, since they are high on a forested ridge overlooking the ocean. **Pros:** fabulous views; bargain prices; serene setting; no kids under 13. **Cons:** very steep road that requires 4WD; must love dogs. 💲 *Rooms from: $70* ⊠ *At Km 148 of Costanera Hwy., head up a rough road for 1.2 km (¾ mile), 4 km (2½ miles) south of Dominical* ☎ *8935–7905, 2200–5428* ⊕ *www.pacificedge.info* ⇋ *4 cabins* ⦿ *No meals.*

$$$
B&B/INN

🖵 **Río Magnolia Nature Lodge.** Hidden away in a spectacular mountain valley, this luxury eco-lodge has the best of everything: a huge stone fireplace inside and an infinity pool outside with distant ocean views from wraparound decks. **Pros:** seclusion; magnificent views; excellent food; lots of books and field guides. **Cons:** very difficult access over rough roads; must love dogs; be prepared for cool mountain nights. 💲 *Rooms from: $205* ⊠ *14 km (8½ miles) northeast of Dominical, off the main hwy. between San Isidro and Dominical, turn at sign for*

LIVING OFF THE GRID

Many hotels in the more remote areas of the South Pacific generate their own electricity, so don't count on air-conditioning, using a hair dryer, calling home, checking your email, or paying with a credit card (unless it's arranged in advance). Some lodges do have contact with the outside world via satellite phone systems you can use in emergencies, but bad weather can often block the satellite signal. On the positive side, you really can get away from it all. Pack as though you are a castaway from modern civilization. Be sure to bring the following:

- Flashlight with extra batteries, or better still, a kinetic flashlight that doesn't need batteries

- Insect repellent (lots of it)

- Sunscreen (ditto)

- After-sun lotion

- All toiletries and medications you could conceivably need, in small travel containers

- Sturdy, breathable hiking shoes and lots of socks (your feet will get wet)

- Waterproof walking sandals

- Binoculars

- Sun hat

- Refillable water bottle

- Portable, battery-operated reading light or a head lamp

- Zip-style baggies of all sizes to keep cameras, snacks, etc., dry and bug-free

La Alfombra ☎ 8493–2506, 8868–5561 ⊕ *www.riomagnolia.com* ⇆ *4 suites, 1 cabin* ⫯❍⫯ *Breakfast.*

$$
B&B/INN
⛨ **Roca Verde.** Small and friendly, this is the only hotel with direct beach access in the area, so it's no surprise it's popular with surfers, anglers, and beach lovers. **Pros:** right on the beach; friendly bar; reasonably priced. **Cons:** can be noisy Friday night if you don't join the party; no phones in rooms. ⑤ *Rooms from: $89* ⊠ *off the Costanera Sur Hwy, on Dominical Beach, 1 km (½ mile) south of Dominical* ☎ 2787–0036 ⇆ *9 rooms* ⫯❍⫯ *Breakfast.*

$$$
B&B/INN
⛨ **Villas Alturas.** One of the best lodging deals on this coast, these seven, no-frills villas are in a sublime, lofty setting, with a large swimming pool and a huge terrace overlooking a million-dollar view of the Pacific. **Pros:** excellent value; fabulous views; personal service. **Cons:** long, steep drive requiring 4WD; long way down to beach and activities. ⑤ *Rooms from: $164* ⊠ *off Costanera Hwy., 7 km (4½ miles) south of Dominical, 800 m up steep hill* ☎ 2200–5440 ⊕ *www.villasalturas.com* ⇆ *7 villas* ⫯❍⫯ *Some meals.*

$$
HOTEL
FAMILY
⛨ **Villas Río Mar.** This upscale yet very affordable hotel is upriver from Dominical beach on exquisitely landscaped grounds filled with orchids, bougainvillea, and hibiscus. **Pros:** huge pool; lovely grounds; excellent restaurant. **Cons:** some rooms lack air-conditioning and TV; 15-minute walk to the main beach. ⑤ *Rooms from: $89* ⊠ *Off main hwy. into town, 1 km (½ mile) west of Dominical* ☎ 2787–0052 ⊕ *www.villasriomar.com* ⇆ *40 rooms, 12 suites* ⫯❍⫯ *Breakfast.*

8

NIGHTLIFE

During the high season, Dominical hops at night, and when the surfers have fled to find bigger waves, there are enough locals around to keep some fun events afloat.

Maracatù World Music Bar. The crowd is young and edgy here, with mostly DJ music and live music some Saturday nights. Check the restaurant window for posters advertising special DJ nights and visiting bands. Wednesday is Ladies' Night. ⊠ *Main street* ☏ *2787–0091.*

Patrón's Bar & Grill. The newest club in town is taking Dominical nightlife to a whole different level, with a huge stage and concert venue, two large bars, and a VIP lounge with its own bar. Concerts with national and international performers attract crowds in the hundreds to thousands. General, standing-space admission is about 8,000 colones ($16) but tickets can run as high as 40,000 colones ($90) for big-name acts. Check Patrón's website for the concert line-up. ⊠ *Dominical main street* ☏ *2787–8010* ⊕ *www.patronscostarica.com.*

FAMILY **Roca Verde.** Friday nights year-round usually feature local bluesy rock band Ben Jammin' and the Howlers, with electric jazz fiddler Nancy Buchan electrifying the happy, upbeat crowd, which consists of a mix of local families, expats, and tourists. Guest artists often join the band. ⊠ *Roca Verde, 1 km (½ mile) south of Dominical* ☏ *2787–0036.*

SHOPPING

Boruca Gallery Gift Shop. If you don't have time to visit the southern Boruca indigenous settlement inland, you can find a huge selection of the carved and painted wooden masks Borucan artisans are famous for, here in the showroom at Pacific Edge. Susie Atkinson has championed and supported the Boruca artists for more than a decade. She has a huge inventory of masks, from small to big, priced at $10 to $120, along with hundreds of woven bags, purses, and belts, colored with traditional, natural dyes. The bulk of the shop proceeds goes to the Borucan artists and artisans. The gallery is open Monday to Saturday, 10 to 4. ⊠ *At Km. 148 on the Costanera, about 4 km (2½ miles) south of Dominical, head up a steep road for 1.2 km (¾ miles), Dominicalito* ☏ *2200–5428, 8935–7905* ⊕ *www.pacificedge.info.*

Mama Toucan's Natural & Organic Foods. Colorful and comfortably air-conditioned, this whole-foods store is a treat to browse in. Along with the fresh organic vegetables, there is a wide selection of gluten-free foods, including bagels and breads. The ice cream, sorbet, and gelato made with coconut milk is delicious whether you are a vegan or an omnivore. The shop also carries hard-to-find, imported specialty foods, spices, and excellent local chocolates. It's open 9 to 8 daily. ⊠ *Pueblo del Río, main street* ☏ *8433–4235.*

BALLENA NATIONAL MARINE PARK

20 km (12 miles) southeast of Dominical.

Named for the whales (*ballenas,* in Spanish) that seasonally migrate here, this park protects marine life in miles of ocean, as well as 10 km (6 miles) of coastline, incorporating four separate beaches, each with its own character. Opportunities abound for fishing, whale- and dolphin-watching tours, kayaking, camping, beachcombing, and swimming. Sunsets here are unbeatable.

GETTING HERE AND AROUND

The park area includes the communities of Uvita, Bahía Ballena, and Ojochal, all easily accessible off the Costanera, a wide, paved highway, now officially called Carretera Nacional Pacifica Fernández. As soon as you get off the highway, however, the roads are often bumpy and dusty. Alternatively, take a taxi or bus from Dominical. Eight buses leave Dominical, starting at 4:45 am until 5:30 pm daily, and there are longer-haul buses that pass along the Costanera and can drop you off in Uvita. Each of the park's four sectors has a small ranger station where you pay your $6 admission.

ESSENTIALS

Hospital Dome Plaza Medical Services. ⊠ *Dome Plaza, 50 m south of the bridge, Uvita* ☎ *2743–8595 doctor, 2743–8418 dentist, 2743–8558 pharmacy.*

Visitor Information Uvita Information Center. ⊠ *On the Costanera Hwy., across from BM Supermarket, Uvita* ☎ *8843–7142, 2743–8889* ⊕ *www.uvita.info.*

EXPLORING

FAMILY **Ballena National Marine Park** (*Parque Nacional Marino Ballena*). Named
Fodor's Choice for the whales who use this area as a nursery, the park has four separate
★ Blue Flag beaches stretching for about 10 km (6 miles) and encompasses a mangrove estuary, a remnant coral reef, and more than 12,350 acres of ocean, home to tropical fish, dolphins, and humpback whales. Playa Uvita is the most popular sector of the park, with the longest stretch of beach and shallow waters calm enough for kids. Restaurants line the road to the Playa Uvita park entrance, but there are no food concessions within the park. Access to each of the four beaches—from north to south, Uvita, Colonia, Ballena, and Piñuela—is off the Costanera Highway. Although the official park offices are open 7 am to 4 pm, visitors can stay on longer, especially to view sunsets or camp. ⊠ *Entrance at Playa Uvita, about 20 km (10 miles) south of Dominical, Uvita* ☎ *2743–8236* ⊡ *$6* ⊙ *Daily 7–4.*

Oro Verde Private Nature Reserve. You'll find excellent bird-watching and hiking in this nature preserve, uphill from the Costanera. Family run, the property has well-groomed trails through a majestic, primary forest reserve. Early-morning, three-hour birding tours start at 6 am ($35) and end with a hearty home-cooked breakfast. In the afternoon, you can set out for a three-hour birding walk. For a totally different perspective on wildlife, join the naturalist-guided night tour, from 6 to 9 pm. The best way to book is through the Uvita Information Center. ⊠ *Off the Costanera Hwy. at Km 159, 3 km (2 miles) uphill from Rancho La Merced, Uvita* ☎ *2743–8889, 8843–8833* ⊙ *By reservation only.*

FAMILY **Rancho La Merced National Wildlife Refuge.** Ride the range on a 1,250-acre property combining forest and pasture ($45) or gallop along the beach at sunset on horseback ($50). Explore the forest on a nature hike ($35) or go bird-watching ($45) with an excellent guide. Riding tours also include a guide and helmets, and kid-size saddles are available. All

Wildlife-Watching Tips

If you're accustomed to nature programs on TV, with visions of wildebeests and zebras swarming across the African savanna, your first visit to a tropical forest can be a bewildering experience. If these forests are so diverse, where are all the animals? Websites, brochures, and books are plastered with lovely descriptions and close-up images of wildlife that give travelers high hopes. Reality is much different but no less fascinating. Here are some tips to make your experience more enjoyable.

■ Don't expect to see rarely sighted animals. It might happen; it might not. Cats (especially jaguars) and tapirs are very rare sightings.

■ Monkeys can be the easiest animals to spot, but although they are as reliable as the tides in some locations, in others they are rare indeed.

■ Remember that nearly all animals spend most of their time avoiding detection.

■ Be quiet! Nothing is more unsettling to a wary animal than 20 *Homo sapiens* conversing as they hike. It's best to treat the forest like a house of worship—quiet reverence is in order.

■ Listen closely. Many visitors are surprised when a flock of parrots overhead is pointed out to them, despite the incredible volume of noise they produce. That low-pitched growl you hear is a howler monkey call, which is obvious if nearby, but easily missed over the din of conversation. Try stopping for a moment and closing your eyes.

■ Slowly observe different levels of the forest. An enormous caterpillar or an exquisitely camouflaged moth may be only a few inches from your face, and the silhouettes in the tree 100 meters (330 feet) away may be howler monkeys. Scan trunks and branches where a sleeping sloth or anteater might curl up. A quick glance farther down the trail may reveal an agouti or peccary crossing your path.

■ In any open area such as a clearing or river, use your binoculars and scan in the distance; scarlet macaws and toucans may be cruising above the treetops.

■ Cultivate some level of interest in the less charismatic denizens of the forest—the plants, insects, and spiders. On a good day in the forest you may see a resplendent quetzal or spider monkey, but should they fail to appear, focus on an intricate spider web, a column of marching army ants, mammal footprints in the mud, or colorful seeds and flowers fallen from high in the canopy.

tours begin at the pleasant reception center, where you can freshen up in clean, modern restrooms. For $6 you can explore the 10 km (6 miles) of hiking trails on your own with a trail map that includes a wildlife picture guide. There's also a night tour with a naturalist guide ($35). ⊠ *Km 159 of Costanera Hwy., north of Uvita, Uvita* ☎ *2743–8032, 8861–5147* ⊕ *www.rancholamerced.com* 🖃 *$35–$50* ⊙ *By reservation only.*

Uvita Market. From 8 am to noon on Saturday, the place to be is this combination farmers' market and weekly gathering place for locals. About 20 vendors show up to sell organic produce, chocolate, homemade cheeses and hot sauces, fresh fish, baked goods, jams, and frozen gourmet dinners and soups to take home. You can also feast on ready-to-eat breakfast burritos, tamales, cakes, cookies, and the freshest, best donuts in the country, made right on the spot. Artists sell painted masks, colorful textiles, and beautiful wildlife photographs. Every third Saturday there's a garage-sale table, too. This is a great place to meet English-speaking locals as they meet and greet. Some weeks, there's live music by local bands. You'll find the market just off the Costanera Highway, across from the Banco de Costa Rica and down a short side road. Just look for all the parked cars. ⊠ *Off Costanera Hwy., across from Banco de Costa Rica, Uvita* ⊙ *Sat. 8–noon.*

OFF THE BEATEN PATH

Finca 6 Museum of the Spheres. The mystery of Costa Rica's pre-Columbian spheres—massive, perfectly round stones uncovered in the 1930s—is explored in this new archaeological museum, built on a recently designated UNESCO World Heritage Site near Sierpe, the port for boats to Drake Bay. Dating from 800 to 1500 AD, these carefully arranged spheres of varying sizes cover acres of land, popping up miles from the source of the rock used to carve them. Anthropologists speculate they may have served as agricultural calendars or as ceremonial sites similar to Stonehenge. All of the theories are outlined, in English and Spanish, along with displays of period pottery, sculpture, and other artifacts in a light and airy new museum, a branch of San José's National Museum. Much of the museum is outdoors, to view archeological sites and see the spheres *in situ*. The sun is hot, so come early and bring along a hat and a water bottle. Squirrel monkeys and birds inhabit the wooded areas along the trails, so it's a good idea to carry binoculars and cameras, too. If you are on your way to the Osa Peninsula, by car or boat, don't miss this opportunity to encounter a surviving vestige of indigenous culture. ⊠ *8 km (5 miles) west of turnoff from Costanera to Palmar Sur, on road to Sierpe; look for Finca 6 sign on left, just before small bridge* ✛ *45 km (28 miles) south of Uvita, on Costanera Hwy., to turnoff for Palmar Sur, then follow signs to airport and Sierpe* ☎ *2100–6000* 🖃 *$6* ⊙ *Tues.–Sun. 8–4.*

8

BEACHES

Playa Ballena. Playa Ballena, 4 km (2½ miles) from Playa Colonia, is a lovely strand backed by lush vegetation and fairly easy to get to from the main highway, along a short, bumpy dirt road. Gas and charcoal barbecues are permitted here, so locals often have barbecues on weekends. There's free parking close to the beach. **Amenities:** showers; toilets. **Best for:** swimming; walking. ⊠ *Ballena National Marine Park, Ojochal* ✛ *off the Costanera, 4 km (2½ miles) south of Playa Colonia access road* 🖃 *$6* ⊙ *7 to 4.*

Playa Colonia. Playa Colonia, 2 km (1¼ miles) south of Playa Uvita along the Costanera Highway, has a safe swimming beach with a view of rocky islands, which you can visit by kayak. The access road is a well-graded dirt road. In high season, vendors sell cold drinks and souvenirs at the beach entrance. It's the only beach where cars can park practically on the beach, and camping is included in the admission price. **Amenities:** food and drink; showers; toilets. **Best for:** swimming. ⊠ *Ballena National Marine Park, Colonia* 🖃 *$6* ⊙ *7 to 4.*

An iguana on Playa Uvita.

Playa Piñuela. Tiny Playa Piñuela is the prettiest of the Ballena National Marine Park beaches, nestled in a deep cove with views of small islands. It's not always the best beach for swimming at high tide, however, since the shore is strewn with large stones and the waves can be a little rough. At low tide, the smooth, sandy beach emerges. The access road is very bumpy but also short. **Amenities:** showers; toilets. **Best for:** walking. ⊠ *Ballena National Marine Park, 3 km (2 miles) south of Colonia, Ojochal* ✛ *turn off Costanera just past Km 172 marker* 🖃 *$6* 🕙 *7 to 4* ☞ *Official hours are 7 to 4, but visitors can remain on the beaches later.*

Fodor's Choice
★ **Playa Uvita.** At the northern end of Ballena National Marine Park, wide, palm-fringed Playa Uvita stretches out along a *tombolo* (a long swath of sand) connecting a former island to the coast. This is the most popular beach, especially on weekends, with shallow waters for swimming. On weekdays you may have it almost to yourself. It's also the launching spot for boat tours and the favorite vantage point for spectacular sunsets. There is no parking at the beach but there are private parking lots along the road leading to the park entrance, charging $4 a day. **Amenities:** food and drink; showers; toilets. **Best for:** sunset; swimming; walking. ⊠ *Ballena National Marine Park, Uvita* 🖃 *$6* 🕙 *7 to 4* ☞ *Official opening hours, but visitors can stay on the beach after hours.*

Playa Ventanas. Just 1½ km (1 mile) south of Ballena National Marine Park, off the Costanera Highway, you'll find a scenic beach with interesting tidal caves, popular for sea kayaking. Coconut palms edge the beach, which is sometimes pebbly, with quite a dramatic surf, especially at high tide when the waves break against huge offshore rock formations. The ocean views are rivaled by the vistas of green, forested mountains rising up behind the beach. You can camp here and use very basic toilets and cold-water showers. There's a new access road to the beach and a guarded parking area ($3 for the day). But it is advisable to not leave anything of value in your car. **Amenities:** parking (fee); toilets; showers. **Best for:** walking. ✉ *1½ km (1 mile) off Costanera, south of Playa Piñuela, Ojochal.*

SPORTS AND THE OUTDOORS

DIVING AND SNORKELING

The best spot for snorkeling in the park is at the north end of Playa Ballena, near the whale's tail.

Bahía Aventuras. Bilingual guides lead half-day tours in covered boats that combine whale- and dolphin-watching with snorkeling for $90. Whale season begins the end of December into March. A boat tour of the Terraba Sierpe Mangrove costs $85. If you want to try your luck, you can fish from a 7-meter (23-foot) boat designed and built locally; a half day costs $750 and a full day around Caño Island costs $950. There is a pleasant waiting room at the tour office, with clean, accessible bathrooms and parking. ✉ *Bahía Ballena* ☎ *2743–8362, 8846–6576* ⊕ *www.bahiaaventuras.com.*

Dolphin Tours of Bahía Ballena. This tried-and-true tour company takes a minimum of two people on four-hour boat tours that combine dolphin- and whale-watching with snorkeling, a visit to ocean caverns, and a rocky island bird sanctuary for $75 per person. All-day fishing trips for snook and red snapper cost $750 for up to four anglers. ☎ *2743–8013, 8825–4031* ⊕ *www.dolphintourcostarica.com.*

Mystic Dive Center. Specializing in dive and snorkel trips to Caño Island, about 50 km (31 miles) offshore, this long-standing dive operation takes a minimum of four divers or eight snorkelers ($130 full-day snorkeling, $170 full-day diving). The tour leaves daily at 7 am and returns around 2:30 pm. Or you can dive or snorkel closer in, only a 15-minute boat ride from Playa Ventanas, morning or afternoon, with a minimum of four people ($90 for snorkelers, $110 for divers). You can also rent surf- and boogie boards or take PADI dive lessons. ✉ *West side of Costanera Hwy., near entrance to Ojochal, Ojochal* ☎ *2786–5217* ⊕ *www.mysticdive.com* ☽ *During rainy season—end of Aug. to Dec. 15.*

ZIP LINING

Osa Canopy Tour. Zip lines are a dime a dozen in Costa Rica, but this relatively new one is getting rave reviews. With 14 platforms and more than 3 km (2 miles) of cable, you will certainly get your money's worth. For the really adventurous, there are also two rappelling stations—one 9 meters (30 feet) high, the other 27 meters (90 feet)—and a Tarzan swing. Count on flying through the forest, 30 meters (100 feet) high at times, for two to three hours, all for $59 per person; $45 for kids under 13. The maximum weight for a zip-liner is 230 pounds. ✉ *Ticket office at Km 196, Costanera Hwy., south of Uvita, Bahía Ballena* ☎ *2788–7555, 8884–1237* ⊕ *www.osacanopytour.com.*

8

WHERE TO EAT

$$$ ✕**Azul Restaurante y Bar.** This intimate restaurant with Mediterranean
MEDITERRANEAN cuisine and an unbeatable view has a sophisticated look and menu. Sun-
sets here are spectacular, overlooking the sea and a picturesque island
on the horizon, with pairs of scarlet macaws winging past at eye level.
But the ultra-chic decor rivals the natural scenery. The restaurant spills
out onto a large terrace, shaded by white sails by day and sparkling
with strings of fairy lights at night. An elegant private room with a
round table for six is illuminated by a unique, eye-catching, driftwood
chandelier. The menu includes delicately fried calamari, goat-cheese
ravioli, and seafood pasta alongside more daring dishes like a delicate
tuna carpaccio and a creamy, tender fish fillet in a saffron sauce studded
with capers. Presentation is creative and delightful. The wine selection
is eclectic and international. Service is a little uneven, but who cares
when you have that view? ⑤ *Average main: $17* ✉ *El Castillo Hotel, off
Costanera Hwy., just past entrance to Ojochal, Ojochal* ☎ *2786–5543.*

$$ ✕**Boca Coronado Bar y Restaurante.** Along the Costanera Highway from
SEAFOOD Dominical to Punta Mala you'll see signs shouting "Ceviche," sold from
carts with cooler chests or in rickety roadside ranchos. If you're interested in trying this local specialty—raw fish and seafood marinated in
lime juice and spiced up with onions and red peppers—try the ceviche,
safely refrigerated, at this breezy, open-air restaurant that's just steps
from the sea. The ceviche is the freshest you'll find: among the various
versions, the shrimp and sea bass marinated in coconut milk is a specialty. But don't stop at the ceviche: the hot dishes are well prepared,
and the excellent chicken curry is a nice nonseafood option. ⑤ *Average
main: $10* ✉ *West side of Costanera Hwy., just south of entrance to
Ojochal, Ojochal* ☎ *2786–5082* ⊙ *Closed Tues.*

$$$ ✕**Citrus Restaurant & Terraza.** Tangy, tart, and refreshing, this ultraso-
ECLECTIC phisticated restaurant lives up to its name, with an inventive fusion
Fodor'sChoice menu that spans the globe. Captained by veteran local chef Marcella
★ Marciano, the culinary voyage careers from classic French escargots
and steak tartare, to Japanese wasabi-spiced, grilled shrimp, to Indian
chicken curry, to Lebanese hummus, with stopovers in Morocco, Mada-
gascar, and Vietnam. Local seafood makes appearances as carpaccio
slices and ceviche cubes; simmering in a piquant, red curry broth; or in
the signature seafood platter of lobster, mussels, calamari, and shrimp,
bathed in a creamy lemon-and-garlic sauce. Local draft beers are on tap,
along with a wide-ranging wine list. Presentation is exquisite. Desserts
are among the best in the country; if you like chocolate, don't pass up
the divine Choco-Choco flourless chocolate cake with vanilla ice cream.
Citrus is now in its third incarnation, starting as a floating boat restau-
rant, then moving to a Moroccan-inspired mansion, and now in a more
intimate, dazzlingly chic and contemporary space, just 200 meters from
its previous location. Open daily for dinner only, from December to
April. Dinner reservations are advised at this very popular restaurant.
⑤ *Average main: $20* ✉ *Ojochal exit off Costanera Hwy., just past
yellow bridge on main road through Ojochal, Ojochal* ☎ *2786–5175,
8304–1717* ⊙ *Closed in Oct.*

$$$ ✕ **Exotica Restaurant.** In the tiny French-Canadian enclave of Ojochal,
FRENCH this intimate and romantic restaurant has just 10 tables encased in
Fodor's Choice greenery under a thatch roof. The menu consists of French-inspired
★ fare with exotic flavors culled from France's colonial past. You'll be
warmly welcomed by Lucy, the restaurant's chic and charming owner.
Start off with a tangy and refreshing avocado, pineapple, lime, and
cilantro appetizer, or an intriguing Tahitian fish carpaccio bathed in
a creamy banana and coconut marinade. Don't miss out on a hearty
serving of fish or shrimp in a banana-curry sauce, or a spicy Vietnamese
chicken soup. French favorites include cognac liver pâté and a pricey
but excellent duck breast with orange sauce. Presentation is artistic,
with garnishes of flowers and sprigs of exotic greenery. The wine list
is international and reasonably priced. Desserts are all homemade and
luscious. Chocoholics won't want to miss the Devil's Fork flourless
chocolate cake, rich and dense, with a hint of chili pepper. For a refresh-
ing finish to a meal, the passion-fruit ice cream with a blackberry coulis
will leave your taste buds tingling. ⑤ *Average main: $18* ✉ *Main road
into Ojochal, off Costanera Hwy., Ojochal* ☎ *2786–5050* ⊙ *Closed
Sun., Nov. to May; Sun. and Mon., May to Oct.; all of Oct. No lunch*
⚐ *Reservations essential.*

$ ✕ **Pancito Café.** Besides crusty baguettes, buttery croissants, and divine
FRENCH pastries to go, this French bakery near the entrance to Ojochal serves
hearty breakfast omelets and does a booming lunch business with a new
menu that includes quiches, croissant sandwiches, crepes, mussels with
french fries, fish soup, and salade Niçoise. Customers perch on high
stools at tables and counters in this casual, thatch-roofed café. Many
have their laptops open, taking advantage of the free Wi-Fi. Get here
early on Tuesday for the popular weekly plat du jour. Take-out dishes
(which are great for picnics) include pork rillettes, smoked trout and
salmon, and stuffed crabs. ⑤ *Average main: $8* ✉ *Plaza de Los Delfines,
off Costanera Hwy. at entrance to Ojochal, Ojochal* ☎ *506/2786–5774,
8729–4115* ▭ *No credit cards* ⊙ *Closed Sun. No dinner.*

$$ ✕ **Pizzeria El Jardín Tortuga.** Pizza is the claim to fame here, baked in a
PIZZA wood-fired clay oven, and served in a casual garden patio and a cool
upstairs rancho. The German pizza baker can make only six individual pizzas at a time, but it's worth the wait for thin-crust pies heaped
with toppings. The menu also includes shrimp, lobster, and paella. For
something a little different, try the German-style pork in beer sauce or
a French meat fondue. While you wait for your meal, you can enjoy
the birds flitting in the garden by day, or in the evening have a drink in
the bar, which is popular with locals. ⑤ *Average main: $12* ✉ *Ojochal,
past supermarket, left on bridge and 1st right, Ballena Marine National
Park* ☎ *2786–5059* ⊕ *www.theturtlesgarden.com* ⊙ *Closed Mon.–Wed.*

$$$ ✕ **Sabor Español.** Authentic paella, made with nutty, saffron-infused
SPANISH Spanish rice and the freshest seafood, is the main reason to wend your
Fodor's Choice way along a rutted dirt road behind Playa Ballena to this jungle outpost
★ of Catalan cuisine. The smallish, open-air rancho is nothing fancy, with
wooden chairs and tables and a few potted palms, but the warm wel-
come along with the expertly executed Catalonian menu quickly dispel
any qualms about the seriousness of this restaurant. There's a classic,

8

spicy, Andalusian gazpacho for starters or tapas to share while you wait the 40 minutes for your cooked-to-order paella. Try the delicate, sweet mussels, bathed in a spicy wine sauce, or the succulent mushrooms marinated in garlic and olive oil. The list of seafood specialties includes whisky-flambéed shrimp and meat-lovers can sink their teeth into sirloin slathered with a wine-and-fresh-grape sauce. Chicken takes on tropical flavors with sauces featuring mango, rum, and curry. The pace is a little leisurely, but a pitcher of excellent sangria, studded with tropical fruit chunks, helps to pass the time enjoyably. There are only five or six tables at this dinner-only restaurant, so reservations are advised. $ *Average main: $16* ⊠ *1 km (½ mile) south of Uvita BM Supermercado along Costanera, Bahía Ballena* ✛ *Turn right at Cabinas Gato sign; look for left-turn Sabor Español sign onto dirt road running parallel to Playa Ballena* ☎ *2743–8312, 8768–9160* ▭ *No credit cards* ☉ *Closed Mon. and Sept. 15–Dec. 15. No lunch.*

$ ✕ **Sibu Coffee & Chocolate.** It's not always easy to find a great cup of cof-
CAFÉ fee around Uvita, especially early in the morning. But the espresso at this new, hip café is excellent—and ready by 7:15 am. Using organic coffee from the high-altitude Dota region, the baristas steam up the best macchiato around. Add in free, high-speed Wi-Fi, divine desserts, and a laid-back vibe, and it's hard to leave this comfortable hangout. On the chocolate side, there's a dark, dense chocolate-and-almond cake with white chocolate icing. But the standout treat is a tart lemon pie with clouds of perfect meringue topping. The café also serves salads, sandwiches, burgers, and pizza. You can buy their coffee beans to take home. $ *Average main: $9* ⊠ *Across from BM supermercado in the center of Uvita, Uvita* ☎ *8526–4974* ☉ *Closed Sun.* ▭ *No credit cards.*

$$ ✕ **Tilapias El Pavón.** To enjoy an authentically Tico day in the country,
COSTA RICAN follow a winding river road up to this family-run tilapia fish farm in the
FAMILY tiny hamlet of Vergel. Look for the restaurant's namesake, the turkey-like Great Curassow (*pavon* in Spanish), in the surrounding forest and carved on the restaurant's handsome doors. You can work up an appetite on a short hike to a spectacular, nearby waterfall with a swimming hole (bring your swimsuit and binoculars for bird-watching), then catch your own tilapia. The cooks at the open-air wooden restaurant overlooking the scenic fishponds will fry up your fish in 10 minutes, presenting it whole or filleted, with rice, salad, yuca, and excellent *patacones* (fried, mashed plantains), plus a pitcher of refreshing fruit naturale, a feast for only $10. There's also chicken for non-fish fans, plus wine and beer. It's open 9–6 weekdays, 9–8 weekends, so it's a good spot for lunch or an early dinner. $ *Average main: $10* ⊠ *2 km (1 mile) south of Ojochal, then just before bridge in Punta Mala, follow a dirt road 4 km (2½ miles) uphill to tiny hamlet of Vergel, Vergel* ☎ *2200–4721* ▭ *No credit cards.*

$$ ✕ **Villa Leonor.** Can't decide between lunch or the beach? You can get
COSTA RICAN both at this cheerful, casual restaurant and beach club, complete with
FAMILY swimming pool and showers, just steps from Playa Ballena. Famous for weekend barbecues, the menu also offers mixed chicken and fish fajitas. Typical *casados* are a bargain, with fish or chicken and lots of sides. Local lobsters, broiled in garlic butter, can be ordered ahead. Chill out

with ice-cold beer, excellent fruit smoothies, and tropical cocktails at the swim-up bar, while the kids play in the pool. Or stroll down to the beach between courses. The covered terrace restaurant has expanded into the garden, with tables under a big-top cover. Dinner is also served daily in high season, generally January to August, until 8 pm. Service is sprightly, and the friendly American owner is usually on hand to greet customers. $ *Average main: $13* ⊠ *Between Km 170 and 171 on Costanera, Bahía Ballena* ✛ *1 km (½ mile) south of road to Hotel Cristal Ballena, turn right on road signed Villa Lenonor* ☎ *2786–5380* ⊟ *No credit cards* ☉ *Sept. to Dec. closed Tues. and no dinner served.*

WHERE TO STAY

$$
RENTAL
FAMILY

⚏ **Diquis del Sur Hotel, Villas & Garden.** At this ideal—and affordable— tropical retreat for the winter-weary, four bungalows are sprinkled around lush grounds with views of both mountains and ocean. **Pros:** reasonable daily rates and weekly bargains; great breakfasts; well-spaced bungalows. **Cons:** some bungalow rooms lack air-conditioning; spare but adequate furnishings; rough road from main highway. $ *Rooms from: $85* ⊠ *Off Costanera Hwy., 1 km (½ mile) up dirt road signed "Calle Papagayo", Ojochal* ☎ *2786–5013* ⊕ *www.diquiscostarica.com* ⟿ *8 bungalow rooms, 5 villas, 2 cabins* ⦿| *Breakfast.*

$$$$
B&B/INN

⚏ **El Castillo.** With perhaps the most spectacular ocean view on the Costa Ballena, this modern "castle" is a luxury boutique hotel with six ultra-chic guest quarters with private terraces. **Pros:** million-dollar view; high design; luxury accommodation; scenic pool with room to swim laps. **Cons:** some noise from trucks on nearby Costanera; stairs to ocean-view rooms and guest deck. $ *Rooms from: $275* ⊠ *Calle Perezoso, off Costanera Hwy,, Ojochal* ✛ *500 m. south of Ojochal* ☎ *2786–5543 hotel, 214/329–9866 U.S.* ⊕ *www.elcastillocr.com* ⟿ *2 suites, 4 rooms* ⦿| *Breakfast.*

$$$$
B&B/INN
FAMILY
Fodor's Choice
★

⚏ **Hotel Cristal Ballena.** High on a hillside with spectacular ocean views framed by giant traveler's palm trees, this Austrian-owned hotel is the most luxurious base for exploring the area, with a 400-square-meter (4,300-square-foot) swimming pool that commands both mountain and sea views. **Pros:** wonderful swimming pool for serious swimmers and loungers; great ocean, mountain, and sky views; luxurious rooms. **Cons:** stairs to manage between rooms and restaurant; steep walk down to beach. $ *Rooms from: $255* ⊠ *Costanera Hwy., 7 km (4 miles) south of Uvita, Uvita* ☎ *2786–5354* ⊕ *www.cristal-ballena.com* ⟿ *19 suites, 2 cabins* ⦿| *Breakfast.*

$$$$
B&B/INN
Fodor's Choice
★

⚏ **Kurá Design Villas.** Stunning contemporary design, high-tech comforts, and a lofty location overlooking the Pacific combine to set a whole new standard of luxury. **Pros:** the ultimate in contemporary design and comfort; saltwater infinity pool; excellent restaurant; no children under 16. **Cons:** the ultimate in price (but worth the splurge); a long, steep drive down to the beach. $ *Rooms from: $690* ⊠ *1 km (½ mile) above Uvita, to parking lot; hotel transport up to Kurá, Bahía Ballena* ☎ *8521–3407, 800–728–0466 toll-free USA* ⊕ *www.kuracostarica.com* ☉ *Closed Oct.* ⟿ *4 villas, 2 junior suites* ⦿| *Breakfast.*

8

$$$ 📺 **La Cusinga.** Along with one of the best sunset views along the coast,
B&B/INN this comfortable eco-lodge on a high cliff bordering Ballena National
FAMILY Marine Park has spacious, airy cabins and a forest trail to a pristine
beach. **Pros:** comfortable cabins; forest and beach access; magnifi-
cent views. **Cons:** steep path between cabins and lodge; Wi-Fi only
in main lodge. ⑤ *Rooms from: $190* ✉ *Between Km 166 and 167 on
the Costanera Hwy., south of Dominical, Bahía Ballena* ☎ *2770–2549
Reservation office, 8318–8598 Lodge* ⊕ *www.lacusingalodge.com* ⤷ *5
cabins, 1 honeymoon cabin, 1 single room, 2 group cabins* �“❘ *Breakfast.*

$ 📺 **Rio Tico Safari Lodge.** You'll feel as though you're on a luxury safari
B&B/INN when you step inside one of these spacious South African–made tents
FAMILY perched on sturdy wooden platforms that are cantilevered over a rush-
ing mountain river. **Pros:** gorgeous natural setting; dry and airy tents;
helpful hosts. **Cons:** steps to climb up and down from main lodge to
tents; no air-conditioning. ⑤ *Rooms from: $60* ✉ *3 km (2 miles) south
of Ojochal on Costanera, turn off just before bridge in Punta Mala, 4
km (2½ miles) up winding dirt road to Vergel de Punta Mala, Vergel de
Punta Mala* ☎ *8996–7935, 4000–0680* ⊕ *www.riotico.com* ⤷ *9 tents,
3 rooms* ❘❘ *No meals.*

$$ 📺 **Villas Gaia.** Conveniently just off the highway, these spacious, tasteful
B&B/INN casitas are hidden behind a ridge overlooking bird-filled forest ravines
leading to Playa Tortuga. **Pros:** easy access off the highway; serene
setting; good restaurant. **Cons:** you must climb some stairs to get to
the villas; pool is small; beach is down a steep path. ⑤ *Rooms from:
$95* ✉ *Off the Costanera Hwy., 15 km (9 miles) south of Uvita, Playa
Tortuga* ☎ *2786–5044, 2241–3393 in San José* ⊕ *www.villasgaia.com*
⤷ *12 casitas, 2 two-bedroom houses* ❘❘ *Breakfast.*

SHOPPING

Green Leaf Arts & Artesania. This well-stocked shop has a great selection
of high-quality local art, indigenous crafts and souvenirs, eclectic home
accessories, and interesting jewelry. Next door at the **Super Feliz** you can
pick up snacks, imported cheeses (including Brie and Gorgonzola), and
treats for a beach picnic, as well as imported beer and the best selection
of wine in the area. Both stores are open daily from 9 to 6. Need some
beach reading? Check out the store's used-book exchange, the **Rainforest Book Trader,** open daily from 9 to 6. ✉ *Plaza Maleku, West side of
Costanera Hwy., next to Mystic Dive Center, Ojochal* ☎ *2786–5221
Green Leaf, 2786–5217 Licorera Feliz.*

THE GOLFO DULCE

One of only three tropical fjords in the world, the Golfo Dulce has
180-meter-deep (600-foot-deep) waters in the center of a usually placid
gulf where you can watch dolphins swim and humpback whales feed.
At Chacarita, 33 km (20 miles) south of Palmar Sur, the southern coast
assumes a split personality. Heading west, you reach the Osa Peninsula
and, eventually, the Pacific Ocean and the wildest region of Costa Rica.
Continuing due south brings you to the Golfo Dulce, which means
"Sweet Gulf," reflecting the usually tranquil waters. This gulf creates
two shorelines: an eastern shore that is accessible only by boat above

Golfito, and a western shore, which is the eastern side of the Osa Peninsula. South of Golfito the coast fronts the Pacific Ocean once again (rather than the calm gulf), with wilder beaches that beckon surfers and nature lovers.

GOLFITO

130 km (81 miles) south of Uvita, 339 km (212 miles) southeast of San José.

Overlooking a small gulf (hence its name) and hemmed in by a steep bank of forest, Golfito has a scenic location. Lodges supply kayaks for paddling the gulf's warm, salty, and crystal-clear waters. When the sun sets behind the rolling silhouette of the Osa Peninsula, you can sometimes spot phosphorescent fish jumping. Fishing, both commercial and for sport, is the main activity here, with lively marinas providing slips to visiting yachts and charter fishing boats.

Golfito was once a thriving banana port—United Fruit arrived in 1938—with elegant housing and lush landscaping for its plantation managers. After United Fruit pulled out in 1985, Golfito slipped into a state of poverty and neglect. The town itself consists of a pleasant, lushly landscaped older residential section and a long strip of scruffy commercial buildings. Visiting U.S. Coast Guard ships dock here, and small cruise ships moor in the harbor. The Costa Rica Coast Guard Academy is also here.

GETTING HERE AND AROUND

From San José the trip used to take eight hours, along paved roads crossing over often-foggy mountains. But with the new toll road from San José, connecting to the paved Costanera Highway, travel time has been cut to five hours. Your best bet, especially if you are visiting a lodge on the gulf, is to fly to Golfito, which takes only about an hour. Direct buses from San José leave twice daily, at 7 am and 3:30 pm, following the longer mountain route; the 6:30 am bus from San José uses the faster Costanera route.

Taxis and boats take you wherever you need to go in and around Golfito. You can hire taxi boats at the city dock in Golfito (about $90 round-trip, often negotiable, to go to area lodges or across the Golfo Dulce to Puerto Jiménez). The only way to reach the remote Golfo Dulce lodges above Golfito is by boat. Early morning is the best time, when the water in the gulf is at its calmest. Most lodges include the boat transport in their rates.

For tour, lodging, and general tourist information, check out ⊕ *www. golfitocostarica.com*, a website managed by longtime Golfito residents.

ESSENTIALS

Banks/ATMs ATH Coopealianza. ✉ *North end of town, across from hospital* ☎ *2775-0025.* **Banco Nacional.** ✉ *South of hospital on main road through Golfito* ☎ *2212-2000.*

Hospital Regional Hospital. ✉ *American Zone, near Deposito* ☎ *2775-7800.*

Pharmacy Farmacia Golfito. ⊠ *Main street, across from city park* ☎ *2775–2442.*

Post Office Correo. ⊠ *Off the main road, south of central park.*

Taxi Taxi service. ⊠ *Taxi stand beside gas station in center of town, near municipal dock* ☎ *2775–2020.*

Visitor Information Land Sea Services. ⊠ *Next to Banana Bay Marina* ☎ *2775–1614* ⊕ *www.golfitocostarica.com.*

EXPLORING

American Zone. The northwestern end of town is the so-called American Zone, full of handsome wooden houses where the expatriate managers of United Fruit lived amid flowering trees imported from all over the world. Many of these vintage houses, built of durable Honduran hardwoods, are now being spruced up. Eccentric garden features, such as a restored railway car, make the neighborhood worth a stroll. If you're on foot, there's also excellent birding in and around the gardens. ⊠ *Golfito.*

Fodor's Choice **Casa Orquideas.** A Garden of Eden with mass plantings of ornamental
★ palms, bromeliads, heliconias, cycads, orchids, flowering gingers, and spice trees, Casa Orquideas has been tended with care for more than 30 years by American owners Ron and Trudy MacAllister. The 2½-hour tour, available Sunday and Thursday at 8:30 am, includes touching, tasting, and smelling, plus spotting toucans and hummingbirds. Trudy is also a font of information on local lore and medicinal plants. Guided tours, given for a minimum of three people, are $10 per person. Self-guided visits, any day but Friday, cost $8. The garden is accessible only by boat; a water taxi to the garden (about $100 round-trip for four or more people) is a tour in itself; most lodges include the garden in their tours. ⊠ *On the Golfo Dulce, north of Golfito* ☎ *8829–1247* ⊑ *$8–$10* ⊙ *Guided tours Thurs. and Sun. at 8:30 am. Closed Fri.*

Piedras Blancas National Park (*Parque Nacional Piedras Blancas*). There is some good birding in the dense forest here, which is also an important wildlife corridor connecting to Corcovado National Park. Follow the main road northwest through the American Zone and past the airstrip and a housing project. The place where a dirt road heads into the rain forest is great for bird-watching. There are no marked trails actually in the park; the best birding is along the road. ⊠ *Adjacent to Golfito National Wildlife Refuge* ☎ *No phone.*

SPORTS AND THE OUTDOORS
FISHING
The open ocean holds plenty of sailfish, marlin, and roosterfish during the dry months, as well as mahimahi, tuna, and wahoo during the rainy season; there's excellent bottom fishing any time of year. Captains are in constant radio contact with one another and tend to share fish finds.

Banana Bay Marina. This marina houses a fleet of four charter fishing boats, fitted with tournament-quality tackle and skippered by English-speaking, world-record-holding captains. A day's fishing for up to four averages $1,450. You can also charter a boat for overnight trips to Drake Bay. ⊠ *Golfito* ☎ *2775–0255, 2775–0003* ⊕ *www. bananabaymarinagolfito.com.*

WHERE TO EAT

$$ ✕ **Banana Bay.** For consistently good American-style food, you can't beat
AMERICAN this breezy marina restaurant with a view of expensive yachts and sport-
fishing boats. Locals complain that the prices are high, but portions are
hefty, and include generous salads, sizzling hamburgers, excellent chicken
fajitas, and a delicious grilled dorado sandwich with a mountain of fries.
Shrimp and fish plates are pricier—$15 to $22—but they couldn't be
fresher, straight off the local boats. It's open for breakfast, too. Try the
signature McBilge sandwich with eggs, cheese, and bacon or sausage.
While you're waiting for your order, take advantage of the free Wi-Fi.
⑤ *Average main: $13* ✉ *Main street, south of town dock* ☎ *2775–0383.*

$$ ✕ **Restaurante Mar y Luna.** This pleasant terrace restaurant jutting out
SEAFOOD over the water has the best harbor view in Golfito, along with jaunty
nautical decor and the coolest breezes in town. The seafood-heavy
lineup includes grilled whole fish served in a variety of ways, including
Caribbean style with coconut milk and a side of patacones (fried green
plantain). Tuna carpaccio and occasional sushi specials add a touch of
sophistication. For a light lunch, the fish tacos are standouts—plenty
of perfectly breaded and lightly fried fish plus fresh slaw and crispy
calamari tossed on top. Salads are also on the menu, along with a few
vegetarian dishes. The bar is a great place to hang out, particularly
during televised sports events when fans gather to watch the two
large flat-screen TVs. During happy hour, from 4 to 7, local beers
are 2 for 1. Inexpensive, motel-style rooms and larger suites with the
same view are available for rent. ⑤ *Average main: $15* ✉ *South end
of main street, north of Hotel Las Gaviotas* ☎ *2775–0192* ⊕ *www.
marylunagolfito.com.*

WHERE TO STAY

The atmosphere of the in-town hotels differs dramatically from that of
the lodges in the delightfully remote east coast of the Golfo Dulce. The
latter is a world of jungle and blue water, birds and fish, and desert-
island beaches, with lodges accessible only by boat from either Golfito
or Puerto Jiménez.

$$$ ⌂ **Casa Roland Marina Resort.** Everything at this luxury resort, designed
HOTEL like an art-deco ocean liner incongruously dry-docked in Golfito's
American Zone, is first-class. **Pros:** style and luxury; excellent service;
resort facilities for bargain price. **Cons:** dark hallways and low ceilings
on lower floor; often deserted and too quiet with few guests. ⑤ *Rooms
from: $165* ✉ *American Zone* ☎ *2775–3405* ⊕ *www.casarolandgolfito.
com* ⌂ *53 rooms, 4 suites* ⏐⊙⏐ *Breakfast.*

$$$$ ⌂ **Esquinas Rainforest Lodge.** This well-managed eco-lodge in a 35-acre
B&B/INN nature preserve bordering Piedras Blancas National Park is run by Aus-
trians who have successfully instilled some sense of Teutonic order
in the jungle (which might be why more than 80% of the guests are
from Germany and Austria). **Pros:** top-notch trails and wildlife-viewing
opportunities in unique natural setting; excellent meals; special, low
rates for children. **Cons:** no air-conditioning and it can get hot here;
some trails are challenging, and you need to be steady on your feet;
lodge is geared to nature lovers who aren't looking for luxury. ⑤ *Rooms
from: $270* ✉ *Near the village of La Gamba, 5 km (3 miles) west of*

8

The view of Gulfo Dulce from the road to Puerto Jiménez.

Villa Briceño turnoff ☎ *2741–8001* ⊕ *www.esquinaslodge.com* ⇥ *14 rooms, 1 two-bedroom villa* ⏐◎⏐ *All meals.*

$$
B&B/INN
FAMILY
⌁ **Hotel Samoa del Sur.** Nautical kitsch at its corniest, this dockside hotel has a large restaurant focused on a ship-shape bar complete with mast, a billowy sail, and a mermaid figurehead. **Pros:** affordable and fun; lively restaurant. **Cons:** can be lots of rambunctious kids in pool; noisy bar some evenings; guard dogs at night may frighten some guests. ⑊ *Rooms from: $85* ✉ *Main street, 1 block north of town dock* ☎ *2775–0233* ⊕ *www.samoadelsur.com* ⇥ *18 rooms* ⏐◎⏐ *Breakfast.*

$$$$
RESORT
Fodor's Choice
★
⌁ **Playa Nicuesa Rainforest Lodge.** Hands down, this is the best eco-lodge on the gulf, combining comfortable, upscale accommodations and great food with an emphasis on adventure on both land and sea. **Pros:** everything you need to have an active vacation; excellent food and service; rate includes boat transport; Wi-Fi. **Cons:** no air-conditioning; cabins are fairly open to nature, so there will be some insects outside the mosquito netting at night. ⑊ *Rooms from: $500* ✉ *Golfo Dulce, accessible only by boat from Golfito or Puerto Jiménez* ☎ *2258–8250 in San José, 2222–0704 in San José, 866/504–8116 in U.S. toll-free* ⊕ *www.nicuesalodge.com* ⊗ *Closed Oct.–Nov. 15* ⇥ *5 cabins, 4 rooms, 1 house* ⏐◎⏐ *All-inclusive.*

NIGHTLIFE

Happy hour is popular in Golfito. The bar at Banana Bay Marina is hopping every day from 5 to 7, when drinks are half price. The lively bar at Samoa del Sur has a mix of Ticos and foreigners, mostly of the hard-drinking, fishermen type. Friday nights there's karaoke and dance music at the huge, high-tech disco-bar by the pool at the Casa Roland Marine Resort.

Fish Hook Marina & Lodge. The curved, polished-wood bar at this marina is cooled by breezes off Golfito Bay. It's a pleasant place to meet locals, tell fish tales, and sit and watch the sunset over the bay. Happy-hour drink specials on local beers and all cocktails are offered from 4 to 7 pm. ⊠ *Main street, south of Banana Bay* ⊕ *fish-hook-marina.com.*

PLAYA ZANCUDO

51 km (32 miles) south of Golfito.

Life here is laid-back and casual, centering on walking the beach, fishing, kayaking, paddleboarding, swimming, and hanging out at the local bars and restaurants. Zancudo has a good surf break at the south end of the beach, but it pales in comparison with Playa Pavones a little to the south. Swimming is especially good two hours before or after high tide, especially at the calmer north end of the beach. The water is always warm.

If you get tired of playing in the surf and sand, you can arrange a boat trip to the nearby mangrove estuary to see birds and crocodiles. Zancudo is also home to one of the area's best sportfishing operations, headquartered at the Zancudo Lodge.

GETTING HERE AND AROUND

The road from Golfito is fully paved for the first 11 km (7 miles), but after the turnoff at El Rodeo, you'll encounter some rough patches. A bridge has finally replaced the ancient cable ferry, making the trip a little shorter, but count on 1½ hours to get here. Instead of driving, you can hire a boat at the municipal dock in Golfito for the 25-minute ride ($60 for two) or take a cheaper collectivo (communal) boat that leaves from Golfito's Samoa del Sur Hotel twice a week; check the schedule at the hotel because it varies throughout the year. A taxi ride from Golfito to Zancudo costs about $85, so the boat is a bargain.

Getting around Playa Zancudo doesn't take much, since there's really only one long, dusty road parallel to the beach. You can rent a bike at Cabinas Sol y Mar or Tres Amigos Supermercado, both on the main road in Zancudo, for about $10 per day.

There is water-taxi service to Golfito ($60 for up to three passengers; $20 each extra) and Puerto Jiménez ($80, up to three people) from Cabinas Los Cocos.

ESSENTIALS
Water Taxi Cabinas Los Cocos. ⊠ *Beach road* ☎ *2776–0012.*

BEACHES
Playa Zancudo. For laid-back beaching involving hammocks strung between palms and nothing more demanding than watching the sunset, you can't beat breezy Playa Zancudo, with its miles of wide, flat beach and romantic views of the Osa Peninsula across the Golfo Dulce. The water is amazingly warm for swimming and except for local holiday times, this beach is pretty much deserted. It isn't picture-perfect: the 10 km (6 miles) of dark, volcanic sand is sometimes strewn with flotsam and jetsam. But there's a constant breeze and a thick cushion of palm and almond trees between the beach and the dirt road running parallel.

8

Away from the beach breezes, be prepared for biting *zancudos* (no-see-ums). **Amenities:** food and drink. **Best for:** sunset; walking; swimming. ⊠ *Playa Zancudo.*

SPORTS AND THE OUTDOORS

FISHING

If you've got your own gear, you can do some good shore fishing from the beach or the mouth of the mangrove estuary, or hire a local boat to take you out into the gulf. The main edible catches are yellowfin tuna, snapper, and snook; catch-and-release fish include marlin, roosterfish, and swordfish.

The Zancudo Lodge. This luxury lodge runs the biggest charter operation in the area, with 16 boats ranging in length from 8½ to 11 meters (28 to 36 feet), including two TwinVee catamarans and two state-of-the-art Contender 32ST. During high season, fishing packages are for guests only. In low season, a day's fishing includes gear, food, and drinks ($975 in standard boats–$1,650 in Contenders for up to three fishers); and nonguests can arrange to be picked up in Golfito or Puerto Jiménez. ⊠ *Main road, north end of town* ☎ 2776–0008 ⊕ *www.zancudolodge.com.*

KAYAKING

The kayaking is great at the beach and along the nearby Río Coto Colorado, lined with mangroves. You can also test your balance on a paddleboard over ocean waves or on the river.

Cabinas Los Cocos. The popular tour ($50 per person, minimum three passengers) takes you for a 1½-hour motorboat ride up the Coto Colorado River, then a magical two-hour kayak tour along a jungly mangrove channel and a relaxing paddle, moving downstream with the current, back to the river mouth. Captain Susan can identify the birds you'll see along the way. The lodge also rents user-friendly sit-on-top kayaks with backrests for $5 per hour, and paddleboards (with instruction) at $15 for two hours. ⊠ *Beach road, north of Cabinas Sol y Mar* ☎ 2776–0012.

WHERE TO EAT

$ | ✕ **Coloso del Mar Restaurant.** Fabulous fish cakes, tasty fish burritos, and a savory fillet of sea bass with a smoky jalapeño cream sauce are a few of the delights at this screened-in-porch restaurant in a bright-yellow clapboard cottage on the beach. Chicken or fish curry is popular with the locals. Attention is paid to sides, too, including creamy mashed potatoes, cheese-topped toasted garlic bread, and perfectly cooked vegetables. Beer and wine by the glass or bottle are available. Service here is with a smile, and everything is cooked to order, so relax—you're at the beach. If you want to try the banana pancakes at breakfast, consider staying at one of the four beachfront cabins, or just come along at breakfast time, 7 to 10 am. ⑤ *Average main: $9* ⊠ *Main road, 200 m north of Soda Tranquilo* ☎ 2776–0050 ⊕ *www.colosodelmar.com* ⊘ *No lunch.*

SEAFOOD

$$$ | ✕ **The Gamefisher Restaurant.** Famous for its sportfishing, the Zancudo Lodge's terrace restaurant excels in cooking fish—all caught by guest fishers that day. Mahimahi, sautéed to crusty perfection on the outside and moist on the inside, might be served with a carrot-ginger broth,

CONTEMPORARY
Fodor's Choice
★

or over a salad of white beans and mixed greens from the lodge's own greenhouse, with a tangy citrus dressing. Carpaccio-thin slices of smoked tuna, sprinkled with finely minced garlic, capers, onions, and parsley, burst with flavor. Meat lovers can indulge in aged New York–style steaks and tender ribs or try the lodge's version of a *casado*: roasted *mojo* pork on a bed of rice and roasted black beans with yuca fries. Nightly four-course dinners ($35–$45, plus tax) have a meat or fish option. There's also a regular menu with salad, shrimp, pasta, burgers (tuna or beef), flaky, meat-filled empanadas, and taco options for diners not hungry enough for the multicourse dinner. Crusty, flavorful breads are baked daily. Desserts are delicious and inventive: try the caramelized *maduro* (sweet banana) à la mode with house-made *dulce de leche* (caramel) ice cream. The setting is ultraluxe: large lanterns and candles illuminate teak tables and chairs and throw shadows on the impressive marlin replica suspended over the chic bar. Service is very attentive and polished. This is simply the best restaurant this remote area has ever seen, and well worth the journey and the price. It's open to the public for lunch and dinner; reservations are a must for dinner. ⑤ *Average main: $17* ✉ *The Zancudo Lodge, North end of town* ☎ *2776–0008* ⊕ *www.zancudolodge.com* ⌖ *Reservations essential.*

$ ✕**Restaurant Sol y Mar.** On a breezy porch with a palm-fringed beach
ECLECTIC   view, this thatch-roofed restaurant has an eclectic menu ranging from spicy quesadillas and burritos to fresh fish with an array of exotic sauces. There's a touch of Thai here, too; one of the most popular dishes is mahimahi in a coconut-curry sauce. For a change from fish, try the thick-cut pork chops slathered in a teriyaki or creamy mushroom sauce. The hearty bar food includes chicken wings, and there are barbecue specials on Monday and Friday night. Homemade desserts are decadent and delicious, including a standout carrot cake, and a key lime pie with a cinnamon cookie crust below and meringue on top. Breakfasts are huge and hearty, featuring giant burritos. Credit cards are accepted but incur an extra 5% fee. ⑤ *Average main: $9* ✉ *Cabinas Sol y Mar, Main road, south of Cabinas Los Cocos* ☎ *2776–0014.*

WHERE TO STAY

$$ ⊡ **Cabinas Los Cocos.** This secluded cluster of self-catering cabins right on
RENTAL   the beach, under palm trees swaying in the breeze, is designed for people who want to kick back and enjoy the beach. **Pros:** like having your own beach house on an idyllic beach; friendly host helps you get the most out of your stay; Wi-Fi in cabins. **Cons:** no air-conditioning, but there are ceiling fans and ocean breezes; no phone in cabins. ⑤ *Rooms from: $85* ✉ *Beach road, north of Cabinas Sol y Mar* ☎ *2776–0012* ⊕ *www. loscocos.com* ⊳ *4 cabins* ⦵ *No meals.*

$ ⊡ **Cabinas Sol y Mar.** Just as the name implies, Cabinas Sol y Mar have
B&B/INN   plenty of sun and sea, as well as a beach fringed by coconut palms and apricot-colored wooden cabinas with porches where you can take in the spectacular views of the Osa Peninsula. **Pros:** beach location; bargain price; lively restaurant and bar; free Wi-Fi. **Cons:** no air-conditioning; bare-bones furniture; no-frills bathrooms. ⑤ *Rooms from: $56* ✉ *Main road, south of Cabinas Los Cocos* ☎ *2776–0014* ⊕ *www.zancudo.com* ⊳ *5 cabinas, 1 house* ⦵ *No meals.*

$$$
RESORT
Fodor's Choice
★

⊞ **The Zancudo Lodge.** Most guests here are well-heeled, avid anglers on all-inclusive sportfishing packages, but the young owners have completely transformed this beachfront property into a top-notch luxury resort that can be enjoyed by those who have never dropped a line. **Pros:** luxurious hotel; excellent fishing boats and captains; air-conditioned, rare in these parts; fiber-optic Wi-Fi. **Cons:** pricey for the area; very quiet evenings since fishers go to bed early in order to rise at 5 am. ⑤ *Rooms from: $250* ⊠ *Main road, northern end of town* ☎ *2776–0008, 800/854–8791 in U.S. toll-free* ⊕ *www.zancudolodge.com* ⇲ *11 rooms, 4 suites* ⦿ *Breakfast.*

PLAYA PAVONES

53 km (33 miles) south of Golfito.

Surfing is the main draw here, especially from April to September when the waves are most reliable. But the dramatic scenery, looking across the Golfo Dulce to the Osa Peninsula, along with a very laid-back vibe, make it a popular destination year-round. The area is not heavily developed but there are some excellent restaurants in town, and nearby Tiskita Jungle Lodge is a birder's paradise.

CAUTION

In the unlikely event that you are bitten by a snake, stay calm, move slowly, and try to remember what the snake looked like, to tell the clinic staff. Allow antivenom to be administered only by trained medical personnel, in case of side effects. Five hours is the window before any tissue loss. To avoid snakebites, stay on trails and wear long, loose pants; in some areas high rubber boots are recommended.

GETTING HERE AND AROUND

There's no avoiding the bumpy road from Golfito to Conte, where the road forks north to Zancudo and south to Pavones. But the dirt road to Pavones is usually well graded. A public bus leaves from Golfito twice a day, and the trip takes about two hours. A taxi from the airstrip in Golfito costs upward of $80.

4X4 Taxi Service. Hire a 4X4 air-conditioned taxi from this outfit for the bumpy ride from Golfito to Pavones, $80. ⊠ *Golfito* ✛ *by phone* ☎ *8874–9325.*

BEACHES

Playa Pavones. Driving along remote Playa Pavones, one of the most scenic beaches in Costa Rica, you catch glimpses through the palms of brilliant blue water, white surf crashing against black rocks, and the soft silhouette of the Osa Peninsula. This area at the southern edge of the mouth of Golfo Dulce attracts serious surfers, but also has pristine black-sand beaches and virgin rain forest. The coast is very rocky, so it's important to ask locals before surfing or swimming. One of the best places to swim is in the Río Claro, under the bridge or at the river mouth (dry season only). The town of Pavones itself is a helter-skelter collection of guesthouses and sodas a few blocks from the beach. **Amenities:** food and drink. **Best for:** surfing; swimming; walking. ⊠ *Pavones.*

SPORTS AND THE OUTDOORS
SURFING

Pavones is famous for one of the longest waves in the world, thanks to the mouth of the Río Claro. The most consistent waves are from April to September, and that's when the surfing crowd heads down here from the Central Pacific beaches. But even at the crest of its surfing season, Pavones is tranquility central compared with the surfing hot spots farther north.

Clear River Sports & Adventures. Down by the beach, this outfit rents surfboards for $15 a day. Bicycles rent for $10 per day, with discounts for longer rentals. There's Wi-Fi access, a library, and rooms for surfers for $15 a night. This outfit also arranges local tours. ⊠ *Main street, north of soccer field, Pavones* ☎ *8629–2508* ⊕ *www.pavonesclearriver.com.*

Sea Kings Surf Shop. You can buy top-of-the-line surfboards and other gear here, along with heavy-duty sunscreen, board wax, and the latest in surfer wear. You can also rent surfboards for $15 a day and boogie boards for $10. ⊠ *Main street, near Café de la Suerte, Pavones* ☎ *2776–2015* ⊕ *www.seakingssurfshop.com.*

WHERE TO EAT

$ ✗ **Café de la Suerte.** Fortunately for food lovers, the "Good Luck Café"
VEGETARIAN serves truly astonishing vegetarian food, along with intriguing exotic juices and thick fruit smoothies. The homemade yogurt is a revelation: light, almost fluffy, and full of flavor, served over a cornucopia of fruits, sprinkled with the café's own granola, and mixed into refreshing fruit-flavor *lassis* (an Indian yogurt-base drink). Healthful sandwiches include excellent hummus, and hot daily specials might include curried hearts of palm or juicy veggie burgers. Don't leave without buying a fudgy brownie or a brown-sugar oatmeal square for the road. Bring your laptop and use the Wi-Fi—the fee of $1 an hour is donated to local community projects. It's open 7 to 5. ⑤ *Average main: $8* ⊠ *Main street, next to soccer field, Pavones* ☎ *2776–2388* ⊕ *www.cafedelasuerte.com* ⊟ *No credit cards* ⊘ *Closed Sun. and Oct. and Nov. No dinner.*

$$ ✗ **Ristorante Italiano La Bruschetta.** This kitschy Italian spot within ear-
ITALIAN shot of the surf serves savory bruschetta and 16 varieties of the town's
FAMILY most authentic pizza: crispy, with a thin crust, Neapolitan-style. The four-seasons pizza is a triumph, with thin, spicy pepperoni, flavorful ham, olives, eggplant, peppers, onion, and zucchini. The medium size is more than big enough for two. Save room for the knockout gnocchi, pillow-soft dumplings made with potatoes and cheese and bathed in olive oil and rosemary. Other choices include tortelloni in cream sauce and filet mignon. Tiramisu, piled high with whipped cream, and key lime pie do dessert duty. Japanese lanterns add a colorful touch, along with fuchsia and lime tablecloths. To find the place, look for the "La Piña" sign. ⑤ *Average main: $15* ⊠ *Main road between Pavones and Punto Banco, north of La Ponderosa Beach and Jungle Resort, Pavones* ☎ *2776–2174* ⊟ *No credit cards.*

WHERE TO STAY

$$
B&B/INN
Fodor'sChoice
★

⌨ **La Ponderosa Beach and Jungle Resort.** The world-famous Playa Pavones surf break is a 10-minute walk from La Ponderosa, the area's only beach resort and several cuts above the usual surfer hangout. **Pros:** affordable rates; close to beach and town; magnificent garden and forest trails. **Cons:** tends to attract a younger crowd; mosquitoes love the garden when there's no breeze. ⑤ *Rooms from: $95* ⊠ *Road betweeen Pavones and Punta Banco, on the beach, Pavones* ☎ *2776–2076, 954/771–9166 in U.S.* ⊕ *www.laponderosapavones.com* ⟿ *7 rooms, 1 2-bedroom house* ⭘ *All meals.*

$$$$
B&B/INN
Fodor'sChoice
★

⌨ **Tiskita Jungle Lodge.** This last-outpost eco-lodge, near the border with Panama, is a draw for bird-watchers as well as nature lovers, yoga enthusiasts, and adventurers who want to really get away from it all in relative comfort. **Pros:** unrivaled wildlife viewing and birding; splendid natural isolation; friendly, knowledgeable owners. **Cons:** some steep walks to cabins in forest; no air-conditioning; not a lot of privacy in joined double and triple cabins, which share verandas. ⑤ *Rooms from: $300* ⊠ *On road between Pavones and Punta Banco, 6 km (4 miles) south of Playa Pavones, Pavones* ☎ *2296–8125* ⊕ *www.tiskita.com* ⊙ *May–Nov., open only to groups of 8 or more* ⟿ *17 rooms arranged in 4 single cabins, 3 duplex cabins, 1 triple cabin, 1 quadruple cabin* ⭘ *Breakfast* ⟿ *All-inclusive package includes all meals.*

THE OSA PENINSULA

If you came to Costa Rica seeking wilderness and adventure, this is it. You'll find the country's most breathtaking scenery and most abundant wildlife on the Osa Peninsula, a third of which is protected by Corcovado National Park. You can hike into the park, take a boat, or fly in on a charter plane. Corcovado also works for day trips from nearby luxury nature lodges, most of which lie within private preserves. And complementing the peninsula's lush forests and pristine beaches is the surrounding sea, with great fishing and some surfing.

There are two sides to the Osa: the gentler Golfo Dulce side, much of it accessible by car, albeit along rocky roads; and the much wilder and dramatic Pacific side, which is accessible only by boat, by plane, or by hiking a sublimely beautiful coastal trail.

PUERTO JIMÉNEZ

130 km (86 miles) west of Golfito, 364 km (226 miles) from San José.

You might not guess it from the rickety bicycles and ancient pickup trucks parked on the main street, but Puerto Jiménez is the largest town on the Osa Peninsula and the main gateway to the rest of the peninsula and to Corcovado National Park. This one-iguana town has a certain frontier charm, with an interesting, funky edge provided by eco-lodge owners and backpacking nature lovers. A bay-side promenade has added a touch of civility, with benches where you can sit and admire the gulf views. At night, elegant street lamps light your way to the restaurants along the waterfront.

CLOSE UP

Scuba and Snorkel Tips

SNORKELING TIPS

■ Never turn your back on the ocean, especially if the waves are big.

■ Ask about riptides before you go in.

■ Enter and exit from a sandy beach area.

■ Avoid snorkeling at dusk and never go in the water after dark.

■ Wear lots of sunscreen, especially on your back and butt cheeks.

■ Don't snorkel too close to the reef. You could get scratched if a wave pushes you.

■ Be mindful of boats.

■ Never dive or snorkel (or swim or surf) alone. Also, never touch the coral or the fish—this is for your own good and the good of the marine life.

DIVING TIPS

■ Make sure your instructor is certified by a known diving agency, such as PADI.

■ Stick to the instructor's guidelines on depth and timing.

■ Never hold your breath.

■ Don't drink alcohol before diving.

■ Never dive while taking medicine unless your doctor tells you it's safe.

■ Diving can be dangerous if you have certain medical problems. Ask your doctor how diving may affect your health.

■ If you don't feel good or if you are in pain after diving, go to the nearest emergency room immediately.

■ Don't fly for 12 hours after a no-decompression dive, even in a pressurized airplane.

8

This is the last civilized outpost on the peninsula. Heading south, you fall off the grid. That means no public electricity or telephones. So make your phone calls, send your email, get cash, and stock up on supplies here. Be prepared for the humidity and mosquitoes—Puerto Jiménez has plenty of both.

If you need a refreshing dip, head southeast of the airport to Playa Platanares, where there is a long stretch of beach with swimmable, warm water. At low tide, you can also walk out onto a narrow, pebbly beach beside the town dock.

The main reason to come to Puerto Jiménez is to spend a night before or after visiting Corcovado National Park, since the town has the best access to the park's two main trailheads and an airstrip with flights from San José. It's also the base for the *colectivo* (public transport via pickup truck) to Carate.

GETTING HERE AND AROUND

Since the drive is grueling and long, most visitors fly to Puerto Jiménez from San José. Driving from Golfito is a little easier these days thanks to the newly paved road all the way from Rincón to Puerto Jiménez; even the formerly potholed road between Chacarita and Rincón has been paved. A faster option from Golfito is the motorboat launches, which make the trip in 45 minutes for only $6, leaving Golfito at 7:30,

The Golfo Dulce and Osa Peninsula

10, 11:30, 1:15, 2:15, and 3:15. Going in the opposite direction, the fast launches to Golfito leave Puerto Jiménez at 6, 8:30, 11:30, and 1:30. The schedule changes frequently, so check before you head to the dock. Be sure to arrive 15 minutes early, because the boats often depart as soon as they are full. You can also hire a private taxi at the city dock in Golfito for about $90, which can drop you off in Puerto Jiménez or at your lodging.

A colectivo taxi—actually an open truck with bench seats—leaves Puerto Jiménez daily at 6 am and 1:30 pm for Cabo Matapalo and Carate. At $8 it's the cheapest way to travel, but the trip is along a bumpy road and is not recommended in rainy season (May through December). It leaves from a stop 200 meters west of the Super 96.

Once you arrive in Puerto Jiménez, you can get around on foot or bicycle.

ESSENTIALS
The new, air-conditioned, modern Barrantes pharmacy also has doctors' offices and a dentist, by appointment.

Bank/ATM Banco Nacional. ⊠ *Main street, south of Super 96* ☎ *2735–5020.*

Hospital Public Clinic and First Aid Station. ⊠ *Main street, west of post office* ☎ *2735–5063.*

Internet CaféNet El Sol/Osa Corcovado Tours. ⊠ *Main street, south of soccer field* ☎ *2735-5719.*

Pharmacy Barrantes Farmacia. ⊠ *Main street, next door to Banco de Costa Rica, diagonally across from Banco Nacional* ☎ *273-5507* ⊕ *www. barrantesyasociados.com.*

Post Office Correo. ⊠ *Main street, west side of soccer field.*

Rental Cars Solid Car Rental. ⊠ *Just past National Parks Service office, road running parallel to airstrip* ☎ *2735-5777* ⊕ *www.solidcarrental.com.*

Visitor Information National Parks Service Headquarters. ⊠ *Road running north, parallel to airstrip* ☎ *2735-5036* ✉ *pncorcovado@gmail.com.*

EXPLORING

FAMILY **Finca Köbö.** Go right to the source to see how cacao grows and becomes chocolate at this organic cacao plantation. The two-hour tour, offered daily at 9 am and 2 pm, includes a naturalist-guided walk around the roughly 50-acre property, which includes gardens, orchards, and both primary and secondary forest. The highlight of the tour is the tasting—dipping an array of tropical fruits grown on-site into a pot of homemade chocolate fondue. If you don't have time for the tour, you can drop in for hot chocolate or coffee with a piece of chocolate cake at the pleasant garden café. You can also buy cocoa nibs and solid, heart-shaped chocolate for making chocolate at home, as well as "chocoholic" T-shirts. Kids under 6 are free; ages 6 to 8, half price. ⊠ *Off main road, 17 km (11 miles) west of Puerto Jiménez, La Palma* ☎ *8398-7604* ⊕ *www. fincakobo.com* ☞ *$32* ⊙ *Mid-Nov.–Sept., daily tours at 9 and 2.*

SPORTS AND THE OUTDOORS
TOUR OPERATOR
Osa Tropical. Isabel Esquivel runs the best general tour operation on the peninsula. Whatever travel question you ask the locals, they will usually reply, "Ask Isabel," whether it's help with arranging flights, ground transportation, hotel rooms, rental houses, guided tours, or car rentals. ⊠ *Main street, across from Banco Nacional* ☎ *2735-5722, 2735-5062* ⊕ *www.osa-tropical.com* ☞ *From $45.*

BIRD-WATCHING
The birding around the Osa Peninsula is world renowned, with more than 400 species. Regional species include Baird's trogon, yellow-billed cotinga, whistling wren, black-cheeked ant tanager, the glorious turquoise cotinga, and, of course, the brilliant, impossible-to-miss scarlet macaws, which make frequent visits to the almond trees around town and all along the coast.

Fodor'sChoice **Bosque del Río Tigre Lodge.** The best English-speaking birding guides are
★ at Bosque del Río Tigre Lodge, just west of Puerto Jiménez. Expert local guides lead birding trips all around the peninsula, including visits to Corcovado National Park. Tours start at $14 per person, per hour (minimum two people) or $22 per hour for a single birder. ⊠ *12 km (7½ miles) northwest of Puerto Jiménez, at the end of a dirt road, and across a shallow river, Dos Brazos del Tigre* ⊕ *www.bosquedelriotigre.com.*

8

Beach views at Drake Bay on the Osa Peninsula

Rincón. One of the best spots on the peninsula to find a rare yellow-billed cotinga is along the north side of the bridge over the river at Rincón. Scan the forested hills above the road. Turquoise cotingas are also spotted here. Make sure to get there before 7 am for the best birding. ⊠ *Main road, 40 km (25 miles) north of Puerto Jiménez, Rincón.*

FISHING

Puerto Jiménez is a major fishing destination, with plenty of billfish, tuna, snapper, and snook, almost all year, with the exception of June and July, when things slow down. The best offshore fishing is between December and April. Charter captains follow the fish up and down the Pacific coast, so ask at your hotel for their recommendation of the best fishing boats currently in town.

Tropic Fins Adventures. Head out onto the Golfo Dulce or the open ocean on a sportfishing adventure aboard a custom-built 8-meter (27-foot) Ocean Runner, equipped with all the latest fishing equipment, a full cooler, plenty of snacks, and a healthy lunch. Captain Cory Craig, a transplanted Canadian, has been fishing these waters for more than a decade. The boat comfortably accommodates four anglers. Half-day excursions are $650; full-day trips, which can last up to nine hours, depending on how the fish are biting, are $950. Or, if you only have two people in your party, try your luck on the smaller SeaPro 6½-meter (21-foot) bay boat for $550 half day and $750 full day. Package tours include flight from San José, plus lodging, meals, and fishing. ⊠ *Playa Platanares* ☎ *8834–6079* ⊕ *www.tropicfins.com.*

HIKING

Fodor's Choice **Osa Aventura.** Many hiking guides have come on the scene since Corcovado made guides compulsory. But this long-standing company has been specializing in multiday hiking adventures into the park for more than a decade. Mike Boston, an ebullient tropical biologist who sounds like Sean Connery and looks like Crocodile Dundee, is the most experienced and most knowledgeable guide in the area. Hikers stay in way-off-the-beaten-track rustic lodges, or in tents in Corcovado National Park. Boston also employs bilingual biologists to lead hikes and conduct scientific research projects in which visitors can sometimes participate. ⊠ *Puerto Jiménez* ☎ *2735–5670, 8372–6135* ⊕ *www.osaaventura.com.*

Osa Wild. The focus here is on sustainable tourism, including horseback-riding treks, nighttime insect tours, and low-impact, low-cost, biologist-guided tours into Corcovado National Park. A three-day, two-night hike into the park starts at $285 per person, minimum two people, and includes transportation, guide, entrance fees, accommodation in tents, and all the necessary camping gear. Reserve at least a month ahead. ⊠ *Main street, north of Banco Nacional* ☎ *2735–5848* ⊕ *www. osawildtravel.com.*

Surcos Tours. The guides in this company are among the most experienced and knowledgeable in the Osa Peninsula, and they are all bilingual. They lead three-day hiking tours into Corcovado National Park, starting from either Los Patos or Carate (from $265 per person, minimum two people; $360 per person with meals). If you have limited time, they offer day tours into the park (from $135 per person; taxi not included), as well as bird-watching and wildlife tours around Matapalo. ⊠ *Puerto Jiménez* ☎ *2227–1484* ✉ *reservations@surcostours.com* ⊕ *www.surcostours.com.*

Tigre Sector. If you have a sturdy vehicle, it's just a 30-minute drive west to the village of Dos Brazos and the Tigre Sector of Corcovado Park. This is the newest official park entrance, with a brand-new ranger station. Few hikers come to this pristine part of the park because it's difficult to access, which means you'll likely have it to yourself. But you must be accompanied by a certified guide and make reservations and pay your entrance fees back in Puerto Jiménez at the National Parks Service Headquarters. The maximum number of visitors a day is 60. ⊠ *Road to Dos Brazos del Tigre, off main hwy. between Rincón and Puerto Jiménez.*

HORSEBACK RIDING

Horseback Tour. Horseback rides in the hills and on the beach near Sandalo, just west of Puerto Jiménez, cost $55 per person with a minimum of two people. There is no sales office in Puerto Jiménez, but most hotels and tour agencies can reserve a spot for you, including Osa Tropical and Osa Wild. ⊠ *Puerto Jiménez* ☎ *8377–6861, 8377–6861.*

KAYAKING

Puerto Jiménez is a good base for sea-kayaking trips on the calm Golfo Dulce and for exploring the nearby mangrove rivers and estuaries.

Aventuras Tropicales Golfo Dulce. Alberto Robleto has amassed an impressive fleet of kayaks with excellent safety equipment at Aventuras

8

Tropicales Golfo Dulce. There are snorkeling, dolphin-watching, and bird-watching tours, but the most popular are the three-hour mangrove tour and the sunset kayaking tour on the gulf, when dolphins are often jumping (each tour $45). A more intense six-hour tour includes sea kayaking, snorkeling, and river kayaking, lunch and snacks included, as well as a motorboat escort to carry all the gear ($90, minimum two people). Outrigger canoe trips ($30 for three hours, minimum six paddlers) are offered at sunset. ⊠ *Road to Playa Platanares, southeast of airport* ☎ *2735–5195* ⊕ *www.aventurastropicales.com.*

Cabinas Jiménez Adventure Boat Tour. If you just want to get out onto the water, this company offers five-hour tours on a covered boat. You can explore the gulf, look for dolphins, do some snorkeling, or try plane boarding. Snacks, fruit, and soft drinks are included ($65 per person, minimum six people). For $25 extra (cash only), you can visit the Osa Wildlife Sanctuary, a refuge for orphaned and injured wildlife. The boat sails at 7:30 am. ⊠ *Cabinas Jiménez, on the waterfront* ☎ *2735–5090* ⊕ *www.cabinasjimenez.com.*

WHERE TO EAT

$$
SEAFOOD
✕ **Corcovado Marisquería, Restaurante y Bar.** If you want to enjoy a little local atmosphere, join the anglers, families, and backpackers at this tiny restaurant that has spilled over into a large waterfront garden. Wooden tables are nattily covered with blue and white tablecloths and are shaded by palm trees. The menu is truly vast, with more than 50 *platos fuertes* (main courses) that run the gamut from seafood rice to whole lobsters to sirloin steaks. You can spend $9 for a plate of grilled fish or $36 on lobster. Wash it down with the only draft beer served in town, and gaze out at Golfo Dulce. An added bonus: there's free Wi-Fi. ⑤ *Average main: $12* ⊠ *On the waterfront, east of city dock* ☎ *2735–5659, 8898–2656.*

$$
ITALIAN
✕ **Il Giardino a la Playa.** Northern Italian–inspired cooking, in the form of tasty risotto, homemade pasta, and excellent salads is on offer at this popular garden spot. The best feature of this restaurant is its waterfront location, taking advantage of the views and fresh breezes off the gulf. Fresh fish rounds out the menu, as well as barbecued meats. Sadly, wood-oven pizzas are not the restaurant's forte, and service can be painfully slow. But sitting under a lime-green umbrella, enjoying the breeze and the view, isn't a hardship. ⑤ *Average main: $15* ⊠ *Waterfront promenade, near the public dock* ☎ *2735–5129* ⊕ *www. ilgiardinoitalianrestaurant.com.*

$
ITALIAN
✕ **Mail It Pizza.** This cheerful, family-run café comes with an authentic pedigree: the Colovattis are from the Italian city of Trieste, and the pizza is simply the best in the area. The crust is toasty crisp on the outside and chewy inside, topped with high-quality fixings and sauce made fresh every day. Calzones and homemade pastas are also on the menu, but pizza reigns supreme. Eat in the dining room—the fresh blue-and-white decor is reminiscent of the owners' hometown on the Adriatic Sea—or order takeout and bring your meal back to your hotel. The restaurant's rather odd name refers to the fact that this building used to be the post office. ⑤ *Average main: $9* ⊠ *Main street, across from soccer field* ☎ *2735–5483* ⊙ *Closed Tues. in low season. No lunch.*

Where Have All the Forests Gone?

The world gives high marks to Costa Rica for its environmental awareness, but accolades don't always match reality. In the last half century more than two-thirds of Costa Rica's original forests have been destroyed. Forests have traditionally been considered unproductive land, and their destruction was for a long time synonymous with development. In the 1970s and 1980s, international and domestic development policies fueled the destruction of large tracts of wilderness. Fortunately, in the 1970s alarmed Costa Rican conservationists began creating what is now the best national park system in Central America. The government has since made progress in curbing deforestation outside the national parks, too.

As you travel through Costa Rica, you see that its predominant landscapes are not cloud and rain forests but the coffee, banana, and pineapple plantations and cattle ranches that have replaced them. Deforestation not only spells disaster for endangered animals like the jaguar and the harpy eagle, but can also have grave consequences for human beings. Forests absorb rain and release water slowly, playing an important role in regulating the flow of rivers—which is why severely deforested regions often suffer twin plagues of floods during the rainy season and drought during the dry months. Tree cover also prevents topsoil erosion, thus keeping the land fertile and productive; in many parts of the country erosion has left once-productive farmland almost worthless. Finally, hidden within Costa Rica's boundless living species are countless unknown or understudied substances that might eventually be extracted to cure diseases. The destruction of this country's forests is a loss for the entire world.

8

$$ ECLECTIC **Fodor's**Choice ★

✕ **Pearl of the Osa.** For the most romantic dining with a dazzling, postcard-perfect beach view, head to this casually chic, open-air restaurant with the most sophisticated menu in the Puerto Jiménez area. It's owned by upscale Iguana Lodge, and its high standards of service apply at this beachfront restaurant. Standouts on the tantalizing menu include a sampler of three soups—cold, spicy gazpacho; zucchini and cilantro; and warm carrot ginger with red-pepper coulis. Fish cakes with sesame-cabbage slaw and ginger marmalade come with heaps of homemade chips. Mahimahi can be prepared tropical style, with a spicy Veracruz sauce, or in garlic butter. If you can't make up your mind, options like shrimp three ways offer a sampling of coconut, garlic, and fried shrimp. Vegetarian options include vegetable stir-fry with tofu, vegetable burritos, and pasta puttanesca. Wines and craft beers, along with exotic fruit drinks, are on tap. Save room for homemade ice cream and brownies. Portions are huge and served with style. $ *Average main: $14* ⊠ *Iguana Lodge grounds, Playa Platanares, 5 km (3 miles) south of airstrip* ☎ *8848–0752* ⊕ *www.iguanalodge.com.*

$ COSTA RICAN

✕ **Restaurante Carolina.** This simple alfresco restaurant in the heart of Puerto Jiménez is the most likely spot to meet locals and run into just about every foreigner in town, making it a good place to pick up information. It serves decent comida típica, salads, pasta, reliably fresh seafood, and excellent fruit smoothies. **⑤** *Average main: $8* ✉ *Main street* ☎ *2735–5185* ▬ *No credit cards.*

WHERE TO STAY

Playa Platanares is only about 6 km (4 miles) outside of Puerto Jiménez, but lodgings there have a different feeling from those in town because they are on a lovely and quiet beach. Bosque del Río Tigre is also outside of town, but inland, in a forested area beside a river, on the northeastern edge of Corcovado Park.

NEED A BREAK?

The best way to beat the heat in Puerto Jiménez is to plop onto a comfortable lounge chair at Jagua Arts & Crafts, 100 meters north of the airstrip, and cool down with a deliciously decadent, personal-sized tub of locally made Jade Luna ice cream. The signature flavor is Aztec chocolate, made with local cacao spiced with chili pepper and cinnamon. There's also a luscious array of refreshingly different dairy-free sorbets, made with coconut milk and coconut water. The creamy ginger and tropical fruit is a revelation.

$$$$
B&B/INN
Fodor's Choice
★

Bosque del Río Tigre Lodge. You can't get any closer to nature than at this off-the-grid lodge, famous for its excellent birding and hiking trails, wedged between forest and the banks of the Río Tigre. **Pros:** a birder's paradise; great hiking trails; fabulous food. **Cons:** shared bathroom and outdoor showers; limited electricity; must love living very close to nature. **⑤** *Rooms from: $340* ✉ *Riverside, in Dos Brazos del Tigre, 12 km (7½ miles) northwest of Puerto Jiménez, Dos Brazos del Tigre ✣ Turn off main hwy. at sign for Dos Brazos and follow dirt road to village and beyond, to the river* ☎ *8705–3729 leave text messages only* ⊕ *www.bosquedelriotigre.com* ☾ *Closed Sept. and Oct.* ⇜ *4 rooms with shared baths, 1 ensuite cabin* ⦿ *All meals.*

$
B&B/INN

Cabinas Jiménez. Overlooking the harbor, these air-conditioned rooms set in a lush garden are the most comfortable in town, and have the best water views. **Pros:** water views; air-conditioning; some rooms with pleasant, private terraces. **Cons:** rooms are on the small side; no food service; some rooms have no view. **⑤** *Rooms from: $60* ✉ *On the waterfront, west of town dock* ☎ *2735–5090* ⊕ *www.cabinasjimenez.com* ⇜ *18 rooms* ⦿ *No meals.*

$
B&B/INN

Cabinas Marcelina. This neat and homey inn is the best bargain hotel in Puerto Jiménez. **Pros:** very affordable; pleasant oasis in middle of town; safe parking. **Cons:** rooms are quite small; some rooms lack a/c. **⑤** *Rooms from: $45* ✉ *Main street, north side of church* ☎ *2735–5007, 2735–5286* ⇜ *6 double rooms, 1 single room* ⦿ *No meals.*

$$
B&B/INN
FAMILY
Fodor's Choice
★

Danta Corcovado Lodge. Follow the giant tapir-footprint signs to this extraordinary, rustic lodge, reminiscent of an Adirondacks camp but with oversized, whimsical wood furniture, all within hiking distance of the western edge of Corcovado National Park. **Pros:** proximity to Corcovado National Park; comfortable rusticity; unique design. **Cons:** no air-conditioning; close encounters of the insect kind in cabins. **⑤** *Rooms from: $125* ✉ *Road from La Palma to Guadalupe, 3 km (2 miles) northwest of La Palma, La Palma* ☎ *2735–1111* ⊕ *www.dantalodge.com* ⇜ *6 cabins, 2 rooms, 1 suite* ⦿ *Breakfast.*

$$$
B&B/INN
Fodor's Choice
★

⊡ **Iguana Lodge.** If a long stretch of deserted beach is your idea of heaven, check out this idyllic lodge with two-story cabins set in an exquisite botanical garden. **Pros:** top-of-the-line accommodation and food in tranquil tropical setting; complimentary kayaks; breakfast and dinner included in casita rooms. **Cons:** no air-conditioning; club rooms are small and can be noisy; be prepared to get friendly with an insect or two. ⑤ *Rooms from: $180* ✉ *Playa Platanares, 5 km (3 miles) south of airport* ☎ *8848–0752* ⊕ *www.iguanalodge.com* ⊷ *8 rooms, 2 duplex casitas with upper and lower separate rooms;, 2 family casitas, 1 beach house* ❍❘ *Some meals.*

NIGHTLIFE

Pearl of the Osa. With pulsing salsa music pumped out by a DJ and a pasta buffet, this beachfront bar attracts a big crowd on Friday nights, starting at 7. There's a mix of ages, and the music is loud and a lot of fun. Tuesday nights there's a barbecue with tiki torches, a bonfire, and tables right on the beach. Come at 5:30 to watch the sun set; it's a good idea to reserve ahead. ✉ *Playa Platanares, next to Iguana Lodge* ☎ *8848–0752.*

SHOPPING

Fodor's Choice
★

Jagua Arts & Crafts. The area's finest arts and crafts are displayed in this impressive shop, including exquisitely detailed bird carvings made by a family in nearby Rincón; mirrors and trivets made by a San José mosaic artist; and indigenous crafts, including mola appliqué work, Boruca carved masks, and real bows and arrows. A gallery features mixed-media nature paintings. The shop is famous for local artisan Karen Herrera's exquisite glass-bead jewelry and miniature glass animals. There's an excellent selection of natural-history field guides and books here, too. For a sweet treat, there is locally made organic chocolate, and Luna Jade ice cream and sorbet at the store's chic, new, open-air lounge. The shop is open daily 6:30 to 5, December to June; till 2 pm July to November; it's closed in October. ✉ *Road beside airport* ✐ *jaguadelbosque@hotmail.com.*

8

CORCOVADO NATIONAL PARK

The crown jewel of the country's national park system, Corcovado is the ultimate in off-the-grid adventure. The only way to see it is on foot, with a certified naturalist guide to interpret the incredible biodiversity that has made this park the most rewarding and challenging natural experience in the country.

GETTING HERE AND AROUND

The easiest way to ⋎visit remote Corcovado National Park is by boat from Drake Bay or on foot from Carate. A 20-minute boat trip from Drake Bay gets you to the San Pedrillo entrance. The boat trip from Drake Bay to Sirena takes 45 minutes to one hour and leaves Drake Bay at 6 am ($25), returning at 1 pm from Sirena. From Carate airfield, where the road and therefore taxis from Puerto Jiménez stop, it's about a 45-minute walk along the beach to La Leona park entrance.

For getting to Corcovado from elsewhere in the country, the most expensive option—but also the easiest way to get into the heart of the park—is flying in on a small charter plane through **Alfa Romeo Aero Taxi** (*Puerto Jiménez Airport,* ☎ 2735–5178).

Less expensive is hiring a taxi in Puerto Jiménez ($100) to take you to Los Patos trailhead or the first crossing of the Río Rincón (where you can hike a few miles upriver to the trailhead). The cheapest, and least convenient, option is to take an 8 am bus from Puerto Jiménez to La Palma (less than $1). You can also take a taxi ($80) to Los Patos entrance. Since all visitors to the park must be accompanied by a guide, transportation to the park is usually included in the cost of a package tour.

EXPLORING

Fodor's Choice **Corcovado National Park** (*Parque Nacional Corcovado*). This is the last
★ and largest outpost of virgin lowland rain forest in Central America, and it's teeming with wildlife. Visitors who tread softly along the park's trails may glimpse howler, spider, and squirrel monkeys, peccaries (wild pigs), poison dart frogs, scarlet macaws, and, very rarely, jaguars and tapirs.

Most first-time visitors to Corcovado come on a daylong boat tour from Drake Bay or hike in from Carate. But to get to the most pristine, wildlife-rich areas, you need to walk, and that means a minimum of three days: one day to walk in, one day to walk out, and one day inside.

There are also new daily limits on the number of visitors who can be in the park, so it's important to book your visit as early as possible. At Sirena Station, the most popular section, there is a maximum of 100 visitors a day and 60 campers overnight. A maximum of 100 people can visit the San Pedrillo sector. The other main sectors each have a limit of 60 visitors per day, but quotas may change. Ranger stations are officially open from 8 am to 4 pm daily, but you can walk in almost any time with a certified guide, as long as you have reserved and paid in advance. For safety reasons, there is no longer any night walking permitted into or out of the park. ⇨ *For more information, see the highlighted listing in this chapter.* ✉ *Corcovado National Park* ⊕ *www. sinac.go.cr/AC/ACOSA/ASPs/PNC* 🖼 *$15 per day.*

SPORTS AND THE OUTDOORS

If your reason for coming to the Osa Peninsula is Corcovado National Park, choose a lodge that has resident naturalist guides. On the Drake Bay and gulf sides of the park, all the lodges arrange guided trips into Corcovado, most with their own guides. Tour operators in Puerto Jiménez and Drake Bay also run guided trips in the park.

HIKING

Corcovado has 13 ecosystems within its boundaries, ranging from mangroves and swamps to lowland rain forest. The park also has more forest giants—trees that stand 50 to 80 meters (165 to 264 feet) high—than anywhere in Central America.

There are two main hiking routes to Corcovado. One begins near La Palma, at Los Patos entrance. The other is a beach trail, an easy, if hot,

3½-km (2¼-mile), 45-minute shore walk from Carate to La Leona entrance, followed by a 16-km (10-mile) walk to La Sirena. The former beach trail from San Pedrillo to La Sirena has been closed for safety reasons. You can hike from Drake Bay to San Pedrillo; it's 14 km (8½ miles) and you need to pay attention to tides and some rocky sections. You can also take a boat to the San Pedrillo station and hike the trails there, as well as camp. There are two other, less-traveled official entrances to the park with ranger stations: Los Planes, inland from Drake Bay, and a new entrance at Dos Brazos del Tigre, west of Puerto Jiménez.

Hiking is always tough in the tropical heat, but the forest route from Los Patos is cooler than the beach hike to La Leona. Although it is possible to hike La Leona at high tide, it's more difficult because you have to walk on a slope rather than the flat part of the beach. The hike between any two stations takes all day.

The hike from La Leona to Sirena requires crossing one big river mouth and a stretch of beach that can be crossed only at low tide. Some guides do it very early in the morning, just before sunrise, to avoid the blistering heat along the beach.

The hike from Los Patos to Sirena is shady all the way; it's 23 km (about 14 miles) and takes about eight hours. Bring plenty of water along. The Sirena ranger station has great trails around it that can easily fill a couple of days.

Swimming on the beach near Sirena is not advised because of rip currents and bull sharks. Also steer clear of the brackish Río Sirena, home to crocs, bull sharks, and snakes. The only advisable swimming area is the Río Claro.

WHERE TO EAT AND STAY

Meals at Sirena have to be arranged and paid for in advance with the National Parks Service office in Puerto Jiménez. There is a maximum capacity of 25 people in the dining room.

Camping in your own tent in Sirena or camping in San Pedrillo are your only options inside the national park. You must reserve camping and prepared meals well in advance. Meals served in the Sirena station are decent but relatively expensive, at $20 for breakfast, $25 for lunch or dinner. Meal times are strict: 6:30 am for breakfast, 11:30 lunch, 5:30 dinner. Camping in Sirena, on two covered platforms for a total of 60 campers per night, costs $4 per person per night. Bring your own tent, gear, and food for camping. At the moment, there are no cooking facilities for campers, so bring along dehydrated meals that can be mixed with water, as well as trail mix and snacks. Drinking water at all the stations is not treated; the only place you can buy bottled water is at the Sirena station. The maximum stay is four nights and five days. Since guides are mandatory, all the gear is usually included in a package tour.

The view from the deck of the Toucan cabina at Bosque del Cabo.

CABO MATAPALO

21 km (14 miles) south of Puerto Jiménez.

The southern tip of the Osa Peninsula, where virgin rain forest meets the sea at a rocky point, retains the kind of natural beauty that people travel halfway across the world to experience. From its ridges you can look out on the blue Golfo Dulce and the Pacific Ocean, sometimes spotting whales in the distance. The forest is tall and dense, with the highest and most diverse tree species in the country, usually draped with thick lianas.

The name Matapalo refers to the strangler fig, which germinates in the branches of other trees and extends its roots downward, eventually smothering the supporting tree by blocking the sunlight. Flocks of brilliant scarlet macaws and troops of monkeys are the other draws here.

GETTING HERE AND AROUND

If you drive one hour south from Puerto Jiménez, be prepared for a bumpy ride and a couple of river crossings. During the height of rainy season, in October and November, cars are sometimes washed out along rivers to the ocean. Most hotels arrange transportation in 4WD taxis or their own trucks. The cheapest—and the roughest—way to travel is by colectivo ($10), which leaves Puerto Jiménez at 6 am and 1 pm. Buses do not serve Cabo Matapalo.

SPORTS AND THE OUTDOORS

TOUR OPERATOR

Fodor'sChoice **Everyday Adventures.** Andy Pruter, an engaging, experienced outfitter,
★ will take you on anything-but-everyday, adrenaline-pumping adventures: rappelling down waterfalls ($95), climbing up a 70-foot strangler fig vine ($65), and rain-forest hiking ($50). Or you can go all out with a combination rappelling and climbing tour for $130. ⊠ *Cabo Matapalo* ☎ *8353–8619* ⊕ *www.psychotours.com.*

SURFING

On the eastern side of Cabo Matapalo, on Pan Dulce beach, waves break over a platform that creates a perfect, very forgiving right, drawing surfers from far and wide, especially beginners.

Pollo Surf School. Local surf expert Oldemar (aka Pollo) Fernandez offers daily lessons at Pan Dulce Beach at his Pollo Surf School. Soft-top boards and rash guards make learning a little less painful. Expect to pay $55 per person for a two-hour group lesson, or $110 for a private lesson. ⊠ *Cabo Matapalo* ☎ *8366–6559, 8363–1481* ⊕ *www. pollosurfschool.com.*

WHERE TO STAY

$$$$ 🏨 **Blue Osa Yoga Retreat & Spa.** Brilliant blue sky, sparkling blue sea, and
B&B/INN bright blue decor make this upscale, beachfront eco-resort and yoga center a true blue heaven. **Pros:** yoga classes and private instruction. **Cons:** check when group yoga retreats are scheduled if yoga isn't your thing. $ *Rooms from: $379* ⊠ *Playa Tamales, 11 km (7 miles) south of Puerto Jiménez* ☎ *No phone* ⊕ *www.blueosa.com* ⟳ *7 triple rooms, 5 doubles, including 1 penthouse* ⊙ *All meals.*

$$$$ 🏨 **Bosque del Cabo.** Atop a cliff at the tip of Cabo Matapalo, this lodge
RESORT has unparalleled views of the Golfo Dulce merging with the endless blue
Fodor'sChoice of the Pacific, as well as hundreds of acres of primary forest, home to
★ plenty of monkeys and peccaries, as well as the occasional puma and ocelot. **Pros:** luxurious bungalows; fabulous trails and guides; congenial atmosphere among guests at cocktail hour and dinner. **Cons:** steep trail to beach and back; limited electricity supply; rates do not include $30 round-trip transfer fee per person. $ *Rooms from: $390* ⊠ *Road to Carate, 22 km (14 miles) south of Puerto Jiménez* ☎ *2735–5206, 8389–2846 at lodge* ⊕ *www.bosquedelcabo.com* ⟳ *10 cabins, 1 family cabin; 1 double cabin with an upper two-bedroom unit and a lower one-bedroom; 4 houses* ⊙ *All meals.*

$$$$ 🏨 **El Remanso.** This tranquil, sophisticated retreat sits in a forest brim-
B&B/INN ming with birds and wildlife, 122 meters (400 feet) above a mostly
Fodor'sChoice deserted beach studded with tide pools. **Pros:** gorgeous natural setting;
★ jungle views; easy access to beach. **Cons:** no air-conditioning; no hair dryers; steep drive down to lodge. $ *Rooms from: $360* ⊠ *Main road to Carate, 22 km (14 miles) south of Puerto Jiménez* ☎ *2735–5569 office, 8814–5775* ⊕ *www.elremanso.com* ⟳ *4 rooms, 2 suites, 6 cabinas* ⊙ *All meals.*

$$$$ 🏨 **Lapa Ríos.** This is the first and still the most spectacular eco-lodge in
B&B/INN Costa Rica, set in a vast, private nature reserve brimming with wildlife.
Fodor'sChoice **Pros:** excellent, professional service; price includes tours and trans-
★ portation and all à la carte meals; retains local flavor with friendly,

8

well-trained staff. **Cons:** many steps to climb to most cabins; steep trail to beach, but there is a shuttle service; most cabins are duplex, attached to one other cabin. ⑤ *Rooms from: $1,056* ✉ *Road to Carate, 20 km (12 miles) south of Puerto Jiménez* ☏ *2735–5130* ⊕ *www.laparios.com* ⇨ *17 cabinas* ⦿ *All-inclusive.*

CARATE

60 km (37 miles) west of Puerto Jiménez.

Carate is literally the end of the road. The black volcanic-sand beach stretches for more than 3 km (2 miles), with dramatically high surf that's perfect for boogie boarding and body surfing. Swimming is best and safest around low tides. The main entertainment at the beach is watching the noisy but magnificent scarlet macaws feasting on nuts in the beach almond trees that edge the shore. Though remote, lodges now have Wi-Fi and some cell-phone coverage.

GETTING HERE AND AROUND

The road from Matapalo to Carate covers 40 suspension-testing km (25 miles); there is a bridge over the Agua Buena River and the road is periodically graded and relatively smooth, but that can all change to a sea of mud with one drenching wet season. You're better off taking the colectivo from Puerto Jiménez *(see Getting Here and Around in Puerto Jiménez, above)*. Or give yourself a break and fly via charter plane to Carate's small airport, which has been upgraded recently; arrange flights through your lodge. From here it's 3 km (2 miles), roughly a 40-minute walk along the beach to La Leona ranger station entrance to Corcovado National Park. In rainy season (May to December) it is sometimes impossible to cross the raging Río Carate that separates the landing strip from the beach path to the park, and you may end up stranded on either side. Parking at the store in Carate is $5 per day.

SPORTS AND THE OUTDOORS

Activities here revolve around Corcovado National Park and its environs. Hiking, horseback riding, canopy tours, and other adventures must be organized through your hotel.

WHERE TO STAY

$$
B&B/INN
Fodor'sChoice
★

⌂ **Finca Exotica.** A garden paradise that lives up to its name, this combination organic farm, botanical garden, and sophisticated eco-lodge is an otherworldly experience. **Pros:** gorgeous gardens; exotically delicious food; charming hosts; affordably priced for this area. **Cons:** no air-conditioning; must enjoy being in a totally natural setting. ⑤ *Rooms from: $150* ✉ *Main road, east of Carate Airstrip* ☏ *4070–0054* ⊕ *www.fincaexotica.com* ⊗ *Closed Oct.* ⇨ *4 one-bedroom cabins, 2 two-bedroom cabins, 7 tents, 1 house* ⦿ *All meals.*

$$$$
B&B/INN
FAMILY

⌂ **Lookout Inn.** This lively, barefoot inn—shoes come off at the bottom step—is set on a precipitous hillside with a spectacular panorama that includes a colorful garden and scarlet macaws foraging in the almond trees that line the beach. **Pros:** proximity to beach and access on foot to Corcovado Park; excellent food; party atmosphere. **Cons:** very steep climb to lodge and down to beach; cabins are quieter than lodge rooms;

stairs to dining room. $ *Rooms from: $270* ⊠ *Main road to Carate, east of Carate landing strip* ☎ *2735–5431* ⊕ *www.lookout-inn.com* ⇆ *2 rooms, 4 tree-house cabins, 2 bungalows, 1 penthouse suite, 2 cabins with shared bath* ❙❍❙ *All meals.*

$$$$
B&B/INN
Fodor's Choice
★

⊡ **Luna Lodge.** Perched on a sublime mountaintop overlooking rain forest and ocean, Luna Lodge is the quintessential yoga retreat, but its remoteness and proximity to wildlife are universally enjoyed. **Pros:** scenic setting for peace, yoga, and therapeutic massage; comfortable lodging and healthful food; excellent birding; free Wi-Fi. **Cons:** extremely steep road up to lodge; beach is quite a hike; large yoga groups come for retreats. $ *Rooms from: $450* ⊠ *2 km (1 mile) up a steep, partially paved road from Carate* ☎ *4070–0010, 888/760–0760 in U.S/Canada.* ⊕ *www.lunalodge.com* ⇆ *8 bungalows, 3 rooms, 5 tents* ❙❍❙ *All meals.*

DRAKE BAY

18 km (11 miles) north of Corcovado, 40 km (25 miles) southwest of Palmar Sur, 310 km (193 miles) south of San José.

This is castaway country, a real tropical adventure, with plenty of hiking and some rough but thrilling boat rides to get here. The rugged coast that stretches south from the mouth of the Río Sierpe to Corcovado probably doesn't look much different from what it did in Sir Francis Drake's day (1540–96), when, as legend has it, the British explorer anchored here. Small, picture-perfect beaches with surf crashing against dark volcanic rocks are backed by steaming, thick jungle. Nature lodges scattered along the coast are hemmed in by the rain forest, which is home to troops of monkeys, sloths, scarlet macaws, and hundreds of other bird species.

The cheapest accommodations in the area can be found in the town of Drake, which is spread out around the bay. A trio of upscale nature lodges—Drake Bay Wilderness Resort, Aguila de Osa Inn, and La Paloma Lodge—are clumped near the Río Agujitas on the bay's southern end. They all offer comprehensive packages, including trips to Corcovado and Caño Island. Lodges farther south, such as Copa del Arbol, Punta Marenco Lodge, and Casa Corcovado, run excursions from even wilder settings.

GETTING HERE AND AROUND
The fastest way to get to Drake Bay is to fly directly to the airstrip. You can also fly to Palmar Sur and take a taxi to Sierpe and then go on a thrilling, if bumpy, boat ride to Drake Bay. From the airport, it's a 25-minute taxi ride to Sierpe. You can pay $15–$20 per person for a seat in a communal boat. These small, open boats leave at low tide, usually 11 to 11:30 am for the one-hour trip to Drake. You need to be at the dock at least an hour early to ensure a seat. There is also boat service from Drake Bay to Sierpe, from the beach, between 7 and 7:30 am, and around 2:30 in the afternoon. Many lodges arrange boat transportation from Drake Bay or Sierpe, and captains will often stop along the way to view wildlife in the river mangroves. From Rincón you can drive to Drake on a 30-km (19-mile) (sometimes) graded dirt road, but only in dry season when the rivers are low enough to cross. Getting here by bus

8

Boat trips are a must to explore the wild Osa Peninsula.

is not easy. Buses leave Puerto Jiménez for La Palma about every two hours from 6 am to 8 pm, connecting in La Palma with buses to Drake Bay at 11:30 am and 4 pm daily, except Sunday. Buses leave Drake at 4:30 am and 1 pm heading for La Palma, to connect with buses in Rincón de Osa to either Puerto Jiménez or San José. These bus schedules often change, so be sure to check with a local source. The drive from San José to Drake is scenic, but an exhausting seven hours long.

SPORTS AND THE OUTDOORS
TOUR OPERATORS

Jinetes de Osa. Experienced guides run popular diving ($115 for a two-tank dive, plus $20 for gear), snorkeling ($80), and dolphin-watching tours ($115), as well as a canopy tour ($65) with some interesting bridge transitions between platforms. ✉ *West side of bay, Drake* ☎ *8996–6161* ⊕ *www.costaricadiving.com.*

FAMILY
Fodor's Choice
★

Night Tour. When you're on the Osa Peninsula, the wildest nightlife is outdoors. Join entomologist Tracie Stice (also known as the Bug Lady) and herpetologist Gianfranco Gomez on their night tour of insects, bats, reptiles, and anything else creeping or crawling around at night. Tracie is a wealth of bug lore, with riveting insect stories from around the world. Top-of-the-line Petzl headlamps help you see in the dark. Tours are $40 per person. Book ahead because these nightly tours, at 5:30 and 7:30 pm, are popular. ✉ *Drake* ☎ *8701–7356* ⊕ *www.thenighttour.com.*

Reel Escape. With its ideal location close to the offshore fish-filled Furuno banks and river mouths along the coast, this charter operation has great fishing options aboard a 35-foot CABO sportfishing boat equipped with

Snorkelers' Paradise

Most of uninhabited 2½-square-km (1-square-mile) **Caño Island Biological Reserve** is covered in evergreen forest that includes fig, locust, and rubber trees. Coastal Indians once used it as a burial ground, and the numerous bits and pieces unearthed here have prompted archaeologists to speculate about pre-Columbian long-distance maritime trade. But virtually nothing remains of indigenous interest. The main attraction is the ocean around the island, offering advanced scuba diving and snorkeling. The snorkeling is best around the rocky points flanking the island's main beach; if you're a certified diver, you'll want to explore Bajo del Diablo and Paraíso, where you're guaranteed to encounter thousands of good-size fish, and if

you're lucky, white-tip, nurse, and trigger sharks. As of this writing, visitors are once again allowed to land on the island, to hike a trail that climbs to the island's summit. But no picnicking is allowed on the beach and there are no toilet facilities owing to runoff that was damaging the surrounding coral.

The only way to get to the island, 19 km (12 miles) due west of the Osa Peninsula, is by boat, arranged by your lodge or a tour company. Reserve well ahead since tour operators have to keep to specific time limits and visitor quotas of 200 visitors per day, split between morning and afternoon. Drake Bay hotels run trips here, as do tour companies in Dominical, Uvita, and Sierpe.

twin 450 CAT engines. There's a full-size galley, bathroom, and shower on board and top-of-the-line fishing gear. Bilingual Capt. Willy Atencio has fished internationally, but has come home to his native Drake Bay. He and his mates will transport you to the boat, take you where the fish are, then clean and fillet your catch. Half-day trips, for one to five fishers, start at $450 (inshore) to $1,800 full-day offshore (lunch included). ⊠ *Drake Bay* ☎ *8824–3036, 855/372–5322 toll-free in US* ⊕ *www.fishdrakebay.com.*

WHERE TO STAY

$$$$
B&B/INN

🗴 **Aguila de Osa Inn.** Formerly a sportfisher's dream lodge, Aguila de Osa now appeals to an up-market crowd, with luxurious, high-ceilinged rooms with handsome, hardwood interiors, king-size beds, and glass-brick-and-granite bathrooms that will please the fussiest traveler. **Pros:** great for fishing enthusiasts; luxurious, spacious rooms; excellent meals. **Cons:** steep climb to rooms; no air-conditioning but rooms have good air circulation, ceiling fans, and screens. ⑤ *Rooms from: $500* ⊠ *South end of town, at mouth of Río Agujitas, Drake* ☎ *2296–2190 in San José, 8840–2929 lodge, 866/924–8452 toll-free in U.S.* ⊕ *www. aguiladeosa.com* ↵ *11 rooms, 2 suites* ⊨◎ *All meals.*

$$$$
B&B/INN
FAMILY
Fodor's Choice
★

🗴 **Casa Corcovado Jungle Lodge.** This hilltop jungle lodge has it all: exquisite bungalows in the closest location to Corcovado National Park; extensive gardens, excellent tours, naturalist guides, and first-class service. **Pros:** unrivaled location adjoining national park; excellent tours, service, and facilities; reasonably priced. **Cons:** an adventure to get here:

8

be prepared for a thrilling, wet landing; no air-conditioning; steep road to beach; steep steps down to cool "adult" pool. ⑤ *Rooms from: $390* ✉ *Northern border of Corcovado, Drake* ☎ *2256–3181, 888/896–6097 in U.S. toll-free, 2206–4611 lodge* ⊕ *www.casacorcovado.com* ⊙ *Closed Sept.–mid-Nov.* ↩ *14 bungalows* ⏄ *All-inclusive.*

$$$$
RESORT
Fodor'sChoice
★

⬚ **Copa de Arbol Beach & Rainforest Resort.** The newest kid on the beach block, Copa de Arbol is ultraluxurious, ultracool (comes with air-conditioning), ultraexpensive, and idyllically sited between crashing ocean surf and dense jungle, right on the Coastal Path walking trail that connects Drake Bay to Corcovado. **Pros:** comfort, hotel-like luxury in the jungle; idyllic location. **Cons:** accessible only by boat (with a wet landing) or on foot; boat transportation and tours not included, making price high, relative to other area lodges; lots of steps to negotiate; cascading pool is dramatic but not very good for swimming. ⑤ *Rooms from: $678* ✉ *Along coastal path, one beach north of Playa Caletas, Drake* ☎ *8935–1212* ⊕ *www.copadearbol.com* ↩ *9 luxury cabins, 2 deluxe duplex suites* ⏄ *All-inclusive.*

$$$
B&B/INN
FAMILY

⬚ **Drake Bay Wilderness Resort.** This breezy, beautifully maintained resort is the best deal in Drake Bay and has the most kid-friendly grounds, with lots of flat, open space for romping, plus a refreshing, saltwater swimming pool and rocky tidal pools to explore. **Pros:** great location; family- and elderly-friendly and affordable; excellent food; free laundry service and free kayaks. **Cons:** not a lot of privacy in the cabins with open screen windows. ⑤ *Rooms from: $250* ✉ *Southern end of bay, at mouth of Río Agujitas, Drake* ☎ *2775–1716* ⊕ *www.drakebay.com* ↩ *20 rooms* ⏄ *All meals.*

$$
B&B/INN

⬚ **Jinetes de Osa.** This small bay-side hotel overlooking the beach and almost hidden behind flowering hedges is the most comfortable and reasonably priced place to stay in the village of Drake. **Pros:** convenient location; affordable rates; adventuresome, active clientele. **Cons:** standard rooms are smallish with no air-conditioning; access is on foot, since the tide washes right up to the lodge steps; steps up to hillside rooms. ⑤ *Rooms from: $96* ✉ *West side of bay, Drake* ☎ *8996–6161 lodge* ⊕ *www.jinetesdeosa.com* ↩ *19 rooms* ⏄ *Breakfast.*

$$$$
B&B/INN
Fodor'sChoice
★

⬚ **La Paloma Lodge.** Sweeping ocean views, impeccably appointed accommodations, and lots of tropical-foliage privacy make this lodge the area's most romantic option. **Pros:** idyllic tropical setting with ocean views and easy access to beach; privacy; great service; interesting guests from all over the world. **Cons:** steep, long climbs to some ranchos; small pool; three-night minimum stay. ⑤ *Rooms from: $550* ✉ *On Drake Bay, near Drake Bay Wilderness Resort, Drake* ☎ *2239–0954 office in San José, 2775–1684 lodge* ⊕ *www.lapalomalodge.com* ⊙ *Closed mid-Sept.–mid-Nov.* ↩ *4 rooms, 7 ranchos* ⏄ *All meals.*

TORTUGUERO AND THE CARIBBEAN COAST

WELCOME TO TORTUGUERO AND THE CARIBBEAN COAST

TOP REASONS TO GO

★ **Dolphin-watching:** Bottlenose, tucuxi, and Atlantic spotted dolphins ply the southern Caribbean coast.

★ **Food and flavors:** Leave *gallo pinto* (rice and beans) behind in favor of mouthwatering *rondón* (meat or fish stew) or *caribeño* (Caribbean) rice and beans, stewed in coconut milk.

★ **Music:** Mix reggae and calypso with your salsa. Rhythms waft in from the far-off Caribbean islands; and homegrown musicians are making names for themselves, too.

★ **Sportfishing:** World-class tarpon and snook attract serious anglers to the shores off Tortuguero National Park.

★ **Turtles:** People from around the world flock to the northern Caribbean for the annual nesting of four sea turtle species.

1 The Sarapiquí Loop. The Sarapiquí Loop circles Braulio Carrillo National Park, rare for its easy-to-access primary rain forest.

2 Northern Lowlands. The Northern Lowlands have little to offer tourists in their own right, but are close to Braulio Carrillo Park and rafting-trip put-in points. The region can be done as a long day trip from San José as well.

3 Tortuguero. The northern Caribbean coast encompasses the coastal jungles and canals leading to and through Tortuguero National Park. Boat and air travel are the only ways to reach this roadless region.

4 Southern Caribbean Coast. The southern Caribbean coast stretches south from port-of-call Limón to Panama. Towns along the coast have an Afro-Caribbean vibe—some are more backpackerish than others. Beaches are fringed with forest, and waters are rough. Surfers make the trip for Salsa Brava.

GETTING ORIENTED

Costa Rica's Caribbean coast is sometimes called its Atlantic coast, so as not to confuse tourists looking for the white sand and clear blue waters of the Caribbean Islands. This Caribbean is different, with sands in shades of brown and black, waters that are rough and murky (but ideal for surfing), dense jungle, heavy and frequent rain, and a less sophisticated, laid-back approach to tourism. It is beautiful and fascinating in its own way, but it's definitely not St. Barts.

9

Tortuguero

Caribbean Sea

Tortuguero National Park

Parismina

Villafranca

Río Jiménez

Boca del Pantano

Hwy Pocora

32

The Guápiles Hwy

32

Limón

2

Siquirres

Westfalia

10

36

CARTAGO

Cahuita National Park

Pandora

4

Cahuita

Puerto Viejo de Talamanca

Bribri

Man

Paraíso

Bratsi

36

LIMÓN

La Amistad National Park

PANAMA

Cerro Chirripó National Park

Cerro Chirripó

CORDILLERA DE TALAMANCA

Mount Eli

Mount Ena

Mount Utyum

Mount Nai

PUNTARENAS

Mount Bine

0   1(

0   10 km

TORTUGUERO NATIONAL PARK

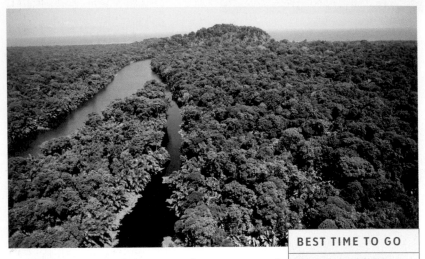

At various times of the year, four species of sea turtles—green, hawksbill, loggerhead, and giant leatherback—lumber up the 35 km (22 miles) of beach to deposit their eggs for safekeeping. This is the best place in Costa Rica to observe these magnificent creatures' nesting and hatching rituals.

In 1975 the Costa Rican government established Tortuguero National Park to protect the sea turtle population, which had been decimated after centuries of being hunted for its eggs and shells. Still, despite preservation efforts, fewer than 1% of the hatchlings will make it to adulthood.

Turtles may be the top draw here, but keep your eyes peeled for other species: tapirs, jaguars, anteaters, ocelots, howler monkeys, capuchin monkeys, three-toed sloths, collared and white-lipped peccaries, coatis, and blue morpho butterflies also populate the park. You can wander the beach when the turtles aren't nesting, but riptides make swimming dangerous, and shark rumors persist.

BEST TIME TO GO

The green turtle's July-through-October nesting season is Tortuguero's most popular time to visit. It rains here (a lot!) year-round, so expect to get wet no matter when you go. February through April and September and October are a tad drier.

FUN FACT

One of nature's mysteries is how turtles find their way back to the same beach where they hatched. It's thought that the sand leaves a biological imprint on the turtle hatchlings during their scurry to the sea, which directs females to return here years later to nest.

BEST WAY TO EXPLORE

BIRD-WATCHING AND WILDLIFE

This is a birder's dream destination. Some of the rarer species you'll find here include the snowy cotinga, palm warbler, and yellow-tailed oriole. Waterbirds and herons abound. On a recent foray, members of the Birding Club of Costa Rica were treated to a close-up view of a wide-eyed rufescent tiger-heron chick sitting in his nest, squawking impatiently for food. You'll also see iguanas, caimans, and sloths. Bird-watching and wildlife spotting sometimes collide: while watching two beautiful agami herons feeding on a muddy bank, birders were shaken up by the sudden splash of a crocodile attacking the herons. Happily, the herons were quicker off the mark than the birders were!

BOAT RIDES

It's not quite *The African Queen,* but a boat ride along the narrow vine-draped canals here is close. Once you're off the main canal, the specially designed, narrow tour boats glide relatively quietly—using mandated electric motors—and slowly, which makes for better wildlife spotting and fewer waves that erode the lagoon banks. Another alternative is to rent a kayak and go at your own speed along the canals.

TOURS

Most visitors opt for a fully escorted tour with one of the big lodges, because you're looked after from the moment you're picked up at your San José hotel until you're dropped off a day or two or seven later. All include a couple of standard tours of the park in their package prices. It's entirely possible to stay at a smaller in-town place and make à la carte arrangements yourself. No matter which way you go, your park tour will be on foot or by boat. Remember: you'll find no four-wheeled vehicles up here.

TOP REASONS TO GO

Luxury in the Jungle
Don't let tales of Tortuguero's isolation dissuade you from making a trip. No question: the place is remote. But the lodges up here package everything (overnight lodging, meals, tours, and, best of all, guided round-trip transportation) into one price in true "leave the driving to them" fashion. You won't lift a finger.

Plane or Boat Only
Whoever coined the old adage "Getting there is half the fun" might have had Tortuguero in mind. Plane and boat are the only ways to get to this no-road sector of Costa Rica. If you have the time, the fully escorted boat trips to and from the jungle give you a real Indiana Jones experience.

Turtles
Tortuguero takes its name from the Spanish word for turtle (*tortuga*), and here you'll get the chance to observe the nesting and hatching of four species of sea turtle, and to ponder one of nature's amazing rituals.

9

CAHUITA NATIONAL PARK

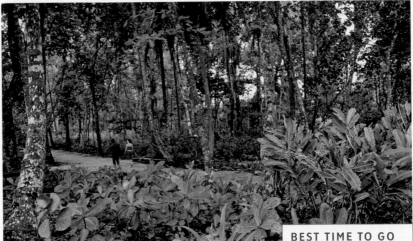

In a land known for its dark-sand beaches, the coral-based white sand of Cahuita National Park (Parque Nacional Cahuita) is a real standout.

The only Costa Rican park jointly administered by the National Parks Service and a community, it starts at the southern edge of the village of Cahuita and runs pristine mile after pristine mile southward. Whereas most of the country's protected areas tender only land-based activities, this park entices you offshore as well.

Roughly parallel to the coastline, a 7-km (4-mile) trail passes through the forest to Cahuita Point. A hike of a few hours along the trail—always easiest in the dry season—lets you spot howler and white-faced capuchin monkeys, coatimundis, armadillos, and raccoons. The coastline is encircled by a 2½-square-km (1-square-mile) coral reef. The park was first created to protect this reef. You'll find superb snorkeling off Cahuita Point, but sadly, the coral reef is slowly being killed by sediment, intensified by deforestation and the erosive effects of the 1991 earthquake that hit the coast.

BEST TIME TO GO

As elsewhere on this coast, you can expect rain here no matter what the time of year. February through April and September and October are drier months, and offer the best visibility for snorkeling; they are the least desirable months if you're here to surf, however.

FUN FACT

Here is Costa Rica's only national park with two-tiered entry fees. You'll pay $5 if you enter in the village of Cahuita. The entrance at Puerto Vargas, several kilometers south of town, charges $10.

BEST WAY TO EXPLORE

BEACHING IT

The waves here are fabulous for bodysurfing along the section of beach at the Puerto Vargas entrance. This wide swath of shoreline is also great for strolling, jogging, or just basking in the Caribbean sun, but be careful of riptides along this stretch of coast. The safest swimming is in front of the camping area.

CYCLING

Cycling makes a pleasant way to see the park in the dry season. Seemingly everybody in Cahuita and Puerto Viejo de Talamanca rents bicycles. (The southern entrance to the park is close enough to Puerto Viejo that it could be your starting point, too.) The park trail gets muddy at times, and you run into logs, river estuaries, and other obstacles.

HIKING

A serious 7-km (4-mile) hiking trail runs from the park entrance at Kelly Creek all the way to Puerto Vargas. Take a bus or catch a ride to Puerto Vargas and hike back around the point in the course of a day. Remember to bring plenty of water, food, and sunscreen.

SNORKELING

Tour operators in Cahuita will bring you to a selection of prime snorkeling spots offshore. If you want to swim out on your own, the best snorkeling spot is off Punta Vargas at the south end of the park. Along with the chance to see some of the 500 or so species of tropical fish that live here, you'll see some amazing coral formations, including impressive elk horn, majestic blue stag horn, and eerie yellow brain corals. When the water is clear and warm, the snorkeling is great. But that warm water also appeals to jellyfish—if you start to feel a tingling sensation on your arms or legs, make a beeline for the shore. Each little sting doesn't hurt much, but accumulated stings can result in a major allergic reaction in some people.

TOP REASONS TO GO

Easy Access
With one of its two entrances sitting in "downtown" Cahuita, access to the park is a snap. But ease of access does not mean the place is overrun with visitors. Fortunately, this is no Manuel Antonio.

Lots of Lodging
Closeness to Cahuita and Puerto Viejo de Talamanca and their spectrum of lodging options means you'll have no trouble finding a place to stay that fits your budget. You can even camp in the park if you're up for roughing it.

Snorkeling
Costa Rica's largest living coral reef just offshore means the snorkeling is phenomenal here. Watch for blue parrot fish and angelfish as they weave their way among equally colorful species of coral, sponges, and seaweeds. Visit during the Caribbean coast's two mini dry seasons for the best visibility.

9

Updated by
Jeffrey Van
Fleet

The tourist brochures tout the country's Caribbean coast as "the other Costa Rica." Everything about this part of Costa Rica seems different: different culture, different history, different climate, and different activities. Expect different prices, too. Your travel dollar goes further here than elsewhere in the country. This region was long ago discovered by European adventure seekers—you're quite likely to hear Dutch, German, and Italian spoken by the visitors here—but is much less known in North American circles.

The ethnic mix differs markedly here, as it does all along the Caribbean coast of Central America. The region was first settled by the British, and then, throughout the 19th century, by the descendants of Afro-Caribbean slaves who came to work on the banana plantations and construct the Atlantic railroad. That makes the Caribbean coast the best place in the country to find English speakers, although the language is disappearing as Spanish takes over.

It is rainier here than in other parts of Costa Rica, and the rain is distributed pretty evenly year-round without a distinct dry season—though October (when the rest of Costa Rica is getting deluged with rain) is the driest month. The region will never draw the typical fun-in-the-sun crowd that frequents the drier Pacific coast, but it does offer a year-round forested lushness and just as many activities at a more reasonable price.

PLANNING

WHEN TO GO
HIGH SEASON: FEBRUARY TO APRIL
Climate is the Caribbean's bugaboo and will forever prevent it from becoming the same high-powered tourist destination that the northern Pacific coast is. (Frankly, we consider that to be a blessing.) The

Caribbean lacks a true dry season, though February to April could be called a "drier" season, with many sunny days and intermittent showers. Yet, despite weather patterns that differ from the rest of Costa Rica, places here charge high-season rates from December to April, just as they do elsewhere in the country. Prices skew a bit lower in the Caribbean, though, than elsewhere in Costa Rica.

LOW SEASON: MAY TO AUGUST AND DECEMBER THROUGH JANUARY

The heaviest rains (and periodic road closures) come in December and January, high season elsewhere in Costa Rica. During the rainiest months visitors are fewer. May through August sees rain, too, although not quite as much. The popularity of this part of the country among European travelers means that July and August become mini high seasons here, often with a slight increase in lodging prices. Tortuguero sets its own seasons, with higher prices the norm during the prime turtle-watching months of July through September.

SHOULDER SEASON: SEPTEMBER TO NOVEMBER

Want in on a little secret? When the rest of Costa Rica settles into the soggiest time of year, the sun comes out and the weather begins to dry up in this part of the country. The Caribbean coast makes the perfect refuge from the insufferably wet months of September and October elsewhere.

PLANNING YOUR TIME

Attractions near Guápiles and Siquirres lend themselves to long day trips from San José. Tour operators also have whirlwind daylong Tortuguero trips from San José. We recommend you avoid these—the area really deserves two or, ideally, three days. Choose a single Caribbean destination and stay put if you have just a few days; Cahuita and Puerto Viejo de Talamanca are ideal for that purpose. If you have a week, you can tackle the north and south coasts.

GETTING HERE AND AROUND

AIR TRAVEL

There are daily flights from San José to the small airport in Limón (LIO) and the airstrip in Tortuguero (TTQ) via Nature Air and SANSA. Both airlines do an early-morning San José–Limón–Tortuguero–San José run. Nature Air also flies daily to the small airport just across the border in Bocas del Toro, Panama (BOC).

Contacts Nature Air. ⊠ *Aeropuerto Juan Santamaría, Pan-American Hwy., San José* ☎ *2299–6000, 800/235–9272 in North America* ⊕ *www.natureair.com.* **SANSA.** ☎ *2290–4100, 877/767–2672 in North America* ⊕ *www.flysansa.com.*

BUS AND SHUTTLE TRAVEL

Grupo Caribeños buses, some snazzy double-deckers, connect San José's Gran Terminal del Caribe with hourly service to Guápiles, Siquirres, and Limón. Autotransportes MEPE, which has a lock on bus service to the south Caribbean coast, has a reputation for being lackadaisical, but is really quite dependable. Its San José buses depart from the capital's Terminal Atlántico Norte. MEPE drivers and ticket sellers are accustomed to dealing with foreigners; even if their English is limited, they'll figure out what you want. MEPE occasionally runs extra buses to Cahuita and Puerto Viejo de Talamanca during the high season. Bus fares to this region are reasonable. From San José, expect to pay $3 to Guápiles, $6 to Limón, $10 to Cahuita, $11 to Puerto Viejo de Talamanca, and $15 to Sixaola on the Panamanian border.

If you prefer a more private form of travel, consider taking a shuttle. Comfortable air-conditioned vans of the nationwide company Interbus or the Caribbean-based Caribe Shuttle depart from San José hotels daily for Cahuita and Puerto Viejo de Talamanca. Reserve tickets ($49 one way) at least a day in advance.

Bus Contacts Autotransportes MEPE. ⌧ *C. 9 and Avda. 12, Downtown* ☎ *2257–8129.* **Caribe Shuttle.** ☎ *2750-0626* ⊕ *www.caribeshuttle.com.* **Grupo Caribeños.** ⌧ *C. Central and Avda. 13, Barrio Tournón* ☎ *2222–0610* ⊕ *www. grupocaribenos.com.* **Interbus.** ☎ *4100–0888* ⊕ *www.interbusonline.com.*

CAR TRAVEL

With the exception of Tortuguero, this region is one of the country's most accessible. The southern coast is a three- to four-hour drive from San José, over mostly decent roads (by Costa Rican standards), and public transportation is frequent and reliable. The highway is undergoing expansion to four lanes between the northern edge of Braulio Carrillo National Park and Limón. Be prepared for occasional construction delays, but when completed—the target date is 2018, assuming all goes well—this region will be easier to reach than ever. Gas stations are plentiful between Guápiles and Limón, but their numbers dwindle to two on the southern coast between Limón and Puerto Viejo de Talamanca. The northern Caribbean coast is another story: the total absence of roads means you have to arrive by plane or boat. Most travelers go with a tour booked through one of the large Tortuguero lodges.

If you're driving here, remember that fog often covers the mountains in Braulio Carrillo National Park, north of San José, by early afternoon. Cross this area in the morning if you can. Always exercise utmost caution on the portion of highway that twists and turns through the park: you'll share the highway with large trucks. Check road conditions before you set out; occasional landslide closures through Braulio Carrillo necessitate leaving San José from the southeast, passing through Cartago, Paraíso, and Turrialba, then rejoining the Caribbean Highway at Siquirres, a route that adds an extra tiring 90–120 minutes onto your trip.

HEALTH AND SAFETY

All the standard tropical precautions apply when traveling in the Caribbean region. This is a very warm part of the country, so carry water, wear a hat, and use plenty of sunscreen. The undertow is dangerous along virtually the entire coast, making swimming risky. Wear mosquito repellent in low-lying coastal areas, where a few cases of dengue and chikungunya have been reported.

MONEY MATTERS

ATMs are becoming more common in this part of the country, although we recommend, if possible, stocking up on cash in San José. You'll find cash machines in Puerto Viejo de Sarapiquí, Guápiles, Guácimo, Siquirres, and several in Limón. Puerto Viejo de Talamanca has two; Cahuita has one; Tortuguero has none. ATMs in smaller towns may run out of cash on weekends. Remember: many smaller places—there are a lot of those here in the Caribbean—do not accept credit cards.

RESTAURANTS

The many open-air dining spots out here provide you with that ultimate tropical dining experience, with Puerto Viejo de Talamanca offering one of Costa Rica's most varied dining scenes. Think seafood, chicken, coconut, and fruits in the Caribbean. Restaurateurs take advantage of the bounty of the land and sea in this part of the country.

HOTELS

The high-rise, glitzy resorts of the Pacific coast are nowhere to be found in the Caribbean. The norm here is small, independent lodgings, usually family owned and operated. Fewer visitors in this region mean plenty of decent lodging at affordable prices most of the year. But tourism *is* growing, so it's risky to show up without reservations. Despite weather patterns that differ from the rest of the country, most Caribbean lodgings charge high-season rates from Christmas through Easter, just like elsewhere in Costa Rica. Many also impose another mini high season in July and August, prime vacation months for the region's predominantly European tourist clientele. Surprisingly few places here have air-conditioning, but sea breezes and ceiling fans usually provide sufficient ventilation. Smaller places frequently don't take credit cards; those that do may give discounts if you pay with cash. *Hotel reviews have been shortened. For full information, visit Fodors.com.*

WHAT IT COSTS IN DOLLARS			
$	$$	$$$	$$$$
Restaurants	under $10	$10–$15	$16–$25	over $25
Hotels	under $75	$75–$150	$151–$250	over $250

Restaurant prices are the average cost of a main course at dinner or, if dinner is not served, at lunch. Hotel prices are the lowest cost of a standard double room in high season.

PACKAGE TOURS

One of Costa Rica's most remote regions is also one of its prime tourist destinations. No roads lead to Tortuguero on the northeast coast, so plane or boat is your only option. If you don't want to bother with logistics, consider booking a package tour with one of the lodges. It will include all transport from San José, overnights, meals, and guided tours. Prices look high at first, but considering all you get, they are quite reasonable. Other types of regional tours are also available: **Horizontes** (☎ 2222–2022 ⊕ *www.horizontes.com*) tours include naturalist guides and transport by 4WD vehicle.

Eco-Lodges in the Caribbean

Development has been slow to come to the Caribbean coast, but that has given the tourism industry here the opportunity to think carefully about what it wants to be. It's opted for a smaller model that preserves the environment and respects local culture.

Almonds & Corals, Gandoca-Manzanillo Wildlife Refuge. Almonds & Corals scatters its comfortable platformed bungalows unobtrusively throughout its forest property and offers myriad environmentally themed activities conducted by local guides. You really do get that "get away from it all" experience with a bit of rustic luxury.

Casa Marbella, Tortuguero. Our favorite in-town lodging provides a far more intimate Tortuguero experience with one-on-one nature tours, rather than big groups, for just a fraction of the cost of the big lodges nearby. The Canadian owner is one of the town's biggest boosters, and we like and appreciate his "transplanted foreigner" model.

Rainforest Lodge, Braulio Carrillo National Park. Although the site is best known for its famous aerial tram, there is accommodation here, and it maintains practices as green and pristine as those of the entire park.

THE SARAPIQUÍ LOOP

The area immediately north of the San José metro area doesn't leap to mind when discussing ecotourism in Costa Rica, but it should. The Sarapiquí River gave its name to this region at the foot of the Cordillera Central mountain range. To the west is the rain forest of Braulio Carrillo National Park, and to the east are Tortuguero National Park and Barra del Colorado National Wildlife Refuge. These splendid national parks share the region with thousands of acres of farmland, including palm, banana, and pineapple plantations, as well as cattle ranching. Cheap land and rich soil brought a wave of Ticos to this area a half century ago. Until the construction of Highway 126 in 1957, which connects the area to San José, this was one of the most isolated parts of Costa Rica, with little or no tourism. Government homesteading projects brought many residents, who cleared massive swaths of the rain forest for cattle grazing and agriculture. Now, old-growth lowland rain forest, montane cloud forest, and wetlands exist only within the borders of the national parks and several adjoining private reserves. A growing selection of nature lodges has set up shop here, and you can enjoy their offerings 60 to 90 minutes after you leave the capital. (Just try getting to the Osa Peninsula on the southern Pacific coast in that same time.)

BRAULIO CARRILLO NATIONAL PARK

30 km (19 miles) north of San José.

One of Central America's largest tracts of primary cloud forest looms just north of the San José metro area. The primary highway to the Caribbean coast passes right through the park, and most visitors see it from their car or van windows.

Sarapiquí Loop

GETTING HERE AND AROUND

From San José, it's a 45-minute drive to the park. Travel northeast on Calle 3, which becomes the Braulio Carrillo Highway (Highway 32), toward Limón. This highway winds through the park, entering at the main ranger station, Zurquí, and exiting at the Quebrada González ranger station. The Barva station is on the west side of the park, north of Zurquí, and is the easiest to access. From Heredia, drive north to Sacramento on Highway 114. The station is 4 km (2½ miles) northeast of Sacramento on a trail that's accessible on foot or by 4WD (except during heavy rains). If you're doing the driving, try to make this a morning trip, as the highway through the park begins to fog over in the afternoon.

A number of tour companies offer one-day tours from San José, and, quite honestly, that is the easiest and safest way to visit the park, and the only method we recommend. Several visitors have become lost over the years trying to do the park on their own. Go with someone who knows the terrain.

EXPLORING

Barva Volcano. This 2,896-meter (9,500-foot) volcanic summit is the highest point in Braulio Carrillo National Park. Dormant for 300 years now, Barva is massive and easily visible from downtown San José: its lower slopes are almost completely planted with coffee fields and hold more than a dozen small towns, nearly all of which are named after saints. On the upper slopes are pastures lined with exotic pines and the occasional native oak or cedar, giving way to the botanical diversity of the cloud forest near the top. The air is usually cool near the summit, which combines with the pines and pastures to evoke European or North American mountain landscapes.

Barva's misty, luxuriant summit is the only part of Braulio Carrillo where camping is allowed, and it's a good place to see the rare resplendent quetzal early in the morning. Because it's somewhat hard to reach, Barva receives a mere fraction of the crowds that flock to the summits of Poás and Irazú. A two- to four-hour hike in from the Barva ranger station takes you to the main crater, which is about 162 meters (540 feet) in diameter. Your efforts should be rewarded by great views (as long as you start before 8 am, to avoid the mist). The almost vertical sides of the crater are covered in *sombrillas de pobre*, a plant that thrives in the highlands, and oak trees laden with epiphytes (nonparasitic plants that grow on other plants). The crater is filled with an otherworldly black lake. Farther down the track into the forest lies a smaller crater lake. Bring rain gear, boots, and a warm shirt. Stay on the trail when hiking anywhere in Braulio Carrillo; even experienced hikers who know the area have lost their way up here, and the rugged terrain makes wandering through the woods very dangerous. In addition, muggings of hikers have been reported in the park (this is the closest national park to San José and its attendant urban problems). Go with a ranger.

For access to the volcano, start from Sacramento, north of Heredia. North of Barva de Heredia the road grows narrow and steep. At Sacramento the paved road turns to dirt, growing worse as it nears the Barva ranger station. We recommend a 4WD vehicle, especially during the rainy season. From the ranger station you can take a 4WD vehicle over the extremely rocky road to the park entrance (dry season only), or hike up on foot. ⊠ *Access via the park's Barva ranger station* ☎ *1192 national parks hotline in Costa Rica* ✉ *$12* ☉ *Tues.–Sun. 7–4.*

Braulio Carrillo National Park (*Parque Nacional Braulio Carrillo*). In a country where deforestation is still rife, hiking through dense, primary tropical cloud forest is an experience to be treasured. The park owes its foundation to the public outcry provoked by the construction of the highway of the same name through this region in the late 1970s—the government bowed to pressure from environmentalists and, somewhat ironically, Braulio Carrillo is the national park that is most accessible from the capital, thanks to the highway. Covering 443 square km (171 square miles), the extremely diverse terrain ranges from 55 meters (180 feet) to about 2,896 meters (9,500 feet) above sea level and extends from the central volcanic range down the Caribbean slope to La Selva research station near Puerto Viejo de Sarapiquí. The park protects a series of ecosystems ranging from the cloud forests on the upper slopes to the tropical wet forest of the Magsasay sector; it is home to 6,000 tree species, 500 bird species, and 135 mammal species.

Despite the park's immense size and proximity to the capital, visitor facilities are extremely limited. Penetrating the park's depths is a project only for the truly intrepid.

The **Zurquí ranger station** is to the right of the highway, ½ km (¼ mile) before the Zurquí Tunnel. Here a short trail loops through the cloud forest. Hikes are steep; wear hiking boots to protect yourself from mud, slippage, and snakes. The main trail through primary forest, 1½ km (1 mile) long, culminates in a *mirador* (lookout point), but alas, the highway mars the view. Monkeys, tapirs, jaguars, kinkajous, sloths, raccoons, margays, and porcupines all live in this forest, and resident birds include the resplendent quetzal and the eagle. Orchids, bromeliads, heliconias, fungi, and mushrooms live closer to the forest floor. Another trail leads into the forest to the right, beginning about 17 km (11 miles) after the tunnel, where it follows the Quebrada González, a stream with a cascade and swimming hole. There are no campsites in this part of the park. The **Carrillo ranger station,** 22 km (14 miles) northeast along the highway from Zurquí, marks the beginning of trails that are less steep. Farther north on this highway, near the park entrance/exit toward Guápiles, is the **Quebrada González** ranger station. To the east of Heredia, a road climbs **Barva Volcano** from San Rafael. ⊠ *Braulio Carrillo National Park* ☎ *2290–8202 Sistemas de Areas de Conservación, 1192 national parks hotline in Costa Rica* 🖅 *$12* ☉ *Daily 7–4.*

OFF THE
BEATEN
PATH

Rain Forest Adventures. Just beyond the northeastern boundary of Braulio Carrillo National Park, about 15 km (9 miles) before the Caribbean-slope town of Guápiles, a 1,200-acre reserve houses a privately owned and operated engineering marvel: a series of gondolas strung together in a modified ski-lift pulley system. (To lessen the impact on the jungle, the support pylons were lowered into place by helicopter.) The 21 gondolas hold five people each, plus a bilingual biologist-guide equipped with a walkie-talkie to request brief stops for snapping pictures. The ride covers 2½ km (1½ miles) in 80 minutes. The $67 price includes a biologist-guided walk through the area for ground-level orientation before or after the tram ride. Several add-ons are possible, too, with frog and butterfly exhibits, a medicinal-plant garden, and a zip-line canopy tour ($57) on-site, as well as a half-day birding tour ($99). There is also on-site lodging. You can arrange a personal pickup in San José for a fee, or there are public buses (on the Guápiles line) every half hour from the Gran Terminal del Caribe in San José. Drivers know the tram as the *teleférico.* Many San José tour operators make a day tour combining the tram with another half-day option; combos with the Britt Coffee Tour, near Heredia, are especially popular. The company also operates parks near Jacó, on the Central Pacific coast, as well as in Panama and the Caribbean-island nations of Jamaica (Ocho Rios), and St. Lucia. ⊠ *Rain Forest Adventures, 10 km (6 miles) northeast of Braulio Carrillo National Park along Rte. 32* ☎ *2257–5961, 866/759–8726 in North America* ⊕ *www.rainforestadventure.com* 🖅 *$67; $112 includes all attractions* ☉ *Tours: Mon. 9–4, Tues.–Sun. 6:30–4. Call for reservations 6 am–9:30 pm.*

9

WHERE TO STAY

$$$$ ☷ **Rainforest Lodge.** Just north of Braulio Carrillo lies a splendid, eco-
B&B/INN minded lodging option whose environmental impact is so unobtrusive
that barely anyone knows it exists—and staying here lets you enjoy
one of the Caribbean region's premier attractions after the day-trippers
have left. **Pros:** eco-friendly; rates include tram and guide. **Cons:** rustic; electricity shuts off after 9 pm. ⑤ *Rooms from: $498* ⊠ *Guápiles
Hwy., north of Braulio Carrillo National Park* ☎ 2257–5961 *in San
José, 866/759–8726 in North America* ⊕ *www.rainforestadventure.com*
🗩 *10 cabins* ⏀ *All meals.*

PUERTO VIEJO DE SARAPIQUÍ

80 km (48 miles) north of San José.

One of Costa Rica's lesser-known eco-destinations has been developing
a growing selection of nature-themed activities in recent years. In the
19th century, Puerto Viejo de Sarapiquí was a thriving river port and the
only link with the coastal lands straight east. Fortunes nose-dived with
the construction of a full-fledged port in the town of Moín near Limón,
and today Puerto Viejo has a slightly run-down air. The activities of the
Nicaraguan Contras made this a danger zone in the 1980s, but now
that the political situation has improved, boats once again ply the old
route up the Sarapiquí River to the San Juan River on the Nicaraguan
border, from where you can travel downstream to Barra del Colorado
or Tortuguero. (Wars of words still occasionally flare up between Costa
Rica and Nicaragua, but they need not concern you as a visitor.) A few
tour companies have Sarapiquí River tours with up to Class III rapids
in the section between Chilamate and La Virgen, with plenty of wildlife
to see. If you prefer to leave the driving to them, many of the lodges
operate boat tours on the tamer sections of the river. Don't confuse
Puerto Viejo de Sarapiquí with Puerto Viejo de Talamanca on the south
Caribbean coast. Locals refer to both as simply "Puerto Viejo." We use
the complete names of both towns to avoid any mix-up.

GETTING HERE AND AROUND

The Braulio Carrillo Highway runs from Calle 3 in San José and passes
the Zurquí and Quebrada González sectors of Braulio Carrillo National
Park. It branches at Santa Clara, north of the park, with the paved
Highway 4 continuing north to Puerto Viejo de Sarapiquí. Alternatively,
an older winding road connects San José with Puerto Viejo de Sarapiquí, passing through Heredia and Vara Blanca. The former route is
easier, with less traffic; the latter route is more scenic but narrow, and
if you are at all prone to motion sickness, the newer road is a safer bet.
Heavy rains sometimes cause landslides that block the newer highway
near the Zurquí Tunnel inside the park, in which case you have to go
via Vara Blanca. Check conditions before you set out. Get an early start;
fog begins to settle in on both routes by the middle of the afternoon.
■ **TIP→** There are gas stations on the Braulio Carrillo Highway at the
turnoff to Puerto Viejo de Sarapiquí, as well as just outside town. Fill
the tank when you get the chance.

Grupo Caribeños buses travel several times daily via both routes—more frequently via the newer route, though—and leave from San José's Gran Terminal del Caribe.

ESSENTIALS

Bank/ATM Banco Nacional. ⊠ *Across from post office* ☎ *2766–6012* ⊕ *www.bncr.fi.cr.*

Medical Clinic Red Cross (*Cruz Roja*). ⊠ *West end of town* ☎ *2766–6901.*

Pharmacy Farmacia Alfa. ⊠ *50 m northeast of Parque Central* ☎ *2766–6348.*

Post Office Correos. ⊠ *Across from Banco Nacional* ⊕ *www.correos.go.cr.*

EXPLORING

Heliconia Island. Some 70 species of the heliconia, a relative of the banana, are among the collections that populate 5 acres of botanical gardens on this island in the Sarapiquí River. Expect to see ample bird- and butterfly life, too. ⊠ *La Chaves, 8 km (5 miles) south of Puerto Viejo de Sarapiquí* ☎ *2764–5220* ⊕ *www.heliconiaisland.com* ▧ *$10, $18 with guide* ☉ *Daily 8–5.*

FAMILY
Fodor's Choice
★

La Selva Biological Station. At the confluence of the Puerto Viejo and Sarapiquí rivers, La Selva packs about 420 bird species, 460 tree species, and 500 butterfly species into just 15 square km (6 square miles). Sightings might include the spider monkey, poison dart frog, agouti, collared peccary, and dozens of other rare creatures. Extensive, well-marked trails and swing bridges, many of which are wheelchair accessible, connect habitats as varied as tropical wet forest, swamps, creeks, rivers, secondary regenerating forest, and pasture. The site is a project of the Organization for Tropical Studies, a research consortium of 63 U.S., Australian, South African, and Latin American universities, and is the oldest of three biological stations OTS operates in Costa Rica. To see the place, take an informative three-hour morning or afternoon nature walk with one of La Selva's bilingual guides, who are among the country's best. Walks start every day at 8 am and 1:30 pm. For a completely different view of the forest, set off on a guided two-hour walk at 5:45 am or the night tour at 6 pm. If you get at least seven people together, you can enroll in the daylong Bird-Watching 101 course, which can be arranged anytime for $80 per person; if you have at least six, you can tag along with one of the resident research scientists for a half day. Young children won't feel left out either, with a very basic nature-identification course geared to them. Even with all the offerings, La Selva can custom design excursions to suit your own special interests, too. Advance reservations are required for the dawn and night walks and any of the courses. ⊠ *Drive 6 km (4 miles) south from Puerto Viejo de Sarapiquí, and look for signs on the west side of the road. La Selva is a $12 taxi ride from Puerto Viejo de Sarapiquí* ☎ *2766–6565, 2524–0607 in San José, 919/684–5774 in North America* ⊕ *www.threepaths.co.cr* ▧ *$45, includes guided walk; dawn or night walk $50* ☉ *Walks daily at 5:45 and 8 am, 1:30 and 6 pm.*

Museum of Indigenous Cultures (*Museo de Culturas Indígenas Doctora María Eugenia Bozzoli*). Costa Rica's indigenous peoples don't get the visibility of those in Guatemala or Mexico, probably because they

9

Insanely steep hills and heavy rainfall make this country a mecca for white-water sports.

number only 40,000 out of a population of 4 million. This museum, part of the Centro Neotrópico Sarapiquís, provides a well-rounded all-under-one-roof introduction to the subject. Nearly 400 artifacts of the Boruca, Bribri, Cabécar, Guaymí, and Maleku peoples are displayed, including masks, musical instruments, and shamanic healing sticks. Start by watching a 17-minute video introduction, *Man and Nature in Pre-Columbian Costa Rica*. A botanical garden next door cultivates medicinal plants still used by many traditional groups. In 1999 researchers discovered an archaeological site on the grounds that contains pre-Columbian tombs and petroglyphs dating from the 15th century. The site is still under study. ⊠ *La Virgen de Sarapiquí, 17 km (11 miles) southwest of Puerto Viejo* 🕾 *2761–1004* ⊕ *www.sarapiquis. com* ✉ *$15 (includes guide)* ⊘ *Daily 9–5.*

FAMILY **Snake Garden.** One of a growing number of Costa Rica's serpentaria, the Snake Garden shows off some 50 species of reptiles, including all the poisonous snakes (and most of the nonpoisonous ones) found in Costa Rica, as well as pythons, anacondas, and rattlesnakes from elsewhere in North and South America. You can handle a few specimens upon request and under supervision. ⊠ *Centro Neotrópico Sarapiquís, La Virgen de Sarapiquí* 🕾 *2761–1004* ⊕ *www.sarapiquis.com* ✉ *$15* ⊘ *Daily 9–5.*

Standard Fruit Company. Curious about the life and times of Costa Rica's most famous yellow fruit? Standard Fruit, which operates as Dole in North America, offers two-hour Banana Tours to guide you through the process from plantation to processing to packing. Visits are best arranged through several San José travel agencies, who will transport you to the site. Options include a longer tour at a plantation here in Sarapiquí or a shorter tour south of the Caribbean port of Limón, which is primarily geared toward cruise-ship passengers. ✉ *Puerto Viejo de Sarapiquí* ☎ *8383–4596* ⊕ *www.bananatourcostarica.com* 💲 *$12* ⊙ *Tours daily at 10.*

Tirimbina Rainforest Center. This working biological research station, 17 km (11 miles) southwest of Puerto Viejo, encompasses 750 acres of primary forest and 8 km (5 miles) of trails, some of them traversing hanging bridges at canopy level. Tours introduce you to bats, frogs, and other common but often misunderstood creatures, and show off the beauty of the forest. Reservations are recommended for all activities, and required for the bat, frog, birding, and night tours. ✉ *La Virgen de Sarapiquí* ☎ *2761–0333* ⊕ *www.tirimbina.org* 💲 *$17, guided tours $24–$30* ⊙ *Daily 7–5; guided nature walks and chocolate tour at 8, 10, 1:30, and 3; birding tour 6 am; night walk 7 pm; frog tour and bat tour 7:30 pm.*

SPORTS AND THE OUTDOORS
TOUR OPERATORS
Hacienda Pozo Azul. This working horse ranch and dairy farm, 17 km (11 miles) southwest of Puerto Viejo, offers a variety of nature-themed excursions. The canopy tour ($56) has 12 zip lines, ranging in height from 18 to 27 meters (60 to 90 feet). Horseback excursions for all experience levels take you through the area around La Virgen. A two-hour tour is $46, a half day is $56. If you're an experienced rider, check out the multiday tours, too. A guided 27-meter (90-foot) river canyon rappelling descent is $46. ✉ *La Virgen de Sarapiquí* ☎ *2438–2616, 877/810–6903 in North America* ⊕ *www.pozoazul.com.*

Hotel Gavilán Río Sarapiquí. The hotel runs wildlife-watching and birding tours from its site on the river near Puerto Viejo de Sarapiquí. ✉ *700 m north of Comando Atlántico (naval command)* ☎ *2766–6743, 2234–9507 in San José* ⊕ *www.gavilanlodge.com* 💲 *Tours from $47.*

RAFTING
The Virgen del Socorro area is one of the most popular put-in points for white-water rafters, and offers both Class II and III rapids. The upper Sarapiquí River gets wilder and woolier with Class IV rapids to navigate. Trips leaving from the Chilamate put-in are more tranquil, with mostly Class I rapids. The put-in point depends on the weather and season. Several operators lead tours on the Sarapiquí River.

Ríos Tropicales. You can raft the Class II–III La Virgen section of the Sarapiquí River as well as the upper river (Class IV) on day excursions from the Arenal area. ✉ *San José* ☎ *2233–6455, 866/722–8273 in North America* ⊕ *www.riostropicales.com* 💲 *Excursions from $90.*

WHERE TO STAY
$ 🛏 **Hotel Gavilán Río Sarapiquí.** Beautiful gardens run down to the river, HOTEL   and colorful tanagers and three types of toucan feast in the citrus trees on the grounds of this two-story lodge, where comfortable, terra-cotta-floor rooms are nicely accented with decorative crafts. **Pros:** lovely gardens; many activities; great for birders. **Cons:** rustic rooms; need a car to stay here; no air-conditioning; patchy Wi-Fi. 💲 *Rooms from: $60* ✉ *700*

9

m north of Comando Atlántico (naval command) ☎ *2766–6743, 2234–9507 in San José* ⊕ *www.gavilanlodge.com* ⇨ *20 rooms* ❑ *Some meals.*

$$ ⊡ **La Selva Biological Station Lodge.** Other lodges provide more luxury
B&B/INN   for the money, but none can match the tropical nature experience
at this working biological-research station where accommodations
are in dorm-style rooms with large bunk beds and lots of screened
windows. **Pros:** many activities included in lodging rate; plenty of
wildlife; ecology-minded staff. **Cons:** bunk beds; cabins are rustic;
no air-conditioning; sometimes difficult to procure overnight space.
⑤ *Rooms from: $124* ⊠ *6 km (4 miles) south of Puerto Viejo de Sara-
piquí* ☎ *2766–6565, 2524–0607 in San José, 919/684–5774 in North
America* ⊕ *www.threepaths.co.cr* ⇨ *60 bunk beds in dorms, 18 cab-
ins, 1 house* ❑ *All meals.*

$ ⊡ **Posada Andrea Cristina.** This basic and comfortable bed-and-breakfast
HOTEL   offers four cabins, two A-frame bungalows, and a rustic treehouse.
Pros: good value; secluded location; attentive owners; Spanish lessons
available. **Cons:** rustic rooms; cash only; mosquitoes; some road noise.
⑤ *Rooms from: $58* ⊠ *½ km (¼ mile) west of town* ☎ *2766–6265*
⊕ *www.andreacristina.com* ⊟ *No credit cards* ⇨ *8 rooms* ❑ *Breakfast.*

$$ ⊡ **Sarapiquís Rainforest Lodge.** Within the Centro Neotrópico Sarapiquís,
HOTEL   an environmental educational center, museum, and garden, you can stay
FAMILY   the night inside indigenous-inspired circular *palenque* (huts) with palm-
thatch roofs. **Pros:** good value; large rooms; private terraces; buffet-style
restaurant. **Cons:** no air-conditioning; sometimes difficult to find space.
⑤ *Rooms from: $105* ⊠ *Centro Neotrópico Sarapiquís, La Virgen de
Sarapiquí, 17 km (11 miles) southwest of Puerto Viejo* ☎ *2761–1004*
⊕ *www.sarapiquis.com* ⇨ *40 rooms* ❑ *Breakfast.*

$$ ⊡ **Selva Verde Lodge.** Built on stilts over the Sarapiquí River on the edge
HOTEL   of a 2-square-km (1-square-mile) private tropical rain-forest reserve,
Fodor's Choice   the lodge caters primarily to those seeking natural-history tours. **Pros:**
★   ecology-minded staff; many activities; great for birders. **Cons:** popu-
lar with tour groups; sometimes difficult to find space in high season;
steep walk to reach a few bungalows. ⑤ *Rooms from: $141* ⊠ *7 km (4
miles) west of Puerto Viejo de Sarapiquí* ☎ *2761–1800, 800/451–7111
in North America* ⊕ *www.selvaverde.com* ⇨ *40 rooms, 5 bungalows*
❑ *All meals.*

$$ ⊡ **Tirimbina Rainforest Lodge.** A variety of comfy lodge accommodations
B&B/INN   put you close to this research complex's many fun nature-themed activi-
ties. **Pros:** access to nature-themed activities; terrific rates for what's
offered. **Cons:** standard rooms are a bit spartan. ⑤ *Rooms from: $89*
⊠ *La Virgen de Sarapiqui, 17 km (11 miles) southwest of Puerto Viejo*
☎ *2761–0333* ⊕ *www.tirimbina.org* ⇨ *18 rooms* ❑ *Breakfast.*

THE NORTHERN LOWLANDS

The lowlands begin about an hour north of San José, after you come
out of Braulio Carrillo National Park. For most visitors, they are merely
a tract of land to pass through on the way to the coast. The Caribbean
does beckon, after all, but a couple of lesser sights here may tempt you
to stop. If you stay on the well-maintained main Guápiles Highway, you

head southeast toward Limón and the Caribbean coast. The highway passes through sultry agricultural lowlands, home to large banana and cacao plantations, but bypasses the region's three main communities: burgeoning Guápiles and the smaller towns of Guácimo and Siquirres.

GUÁPILES

60 km (38 miles) northeast of San José.

The hub towns of Guápiles and Guácimo aren't destinations in their own right, but rather the nucleus for a few on-the-way-to-the-Caribbean activities. Guápiles, one of the country's fastest-growing cities, is the hub of northeastern Costa Rica, and with all the facilities in town, residents of the region barely need to trek to San José anymore. The smaller town of Guácimo lies 12 km (7 miles) east on the Guápiles Highway.

GETTING HERE AND AROUND

Guápiles lies just north of Braulio Carrillo National Park and straddles the highway to the Caribbean. It's an easy one-hour drive from San José just 60 km (38 miles) to the southwest, or Limón 84 km (50 miles) to the east. Grupo Caribeños buses connect San José's Gran Terminal del Caribe with Guápiles every half hour from early morning until late evening, and provide service seven times daily to Guácimo. The Guápiles terminal is 200 meters south of the stadium. San José's bus terminals are in sketchy neighborhoods, so take care if this is your mode of transportation.

ESSENTIALS

Banks/ATMs BAC San José. ⊠ *Across from Casa de la Cultura* ☎ *2710–7434* ⊕ *www.bac.net.* **Banco Nacional.** ⊠ *200 m north of Ebal Rodríguez stadium* ☎ *2713–2000* ⊕ *www.bncr.fi.cr.*

Hospital Hospital de Guápiles. ⊠ *90 m south of fire station* ☎ *2710–6801.*

Pharmacy Farmacia Santa Marta. ⊠ *Across from Banco Nacional* ☎ *2710–6253.*

Post Office Correos. ⊠ *North of MUCAP* ⊕ *www.correos.go.cr.*

Visitor Information Instituto Costarricense de Turismo. ⊠ *Next to Bancrédito* ☎ *2710–7516* ⊕ *www.visitcostarica.com.*

EXPLORING

EARTH. The nonprofit university called EARTH (Escuela de Agricultura de la Región Tropical Húmeda, or Agricultural School of the Humid Tropical Region) researches medicinal plants and forms of sustainable tropical agriculture, including the production of bananas that are less pesticide dependent. The university graduates some 100 students from Latin America and Africa each year. EARTH's elegant stationery, calendars, and other paper products are made from banana stems, tobacco leaves, and coffee leaves and grounds, and are sold at the on-site Oropéndola store and in many tourist shops around the country. The property encompasses a banana plantation and a forest reserve with nature trails, and it's a bird-watchers' favorite; some 250 species have been spotted

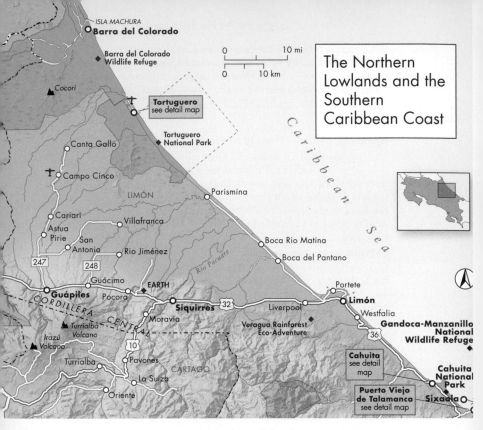

here. Lunch is available ($13). Though priority is given to researchers and conference groups, you're welcome to stay in the school's 50-person lodging facility, with private bathrooms, hot water, and ceiling fans, for $85 a night, which includes the use of a swimming pool and exercise equipment. Reservations are required for tours or accommodations. ⊠ *Pocora de Guácimo, 15 km (9 miles) east of Guápiles on Guápiles Hwy.* ☎ *2713–0000, 404/995–1230 in North America* ⊕ *www.earth. ac.cr* 🖃 *$25 half-day tour; $35 full day* ☉ *By reservation.*

SIQUIRRES

28 km (17 miles) east of Guápiles.

Siquirres anchors a fertile banana- and pineapple-growing region, and marks the transition point between the agricultural lowlands and the tropical, palm-laden coast. The odd name is a corruption of the words *Si quieres* (if you want), fittingly impassive for this lackluster town. Siquirres has the unfortunate historical distinction of having once been the westernmost point to which Afro-Caribbean people could migrate. Costa Rica implemented the law in the late 1880s—when large numbers of Afro-Caribbeans immigrated (mainly from Jamaica) to construct the Atlantic Railroad—but abolished it in the 1949 constitution.

GETTING HERE AND AROUND
Siquirres lies just off the main highway and is easily accessible from the east, west, or south (if you're arriving from Turrialba). Grupo Caribeños buses connect San José's Gran Terminal del Caribe with Siquirres several times daily.

ESSENTIALS
Bank/ATM Banco Nacional. ⊠ *50 m south of Acón gas station* ☏ *2768–8128* ⊕ *www.bncr.fi.cr.*

Medical Clinic Centro de Salud de Siquirres. ⊠ *West side of soccer field* ☏ *2768–6138.*

Pharmacy Farmacia Santa Lucía. ⊠ *50 m east of fire station* ☏ *2768–9304.*

Post Office Correos. ⊠ *Across from Guardia Rural* ⊕ *www.correos.go.cr.*

SPORTS AND THE OUTDOORS
RAFTING
Siquirres's proximity to the put-in sites of several classic rafting excursions makes it an ideal place to begin a trip.

Ríos Tropicales. Old standby Ríos Tropicales has tours on a Class III–IV section of the Pacuare River between Siquirres and San Martín, as well as the equally difficult section between Tres Equis and Siquirres. Not quite so wild is the nearby El Carmen section (billed as Class II+) of the Reventazón. Day excursions normally begin in San José, but if you're out in this part of the country, you can kick off your outing here at the company's operations center in Siquirres. Ríos Tropicales also offers multiday rafting excursions of the rivers in this part of the country. ⊠ *On the hwy.* ☏ *2233–6455, 866/722–8273 in North America* ⊕ *www.riostropicales.com* ✉ *$99 day trip, including transportation from San José, breakfast, and lunch; 4 days (3 nights) from $420.*

TORTUGUERO

30 mins by air and 4 hrs by road and boat northeast of San José.

Some compare these dense layers of green set off by brilliantly colored flowers—a vision doubled by the jungle's reflection in mirror-smooth canals—to the Amazon. That might be stretching it, but there's still an Indiana Jones mystique to the journey up here, especially when you get off the main canals and into the narrower lagoons. The region remains one of those Costa Rican anomalies: roadless and remote, it's nevertheless one of the country's most visited places. The tourism seasons here are defined not by the rains or lack thereof (with 200 inches of rain annually, Tortuguero is wet most of the year) but by the months of prime turtle hatching.

The stretch of beach between the Colorado and Matina rivers was first mentioned as a nesting ground for sea turtles in a 1592 Dutch chronicle. Nearly a century earlier, Christopher Columbus compared traversing the north Caribbean coast and its swimming turtles to navigating through rocks. Because the area is so isolated—there's no road here to this day—the turtles nested undisturbed for centuries. By the

NICARAGUA CANAL?

During the 1840s' California gold rush, the Río San Juan, which forms much of the border between Costa Rica and Nicaragua, became an important crossroads allowing miners and gold to move between New York and San Francisco some 70 years before the Panama Canal opened. Cornelius Vanderbilt financed the dredging of the waterway to allow ships to pass up the river to Lake Nicaragua. From here a rail line connected to the Pacific Ocean. While the Panama Canal is undergoing a much-needed expansion as it marks its centennial, plans are moving ahead to construct a full-fledged canal farther north through Nicaragua. A Chinese-backed investment group has announced plans to finance the $40 billion project, and ground has been broken, but a completion date is still anyone's guess. Shock waves in the Chinese economy during 2016 have dimmed hopes that the project can be completed on schedule. Stay tuned.

mid-1900s, however, the harvesting of eggs and poaching of turtles had reached such a level that these creatures faced extinction. In 1963 an executive decree regulated the hunting of turtles and the gathering of eggs, and in 1970 the government established Tortuguero National Park; modern Tortuguero bases its economy on tourism.

In 1970 a system of canals running parallel to the shoreline was constructed to provide safer access to the region than the dangerous journey up the seacoast. You can continue up the canals, natural and man-made, that begin in Moín, near Limón, and run all the way to Tortuguero. Or you can embark at various points north of Guápiles and Siquirres, as do public transportation and most of the package tours. (The lodges' minivans bring you from San José to the put-in point, where you continue your journey by boat.)

North of the national park of the same name, the hamlet of Tortuguero is a pleasant little place with 600 inhabitants, two churches, three bars, a handful of souvenir shops, and a small selection of inexpensive lodgings. And one more plus: there are no motor vehicles here, a refreshing change from the traffic woes that plague the rest of Costa Rica. You can also take a stroll on the 32-km (20-mile) beach, but avoid swimming here because of strong riptides and large numbers of bull sharks and barracuda.

GETTING HERE AND AROUND

It's easier than you'd think to get to remote Tortuguero. Flying is the quickest (and most expensive) option. Nature Air and SANSA provide early-morning flights to and from San José. Both flights stop in Limón on their way up here, but fly nonstop back to San José.

If you're staying at one of the lodges, its boat will meet you at the airstrip.

The big lodges all have packages that include transportation from and back to San José, along with lodging, meals, and tours. Guide-staffed minivans pick you up at your San José hotel and drive you to their own put-in site, usually somewhere north of Siquirres, where you board a covered boat for the final leg on the canals to Tortuguero. The trip entails sightseeing and animal viewing. The trip back to San José stops only for a lunch break. This is the classic "leave the driving to them" way to get to Tortuguero.

A boat from the port of Moín, near Limón, is the traditional budget method of getting to Tortuguero if you are already on the Caribbean coast. Arrive at the docks before 10 am and you should be able to find someone to take you there. The going price is $40 per person each way, and travel time is about three hours.

If you arrive in Moín in your own vehicle, JAPDEVA, Costa Rica's Atlantic port authority, operates a secure, guarded parking facility for your car while you are in Tortuguero.

San José–based Jungle Tom Safaris offers one-way van-boat shuttle service between the capital and Tortuguero ($45), as well as to and from Cahuita, Puerto Viejo de Talamanca, and La Fortuna. Meal stops along the way are at your expense.

It's entirely possible to make the trip independently via public transportation from San José, and it's a good option if you are staying in the village rather than at a lodge. A direct bus departs from San José's Gran Terminal del Caribe to Cariari, north of Guápiles, at 9 am. At Cariari, disembark and walk five blocks to the local terminal, where you can board an 11:30 am bus for the small crossroads of La Pavona. From here, boats leave at 1 pm to take you to Tortuguero, arriving around 3 pm. La Pavona has secure parking facilities. The charge is $10 per night. The Cariari–La Pavona–Tortuguero bus-boat service is provided by COOPETRACA or Viajes Clic-Clic for $10 one way. They operate jointly, alternating days, and honor one another's tickets. Cariari has only spartan accommodation; La Pavona has none.

Bus Contacts COOPETRACA. ☎ *2767–7137.* **Jungle Tom Safaris.** ☎ *2221–7878* ⊕ *www.jungletomsafaris.com.* **Viajes Clic-Clic.** ☎ *2709–8155, 8844–0463, 8308–2006.*

■**TIP➔ If you can, avoid Rubén Bananero, a company that provides bus-boat transportation from Cariari.** Its aggressive agents begin to hustle you the minute you get off the bus in Cariari (Bananero even maintains an information booth at the Gran Terminal del Caribe bus station in San José). They'll pressure you into buying a round-trip ticket, limiting your return options, and do everything they can to steer you toward hotels that pay them a commission. Others will also try to take you to their own dedicated "information dock" in the village, steering you toward their own guides. If you've made advance reservations for guides or hotels, be firm and say, *"No, gracias."*

Water taxis provide transportation from multiple points in the village to the lodges. Expect to pay about $3 to $5 per trip.

ESSENTIALS

This unstaffed kiosk with free brochures offers information on the town's history, the park, turtles, and other wildlife.

Visitor Information Kiosk. ⊠ *Town center.*

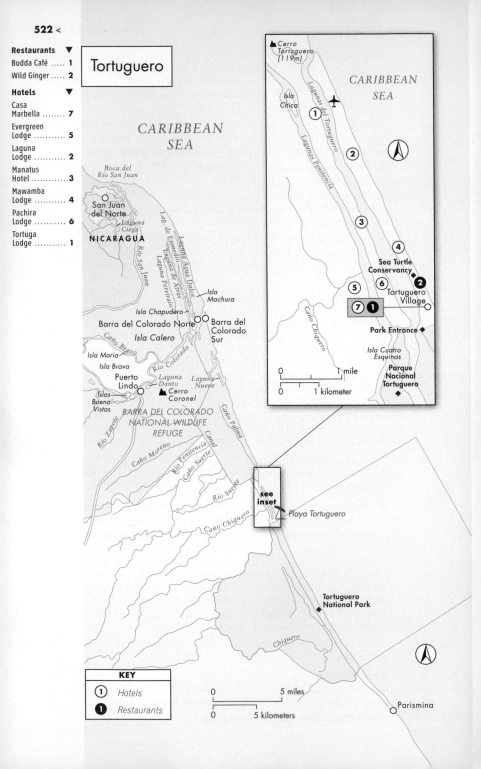

EXPLORING

Sea Turtle Conservancy. Florida's Sea Turtle Conservancy runs a visitor center and a museum with excellent animal photos, a video narrating local and natural history, and detailed discussions of the latest ecological goings-on and what you can do to help. There's a souvenir shop next door. For the committed ecotourist, the **John H. Phipps Biological Field Station,** which is affiliated with the conservancy and has been operating in Tortuguero since 1959, has camping areas and dorm-style quarters with a communal kitchen. If you want to get involved in the life of the turtles, helping researchers to track turtle migration (current research, using satellite technology, has tracked turtles as far as the Florida Keys), or want to help catalog the population of neotropical migrant birds, arrange a stay in advance through the center's offices in Florida. ⊠ *From beach at north end of village, walk north along path and watch for sign* ☎ *2709– 8091, 352/373–6441 in North America* ⊕ *www.conserveturtles.org* 🖃 *$1* ⊙ *Mon.–Sat. 8–4, Sun. 9–5.*

> **DID YOU KNOW?**
>
> Some people still believe turtle eggs to be an aphrodisiacal delicacy, and some bars around Costa Rica (illegally) serve them as snacks. It's a big part of the human contribution to the turtles' disappearance.

FAMILY
Fodor's Choice
★

Tortuguero National Park (*Parque Nacional Tortuguero*). There is no better place in Costa Rica to observe sea turtles nesting, hatching, and scurrying to the ocean. The July–October nesting season for the green turtle is Tortuguero's most popular time to visit. Toss in the hawksbill, loggerhead, and leatherback—the three other species of sea turtle that nest here, although to a lesser extent—and you expand the season from February through October. You can undertake night tours only with an authorized guide, who will be the only person in your party with a light, and that will be a light with a red covering. Photography, flash or otherwise, is strictly prohibited. The sight of a mother turtle furiously digging in the sand to bury her eggs is amazing, even from several yards away, and the spectacle of a wave of hatchlings scurrying out to sea is simply magnificent. *For more information see the highlighted listing in this chapter.* ⊠ *Tortuguero* ⊹ *south of village* ☎ *2710–2929* 🖃 *$15* ⊙ *Daily 6–6.*

BEACHES

Playa Tortuguero. The crashing waves and misty air (it rains a lot in Tortuguero) give you the unsettling feeling that you're standing at the edge of the world. Swimming and surfing are simply not possible here— sharks can be an issue along this stretch of coast, for one thing—but by night, depending on the season, this beach comes alive with the age-old ritual of Tortuguero's four species of sea turtles laying and burying their eggs. They then hatch and the baby turtles scurry out to sea, a spectacle that's viewable only in the company of a licensed guide. Sunbathing? People-watching? Who needs that when this is the real show? **Amenities:** none. **Best for:** solitude; sunrise; walking. ⊠ *North of Tortuguero village.*

SPORTS AND THE OUTDOORS

TOUR GUIDES AND OPERATORS

Tortuguero is one of those "everybody's a guide" places. Quality varies, but most guides are quite knowledgeable. If you stay at one of the lodges, guided tours are usually included in your package price (check when you book). If you hire a private guide, $15–$20 per person per hour is the going rate depending on the excursion, with most lasting three hours.

Daryl Loth. Canadian-born naturalist Daryl Loth has a wealth of information about the area and conducts boat excursions on the canals and, with advance notice, responsible turtle-watching tours in season. ⊠ *Tortuguero* ☎ *8833–0827, 2709–8011* ✉ *safari@racsa.co.cr.*

Riverboat Francesca. Local indigenous Miskito guide Modesto Watson is legendary for his bird- and animal-spotting skills as well as for his howler-monkey imitations. The family's riverboat, *Francesca,* can take you up the canals for two-day, one-night excursions to Tortuguero for $200–$220 per person, depending on the lodge used. As with all Tortuguero excursions, Watson offers a more leisurely three-day, two-night trip as well. If you're interested only in seeing the canals, a four-hour tour ($75) includes lunch. Trips begin at the Caribbean port of Moín, 5 km (3 miles) northwest of Limón. ☎ *2226–0986 in San José, 8843–8504, 810/433–1410 in North America* ⊕ *www.tortuguerocanals.com.*

Sea Turtle Conservancy. Call or stop by the visitor center at the Sea Turtle Conservancy to get a recommendation for good local guides. ⊠ *Tortuguero* ☎ *2709–8091, 352/373–6441 in North America* ⊕ *www. conserveturtles.org.*

Victor Barrantes. Local guide and area expert Victor Barrantes conducts hiking and boating tours around the area. ⊠ *Tortuguero* ☎ *2709–8055, 8928–1169* ✉ *tortuguero_info@racsa.co.cr.*

FISHING

You have your choice of mackerel, tarpon, snook, and snapper if you fish in the ocean; snook and calba if you fish in the canals. If you opt for the latter, the National Parks Service levies a $30 license fee (you are fishing in the confines of Tortuguero National Park), good for one month. Operators include the fee in your tour price.

Eddie Brown. Longtime area fishing expert Eddie Brown and his brother Roberto are based out of Tortuga Lodge and have half-day fishing packages for $298; daylong excursions are $600. ⊠ *Tortuguero* ☎ *2709–8136* ⊕ *www.tortugalodge.com.*

Tortuguero Sport Fishing. Known as "Primo" to everyone in town, Elvin Gutiérrez takes two passengers out on the ocean for two hours or more, at $75 per hour, or for a full nine-hour day ($500). Prices include boat, guide, and refreshments. ⊠ *Tortuguero* ☎ *2709–8115* ⊕ *www. tortuguerosportfish.com.*

TURTLE-WATCHING

If you want to watch the *deshove* (egg laying), contact your hotel or the parks office to hire a certified local guide, required on turtle-watching excursions. The Turtle Scout Program, affiliated with the Sea Turtle

9

The magnificent Emerald Basilisk is just one of the creatures found in Tortuguero Park.

Conservancy, maintains a network of knowledgeable guides and has cut out a route of less obtrusive trails that minimize long walks on the beach, all to the benefit of the turtles. Note that you won't be allowed to use a camera—flash or nonflash—on the beach, and only your guide is permitted to use a flashlight (and that must be covered with red plastic), because lights can deter the turtles from nesting. Wear dark clothing if you can and avoid loud talking. Smoking is prohibited on the tours. ■TIP➜ A few unscrupulous locals will offer to take you on a turtle-watching tour outside the allowed February-through-November season, disturbing sensitive nesting sites in the process. If it's not the season, don't go on a turtle excursion. As the signs around town admonish: "Don't become another predator."

WHERE TO EAT

If you stay at one of the big lodges up here, your meals will be included in your package price, both in Tortuguero and on your way to and from. Usually *not* included in package prices are alcoholic beverages, soda, and bottled water. Ask to be sure.

If you're staying in town, you have a few simple, but satisfying, restaurant options.

$ ✕ **Budda Café.** Pizza, crepes, pastas, and fresh fish are on the menu at
ITALIAN this small, canal-side café in the center of town. Lattice wood over the windows, a thatched roof, and, not surprisingly, a Buddha statue make up the furnishings. Jazzy cha-cha or a Dean Martin ballad might be

playing in the background. ⑤ *Average main: $8* ✉ *Next to ICE Bldg.* ☎ *2709–8084* ⊕ *www.buddacafe.com* ⊟ *No credit cards.*

$$$
COSTA RICAN
Fodor'sChoice
★

✕ **Wild Ginger.** The owners of this small place at the north end of the village call their cuisine "California–Costa Rican fusion." This is the area's most upscale dining option, but it's still Tortuguero, so surroundings are pretty simple. You'll be seated at tables (with tablecloths—not common up here) indoors or on a pleasant terrace overlooking the garden. Start out with an appetizer or ceviche (fish marinated in lemon juice), or plantains in a black-bean dip. Move on to main courses such as chicken breast with apple curry or lobster in ginger-garlic sauce. Finish things off with the sole item on the dessert menu, the *volcán,* a rich chocolate-espresso cake with fruit and caramel sauce on the side. These folks also operate the Wild Ginger Café, near the center of the village, with a selection of coffees, sundaes, milk shakes, smoothies, and brownies. ⑤ *Average main: $18* ✉ *North end of village* ☎ *2709–8240* ⊕ *www.wildgingercr.com* ⊗ *Closed Tues. No lunch* ⊟ *No credit cards.*

WHERE TO STAY

The big lodges here offer one- or two-night excursion packages, and, given the choreography it takes to get up here, you should opt for a more leisurely two-night stay if you can. Rates look expensive at first glance, but prices include everything from guides, tours, meals, and snacks to minivan and boat transportation, and in some cases air travel from and back to San José. The $15 entrance fee to Tortuguero National Park may or may not be included in the package price; ask to make sure. If you calculate what you get, the price is actually quite reasonable, and the tours are undeniably great fun. Few of the lodges have phones, although all have radio contact with the outside world. All reservations must be made with their offices in San José. Be sure to travel light; you get a baggage allowance of 25 pounds, strictly enforced. There's simply no space in the boats for you to bring more. Since you're likely returning to San José at the completion of your Tortuguero tour, your hotel in the capital may allow you to store your bigger bags there. Ask ahead of time.

$
B&B/INN
Fodor'sChoice
★

🛏 **Casa Marbella.** This B&B, the best of the in-town lodgings, is a real find, and the owner, Canadian-born naturalist Daryl Loth, is a virtual encyclopedia of all things Tortuguero and one of the community's biggest boosters. **Pros:** knowledgeable, enthusiastic owner; immaculate rooms. **Cons:** some pedestrian street noise; no access to lodge-package amenities of big lodges; can be difficult to find availability. ⑤ *Rooms from: $45* ✉ *Across from Catholic church* ☎ *2709–8011* ⊕ *casamarbella.tripod.com* ⊟ *No credit cards* ➦ *11 rooms* ⑩ *Breakfast.*

$$$$
RESORT
Fodor'sChoice
★

🛏 **Evergreen Lodge.** The Evergreen offers an entirely different (and intimate) concept in Tortuguero lodging: whereas other lodges have cabins arranged around a clearing, at Evergreen they penetrate deep into the forest. **Pros:** seclusion from other lodges; lush wooded setting. **Cons:** rustic rooms; farther from town than other lodges. ⑤ *Rooms from: $458* ✉ *2 km (1 mile) from Tortuguero village on Canal Penitencia*

9

☎ 2222–6841 *in San José, 800/644–7438 in North America* ⊕ *www. evergreentortuguero.com* ⊲ *55 cabins* ⦿ *All-inclusive.*

$$$$ ⊞ **Laguna Lodge.** Laguna is the largest of the Tortuguero lodges, with a
RESORT mix of concrete and wood buildings spread out over 12 acres of grounds on a thin sliver of land between the ocean and the first canal inland, and it hums with activity. **Pros:** many activities; unique architecture. **Cons:** large numbers of guests; not for those who crave solitude. ⑤ *Rooms from: $479* ⊠ *Between ocean and first canal inland* ☎ *2709–8082, 2272–4943 in San José, 888/259–5615 in North America* ⊕ *www. lagunatortuguero.com* ⊲ *110 rooms* ⦿ *All-inclusive.*

$$$$ ⊞ **Manatus Hotel.** Amenities such as air-conditioning, satellite television,
RESORT fitness centers, Wi-Fi, and spa treatments are typically not found in Tortuguero, but the area's most luxurious hotel has them all. **Pros:** intimate surroundings; numerous creature comforts not ordinarily found here. **Cons:** fills up quickly in high season; degree of luxury may feel out of place in Tortuguero. ⑤ *Rooms from: $540* ⊠ *Across river, about 1 km (½ mile) north of village* ☎ *2709–8197, 2239–4854 in San José* ⊕ *www. manatuscostarica.com* ⊲ *12 rooms* ⦿ *All-inclusive.*

$$$$ ⊞ **Mawamba Lodge.** Nestled between the river and the ocean, Mawamba
RESORT is the perfect place to kick back and relax, and it is also the only jungle lodge within walking distance (about 10 minutes) of town. **Pros:** many activities; walking distance to village. **Cons:** rustic rooms; not for those who crave solitude. ⑤ *Rooms from: $460* ⊠ *½ km (¼ mile) north of Tortuguero on ocean side of canal* ☎ *2709–8181, 2293–8181 in San José* ⊕ *www.grupomawamba.com* ⊲ *58 cabinas* ⦿ *All-inclusive.*

$$$$ ⊞ **Pachira Lodge.** This is the prettiest of Tortuguero's lodges, but not
RESORT the costliest—the owners here market competitively and keep prices
Fodor's Choice reasonable. **Pros:** many activities; good value; beautiful surroundings;
★ turtle-shaped pool. **Cons:** large numbers of guests; can be difficult to find space; not for those who crave solitude. ⑤ *Rooms from: $458* ⊠ *Across river from Sea Turtle Conservancy* ☎ *8830–9956, 2257–2242 in San José, 800/644–7438 in North America* ⊕ *www.pachiralodge.com* ⊲ *88 rooms* ⦿ *All-inclusive.*

$$$$ ⊞ **Tortuga Lodge.** Lush lawns, orchids, and tropical trees surround
RESORT this thatched riverside lodge owned by Costa Rica Expeditions and
Fodor's Choice renowned for its nature packages and top-notch, personalized service.
★ **Pros:** many activities; seclusion from other lodges; top-notch guides; air transfers via chartered flights; upscale clientele. **Cons:** rustic rooms; this is farther from the park than most lodges in the area. ⑤ *Rooms from: $356* ⊠ *Across the river from airstrip, 2 km (1 mile) from village* ☎ *2709–8136, 2257–0766 in San José* ⊕ *www.tortugalodge.com* ⊲ *27 rooms* ⦿ *All-inclusive.*

SOUTHERN CARIBBEAN COAST

The landscape along the Guápiles Highway changes from farmland to tropics as you approach the port city of Limón. Place names change, too. You'll see signs to towns called Bristol, Stratford, and Liverpool, reflecting the region's British Caribbean heritage. At first look, tourist havens par excellence Cahuita and Puerto Viejo de Talamanca still

Fish You'll Find

GASPAR (alligator gar), found in Barra del Colorado River and Lake Arenal, look like a holdover from prehistoric times and have long narrow snouts full of sharp teeth; they make great sport on light tackle. Gar meat is firm and sweet (some say shrimplike), but the eggs are toxic to humans.

MARLIN AND SAILFISH migrate northward through the year, beginning about November, when they are plentiful in the Golfito region. From December into April they spread north to Quepos, which has some of the country's best deep-sea fishing, and are present in large numbers along the Nicoya Peninsula at Carrillo and Sámara from February to April, and near Tamarindo and Flamingo from May to September. Pacific sailfish average more than 45 kilos (100 pounds), and are usually fought on a 15-pound line or less. Costa Rican laws require that all sailfish be released and bans sportsfishers from bringing them on board for photo ops.

GUAPOTE (rainbow bass) make their home in Lake Arenal. It's a hard-hitting catch: 5- to 6-pounders are common. Taxonomically, guapote are not related to bass, but are caught similarly, by casting or flipping plugs or spinner bait. Streams near the Cerro de la Muerte, off the Pan-American Highway leading south from San José, are stocked with guapote. The fish tend to be small, but the scenery makes a day here worthwhile.

TARPON AND SNOOK fishing are big on the Caribbean coast, centered at the mouth of the Barra del Colorado River. The acrobatic tarpon, which averages about 38 kilos (85 pounds) here, is able to swim freely between salt water and freshwater and is considered by many to be the most exciting catch on earth. Tarpon sometimes strike like a rocket, hurtling 5 meters (16 feet) into the air, flipping, and twisting left and right. Anglers say the success rate of experts is to land about 1 out of every 10 tarpon hooked. In the Colorado, schools of up to 100 tarpon following and feeding on schools of titi (small, sardinelike fish) travel for more than 160 km (100 miles) to Lake Nicaragua. The long-standing International Game Fishing Association all-tackle record was taken in this area.

9

resemble the cluttered beach towns first discovered by European backpackers more than two decades ago. But both have grown up and now offer a terrific selection of fine dining and gracious lodging to complement the beaches, surfing, partying, and nature for which this area has long been known.

LIMÓN

100 km (62 miles) southeast of Guápiles, 160 km (100 miles) north and east of San José.

The colorful Afro-Caribbean flavor of one of Costa Rica's most important ports (population 90,000) is the first sign of life for seafaring visitors to Costa Rica's east coast. Limón (sometimes called "Puerto Limón") is a lively, if shabby, town with a 24-hour street life. Most travelers do not stop here, heading immediately to Cahuita and Puerto

Viejo de Talamanca farther south. The wooden houses are brightly painted, but the grid-plan streets look rather worn, partly because of the damage caused by a 1991 earthquake. Street crime, including pick-pocketing and nighttime mugging, is not uncommon here. Long charged with neglecting the city, the national government continually promises to turn new attention to Limón, although the results never match residents' expectations.

Limón receives thousands of visitors every year, owing in large part to its newest incarnation as a port of call. Azamara, Carnival, Celebrity, Cunard, Holland America, Norwegian, Oceania, P&O, Princess, Pullmantur, Regent Seven Seas, and Silversea cruise ships all dock here on select Panama Canal or western Caribbean itineraries. (Pullmantur offers the option to begin and end your cruise in Limón.) The downtown Terminal de Cruceros hums with activity between October and May, with one or two boats daily during the peak season (December through March). This is the place to find telephones, Internet cafés, manicurists (they do quite a brisk business), a tourist-information booth, and tour-operator stands, too. The terminal contains souvenir stands staffed by low-key vendors who invite you to look, but they don't pester you if your answer is *"No, gracias."* Much to the chagrin of local businesses, most cruise passengers exit their ships and head out on organized shore excursions, seeing the town only through the windows of their tour vans. This has become an increasingly common complaint among residents of Costa Rica's ports of call who were promised an economic boom when the ships arrived.

GETTING HERE AND AROUND

If you're driving to the Caribbean coast, you'll pass through Limón. The Guápiles Highway that began in San José ends here at the ocean but bypasses the heart of downtown by a couple of blocks. Budget about 3½ hours for the trip. Just after the sign to "Sixaola" and the coastal highway south to Cahuita and Puerto Viejo de Talamanca is the city center. The Autotransportes Caribeños bus terminal lies at Avenida 2 and Calle 8, across from the soccer stadium, and serves routes from San José, Guápiles, and Siquirres, with buses arriving several times daily from each. Opt for the *directo* (express) service from San José rather than the *corriente* buses, which make many stops along the route. Buses to Cahuita and Puerto Viejo de Talamanca and all points on the south coast arrive and depart at the Autotransportes MEPE terminal, 200 meters east of the turnoff to the southern coastal highway.

Both Nature Air and SANSA fly daily nonstop from San José to the small airport just south of Limón on the highway to Cahuita and Puerto Viejo de Talamanca. The return flight stops in Tortuguero before returning to the capital.

Avenidas (avenues) run east and west, and *calles* (streets) north and south, but Limón's street-numbering system differs from that of other Costa Rican cities. "Number one" of each avenida and calle begins at the water, and numbers increase sequentially as you move inland, unlike the evens-on-one-side, odds-on-the-other scheme used in San José. But the scarcity of street signs means everyone uses landmarks anyway.

Official red taxis ply the streets or wait at designated taxi stands near Parque Vargas, the Mercado Municipal, and, naturally, the cruise-ship terminal.

ESSENTIALS

Banks/ATMs BAC San José. ⊠ *Avda. 3, Cs. 2–3* ☎ *2798-0155* ⊕ *www.bac.net.* **Banco Nacional.** ⊠ *Avda. 2, Cs. 3–4* ☎ *2758-0094* ⊕ *www.bncr.fi.cr.* **Scotiabank.** ⊠ *Avda. 3 and C. 2* ☎ *2798-0009* ⊕ *www.scotiabankcr.com.*

Hospital Hospital Dr. Tony Facio. ⊠ *Hwy. to Portete* ☎ *2758-2222.*

Pharmacy Farmacia Británica. ⊠ *East side of Maxi Bodega* ☎ *2798-1671.*

Post Office Correos. ⊠ *Avda. 2 and C. 4* ⊕ *www.correos.go.cr.*

Visitor Information JAPDEVA (*Atlantic Port Authority*). ⊠ *Terminal de Cruceros* ⊕ *www.japdeva.go.cr.*

EXPLORING

Cemetery. On the left side of the highway as you enter Limón is a large cemetery. A glance as you pass by is probably enough, but notice the "Colonia China" ("Chinese colony") and corresponding sign in Chinese on the hill in the cemetery: Chinese workers made up a large part of the 1880s railroad-construction team that worked here. Thousands died of malaria and yellow fever. ⊠ *Limón.*

Municipal Market (*Mercado Municipal*). A couple of blocks west of the north side of Parque Vargas is the lively enclosed Municipal Market, where you can buy fruit for the road ahead and experience the sights, sounds, and smells of a Central American market. The hustle and bustle of a crowded market always means a risk of pickpockets. Watch your things. ⊠ *Pedestrian mall, Avda. 2, Cs. 3–4.*

Parque Vargas. The aquamarine wooden port building faces the cruise terminal, and just to the east lies the city's palm-lined seaside park, Parque Vargas. From the promenade facing the ocean you can see the raised dead coral left stranded by the 1991 earthquake. Ten or so Hoffman's two-toed sloths live in the trees of Parque Vargas; ask a passerby to point them out, as spotting them requires a trained eye. ⊠ *Limón.*

Standard Fruit Company. The ins and outs of Costa Rica's favorite yellow fruit are on display at this banana plantation and packing plant in Bananito, just south of Limón. The hour-long tour is geared primarily toward cruise passengers. A longer tour takes place at a larger installation near Puerto Viejo de Sarapiquí in northern Costa Rica. Standard Fruit does business as "Dole" in North America. ⊠ *Bananito* ☎ *8383-4596* ⊕ *www.bananatourcostarica.com* ☉ *By reservation.*

FAMILY
Fodor'sChoice
★
Veragua Rainforest Eco-Adventure. Limón's hottest attraction is a 4,000-acre nature theme park, about 30 minutes west of the city. It's popular with cruise-ship passengers in port for the day and is well worth a stop if you're in the area. Veragua's great strength is its small army of enthusiastic, super-informed guides who take you through a network of nature trails and exhibits of hummingbirds, snakes, frogs, butterflies, and other insects. A gondola ride overlooks the complex and transports you through the rain-forest canopy. A branch of the Original Canopy Tour, with nine platforms rising 46 meters (150 feet) above the forest

floor, is here. The zip-line tour is not included in the basic admission to the park. Packages including transportation (a minimum of two people) can be arranged to and from San José (admittedly a very long trip), to and from Puerto Viejo de Talamanca, or starting out at one and ending at the other. ✉ *Veragua de Liverpool, 15 km (9 miles) west of Limón* ☎ *2296–5056 in San José, 4000–0949* ⊕ *www.veraguarainforest.com* ✆ *Full-day tour $66; with canopy tour $99; with transportation (does not include canopy tour): from San José $149; from Puerto Viejo de Talamanca $99* ⊙ *Tues.–Sun. 8–3 and Mondays when cruise ships are in port in Limón.*

SPORTS AND THE OUTDOORS
TOUR OPERATOR
Mambo Tour. In addition to horseback riding, white-water rafting, and snorkeling or scuba diving, these folks can take you on three- to eight-hour excursions around the region, and even on an all-day trip to the Rain Forest Aerial Tram or San José. ✉ *Terminal de Cruceros* ☎ *8997– 4198* ⊕ *www.mambotour.com* ✆ *From $30.*

SHOPPING
The cruise-ship terminal contains an orderly maze of souvenir stands. Vendors are friendly; there's no pressure to buy.

Congo. The small Congo chain of gift shops has an outlet at the Veragua Rainforest Eco-Adventure park, with a good selection of crafts made by Costa Rican artisans. The shop is accessible only if you've paid admission to the park. ✉ *Veragua de Liverpool, 15 km (9 miles) west of Limón* ⊕ *www.costaricacongo.com* ⊙ *Tues.–Sun. 9–3.*

CAHUITA

44 km (26 miles) southeast of Limón.

Dusty Cahuita (pronounced *cah-WEE-tah*), its main street flanked by wooden-slat cabins, is a backpackers' vacation town—a hippie hangout with a dash of Afro-Caribbean spice tossed in. Tucked in among the backpackers' digs are a few surprisingly nice get-away-from-it-all lodgings, and restaurants with some tasty cuisine at decent prices. After years of negative crime-related publicity, Cahuita has beefed up security—this is one of the few places in the country where you will be conscious of a visible and reassuring, though not oppressive, police presence—and has made a well-deserved comeback on the tourist circuit. No question that nearby Puerto Viejo de Talamanca has overtaken Cahuita and become the hottest spot on the southern Caribbean coast. But as Puerto Viejo grows exponentially, Cahuita's appeal is that it remains small and manageable. It's well worth a look.

GETTING HERE AND AROUND
Autotransportes MEPE buses travel from San José's Terminal Atlántico Norte four times a day, and approximately hourly throughout the day from Limón and Puerto Viejo de Talamanca. The bus terminal sits at the entrance to Cahuita, about four blocks from the town center. You can give yourself a wider selection of times than the four daily San José–Cahuita services: hourly Grupo Caribeños buses connect San José

with Limón, and hourly MEPE buses connect Limón with Cahuita. The MEPE and Caribeños terminals are one block apart in Limón. Walking could be an option if you're not laden with bags and if it's still light out. Unlike MEPE vehicles, Caribeños buses are air-conditioned.

Car travel is straightforward: watch for signs in Limón and head 45 minutes south on the coastal highway. Road conditions fluctuate with the severity of the previous year's rains and with the speed at which highway crews patch the potholes (the road's blacktop surface makes it a never-ending battle). Cahuita has three entrances from the highway: the first takes you to the far north end of the Playa Negra road, near the Magellan Inn; the second, to the middle section of Playa Negra, near the Atlántida Lodge; and the third, to the tiny downtown.

The proximity of the Panamanian border means added police vigilance on the coastal highway. No matter what your mode of travel, expect a passport inspection and cursory vehicle search at a police checkpoint just north of Cahuita. If you're on public transportation, you may be required to disembark from the bus while it is searched.

NAVIGATING CAHUITA Cahuita's tiny center is quite walkable, if dusty in the dry season and muddy in the wet season once you get off the few paved streets. It's about a 30-minute walk to the end of the Playa Negra road to Hotel La Diosa. Always take a taxi to or from Playa Negra and Playa Grande after dark. Cahuita has a couple of officially licensed red taxis, but most transportation is provided informally by private individuals. To be on the safe side, have your hotel or restaurant call a driver for you.

Bicycles are a popular means of utilitarian transportation in Cahuita. Seemingly everyone rents basic touring bikes for $10 per day, but quality varies widely—and note that no one rents helmets.

ESSENTIALS

Bank/ATM Banco de Costa Rica. ⊠ *Bus terminal at entrance to town* ☏ *2755–0401.*

Pharmacy Farmacia Cahuita. ⊠ *Bus terminal* ☏ *2755–0505.*

Post Office Correos. ⊠ *Bus terminal* ⊕ *www.correos.go.cr.*

EXPLORING

FAMILY Fodor's Choice ★ **Sloth Sanctuary of Costa Rica.** A full-fledged nature center a few miles northwest of Cahuita is well worth a stop. Many of the sloths that live on the premises are here because of illness or injury and are not on display to the public, but Buttercup, the very first of their charges, holds court in the nature-focused gift shop. She has been joined by Leno, a Bradypus male—that's one of the two sloth species found in Costa Rica—who can be found in the aquarium. A visit is a good way to learn about these little-known animals, though numerous requests from visitors to hold or pet the sloths have to be turned down. Your admission includes a two-hour tour (no reservations are needed) and contributes to further care and research by the good-hearted folks who operate the facility. Reservations are required for a special insider's tour that takes you behind the scenes into the sloth clinic and nursery. ⊠ *9 km (5 miles) northwest of Cahuita, follow signs on Río Estrella delta*

9

CLOSE UP

The Old Atlantic Railroad

Christopher Columbus became the Caribbean's (and the country's) first tourist when he landed at Uvita Island near Limón during his fourth voyage to the New World in 1502. But the region was already home to thriving, if small, communities of Kekoldi, Bribri, and Cabécar indigenous peoples. If Costa Rica was an isolated backwater, its Caribbean coastal region remained even more remote from colonial times through most of the 19th century.

New York industrialist Minor Keith changed all that in 1871 with his plan to launch the British-funded Atlantic Railroad, a mode of transportation that would permit easier export of coffee and bananas to Europe. Such a project required a massive labor force, and thousands of West Indians, Asians, and Italians were brought to Costa Rica to construct the 522-km (335-mile) railroad from Limón to San José. Thousands are reputed to have died of yellow fever, malaria, and snakebite during construction of the project. Those who survived were paid relatively well, however, and by the 1930s many Afro-Caribbean residents owned their own small plots of land. When the price of cacao rose in the 1950s, they emerged as comfortable

landowners. Not that they had much choice about going elsewhere: until the Civil War of 1948, black Costa Ricans were forbidden from crossing into the Central Valley lest they upset the country's racial balance, and they were thus prevented from moving when United Fruit abandoned many of its blight-ridden northern Caribbean plantations in the 1930s for green-field sites on the Pacific plain.

Costly upkeep of rail service, construction of the Braulio Carrillo Highway to the coast, declining banana production, and an earthquake that rocked the region in 1991 all sounded the death knell for the railroad. The earthquake was also a wake-up call for many here. The time it took for aid to reach stricken areas symbolized the central government's historic neglect of the region. Development has been slow to reach this part of the country. As elsewhere in the country, communities now look to tourism to put colones in the coffers. San José has resurrected commuter-rail service within the metro area, and a few folks out here hold out faint hopes that Caribbean train service will start up once again, but that's likely a long way off.

☎ 2750–0775 ⊕ www.slothsanctuary.com ✉ $30, including 2-hr tour; Insider Tour $150 ⊙ Tues.–Sun. 8–2:30.

FAMILY **Tree of Life Wildlife Rescue Center** (*El Árbol de Vida*). Capuchin and howler monkeys, peccaries, sloths, iguanas, raccoons—they're all here at this wildlife sanctuary just off the Playa Negra road. As much as possible, the goal is to reintroduce these rescued animals back to nature, although the fragile condition of some means this will be their permanent home. Your admission supports the good work these folks do. ⊠ 3 km (2 miles) north of town at end of Playa Negra road ☎ 2755–0014 ⊕ www.treeoflifecostarica.com ✉ $15 ⊙ Nov.–Easter and July–Aug. by guided tour at 11.

BEACHES

Playa Blanca (*White Beach*). Costa Rica's Caribbean coast has no true white-sand beaches, but Cahuita's in-town beach is as close as it gets (*blanca* means "white" in Spanish). Right at the town entrance to the national park, you're a few steps from local eateries. The park's jungle comes right up to the beach's edge, creating one of those postcard-perfect views. The undertow can be strong here; swimmers are more likely to venture out near the center of the beach. Use caution in any case. **Amenities:** food and drink. **Best for:** sunrise; walking. ⊠ *Town center.*

Playa Grande. Beyond the Atlántida Lodge, Playa Negra's black sand lightens to a dark brown. Whether this constitutes a separate beach or not is open for debate, but the lodgings out here distinguish their stretch of sand as "Playa Grande." You're much farther from town here; the beach feels even more isolated. Do be careful. As with all beaches on this coast, the undertow makes swimming risky. **Amenities:** none. **Best for:** sunrise; walking. ⊠ *Cahuita.*

Playa Negra (*Black Beach*). Cahuita's Playa Negra—it's not the same as the beach of the same name in Puerto Viejo de Talamanca—fronts a narrow road heading north out of the town center. Depending on the stretch of sand, it puts you a few steps from eateries. Your fellow beachgoers are likely to be surfers. Remember: the waves that make for good surfing conditions cause problems for swimming. Most stretches of black-sand Playa Negra feel isolated. If there aren't visitors around, don't linger. **Amenities:** food and drink. **Best for:** sunrise; surfing; walking. ⊠ *Cahuita.*

SPORTS AND THE OUTDOORS

Cahuita is small enough that its tour operators don't focus simply on the town and nearby national park, but instead line up excursions around the region, even as far away as the Tortuguero canals to the north and Bocas del Toro, Panama, to the south.

Brigitte. Here you can rent good bikes for $10 per day, as well as take part in a daylong or multiday horse-riding excursion. Brigitte also offers tours to a nearby indigenous community. ⊠ *Playa Negra road, 1½ km (1 mile) from town* ☎ *2755–0053* ⊕ *www.brigittecahuita.com* ⊠ *Tours from $35.*

Willie's Tours. The town's largest tour operator can set you up with a variety of adventures, including rafting, kayaking, hiking the national park, and visiting indigenous reserves for a glimpse into traditional life. Willie's also offers tours that take you farther afield, north to Tortuguero and south to Bocas del Toro, Panama. ⊠ *Main St., 100 m north of Coco's Bar* ☎ *2755–1024* ⊕ *www.williestourscostarica.com* ⊠ *From $25.*

WHERE TO EAT

$ × **Brigitte.** Fuel up for the day's activities at this informal, open-air café
CAFÉ on the Playa Negra road. A hearty breakfast—served until noon—of banana pancakes and fruit with honey or pineapple jam does the trick. Gallo pinto is on the menu, though most travelers have had their fill of that ubiquitous dish by the time they get to the Caribbean. Omelets, toast, and American-style cereals round out the offerings. ⑤ *Average main: $6* ⊠ *Playa Negra road, 1½ km (1 mile) from town* ☎ *2755–0053* ⊕ *www.brigittecahuita.com* ⊟ *No credit cards* ☉ *No lunch or dinner.*

$ × **Miss Edith.** Miss Edith is revered for her flavorful Caribbean cooking,
CARIBBEAN vegetarian meals, and herbal teas for whatever ails you. She dishes up food at her semi-open-air restaurant on an easy-to-miss street at the north end of town. Jerk chicken and *rondón*, a fish stew, are specialties (the latter is quite labor-intensive; stop by in the afternoon to see if it will be on the menu that night). There is a bit of Christian overlay here—a *Jesús te ama* ("Jesus loves you") sign greets you at the entrance—but nothing about the place crosses a line into proselytizing. ⑤ *Average main: $9* ⊠ *75 m east of police station* ☎ *2755–0248* ⊟ *No credit cards.*

$ × **Pizzeria Cahuita.** Pastas and meat entrées are on the menu, but the real
PIZZA draw here is the 30 varieties of thin-crust pizza whipped up and served with style by a gregarious Italian family from Ravenna. The Cuatro Quesos ("four cheeses") with mozzarella, Gorgonzola, Parmesan, and fontina is the most popular. These folks do a brisk carry-out business, too. ⑤ *Average main: $9* ⊠ *50 m east of police station* ☎ *2755–0179* ☉ *Closed Thurs. No lunch.*

$$ × **Sobre Las Olas.** The name means "over the waves," and this is one
SEAFOOD of the few dining spots in Cahuita perched this close to the shore. Set

along the less busy stretch of Playa Negra (as you head out of town), the admittedly spartan dining area features terrific ocean views that perfectly complement the house specialty, red snapper, as well as a variety of other seafood and pasta dishes. Lunch includes sandwiches and lighter fare. The menu has a good selection of wine and natural fruit juices. $ *Average main: $13* ✉ *Playa Negra road, just north of El Encanto* ☎ *2755–0109* ⊘ *Closed Tues.*

> **RECYCLE!**
>
> Unfortunately, it's difficult to recycle in most places in Costa Rica, but Cahuita and Puerto Viejo de Talamanca have made it a breeze. Separate and deposit your aluminum cans and glass and plastic beverage bottles in the *Recicaribe* barrels you'll see in either community.

WHERE TO STAY

$ **Atlántida Lodge.** Attractively landscaped grounds, the beach across the
HOTEL road, and a large pool are Atlántida's main assets. **Pros:** good value; decent pool. **Cons:** some dark rooms; lackluster staff. $ *Rooms from: $62* ✉ *Next to soccer field at Playa Negra* ☎ *2755–0115* ⟟ *32 rooms, 2 suites* ⵏ⚬ⵏ *No meals.*

$ **Bungalows Aché.** Aché has wooden bungalows—three octagonal struc-
B&B/INN tures in this case—nestled amid wooded grounds that make the close-by town center seem far away. **Pros:** central location; friendly staff. **Cons:** small and spartan rooms. $ *Rooms from: $50* ✉ *180 m west of national park entrance* ☎ *2755–0119* ⊕ *www.bungalowsache.com* ▭ *No credit cards* ⟟ *3 bungalows* ⵏ⚬ⵏ *No meals.*

$$ **El Encanto Hotel and Spa.** Cahuita doesn't get more serene than these
B&B/INN lodgings spread out in a garden with an extensive bromeliad collection.
Fodor's Choice **Pros:** friendly owners; good value for what's offered; central location
★ without being right in the heart of things. **Cons:** not for young travelers looking for a scene. $ *Rooms from: $90* ✉ *200 m west of police station on Playa Negra road* ☎ *2755–0113* ⊕ *www.elencantocahuita.com* ⟟ *2 rooms, 2 suites, 1 apartment, 3 bungalows* ⵏ⚬ⵏ *Breakfast.*

$$ **Hotel La Diosa.** Brightly painted stone or wood cabins—a few have
HOTEL air-conditioning, a rarity here—are scattered around the grounds at this place on the far north end of Playa Grande. **Pros:** seclusion; air-conditioning available. **Cons:** far from sights; small rooms. $ *Rooms from: $85* ✉ *2 km (1 mile) north of town at end of Playa Negra road* ☎ *2755–0055, 800/854–7761 in North America* ⊕ *www.hotelladiosa.com* ⟟ *10 cabins* ⵏ⚬ⵏ *Breakfast.*

$ **Kelly Creek Hotel & Restaurante.** This wonderful budget option in a
B&B/INN handsome wooden hotel has a terrific Spanish restaurant on the creek bank across a short pedestrian bridge from the Cahuita National Park entrance. **Pros:** good value; terrific Spanish restaurant; friendly owners. **Cons:** dark rooms; occasional, but rare, street noise. $ *Rooms from: $65* ✉ *Next to park entrance* ☎ *2755–0007* ⊕ *www.hotelkellycreek.com* ⟟ *4 rooms* ⵏ⚬ⵏ *No meals.*

$$ **Kenaki Lodge.** The rooms and bungalows at this serene lodge have
B&B/INN dark hardwood floors and vaulted ceilings and are decorated with bright tropical colors. **Pros:** quiet seclusion; good value for what's offered.

9

Adventurous anglers flock to Costa Rica to test their will against saltwater fish like this dorado (mahi-mahi).

Cons: far from town and sights; events may create commotion in dining area; breakfast not included in bungalow prices. ⑤ *Rooms from: $100 ✉ Playa Grande, far north end of Playa Negra road ☎ 2755–0485 ⊕ www.kenakilodge.com ⥯ 4 rooms, 2 bungalows* ⑩ *No meals.*

$ **☷ Magellan Inn.** One of Cahuita's most elegant lodgings, this group of
B&B/INN bungalows is graced with tile-floor terraces facing a pool and gardens growing on an ancient coral reef. **Pros:** seclusion; good value; scrumptious dinners; air-conditioning in some rooms. **Cons:** far from sights; staff can be too businesslike. ⑤ *Rooms from: $65 ✉ 2 km (1 mile) north of town at end of Playa Negra road ☎ 2755–0035 ⊕ www.magellaninn. com ⥯ 6 rooms* ⑩ *Breakfast.*

$$ **☷ Playa Negra Guesthouse.** This gracious, Québécois-owned lodging set
HOTEL in lush, hibiscus-strewn gardens has become a Cahuita favorite. **Pros:**
Fodor's Choice stylish surroundings; attentive owners; terrific rates for what's offered.
★ **Cons:** friendly dogs on-site, so not a place to stay if canines aren't your thing. ⑤ *Rooms from: $79 ✉ Playa Negro road, 50 m north of soccer field ☎ 2755–0127 ⊕ www.playanegra.cr ⥯ 4 rooms, 3 cottages* ⑩ *Breakfast.*

NIGHTLIFE
Aside from the local bars, Cahuita's nightlife centers on restaurants, all pleasant places to linger over dinner for the evening.

Chao's Paradise. If you're out this way, Chao's makes for a pleasant, open-air space for a beer and some seafood and fries. After dark, get here and back by taxi. ✉ *Playa Negra road, 50 m north of soccer field ☎ 2755–0284.*

Coco's Bar. Lively reggae, soca, and samba blast weekend evenings from the turquoise Coco's Bar. The assemblage of dogs dozing on its veranda during the day illustrates the rhythm of local life. ⊠ *Main road* ☎ *2755-0437.*

Cocorico. Italian eatery Cocrico shows movies on DVD many evenings at 7:30. ⊠ *Main road* ⊘ *Closed Tues.*

Reggae Bar. As befits the name of the place, reggae music is on tap here a few evenings of the week. You're bound to hear "No Woman, No Cry" and all the other anthems. After dark, take a taxi to and from here. ⊠ *Playa Negra road, 50 m north of soccer field* ☎ *2755-0209.*

Ricky's Bar. Quieter than Coco's across the street (although if Coco's is hosting live music, you'll hear it from here, too), Ricky's is a good place to kick back with a beer and watch the passing parade on the main street. It's "Ricky's" or "Rikki's," depending on which sign you look at. ⊠ *Main road.*

> **A TOWN THAT WON'T LET YOU DOWN**
>
> Cahuita's first tourist of note was Costa Rican president Alfredo González, whose boat shipwrecked on this stretch of coast in 1915. The president was so grateful for the aid settlers gave him that he purchased a tract of land here and donated it to them to construct a town.

CAHUITA NATIONAL PARK

Just south of Cahuita.

A perfect, white-sand beach with palm trees lining its edge sits just outside downtown Cahuita and will be your first glimpse of Cahuita National Park. (There's also a southern entrance halfway to Puerto Viejo de Talamanca.) The reserve's true reason for existence is to protect a coral reef just off the coast, and that ensures the best of both land and marine wildlife here. The location means you'll find a great selection of in-town dining and lodging options within a few blocks of the park's northern entrance, making this one of the country's easiest protected areas to visit. However, don't be worried about development encroaching on the park itself.

GETTING HERE AND AROUND

Choose from two park entrances: one is in downtown Cahuita; the other is at Puerto Vargas, just off the main road, 5 km (3 miles) south of town. If you don't have a car, you can get here easily via bike or taxi.

EXPLORING

Cahuita National Park (*Parque Nacional Cahuita*). With its rain forest extending right to the edge of its curving, utterly undeveloped 3-km (2-mile) white (or "whitish") sand beach, one of Costa Rica's most popular national parks is the stuff of picture postcards. The park was created to protect the 2½-square-km (1-square-mile) coral reef that encircles the coast and offers excellent snorkeling off Cahuita Point. Trails into the rain forest reveal a wealth of wildlife. February through April and September and October are slightly drier months, and offer

Wildlife-watching in Cahuita National Park

the best visibility for snorkeling. *For more information see the highlighted listing in this chapter.* ⊠ *Southern end of Cahuita, Cahuita* ☎ *2755–0461 Cahuita entrance, 2755–0302 Puerto Vargas entrance* 🖭 *$5 at Cahuita entrance; $10 at Puerto Vargas entrance* ⊙ *Daily 6–5 Cahuita entrance, daily 7–4 Puerto Vargas entrance.*

SPORTS AND THE OUTDOORS

TOUR OPERATORS

Operators in Cahuita or Puerto Viejo de Talamanca can hook you up with excursions to and in the park, or you can go on your own, especially if you use the entrance at the southern edge of the village.

SNORKELING

Cahuita's reefs are just one of several high-quality snorkeling spots in the region. Rent snorkeling gear in Cahuita or Puerto Viejo de Talamanca or through your hotel; most hotels also organize trips. It's wise to work with a guide, as the number of good snorkeling spots is limited and they're not always easily accessible. Cahuita established a community lifeguard team in 2002, unusual in Costa Rica. ■TIP→ As elsewhere up and down the Caribbean coast, the undertow poses risks for even experienced swimmers. Use extreme caution and never swim alone.

PUERTO VIEJO DE TALAMANCA

16 km (10 miles) south of Cahuita.

This muddy, colorful little town is one of the hottest spots on the international budget-travel circuit, and swarms with backpackers, surfers, and New Agers. For better or for worse, though, Puerto Viejo de Talamanca has outgrown its surfer roots and you'll find plenty of more "grown-up" offerings on the road heading southeast and northwest out of town.

At the last count, some 50 nationalities were represented in this tiny community, and most are united in concern for the environment and orderly development of tourism—few want to see the place become just another Costa Rican resort community. Some locals bemoan the loss of their town's innocence, as drugs and other evils have surfaced, but this is still a fun town to visit, with a great variety of hotels, cabinas, and restaurants in every price range. Unlike some other parts of Costa Rica, no one has been priced out of the market here.

Locals shorten the name to just "Puerto Viejo"—British settlers called the area "Old Harbour"—but we use the complete name to avoid confusion with the other Puerto Viejo: Puerto Viejo de Sarapiquí in northern Costa Rica. (Note that you may also see this Caribbean town referred to as "Puerto Viejo de Limón.") You have access to the beach right in town, and the Salsa Brava, famed in surfers' circles for its pounding waves, is here off the coast, too. The best strands of Caribbean sand are outside the village: Playa Cocles, Playa Chiquita (technically a series of beaches), and Punta Uva, all dark-sand beaches, line the road heading southeast from town. Playa Negra—not to be confused with the Playa Negra near Cahuita—is a black-sand beach northwest of town. Punta Uva, with fewer hotels and the farthest from the village, sees fewer crowds and more tranquility. Playa Negra shares that distinction, too—for now—but developers have eyed the beach as the next area for expansion.

GETTING HERE AND AROUND

The turnoff to Puerto Viejo de Talamanca is 10 km (6 miles) down the coastal highway south of Cahuita (the highway then continues south to Bribri and Sixaola at the Panamanian border). The village lies another 5 km (3 miles) beyond the turnoff. The paved road passes through town and continues to Playas Cocles and Chiquita and Punta Uva all the way to the village of Manzanillo. "Periodically potholed" describes the condition of the road from the highway into town and as far as Playa Cocles. The newer paved sections beyond Cocles haven't disintegrated—yet. Autotransportes MEPE buses travel from San José's Terminal Atlántico Norte four times a day, and approximately hourly throughout the day from Limón and Cahuita. The town has no bus terminal. If you arrive on public transportation, you disembark at a bus shelter strewn with a few beer bottles on the street fronting the beach. (It makes an awful first impression, but this is a fun town, so keep your disappointment in check.) The MEPE ticket office is about a half block away. All buses from San José go into Puerto Viejo de Talamanca; most, though not all, Limón-originating buses do as well, but a couple drop you off on the highway. Check if you board in Limón. You can give yourself a wider selection of times than the four daily San José–Puerto Viejo services. Hourly Grupo Caribeños buses connect San José with Limón, and hourly MEPE buses connect Limón with Puerto Viejo. The MEPE and Caribeños terminals are one block apart in Limón. Walking could

9

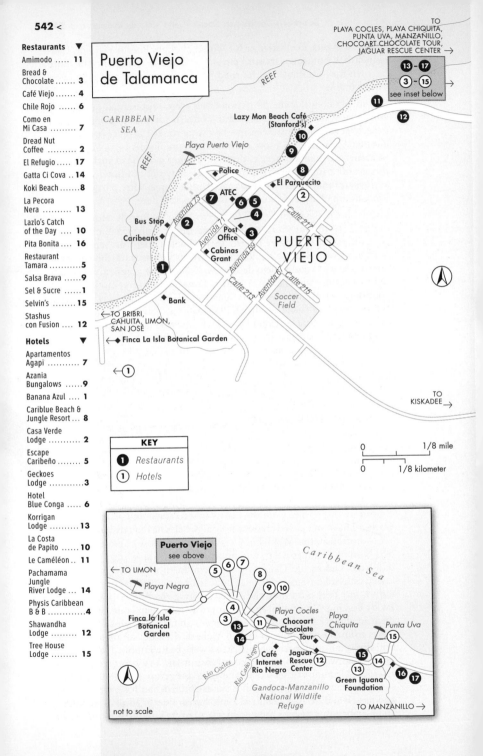

Restaurants ▼

Amimodo 11

Bread &
Chocolate 3

Café Viejo 4

Chile Rojo 6

Como en
Mi Casa 7

Dread Nut
Coffee 2

El Refugio 17

Gatta Ci Cova .. 14

Koki Beach 8

La Pecora
Nera 13

Lazlo's Catch
of the Day 10

Pita Bonita 16

Restaurant
Tamara 5

Salsa Brava 9

Sel & Sucre 1

Selvin's 15

Stashus
con Fusion 12

Hotels ▼

Apartamentos
Agapi 7

Azania
Bungalows 9

Banana Azul 1

Cariblue Beach &
Jungle Resort ... 8

Casa Verde
Lodge 2

Escape
Caribeño 5

Geckoes
Lodge 3

Hotel
Blue Conga 6

Korrigan
Lodge 13

La Costa
de Papito 10

Le Caméléon .. 11

Pachamama
Jungle
River Lodge ... 14

Physis Caribbean
B & B 4

Shawandha
Lodge 12

Tree House
Lodge 15

be an option if you're not weighed down with bags and if it's still light out. Unlike MEPE vehicles, Caribeños buses are air-conditioned.

Local buses ply the 15-km (9-mile) paved road between Puerto Viejo and Manzanillo every two hours during the day. Unless your schedule meshes exactly with theirs, you're better off biking or taking a taxi to and from the far-flung beaches along the way. Taxis charge $6 to Playa Cocles or Playa Negra, $10 to Playa Chiquita, $14 to Punta Uva, and $20 to Manzanillo.

> **SAFETY**
>
> Swimming alone at the beach is never safe, and walking alone on the beach here is not safe either. The forest comes right up to the edge of many of the stretches of sand. Stick to areas where other people congregate, and you can have a safe, secure time in Puerto Viejo.

You can manage the town center quite easily on foot, though it is dusty in the dry season and muddy when it rains. The main street is, thankfully, paved. Everyone gets around by bike here, and seemingly everyone has one for rent (invariably without a helmet). Quality varies widely, but we recommend renting from Cabinas Grant or Casa Verde Lodge. Expect to pay $10 per day for a good bike.

Cabinas Grant. Here you'll find the best selection of quality bikes in town. ⊠ *100 m south of bus stop* ☎ *2750–0292.*

Casa Verde Lodge. Priority is given to guests at Casa Verde Lodge, but they usually have extra bikes that you can rent for a half or full day even if you're not staying there. ⊠ *200 m south and 200 m east of bus stop* ☎ *2750–0015* ⊕ *www.cabinascasaverde.com.*

ESSENTIALS

Banks/ATMs Banco de Costa Rica. ⊠ *50 m south of bridge at entrance to town* ☎ *2750-0707* ⊕ *www.bancobcr.com.* **Banco Nacional.** ⊠ *25 m south of Correos* ⊕ *www.bncr.fi.cr.*

Internet ATEC (*Talamancan Association of Ecotourism and Conservation*). ⊠ *Across from Restaurant Tamara* ☎ *2750-0191* ⊕ *www.ateccr.org.*

Pharmacy Farmacia Caribe. ⊠ *Next to Banco de Costa Rica* ☎ *2750-0698.*

Post Office Correos. ⊠ *Next to Banco de Costa Rica* ⊕ *www.correos.go.cr.*

Visitor Information ATEC (*Talamancan Association of Ecotourism and Conservation*). ⊠ *Across from Restaurant Tamara* ☎ *2750-0191* ⊕ *www.ateccr.org.*

EXPLORING

Finca la Isla Botanical Garden (*Jardín Botánico Finca la Isla*). At the Finca la Isla Botanical Garden, you can explore a working tropical-fruit, spice, and ornamental-plant farm. Sloths abound, and you might see a few poison dart frogs. A guided tour—there is a three-person minimum, and tours must be reserved in advance—lasts two hours and includes admission and a glass of the farm's homemade fruit juice. You get the fruit juice if you wander around on your own, too (a $1 self-guiding tour book is available in English, Spanish, French, and German). Watch the demonstration showing how cacao beans are turned into chocolate, and sample some of the product at the end of the tour. ⊠ *½ km (¼ mile)*

9

west of Puerto Viejo at Playa Negra ☎ 8886–8530 ⬚ $6, guided tour $10 ☉ Fri.–Mon. 10–4.

FAMILY **Green Iguana Foundation** (*Fundación Iguana Verde*). You'll no doubt see Costa Rica's ubiquitous iguanas scurrying across roads on your travels around the country. A project of the nearby Tree House Lodge acquaints you with the lives of these fascinating animals. The green iguana—one of eight species and the most common found on the Caribbean coast—grows up to six feet in length, with two-thirds of that span consisting of the tail. The goal here is the breeding and raising of iguanas with their release into the wild in the adjoining Gandoca-Manzanillo Wildlife Refuge. Admission goes to support that work. ⊠ *Puerto Viejo de Talamanca* ✛ *Punta Uva* ☎ 2750-0706 ⊕ *www.iguanaverde.com* ⬚ *$15* ☉ *Tours Tues., Thurs., Sat. 10 am.*

FAMILY
Fodor's Choice
★
Jaguar Rescue Center (*Centro de Rescate Jaguar*). Many regard a visit to the Jaguar Rescue Center as the highlight of their trip to Puerto Viejo. The name is a bit misleading. The original rescued animal here was an orphaned, injured jaguar cub that ultimately did not survive. His memory lives on in the facility's name, even if there are no other jaguars on-site. Primarily howler monkeys, sloths, and lots of snakes make up the charges of the capable staff here. The goal, of course, is to return the animals to the wild, but those that are too frail are assured a permanent home here. Your admission fee for the 90-minute tour (English or Spanish) helps fund the rescue work. ⊠ *3 km (2 miles) southeast of Puerto Viejo between Playa Cocles and Playa Chiquita* ☎ 2750–0710 ⊕ *www.jaguarrescue.com* ⬚ *$15* ☉ *Mon.–Sat. tours at 9:30 and 11:30.*

BEACHES

Playa Chiquita. Nothing against Puerto Viejo, but the farther you get from town, the quieter things get—to put it bluntly, the "riff-raff" factor lessens out here. The downside is that you'll find fewer visitors congregating on dark-sand Chiquita, and isolated stretches of beach can spell trouble. Stay only if you see a lot of other people around. The undertow is strong out here. Swim at your own risk, preferably in company, and don't venture out too far. **Amenities:** none. **Best for:** sunrise; surfing; walking. ⊠ *6 km (4 miles) southeast of Puerto Viejo de Talamanca.*

Playa Cocles. The sand gets a bit lighter and the crowd slightly more upscale—it is still Puerto Viejo, though—a couple of kilometers outside of town. Fewer vendors will pester you here than in the town itself, and it'll be mostly you and other travelers. (If there's nobody around, don't linger. There's always safety in numbers.) As with all Puerto Viejo area beaches, the undertow can be strong on Cocles. Never venture out too far. **Amenities:** food and drink. **Best for:** partiers; sunrise; surfing, walking. ⊠ *2 km (1 mile) southeast of Puerto Viejo de Talamanca.*

NEED A
BREAK?
Caribeans. At first glance, this small café could use a spelling lesson, but since Caribeans deals in coffee, the play on words is apt. Treat yourself to a latte, mocha, or coconut cappuccino, all made from organic, fair-trade coffee from the Turrialba region in the far-eastern Central Valley, and roasted here. ⊠ *2 km (1 mile) southeast of town at Playa Cocles* ☎ *8836–8930* ⊕ *www.caribeanscr.com* ☉ *Closed Tues.*

Reefs at Risk

One of the most complex organisms in the marine world, a coral reef is an extraordinary and extraordinarily delicate habitat. Coral reefs are the result of the symbiotic relationship between single-cell organisms called zooxanthellae and coral polyps. The zooxanthellae grow inside the cells of the polyps, producing oxygen and nutrients that are released into the coral tissues. Corals secrete calcium carbonate (limestone) that, over time, forms the vast coral reef "superstructure." Zooxanthellae require exposure to sunlight to thrive. The healthiest coral reefs are in clear, clean, tropical seawater at a temperature of 20°C to 25°C (70°F to 80°F). Healthy coral reefs are biologically rich gardens occupied by a diverse selection of life-forms, from microscopic unicellular algae and phytoplankton to a wide range of fish.

Unfortunately, coral reefs in Costa Rica are in danger. Dirt and sediment from banana plantations and logging areas, as well as runoff from pesticide use, are killing them. The dirty runoff literally clogs the pores of the zooxanthellae and smothers them. In the southern Pacific coast's Golfo Dulce, 98% of one of the oldest reefs in Costa Rica has been destroyed by this sedimentation. Many of the once-enormous reefs of Cahuita are almost entirely gone.

Human visitors, including careless snorkelers, have also damaged reefs. Simply touching a reef damages it. When exploring a coral reef, look but don't touch, and snorkel only on its outer side, preferably in calm weather. Can the reefs be saved? With commitment and time, yes. Coral is resilient, and will grow back—if the Costa Rican government makes it a priority.

Playa Negra (*Black Beach*). Not to be confused with Cahuita's beach of the same name, Puerto Viejo's black-sand Playa Negra lies close to town but is relatively undeveloped. That situation is expected to change in coming years, but, for now, you'll likely have this stretch of sand north of town to yourself. While this sounds idyllic, remember that there's always safety in numbers on beaches in this area. Be careful about going into the water; the undertow can be strong. **Amenities:** none. **Best for:** sunrise; surfing; walking. ⊠ *1 km (½ mile) north of Puerto Viejo de Talamanca.*

Playa Puerto Viejo. You can do much better than Puerto Viejo's unnamed, in-town, cluttered, dark-sand beach. Locals, friendly and occasionally a bit sketchy, gather here. The strong undertow makes swimming risky along this stretch, but surfers delight in the consistently good waves. The upside is that you're just a few steps from the in-town restaurants. **Amenities:** food and drink. **Best for:** partiers; sunrise; surfing; walking. ⊠ *In town.*

Punta Uva. The area's most beautiful beach—with dark sand like all the area strands—lies a long way from Puerto Viejo and offers splendid isolation from the commotion of town. *Uva* means "grape" in Spanish, and the beach gets its name from the sea-grape trees found out here. A few nearby restaurants can take care of your culinary needs. As always here, there's the undertow to contend with. Be careful and never venture too far out into the water. **Amenities:** food and drink. **Best for:** sunrise; surfing; walking. ⊠ *9 km (5½ miles) south of Puerto Viejo de Talamanca.*

SPORTS AND THE OUTDOORS

TOUR OPERATORS

As in Cahuita, tour operators and outfitters here can set up tours and activities anywhere on the south Caribbean coast.

> **CAUTION**
>
> The conditions that make the Caribbean so popular among surfers spell danger for swimmers. A few drownings occur each year. Strong riptides can pull you out to sea, even in waist-deep water, before you realize what's happening. Never swim alone in these parts—good advice anywhere.

ATEC (*Talamancan Association of Ecotourism and Conservation*). Tours with ATEC have an environmental or cultural bent, such as Afro-Caribbean or indigenous-culture walks—tours to the nearby Kekoldi indigenous reserve are especially popular—rain-forest hikes, coral-reef snorkeling trips, fishing trips, bird-watching tours, night walks, adventure treks, and dance lessons. Local organizations and wildlife refuges receive 15% to 20% of ATEC's proceeds. ⊠ *Across from Restaurant Tamara* ☎ *2750–0191* ⊕ *www. ateccr.org* ⊠ *Tours from $26.*

Terraventuras. This well-established operator can lead you around Puerto Viejo de Talamanca and Cahuita, or take you on excursions to Tortuguero, the Gandoca-Manzanillo Wildlife Refuge, and Bocas del Toro in Panama. It also rents good-quality surfboards, bicycles, boogie boards, and snorkeling gear. ⊠ *100 m south of bus stop* ☎ *2750–0750* ⊕ *www. terraventuras.com* ⊠ *Tours from $45.*

RAFTING

Exploradores Outdoors. Rafting excursions lie about two hours away, but one San José–based outfitter has an office here. Exploradores Outdoors is highly regarded and has one- or two-day excursions on the Pacuare River, with a pickup point here or in San José, and the option to start in one place and be dropped off at the other. The outfitter also offers sea-kayaking excursions off the coast of the Gandoca-Manzanillo Wildlife Refuge. ⊠ *100 m east of Lazy Mon Beach Cafe (aka Stanford's)* ☎ *2750–2020, 2222–6262 in San José, 646/205–0828 in North America* ⊕ *www.exploradoresoutdoors.com.*

SURFING

Surfing is the name of the game in Puerto Viejo, for everyone from newbies to Kelly Slaters. The best conditions are late December through March, but there's action all year. Longtime surfers compare the south Caribbean with Hawaii, but without the "who-do-you-think-you-are?" attitude. There are a number of breaks here, most famously **Salsa Brava**, which translates to "wild sauce." It breaks fairly far offshore and requires maneuvering past some tricky currents and a shallow reef. Hollow and primarily right breaking, Salsa Brava is one gnarly wave when it gets big. If it gets *too* big, or not big enough, check out the breaks at Punta Uva, Punta Cocles, or Playa Chiquita. Boogie boarders and bodysurfers can also dig the beach-break waves at various points along this tantalizingly beautiful coast.

Aventuras Bravas. If you've always wanted to try surfing, consider the friendly, 90-minute $40 surf school at Aventuras Bravas. They'll start you out with a small wave near the bus stop. A two-hour private lesson will run you $50. You can also rent equipment here. ✉ *Inside Rockin' J's hostel, 1 km (½ mile) southeast of Lazy Mon Beach Cafe (aka Stanford's)* ☎ *2750–0626* ⊕ *www.rockingjs.com.*

WHERE TO EAT

$$ ✗ **Amimodo.** The name translates to "my way," and the exuberant Italian owners really do it their way, combining the cuisine of their native northern Italy with Caribbean flavors. Your antipasto might be classic bruschetta or *jamón de tiburón* (shark ham with avocado dressing), and your ravioli might be stuffed with tropical shrimp, pineapple, and curry, with avocado sauce on the side. The tropical veranda with gingerbread trim spills over onto the beach with abundant greenery, and the restaurant is a popular gathering place for Puerto Viejo's Italian community. ⑤ *Average main: $14* ✉ *200 m east of Lazy Mon Beach Cafe (aka Stanford's)* ☎ *2750–0257.*

ITALIAN

$ ✗ **Bread & Chocolate.** The takeaway line for brownies forms at the gate before this place opens at 6:30 am, but stick around for a hearty breakfast of cinnamon-oatmeal pancakes, French toast, or creamy scrambled eggs, washed down with a cup of French-press coffee. Lunch brings jerk chicken, roasted red peppers, and chocolate truffles. Everything is homemade, right down to the mayonnaise. This is one of several bakery-slash-breakfast-and-lunch cafés open in town; the friendly owners and staff give this place the edge. ⑤ *Average main: $6* ✉ *50 m south of post office* ☎ *2750–0723* ▭ *No credit cards* ☾ *Closed Tues. May–Nov. No dinner.*

CAFÉ

$$ ✗ **Café Viejo.** This is the hot place to see and be seen on Puerto Viejo's main drag. The owners learned to cook at the knee of their Italian grandmother back in Rimini, and have concocted a menu, several pages long, of pizzas and handmade pastas. Recorded reggae and mambo music bops in the background. ⑤ *Average main: $11* ✉ *Across from ATEC* ☎ *2750–0817* ⊕ *www.cafeviejo.com* ☾ *Closed Tues. No lunch.*

ITALIAN

$ ✗ **Chile Rojo.** There's not a thing about the name or furnishings to reflect its Thai and Middle Eastern offerings, but this restaurant does a brisk business. Choose from Thai grilled tuna, falafel, hummus, and samosas. Sushi is available on Saturday. The spacious, open second-floor setting catches the breezes and lets you watch the passersby on Puerto Viejo's main drag down below. You'll have plenty of time for people-watching; service tends to be slow here. ⑤ *Average main: $9* ✉ *Across from ATEC* ☎ *2750–0319* ☾ *Closed Mon.*

THAI

$ ✗ **Como en Mi Casa.** Everything is made on-site at this small, second-floor café. Start off the day with an order of vegan pancakes or ease into lunch with veggie burritos and a tomato, oregano, and olive oil bruschetta. You'll find some gluten-free options on the menu, too. Bopping tunes make for an upbeat vibe, and there is a nice balcony for dining outdoors. ⑤ *Average main: $5* ✉ *100 m east of bus stop* ☎ *6069–6319* ▭ *No credit cards* ☾ *Closed Wed. No dinner.*

VEGETARIAN

9

$
CARIBBEAN

✗ **Dread Nut Coffee.** An easy-to-miss Caribbean-style clapboard house near the bus stop makes a great place to fortify yourself for a day of sightseeing. The industrious staff here starts the day with omelets and freshly baked banana bread and pastries. Lunch gives way to a variety of sandwiches—you choose from ingredients to construct your own. Organic coffee, tropical fruit drinks, and homemade ice cream round out the offerings. ⑤ *Average main: $6 ⊠ 50 m east of bus stop ☎ 8995-6103 ⊘ Closed Sun. No dinner ⊟ No credit cards.*

$$$
ARGENTINE
Fodor's Choice
★

✗ **El Refugio.** This unexpected place in the middle of a forest clearing is one of the country's top Argentine restaurants. The restaurant is tiny, with a scant five tables in a lovely rancho in a wooded setting, making it one of the Caribbean coast's most intimate dining experiences. The menu varies throughout the year and might consist of beef in chimichurri sauce, spinach crepes, curried shrimp, mussels in white wine, or *milanesa de corvina* (seabass cutlet). All meals here kick off with homemade chips and guacamole, a house specialty. The place feels remote and, indeed, you're a long way from most lodgings when you're out here in Punta Uva. Take a taxi to and from if you're without your own wheels. ⑤ *Average main: $16 ⊠ Puerto Viejo de Talamanca ☎ 2759-9007 ⊘ Closed Wed. No lunch ⚄ Reservations essential ⊟ No credit cards.*

$$
ITALIAN

✗ **Gatta Ci Cova.** This restaurant, whose name comes from an Italian expression meaning "things kept secret," provides an informal, inexpensive dining experience that still has flair and fun. (The same chef owns the more upscale La Pecora Nera restaurant, 100 meters away.) Lunch offerings focus on the $10 *plato del día,* a bargain with appetizer, salad, a rotating selection of pastas, dessert, and a glass of wine. ⑤ *Average main: $11 ⊠ 3 km (2 miles) southeast of town at Playa Cocles ☎ 2750-0730 ⊘ Closed Mon.*

$$
ECLECTIC

✗ **Koki Beach.** This slightly elevated terrace restaurant with colorful furniture (and colorful characters) is visible to all who walk by. The tradeoff for being on display while you eat is the chance to watch Puerto Viejo's parade of evening passersby and the ocean waves lapping on the beach across the street. The mostly surf-and-turf menu means lots of shrimp and sea bass and lots of beef and chicken, all served on or off skewers according to your preference. A great selection of drinks rounds out the offerings. Live music gets under way many evenings, usually in the later hours. ⑤ *Average main: $13 ⊠ 100 m west of Lazy Mon Beach Cafe (aka Stanford's) ☎ 2750-0902 ⊕ kokibeach.blogspot. com ⊘ No lunch.*

$$$
ITALIAN
Fodor's Choice
★

✗ **La Pecora Nera.** Though the name means "black sheep" in Italian, there's nothing shameful about this thatch-roof roadside restaurant. There's always a lot more to choose from than you'll see on the sparse-looking menu. Wait for the owner-chef to come out of the kitchen and triumphantly announce—with flair worthy of an Italian opera—which additional light Tuscan entrées, appetizers, and desserts they've concocted that day. Be prepared for a long, leisurely dining experience with attentive service. It's worth the wait; this is one of the country's top Italian restaurants. ⑤ *Average main: $24 ⊠ 3 km (2 miles) southeast of town at Playa Cocles ☎ 2750-0490 ⊘ Closed Mon. No lunch.*

$$$
SEAFOOD
Fodor'sChoice
★
✕ **Lazlo's Catch of the Day.** This dining spot thrives despite having no menu, no fixed hours, no sign, and no official name. A transplanted Hungarian family fishes by day and cooks and serves their catch to the public by night. Dinner is frequently red snapper or seabass or tuna steaks. It all depends on what Lazlo and company came home with that day. French fries and veggies complete your plate for a fixed $16; beer and cocktails are extra. The entire production takes place only on some days, and there's the kicker: the premise here makes it difficult to plan any more than a few hours in advance. Your best bet is to have your hotel call to see if anything is going on that evening. If Lazlo's and your schedule coincide, go and enjoy the fun informality of it all. Get there by 6; when the fish is gone, it's gone. $ *Average main: $16* ✉ *Puerto Viejo de Talamanca* ☎ *No phone* ⊗ *No lunch, irregular hours* 🗖 *No credit cards.*

$$
MIDDLE EASTERN
✕ **Pita Bonita.** The area's only Middle Eastern dining spot is an open-air restaurant with cool breezes in Punta Uva. What the menu here lacks in quantity it makes up for in quality. Lamb kebabs, chicken shawarma, and *shakshouka* (a Tunisian dish with eggs poached in tomato, pepper, and onion) are the specialties here. All can be jazzed up if you like with a homemade Yemeni hot sauce (beware: it packs a punch). The wine selection here includes the standard Chilean and Argentine varieties you see elsewhere around Costa Rica, with a few interesting Spanish and Israeli ones to boot, and you can top off your meal with a Turkish coffee. Pita Bonita's handmade hummus and freshly baked pita bread are also sold in a few stores around town. $ *Average main: $12* ✉ *Puerto Viejo de Talamanca* ☎ *2756-8173* ⊗ *Closed Sun.*

$
CARIBBEAN
✕ **Restaurant Tamara.** Once upon a time, this unpretentious two-story place was the only restaurant in town. The Caribbean food is tasty and authentic: you can't lose with the chicken in Caribbean sauce or virtually any of the fresh fish dishes. In the nondescript indoor seating area you're cooled by a fan and entertained by TV; the outdoor seating area has a palpable Jamaican motif and is a great place for people-watching. $ *Average main: $9* ✉ *Across from ATEC* ☎ *2750–0148* ⊗ *Closed Tues. May–Nov.*

$
SEAFOOD
✕ **Salsa Brava.** The restaurant overlooking the Salsa Brava break—with sublime surf vistas—has taken the name of this famed surfing spot. Opt for casual counter service or grab a seat at one of the colorful beachside tables. Lunch centers on grilled fish and meat. Try the red snapper prepared in olive oil, garlic, and cayenne pepper—it's a specialty. $ *Average main: $9* ✉ *100 m east of Lazy Mon Beach Cafe (aka Stanford's)* ☎ *2750–0241* ⊗ *Closed Mon. and Tues.*

$
FRENCH
✕ **Sel & Sucre.** The *sel* (salt) in this restaurant's name reflects the ham, chicken, spinach, goat cheese, and roasted almonds you'll find as ingredients in a huge selection of crepes. *Sucre* (sugar) shows up in the sweet versions of crepes, with the Grand Marnier a special standout. Light side salads, waffles, and cheese fondue round out the menu. Top it all off with a gourmet coffee or fruit smoothie. $ *Average main: $8* ✉ *120 m south of bus stop* ☎ *2750–0636* ⊕ *www.seletsucrecr.com* 🗖 *No credit cards* ⊗ *Closed Mon.*

9

$ ✕ **Selvin's.** An old standby at Punta Uva, Selvin's keeps limited, some-
CARIBBEAN times irregular, hours, especially in the off-season, so always call ahead
and head out here if you're fortunate enough to be in town when it's
open. The owner, known to everyone in town as "Blanca," cooks up a
menu of rondón, rice and beans, lobster, shrimp, and chicken with sweet
mole sauce. ⑤ *Average main: $8* ⊠ *7 km (4½ miles) southeast of town
at Punta Uva* ☎ *2750–0664* ▭ *No credit cards* ⊘ *Closed Mon.–Wed.;
may be closed other days May, June, and Sept.–Nov.*

$$ ✕ **Stashus con Fusion.** This restaurant epitomizes Puerto Viejo: lively,
ECLECTIC organic, all the rage, but confident enough not to seek trendiness.
Fodor'sChoice Ordering is by sauces: Thai peanut, Indonesian-Caribbean curry, Mexi-
★ can chipotle, Jamaican jerk-style, or Malaysian-guayaba curry. Then
select vegetables, chicken, shrimp, or fish (marlin or tuna). Live music
gets going later on Sunday evenings, although the place closes at 10.
⑤ *Average main: $13* ⊠ *200 m south of Lazy Mon Beach Cafe (aka
Stanford's)* ☎ *2750–0530* ⊘ *Closed Wed. No lunch.*

WHERE TO STAY

$ ⊞ **Apartamentos Agapi.** Agapi means "love" in Greek, and the Costa
HOTEL Rican–Greek owners lovingly watch over their guests with attentive ser-
vice at these furnished apartments overlooking the beach. **Pros:** kitchens
ideal for housekeeping vacation; central location just outside of town;
great value. **Cons:** not for travelers who want anonymity; first-floor
rooms can be dark. ⑤ *Rooms from: $73* ⊠ *1 km (½ mile) southeast of
Lazy Mon Beach Cafe (aka Stanford's)* ☎ *2750–0446* ⊕ *www.agapisite.
com* ⤸ *5 rooms, 12 apartments* ⦿| *Breakfast.*

$$ ⊞ **Azania Bungalows.** Ten thatched-roof, A-frame bungalows are spread
B&B/INN around Azania's ample gardens, and each sleeps four. **Pros:** good value;
good Argentine restaurant. **Cons:** difficult to make reservations; bungalows are dark inside. ⑤ *Rooms from: $100* ⊠ *1½ km (1 mile) southeast
of town at Playa Cocles* ☎ *2750–0540* ⊕ *www.azania-costarica.com*
⤸ *10 bungalows* ⦿| *Breakfast.*

$$ ⊞ **Banana Azul.** Hardwood furnishings are abundant at this gay-friendly
RESORT (but by no means exclusive) hotel at the secluded far end of Playa Negra.
Pros: friendly management and staff; seclusion, set away from hubbub
of town; great ocean views. **Cons:** no kids allowed, so not an option
for families. ⑤ *Rooms from: $89* ⊠ *1½ km (1 mile) north of Puerto
Viejo at end of Playa Negra* ☎ *2750–2035* ⊕ *www.bananaazul.com*
⤸ *12 rooms* ⦿| *Breakfast.*

$$ ⊞ **Cariblue Beach & Jungle Resort.** The youthful Italian owners came here
HOTEL to surf years ago, stayed on, and built a lodging that combines refine-
Fodor'sChoice ment with that hip Puerto Viejo vibe in exactly the right proportions.
★ **Pros:** friendly owners; good restaurant; air-conditioning. **Cons:** ideal to
have a car to stay here. ⑤ *Rooms from: $115* ⊠ *2 km (1 mile) south-
east of town at Playa Cocles* ☎ *2750–0035* ⊕ *www.cariblue.com* ⤸ *12
rooms, 8 suites, 23 bungalows* ⦿| *Breakfast.*

$ ⊞ **Casa Verde Lodge.** If you've graduated from your backpacker days
HOTEL and are a bit more flush with cash but still want to be near the action,
this old standby on a quiet street a couple of blocks from the center of
town is ideal. **Pros:** good value; immaculately kept up; nicest in-town
lodging. **Cons:** difficult to find vacancies; businesslike staff. ⑤ *Rooms*

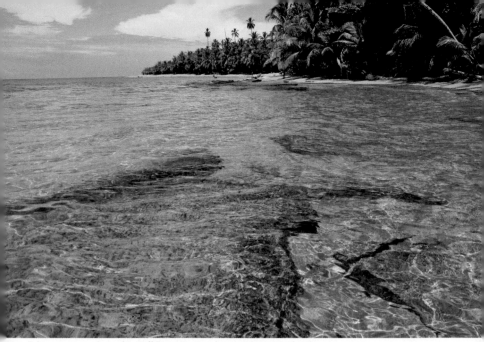

Calm waters over the reef just off Punta Uva Beach near Puerto Viejo de Talamanca

from: $68 ✉ 200 m south and 200 m east of bus stop ☎ 2750–0015 ⊕ www.cabinascasaverde.com ⤴ 17 rooms, 2 apartments ⦿ No meals.

$$
B&B/INN

⌂ **Escape Caribeño.** The wonderfully friendly Italian owners—who treat you like family—are what make this place, with immaculate hardwood bungalows lining a pleasant garden amply populated with hummingbirds, just outside town. **Pros:** central location without being right in town; gregarious owners. **Cons:** some small, spartan rooms. ⑤ *Rooms from: $75 ✉ 400 m southeast of Lazy Mon Beach Cafe (aka Stanford's) ☎ 2750–0103 ⊕ www.escapecaribeno.com ⤴ 18 cabins ⦿ No meals.*

$$$$
B&B/INN
Fodor's Choice
★

⌂ **Geckoes Lodge.** Impeccable service gives this place an edge among the area's handful of set-back-in-the-woods lodgings, and the Wi-Fi, private plunge pool, and barbecue that come with each house are unexpected touches in a setting such as this. **Pros:** wonderful, personalized service; lush, sumptuous surroundings; careful attention to environment. **Cons:** can be difficult to find; only two accommodations. ⑤ *Rooms from: $250 ✉ 3 km (2 miles) southeast of town and 1 km (½ mile) inland at Playa Cocles ☎ 2750–0908 ⊕ www.geckoeslodge.com ⤴ 2 houses ⦿ No meals.*

$
HOTEL

⌂ **Hotel Blue Conga.** You generally have to get farther out of Puerto Viejo to enjoy the area's garden-style lodgings, but Blue Conga offers lush surroundings (and air-conditioning—a real rarity here on the coast) close to town. **Pros:** attentive owner; air-conditioning; quiet surroundings set back from the road. **Cons:** first-floor rooms have less privacy. ⑤ *Rooms from: $70 ✉ 600 m south of Lazy Mon Beach Cafe (aka Stanford's) ☎ 2750–0681 ⊕ www.hotelblueconga.com ⤴ 14 rooms ⦿ Breakfast.*

9

$$ 🖫 **Korrigan Lodge.** Four octagonal wood bungalows are scattered around
B&B/INN the secluded wooded property here with its wonderfully cool surround-
ings (no air-conditioning is needed). Pros: lush, green setting; attentive
service. Cons: can be difficult to find; dogs on-site so not a place to
stay if you dislike canines. ⑤ *Rooms from: $106* ✉ *Punta Uva, 8 km
(5 miles) south of Puerto Viejo de Talamanca* 🕾 *2759–9103* ⊕ *www.
korriganlodge.com* ↩ *4 bungalows* ⎮⊙⎮ *Breakfast.*

$$ 🖫 **La Costa de Papito.** Papito's raised cabins are deep in the property's
HOTEL wooded grounds and furnished with whimsical, bright, tropical-blue-
and-zebra-stripe prints. Pros: good value; friendly owner. Cons: need
a car to stay here; some noise from bar area. ⑤ *Rooms from: $107*
✉ *2 km (1 mile) southeast of town at Playa Cocles* 🕾 *2750–0704,
516/252–4509 in North America* ⊕ *www.lacostadepapito.com* ↩ *13
cabins* ⎮⊙⎮ *No meals.*

$$$ 🖫 **Le Caméléon.** This boutique hotel fronting Playa Cocles is decidedly
HOTEL un-Puerto Viejo in its luxury, but if you're in the mood for a splurge here
on the coast, this is the spot. Pros: stylish luxury; attentive staff; many
amenities. Cons: such luxury might seem out of place in Puerto Viejo.
⑤ *Rooms from: $240* ✉ *Playa Cocles, 200 m east of soccer field* 🕾 *2750–
0501* ⊕ *www.lecameleonhotel.com* ↩ *22 rooms, 1 suite* ⎮⊙⎮ *Breakfast.*

$$ 🖫 **Pachamama Jungle River Lodge.** Though still within sight of the Puerto
B&B/INN Viejo–Manzanillo road, this French-owned place delivers a get-away-
from-it-all nature experience, within the confines of the Gandoca-
Manzanillo Wildlife Refuge, at a fraction of the cost of other Costa
Rican eco-lodges. Pros: wonderful seclusion; friendly owners. Cons:
far from sights; need a car to stay here. ⑤ *Rooms from: $100* ✉ *9 km
(5½ miles) southeast of town at Punta Uva* 🕾 *8531–4845* ⊕ *www.
pachamamacaribe.com* ▤ *No credit cards* ↩ *3 bungalows, 2 houses*
⎮⊙⎮ *No meals; Breakfast.*

$$ 🖫 **Physis Caribbean B&B.** If you want to experience the area's well-known
B&B/INN vibe but have outgrown Puerto Viejo's backpacker digs, this lodging
Fodor'sChoice owned by a fun, transplanted California couple is the ticket. Pros: hip,
★ knowledgeable owners; impeccable service; immaculate rooms. Cons:
friendly dogs on-site, so not ideal if you dislike canines. ⑤ *Rooms from:
$105* ✉ *1½ km (1 mile) southeast of town at Playa Cocles* 🕾 *2750–
0941, 916/350–4698 in North America* ⊕ *www.physiscaribbean.net*
↩ *4 rooms* ⎮⊙⎮ *Breakfast.*

$$ 🖫 **Shawandha Lodge.** The service is personalized and friendly at Shawa-
RESORT ndha, where spacious, beautifully designed bungalows are well back
Fodor'sChoice from the road at Playa Chiquita. Pros: elegant bungalows; sumptuous
★ restaurant; near white-sand beach. Cons: far from sights; easiest to stay
here with a car. ⑤ *Rooms from: $140* ✉ *6 km (4 miles) southeast of
town at Playa Chiquita* 🕾 *2750–0018* ↩ *13 bungalows* ⎮⊙⎮ *Breakfast.*

$$$ 🖫 **Tree House Lodge.** This lodging complex among forested ground con-
HOTEL tains four large, stylish houses, all at ground level, one of which is built
around a tree (that's the Tree House). Pros: attention to style in fur-
nishings; romantic seclusion. Cons: far from sights; easiest to stay here
if you have a car. ⑤ *Rooms from: $177* ✉ *Punta Uva* 🕾 *2750–0706,
415/878–3786 in North America* ⊕ *www.costaricatreehouse.com* ↩ *1
suite, 3 houses* ⎮⊙⎮ *Breakfast.*

NIGHTLIFE

The distinction between dining spot and nightspot blurs as the evening progresses, as many restaurants become pleasant places to linger after dinner. You'll also find bars with live music on certain nights. The town's main drag is packed with pedestrians, bicycles, and a few cars most evenings, the block between Café Viejo and Hot Rocks getting the most action. Wander around; something is bound to entice you in. Be aware that some of the strictly local hangouts get pretty rough around the edges at night. The Lazy Mon Beach Café, which everyone knows by its former name, Stanford's, is used as a landmark for finding addresses on the road heading out of town toward Playa Cocles, but it's one of those rough places. We do not recommend it. ■TIP→ When out after dark, ask a staff member at the restaurant, bar, or club to call you a taxi when you're ready to call it an evening.

A BAD RAP

The Caribbean has a reputation among Costa Ricans for being crime-ridden, mainly because of a few high-profile cases here years ago, the nearness of the Panamanian border, and the fact that this is an impoverished region compared with other parts of the country. In actuality, the problem is no better or worse here than elsewhere. Take the standard precautions you would when you travel anywhere and do stick to well-traveled tourist paths.

BARS

Hot Rocks. A wonderful breeze wafts through this huge, semi-open-air, U-shaped bar just off the beach. Nights are dedicated variously to bingo, karaoke, live music, and open-mike performances. ⊠ *Puerto Viejo de Talamanca* ✛ *50 m east of ATEC* ☎ *No phone.*

Tasty Waves Cantina. Tuesday is $2 taco night at the lively, sometimes rowdy, Tasty Waves Cantina. Movies get under way at 7:30 pm on Monday evening and several other nights a week as well. ⊠ *Playa Cocles, 1 km (½ mile) southeast of town* ☎ *2750–0507* ⊙ *Thurs.–Tues. noon–midnight.*

DANCE CLUB

Mango Sunset. A lively mix of expats and tourists holds court at Mango Sunset each evening. ⊠ *20 m south of bus stop* ☎ *8691–0756* ⊙ *Daily 6–midnight.*

LIVE MUSIC

Stashus con Fusion. You can hear live music on Sunday evenings at this organic-food restaurant. ⊠ *200 m south of Lazy Mon Beach Cafe (aka Stanford's)* ☎ *2750–0263* ⊙ *Thurs.–Tues. 5–10.*

SHOPPING

Vendors set up stands at night on the beach road heading out of town toward Playa Cocles, cheap jewelry being the prime fare. But the town counts a couple of honest-to-goodness souvenir shops, too.

Feria Agrícola. Puerto Viejo's Saturday-morning farmers' market is a good place to stock up on fresh fruits and veggies for that weekend beach picnic. It takes place in a building just south of the bus stop. ⊠ *50 m south of bus stop* ⊙ *Sat. 6–noon.*

9

Luluberlu. Puerto Viejo's nicest shop sells a wonderful selection of local indigenous carvings—balsa and *chonta* wood are especially popular—as well as jewelry, paintings, and ceramics by 30 artists from the region. Prices run a tad higher here than other places around town, but you're assured of good quality. ✉ *200 m south and 50 m east of bus stop* ☎ *2750–0394.*

Tienda del Mar. Really two stores in one, Tienda del Mar sprawls around a street corner in the center of town and specializes in bright, colorful batik clothing of all sizes, as well as more run-of-the-mill T-shirts, sandals, wood carvings, and postcards. ✉ *Next to Restaurant Tamara* ☎ *No phone.*

GANDOCA-MANZANILLO NATIONAL WILDLIFE REFUGE

15 km (9 miles) southeast of Puerto Viejo.

The boundaries of the southern Caribbean coast's preeminent wildlife refuge aren't well defined. You'll pass in and out of the forested reserve as you drive southeast from Puerto Viejo de Talamanca. The village of Manzanillo remains an "end-of-the-world" kind of place. Tourism is still in its infancy this far down the coast, though with the road paved all the way here, the town is a popular destination among people from Limón for weekend day trips. The rest of the week, you'll likely have the place to yourself.

GETTING HERE AND AROUND

The paved road from Puerto Viejo de Talamanca ends at the entrance to the village of Manzanillo. Buses connect the two every two hours during the day. Taxis are a much easier proposition. Drivers in Puerto Viejo charge $18 for the trip here.

EXPLORING

Gandoca-Manzanillo National Wildlife Refuge (*Refugio Nacional de Vida Silvestre Gandoca-Manzanillo*). The refuge stretches along the southeastern coast from southeast of Puerto Viejo de Talamanca to the town of Manzanillo and on to the Panamanian border. Its limits are not clearly defined. Because of weak laws governing the conservation of refuges and the rising value of coastal land in this area, Gandoca-Manzanillo is less pristine than Cahuita National Park and continues to be developed. (Development thins out the farther you get from Puerto Viejo and the closer you get to the village of Manzanillo.) However, the refuge still has plenty of rain forest, *orey* (a dark tropical wood) and jolillo swamps, 10 km (6 miles) of beach where four species of turtles lay their eggs, and almost 3 square km (1 square mile) of *cativo* (a tropical hardwood) forest and coral reef. The Gandoca estuary is a nursery for tarpon and a wallowing spot for crocodiles and caimans.

The easiest way to explore the refuge is to hike along the coast south of Manzanillo. You can hike back out the way you came in or arrange (in Puerto Viejo de Talamanca) to have a boat pick you up at Punta Mono (Monkey Point), a three- to four-hour walk from Manzanillo, where you find secluded beaches hidden by tall cliffs of fossilized coral. The mangroves of Gandoca, with abundant caimans, iguanas, and

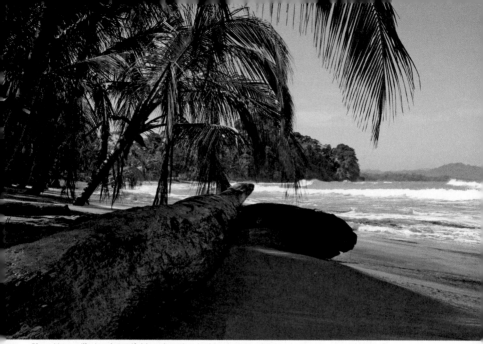
Playa Manzanillo is a beautiful beach with a laid-back atmosphere.

waterfowl, lie six to eight hours away. Park administrators can tell you more and recommend a local guide; inquire when you enter Manzanillo village and the locals will point you toward them. ✉ *15 km (9 miles) southeast of Puerto Viejo de Talamanca* ☎ *2750–0398 for ATEC* 🎫 *Free* ⏰ *Daily 7–4.*

BEACHES
Playa Manzanillo. Ensconced within the Gandoca-Manzanillo Wildlife Refuge, this beach comes close to being picture-perfect with the lush green forest—and its resident howler monkeys—bordering the edge of the sand. The in-town stretches put you close to food and drink. A few reports of bag snatchings have occurred here when visitors weren't paying attention. As always on this stretch of coast, avoid walking on the beach alone and be careful about going into the water, where the undertow can be strong. **Amenities:** food and drink. **Best for:** snorkeling; sunrise; surfing; walking. ✉ *Manzanillo village.*

SPORTS AND THE OUTDOORS
TOUR OPERATORS
A guide can help you get the most out of this relatively unexplored corner of the country.

Association of Indigenous Naturalist Guides of Manzanillo. This consortium of high-quality, knowledgeable local guides knows the area well and leads a variety of half- and full-day tours, thanks to the U.S. Agency for International Development, who planted the seed money to get the project going. They can take you for a hike in the reserve or out to Monkey Point, with a return trip by boat. They also have horseback riding;

9

bird-, dolphin-, and turtle-watching; and traditional fishing excursions. ✉ *Main road, Manzanillo* ☎ *2759–9064* ✐ *guiasmant@yahoo.com.mx.*

DIVING AND SNORKELING

Companies in Puerto Viejo de Talamanca can arrange boat trips to dive spots and beaches in the refuge as well.

Aquamor Talamanca Adventures. The friendly staff at Aquamor Talamanca Adventures specializes in land- and ocean-focused tours of the Gandoca-Manzanillo Wildlife Refuge, and can tend to all your water-sporting needs in these parts, with guided kayaking, snorkeling, and scuba-diving tours, as well as equipment rental. ✉ *Main road, Manzanillo* ☎ *2759–9012* ⊕ *www.greencoast.com/aquamor.htm* ⌨ *Tours from $25.*

WHERE TO EAT AND STAY

$$
CARIBBEAN
✕ **Cool & Calm Café.** You might drive right by this small, semi-open-air joint with plastic chairs and tables—it isn't much to look at—but the menu satisfies with dishes such as spicy Caribbean chicken, red snapper, and curried vegetables and rice. Views of the beach (just across the road) are another plus. You can rinse off the sand at the outdoor shower next to the restaurant if you've just walked over from the beach. ⑤ *Average main: $11* ✉ *50 m west of bus stop, Manzanillo* ☎ *8843–7460* ▬ *No credit cards* ☽ *Closed Tues. No lunch Mon.*

$
SEAFOOD
✕ **Restaurant Maxi's.** Cooled by sea breezes and shaded by tall, stately palms, this two-story, brightly painted wooden building offers weary travelers cold beer, potent cocktails, and great seafood at unbeatable prices after a day's hike in the refuge. Locals and expatriates alike come here for their lobster fix, and the fresh fish is wonderful, too. Sundays get very crowded here as people drive out for lunch from as far away as Limón. Locals tend to congregate in the rowdy but pleasant downstairs bar, where reggae beats into the wee hours. ⑤ *Average main: $9* ✉ *Main road, Manzanillo* ☎ *2759–9073* ▬ *No credit cards.*

$$$
RESORT
☷ **Almonds & Corals** (*Almendros y Corales*). Hidden in a beachfront jungle within the Gandoca-Manzanillo Wildlife Refuge, Almonds & Corals features scattered bungalows raised on stilts and linked by boardwalks lighted by kerosene lamps. **Pros:** rustic comfort; lots of activities. **Cons:** far from sights; need a car to stay here. ⑤ *Rooms from: $195* ✉ *Near end of road to Manzanillo* ☎ *2759–9056, 2271–3000 in San José, 888/373–9042 in North America* ⊕ *www.almondsandcorals.com* ⇆ *24 bungalows* ⏀ *Some meals.*

$$$
B&B/INN
☷ **Nature Observatorio.** If you're looking for some "Guess where we stayed!" bragging rights following your return from Costa Rica, this lodging option high in a tree provides them. **Pros:** definitely has the "wow" factor; the ultimate in seclusion. **Cons:** not for those with fear of heights; cannot come and go as you please; hoisting to the platform requires physical strength. ⑤ *Rooms from: $200* ✉ *Gandoca-Manzanillo National Wildlife Refuge* ✛ *South of Manzanillo village* ☎ *8628–2663* ⊕ *www.natureobservatorio.com* ⇆ *1 platform* ⏀ *All meals.*

CLOSE UP: Crossing into Panama at Sixaola

The border crossings are open daily 7 am to 5 pm (8 am to 6 pm Panamanian time). Set your watch one hour ahead when you enter Panama.

Costa Rican rental vehicles may not leave the country, so crossing into Panama as a tourist is an option only via public transportation. The public bus route from San José to Cahuita and Puerto Viejo de Talamanca terminates here at the border approximately six hours after leaving the capital. Taxis in Puerto Viejo de Talamanca charge about $75 for the jaunt to the border, a much quicker and reasonable option if you can split the fare among a group.

Disembark and head for the Costa Rican immigration office ☎ 2754–2044 down a flight of stairs from the west end of a former railroad bridge. Officials place an exit stamp in your passport, after which you walk across the bridge and present your passport to Panamanian immigration ☎ 507/759-7019. A larger, more modern bridge nearby is open to private vehicles only. U.S. visitors must also purchase a $5 tourist card for entry into the country. ■TIP→ Although some local residents here make the crossing without going through border formalities, you cannot. Make sure you exit and enter Costa Rica and Panama properly in either direction.

Taxis wait on the Panamanian side to transport you to the small city of Changuinola, the first community of any size inside the country, from which there are bus and air connections for travel farther into Panama. Taxis can also take you to Almirante, where you'll find boat launches to Bocas del Toro.

■TIP→ Whatever your destination in Panama, come armed with dollars. Panama uses U.S. currency, but refers to the dollar as the *balboa*. (It does mint its own coins, all the same size as their U.S. counterparts.) No one anywhere will accept or exchange your Costa Rican colones.

9

CROSSING INTO BOCAS DEL TORO, PANAMA VIA SIXAOLA

Costa Rica's sleepy border post at Sixaola fronts Guabito, Panama's equally quiet border crossing, 44 km (26 miles) south of the turnoff to Puerto Viejo de Talamanca. Both are merely collections of banana-plantation stilt houses and a few stores and bars; neither has any lodging or dining options, but this is a much more low-key crossing into Panama than the busy border post at Paso Canoas on the Pan-American Highway near the Pacific coast. If you've come this far, you're likely headed to **Bocas del Toro,** the real attraction in the northwestern part of Panama. This archipelago of 68 islands continues the Afro-Caribbean and indigenous themes seen on Costa Rica's Atlantic coast, and has opportunities for diving, snorkeling, swimming, and wildlife viewing. The larger islands are home to a growing selection of hotels and restaurants—everything from funky to fabulous. "Bocas" has acquired a cult following among long-term foreign visitors to Costa Rica, who find it a convenient place to travel when their permitted three-month status as a tourist has expired, since a quick 72-hour jaunt out of the country gets you another 90 days in Costa Rica.

Consulate of Panama. The Panamanian consulate in San José can provide more information about travel in Panama. ⊠ *San José* ☎ *2281–2442* ⊕ *www.panamaenelexterior.gob.pa/costa-rica* ⊗ *Weekdays 9–3.*

A few tour operators in Cahuita and Puerto Viejo de Talamanca can set you up with shuttle transportation to Bocas del Toro. They also offer day tours to the islands, but travel time and border formalities eat up a huge chunk of that day. Bocas is a fun destination in its own right and worth spending a couple of nights. You can forego land travel completely if you like. Nature Air flies daily from San José to Bocas del Toro, about a 60-minute flight.

For more information about Bocas del Toro and Panama than we can supply here, pick up a copy of *Fodor's In Focus Panama.*

Caribe Shuttle. This company offers daily van/boat-shuttle service between Puerto Viejo de Talamanca and Bocas del Toro for $32 one way. Caribe also offers multiday packages from Puerto Viejo to Bocas that include accommodations. ⊠ *Inside Rockin' J's hostel, 1 km (½ mile) southeast of Puerto Viejo de Talamanca, San José* ☎ *2750–0626* ⊕ *www.caribeshuttle.com.*

Willie's Tours. The folks here can set you up with one- or multi-day tours starting at $150 from Cahuita to Bocas del Toro, as well as basic shuttle transportation for $35 one way. ⊠ *Main street, 100 m north of Coco's Bar, Cahuita* ☎ *2755-1024* ⊕ *www.williestourscostarica.com.*

UNDERSTANDING COSTA RICA

COSTA RICA AT A GLANCE

**WILDLIFE AND
PLANT GLOSSARY**

MENU GUIDE

VOCABULARY

COSTA RICA AT A GLANCE

FAST FACTS

Capital: San José

Type of government: Democratic republic

Independence: September 15, 1821 (from Spain)

Population: 4,814,144

Population density: 84 persons per square km (220 persons per square mile)

Literacy: 96.3%

Language: Spanish (official); English spoken by most in the tourism industry

Ethnic groups: White (including mestizo) 83.6%, mulato 6.7%, indigenous 2.4%, black of African descent 1.1%, other 1.1%, none 2.9%, unspecified 2.2%

Religion: Roman Catholic 76.3%, Evangelical 13.7%, Jehovah's Witnesses 1.3%, other Protestant 0.7%, other 4.8%, none 3.2%

GEOGRAPHY AND ENVIRONMENT

Land area: 51,100 square km (19,730 square miles); slightly smaller than the U.S. state of West Virginia

Coastline: 1,290 km (802 miles)

Terrain: Rugged central range with 112 volcanic craters that separate the eastern and western coastal plains

Natural resources: Hydroelectric power, forest products, fisheries products

Natural hazards: Droughts, flash floods, thunderstorms, earthquakes, hurricanes, active volcanoes, landslides

Flora: 9,000 species, including 1,200 orchid species and 800 fern species; tidal mangrove swamps, tropical rain forest, subalpine forest

Fauna: 36,518 species, including 34,000 species of insects and 2,000 species of butterflies

Environmental issues: Deforestation, rapid industrialization and urbanization, air and water pollution, soil degradation, plastic waste, fisheries protection

ECONOMY

Currency: Colón, (*pl.*) colones

GDP: $49.55 billion

Per capita income: $12,900

Unemployment: 8.6%

Major industries: Microprocessors, tourism, food processing, textiles and clothing, construction materials, fertilizer, plastic products

Agricultural products: Bananas, coffee, pineapples, sugarcane, corn, rice, beans, potatoes, beef

Exports: $11.1 billion

Major export products: Bananas, coffee, pineapples, electronic components, fertilizers, sugar, textiles, electricity, ornamental plants, medical equipment

Export partners: (in order of volume) United States, Netherlands, Panama, China, Nicaragua

Imports: $16.4 billion

Major import products: Chemicals, consumer goods, electronic components, machinery, petroleum products, vehicles

Import partners: United States (44%), China (10%), Mexico (7%)

DID YOU KNOW?

■ Tourism earns more foreign exchange than bananas and coffee combined.

■ Costa Rica did away with its military in 1949.

■ Five percent of the world's identified plant and animal species are found in this country.

■ Costa Rica is the home of five active volcanoes.

WILDLIFE AND PLANT GLOSSARY

Here is a rundown of some of the most common and attention-grabbing mammals, birds, reptiles, amphibians, plants, and even a few insects that you might encounter. We give the common Costa Rican names, so you can understand the local lingo, followed by the latest scientific terms.

Fauna

Agouti (*guatusa*; *Dasyprocta punctata*): A 20-inch, tailless rodent with small ears and a large muzzle, the agouti is reddish brown on the Pacific side, more of a tawny orange on the Caribbean slope. It sits on its haunches to eat large seeds and fruit and resembles a large rabbit without the long ears.

Anteater (*Oso hormiguero*): Three species of anteater inhabit Costa Rica—the very rare giant (*Myrmecophaga tridactyla*), the nocturnal silky (*Cyclopes didactylus*), and the collared, or vested (*Tamandua mexicana*). Only the last is commonly seen, and too often as roadkill. This medium-size anteater, 30 inches long with an 18-inch tail, laps up ants and termites with its long, sticky tongue and has long, sharp claws for ripping into insect nests.

Armadillo (*cusuco*; *Dasypus novemcinctus*): The nine-banded armadillo is widespread in Costa Rica and also found in the southern United States. This nocturnal and solitary edentate roots in soil with a long muzzle for a varied diet of insects, small animals, and plant material.

Baird's Tapir (*danta*; *Tapirus bairdii*): The largest land mammal in Costa Rica (to 6½ feet), Baird's tapir is something like a small rhinoceros without armor. Adapted to a wide range of habitats, it's nocturnal, seldom seen, but said to defecate and sometimes sleep in water. Tapirs are herbivorous and use their prehensile snouts to harvest vegetation. The best opportunities for viewing wild tapirs are in Corcovado National Park.

Bat (*murciélago*): With more than 100 species, Costa Rica's bats can be found eating fruit, insects, fish, small vertebrates, nectar, and even blood, in the case of the infamous vampire bat (*vampiro*, *Desmodus rotundus*), which far prefers cattle blood to that of any tourist. As a group, bats are extremely important ecologically, and are essential to seed dispersal, pollination, and controlling insect populations.

Butterfly (*mariposa*): Estimates of the number of butterfly species in Costa Rica vary, but all range in the thousands. The growing number of butterfly gardens popping up around the country is testament to their popularity among visitors. Three Costa Rican morpho species—spectacular, large butterflies—have a brilliant blue upper-wing surface, giving them their local nickname of *pedazos de ciel* (pieces of sky). The blue morpho (*Morpho peleides*), arguably the most distinctive, is common in moister areas and has an intense ultraviolet upper surface. Adults feed on fermenting fruit; they never visit flowers.

Caiman (*caimán*): The spectacled caiman (*Caiman crocodilus*) is a small crocodilian (to 7 feet) inhabiting freshwater, subsisting mainly on fish. Most active at night (it has bright red eye shine), it basks by day. It is distinguished from the American crocodile by a sloping brow and smooth back scales.

Coati (*pizote*; *Nasua narica*): This is a long-nose relative of the raccoon, its long tail often held straight up. Lone males or groups of females with young are active during the day, on the ground, or in trees. Omnivorous coatis feed on fruit, invertebrates, and small vertebrates. Unfortunately, many have learned to beg from tourists, especially in Monteverde and on the roads around Arenal.

Cougar (*puma*; *Felis concolor*): Mountain lions are the largest unspotted cats (to 8 feet, including the tail) in Costa Rica. Widespread but rare, they live in essentially all-wild habitats and feed on vertebrates ranging from snakes to deer.

Crocodile (*lagarto*; *Crocodylus acutus*): The American crocodile, up to 16 feet in length, is found in most major river systems, particularly the Tempisque and Tárcoles estuaries. It seldom attacks humans, preferring fish and birds. It's distinguished from the caiman by size, a flat head, narrow snout, and spiky scales.

Ctenosaur (*garrobo; Ctenosaura similis*): Also known as the black, or spiny-tailed, iguana, this is a large (up to 18 inches long with an 18-inch tail) tan lizard with four dark bands on its body and a tail ringed with sharp, curved spines, reminiscent of a dinosaur. Terrestrial and arboreal, it sleeps in burrows or tree hollows. It lives along the coast in the dry northwest and in wetter areas farther south. The fastest known reptile (clocked on land), the ctenosaur has been recorded moving at 21.7 miles per hour.

Dolphin (*delfín*): Several species, including bottlenose dolphins (*Tursiops truncatus*), frolic in Costa Rican waters. Often seen off Pacific shores are spotted dolphins (*Stenella attenuata*), which are small (up to 6 feet) with pale spots on the posterior half of the body; they commonly travel in groups of 20 or more and play around vessels and in bow wakes. Tucuxi dolphins (*Sotalia fluviatilis*) have also been spotted in small groups off the southern Caribbean coast, frequently with bottlenose dolphins.

Frog and Toad (*rana,* frog; *sapo,* toad): Some 120 species of frog exist in Costa Rica; many are nocturnal. The most colorful daytime amphibians are the tiny strawberry poison dart frog (*Dendrobates pumilio*) and green-and-black poison dart frog. The bright coloration of these two species, either red with blue or green hind legs or charcoal black with fluorescent green markings, warns potential predators of their toxicity. The red-eyed leaf frog (*Agalychnis callidryas*) is among the showiest of nocturnal species. The large, brown marine toad (*Bufo marinus*), also called cane toad or giant toad, comes out at night.

Howler Monkey (*mono congo; Alouatta palliata*): These dark, chunky-bodied monkeys (to 22 inches long with a 24-inch tail) with black faces travel in troops of up to 20. Lethargic mammals, they eat leaves, fruits, and flowers. The males' deep, resounding howls sound like lions roaring, but actually serve as communication among and between troops.

Hummingbird (*colibrí; Trochilidae*): Weighing just a fraction of an ounce, hummingbirds are nonetheless some of the most notable residents of tropical forests. At least 50 varieties can be found in Costa Rica, visiting typically red tubular flowers in their seemingly endless search for energy-rich nectar. Because of their assortment of iridescent colors and bizarre bills and tail shapes, watching them can be a spectator sport. Best bets are hummingbird feeders and anywhere with great numbers of flowers.

Iguana (*iguana*): Mostly arboreal but good at swimming, the iguana is Costa Rica's largest lizard: males can grow to 10 feet, including tail. Only young green iguanas (*Iguana iguana*) are bright green; adults are much duller, females dark grayish and males olive (with orangish heads in breeding season). All have round cheek scales and smooth tails.

Jaguar (*tigre; Panthera onca*): The largest New World feline (to 6 feet, with a 2-foot tail), this top-of-the-line predator is exceedingly rare but lives in a wide variety of habitats, from dry forest to cloud forest. It's most common in the vast Amistad Biosphere Reserve, but it is almost never seen in the wild.

Jesus Christ Lizard (*gallego*): Flaps of skin on long toes enable this spectacular lizard to run across water. Costa Rica has three species of this lizard, which is more properly called the basilisk: lineated (*Basiliscus basiliscus*) on the Pacific side is brown with pale lateral stripes; in the Caribbean, emerald (*Basiliscus plumifrons*) is marked with turquoise and black on a green body; and striped (*Basiliscus vittatus*), also on the Caribbean side, resembles the lineated basilisk. Adult males grow to 3 feet (mostly tail), with crests on the head, back, and base of the tail.

Leaf-Cutter Ant (*zompopas; Atta* spp.): Found in all lowland habitats, these are the most commonly noticed neotropical ants, and one of the country's most fascinating animal phenomena. Columns of ants carrying bits of leaves twice their size sometimes extend for several hundred yards from an underground nest to plants being harvested. The ants don't eat the leaves; their food is a fungus they cultivate on the leaves.

Macaw (*lapas*): Costa Rica's two species are the scarlet macaw (*Ara macao*), on the Pacific side (Osa Peninsula and Carara Biological Reserve), and the severely threatened great green macaw (*Ara ambigua*), on the Caribbean side. These are huge, raucous parrots with long tails; their immense bills are used to rip fruit apart to reach the seeds. They nest in hollow trees and are victimized by pet-trade poachers and deforestation.

Magnificent Frigatebird (*tijereta del mar; Fregata magnificens*): A large, black soaring bird with slender wings and forked tail, this is one of the most effortless and agile flyers in the avian world. More common on the Pacific coast, it doesn't dive or swim but swoops to pluck its food, often from the mouths of other birds.

Manatee (*manatí; Trichechus manatus*): Although endangered throughout its range, the West Indian manatee can be spotted in Tortuguero, meandering along in shallow water, browsing on submerged vegetation. The moniker "sea cow" is apt, as they spend nearly all their time resting or feeding. Their large, somewhat amorphous bodies won't win any beauty contests, but they do appear quite graceful.

Margay (*caucel; Felis wiedii*): Fairly small, this spotted nocturnal cat (22 inches long, with an 18-inch tail) is similar to the ocelot but has a longer tail and is far more

arboreal: mobile ankle joints allow it to climb down trunks head first. It eats small vertebrates.

Motmot (*pájaro bobo; Momotus momota*): These handsome, turquoise-and-rufous birds of the understory have racket-shaped tails. Nesting in burrows, they sit patiently while scanning for large insect prey or small vertebrates. Costa Rica has six species.

Northern Jacana (*gallito de agua; Jacana spinosa*): These birds are sometimes called "lily trotters" because their long toes allow them to walk on floating vegetation. Feeding on aquatic organisms and plants, they're found in almost any body of water. They expose yellow wing feathers in flight. Sex roles are reversed; "liberated" females are larger and compete for mates (often more than one), whereas the males tend to the nest and care for the young.

Ocelot (*manigordo; Felis pardalis*): Mostly terrestrial, this medium-size spotted cat (33 inches long, with a 16-inch tail) is active night and day and feeds on rodents and other vertebrates. Forepaws are rather large in relation to the body, hence the local name *manigordo*, which means "fat hand."

Opossum (*zorro pelón; Didelphis marsupialis*): Like the kangaroo, the common opossum belongs to that rare breed of mammal known as marsupials, distinguished by their brief gestation period and completion of development and nourishment following birth in the mother's pouch. The Costa Rican incarnation does not "play possum," and will bite if cornered rather than pretend to be dead.

Oropendola (*oropéndola; Psarocolius* spp.): These crow-size birds in the oriole family have a bright-yellow tail and nest in colonies in pendulous nests (up to 6 feet long) built by females in isolated trees. The Montezuma species has an orange beak and blue cheeks; the chestnut-headed has a yellow beak. Males make an unmistakable, loud, gurgling-liquid call. The bird is far more numerous on the Caribbean side.

Parakeet and Parrot (*pericos*, parakeets; *loros*, parrots): There are 15 species in Costa Rica (plus two macaws), all clad in green, most with a splash of a primary color or two on the head or wings. They travel in boisterous flocks, prey on immature seeds, and nest in cavities.

Peccary (*Tayassuidea*): Piglike animals with thin legs and thick necks, peccaries travel in small groups (larger where the population is still numerous); root in soil for fruit, seeds, and small creatures; and have a strong musk odor. You'll usually smell them before you see them. Costa Rica has two species: the collared peccary (*saíno*; *Tayassu tajacu*) and the white-lipped peccary (*chancho de monte*; *Tayassu pecari*). The latter is now nearly extinct.

Pelican (*pelícano*): Large size, a big bill, and a throat pouch make the brown pelican (*Pelecanus occidentalis*) unmistakable in coastal areas (it's far more abundant on the Pacific side). Pelicans often fly in V formations and dive for fish.

Quetzal (*Pharomachrus mocinno*): One of the world's most exquisite birds, the resplendent quetzal was revered by the Maya. Glittering green plumage and the male's long tail coverts draw thousands of people to highland cloud forests for sightings from February to April.

Roseate Spoonbill (*garza rosada*; *Ajaja ajaja*): Pink plumage and a spatulate bill set this wader apart from all other wetland birds; it feeds by swishing its bill back and forth in water while using its feet to stir up bottom-dwelling creatures. Spoonbills are most common around Palo Verde and Caño Negro.

Sloth (*perezoso*): Costa Rica is home to the brown-throated, three-toed sloth (*Bradypus variegatus*) and Hoffmann's two-toed sloth (*Choloepus hoffmanni*). Both grow to 2 feet, but two-toed (check forelegs) sloths often look bigger because of longer fur and are the only species in the highlands. Sloths are herbivorous, accustomed to a low-energy diet, and well camouflaged.

Snake (*culebra*): Costa Rica's serpents can be found in trees, above- and belowground, and even in the sea on the Pacific coast. Most of the more than 125 species are harmless, but are best appreciated from a distance. Costa Rica's largest snake, the boa constrictor (*Boa constrictor*), reaches up to 15 feet. The fer-de-lance (*terciopelo*; *Bothrops asper*) is a much smaller (up to 6 feet) but far more dangerous viper.

Spider Monkey (*mono colorado, mono araña*): Lanky and long tailed, the black-handed spider monkey (*Ateles geoffroyi*) is the largest monkey in Costa Rica (to 24 inches, with a 32-inch tail). Moving in groups of two to four, they eat ripe fruit, leaves, and flowers. Incredible aerialists, they can swing effortlessly through branches using long arms and legs and prehensile tails. They are quite aggressive and will challenge onlookers and often throw down branches. Caribbean and southern Pacific populations are dark reddish brown; northwesterners are blond.

Squirrel Monkey (*mono titi*): The smallest of four Costa Rican monkeys (11 inches, with a 15-inch tail), the red-backed squirrel monkey (*Saimiri oerstedii*) has a distinctive facial pattern (black cap and muzzle, white mask) and gold-orange coloration on its back. It is the only Costa Rican monkey without a prehensile tail. The species travels in noisy, active groups of 20 or more, feeding on fruit and insects. Numbers of this endangered species have been estimated between 2,000 and 4,000 individuals. Most squirrel monkeys in Costa Rica are found in Manuel Antonio National Park, in parts of the Osa Peninsula, and around the Golfo Dulce.

Three-Wattled Bellbird (*pájaro campana*; *Procnias tricarunculata*): Although endangered, the bellbird can be readily identified in cloud forests (around Monteverde, for example), where it breeds by its extraordinary call, a bold and aggressive "bonk," unlike any other creature in the forest. If you spot a male calling, look for the three pendulous wattles at the base of its beak.

Toucan (*tucán, tucancillo*): The keel-billed toucan (*Ramphastos sulfuratus*) with the rainbow-colored beak is familiar to anyone who's seen a box of Froot Loops cereal. Chestnut-mandibled toucans (*Ramphastos swainsonii*) are the largest (18 inches and 22 inches); as the name implies, their lower beaks are brown. The smaller, stouter emerald toucanet (*Aulacorhynchus prasinus*) and yellow-eared toucanet (*Selenidera spectabilis*) are aptly named. Aracaris (*Pteroglossus* spp.) are similar to toucans, but colored orange and yellow with the trademark toucan bill.

Turtles (*tortuga*): Observing the nesting rituals of the five species of marine turtles here is one of those truly memorable Costa Rican experiences. Each species has its own nesting season and locale. The olive ridley (*lora; Lepidochelys olivacea*) is the smallest of the sea turtles (average carapace, or hardback shell, is 21–29 inches) and the least shy. Thousands engage in nighttime group-nesting rituals on the North Pacific's Ostional. At the other extreme, but only slightly farther north on Playa Grande, nests the leatherback (*baula; Dermochelys coriacea*) with its 5-foot-long shell. On the north Caribbean coast, Tortuguero hosts four of them: the leatherback, the hawksbill (*carey; Eretmochelys imbricata*), the loggerhead (*caguama; Caretta caretta*), and the green (*tortuga verde; Chelonia mydas*), with its long nesting season (June–October) that draws the most visitors and researchers.

Whales (*ballena*): Humpback whales (*Megaptera novaeanglia*) appear off the Pacific coast between November and February; they migrate from California and

as far as Hawaii. You can also spot sei whales, Bryde's whales, and farther out to sea, blue whales and sperm whales. On the Caribbean side, there are smaller (12 to 14 feet) Koiga whales.

White-Faced Capuchin Monkey (*mono cara blanca; Cebus capuchinus*): Medium-size and omnivorous, this monkey (to 18 inches, with a 20-inch tail) has black fur and a pink face surrounded by a whitish bib. Extremely active foragers, they move singly or in groups of up to 20, examining the environment closely and even coming to the ground. It's the most commonly seen monkey in Costa Rica. It's also the most often fed by visitors, to the point where some monkey populations now have elevated cholesterol levels.

White-Tailed Deer (*venado; Odocoileus virginianus*): Bambi would feel at home in Costa Rica, although his counterparts here are slightly smaller. As befits the name, these animals possess the distinctive white underside to their tail (and to their bellies). They are seen in drier parts of the country, especially in the northwest province of Guanacaste.

White-Throated Magpie-jay (*urraca; Calocitta formosa*): This southern relative of the blue jay, with a long tail and distinctive topknot (crest of forward-curved feathers), is found in the dry northwest. Bold and inquisitive, with amazingly varied vocalizations, these birds travel in noisy groups of four or more.

Flora

Ant-acacia (*acacia; Acacia* spp.): If you'll be in the tropical dry forest of Guanacaste, learn to avoid this plant. As if its sharp thorns weren't enough, acacias exhibit an intense symbiosis with various ant species (*Pseudomyrmex* spp.) that will attack anything—herbivores, other plants, and unaware human visitors that come in contact with the tree. The ants and the acacias have an intriguing relationship, though, so do look, but don't touch.

Bromeliad (*piña silvestre*): Members of the family *Bromeliaceae* are epiphytes, living on the trunk and branches of trees. They are not parasitic, however, and so have adapted to acquire all the necessary water and nutrients from what falls into the central "tank" formed by the leaf structure. Amphibians and insects also use the water held in bromeliads to reproduce, forming small aquatic communities perched atop tree branches. In especially wet areas, small bromeliads can even be found on power lines. Their spectacular, colorful efflorescences make popular—and expensive—houseplants in northern climes.

Heliconia (*heliconia; Heliconia* spp.): It's hard to miss these stunning plants, many of which have huge inflorescences of red, orange, and yellow, sometimes shaped like lobster claws, and leaves very much the size and shape of a banana plant. With luck, you'll catch a visiting hummingbird with a beak specially designed to delve into a heliconia flower—truly a visual treat.

Mangroves (*manglares*): Taken together, this handful of salt-tolerant trees with tangled, aboveground roots makes up its own distinct ecosystem. Buttressing the land against the sea, the trees serve as nurseries for countless species of fish, crab, and other marine animals and provide roosting habitat for marine birds. Mangroves are found on the coast in protected areas such as bays and estuaries.

Naked Indian Tree (*indio desnudo; Bursera simaruba*): This tree can be found in forests throughout Costa Rica, often forming living fences, and is instantly identifiable by its orange bark that continually sloughs off, giving rise to another common name, the sunburned tourist tree. One theory suggests that the shedding of its bark aids in removing parasites from the tree's exterior.

Orchid (*orquídea*): The huge Orchidaceae family has more than 1,200 representatives in Costa Rica alone, with nearly 90% living as epiphytes on other plants. The great diversity of the group includes not only examples of great beauty but exquisite adaptations between flowers and their insect pollinators. With a combination of rewards (nectar) and trickery (visual and chemical cues), orchids exhibit myriad ways of enticing insects to cooperate.

Strangler Fig (*matapalo; Ficus* spp.): Starting as seedlings high in the canopy, these aggressive plants grow both up toward the light and down to the soil, slowly taking over the host tree. Eventually they encircle and appear to "strangle" the host, actually killing it by hogging all the available sunlight, leaving a ring of fig trunk around an empty interior. Figs with ripe fruit are excellent places for wildlife spotting, as they attract monkeys, birds, and an assortment of other creatures.

MENU GUIDE

Rice and beans are the heart of Costa Rica's *comida típica* (typical food). It's possible to order everything from sushi to crepes in and around San José, but most Ticos have a simple diet built around rice, beans, and the myriad fruits and vegetables that flourish here. Costa Rican food isn't spicy, and many dishes are seasoned with the same five ingredients—onion, salt, garlic, cilantro, and red bell pepper.

SPANISH	ENGLISH
GENERAL DINING	
Almuerzo	Lunch
Bocas	Appetizers or snacks (literally "mouthfuls") served with drinks in the tradition of Spanish tapas
Casado	Heaping plate of rice, beans, fried plantains, cabbage salad, tomatoes, *macarrones* (noodles), and fish, chicken, or meat—or any variation thereof
Cena	Dinner
Desayuno	Breakfast
Plato del día	Plate of the day
Soda	An inexpensive café; casados are always found at sodas.
ESPECIALIDADES (SPECIALTIES)	
Arreglados	Sandwiches or meat and vegetable puff pastry
Arroz con mariscos	Fried rice with fish, shrimp, octopus, and clams, or whatever's fresh that day
Arroz con pollo	Chicken with rice
Camarones	Shrimp
Ceviche	Chilled, raw seafood marinated in lime juice, served with chopped onion and garlic
Chilaquiles	Meat-stuffed tortillas
Chorreados	Corn pancakes, served with *natilla* (sour cream)
Corvina	Sea bass
Empanadas	Savory or sweet pastry turnover filled with fruit or meat and vegetables

SPANISH	ENGLISH
Empanaditas	Small empanadas
Gallo pinto	Rice sautéed with black beans (literally, "spotted rooster"), often served for breakfast
Langosta	Lobster
Langostino	Prawns
Olla de carne	Soup of beef, chayote squash, corn, yuca (a tuber), and potatoes
Palmitos	Hearts of palm, served in salads or as a side dish
Pejibaye	A nutty, orange-color palm fruit eaten in salads, soups, and as a snack
Pescado ahumado	Smoked marlin
Picadillo	Chayote squash, potatoes, carrots, or other vegetables chopped into small cubes and combined with onions, garlic, and ground beef
Pozol	Corn soup
Salsa caribeño	A combination of tomatoes, onions, and spices that accompanies most fish dishes on the Caribbean coast

POSTRES (DESSERTS) AND DULCES (SWEETS)

Cajeta	Molasses-flavored fudge
Cajeta de coco	Fudge made with coconut and orange peel
Dulce de leche	Thick syrup of boiled milk and sugar
Flan	Caramel-topped egg custard
Mazamorra	Cornstarch pudding
Pan de maíz	Sweet corn bread
Torta chilena	Flaky, multilayer cake with dulce de leche filling
Tres leches	"Three milks" cake, made with condensed and evaporated milk and cream

SPANISH	ENGLISH
FRUTAS (FRUITS)	
Aguacate	Avocado
Anón	Sugar apple; sweet white flesh; resembles an artichoke with a thick rind
Banano	Banana
Bilimbi	Looks like a miniature cucumber crossed with a star fruit; ground into a savory relish
Carambola	Star fruit
Cas	A smaller guava
Fresa	Strawberry
Granadilla	Passion fruit
Guanábana	Soursop; large, spiky yellow fruit with white flesh and a musky taste
Guayaba	Guava
Mamón chino	Rambutan; red spiky ball protecting a white fruit similar to a lychee
Mango	Many varieties, from sour green to succulently sweet oro (golden); March is the height of mango season
Manzana de agua	Water apple, shaped like a pear; juicy but not very sweet
Marañón	Cashew fruit; used in juices
Melón	Cantaloupe
Mora	Blackberry
Palmito	Heart of palm
Papaya	One of the most popular and ubiquitous fruits
Piña	Pineapple
Pipa	Green coconut; sold at roadside stands with ends chopped off and straws stuck inside
Sandía	Watermelon

SPANISH	ENGLISH

BEBIDAS (BEVERAGES)

Agua dulce	Hot water sweetened with raw sugarcane
Batido	Fruit shake made with milk (con leche) or water (con agua)
Café con leche	Coffee with hot milk
Café negro	Black coffee
Cerveza	Beer
Fresco natural	Fresh-squeezed juice
Gaseosa	Any carbonated beverage
Guaro	Harsh, clear spirit distilled from fermented sugarcane
Horchata	Cinnamon-flavor rice drink
Refresco	Tropical fruit smoothie with ice and sugar
Ron	Rum

VOCABULARY

ENGLISH	SPANISH	PRONUNCIATION

BASIC PHRASES

ENGLISH	SPANISH	PRONUNCIATION
Yes/no	Sí/no	see/no
OK.	De acuerdo.	de a- **kwer**-doe
Please.	Por favor.	pore fah- **vore**
May I?	¿Me permite?	may pair- **mee**-tay
Thank you (very much).	(Muchas) gracias.	(**moo**-chas) **grah**-see-as
You're welcome.	Con mucho gusto.*	con **moo**-cho **goose**-toe
Excuse me.	Con permiso.	con pair- **mee**-so
Pardon me.	¿Perdón?	pair- **dohn**
Could you tell me?	¿Podría decirme?	po-dree-ah deh- **seer**-meh
I'm sorry.	Disculpe.	dee- **skool**-peh
Good morning!	¡Buenos días!	**bway**-nohs **dee**-ahs
Good afternoon!	¡Buenas tardes!	**bway**-nahs **tar**-dess
Good evening!	¡Buenas noches!	**bway**-nahs **no**-chess
Goodbye!	¡Adiós!/¡Hasta luego!	ah-dee- **ohss** / **ah**-stah-lwe-go
Mr./Mrs.	Señor/Señora	sen- **yor** /sen- **yohr**-ah
Miss	Señorita	sen-yo- **ree**-tah
Pleased to meet you.	Mucho gusto.	**moo**-cho **goose**-toe
How are you?	¿Cómo está usted?	**ko**-mo es- **tah** oo- **sted**
Very well, thank you.	Muy bien, gracias.	**moo**-ee bee- **en**, **grah**-see-as
And you?	¿Y usted?	ee oos- **ted**

*Other Spanish speakers use "De nada" (It's nothing) to say "You're welcome." The Costa Rican phrase translates as "With much pleasure."

DAYS OF THE WEEK

ENGLISH	SPANISH	PRONUNCIATION
Sunday	domingo	doe- **meen**-goh
Monday	lunes	**loo**-ness
Tuesday	martes	**mahr**-tess
Wednesday	miércoles	me- **air**-koh-less
Thursday	jueves	hoo- **ev**-ess

ENGLISH	SPANISH	PRONUNCIATION
Friday	viernes	vee- **air**-ness
Saturday	sábado	**sah**-bah-doh

USEFUL PHRASES

Do you speak English?	¿Habla usted inglés?	**ah**-blah oos- **ted** in- **glehs**
I don't speak Spanish.	No hablo español.	no **ah**-bloh es-pahn- **yol**
I don't understand (you).	No entiendo.	no en-tee- **en**-doh
I understand (you).	Entiendo.	en-tee- **en**-doh
I don't know.	No sé.	no seh
I am American/British.	Soy americano (americana)/inglés(a).	soy ah-meh-ree- **kah**-no (ah-meh-ree- **kah**-nah)/ in- **glehs (ah)**
What's your name?	¿Cómo se llama usted?	koh-mo seh **yah**-mah **oos**-ted
My name is . . .	Me llamo . . .	may **yah**-moh
What time is it?	¿Qué hora es?	keh **o**-rah es
It is one, two, three . . . o'clock.	Es la una. . . . Son las dos, tres.	es la **oo**-nah/sohn lahs dohs, tress
How?	¿Cómo?	**koh**-mo
When?	¿Cuándo?	**kwahn**-doh
This/Next week	Esta semana/la semana que entra	**es**-teh seh- **mah**-nah/ lah seh- **mah**-nah keh **en**-trah
This/Next month	Este mes/el próximo mes	**es**-teh mehs/el **proke**-see-mo mehs
This/Next year	Este año/el año que viene	**es**-teh **ahn**-yo/el **ahn**-yo keh vee- **yen**-ay
Yesterday/today/ tomorrow	Ayer/hoy/mañana	ah- **yehr** /oy/ mahn- **yah**-nah
This morning/ afternoon	Esta mañana/tarde	**es**-tah mahn- **yah**-nah/ **tar**-deh
Tonight	Esta noche	**es**-tah **no**-cheh
What?	¿Qué?	keh
What is it?	¿Qué es esto?	keh es **es**-toh
Why?	¿Por qué?	pore **keh**

ENGLISH	SPANISH	PRONUNCIATION
Who?	¿Quién?	kee-**yen**
Where is . . . ?	¿Dónde está . . . ?	**dohn**-deh es-**tah**
the bus stop?	la parada del bus?	la pah-**rah**-dah del **boos**
the post office?	la oficina de correos?	la oh-fee-**see**-nah deh koh-**reh**-os
the museum?	el museo?	el moo-**seh**-oh
the hospital?	el hospital?	el ohss-pee-**tal**
the bathroom?	el baño?	el **bahn**-yoh
Here/there	Aquí/allá	ah-**key** /ah-**yah**
Open/closed	Abierto/cerrado	ah-bee-**er**-toh/ ser-**ah**-doh
Left/right	Izquierda/derecha	iss-key-**er**-dah/ dare-**eh**-chah
Straight ahead	Derecho	dare-**eh**-choh
Is it near/far?	¿Está cerca/lejos?	es-**tah sehr**-kah/ **leh**-hoss
I'd like . . .	Quisiera . . .	kee-see-ehr-ah
a room.	un cuarto/una habitación.	oon **kwahr**-toh/ **oo**-nah ah-bee-tah-see-**on**
the key.	la llave.	lah **yah**-veh
a newspaper.	un periódico.	oon pehr-ee-**oh**-dee-koh
a stamp.	una estampilla.	**oo**-nah es-stahm-**pee**-yah
I'd like to buy . . .	Quisiera comprar . . .	kee-see-**ehr**-ah kohm-**prahr**
a dictionary.	un diccionario.	oon deek-see-oh-**nah**-ree-oh
soap.	jabón.	hah-**bohn**
suntan lotion.	loción bronceadora.	loh-see-**ohn** brohn-seh-ah-**do**-rah
a map.	un mapa.	oon **mah**-pah
a magazine.	una revista.	**oon**-ah reh-**veess**-tah
a postcard.	una tarjeta postal.	**oon**-ah tar-**het**-ah post-**ahl**
How much is it?	¿Cuánto cuesta?	**kwahn**-toh **kwes**-tah
Telephone	Teléfono	tel-**ef**-oh-no

ENGLISH	SPANISH	PRONUNCIATION
Help!	¡Auxilio!	owk- **see**-lee-oh
	¡Ayuda!	ah- **yoo**-dah
	¡Socorro!	soh- **kohr**-roh
Fire!	¡Incendio!	en- **sen**-dee-oo
Caution!/Look out!	¡Cuidado!	kwee- **dah**-doh

SALUD (HEALTH)

I am ill.	Estoy enfermo(a).	es- **toy** en- **fehr**- moh(mah)
Please call a doctor.	Por favor llame a un médico.	pohr fah- **vor ya**-meh ah oon **med**-ee-koh
acetaminophen	acetaminofeno	a-say-ta- **mee**-no-fen-oh
ambulance	ambulancia	ahm-boo- **lahn**-see-a
antibiotic	antibiótico	ahn-tee-bee- **oh**-tee-co
aspirin	aspirina	ah-spi- **ree**-na
capsule	cápsula	**cahp**-soo-la
clinic	clínica	**clee**-nee-ca
cold	resfriado	rays-free- **ah**-do
cough	tos	toess
diarrhea	diarrea	dee-ah- **ray**-a
fever	fiebre	fee- **ay**-bray
flu	gripe	**gree**-pay
headache	dolor de cabeza	doh- **lor** day cah- **bay**-sa
hospital	hospital	oh-spee- **tahl**
medication	medicamento	meh-dee-cah- **men**-to
pain	dolor	doh- **lor**
pharmacy	farmacia	fahr- **mah**-see-a
physician	médico	**meh**-dee-co
prescription	receta	ray- **say**-ta
stomachache	dolor de estómago	doh- **lor** day eh- **sto**-mah-go

TRAVEL SMART
COSTA RICA

GETTING HERE AND AROUND

■ AIR TRAVEL

If you are visiting several regions of the country, flying into San José, in the center of Costa Rica, is your best option. Flying into Liberia, in northwest Costa Rica, makes more sense if you are planning to spend your vacation entirely in the North Pacific. Fares are usually lower to San José than to Liberia. San José also has many more flights each day, making it easier if you miss a flight or have some other unexpected mishap.

Rarely does an international flight arrive in San José early enough to make a domestic connection, particularly in the rainy season, as the weather is typically unsuitable for flying in the afternoon. So you'll likely end up spending your first night in San José, leaving for your domestic destination the next morning.

It's rare, but afternoon and evening storms during the May-to-November rainy season occasionally cause flights coming into San José to be rerouted to Panama City, where you may be forced to spend the night. October, with its frequent evening fog, tends to be the worst month for reroutes. ■TIP➔ In the rainy season, try to book a flight with the earliest arrival time available.

Once you're in Costa Rica, some airlines recommend that you call them about three days before your return flight to reconfirm. Others explicitly say it's not necessary. It's always a good idea to check the day before you are scheduled to depart to make sure your flight time hasn't changed.

If you arrive in Costa Rica and your baggage doesn't, the first thing you should do is go to the baggage claims counter and file an official report. Then contact your airline to let them know where you will be staying. Bags are usually located within two days and can be sent to you just about anywhere in the country. Don't expect too much from local agents; try to get updates directly from your airline.

If your bag has been searched and contents are missing or damaged, file a claim with the Transportation Security Administration's Consumer Response Center as soon as possible. If your bags arrive damaged or fail to arrive at all, file a written report with the airline before leaving the airport.

Costa Rica levies a $29 airport departure tax, payable in dollars or the equivalent in colones. At this writing, it is slowly moving to a system of bundling the tax into ticket prices. You'll need to check with your airline. If not already included, you pay the tax at the airport upon departure. Paying with a MasterCard or Visa credit card means the transaction will be processed as a cash advance and incur additional fees. A few hotels will collect the tax for you as well.

Airline Security Issues Transportation Security Administration. ⊕ *www.tsa.gov.*

AIRPORTS

Costa Rica has two international airports. Aeropuerto Internacional Juan Santamaría (SJO) is the country's main airport, about 17 km (10 miles), northwest of downtown San José, just outside the city of Alajuela. The drive takes about 30 minutes. Domestic airlines SANSA and Nature Air—most of its routes—operate from here, SANSA in its own terminal and Nature Air inside the main building. The country's other international airport is Aeropuerto Internacional Daniel Oduber Quirós (LIR), a small airport near the city of Liberia in the North Pacific. It's about 13 km (8 miles) west of the city.

The small Aeropuerto Tobías Bolaños, in the Pavas district on San José's west side, serves a couple of Nature Air routes and several charter flights.

Other places where planes land in Costa Rica aren't exactly airports. They're more like carports with landing strips, and airline representatives arrive a few minutes before a plane is due to land or take off. Most international flights arrive in the evening and depart early in the morning. Prepare yourself for long waits at immigration and customs. When you're departing the country, prepare for security checkpoints at both airports. Liquids and gels of more than 3 ounces are not permitted. Carry-on bags are searched again at the gates for flights to the United States. Get to the airport three hours before your flight.

Airport Information Aeropuerto Internacional Daniel Oduber Quirós (LIR). ⊠ Liberia ☎ 2668–1010 in Costa Rica. **Aeropuerto Internacional Juan Santamaría (SJO).** ⊠ Alajuela ☎ 2437–2400, 2437–2626 in Costa Rica for departure and arrival info ⊕ www.fly2sanjose.com. **Aeropuerto Tobías Bolaños (SYQ).** ⊠ Pavas ☎ 2232–2820.

GROUND TRANSPORTATION
At Aeropuerto Internacional Juan Santamaría, you exit the terminal into a fume-filled parking area flanked by hordes of taxis and tour vans. If you're with a tour, you need only look for a tour company representative with a sign that bears your name. If you need a taxi, a uniformed agent will escort you to one of the orange Taxi Aeropuerto cabs (no other taxis are allowed in the arrivals area). The metered fare to most areas of San José is $25 to $35.

Transportation at Aeropuerto Internacional Daniel Oduber Quirós is also a mix of taxis and tour vans. The big Pacific-coast resorts provide transportation, but always check with your lodging for recommendations on the best way to arrive.

FLIGHTS
From North America to San José: American flies from Miami, Dallas and Charlotte and, from November to April, from New York (JFK) and Phoenix; United flies from Houston (IAH), Newark, Chicago O'Hare, and Washington Dulles (IAD) and, from December to April, from Denver; Delta flies from Atlanta and Los Angeles and, from December to April, from Minneapolis and New York (JFK); Alaska flies from Los Angeles; Spirit flies from Fort Lauderdale and Houston (IAH); JetBlue flies from Orlando and Fort Lauderdale; Southwest flies from Baltimore and Houston Hobby (HOU); Air Canada Rouge, the leisure division of Air Canada, flies from Toronto; WestJet flies from Toronto from December to April; Avianca offers connections from several U.S. airports through its hubs in San Salvador, El Salvador, or Bogotá, Colombia. Mexico's AeroMéxico does the same via its hub in Mexico City, and Panama's Copa also offers connections through its hub in Panama City.

From New York or Los Angeles, nonstop flights to San José are 5½ hours. San José is 2½ hours from Miami, 3½ hours from Houston, and 4 hours from Charlotte and Dallas. In general, nonstop flights aren't that much more expensive. Ticket prices from hubs such as New York, Los Angeles, and Miami hover between $500 and $600, although the range varies widely.

From North America to Liberia: American flies from Dallas, Charlotte, and Miami; Delta flies from Atlanta, and, from December through April, from Los Angeles, Minneapolis, and New York (JFK); United flies from Houston, and, from December through April, from Chicago, Houston (IAH), and Newark; JetBlue flies from New York (JFK) and, from December through April, from Boston; Alaska flies from Los Angeles; Southwest flies from Baltimore, Los Angeles, and Houston Hobby (HOU); Air Canada Rouge flies from Toronto; Air Canada also flies from Montreal (December to April); and WestJet flies from Toronto, and, from December through April, from Calgary. Avianca and Copa connect their U.S. gateways to

Liberia via their hubs in San Salvador and Panama City, respectively.

Avianca and Copa connect San José with other Central American cities. Nature Air flies from Managua, Nicaragua, and from Bocas del Toro, Panama.

Given Costa Rica's often-difficult driving conditions, domestic flights are a desirable and practical option. The informality of domestic air service—"airports" other than Liberia and San José usually consist of only an airstrip with no central building at which to buy tickets—means you might want to purchase your domestic airplane tickets in advance. You can also buy them at travel agencies once you're in the country. We recommend grabbing a seat as soon as you know your itinerary.

There are two major domestic commercial airlines, SANSA and Nature Air, and most of their flights leave from the San José area. You can buy tickets online, over the phone, and at most travel agencies in Costa Rica. The tiny, domestic passenger planes in Costa Rica require that you pack light. A luggage weight limit of 30 pounds is imposed by SANSA; Nature Air allows 15–40 pounds, depending on the fare. Extra luggage is sometimes allowed, but costs $1 to $3 per pound and will go standby. Neither airline can store extra baggage, but hotels and lodges may be able to store your luggage—ask ahead and bring a smaller bag for your domestic travels. Neither SANSA nor Nature Air has interline ticketing or baggage transfer with the international airlines serving Costa Rica.

Charter flights within Costa Rica are not as expensive as you might think, and can be a good deal if you are traveling in a group. The price per person will be only slightly more than taking a regularly scheduled domestic flight, and you can set your own departure time. The country has dozens of airstrips that are accessible only by charter planes. Charter planes are most often booked through tour operators,

travel agents, or remote lodges. Most charter planes are smaller than domestic commercial planes.

■TIP→ Don't book a domestic flight for the day you arrive in or leave Costa Rica; connections are extremely tight, and you'll be at the mercy of the weather.

Airline Contacts AeroMéxico. ☎ 800/237–6639 in North America, 2331–6834 ⊕ www. aeromexico.com. **Air Canada/Air Canada Rouge.** ☎ 888/247–2262 in North America, 0800/052–1988 in Costa Rica ⊕ www. aircanada.com. **Alaska Airlines.** ☎ 800/252–7522 in North America. **American Airlines.** ☎ 800/433–7300 in North America, 2248–9010 in Costa Rica ⊕ www.aa.com. **Avianca.** ☎ 800/284–2622 in North America, 2299–8222 in Costa Rica ⊕ www.avianca.com. **Copa.** ☎ 800/359–2672 in North America, 2223–2672 in Costa Rica ⊕ www.copaair.com. **Delta Airlines.** ☎ 800/241–4141 for international reservations, 0800/056–2002 in Costa Rica ⊕ www.delta.com. **JetBlue.** ☎ 800/538–2583 in North America, 0800/012–1666 in Costa Rica ⊕ www.jetblue.com. **Southwest.** ☎ 800/435–9792 in North America ⊕ www. southwest.com. **Spirit Airlines.** ☎ 801/401–2222 in North America, 4000–1887 in Costa Rica ⊕ www.spiritair.com. **United Airlines.** ☎ 800/864–8331 in North America, 0800/044–0005 In Costa Rica ⊕ www.united.com. **WestJet.** ☎ 888/937–8538 in North America, 800/5381–5696 in Costa Rica ⊕ www.westjet.com.

Domestic and Charter Airlines Aerobell Air Charter. ✉ Pavas ☎ 888/359–1359 in North America, 2291–7979 in Costa Rica ⊕ www. aerobell.com. **Nature Air.** ☎ 800/235–9272 in North America, 2299–6000 in Costa Rica ⊕ www.natureair.com. **SANSA.** ☎ 2290–4100 in Costa Rica, 877/767–2672 in North America ⊕ www.flysansa.com.

▮ BUS TRAVEL

Tica Bus has daily service to Panama and Nicaragua, with connections to Honduras, El Salvador, Guatemala, and southern Mexico. Transnica serves Nicaragua and Honduras. Central Line offers service to Nicaragua. We recommend Tica Bus—it's more established and serves more destinations—but Transnica and Central Line are acceptable too. All three companies have comfortable, air-conditioned coaches with videos and onboard toilets, and help with border procedures.

All Costa Rican towns are connected by regular bus service that's reliable, comprehensive, and inexpensive. Buses between major cities are modern, but in rural areas you may get a converted school bus without air-conditioning. On longer routes, buses stop midway at modest restaurants. Near their destinations many buses turn into large taxis, dropping passengers off one by one along the way. To save time, take a *directo* (express) bus, which still might make a few stops. Be prepared for bus-company employees and bus drivers to speak only Spanish.

The main inconvenience of long-distance buses is the time spent getting there. For example, a bus from San José to the Osa Peninsula is nine hours or more, whereas the flight is one hour. Shorter distances reduce the difference—the bus to Quepos is 3½ hours, while the flight is 30 minutes. There is no central bus station in San José; buses leave from a variety of departure points, depending on the region they serve. You frequently have to return to San José to travel between outlying regions.

▮TIP➔ Avoid putting your belongings in the overhead bin. If you must, keep your eye on them. If anyone—even someone who looks like a bus employee—offers to put your things in the luggage compartment, politely decline. If you must put your luggage underneath the bus, get off quickly when you arrive to retrieve it.

Most bus companies don't have printed schedules, although departure times may be posted on a sign at the ticket window. Phones are usually busy or go unanswered. ▮TIP➔ For the most reliable schedules, go to the bus station a day before your departure. The official tourism board, the Instituto Costarricense de Turismo (ICT), provides bus schedules on its website, but the information is updated infrequently. Hotel employees can usually give you the information you need.

Buses usually depart and arrive on time; they may even leave a few minutes early if they are full. Tickets are sold at bus stations and on the buses themselves; reservations aren't accepted, and you must pay in person with cash. Be sure to have loose change and small bills handy; employees won't have change for a 10,000-colón bill. Buses to popular beach and mountain destinations often sell out on weekends and holidays. It's difficult to get tickets to San José on Sunday afternoon. Some companies won't sell you a round-trip ticket from the departure point; if that's the case, make sure the first thing you do on arrival in your destination is to buy a return ticket. Sometimes tickets include seat numbers, which are usually printed on the tops of the seats or above the windows. Smoking is not permitted.

Two private bus companies, Gray Line and Interbus, travel to the most popular tourist destinations in modern, air-conditioned vans. Vehicles for both companies seat 10 to 20 people. (Interbus can also supply coaches for large groups.) Costs range from $42 to $99 one way, but can take hours off your trip. Reservations must always be made at least 24 hours in advance. Gray Line offers a weekly pass ($198) good for unlimited travel. Interbus offers three- to seven-trip Flexipasses; they cost $125 to $275 and are good for one month, but not on every route served. Be sure to double-check information on the websites—published prices do change and routes may be discontinued. Costa Rica Shuttle offers minivan service that's great if you're traveling in a group. Rates range from $65 to $465 for up to five people.

Bus Information Central Line. ✉ *Avda. 7, C. 10, Barrio La Merced* ☎ *2221-9115* ⊕ *www. transportescentralline.com.* **Tica Bus.** ✉ *Avda. 3 and C. 26, 200 m north and 100 m west of Torre Mercedes, Paseo Colón* ☎⊕ *www. ticabus.com.* **TransNica.** ✉ *C. 22, Avdas. 3–5, San José* ☎ *2223-4920* ⊕ *www.transnica.com.*

Shuttle-Van Services Costa Rica Shuttle. ☎ *2289–4292, 800/849–9403 in North America* ⊕ *www.costaricashuttle.com.* **Gray Line.** ☎ *2291–2222, 800/719–3905 in North America* ⊕ *www.graylinecostarica.com.* **Inter-bus.** ☎ *4100–0888* ⊕ *www.interbusonline.com.*

■ CAR TRAVEL

Hiring a car with a driver makes the most sense for sightseeing in and around San José. You can also usually hire a taxi driver to ferry you around; most will stick to the meter, which will tick at a rate of about $20 for each hour the driver spends waiting for you. At $100 to $130 per day plus the driver's food, hiring a driver for areas outside the San José area costs almost the same as renting a four-wheel-drive vehicle, but is more expensive for multiday trips because you also have to pay for the driver's lodging. Some drivers are also knowledgeable guides; others just drive. Unless they're driving large passenger vans for established companies, it's doubtful that drivers have any special training or licensing.

Hotels can usually direct you to trusted drivers. Alamo provides professional car-and-driver services for a minimum of three days. On top of the rental fee, you pay $80 for the driver, plus food and lodging.

GASOLINE

You'll usually find 24-hour stations only in San José or along the Pan-American Highway. Most stations are open 7 to 7, although some are open until midnight. Regular unleaded gasoline is called *regular,* and high-octane unleaded, required in most modern vehicles, is called *súper.* Gas is sold by the liter.

Try to fill your tank in cities—gas is more expensive (and more likely to be dirtier) at informal fill-up places in rural areas, where gas stations can be few and far between. Major credit cards are widely accepted. There are no self-service gas stations in Costa Rica. It is not customary to tip attendants. If you want a *factura* (receipt), ask for it.

PARKING

On-street parking is scarce in downtown San José. Where you find a spot, you'll also find *guachimanes* ("watchmen," informal, usually self-appointed guards). They won't actually get involved if someone tries something with your car, but it's best to give them a couple of hundred colones per hour anyway. It's illegal to park in zones marked by yellow curb paint, or in front of garage doors or driveways, usually marked *no estacionar* (no parking). Downtown parking laws are strictly enforced; the fine for illegal parking is 5,000 colones (about $10). In places like San José, Alajuela, and Heredia, you'll find signs with a large E in a red circle, and the words *con boleto* (with a ticket). These tickets can be bought for ½-hour (250 colones), one-hour (500 colones), or two-hour (1,000 colones) increments.

Safer and ubiquitous are the public lots (*parqueos*), which average about $2 per hour. Most are open late, especially near hopping nightspots or theaters, but check beforehand. Never leave anything inside the car.

Outside San José and the surrounding communities, parking rules are far more lax. Guarded hotel or restaurant parking lots are the rule, with few public lots.

RENTAL CARS

When you reserve a car, ask about cancellation penalties, taxes, drop-off charges (if you're planning to pick up the car in one city and leave it in another), insurance, and surcharges (for being under or over a certain age, for additional drivers, or for driving beyond a specific distance). All these things can add substantially to your costs. Request such extras as car seats and GPS devices when you book.

Rates are sometimes—but not always—better if you book in advance or reserve through a rental agency's website. Book ahead during the busier times of the year and to ensure that you get a certain type of vehicle (a van, SUV, or sports car, for instance).

■ TIP➔ If you're only visiting one or two major areas, taking a shuttle van or a domestic flight is cheaper and more convenient than driving. Renting is a good choice if you're destination hopping, staying at a hotel outside town, or going well off the beaten path. Car trips to northern Guanacaste from San José can take an entire day, so flying is a better option if you don't have a lot of time. Flying is definitely better than driving for visiting the South Pacific.

A standard vehicle is fine for most destinations, but a *doble-tracción* (four-wheel-drive vehicle) is often essential to reach the remote parts of the country, especially during the rainy season. Even in the dry season, a 4WD vehicle is necessary to reach Monteverde and some off-the-beaten-path destinations on the North and South Pacific coasts. The biggest 4WD vehicles can cost twice as much as an economy car, but compact 4WDs are more reasonable.

Most cars in Costa Rica have manual transmissions. ■ TIP➔ Specify when making a reservation if you want automatic transmission; it usually costs $5 to $10 more per day. If you plan to rent a car between December 15 and January 3 or during the week leading up to Easter—when most Costa Ricans are on vacation—reserve several months ahead of time.

Costa Rica has around 30 car-rental firms. Most local firms are affiliated with international chains and offer the same guarantees and services. Tricolor, a local company, gets high marks from travelers on ⊕ *www.fodors.com*. Renting in or near San José is by far the easiest way to go. At least a dozen rental offices line San José's Paseo Colón. It's getting easier to rent outside San José, particularly on the Pacific coast. Several rental companies have set up branches in Liberia, Quepos, Manuel Antonio, Jacó, Tamarindo, and La Fortuna. In most other places across the country, it's either impossible or very difficult and expensive to rent a car.

Rental cars may not be driven across borders to Nicaragua and Panama. For a $50 fee, Alamo will let you drop off a Costa Rican rental car at the Nicaragua border at Peñas Blancas and provide you with a Nicaraguan rental on the other side. Fuel-efficiency measures restrict cars from much of San José and the neighboring suburb of San Pedro between 6 am and 7 pm once a week, according to the final license-plate number (plates that end in 1 and 2 are restricted on Monday; 3 and 4, on Tuesday; 5 and 6, on Wednesday; 7 and 8, on Thursday; and 9 and 0 on Friday). This also applies to rental cars.

To rent a car, you need a driver's license, a valid passport, and a credit card. The minimum age varies; agencies such as Economy, Budget, and Alamo rent to anyone over 21; Avis sets the limit at 23, Hertz at 25. If you are under 25 and the firm will rent to you, you may pay a higher rate. Though it's rare, some agencies have a maximum age limit.

High-season rates in San José begin at $60 a day and $220 a week for an economy car with air-conditioning, manual transmission, and unlimited mileage, along with obligatory insurance. Rates fluctuate considerably according to demand, season, and company. Rates for a 4WD vehicle during high season are $80 to $100 a day and $500 to $600 per week. Companies often require a $1,000 deposit, payable by credit card.

Cars picked up at or returned to San José's Aeropuerto Internacional Juan

Santamaría incur a 12% surcharge. You can pick up cars directly at the Liberia airport, but a range of firms have offices nearby and transport you from the airport free of charge—and with no surcharge for an airport pickup. Check cars thoroughly for damage before you sign the contract. Even tough-looking 4WD vehicles should be coddled. ■TIP➔ Repair charges levied by rental companies for damage—no matter how minor—are outrageous even by U.S. or European standards. One-way service surcharges are $50 to $150, depending on the drop-off point; National allows travelers free car drop-off at any of its offices with a minimum three-day rental. To avoid a hefty refueling fee, fill the tank just before you return the car. It's almost never a good deal to buy the tank of gas that's in the car when you rent it; the understanding is that you'll return it empty, but some fuel usually remains. Additional drivers can cost $10 per day. Almost all agencies have cell-phone rental; prices range between $5 and $10 per day, with national per-minute costs between 50¢ and $2.

It's wise to opt for full insurance coverage. Auto insurance in Costa Rica is a government monopoly. At a minimum, you are required to purchase collision-damage waiver as well as third-party liability insurance through the rental agency to cover damages to other persons and vehicles. Your own credit-card coverage does not exempt you from this charge. Some rental agencies include such costs in your quoted rates. Many do not, however, and we hear numerous tales of clients shocked at the final tally when they pick up the car. Always ask what is included when you reserve.

International driving permits (IDPs), which translate your license into 10 languages, are not necessary in Costa Rica. Your own driver's license is good for the length of your initial tourist visa. You must carry your passport, or a copy of it with the entry stamp, to prove when you entered the country.

Local Agencies Economy. ☏ 877/326-7368 in North America, 2299-2000 in Costa Rica ⊕ www.economyrentacar.com. **Tricolor.** ☏ 800/949-0234 in North America, 2440-3333 in Costa Rica ⊕ www.tricolorcarrental.com. **Vamos.** ☏ 4000-0557 in Costa Rica, 800/950-8426 in North America ⊕ www.vamosrentacar.com.

Major Agencies Alamo. ☏ 2242-7733 in Costa Rica, 877/222-9075 in North America ⊕ www.alamocostarica.com. **Avis.** ☏ 2293-2222 in Costa Rica, 800/331-1084 in North America ⊕ www.avis.cr. **Budget.** ☏ 2436-2000 in Costa Rica, 800/424-5431 in North America ⊕ www.budget.co.cr. **Dollar.** ☏ 877/767-8651 in North America, 2443-2950 in Costa Rica ⊕ www.dollarcostarica.com. **Enterprise.** ☏ 855/266-9289 in North America, 2242-7800 in Costa Rica ⊕ www.enterprise.com. **Hertz.** ☏ 800/654-3001 in North America, 2221-1818 in Costa Rica ⊕ www.hertzcostarica.com. **National Car Rental.** ☏ 877/862-8227 in North America, 2242-7878 in Costa Rica ⊕ www.natcar.com.

ROAD CONDITIONS

Many travelers shy away from renting a car in Costa Rica. Indeed, this is not an ideal place to drive. In San José, traffic is bad and car theft is rampant (look for guarded lots or hotels with parking). Roads in rural areas are often unpaved or potholed—and tires usually aren't covered by the basic insurance. And Ticos are reckless drivers—with one of the highest accident rates in the world. But although driving can be a challenge, it's a great way to explore certain regions, especially the North Pacific, the Northern Lowlands, and the Caribbean coast (apart from roadless Tortuguero). Keep in mind that winding roads and poor conditions make most trips longer than you'd normally expect.

The winding Pan-American Highway south of the capital is notorious for long snakes of traffic stuck behind slow-moving trucks. Look out for potholes, even in the smoothest sections of the best roads. Also watch for unmarked speed bumps where you'd least expect them, particularly on main thoroughfares in rural areas. During the rainy season, roads are in much worse shape. Check with your destination before setting out; roads, especially in Limón Province, are prone to washouts and landslides.

San José is terribly congested during weekday rush hours (7 to 9 am and 4 to 6 pm). Try to avoid returning to the city on Sunday evening, when traffic from the beaches can be backed up for miles. Frequent fender benders tie up traffic. Keep your windows rolled up in the center of the city, because thieves may reach into your car at stoplights and snatch purses, jewelry, and valuables.

Signage is notoriously bad off main highways, but improving. Distances are given in kilometers (1 km = 0.6 miles). Watch carefully for *"No Hay Paso"* ("Do Not Enter") signs; one-way streets are common, and it's not unusual for a two-way street to suddenly become one way. Single-lane bridges are common in rural areas. A *"Ceda El Paso"* ("Yield") sign facing you means just that: let oncoming traffic proceed before you enter the bridge.

Highways are numbered on signs and maps, but few people use or even know the numbering system. Asking for directions to "Highway 27" will probably be met with a blank stare. Everyone calls it the "Carretera a Caldera" (highway to Caldera, on the Pacific coast) instead. Outside San José you may run into long stretches of unpaved road. Look out for potholes, landslides during the rainy season, and cattle on the roads. Drunk drivers are a hazard on weekend nights. Driving at night outside cities and towns is not recommended, because roads are poorly lighted and many don't have painted center lines or shoulder lines. The sun sets here around 5:30 pm all year long. Make a point to arrive at your destination before then.

ROADSIDE EMERGENCIES

Costa Rica has no highway emergency service organization. In Costa Rica, 911 is the nationwide number for accidents and all emergencies. Traffic Police (*tránsitos*) are scattered around the country, but Costa Ricans are very good about stopping for people with car trouble. Whatever happens, don't move the car after an accident, even if a monstrous traffic jam ensues. Call 911 first if the accident is serious (nearly everyone has a cell phone), then call the emergency number of your car-rental agency.

Emergency Services Ambulance and Police. 🖀 *911.* **Traffic Police** (*Policía de Tránsito*). 🖀 *911.*

RULES OF THE ROAD

■ **TIP➜ Obey traffic laws religiously, even if Costa Ricans don't.** Fines are frightfully high—a speeding ticket could set you back $580—and evidence exists that transit police target foreigners. Don't get too complacent if you don't see any police; cameras monitor traffic on the highways around San José. Your rental agency may charge you for a speeding ticket it receives after your return home.

Driving is on the right side of the road in Costa Rica. The highway speed limit is usually 90 kph (54 mph), which drops to 60 kph (36 mph) in residential areas. In towns, limits range from 30 to 50 kph (18 to 31 mph). Speed limits are enforced in all regions of the country. *"Alto"* means "stop" and *"Ceda el Paso"* means "yield." Right turns on red are permitted except where signs indicate otherwise, but in San José this is usually not possible because of one-way streets and pedestrian crossings.

Local drunk driving laws are strict. You'll get nailed with a $580 fine if you're caught driving in a "predrunk" state (blood alcohol levels of 0.05% to 0.075%). If your level is higher than that, the car will be confiscated, your license will be taken away, and you risk jail time. Police officers who stop drivers for speeding and drunk driving are often looking for payment on the spot—essentially a bribe. Asking for a ticket instead of paying the bribe discourages corruption and does not compromise your safety. You can generally pay the ticket at your car-rental company, which will pay it on your behalf.

Seat-belt use is mandatory. Car seats are required for children ages four and under. Children over 12 are allowed in the front seat. Drivers are prohibited from texting or using handheld cell phones. Any such infraction means a $390 fine.

CRUISE-SHIP TRAVEL

Costa Rica is a popular cruise destination on many Panama Canal and Western Caribbean itineraries during a season that runs August–May. Most large cruises stop in the country only once. Smaller ships, including those of Windstar Cruises (capacity 148 guests), Paul Gauguin Cruises (88 guests), Variety Cruises (72 guests), and highly recommended, conservation-minded Lindblad Expeditions (62 guests) offer Costa Rica–focused cruises along the Pacific coast that may include calls in neighboring Panama or Nicaragua. Azamara Club and Pullmantur also offer the opportunity to begin and/or end your cruise in Costa Rica.

Cruise Lines Azamara Club Cruises. 877/999-9553 in North America ⊕ www.azamaraclubcruises.com. **Carnival.** 800/764-7419 in North America ⊕ www.carnival.com. **Celebrity.** 800/647-2251 in North America ⊕ www.celebritycruises.com. **Crystal.** 888/722-0021 in North America ⊕ www.crystalcruises.com. **Cunard.** 800/728-6273 in North America ⊕ www.cunard.com. **Holland America.** 877/932-4259 in North America ⊕ www.hollandamerica.com. **Lindblad Expeditions.** 800/397-3348 in North America ⊕ www.expeditions.com. **Norwegian.** 866/234-7350 in North America ⊕ www.ncl.com. **Oceania.** 855/623-2642 in North America ⊕ www.oceaniacruises.com. **P&O Cruises.**

877/828-4728 ⊕ www.poamericas.com. **Paul Gauguin Cruises.** 800/848-6172 in North America ⊕ www.pgcruises.com. **Princess.** 800/774-6237 in North America ⊕ www.princess.com. **Pullmantur Cruises.** 888/381-4656 ⊕ www.pullmanturcruiseline.com. **Regent Seven Seas.** 844/473-4368 in North America ⊕ www.rssc.com. **Royal Caribbean.** 866/562-7625 in North America ⊕ www.royalcaribbean.com. **Silversea.** 888/978-4070 in North America ⊕ www.silversea.com. **Variety Cruises.** 800/319-7776 ⊕ www.varietycruises.com. **Windstar Cruises.** 888/216-9373 ⊕ www.windstarcruises.com.

TAXI TRAVEL

Taxis are cheap and your best bet for getting around San José. Just about every driver is friendly and eager to use a few English words to tell you about a cousin or sister in New Jersey; however, cabbies truly conversant in English are scarce. Tipping is not expected, but a good idea when you've had some extra help, especially with your bags. Taxis are not shared with strangers here; the ride is for you and your party only.

Cabs are red, usually with a yellow light on top. To hail one, extend your hand and wave it at about hip height. If it's available, the driver will often flick his headlights before pulling over. The city is dotted with *paradas de taxi,* taxi queues where you stand the best chance of grabbing one. Taxis generally congregate around the central park in most other cities and towns. Your hotel can usually call you a reputable taxi or private car service, and when you're out to dinner or on the town, ask the manager to call you a cab—it's much easier than hailing one on the street, and safer, too.

■TIP➔ Taxi drivers are infamous for "not having change." If it's just a few hundred colones, you may as well round up. If it's a lot, ask to go to a store or gas station where you can make change. To avoid this situation, never use a 10,000-colón bill in a taxi, and avoid paying with 5,000-colón bills unless you've run up almost that much in fares. Drivers will round the fare up to the nearest 100 colones.

Outside the capital area, drivers often use their odometers to creatively calculate fares. Manuel Antonio drivers are notorious for overcharging. It's illegal, but taxis charge up to double for hotel pickups or fares that take them out of the province (such as San José to Alajuela). Ask the manager at your hotel about the going rate. Outside the capital, try to avoid taking an unofficial taxi (*pirata*), although it's sometimes the only option. It's better to ask your hotel for recommendations.

The ride service Uber operates in Costa Rica with service primarily in San José and the metro area. Uber also offers rides to a few destinations elsewhere in the country for fixed rates.

Uber. ⊕ *www.uber.com/cities/san-jose.*

ESSENTIALS

■ ACCOMMODATIONS

Costa Rica excels in its selection of boutique hotels, tasteful bungalows, and bed-and-breakfasts, which offer a high degree of personalized service. Because they're generally small, you may have to book one or two months ahead, and up to six months in the high season, especially around Christmas or Easter. Reserving through an association or agency can significantly reduce the time you spend scanning the Internet, but you can often get a better deal and negotiate longer-stay or low-season discounts directly with the hotel.

High-end accommodations range from luxury tents to exquisite hotels to villa rentals. You'll find all the amenities you expect at such areas, with one notable exception: the roads and routes to even five-star villas can be atrocious. Resorts are generally one of two kinds: luxurious privileged gateways to the best of the country (such as Punta Islita) or generic medium-budget all-inclusives (such as the Spanish hotel chain Barceló). Several chain hotels have franchises in Costa Rica, and they are rarely booked solid.

Nature lodges in the South Pacific may be less expensive than they initially appear, as the nightly rate usually includes three hearty meals and sometimes even guided hikes. Internet access isn't a given, even if a place has a website. Many have an eco-friendly approach (even to luxury), so air-conditioning might not be included. Consider how isolated you want to be; some lodges are miles from neighbors and have few rainy-day diversions. The ICT's voluntary "green leaf" rating system evaluates eco-friendly lodgings. A listing can be found at ⊕ *www.turismo-sostenible.co.cr.*

Be sure to reserve well in advance for the dry season (mid-December to April everywhere except the Caribbean coast, which has a short September to October "dry" season). ■TIP➔ If you're having trouble finding accommodations, consider contacting a tour operator. Because they reserve blocks of rooms, you might have better luck. During the rainy season (May to mid-November except on the Caribbean coast, where it's almost always rainy) most hotels drop their rates considerably, which sometimes sends them into a lower price category than the one we indicate.

Most hotels and other lodgings require you to give your credit-card details before confirming your reservation. Get confirmation in writing and have a copy of it handy when you check in.

Be sure you understand the hotel's cancellation policy. Some places allow you to cancel without any kind of penalty— even if you prepaid to secure a discounted rate—if you cancel at least 24 hours in advance. Others require you to cancel a week in advance or penalize you the cost of one night. Small inns and bed-and-breakfasts are most likely to require you to cancel far in advance. Most hotels allow children under a certain age to stay in their parents' room at no extra charge, but others charge for them as extra adults; find out the cutoff age for discounts.

The lodgings we list are Costa Rica's cream of the crop in each price category. When pricing accommodations, always ask what's included and what costs extra. Keep in mind that prices don't include 16.4% service and tax. Smoking is prohibited in all hotels, both in rooms and public areas. *Our local writers vet every hotel to recommend the best overnights in each price category, from budget to expensive. Unless otherwise specified, you can expect private bath, phone, and TV in your room. Hotel reviews have been shortened. For full information, visit Fodors.com.*

APARTMENT AND HOUSE RENTALS

Rental houses are common all over Costa Rica, particularly in the Pacific coast destinations of Manuel Antonio, Tamarindo, Ocotal, and Jacó. Homes can accommodate whole families, often for less money and at a higher comfort level than a hotel. Properties are often owned by foreigners, most of them based in the United States, with property managers in Costa Rica.

Resort communities with villa-style lodgings are also growing. Nosara Beach Rentals lists apartments and villas on the Nicoya Peninsula. Escape Villas Costa Rica lists rentals in Manuel Antonio, Dominical, Jacó, Playa Flamingo, Tamarindo, Nosara, Sámara, Arenal, and Puerto Viejo de Talamanca. Villas & Apartments Abroad has a good selection of rentals on the North and Central Pacific coasts. Villas International has an extensive list of properties in the Central Valley, Tamarindo, Quepos, Jacó, and Dominical. Villas Caribe offers a variety of rentals up and down the Pacific coast. For the southern Nicoya Peninsula and Playa Hermosa on the North Pacific coast, check Costa Rica Beach Rentals.

The rental clearinghouse airbnb lists lodgings countrywide with prices ranging from $30 to $350.

Contacts Costa Rica Beach Rentals.
☎ 8340–3842, 973/917–8046 in North America ⊕ www.costarica-beachrentals.com. **Escape Villas Costa Rica.** ☎ 2203–2158, 888/771–2976 in North America ⊕ www. villascostarica.com. **Nosara Beach Rentals.** ☎ 2682–0153 ⊕ www.nosarabeachrentals.com. **Villas & Apartments Abroad.** ✉ 183 Madison Ave., Suite 1111, New York ☎ 212/213–6435 in North America ⊕ www.vaanyc.com. **Villas Caribe.** ☎ 800/645–7498 ⊕ www.villascaribe. com. **Villas International.** ✉ 17 Fox La., San Anselmo ☎ 415/499–9490 in North America, 800/221–2260 ⊕ www.villasintl.com.

BED-AND-BREAKFASTS

A number of quintessential bed-and-breakfasts—small and homey—are clustered in the Central Valley, generally offering hearty breakfasts and friendly inside information for $50 to $100 per night. You'll also find them scattered through the rest of the country, mixed in with other self-titled bed-and-breakfasts that range from small cabins in the mountains to luxurious boutique-hotel-style digs in the North Pacific region.

HOME EXCHANGES

With a direct home exchange you stay in someone else's home while they stay in yours. Some outfits also deal with vacation homes, so you're not actually staying in someone's full-time residence, just their vacant weekend place.

Home exchanges are an excellent way to immerse yourself in the true Costa Rica, particularly if you've been here before. Drawbacks include restricted options and dates. Many companies list home exchanges, but we've found Home Exchange, which lists a handful of jazzy houses around Costa Rica, to be the most reliable.

Exchange Clubs Home Exchange.
☎ 800/877–8723 ⊕ www.homeexchange.com.

▌ADDRESSES

In Costa Rica addresses are usually given in terms of how many meters the place is from a landmark. Street names and building numbers are not commonly used. Churches, stores, even large trees that no longer exist—almost anything can be a landmark, as long as everyone knows where it is, or where it used to be. A typical address in San José is *100 metros este y 100 metros sur del supermercado* (100 meters east and 100 meters south from the supermarket). ▌**TIP→ In Costa Rica, each block is assumed to be 100 meters, although some blocks may be much longer and some may be shorter.**

Ticos, as Costa Ricans call themselves, are generally happy to help lost visitors, and they spend a lot of time describing where things are. But be warned—even if they don't know where something is, Ticos will often give uncertain or even wrong information rather than seem unhelpful. Ask at least two people in quick succession to avoid getting hopelessly lost. Key direction terms are *lugar* (place), *calle* (street), *avenida* (avenue), *puente* (bridge), *piso* (floor), *edificio* (building), *cruce* (intersection), *semáforo* (traffic light), *rotonda* (traffic circle), and *cuadra* (block).

▌COMMUNICATIONS

INTERNET
With the advent of smartphones, Internet cafés are dwindling in number. Downtown San José still has a few with high-speed connections; prices are usually less than $1 per hour. As you move away from the capital, prices rise to $2 to $4 per hour and connections become less reliable. Wildly expensive satellite Internet is available at some exclusive hotels in remote areas. Most major hotels have free wireless access or use of a wired computer. Denny's, McDonald's, and a number of upscale cafés have Wi-Fi, although a few travelers have been robbed of their laptops and tablets in restaurants. (Smartphones are generally safe.)

Internet access via your smartphone should work in most cities of any size, but we recommend always looking for a Wi-Fi signal to avoid surprises on your bill after you return home. Data charges are high.

PHONES
The good news is that you can now make a direct-dial telephone call from virtually any point on Earth. The bad news? You can't always do so cheaply. Calling from a hotel is almost always the most expensive option; hotels usually add huge surcharges to all calls, particularly international ones. Calling cards usually keep costs to a minimum, but only if you purchase them locally.

CALLING WITHIN COSTA RICA
All phone numbers have eight digits. Landline numbers begin with 2; cell numbers begin with 4, 5, 6, 7, or 8. There are no area codes in Costa Rica, so you need only dial the eight-digit number, without the 506 country code. Coin-operated phones have been phased out in favor of those that use local calling cards.

CALLING OUTSIDE COSTA RICA
The country code for the United States is 1.

Internet phone services such as Skype are by far the cheapest way to call home; it is a viable option in the Central Valley and major tourist hubs. For other regions or for more privacy, a pay phone using an international phone card is the next step up; you can also call from a pay phone using your own long-distance calling card. Dialing directly from a hotel room is very expensive, as is recruiting an international operator to connect you. ■TIP→ Watch out for pay phones marked "Call USA/Canada with a credit card." They are wildly expensive.

To call overseas directly, dial 00, then the country code (dial 1 for the United States and Canada), the area code, and the number.

AT&T and Sprint access codes make calling long distance relatively convenient but can be very expensive. When requesting a calling card from your phone provider, ask specifically about calls from Costa Rica. Most don't work in Costa Rica. Callingcards.com is a great resource for prepaid international calling cards. It lists a calling-card company with a rate of 87¢ per each block of three minutes for calls from Costa Rica to the United States.

You may find your phone company's local access number blocked in many hotel rooms. If the hotel balks, ask for an international operator, or dial the international operator yourself. One way to improve your odds of getting connected to your long-distance carrier is to sign up with more than one company: a hotel may block Sprint, for example, but not MCI. If all else fails, call from a pay phone.

Phone Resources AT&T. ☎ *0800/011-4114 in Costa Rica.* **Callingcards.com.** ☎ *866/299–3937* ⊕ *www.callingcards.com.* **International information.** ☎ *1024.* **International operator.** ☎ *1116.* **Local information.** ☎ *1113.* **Sprint.** ☎ *0800/013-0123 in Costa Rica.* **Skype.** ⊕ *www.skype.com.*

CALLING CARDS

Phone cards can be used from any telephone in Costa Rica, including residential phones, cell phones, and hotel phones. It's rare to be charged a per-minute rate for the mere use of the phone in a hotel. Phone cards are sold in any business displaying the gold-and-blue *"tarjetas telefónicas"* sign. International cards tend to be easier to find in downtown San José and in popular tourist areas.

Tarjetas para llamadas nacionales (domestic calling cards) are available in denominations of 500 colones and 1,000 colones. Phone-card rates are standard throughout the country, about 1¢ per minute for local calls; a 500-colón card provides about 100 minutes of landline calls. *Tarjetas para llamadas internacionales* (international calling cards) are sold in $10, $20, 2,500-colón, 5,000-colón, and 10,000-colón amounts (denominations are inexplicably split between dollars and colones). In busy spots, roaming card-hawkers abound; feel free to take advantage of the convenience—they're legit.

To use the international card, dial 1199. Select Spanish or English, then key in the PIN on the back of your card (revealed after scratching off a protective coating), then dial the phone number as you would a direct long-distance call.

CELL PHONES

If you have an unblocked phone (some countries use different frequencies than what's used in the United States) and your service provider uses the world-standard GSM network (as do T-Mobile, Cingular, and Verizon), you can probably use your phone abroad. ■TIP→ If you travel internationally frequently, save one of your old cell phones or buy a cheap one on the Internet; ask your cell-phone company to unlock it for you, and take it with you as a travel phone, buying a new SIM card with pay-as-you-go service in each destination.

If your cell-phone company has service to Costa Rica, theoretically you can use it here, but expect reception to be impossibly bad in many areas of this mountainous country. Costa Rica works on an 1,800 MHz system—a tri- or quad-band cell phone is your best bet. Note that roaming fees can be steep.

Most car-rental agencies have good deals on cell phones, often better than the companies that specialize in cell-phone rental. Rates range from $5 to $15 per day, plus varying rates for local or international coverage and minimum usage charges. Local calls average 70¢ per minute, international $1 to $1.50. You'll need your passport, a credit card, and a deposit, which varies per phone and service but averages $300 to $400; some rent only to those over 21.

Friendly and professional, Cell Service Costa Rica will get you hooked up and provides door-to-door service.

Contacts Cell Service Costa Rica. ☎ *2296–5553* ⊕ *www.cellservicecr.com.*

■ CUSTOMS AND DUTIES

You're always allowed to bring goods of a certain value back home without having to pay any duty or import tax. But there's a limit on the amount of tobacco and liquor you can bring back duty-free, and some countries have separate limits for perfumes; for exact figures, check with your customs department. The values of so-called duty-free goods are included in these amounts. When you shop abroad, save all your receipts, as customs inspectors may ask to see them as well as the items you purchased. If the total value of your goods is more than the duty-free limit, you'll have to pay a tax (most often a flat percentage) on the value of everything beyond that limit.

When shopping in Costa Rica, keep receipts for all purchases. Be ready to show customs (*aduanas*) officials what you've bought. Pack purchases together in an easily accessible place. The only orchids you can take home are packaged in a tube and come with an export permit.

If you think a duty is incorrect, appeal the assessment. If you object to the way your clearance was handled, note the inspector's badge number. In either case, first ask to see a supervisor. If the problem isn't resolved, write to the appropriate authorities, beginning with the port director at your point of entry.

Visitors entering Costa Rica may bring in 500 grams of tobacco, 5 liters of wine or spirits, 2 kilograms of sweets and chocolates, and the equivalent of $500 worth of merchandise. You can also bring one camera and one video camera, six rolls of film, binoculars, and electrical items for personal use only, including laptops and other electronics. Make sure you have personalized prescriptions for any medication you are taking. Customs officials at San José's international airport rarely examine tourists' luggage by hand, although all incoming bags are x-rayed. If you enter by land, they'll probably look through your bags. Officers at the airport generally speak English and are generally your best (only, really) option for resolving any problem. It usually takes about 30 minutes to clear immigration and customs when arriving in Costa Rica.

Pets (cats or dogs only) with updated health and vaccination certificates are welcome in Costa Rica; no prior authorization is required if bringing a dog or cat that has up-to-date (within two weeks of departure) health and vaccination cards. The Servicio Nacional de Salud Animal can provide more info.

Information in Costa Rica Costa Rica Customs (*Servicio Nacional de Aduanas*). ☎ 2522–9000 *in Costa Rica* ⊕ *www.hacienda. go.cr.* **Servicio Nacional de Salud Animal** (*SENASA*). ☎ 2587–1600 *in Costa Rica* ⊕ *www.senasa.go.cr.*

U.S. Information U.S. Customs and Border Protection. ⊕ *www.cbp.gov.*

■ EATING OUT

Dining options around Costa Rica run the spectrum from elegant and formal to beachy and casual. San José and popular tourist centers, especially Manuel Antonio, offer a wide variety of cuisine types. Farther off the beaten track, expect hearty, filling local cuisine. Increasingly common as you move away from San José are the thatched conical roofs of the round, open *rancho* restaurants that serve a combination of traditional staples with simple international fare.

Every town has at least one *soda*—that's Costa Rican Spanish for a small, family-run restaurant frequented by locals. Don't expect anything as fancy as a menu. A board usually lists specials of the day. The lunchtime *casado* (literally, "married")—a "marriage" of chicken, pork, or beef with rice, beans, cabbage salad, and natural fruit drink—sets you back about $3. No one will bring you a bill; just pay the cashier when you're finished. Having a meal at your local soda always provides a good opportunity to practice your Spanish.

MEALS AND MEALTIMES

In San José and surrounding cities, most sodas are open daily 7 am to early evening, though some close Sunday. Other restaurants are usually open 11 am to 9 pm, and in resort areas some restaurants may stay open later. Normal dining hours in Costa Rica are noon to 3 and 6 to 9. *Desayuno* (breakfast) is served at most sodas and hotels. The traditional breakfast is *gallo pinto*, which includes eggs, plantains, and fried cheese; hotel breakfasts vary widely and generally offer lighter international options in addition to the local stick-to-your-ribs plate. *Almuerzo* (lunch) is the biggest meal of the day for Costa Ricans, and savvy travelers know that lunch specials are often a great bargain. *Cena* (dinner or supper) runs the gamut.

Except for those in hotels, many restaurants close between Christmas and New Year's Day and during Holy Week (Palm Sunday to Easter Sunday). Unless otherwise noted, the restaurants listed in this guide are open daily for lunch and dinner. Credit cards are not accepted at many rural restaurants. Always ask before you order to find out if your credit card will be accepted. Visa and MasterCard are the most commonly accepted cards; American Express and Diners Club are less widely accepted. The Discover card is increasingly accepted. ■TIP➔ Remember that 25% is added to all menu prices: 15% for tax and 10% for tip. Legally, menus are required to show after-tax, after-tip prices in colones; in practice, many tourist-oriented places do not. Because a gratuity (*propina*) is included, there's no need to tip, but if your service is good, it's nice to add a little money to the obligatory 10%.

RESERVATIONS AND DRESS

Costa Ricans generally dress more formally than North Americans. For dinner at an upscale restaurant, long pants and closed-toe shoes are standard for men except in beach locations, and women tend to wear high heels and dressy clothes that show off their figures. Shorts, flip-flops, and tank tops are not acceptable, except at inexpensive restaurants in beach towns.

VEGETARIAN OPTIONS

Vegetarians sticking to lower-budget establishments won't go hungry, but may develop a love-hate relationship with rice, beans, and fried cheese. A simple *sin carne* (no meat) request is often interpreted as "no beef," so specify *solo vegetales* (only vegetables), and for good measure, *nada de cerdo, pollo, o pescado* (no pork, chicken, or fish). More cosmopolitan restaurants are more conscious of vegetarians—upscale Asian restaurants often offer vegetarian options.

WINES, BEER, AND SPIRITS

The ubiquitous sodas generally don't have liquor licenses, but getting a drink in any other eatery isn't usually a problem. Don't let Holy Thursday and Good Friday catch you off guard; both are legally dry days. In general, restaurant prices for imported alcohol—which includes just about everything except local beer, rum, and *guaro*, the local sugarcane firewater—may be more than what you'd like to pay.

■ ELECTRICITY

North American appliances are compatible with Costa Rica's electrical system (110 volts) and outlets (parallel two-prong). Australian and European appliances require a two-prong adapter and a 220-volt to 110-volt transformer. Never use an outlet that specifically warns against using higher-voltage appliances without a transformer. Dual-voltage appliances (i.e., they operate equally well on 110 and 220 volts) such as most laptops, phone chargers, and hair dryers, need only a two-prong adapter, but you should bring a surge protector for your computer.

Contacts
Walkabout Travel Gear. ☎ *800/852–7085* ⊕ *www.walkabouttravelgear.com.*

■ EMERGENCIES

Dial 911 for an ambulance, the fire department, or the police. Costa Ricans are usually quick to respond to emergencies. In a hotel or restaurant, the staff will usually offer immediate assistance, and in a public area passersby can be counted on to stop and help.

For emergencies ranging from health problems to lost passports, contact your embassy.

U.S. Embassy United States Embassy
(*Embajada de los Estados Unidos*). ⊠ *C. 120 and Avda. 0, Pavas* ☎ *2519–2000* ⊕ *costarica. usembassy.gov.*

▌ HEALTH

Most travelers to Costa Rica do not get any vaccinations or take any special medications. The U.S. Centers for Disease Control and Prevention recommends that all travelers to Costa Rica be up to date on routine immunizations, namely seasonal influenza, tetanus, diphtheria, and pertussis (whooping cough). Children traveling to Costa Rica should be up to date on all routine immunizations as well. The CDC also suggests being immunized against typhoid and hepatitis A, especially if you're headed off the beaten path or staying a few weeks. The agency no longer recommends malaria prophylaxis for travel to Costa Rica.

SPECIFIC ISSUES IN COSTA RICA

Costa Rica is one of several Latin American countries where transmission of the mosquito-borne Zika virus has been identified. Because risks to fetal development during any trimester of pregnancy have been reported, the CDC recommends that pregnant women consider postponing travel to any area of transmission. If travel is necessary, take strict steps to avoid mosquito bites.

The CDC marks Costa Rica as an area infested by the *Aedes aegypti* (dengue-carrier) mosquito, but not as an epidemic region. The highest-risk area is the Caribbean, especially in the rainy season. The mosquito-borne chikungunya virus began appearing in Costa Rica in 2015. In areas with Zika, chikungunya, and dengue, use mosquito nets, wear clothing that covers your whole body, and use *repelente* (insect repellent) and *espirales* (mosquito coils), sold in supermarkets, pharmacies, and, sometimes, small country stores.
■TIP➔ **Repellents made with DEET or picaridin are most effective.** Perfume and aftershave can actually attract mosquitoes.

It's unlikely that you will contract chikungunya or dengue, but if you start suffering from high fever, the shakes, or joint pain, make sure you ask to be tested for these diseases at a local clinic. Your embassy can provide you with a list of recommended doctors and dentists. Such symptoms in the weeks following your return should also spark concern.

Poisonous snakes, scorpions, and other pests pose a small threat in Costa Rica.

Water is generally safe to drink, especially around San José, but the quality can vary; to be safe, drink bottled water. In rural areas you run a mild risk of encountering drinking water, fresh fruit, and vegetables contaminated by fecal matter, which in most cases causes a bit of traveler's diarrhea but can cause leptospirosis (which can be treated by antibiotics if detected early). Stay on the safe side by avoiding uncooked food, unpasteurized milk, and ice—ask for drinks *sin hielo* (without ice). Ceviche, raw fish cured in lemon juice—a favorite appetizer, especially at seaside resorts—is generally safe to eat.

Mild cases of diarrhea may respond to Imodium (known generically as loperamide) or Pepto-Bismol, both of which can be purchased over the counter. Drink plenty of purified water or tea; chamomile (*manzanilla* in Spanish) is a good folk remedy. In severe cases, rehydrate yourself with a salt-sugar solution (½ teaspoon salt and 4 tablespoons sugar per quart of water).

Heatstroke and dehydration are real dangers, especially for hikers, so drink lots of water. Take at least 1 liter per person for every hour you plan to be on the trail. Sunburn is the most common traveler's health problem. Use sunscreen with SPF 30 or higher. Most pharmacies and supermarkets carry sunscreen in a wide range of SPFs, though it is relatively pricey.

The greatest danger to your person actually lies off Costa Rica's popular beaches—riptides are common wherever there are waves, and tourists run into serious difficulties in them every year. If you see waves, ask the locals where it's safe to swim; and if you're uncertain, don't go in deeper than your waist. If you get caught in a rip current, swim parallel to the beach until you're free of it, and then swim back to shore. ■TIP→ Avoid swimming where a town's main river opens up to the sea. Septic tanks aren't common. Do not fly within 24 hours of scuba diving.

OVER-THE-COUNTER REMEDIES

Farmacia is Spanish for pharmacy, and the names for common drugs like *aspirina, ibuprofen,* and *acetaminofina* (Tylenol) are basically the same as they are in English. Many drugs for which you need a prescription back home are sold over the counter in Costa Rica. Pharmacies throughout the country are generally open from 8 to 8. Some pharmacies in San José stay open 24 hours.

Government facilities—the so-called Caja hospitals (short for Caja Costarricense de Seguro Social, or Costa Rican Social Security System)—and clinics are of acceptable quality, but notoriously overburdened. Private hospitals are more accustomed to serving foreigners.

Centers for Disease Control and Prevention. ⊕ *www.cdc.gov.*

■ HOURS OF OPERATION

Like the rest of the world, Costa Rica's business hours have been expanding. Megamalls are usually open seven days a week, opening around 10 am and closing around 9 pm. Some government offices and smaller businesses close for lunch, especially in rural areas, but *jornada continúa* (without the lunch break) is becoming more common in San José. Larger museums usually keep a Monday-to-Sunday schedule, and smaller ones are open weekdays. National parks often close one day a week; for example, Manuel Antonio is closed Monday. Eateries in beach towns and other tourist areas often stay open seven days a week, while those in the cities close Sunday and sometimes Monday. Bars and nightclubs are generally open until 1 or 2 am. Last calls vary from place to place.

Three public holidays (April 11, July 25, and October 12) are usually observed on the following Monday. Government offices and commercial establishments observe all the holidays. The only days the country truly shuts down are Holy Thursday and Good Friday; some buses still run, but no alcohol can be purchased, and most restaurants and all stores are closed.

HOLIDAYS

January 1: New Year (*Año Nuevo*)

April 11: Juan Santamaría Day (*Día de Juan Santamaría*)

Easter Week: Holy Thursday and Good Friday, religious activities (*Semana Santa*)

May 1: International Labor Day (*Día del Trabajador*)

July 25: Annexation of Guanacaste Province (*Anexión de Guanacaste*)

August 2: Day of the Virgin of Los Angeles (*Virgen de los Ángeles*), patron saint of Costa Rica

August 15: Mother's Day (*Día de la Madre*)

September 15: Independence Day (*Día de Independencia*)

October 12: Culture Day (*Día de las Culturas*)

December 25: Christmas (*Navidad*)

■ MAIL

The Spanish word for post office is *correo*. Mail from the United States can take up to two to three weeks to arrive in Costa Rica (occasionally it never arrives at all). Within the country, mail service is even less reliable. Outgoing mail is marginally quicker, with delivery to North America in about 10 days, especially when sent from San José. It's worth registering mail; prices are only slightly higher. All overseas cards and letters will automatically be sent airmail. Mail theft is a chronic problem, so do not mail checks, cash, or anything else of value.

Minimum postage for postcards and letters under 20 grams from Costa Rica to the United States and Canada costs the equivalent of U.S. $1.10.

You can have mail sent *poste restante* (*lista de correos*) to any Costa Rican post office (specify Correo Central to make sure it goes to the main downtown office). In written addresses, *apartado*, abbreviated *apdo.*, indicates a post-office box.

Post offices are generally open weekdays 7:30 to 5:30 and Saturday 8 to noon. Stamps can be purchased at post offices and a very few hotels and souvenir shops. These vendors will also accept the mail you wish to send; don't bother looking for a mailbox, as there are only a handful (usually in rural areas with no post office).

SHIPPING PACKAGES

Shipping parcels through the post office is not for those in a hurry because packages to the United States and Canada can take weeks. Also, packages may be pilfered. However, post-office shipping is the cheapest way to go, with rates starting at $5 per kilogram.

Some stores offer shipping, but it is usually quite expensive. If you can, carry your packages home with you.

UPS has offices in San José, Santa Ana, Tamarindo, Liberia, Jacó, Manuel Antonio, Sarchí, Nuevo Arenal, La Fortuna, and Limón. DHL has drop-offs in San José (Rohrmoser, Paseo Colón), Curridabat, Escazú, Heredia, Liberia, Limón, Ciudad Quesada, Jacó, Quepos, and San Isidro de El General. FedEx has offices in San José and Heredia; it offers package pickup service in San José and other centers, such as Limón. All three have central information numbers with English-speaking staff. Prices are about 10 times what you'd pay at the post office, but packages arrive in a matter of days. "Overnight" is usually

a misnomer—shipments to most North American cities take two business days.

Express Services Main Offices DHL.
✉ *Paseo Colón, next to Budget car rental, Paseo Colón* ☏ *2209-6000 in Costa Rica* ⊕ *www.dhl.co.cr.* **FedEx.** ✉ *Paseo Colón and C. 40, 100 m east of León Cortés statue, San José* ☏ *800/463-3339 in Costa Rica* ⊕ *www.fedex.com.* **UPS.** ✉ *Pavas Hwy., 50 m east of Pizza Hut, Pavas* ☏ *2290-2828 in Costa Rica* ⊕ *www.ups.com.*

∎ MONEY

In general, Costa Rica is cheaper than North America or Europe, but travelers looking for dirt-cheap developing-nation deals may find it's more expensive than they bargained for—and prices are rising as more foreigners visit.

The tourism industry quotes prices in dollars. You may certainly pay for hotels and tours in local currency, but they will be priced at that day's equivalent colón exchange rate.

Food in modest restaurants and public transportation are inexpensive. A 2-km (1-mile) taxi ride costs about $2.

ATMS AND BANKS

Costa Rica's four state-owned banks (Banco Nacional, Banco de Costa Rica, Bancrédito, and Banco Popular) come complete with horrendous lines, although many branches have chairs for sitting while you wait for your number to be called. Private banks (BAC San José, Citi, and Scotiabank) are quicker options in larger cities. Better yet, get your spending money at a *cajero automático* (automatic teller machine). If you do use the bank, remember that Monday, Friday, and the first, last, and 15th days of the month are the busiest days. For security reasons, all banks prohibit cell and smartphone use while inside.

Although they are springing up at a healthy rate, don't count on using an ATM outside San José. Though not exhaustive, the A Toda Hora website lists locations of its ATH cash machines, and notes which ones offer colones (usually in increments of 10,000 colones), dollars (in increments of $20), or both; choose your region or city in the box on the homepage called *Búsqueda de Cajeros.*

For reasons of security, a growing number of ATMs shut down at 10 pm and begin working again at 6 am. In addition to banks, you'll find them in major grocery stores, some hotels, gas-station convenience stores, and even a few McDonald's. ATH, Red Total, and Scotiabank machines supposedly accept both Cirrus (a partner with MasterCard) and Plus (a partner with Visa) cards, but sometimes don't. If you'll be spending time away from major tourist centers, particularly in the Caribbean, get all the cash you need in San José and carry a few U.S. dollars in case you run out of colones. It's helpful to have both a Visa and a MasterCard—even in San José—as a few machines accept only one or the other. Both companies have sites with fairly comprehensive lists of accessible ATMs around the world.

ATMs are occasionally out of order and sometimes run out of cash on weekends. ■ TIP➔ PIN codes with more than four digits are not recognized at Costa Rican ATMs. If you have a five-digit PIN, change it with your bank before you travel. Although it seems counterintuitive, try to use ATMs only during bank business hours. If an ATM "eats" your card, you can go inside to retrieve it or get cash from a teller.

The Credomatic office, housed in the BAC San José central offices on Calle Central between Avenidas 3 and 5, is the local representative for most major credit cards; get cash advances here, or at any bank (Banco Nacional and BAC San José are good for both MasterCard and Visa; Banco Popular and Banco de Costa Rica always accept Visa).

State banks have branches with slightly staggered hours; core times are weekdays 9 to 4, and very few are open Saturday morning. A few branches of Banco Nacional are open until 6, or occasionally 7.

Private banks tend to keep longer hours and are usually the best places to change U.S. dollars and travelers' checks; rates may be marginally better in state banks, but the long waits cancel out any benefit. Multinational banks like Citi and Scotiabank have branches here, but none has any link to your back-home account except via your ATM card. The BAC San José in the check-in area at Aeropuerto Internacional Juan Santamaría is open daily 5 am to 10 pm.

Resources A Toda Hora (*ATH*). ☎ *2211–4500* ⊕ *www.ath.com.* **MasterCard.** ⊕ *www. mastercard.com/cr.* **Visa.** ⊕ *www.visa.com.*

CREDIT CARDS

It's a good idea to inform your credit-card company before you travel, especially if you're going abroad and don't travel internationally very often. Record all your credit-card numbers—as well as the phone numbers to call if your cards are lost or stolen—in a safe place. Both MasterCard and Visa have general numbers you can call (collect if you're abroad) if your card is lost, but you're better off calling the number of your issuing bank, since MasterCard and Visa usually just transfer you to your bank; your bank's number is printed on your card.

Major credit cards are accepted at most hotels and restaurants in this book; Visa and MasterCard have the widest acceptance, with American Express, Discover, and Diners Club somewhat less so. As the phone system improves, many budget hotels, restaurants, and other businesses have begun to accept plastic; but plenty of places still require payment in cash. ■ TIP➔ Carry enough cash, including smaller denominations, to patronize the many businesses without credit-card capability. Note that some hotels, restaurants, tour companies, and other businesses add a surcharge (around 5%) to the bill if you pay with a credit card, or give you a 5% to 10% discount if you pay in cash. It's always a good idea to pay for large purchases with a major credit card

LOCAL DO'S AND TABOOS

CUSTOMS OF THE COUNTRY

Ticos prefer formal Spanish, for example, *con mucho gusto* (with much pleasure) instead of the typical *de nada* for "you're welcome." Family is important in Costa Rica. It is considered polite to ask about marital status and family.

Ticos can be disarmingly direct; don't be surprised if locals pick up on a physical trait and give you a nickname, meant affectionately. In other situations, a circumspect approach is advised; straightforwardness often comes across as abrupt. Preceding requests with a bit of small talk goes a long way. Costa Ricans don't like to say no, and will often avoid answering a question or simply say *gracias* when they really mean no.

Many Costa Rican men have a habit of ogling or making comments when young women pass on the street.

Transportation, theaters, government, and major businesses tend to stick to official schedules. Everything else is on "Tico time", so build in a little buffer time and slide into the tropical groove.

GREETINGS

Costa Ricans are extremely polite, quick to shake hands with a light squeeze and place a kiss on the right cheek. The formal pronoun *usted* (you) is used almost exclusively; the slangier *vos* is thrown about among close friends and relatives.

SIGHTSEEING

As you would anywhere, dress and behave respectfully when visiting churches. Do not wear shorts, sleeveless shirts, or sandals. Bathing suits and short shorts are inappropriate city wear, but tend to be the uniform in beach towns.

Panhandlers are not a major problem, but if you're in San José, you'll come across a few. It's always better to give to an established organization, but even a couple of hundred colones will be appreciated.

Banks and other offices allow pregnant women and the elderly to move immediately to the front of the line, and this respect is carried over to other establishments and crowded buses. If you're in a crowd and need to step in front of them, murmur *"Con permiso"* ("Excuse me").

OUT ON THE TOWN

Locals tend to dress up to go out, whatever the activity: a snazzy (but not too dressy) outfit will serve you well in San José. To catch a waiter's attention, wave discreetly or say, *"Disculpe, señor"* (or *señora* for women). For the bill, ask for *"La cuenta, por favor."* (No one will bring the check to you until you ask.) Smoking is prohibited in bars and restaurants. Excessive displays of affection draw frowns. If invited to someone's home, bring flowers or a bottle of wine or some trinket from your home country. If offered food at someone's home, it's polite to accept it and eat it (even if you aren't hungry).

LANGUAGE

It's always a good idea to learn a little of the local language. Mastering a few basic words is bound to make chatting with the locals more rewarding. Learn the rudiments of polite conversation—using *por favor* (please) and *gracias* (thank you) will be appreciated. ⇨ *For more words and phrases, see the Spanish glossary in the back of the book.* In the Caribbean province of Limón, a Creole English called Mekatelyu is spoken by older generations. English is understood by many people in these parts.

An open-ended *"¿Dónde está . . . ?"* ("Where is . . . ?") may result in a wall of rapid-fire Spanish. Avoid language as much as possible when asking for directions. Keep a good map handy, and ask for a nearby town on your itinerary rather than the final destination.

You can't go wrong with an amiable *"Pura vida,"* which serves as "hello," "good-bye," "thanks," "cool," etc.

so you can cancel payment or get reimbursed if there's a problem.

CURRENCY AND EXCHANGE

Costa Rica's currency is the colón. (The plural is colones.) Prices are shown with a "¢" sign in front of the number. At this writing, the colón is about 535 to the U.S. dollar and 590 to the euro. After years of unstable exchange rates, the colón has settled into the mid-500s in relation to the dollar. Coins come in denominations of 5, 10, 25, 50, 100, and 500 colones. Be careful not to mix up the very similar 100- and 500-colón coins. Bills come in denominations of 1,000 (red), 2,000 (blue), 5,000 (yellow), 10,000 (green), 20,000 (orange), and 50,000 (purple) colones. As you'd expect, prices have a lot of zeroes. If you want to approximate a colón price in dollars, lop off the last two digits and divide by 5. You'll be pretty close (2,500 colones = about $5). Avoid using larger-denomination bills in taxis, on buses, or in small stores. Many tourist-oriented businesses accept U.S. dollars, although the exchange rate might not be favorable to you. Make sure your dollars are in good condition—no tears or writing—and don't use anything larger than a $20. Many counterfeit $50 and $100 bills circulate here.

Assuming you can find them at all, Costa Rican colones are sold abroad at terrible rates, so wait until you arrive in Costa Rica to get local currency. U.S. dollars are still the easiest to exchange, but euros can be exchanged for colones at just about any Banco Nacional office and at the San José and Escazú branches of other banks. Private banks—Scotiabank and BAC San José—are the best places to change U.S. dollars and travelers' checks. The arrivals area of the international airports in San José and Liberia both have ATMs and are your best bet for getting cash after you land. There is a branch of the BAC San José upstairs in the check-in area of Juan Santamaría airport where you can exchange money when you arrive or depart—it's a much better deal than the Global Exchange counter in the baggage-claim area or at the departure gates. Airport taxi and van drivers accept U.S. dollars. Outdoor money changers are rarely seen on the street, but avoid them if they approach; you will most certainly get a bad deal, and you risk robbery by pulling out wads of cash.

■ TIP➜ Even if a currency-exchange booth has a sign promising no commission, rest assured that there's some kind of huge, hidden fee. (Oh . . . that's right. The sign didn't say no fee). And as for rates, you're almost always better off getting foreign currency at an ATM or exchanging money at a bank.

▮ PACKING

Travel light, and make sure you can carry your luggage without assistance. Even if you're planning to stay only in luxury resorts, odds are that at least once you'll have to haul your stuff a distance from bus stops, the shuttle drop-off, or the airport. Another incentive to pack light: domestic airlines have tight weight restrictions—at this writing 11 to 13 kilograms, or 25 to 30 pounds—and not all buses have luggage compartments. Frameless backpacks and duffel bags can be squeezed into tight spaces and are less conspicuous than fancier luggage.

Bring comfortable, hand-washable clothing. T-shirts and shorts are acceptable near the beach and in tourist areas; long-sleeve shirts and pants protect your skin from ferocious sun and, in coastal regions, mosquitoes. Leave your jeans behind—they take forever to dry. Pack a waterproof, lightweight jacket and a light sweater for cool nights, early mornings, and trips up volcanoes; you'll need even warmer clothes for trips to Chirripó National Park or Cerro de la Muerte and overnight stays in San Gerardo de Dota or on the slopes of Poás Volcano. Bring at least one good (and wrinkle-free) outfit for going out at night.

It's sometimes tough to find tampons, so bring your own and, since septic systems here generally cannot handle them, refrain from flushing down the toilet. For almost all toiletries, including contact lens supplies, a pharmacy is your best bet. Don't forget sunblock, and expect to sweat it off and reapply regularly in the high humidity. Definitely bring batteries, because they're expensive here.

Snorkelers staying at budget hotels should consider bringing their own equipment; otherwise, you can rent gear at most beach resorts.

You have to get down and dirty—well, more like wet and muddy—to see many of the country's natural wonders. The following packing list is not comprehensive; it's a guide to some of the things you might not think to bring. For your main piece of luggage, a sturdy internal-frame backpack is great, but a duffel bag works, too. You can get by with a rolling suitcase, but then bring a smaller backpack as well.

PACKING LIST FOR COSTA RICA

Quick-drying synthetic-fiber shirts and socks

Hiking boots or shoes that can get muddy and wet

Waterproof sport sandals (especially in the Osa Peninsula, where most transportation is by boat, and often there are no docks)

Knee-high socks for the rubber boots that are supplied at many lodges

A pair of lightweight pants (fire ants, mosquitoes, and other pests make covering yourself a necessity on deep-forest hikes)

Pants for horseback riding (if that's on your itinerary)

Waterproof, lightweight jacket, windbreaker, or poncho

Day pack for hikes

Sweater for cool nights and early mornings

Swimsuit

Insect repellent (with DEET, for forested areas and especially on the northern Caribbean coast, where there are pockets of malaria)

Flashlight or headlamp with spare batteries (for occasional power outages or inadequately lighted walkways at lodges)

Sunscreen with a minimum of SPF 30 (waterproof sunscreens are best; even if you're not swimming, you might be swimming in perspiration)

Large, portable water bottle

Hat and/or bandannas (not only do they provide shade, but they prevent perspiration from dripping down your face)

Binoculars (with carrying strap)

Camera (waterproof, or with a waterproof case or dry bag, sold in outdoor-equipment stores)

Imodium and Pepto-Bismol (tablet form is best)

Swiss Army knife (and remember to pack it in your checked luggage, never your carry-on—even on domestic flights in Costa Rica)

Zip-style plastic bags (they always come in handy)

Travel alarm clock or watch with an alarm (don't count on wake-up calls)

Nonelectric shaving utensils

Toilet paper (rarely provided in public bathrooms)

▌PASSPORTS

U.S. citizens need only a passport to enter Costa Rica and a return plane ticket home or to another country for stays of up to 90 days. Make sure it's up to date. We've received much conflicting information, even within officialdom, about how long your passport must be valid—government officials, passport officers, and airline check-in agents seem to interpret the rules differently. To be on the safe side, △ **make sure your passport is valid for at least six months.** Renew it before your trip if it is not. Spending 72 hours outside the country—Nicaragua or Panama are popular options—gets you another 90 days, but don't expect to do that undetected more than a couple of times. Customs forms ask how many visits you've made to Costa Rica in the past year.

Costa Rica has one of the highest rates of U.S.-passport theft in the world. Travelers in Costa Rica are not required to carry their original documents with them at all times, although you must have easy access to them. Photocopies of the data page and your entry stamp are sufficient; those, at least, must be with you at all times. Although there have been reports from around the world about security problems with in-room safes, if your hotel doesn't have a safe in reception, locking a passport in a hotel-room safe is better than leaving it in an unlocked hiding place or carrying it with you.

■ TIP→ For easy retrieval in the event of a lost or stolen passport, before you leave home scan your passport into a portable storage device (like an iPod) that you're carrying with you or email the scanned image to yourself.

If your passport is lost or stolen, first call the police—having the police report can make replacement easier—and then call your embassy. You'll get a temporary Emergency Travel Document that will need to be replaced once you return home. Fees vary according to how fast you need the passport; in some cases the fee covers your permanent replacement as well. The new document will not have your entry stamps; ask if your embassy takes care of this, or whether it's your responsibility to get the necessary immigration authorization.

GENERAL REQUIREMENTS FOR COSTA RICA	
Passport	Make sure it is valid for 6 months after date of arrival
Visa	Free upon entry for Americans
Vaccinations	None required
Driving	International driver's license not required
Departure Tax	$29, usually included in ticket price

▌RESTROOMS

When nature calls, look for signs that say *"servicios sanitarios"* or simply *"sanitarios."* In smaller venues, toilet paper is tossed into a trash bin rather than into the toilet. Septic systems are delicate and the paper will clog the toilet. At some public restrooms you might have to pay 50¢ or so for a few sheets of toilet paper. At others, there may not be any toilet paper at all. It's always a good idea to have some tissues at the ready. Gas stations generally have facilities, but you may decide not to be a slave to your bladder once you get a look at them. On car trips, watch for parked buses; generally this indicates some sort of better-kept public facilities.

▌SAFETY

Violent crime is not a serious problem in Costa Rica, but thieves can easily prey on tourists, so be alert. The government has created a Tourism Police unit whose more than 250 officers can be seen on bikes or motorcycles patrolling areas in Guanacaste, San José, and the Arenal area.

For many English-speaking tourists, standing out like a sore thumb can't be avoided. But there are some precautions you can take:

■ Don't bring anything you can't stand to lose.

■ Don't flash expensive jewelry or watches.

■ In cities, don't carry expensive cameras or lots of cash.

■ Wear backpacks on your front; thieves can slit your backpack and run away with its contents before you notice.

■ Don't wear a waist pack, because thieves can cut the strap.

■ Distribute your cash and any valuables (including credit cards and passport) between a deep front pocket, an inside jacket or vest pocket, and a hidden money belt. (If you use a money belt, have some small bills handy so you don't have to reach for it in public.)

■ Keep your hand on your wallet if you are in a crowd or on a bus.

■ Don't let your purse dangle from your shoulder; always hold on to it with your hand for added security.

■ Keep car windows rolled up and car doors locked at all times in cities.

■ Park in designated lots—car theft is common—or if that's not possible, accept the offer of the *guachimán* (a term adopted from English, pronounced "watchie man")—men or boys who watch your car while you're gone. Give them the equivalent of a dollar an hour when you return.

■ Never leave valuables in a car, even in an attended parking lot.

■ Padlock your luggage.

■ Talk with locals or your hotel staff about any areas you should avoid. Never leave a drink unattended in a club or bar: scams involving date-rape drugs have been reported, targeting both men and women.

■ Never leave your belongings unattended, including at the beach or in a tent.

■ Use your hotel room's safe, even if there's an extra charge. If your room doesn't have one, ask the manager to put your valuables in the hotel safe and ask him or her to sign a list of what you are storing.

■ If someone does try to rob you, immediately surrender your possessions and don't try to be a hero.

Scams occur in San José. A distraction artist might squirt you with something, or spill something on you, then try to clean you off while his partner steals your backpack. Pickpockets and bag slashers work buses and crowds. Beware of anyone who seems overly friendly, aggressively helpful, or disrespectful of your personal space. Be particularly vigilant around San José's Coca-Cola bus terminal, one of the dicier areas but a central transportation hub.

A few tourists have been hit with the slashed-tire scam: someone punctures the tires of your rental car (often right at the airport, when you arrive) and then comes to your "aid" when you pull off to the side of the road and robs you. Forget about the rims: always drive to the nearest open gas station or service center if you get a flat.

Lone women travelers will get a fair amount of attention from men; to minimize hassles, avoid wearing short shorts or skirts. On the bus, try to take a seat next to a woman. Women should not walk alone in San José at night. Ask at your hotel which neighborhoods to avoid. Ignore unwanted comments. If you are being harassed on a bus, at a restaurant, or in some other public place, tell the manager. In taxis, sit in the back seat. If you want to fend off an earnest but decent admirer in a bar, you can politely say, *"Por favor, necesito un tiempo a solas"* (I'd like some time on my own, please). Stronger is *"Por favor, no me moleste"* (Please, stop bothering me), and for real pests the simple *"Váyase!"* (Go away!) is usually effective.

▌ TAXES

The airport departure tax for tourists is $29, payable in cash (dollars or colones) or with Visa or MasterCard. At this writing, some airlines have begun including the tax in the ticket price. All Costa Rican businesses charge a 15% sales tax, called the IVA. It is included in the shelf price you see. Hotels charge a 16.4% fee covering service and tax, usually on top of their posted rates. Restaurants add the 15% IVA tax and 10% service fee to meals. By law, menu prices are supposed to reflect the final price you pay; many tourist-oriented dining spots ignore the requirement. Tourists are not refunded for taxes paid in Costa Rica.

▌ TIME

Costa Rica does not observe daylight saving time, so from November to March it's the equivalent of Central Time in the United States (one hour behind New York). The rest of the year, it is the equivalent of Mountain Time in the United States (two hours behind New York). This close to the equator, days and nights are roughly the same length all year. Sunrise is about 5:30 am; sunset is about 5:30 pm with about 15 minutes' variation either way.

Time Zones Timeanddate.com.
⊕ *www.timeanddate.com/worldclock.*

▌TIPPING

Costa Rica doesn't have a tipping culture, but positive reinforcement goes a long way to fostering a culture of good service; good intentions are usually there, but execution can be hit or miss. Tip only for good service. ▌TIP➔ Tipping in colones is best. Never tip with U.S. coins, because there's no way for locals to exchange them.

TIPPING	
Bellhop	$1–$5 or 500 colones per bag, depending on the level of the hotel
Hotel Concierge	$5 or more, if he or she performs a service for you
Hotel Doorman	$1–$2 if he helps you get a cab
Hotel Maid	$1–$3 or 500 to 1,500 colones per day (either daily or at the end of your stay, in cash)
Hotel Room-Service Waiter	$1–$2 or 500 to 1,000 colones per delivery, even if a service charge has been added
Tour Guide	$10 or 5,000 colones per group member per day
Hired Driver	10% of the rental
Waiter	10%–15%, with 15% being the norm at high-end restaurants; nothing additional if a service charge is added to the bill
Bartender	200 colones
Restroom Attendant	$1
Coat-check	$1–$2 per item checked unless there is a fee, then nothing
Taxi Driver	200–300 colones if they've helped you navigate a complicated set of directions, or 500 colones if they've helped you with luggage, otherwise nothing

▌TOURS

BIKING
Costa Rica is mountainous and rough around the edges. It's a rare bird who attempts a road-biking tour here. But the payoff for the ungroomed, tire-munching terrain is uncrowded, wildly beautiful off-road routes. Most bike-tour operators want to make sure you're in moderately good shape and do some biking at home. Operators generally provide top-notch equipment, including bikes and helmets, but welcome serious mountain bikers who bring their own ride. Operators usually meet you at the airport and take care of all logistics.

Useful topographical maps (not biking maps per se) are generally provided as part of the tour, and include unpaved roads. If you're striking out on your own, these maps can usually be found at downtown San José's Lehmann bookstore for about $5. Some basic Spanish is highly recommended if you're going to do it yourself.

▌TIP➔ Check with individual airlines about bike-packing requirements. Cardboard bike boxes can be found at bike shops for about $15; more secure options start at $40. International travelers often can substitute a bike for a piece of checked luggage at no charge (if the box conforms to regular baggage dimensions), but U.S. airlines will sometimes charge a $100 to $200 handling fee each way.

Bike Arenal. Biking packages in the Arenal area and around the country are suitable for all skill levels, with short and long ride options for each day. ☎2479–9020, 866/465–4114 in North America ⊕ *www.bikearenal.com* ✉ *From $85 for half-day tour.*

Coast to Coast Adventures. Multiday cycling tours are available for a variety of skill levels, some easier than the jaunts other outfitters do. ☎2280–8054 in Costa Rica ⊕ *www.coasttocoastadventures.com* ✉ *From $990 for eight-day tour.*

BIRD-WATCHING

You will get more out of your time in Costa Rica by taking a tour rather than trying to find birds on your own. Bring your own binoculars, but don't worry about a spotting scope; if you go with a company that specializes in birding tours, your guide will have one. Expect to see about 300 species during a weeklong tour. Many U.S. travel companies subcontract with Costa Rican tour operators. By arranging your tour directly with local companies, you save money.

Birdwatching Costa Rica. Comprehensive multiday birding tours are offered by this company, with eight options in various regions of Costa Rica as well as tours customized to your own requirements. ☎ 2771–4582 in Costa Rica ⊕ www.birdwatchingcostarica.com ✉ From $1,288.

DIVING

Costa Rica's remote Cocos Island—one of the world's best dive spots—can be visited only on multiday scuba safaris, but Guanacaste, the South Pacific, and, to a lesser extent, the Caribbean offer some respectable underwater adventures. Also in the south lies Caño Island, a good alternative to Cocos Island, particularly in the rainy season, when dive sites closer to shore are clouded by river runoff.

Aggressor. The *Okeanos Aggressor I* and *II* visit Cocos Island several times throughout the year on multiday diving excursions, in which you live on board and explore waters that are home to some exciting species. Hiking trips ashore are also included, weather permitting. ☎ 800/348–2628 in North America ⊕ www.aggressor.com ✉ From $2,795.

Bill Beard's Costa Rica. This Gulf of Papagayo outfitter pioneered Costa Rican diving tours and offers several Pacific-coast options. ☎ 877/853–0538 in North America ⊕ www.billbeardcostarica.com ✉ From $1,463 for three full diving days in multi-day packages.

Costa Rica Adventure Divers. In the South Pacific, Costa Rica Adventure Divers arranges multiday diving trips in the Drake Bay area, as well as offering the full range of PADI courses. ☎ 2231–5806, 866/553–7073 in North America ⊕ www. costaricadiving.com ✉ Dives from $115.

Sirenas Diving Costa Rica. Based in Playa Hermosa, Sirenas Diving has trips to all the dive sites in Guanacaste and the North Pacific coast, as well as the complete range of PADI courses. ☎ 8387–4710 in Costa Rica ⊕ www.sirenasdivingcostarica.com ✉ From $125.

Undersea Hunter. The *Argo*, *Sea Hunter*, and *Undersea Hunter* make 10-day, 9-night excursions several times a year to Cocos Island, with six full days of diving. ☎ 2228–6613, 800/203–2120 in North America ⊕ www.underseahunter.com ✉ From $5,645.

FISHING

If fishing is your primary objective in Costa Rica, you are best off booking a package. During peak season you may not even be able to find a hotel room in the hot fishing spots, let alone one of the top boats and skippers. The major fish populations move along the Pacific coast through the year, and tarpon and snook fishing on the Caribbean is subject to the vagaries of seasonal wind and weather but viable year-round.

Costa Rica Outdoors. San José–based Costa Rica Outdoors is one of the best bets for full service and honest advice about where to go and works with the widest range of operators around the country. ☎ 2231–0306, 800/308–3394 in North America ⊕ www.costaricaoutdoors.com.

J.P. Sportfishing Tours. This longtime operator is the place to get hooked up for fishing in Quepos and the Central Pacific coast. Experienced skippers are fluent in English and, depending on the season, offer the chance to catch marlin, dorado, Pacific sailfish, snapper, yellowfin, or roosterfish. You'll need to obtain your own fishing license. ☎2777–1613, 866/620–4188 in North America ⊕ www. jpsportfishing.com ✉ From $675 for 1–4 anglers for half day.

Kingfisher Sportfishing. Anglers in the know recommend Kingfisher Sportfishing in Playa Carrillo, Guanacaste. Trips to suit experienced anglers and novices of all ages are available. ☎2656–0091 in Costa Rica, 800/783–3817 in North America ⊕ www.costaricabillfishing.com ✉ From $900 for 2–4 anglers for half day.

Río Colorado Lodge. This is the best known of the fishing lodges in Barra del Colorado, north of Tortuguero on the northern Caribbean coast, specializing in tarpon, snook, and light-tackle game fish. Accommodations are in an air-conditioned lodge with good amenities. ☎2232–4063, 800/243–9777 in North America ⊕ www.riocoloradolodge.com ✉ From $2,500 for 6 days, 5 nights, with 3 full days of fishing.

The Zancudo Lodge. Near Golfito on the South Pacific coast, this lodge mixes sportfishing with upscale accommodations and a variety of other activities. ☎2776–0008, 800/854–8791 in North America ⊕ www. zancudolodge.com ✉ From $2,795 for 3 days fishing, accommodations, and meals.

GOLF

Putting on a green against a dramatic Pacific backdrop isn't the first image that springs to mind for Costa Rican vacations, but the increase in luxury resorts and upscale tourism has created a respectable, albeit small, golfing circuit in the Central Valley and along the Pacific coast. Most packages maximize links time with side excursions to explore the country's natural riches.

Costa Rica Golf Adventures. Multiday golf tours include accommodations at four- and five-star lodgings and a choice of six courses, including some of Central America's finest. ☎888/536–8510 in North America ⊕ www.golfcr.com ✉ From $599 (3 days of golf, including lodging).

HIKING

Most nature-tour companies include hiking as part of their itineraries, but these hikes may not be strenuous enough for serious hikers. Ask many questions about hike lengths and difficulty levels before booking the tour or you may be disappointed with the amount of time you get to spend on the trails. Serendipity Adventures is one that caters to both moderate and serious hikers.

Serendipity Adventures. Customized multiday excursions include camping in areas not normally open to the public. ☎877/507–1358 in North America, 2556–2222 in Costa Rica ⊕ www. serendipityadventures.com ✉ Multiday tours from $2,180.

SURFING

Most Costa Rican travel agencies have packages that ferry both veterans and newcomers between the country's famed bicoastal breaks.

Del Mar Surf Camp. With branches in Jacó and Nosara, this company offers a variety of surf lessons, including women-only classes, and seven-day packages with daily surfing sessions and accommodations. ☎2643–3197 in Costa Rica, 855/833–5627 in North America ⊕ www.delmarsurfcamp.com ✉ From $1,350 for 7 days.

SPANISH-LANGUAGE PROGRAMS

Thousands of people travel to Costa Rica every year to study Spanish. Dozens of schools in and around San José offer professional instruction and homestays, and there are several smaller schools outside the capital. Bundling a homestay with a local family into the course is always a way to increase your progress.

Conversa. This school in Santa Ana, in the west Central Valley, offers hourly classes as well as "Intense" (4 hours a day) and "Super Intense" (5½ hours per day) programs ranging from a week to a month (with further add-on weeks available).

☎ *4001–2497, 888/669–1664 in North America* ⊕ *www.conversa.com* ✉ *From $815 for 1 wk.*

CPI Spanish Immersion School. You can sign up for four or five hours per day of study at CPI's schools in Heredia, Monteverde, and Playa Flamingo. ☎ *2265–6306, 877/373–3116 in North America* ⊕ *www. cpi-edu.com* ✉ *From $460 (1 wk).*

ILISA. Cultural immersion classes are based in San Pedro, San José's preeminent eastside suburb. ☎ *2280–0700, 800/454–7248 in North America* ⊕ *www.ilisa.com* ✉ *From $440 (1 wk).*

Institute for Central American Development Studies (*ICADS*). Language programs here include optional academic seminars in English about Central America's political, social, and economic conditions. ☎ *2225–0508* ⊕ *www.icads.org* ✉ *From $1,790 (4 wks).*

La Academia de Español d'Amore. In beautiful Manuel Antonio, this is one of Costa Rica's prime places to combine language study and beach time. ☎ *2777–0233, 877/434–7290 in North America* ⊕ *www.academiadamore.com* ✉ *From $850 (2 wks).*

VOLUNTEER PROGRAMS

In recent years more and more Costa Ricans have realized the need to preserve their country's precious biodiversity. Both Ticos and far-flung environmentalists have founded volunteer and educational concerns to this end.

Volunteer opportunities span a range of diverse interests. You can tag sea turtles as part of a research project, build trails in a national park, or volunteer at an orphanage. Many of the organizations require at least rudimentary Spanish. Beach cleanups, recycling, and some wildlife projects don't require proficiency in Spanish.

Costa Rican Humanitarian Foundation (*Fundación Humanitaria*). Volunteer opportunities include working with indigenous communities, women, street kids, community-based clinics, and education centers.

☎ *8390–4192 in Costa Rica* ⊕ *www.crhf. org* ✉ *From $500.*

Earthwatch Institute. Science-based trips led by Earthwatch include studying monkeys, turtles, dolphins, rain forests, and climate change. ☎ *800/776–0188 in North America* ⊕ *www.earthwatch.org* ✉ *From $1,950.*

Institute for Central American Development Studies (*ICADS*). The Institute delves into development and social justice in a variety of volunteer programs that let you work with schools and disadvantaged communities. ☎ *2225–0508 in Costa Rica* ⊕ *www.icads.org* ✉ *From $1,990 (4 wks).*

Sea Turtle Conservancy. This conservancy, in Tortuguero on the northern Caribbean coast, is devoted to the preservation of endangered sea turtles. You can sign up as an eco-volunteer for one, two, or three weeks, with all-inclusive accommodations, and take part in nighttime turtle patrols and hands-on conservation projects. ☎ *352/373–6441 in North America* ⊕ *www.conserveturtles.org* ✉ *From $1,508.*

Talamancan Association of Ecotourism and Conservation (*ATEC*). As well as designing short group and individual outings centered on Costa Rican wildlife and indigenous culture, ATEC keeps an updated list of up to 30 Caribbean-based organizations that welcome volunteers. A two-month commitment is required. ☎ *2750–0398 in Costa Rica* ⊕ *www.ateccr.org.*

▌VISITOR INFORMATION

The official tourism board, the Instituto Costarricense de Turismo (ICT), has an office on Avenida Central in San José and a small desk in the baggage claim area at Juan Santamaría airport. The airport counter contains a few brochures but is staffed only sporadically. Visitor information is provided by the Costa Rica Tourist Board in the United States.

Contacts Instituto Costarricense de Turismo (*ICT*). ☎ *2299–5800, 866/267–8274 in North America* ⊕ *www.visitcostarica.com*.

ONLINE TRAVEL TOOLS

The REAL Costa Rica slips in a bit of attitude with its information, and is a bit lax on updating, but scores high marks for overall accuracy. Scope out detailed maps, driving distances, and pictorial guides to the locations of hotels and businesses in some communities at CostaRicaMap.com. The Association of Residents of Costa Rica online forums are some of the region's most active and informed, with topics ranging from business and pleasure trips to the real-estate market, with loads of information if you're interested in moving to the country. *The Tico Times* publishes news about Costa Rica, much of it of interest to visitors.

Contacts Association of Residents of Costa Rica (*ARCR*). ⊕ *www.arcr.net*. **CostaRicaMap. com.** ⊕ *www.costaricamap.com*. **The REAL Costa Rica.** ⊕ *www.therealcostarica.com*. **The Tico Times.** ⊕ *www.ticotimes.net*.

INDEX

PHOTO CREDITS

Front cover: DanitaDelimont / AWL Images [Description: A wild Fiery-billed Aracari sits on a branch in the Costa Rican jungle]. 1, kallielukasik, Fodors.com member. 2, Mlenny Photography/iStockphoto. Chapter 1: Experience Costa Rica: 8-9, Robert Harding Travel/photolibrary.com. 14 (left), Nickolay Stanev / Shutterstock. 14 (top center), Arhen / iStockphoto. 14 (top right), raquel_z, Fodors.com member. 14 (bottom right), Highwind1, Fodors.com member. 15 (top left), RuthChoi/Shutterstock. 15 (bottom left), Pablo Arroyo and Margaret Kalacska. 15 (top center), Juan Amighetti/Costa Rica Tourist Board (ICT). 15 (right), Pablo Arroyo and Margaret Kalacska. Chapter 2: Biodiversity: 47, Justin Hubbell, Fodors.com member. 48, Jaimi DeFeo, Fodors.com member. 49, Costa Rica Tourist Board (ICT). 52-53, urosr/Shutterstock. 54 (top), Martin Shields/Alamy. 54 (bottom), danmike, Fodors.com member. 55, Costa Rica Tourism. 56 (top), Dennis Frates/Alamy. 56 (2nd from top), Philipp Weigell/wikipedia. org. 56 (3rd from top). blickwinkel/Alamy. 56 (bottom), O. Baudys/wikipedia.org. 57 (top), wikipedia. org. 57 (2nd from top), EML/Shutterstock. 57 (3rd from top), Ben Lunsford/wikipedia.org. 57 (bottom), Stefa Laube/wikipedia.org. 58-59, Sylvain Grandadam/age fotostock. 60 (top), piper35w, Fodors. com member. 60 (bottom), Marco13, Fodors.com member. 61, Nik Wheeler/Alamy. 62 (top), Jason Kremkau. 62 (2nd from top), wikipedia.org. 62 (3rd from top), Peter Arnold, Inc./Alamy. 62 (bottom), Túrelio/wikipedia.org. 63 (top), Danita Delimont/Alamy. 63 (2nd from top), Ken Thornsley/NASA/ wikipedia.org. 63 (3rd from top), wikipedia.org. 63 (bottom), Danita Delimont/Alamy. 64-65, Alvaro Leiva/age fotostock. 66 (top), maddytem, Fodors.com member. 66 (bottom), Martin Rugner/age fotostock. 67, Ronald Reyes. 68 (top), Orchi/wikipedia.org. 68 (2nd from top), PeterArnold, Inc./Alamy. 68 (3rd from top), John Seiler/iStockphoto. 68 (bottom), Peter Arnold, Inc./Alamy. 69 (top), Danita Delimont/Alamy. 69 (2nd from top), Papilio/Alamy. 69 (3rd from top), worldswildlifewonders/Shutterstock. 69 (bottom), Erlaubnis des Autors/wikipedia.org. 70-71, Alvaro Leiva/age fotostock. 72 (top), reedjoella, Fodors.com member. 72 (bottom), frans lemmens/Alamy. 73, Costa Rica Tourist Board (ICT). 74 (top), Cody Hinchliff/wikipedia.org. 74 (2nd from top), plumboy, Fodors.com member. 74 (3rd from top), Avancari/wikipedia.org. 74 (bottom), Louise Wolff/wikipedia.org. 75 (top), Jerry Oldenettel/wikipedia.org. 75 (2nd from top), matt knoth/wikipedia.org. 75 (3rd from top), Andrew Hewitt/ Alamy. 75 (bottom), David Jensen (Storkk)/wikipedia.org. 76-77, Andoni Canela/age fotostock. 78 (top), Liz Stuart, Fodors.com member. 78 (bottom), StupFD, Fodors.com member. 79, Thornton Cohen. 80 (top), Florida Images/Alamy. 80 (2nd from top), Arco Images GmbH/Alamy. 80 (3rd from top), Wibowo Djatmiko/wikipedia.org. 80 (bottom), William Tait/Alamy. 81 (top), Mehmet Karatay/ wikipedia.org. 81 (2nd from top), Mike Baird/wikipedia.org. 81 (3rd from top), Steven G. Johnson/ wikipedia.org. 81 (bottom), WaterFrame/Alamy. 82-83, Alvaro Leiva/age fotostock. 84 (top), Toronto-Jeff, Fodors.com member. 84 (bottom), Justin Hubbell, Fodors.com member. 85, Juan Amighetti/Costa Rica Tourist Board (ICT). 86 (top), wikipedia.org. 86 (2nd from top), Andrewtappert/wikipedia.org. 86 (3rd from top), Daniel J. Cox/Alamy. 86 (bottom), Wilfredo Rodríguez/wikipedia.org. 87 (top), Dori (http://dori.merr.info)/wikipedia.org. 87 (2nd from top), Jim Lebster/wikipedia.org. 87 (3rd from top), Thierry Caro/wikipedia.org. 87 (bottom), Patrick Verdier/wikipedia.org. 88, pilesasmiles/iStockphoto. Chapter 3: San José: 89, R1/Alamy. 90, Lindy Drew. 91 (top), R1/Alamy. 91 (bottom), Costa Rica Tourist Board (ICT). 92 and 93 (both), Lindy Drew. 94, Ronald Reyes. 100, Pietro Scozzari/age fotostock. 110, R1/Alamy. 114, Dchulov l Dreamstime.com. 126, Liz Stuart, Fodors.com member. 131, Neil McAllister/Alamy. Chapter 4: The Central Valley: 135, jvcostarica, Fodors.com member. 136, Pablo Arroyo and Margaret Kalacska. 137 (top and bottom), Costa Rica Tourist Board (ICT). 138, mrsviv07, Fodors.com member. 139 (top), Alvaro Leiva/age fotostock. 139 (bottom), R1/Alamy. 140, Jason Kremkau. 141 (top), Ginita215, Fodors.com member. 141 (bottom), Fernando Ramírez/age fotostock. 142, mrsviv07, Fodors.com member. 143 (top), Alvaro Leiva/age fotostock. 143 (bottom), R1/Alamy. 144, Brian Allen, Fodors.com member. 152, Lindy Drew. 170, travelib costa rica/Alamy. 172, Gay Bumgarner/Alamy. 179 and 183, Lindy Drew. 185, Ronald Reyes. 188, Neil McAllister/Alamy. 195, Linda137, Fodors.com member. Chapter 5: Arenal, Monteverde, and the Northern Lowlands: 197, Msoberma, Fodors.com member. 199 (top), Leethal33, Fodors.com member. 199 (bottom), Costa Rica Tourist Board (ICT). 200, Colin D. Young/Shutterstock. 201 (top), vogelmutter, Fodors.com member. 201 (bottom), racegirl, Fodors.com member. 202, robrick, Fodors.com member. 203 (top), imagebroker/Alamy. 203 (bottom), Jordi Camí /Alamy. 204, Lindy Drew. 211, sportster, Fodors.com member. 220, Sylvain Grandadam/age fotostock. 225, tiffnco, Fodors.com member. 227, Inger Hogstrom / age fotostock. 230, Jan Csernoch/Alamy. Chapter 6: Guanacaste and the Nicoya Peninsula: 245, Carver Mostardi / Alamy. 246, Thornton Cohen. 247, Gpkbrand, Fodors.com member. 248, imagebroker/ Alamy. 249 (top), Sylvia Cordaiy Photo Library Ltd/Alamy. 249 (bottom), R1/Alamy. 250, Danita Delimont/Alamy. 251 (top), Zach Holmes/Alamy. 251 (bottom). Catherine Scott/iStockphoto. 252, Thornton Cohen/Alamy. 253 (top), Mark Gabrenya/Shutterstock. 253 (bottom), Kevin Schafer/Alamy. 254,

PDSF, Fodors.com member. 271, Luis Alberto Aldonza/age fotostock. 290, Eyal Nah-Fodo_mias/ Alamy. 296, Guillen Photography/UW/Costa Rica/Alamy. 302, Jason Bazzano/age fotostock. 310, Yadid Levy/Alamy. 323, Gusto Beach Samara ImageSync Ltd/Alamy. 336, Jon Arnold Images Ltd/ Alamy. 351, Hemis/Alamy. 362, Yadid Levy/Alamy. Chapter 7: Manuel Antonio and the Central Pacific Coast: 367, Gwendolyn Morris, Fodors.com member. 369 (top left) Ruthalan, Fodors.com member. 369 (top right), TorontoJeff, Fodors.com member. 369 (bottom), Plumboy, Fodors.com member. 370, volcanogirl, Fodors.com member. 371 (top), LynneL, Fodors.com member. 371 (bottom), kjorgen / iStockphoto. 372, esp05, Fodors.com member. 388, Leethal33, Fodors.com member. 392-393, Chris Cheadle/age fotostock. 403, Colleen George, Fodors.com member. 408, Antonio Jorge Nunes/Shutterstock. 414, Sylvain Grandadam/age fotostock. Chapter 8: The Osa Peninsula and the South Pacific: 417, Chad Clark, Fodors.com member. 418, Volcanogirl, Fodors.com member. 419 (top), Cutestcookie, Fodors.com member. 419 (bottom), buckscofamily, Fodors.com member. 420, Roberto-Ramos/ Costa Rica Tourist Board (ICT). 421 (top), Justin Hubbell, Fodors.com member. 421 (bottom), Danita Delimont/Alamy. 422, Claude Huot/Shutterstock. 423 (top), Jason Kremkau. 423 (bottom), David South/Alamy. 424, Highwind1, Fodors.com member. 425 (top), Timur Kulgarin/Shutterstock. 425 (bottom), drs, Fodors.com member. 426, Ronald Reyes. 435, Danita Delimont/Alamy. 444, Genevieve Vallee / Alamy. 450, Richard Bueno, Fodors.com member. 460, Justin Hubbell, Fodors.com member. 470, jamie722, Fodors.com member. 480-481, Dirscherl Reinhard/age fotostock. 482, Loetscher Chlaus/Alamy. 490, Monica Richards, Fodors.com member. 494, ticopix/Alamy. Chapter 9: Tortuguero and the Caribbean Coast: 497, John Cancalosi/age fotostock. 498 and 499, Costa Rica Tourist Board (ICT). 500, Wendler/age fotostock. 501 (top), Andoni Canela/age fotostock. 501 (bottom), Stjerne, Fodors.com member. 502, Costa Rica Tourist Board (ICT). 503 (top), jhubson1, Fodors.com member. 503 (bottom), Costa Rica Tourist Board (ICT). 504, JuanAmighetti/Costa Rica Tourist Board (ICT). 514, Erro/Barrantes/Costa Rica Tourist Board (ICT). 524, Jordi Camí/age fotostock. 526, Liz Stuart, Fodors.com member. 538, janenicole, Fodors.com member. 540, Rodrigo Montenegro/Costa Rica Tourist Board (ICT). 551, Ronald Reyes. 555, dgray, Fodors.com member. Back cover, from left to right: Timur Kulgarin/Shutterstock; EML/Shutterstock; Korzeniewski | Dreamstime.com. Spine: Jodi Jacobson/iStockphoto. About Our Writers: All photos are courtesy of the writers except for the following: Marlise Kast-Myers, courtesy of Benjamin Myers.

NOTES

NOTES

NOTES

NOTES

NOTES

NOTES